United Kingdom National Accounts

The Blue Book 2001

Editor: Jennie Tse

London: The Stationery Office

© Crown copyright 2001.
Published with the permission of the Controller of Her Majesty's Stationery Office (HMSO).

ISBN 0 11 621470 8
ISSN 0267–8691

Applications for reproduction should be submitted to HMSO under HMSO's Class Licence:
www.clickanduse.hmso.gov.uk

Alternatively applications can be made in writing to:
HMSO Licensing Division
St Clement's House
2-16 Colegate
Norwich NR3 1BQ

Contact points
For enquiries about this publication, contact
Jennie Tse
Tel: 020 7533 6031
E-mail: jennie.tse@ons.gov.uk

To order this publication, call The Stationery Office on **0870 600 5522**. See also back cover.

For general enquiries, contact the National Statistics Public Enquiry Service on **0845 601 3034**
(minicom: 01633 812399)
E-mail: info@statistics.gov.uk
Fax: 01633 652747
Letters: Room 1.001, Government Buildings, Cardiff Road, Newport NP10 8XG

You can also find National Statistics on the internet - go to **www.statistics.gov.uk**

About the Office for National Statistics
The Office for National Statistics (ONS) is the government agency responsible for compiling, analysing and disseminating many of the United Kingdom's economic, social and demographic statistics, including the retail prices index, trade figures and labour market data, as well as the periodic census of the population and health statistics. The Director of ONS is also the National Statistician and the Registrar General for England and Wales, and the agency administers the statutory registration of births, marriages and deaths there.

A National Statistics publication
Official statistics bearing the National Statistics logo are produced to high professional standards set out in the National Statistics Code of Practice. They undergo regular quality assurance reviews to ensure that they meet customer needs. They are produced free from any political interference.

Contents

Page

Preface 7
Introduction 8
Calendar of Economic Events 18

Part 1 Main aggregates and summary accounts
Chapter 1 : Main aggregates and summary accounts
    The National Accounts at a glance 22
    Explanation of main aggregates and summary accounts 25
    Changes since last year's Blue Book 33
    1.1   Main aggregates : index numbers and values, 1982-2000 36
    1.2   Gross domestic product and national income, 1982-2000 38
    1.3   Gross domestic product at constant 1995 prices, 1982-2000 40
    1.4   Indices of value, volume, prices and costs, 1982-2000 42
    1.5   Population, employment and GDP per head, 1992-2000 44
    1.6   United Kingdom summary accounts, 1992-2000 45
    1.7   Summary analysis by sector, 1997-2000 56
    1.7.1 Detailed analysis by sector, 1999 64

Part 2 The industrial analyses
Chapter 2 : The industrial analyses
    The industrial analyses at a glance 86
    Explanation of industrial analyses 87
    2.1   Input-Output Supply and Use Tables, 1992-1999 94
    2.2   Gross value added at current basic prices, by industry and type of income, 1992-2000 110
    2.3   Gross value added at current basic prices, by industry, 1992-2000 111
    2.4   Gross value added at constant 1995 basic prices, by industry (index numbers), 1992-2000 112
    2.5   Employment by industry, 1992-2000 116

Part 3 The sector accounts
    The sector accounts at a glance 118
    Sector accounts key indicators 120
    Explanation of the sector accounts 121

Chapter 3 : Non-financial corporations
    3.1   Non-financial corporations 127
    3.2   Public non-financial corporations 135
    3.3   Private non-financial corporations 143

Chapter 4 : Financial corporations
    4.1   Financial corporations 153
    4.2   Monetary financial institutions 161
    4.3   Other financial intermediaries and financial auxiliaries 169
    4.4   Insurance corporations and pension funds 177
    4.5   Financial derivatives 184

Chapter 5 : General government
    5.1   General government 189
    5.2   Central government 198
    5.3   Local government 208

Chapter 6 : Households and Non-profit institutions serving households (NPISH)
    6.1   Combined households and NPISH sector 220
    6.2   Household final consumption expenditure at current market prices classified by commodity 230
    6.3   Household final consumption expenditure at 1995 market prices classified by commodity 231
    6.4   Individual consumption expenditure at current market prices by households, NPISH and general government 232
    6.5   Individual consumption expenditure at 1995 market prices by households, NPISH and general government 234

Chapter 7 : Rest of the world
    7.1   Rest of the world 239

Contents

Part 4 Other analyses and derived statistics

Chapter 8 : Percentage distributions and growth rates

- 8.1 Composition of UK gross domestic product at current market prices by category of expenditure 252
- 8.2 Composition of UK gross domestic product at current market prices by category of income 252
- 8.3 Value added at current basic prices analysed by industry 253
- 8.4 Annual increases in categories of expenditure at 1995 prices 253
- 8.5 Some aggregates related to the gross national income 253
- 8.6 Rates of change of GDP at current market prices 254
- 8.7 Rates of change of GDP at constant 1995 market prices 255
- 8.8 Rates of change of GDP at current market prices per capita 256
- 8.9 Rates of change of GDP at constant 1995 market prices per capita 256
- 8.10 Rates of change of real household disposable income at constant 1995 prices 257
- 8.11 Rates of change of real household disposable income at constant 1995 prices per capita 258

Chapter 9: Fixed capital formation supplementary tables

- 9.1 Analysis of gross fixed capital formation at current purchasers' prices by type of asset and sector 260
- 9.2 Analysis of gross fixed capital formation at current purchasers' prices by broad sector and type of asset 261
- 9.3 Analysis of gross fixed capital formation at current purchasers' prices by type of asset 261
- 9.4 Analysis of gross fixed capital formation at 1995 purchasers' prices by broad sector and type of asset 262
- 9.5 Analysis of gross fixed capital formation at 1995 purchasers' prices by type of asset 262
- 9.6 Analysis of fixed capital consumption at current prices by industry 263
- 9.7 Analysis of fixed capital consumption at constant 1995 prices by industry 263
- 9.8 Analysis of fixed capital consumption at current prices by sector 264
- 9.9 Analysis of net capital stock at current prices by sector and type of asset 265
- 9.10 Analysis of gross capital stock at constant 1995 prices by industry 266
- 9.11 Analysis of gross capital stock at constant 1995 prices by type of asset 266

Chapter 10: Non-financial balance sheets

- Explanation of non-financial balance sheets 268
- 10.1 National balance sheet sector totals 269
- 10.2 National balance sheet asset totals 269
- 10.3 Non-financial corporations 270
- 10.4 Public non-financial corporations 270
- 10.5 Private non-financial corporations 271
- 10.6 Financial corporations 271
- 10.7 General government 272
- 10.8 Central government 272
- 10.9 Local government 273
- 10.10 Households & non-profit institutions serving households (NPISH) 273
- 10.11 Public sector 274

Chapter 11: General government supplementary tables

- Explanation of general government supplementary tables 276
- 11.1 Taxes paid by UK residents to general government and the European Union 278
- 11.2 General government: analysis of total outlays by classification of function of government (COFOG) 280
- 11.3 Public sector: key fiscal balances and expenditure indicators 283
- 11.4 General government: reconciliation of financial transactions and balance 284
- 11.5 Central government: reconciliation of financial transactions and balance 284
- 11.6 Local government: reconciliation of financial transactions and balance 285
- 11.7 Housing operating account 285

Chapter 12 : Statistics for European Union purposes

- Explanation of statistics for European Union purposes 288
- 12.1 UK gross domestic and national product ESA79 compiled for EU budgetary purposes 289
- 12.2 UK official transactions with institutions of the EU 290

Contents

Part 5 Environmental accounts

Chapter 13 : UK Environmental Accounts

	The UK Environmental Accounts at a glance	292
	Explanation of the UK Environmental Accounts	294
13.1	Estimates of oil and gas reserves	303
13.2	Monetary balance sheets for oil and gas reserves	304
13.3	Energy consumption (on an energy supplied basis)	305
13.4	Atmospheric emissions, 1999	306
13.5	Greenhouse gas and acid rain precursor emissions	306
13.6	Total waste arisings in the UK 1998/99	307
13.7	Material flows in the UK	308
13.8	Government revenues from environmental taxes	309
13.9	UK environmental protection expenditure, 1999	309
13.10	Land cover account, Great Britain 1990-1998	310

Glossary of terms ... 311
Index ... 319

Preface

The annual National Statistics *Blue Book* contains the estimates of the domestic and national product, income and expenditure of the United Kingdom.

The presentation of accounts is based on the European System of Accounts 1995 (ESA95), which is itself based on the System of National Accounts 1993 (SNA93). SNA93 has been adopted world wide.

This edition of the Blue Book contains a number of significant changes and data revisions arising from the development of new methodology; new classifications; and new and enhanced data sources. In addition, there are a few changes that are the result of the implementation of further work to ensure consistency with ESA95. Although the programme of work to present these accounts on a ESA95 basis was largely completed for the 1998 edition of the Blue Book, the timetable for the full implementation of ESA95 extends to 2005. All of these changes have been taken back as far as data exists, which in some cases, is 1948.

Reliability of the estimates

All the value estimates are calculated as accurately as possible, however they cannot always be regarded as being absolutely precise to the last digit shown. Similarly, the index numbers are not necessarily absolutely precise to the last digit shown. Some figures are provisional and may be revised later; this applies particularly to many of the detailed figures for 1999 and 2000.

Quarterly estimates

Quarterly estimates of the main components of the National Accounts for the last few years are published in National Statistics First Releases and, in more detail with commentary, in *UK Economic Accounts*.

Long run quarterly and annual estimates consistent with the *Blue Book* are published in the *Economic Trends Annual Supplement*. The latest estimates are also given in summary form in the *Monthly Digest of Statistics* and the quarterly income, capital and financial accounts for each sector are published regularly in *Financial Statistics*.

Blue Book data in computer-readable form

This publication is available in electronic format via the National Statistics DataBank Service and StatBase®. The DataBank Service provides electronic versions of various National Statistics business and economic publications and press notices on diskette, or as files downloadable via the internet. A DataBank catalogue can be downloaded from the DataBank web-page (http://www.statistics.gov.uk/databank/dbcatalog.asp) which is hosted on the National Statistics web-site (http://www.statistics.gov.uk/). There is also a shortcut to national accounts information: (http://www.statistics.gov.uk/nationalaccounts). StatBase® provides free on-line access to individual and groups of time series, cross sectional data and metadata. StatBase® is also held on the National Statistics web-site: (http://www.statistics.gov.uk/statbase/mainmenu.asp).

For more details of these services please contact:
Online Services Branch
B1/12, 1 Drummond Gate
LONDON SW1V 2QQ
(Tel: 020 7533 5675 Fax: 020 7533 5688
Email: on-line.services.branch@statistics.gov.uk).

National Statistics looks forward to receiving comments on its publications. Suggestions for improvements or alterations to the *Blue Book* can be sent in writing to:
Jennie Tse
Blue Book Editor
D3/11, 1 Drummond Gate
LONDON SW1V 2QQ
(Tel: 020 7533 6031 Fax: 020 7533 5937
Email: jennie.tse@ons.gov.uk).

Enquiries regarding National Accounts should be directed to the following:

National Accounts/Sector Accounts:
Jon Beadle 020 7533 5938 (jon.beadle@ons.gov.uk)
Household final consumption expenditure:
Margaret Dolling 020 7533 5996 (margaret.dolling@ons.gov.uk)
General government and public sector:
Martin Kellaway 020 7533 5987 (martin.kellaway@ons.gov.uk)
Gross capital formation:
Adrian Chesson 01633 652537 (adrian.chesson@ons.gov.uk)
Capital stock and non-financial balance sheets:
Graham Jenkinson 020 7533 6297 (graham.jenkinson@ons.gov.uk)
Exports and imports of goods:
David Ruffles 020 7533 6070 (david.ruffles@ons.gov.uk)
Exports and imports of services:
Jennie Tse 020 7533 6095 (jennie.tse@ons.gov.uk)
Gross value added by industry:
Geoff Reed 020 7533 5966 (geoff.reed@ons.gov.uk)
Input-Output Supply and Use Tables/Production accounts:
Sanjiv Mahajan 020 7533 5954 (sanjiv.mahajan@ons.gov.uk)
Households and NPISH sector:
Roger Ward 020 7533 6002 (roger.ward@ons.gov.uk)
Non-financial corporations:
Ian Hill 020 7533 6019 (ian.hill@ons.gov.uk)
Financial corporations:
Richard Dagnall 020 7533 6055 (richard.dagnall@ons.gov.uk)
Rest of the world:
Simon Humphries 020 7533 6075 (simon.humphries@ons.gov.uk)
Environmental accounts:
Rocky Harris 020 7533 5916 (rocky.harris@ons.gov.uk)

The *Blue Book* is a collaborative effort. National Statistics is grateful for the assistance provided by the various government departments and organisations that have contributed to this book.

Introduction

An introduction to the United Kingdom National Accounts

The *Blue Book* presents the full system of the UK accounts, revealing a highly articulated system that embraces a vast amount of economic information. It presents estimates of the UK domestic and national product, income and expenditure. It covers the calendar years 1992-2000. The tables of the main aggregates are extended to cover 1983-1991 on a consistent basis. Data for 2000 are not yet available for the production account, the generation of income account, Input-Output Supply and Use Tables and for the full detailed industrial analysis of gross value added and its income components.

The National Accounts are the economic accounts for the United Kingdom. These accounts, which comprise a great wealth of economic series, are compiled by the Office for National Statistics. They record and describe economic activity in the United Kingdom and as such are used to support the formulation and monitoring of economic and social policies.

The accounts are based on the European System of Accounts 1995 (ESA95)[1], itself based on the System of National Accounts 1993 (SNA93)[2], which is being adopted by national statistical offices throughout the world. The UK National Accounts have been based on ESA95 since September 1998. The 1998 edition of the *Blue Book* explains the main changes; a more detailed explanation of changes can be found in *Introducing the ESA95 in the UK*[3]. A detailed description of the structure for the accounts is provided in a separate National Statistics publication *UK National Accounts Concepts, Sources and Methods*[4].

This introduction gives a brief overview of the accounts, explains their framework and sets out the changes included in this edition of the *Blue Book*. Definitions of terms used throughout the accounts are included in the glossary. Explanations of more specific concepts are provided within the relevant parts.

The *Blue Book* comprises five parts:

- *Part 1* provides a summary of the UK accounts along with explanations and tables that cover the main national and domestic aggregates, for example gross domestic product (GDP) at current and constant market prices and the GDP deflator; gross value added (GVA) at basic prices; gross national income (GNI); gross national disposable income (GNDI); and where appropriate their equivalents net of capital consumption; population estimates; employment estimates and GDP per head; and the UK summary accounts (the goods and services account, production accounts, distribution and use of income accounts and accumulation accounts). It also includes details of revisions to the data.

- *Part 2* includes Input-Output Supply and Use Tables and analyses of current and constant price gross value added, capital formation and employment, by industry.

- *Part 3* provides a description of the institutional sectors as well as explaining different types of transactions, the sequence of the accounts and the balance sheets. Explanation is also given of the statistical adjustment items needed to reconcile the accounts. This part comprises the full set of accounts showing transactions by sectors and appropriate sub-sectors of the economy (including the rest of the world).

- *Part 4* covers other additional analyses. It includes tables showing the percentage growth rates of the main aggregates and supplementary tables for capital consumption, gross fixed capital formation, capital stock, non-financial balance sheets, government data, and GDP and GNP consistent with ESA79 compiled for EU budgetary purposes.

- *Part 5* covers environmental accounts.

Overview of the accounts

In the United Kingdom the general approach essentially begins with the quarterly economic accounts and the production of a single estimate of GDP using the income, production and expenditure data. The income analysis is available at current prices, expenditure is available at both current and constant prices and value added on a quarterly basis is compiled in constant prices only. Income, capital and financial accounts are also produced for each of the institutional sectors: non-financial corporations, financial corporations, general government and the combined households and non-profit institutions serving households sector. The accounts are fully integrated, but with a statistical discrepancy, known as the statistical adjustment, shown for each sector account (which reflects the difference between the sector net borrowing or lending from the capital account and the identified borrowing or lending in the financial accounts which should theoretically be equal). Financial transactions and balance sheets are also produced for the rest of the world sector in respect of its dealings with the United Kingdom.

Summary of Changes

Section 4 has an annex this year. The annex shows Financial Derivatives positions data by currency and main sector.

The basic framework of the UK National Accounts

The accounting framework provides for a systematic and detailed description of the UK economy. It includes the sector accounts, which provide, by institutional sector, a description of the different stages of the economic process from production through income generation, distribution and use of income to capital accumulation and financing; and the Input-Output framework, which describes the production process in more detail. It contains all the elements required to compile aggregate measures such as GDP, gross national income (previously known as gross national product), saving and the current external balance (the balance of payments). The economic accounts provide the framework for a system of volume and price indices, so that constant price measures of aggregates such as GDP can be produced. It should be noted that, in this system, value added, from the production approach, is measured at basic prices (including taxes and subsidies on production but not on products) rather than at factor cost (which excludes all taxes and subsidies on production). The system also encompasses measures of population and employment.

The whole economy is subdivided into institutional sectors. For each sector, current price accounts run in sequence from the production account through to the balance sheet.

The accounts for the whole UK economy and its counterpart, the rest of the world, follow a similar structure to the UK sectors, although several of the rest of the world accounts are collapsed into a single account because they can never be complete when viewed from a UK perspective. For the UK, there is an extra, separate account at the beginning of the system for goods and services used (UK imports) and produced (UK exports) in the economy (Account 0). A similar account is shown for the rest of the world.

The table numbering system is designed to show the relationships between the UK, its sectors and the rest of the world. A three part numbering system (eg. 5.2.7) has been adopted for the accounts drawn directly from the ESA95. The first two digits denote the sector; the third digit denotes the ESA account. In this way for example, 5.2.1 is the central government production account, 5.3.1 is the local government production account and 5.3.2 is the local government generation of income account. Not all sectors can have all types of account, so the numbering is not necessarily consecutive within each sector's chapter. For the rest of the world, the identified components of accounts 2-6 inclusive are given in a single account numbered 2. The UK whole economy ESA95 accounts are given in section 1.6. as a time series and in 1.7. for the year 1999 in detailed matrix format with all sectors, the rest of the world, and the UK total identified.

The ESA95 code for each series is shown in the left hand column. The ESA95 codes use the prefix 'S' for the classification of institutional sectors. The ESA95 classification of transactions and other flows comprises transactions in products (prefix P), distributive transactions (prefix D), transactions in financial instruments (prefix F) and other accumulation entries (prefix K). Balancing items are classified using the prefix B. Within the financial balance sheets, financial assets/liabilities are classified using the prefix AF and non-financial assets/liabilities using the prefix AN.

What is an account? What is its purpose?

An account records and displays all of the flows and stocks for a given aspect of economic life. The sum of resources is equal to the sum of uses with a *balancing item* to ensure this equality. Normally the balancing item will be an economic measure which is itself of interest.

By employing a system of economic accounts we can build up accounts for different areas of the economy which highlight, for example, production, income and financial transactions. In many cases these accounts can be elaborated and set out for different institutional units and groups of units (or sectors). Usually a balancing item has to be introduced between the total resources and total uses of these units or sectors and, when summed across the whole economy, these balancing items constitute significant aggregates. Table A below provides the structure of the accounts and shows how GDP estimates are derived as the balancing items.

The integrated economic accounts

The integrated economic accounts of the UK provide an overall view of the economy. The sequence of accounts is shown in Figure 1 below. Figure 1 presents a summary view of the accounts, balancing items and main aggregates and shows how they are expressed.

The accounting structure is uniform throughout the system and applies to all units in the economy, whether they are institutional units, sub-sectors, sectors or the whole economy, though some accounts (or transactions) may not be relevant for some sectors.

The accounts are grouped into four main categories: goods and services account, current accounts, accumulation accounts and balance sheets.

The goods and services account (Account 0)

The goods and services account is a transactions account which balances total resources, from output and imports, against the uses of these resources in consumption, investment, inventories and exports. Because the resources are simply balanced with the uses, there is no balancing item. The goods and services account is discussed in detail in Chapters 3 and 12 of *UK National Accounts Concepts, Sources and Methods*[4]. A summary analysis of the goods and services account is shown in the form of Input-Output Supply and Use Tables in Chapter 2; a separate publication, *United Kingdom Input-Output Analyses, 2001 edition*[5] gives more detail.

Current accounts: the production accounts and the distribution of income accounts

Current accounts deal with production, distribution of income and use of income.

Introduction

A UK summary accounts
1995
Total economy: all sectors and the rest of the world

£ million

		INCOME Non-financial corporations S.11	Financial corporations S.12	General government S.13	Households & NPISH S.14+S.15	Not sector -ised S.N	Rest of the world S.2	UK total economy S.1
	PRODUCTION							
P.1	Output at basic prices	920 290	84 975	149 097	209 172			1 363 534
-P.2	*less* Intermediate consumption	–483 315	–46 588	–81 127	–89 381	–23 215		–723 626
D.21-D.31	Taxes *less* subsidies on products					79 268		79 268
	Gross value added at basic prices /							
B.1g	**gross domestic product at market prices**	**436 975**	**38 387**	**67 970**	**119 791**	**56 053**		**719 176**
	GENERATION OF INCOME							
D.1	Compensation of employees							
B.2g	Operating surplus, gross							
B.3g	Mixed income, gross							
	Gross value added at factor cost							
D.2	Taxes on production							
-D.3	*less* Subsidies on production							
di	Statistical discrepancy, income components							
	Gross value added at basic prices /							
B.1g	**gross domestic product at market prices**							
	ALLOCATION OF INCOME							
D.1	Compensation of employees, received				386 422		1 183	386 422
B.2g	Operating surplus, gross	153 152	17 838	6 447	38 165	–23 215		192 387
B.3g	Mixed income, gross				46 647			46 647
D.2	Taxes on production, received			94 275			7 358	94 275
-D.3	*less* Subsidies on production, paid			–5 778			–2 431	–5 778
	EXPENDITURE							
P.4	Actual final consumption							
P.6	Exports of goods and services							
-P.7	*less* Imports of goods and services							
P.51	Gross fixed capital formation							
-K.1	*less* Fixed capital consumption							
P.52	Changes in inventories							
P.53	Acquisitions less disposals of valuables							
di	Statistical discrepancy, income components							
B.1n	**Net domestic product at market prices**							
K.1	*plus* Fixed capital consumption							
B.1g	**Gross domestic product at market prices**							
	DISTRIBUTIVE TRANSACTIONS: RESOURCES							
D.4	Property income							
D.41	Interest	9 337	153 969	8 553	26 454		66 376	264 689
D.42	Distributed income of corporations	22 367	30 302	6 915	32 544		12 310	104 438
D.43	Reinvested earnings on direct foreign investment	11 376	3 002		–		5 254	19 632
D.44	Property income attributed to insurance policy holders	395	74	32	42 358		795	43 654
D.45	Rent	110	28	684	99			921
	Adjustment to property income							
-P.119	for financial services (FISIM)		–23 215			23 215		
	Other current transfers							
D.51	Taxes on income			95 042			557	95 599
D.59	Other current taxes			11 937				11 937
D.61	Social contributions	3 329	47 220	53 828	455		–	104 832
D.62	Social benefits				149 151		1 044	150 195
D.63	Social transfers in kind				97 574			97 574
D.7	Other current transfers	5 210	25 967	60 658	31 845		11 168	134 848
D.8	Adjustment for change in households' net equity							
	in pension funds				11 690		–2	11 688
D.9	Capital transfers							
D.91	Capital taxes			1 441				1 441
D.92	Investment grants	3 274	–	2 793	3 968		149	10 184
D.99	Other capital transfers	1 604	–	138	678		481	2 901
	Acquisition less disposals of							
K.2	**non-produced non-financial assets**							
B.9	Net lending(+) / net borrowing(-)							
	Total income	647 129	293 572	404 935	987 841	56 053	104 242	

Introduction

A UK summary accounts 1995
continued **Total economy: all sectors and the rest of the world**

£ million

		EXPENDITURE Non-financial corporations S.11	Financial corporations S.12	General government S.13	Households & NPISH S.14+S.15	Not sector -ised S.N	Rest of the world S.2	Total
P.1	**PRODUCTION** Output at basic prices							
-P.2	less Intermediate consumption							
D.21-D.31	Taxes less subsidies on products							
	Gross value added at basic prices /							
B.1g	gross domestic product at market prices							
	GENERATION OF INCOME							
D.1	Compensation of employees	272 489	19 219	59 839	35 171		887	386 718
B.2g	Operating surplus, gross	153 152	17 838	6 447	38 165	−23 215		192 387
B.3g	Mixed income, gross				46 647			46 647
	Gross value added at factor cost	425 641	37 057	66 286	119 983	−23 215		625 752
D.2	Taxes on production	12 099	1 330	1 684	101	86 419	−	101 633
-D.3	less Subsidies on production	−765	−	−	−293	−7 151		−8 209
di	Statistical discrepancy, income components					−		
	Gross value added at basic prices /							
B.1g	gross domestic product at market prices	436 975	38 387	67 970	119 791	56 053		719 176
	ALLOCATION OF INCOME							
D.1	Compensation of employees, received							
B.2g	Operating surplus, gross							
B.3g	Mixed income, gross							
D.2	Taxes on production, received							
-D.3	less Subsidies on production, paid							
	EXPENDITURE							
P.4	Actual final consumption			59 938	540 941			600 879
P.6	Exports of goods and services						203 509	203 509
-P.7	less Imports of goods and services						−207 051	−207 051
P.51	Gross fixed capital formation	70 220	5 590	14 056	27 582			117 448
-K.1	less Fixed capital consumption	−57 527	−4 063	−6 447	−18 922			−86 959
P.52	Changes in inventories	4 384	20	−154	262			4 512
P.53	Acquisitions less disposals of valuables	−52	−93	−	24			−121
de	Statistical discrepancy, expenditure components					−		−
B.1n	**Net domestic product at market prices**	17 025	1 454	148 486	468 794		−3 542	632 217
K.1	plus Fixed capital consumption	57 527	4 063	6 447	18 922			86 959
B.1g	**Gross domestic product at market prices**	74 552	5 517	154 933	487 716		−3 542	719 176
	DISTRIBUTIVE TRANSACTIONS: USES							
D.4	Property income							
D.41	Interest	26 575	109 685	30 077	40 288		58 064	264 689
D.42	Distributed income of corporations	71 532	18 216				14 690	104 438
D.43	Reinvested earnings on direct foreign investment	4 662	592				14 378	19 632
D.44	Property income attributed to insurance policy holders		43 654					43 654
D.45	Rent	719	−		202			921
-P.119	Adjustment to property income for financial services (FISIM)							
	Other current transfers							
D.51	Taxes on income	19 005	1 532		74 590		472	95 599
D.59	Other current taxes				11 937			11 937
D.61	Social contributions				104 737		95	104 832
D.62	Social benefits	3 329	35 532	110 409	925		755	150 950
D.63	Social transfers in kind			81 093	16 481			97 574
D.7	Other current transfers	5 059	26 032	71 802	22 402		9 553	134 848
D.8	Adjustment for change in households' net equity in pension funds		11 688				−	11 688
D.9	Capital transfers							
D.91	Capital taxes	−	−		1 441			1 441
D.92	Investment grants			9 699			485	10 184
D.99	Other capital transfers	144	−	1 626	453		678	2 901
K.2	Acquisition less disposals of non-produced non-financial assets	301	−77	−143	−81		−	−
B.9	**Net lending(+)/net borrowing(-)**	4 276	2 814	−41 438	25 866	−	8 482	−
	Total expenditure	647 129	293 572	404 935	987 841	56 053	104 997	1 438 352
	NET FINANCIAL TRANSACTIONS: (Assets less liabilities)							
F.1	Monetary gold and SDRs			−120			120	−
F.2	Currency and deposits	9 731	−30 501	−1 900	31 396		−8 726	−
F.3	Securities other than shares	−9 291	40 521	−34 704	2 953		521	−
F.4	Loans	−13 122	21 906	−2 198	−24 057		17 471	−
F.5	Shares and other equity	13 760	7 685	−2 369	−11 269		−7 807	−
F.6	Insurance technical reserves	920	−35 092	73	33 128		971	−
F.7	Other accounts receivable	−1 521	4 378	−460	−1 477		−920	−
dB.9f	Statistical adjustment	3 799	−6 083	240	−4 808	−	6 852	
B.9	Net lending (+)/ net borrowing	4 276	2 814	−41 438	25 866	−	8 482	

United Kingdom National Accounts 2001, © Crown copyright 2001

Introduction

Figure 1 Synoptic presentation of the accounts, balancing items and main aggregates

Accounts					Balancing items		Main aggregates [1]
Full sequence of accounts for institutional sectors							
Current accounts	I.	Production account			B.1	Value added	Domestic product (GDP/NDP)
	II.	Distribution and use of income accounts	II.1.	Primary distribution of income accounts	B.2 B.3 B.5	Operating surplus Mixed income Balance of primary incomes	National income (GNI, NNI)
			II.1.1. II.1.2.	Generation of income account II Allocation of primary income account			
			II.2. II.3.	Secondary distribution of income account Redistribution of income in kind account	B.6	Disposable income	National disposable income
			II.4. II.4.1. II.4.2.	Use of income account Use of disposable income account Use of adjusted disposable income account	B.7 B.8	Adjusted disposable income Saving	National saving
Accumulation accounts	III.	Accumulation accounts	III.1.	Capital account	B.10.1 B.9 B.9	(Changes in net worth, due to saving and capital transfers) Net lending/Net borrowing Net lending/Net borrowing	
			III.2.	Financial account			
Balance sheets	IV.	Financial balance sheets	IV.3.	Closing balance sheet	B.90	Financial net worth	
Transaction accounts							
Goods and services account	0	Goods and services account					National expenditure
Rest of the world account (external transactions account)							
Current accounts	V.	Rest of the world account	V.I. V.II.	External account of goods and services External account of primary income and current transfers	B.11 B.12	External balance of goods and services Current external balance	External balance of goods and services Current external balance
Accumulation accounts			V.III.	External accumulation accounts	B.10.1 B.9 B.9	(Changes in net worth due to current external balance and capital transfers) Net lending/Net borrowing Net lending/Net borrowing	Net lending/Net borrowing of the nation
			V.III.1. V.III.2.	Capital account Financial account			
Balance sheets			V.IV.	External assets and liabilities account	B.90	Net worth	
			V.IV.3.	Closing balance sheet	B.10 B.90	Changes in net worth Net worth	

1/ Most balancing items and aggregates may be calculated gross or net.

Introduction

The production account (Account I)

The production account displays the transactions involved in the generation of income by the activity of producing goods and services. In this case the balancing item is *value added* (B.1). For the nation's accounts, the balancing item (the sum of value added for all industries) is, after the addition of net taxes on products, gross domestic product (GDP) at market prices or net domestic product when measured net of capital consumption. The production accounts are also shown for each institutional sector. The production accounts are discussed in detail in Chapters 4 and 13 of *Concepts, Sources and Methods*[4].

Distribution and use of income account (Account II)

The distribution and use of income account shows the distribution of current income (in this case value added) carried forward from the production account, and has as its balancing item *saving* (B.8), which is the difference between income (disposable income) and expenditure (or final consumption). There are three sub-accounts which break down the distribution of income into the primary distribution of income, the secondary distribution of income and the redistribution of income in kind.

Primary incomes are those that accrue to institutional units as a consequence of their involvement in production or ownership of productive assets. They include property income (from lending or renting assets) and taxes on production and imports, but exclude taxes on income or wealth, social contributions or benefits and other current transfers. The primary distribution of income shows the way these are distributed among institutional units and sectors.

The secondary distribution of income account shows how the balance of primary incomes for an institutional unit or sector is transformed into its disposable income by the receipt and payment of current transfers (excluding social transfers in kind). The primary distribution account is itself divided into two sub accounts - the generation and the allocation of primary incomes - but ESA 95's further breakdown of the allocation of primary income account into an entrepreneurial income account and an allocation of other primary income account has not been adopted in the United Kingdom. A further two sub-accounts - the use of disposable income and the use of adjusted disposable income - look at the use of income for either consumption or saving. These accounts are examined in detail in Chapters 5 and 14 of *Concepts, Sources and Methods*[4].

Aggregated across the whole economy the balance of the primary distribution of income provides *national income* (B.5) (which can be measured net or gross), the balance of the secondary distribution of income in kind provides *national disposable income* (B.6), and the balance of the use of income accounts provides *national saving* (B.8). These are shown in Figure 1.

The accumulation account

The accumulation account covers all changes in assets, liabilities and net worth (the difference for any sector between its assets and liabilities). The accounts are structured to allow various types of change in these elements to be distinguished.

The first group of accounts covers transactions which would correspond to all changes in assets/liabilities and net worth which result from transactions e.g. savings and voluntary transfers of wealth (capital transfers). These accounts are the *capital account* and *financial account* which are distinguished in order to show the balancing item *net lending/ borrowing* (B.9). The second group of accounts relates to changes in assets, liabilities and net worth due to other factors (for example the discovery or re-evaluation of mineral reserves, or the reclassification of a body from one sector to another). Within this second group, the *other changes in assets* accounts, has not yet been implemented in the United Kingdom.

Capital account (Account III.1)

The capital account concerns the acquisition of non-financial assets (some of which will be income creating and others which are wealth only) such as fixed assets or inventories, financed out of saving, and capital transfers involving the redistribution of wealth. Capital transfers include, for example, capital grants from private corporations to public corporations (e.g. private sector contributions to the extension of the Jubilee line). This account shows how saving finances investment in the economy. In addition to gross fixed capital formation and changes in inventories, it shows the redistribution of capital assets between sectors of the economy and the rest of the world. The balance on the capital account, if negative, is designated *net borrowing*, and measures the net amount a unit or sector is obliged to borrow from others; if positive the balance is described as *net lending*, the amount the United Kingdom or a sector has available to lend to others. This balance is also referred to as the financial surplus or deficit and the net aggregate for the five sectors of the economy equals net lending/borrowing from the rest of the world.

Financial account (Account III.2)

The financial account shows how net lending and borrowing are achieved by transactions in financial instruments. The net acquisitions of financial assets are shown separately from the net incurrence of liabilities. The balancing item is again *net lending* or *borrowing*.

In principle net lending or borrowing in the capital account should be identical to net lending or borrowing on the financial account. However in practice, because of errors and omissions, this identity is very difficult to achieve for the sectors and the economy as a whole. The difference is known as the *statistical discrepancy* (previously known as the balancing item).

Introduction

The balance sheet (Account IV)

The second group of accounts within the accumulation accounts completes the full set of accounts in the system. These include the balance sheets and a reconciliation of the changes that have brought about the change in net worth between the beginning and the end of the accounting period.

The opening and closing balance sheets show how total holdings of assets by the UK or its sectors match total liabilities and net worth (the balancing item). In detailed presentations of the balance sheets the various types of asset and liability can be shown. Changes between the opening and closing balance sheets for each group of assets and liabilities result from transactions and other flows recorded in the accumulation accounts, or reclassifications and revaluations. Net worth equals changes in assets *less* changes in liabilities.

Rest of the world account (Account V)

This account covers the transactions between resident and non-resident institutional units and the related stocks of assets and liabilities. The rest of the world plays a similar role to an institutional sector and the account is written from the point of view of the rest of the world. This account is discussed in detail in Chapter 24 of *Concepts, Sources and Methods*[4].

Satellite accounts

Satellite accounts are accounts which involve areas or activities not dealt with in the central framework above, either because they add additional detail to an already complex system or because they actually conflict with the conceptual framework. The UK has begun work on a number of satellite accounts and one such - the UK environmental accounts - links environmental and economic data in order to show the interactions between the economy and the environment. Summary information from the environmental accounts is presented in Part 5. More detailed information on the environmental accounts is available from the National Statistics website or *UK Environmental Accounts* 1998[6].

Some Definitions

The text within Sections 1-3 explains the sources and methods used in the estimation of the UK economic accounts, but it is sensible to precede them with an explanation of some of the basic concepts and their 'UK specific' definitions, namely:

- the limits of the UK national economy: economic territory, residency and centre of economic interest
- economic activity: what production is included - the production boundary
- what price is used to value the products of economic activity
- estimation or imputation of values for non-monetary transactions
- the rest of the world: national and domestic.

A full description of the accounting rules is provided in Chapter 2 of *Concepts, Sources and Methods*[4].

The limits of the national economy: economic territory, residence and centre of economic interest

The economy of the United Kingdom is made up of institutional units (*see* Chapter 10 of *Concepts, Sources and Methods*[4]) which have a centre of economic interest in the UK economic territory. These units are known as resident units and it is their transactions which are recorded in the UK National Accounts. The definitions of these terms are given below:

The UK economic territory is made up of:

> Great Britain and Northern Ireland (the geographic territory administered by the UK government within which persons, goods, services and capital move freely);
>
> any free zones, including bonded warehouses and factories under UK customs control;
>
> the national airspace, UK territorial waters and the UK sector of the continental shelf.

It excludes the offshore islands - the Channel Islands and the Isle of Man - which are not members of the European Union and are therefore not subject to the same fiscal and monetary authorities as the rest of the United Kingdom.

Within ESA 95 the definition of economic territory also includes:

territorial enclaves in the rest of the world (like embassies, military bases, scientific stations, information or immigration offices, aid agencies, etc., used by the British government with the formal political agreement of the governments in which these units are located),

but excludes:

any extraterritorial enclaves (i.e. parts of the UK geographic territory like embassies and US military bases used by general government agencies of other countries, by the institutions of the European Union or by international organisations under treaties or by agreement).

Centre of economic interest and residency

An institutional unit has a centre of economic interest and is a resident of the UK when, from a location (for example a dwelling, place of production or premises) within the UK economic territory, it engages and intends to continue engaging (indefinitely or for a finite period; one year or more is

Introduction

used as a guideline) in economic activities on a significant scale. It follows that if a unit carries out transactions on the economic territory of several countries it has a centre of economic interest in each of them (for example BP has an interest in many countries where it is involved in the exploration and production of oil and gas). Ownership of land and structures in the UK is enough to qualify the owner to have a centre of interest here.

Within the definition given above resident units are basically households, legal and social entities such as corporations and quasi corporations (for example branches of foreign investors), non-profit institutions and government. Also included here however are so called 'notional residents'.

Travellers, cross border and seasonal workers, crews of ships and aircraft and students studying overseas are all residents of their home countries and remain members of their households. However an individual who leaves the UK for a year or more (except students and patients receiving medical treatment) ceases to be a member of a resident household and becomes a non-resident even on home visits.

Economic activity: what production is included?

As GDP is defined as the sum of all economic activity taking place in UK territory, having defined the economic territory it is important to be clear about what is defined as economic activity. In its widest sense it could cover all activities resulting in the production of goods or services and so encompass some activities which are very difficult to measure. For example, estimates of smuggling of alcoholic drink and tobacco products, and the output, expenditure and income directly generated by that activity, are included for the first time in this edition of the Blue Book.

In practice a 'production boundary' is defined, inside which are all the economic activities taken to contribute to economic performance. This economic production may be defined as activity carried out under the control of an institutional unit that uses inputs of labour or capital and goods and services to produce outputs of other goods and services. These activities range from agriculture and manufacturing through service-producing activities (for example financial services and hotels and catering) to the provision of health, education, public administration and defence; they are all activities where an output is owned and produced by an institutional unit, for which payment or other compensation has to be made to enable a change of ownership to take place. This omits purely natural processes.

Basically the decision whether to include a particular activity within the production boundary takes into account the following:

- does the activity produce a useful output?
- is the product or activity marketable and does it have a market value?
- if the product does not have a meaningful market value can a market value be assigned (i.e. can a value be imputed)?
- would exclusion (or inclusion) of the product of the activity make comparisons between countries or over time more meaningful?

In practice under ESA95 the production boundary can be summarised as follows:

The production of all **goods** whether supplied to other units or retained by the producer for own final consumption or gross capital formation, and **services** only in so far as they are exchanged in the market and/or generate income for other economic units.

For households this has the result of including the production of goods on own-account, for example the produce of farms consumed by the farmer's own household (however, in practice produce from gardens or allotments has proved impossible to estimate in the United Kingdom so far). The boundary excludes the production of services for own final consumption (household domestic and personal services like cleaning, cooking, ironing and the care of children and the sick or infirm). Although the production of these services does take a considerable time and effort, the activities are self-contained with limited repercussions for the rest of the economy and, as the vast majority of household domestic and personal services are not produced for the market, it is very difficult to value the services in a meaningful way.

What price is used to value the products of economic activity?

In the UK there are a number of different prices used to value inputs and outputs depending on the treatment of taxes and subsidies on products and trade and transport margins. These prices - purchasers' (or market) prices, basic prices and producers' prices - are looked at in turn below. Although the factor cost valuation (see explanation in Part 1) is not required under SNA93 or ESA95, ONS will continue to provide figures for gross value added at factor cost for as long as customers continue to find this analysis useful.

The 'market price', the price agreed and paid by transactors, is the main reference for the valuation of transactions in the accounts. However the market prices of products include indirect taxes (for instance VAT) paid to the government and are reduced by subsidies paid to producers by the government. As a result, the producer and user of a product will usually perceive the value of the product differently. This has resulted in two distinctions in the valuation of products: output prices received by producers, and prices paid as products are acquired.

Basic prices

These prices are the preferred method of valuing output as they reflect the amount received by the producer for a unit of goods or services, *minus* any taxes payable, and plus any subsidy receivable on that unit as a consequence of production or sale (i.e. the cost of production including

Introduction

subsidies). As a result the only taxes included in the price will be taxes on the output process - for example business rates and vehicle excise duty - which are not specifically levied on the production of a unit of output. Basic prices exclude any transport charges invoiced separately by the producer. When a valuation at basic prices is not feasible producers' prices may be used.

Producers' prices

Producers' prices equals basic prices *plus* those taxes paid (other than VAT or similar deductible taxes invoiced for the output sold) per unit of output *less* any subsidies received per unit of output.

Purchasers' or Market prices

Essentially these are the prices paid by the purchaser and include transport costs, trade margins and taxes (unless the taxes are deductible by the purchaser), i.e.

Purchasers' price equals producers' price *plus* any non-deductible VAT or similar tax payable by the purchaser *plus* transport prices paid separately by the purchaser and not included in the producers' price. 'Purchaser's prices' are also referred to as 'market prices', for example 'GDP at market prices'.

The rest of the world: national and domestic

Domestic product (or income) includes production (or primary incomes generated and distributed) resulting from all activities taking place 'at home' or in the UK domestic territory. This will include production by any foreign-owned company in the United Kingdom but exclude any income earned by UK residents from production taking place outside the domestic territory. Thus gross domestic product is also equal to the sum of primary incomes distributed by resident producer units.

The definition of gross national income can be introduced by considering the primary incomes distributed by the resident producer units above. These primary incomes, generated in the production activity of resident producer units, are distributed mostly to other residents institutional units. For example, when a resident producer unit is owned by a foreign company, some of the primary incomes generated by the producer unit are likely to be paid abroad. Similarly, some primary incomes generated in the rest of the world may go to resident units. Thus, when looking at the income of the nation, it is necessary to exclude that part of resident producer's primary income paid abroad, but include the primary incomes generated abroad but paid to resident units; i.e.

Gross domestic product (or income)
    less
    primary incomes payable to non-resident units
    plus
    primary incomes receivable from the rest of the world
    equals
    Gross national income

Thus gross national income (GNI) at market prices is the sum of gross primary incomes receivable by resident institutional units/sectors. National income includes income earned by residents of the national territory, remitted (or deemed to be remitted in the case of direct investment) to the national territory, no matter where the income is earned.

GDP at constant market prices
    less
    trading gain
    equals
    Real gross domestic income (RGDI)

Real gross domestic income (RGDI)
    plus
    real primary incomes receivable from abroad
    less
    real primary incomes payable abroad
    equals
    Gross national income (GNI) at constant market prices

Real GNI at constant market prices
    plus
    real current transfers from abroad
    less
    real current transfers abroad
    equals
    Gross national disposable inome (GNDI) at constant market prices

Receivables and transfers of primary incomes, and transfers to and from abroad are deflated using the index of gross domestic final expenditure.

Gross domestic product: the concept of net and gross

The term *gross* refers to the fact that when measuring domestic production we have not allowed for an important phenomenon: capital consumption or depreciation. Capital goods are different from the materials and fuels used up in the production process because they are not used up in the period of account but are instrumental in allowing that process to take place. However, over time capital goods do wear out or become obsolete and in this sense gross domestic product does not give a true picture of value added in the economy. In other words, in calculating value added as the difference between output and costs we should include as a current cost that part of the capital goods used up in the production process; that is, the depreciation of the capital assets.

Net concepts are net of this capital depreciation, for example:
Gross domestic product
>minus
>consumption of fixed capital
>equals
>*Net* domestic product

However, because of the difficulties in obtaining reliable estimates of the consumption of fixed capital (depreciation), gross domestic product remains the most widely used measure of economic activity.

Symbols and conventions used

Symbols   In general, the following symbols are used:
- ..   not available
- -   nil or less than £500,000

In practice, in this edition, there may be some inconsistency in the use of these two symbols, with 'nil' appearing against certain items which should really be marked 'not available'.

£billion denotes £1,000 million.

Sign conventions

Resources and Uses

>Increase shown positive
>Decrease shown negative

Capital account

>Liabilities, net worth and Assets:

>Increase shown positive
>Decrease shown negative

Financial account

>Assets: net acquisition shown positive
>   net disposal shown negative
>Liabilities: net acquisition shown positive
>   net disposal shown negative

Balance sheet

>Assets and liabilities each shown positive
>Balance shown positive if net asset, negative if net liability

References:

1. *European System of Accounts 1995 (ESA 95)*, Eurostat
   ISBN 92 827 7954 8
2. *System of National Accounts 1993* (SNA 93); UN, OECD, IMF, EU
   ISBN 92 1 161352 3
3. *Introducing the ESA95 in the UK*   ISBN 0 11 621061 3
4. *National Accounts Concepts, Sources and Methods*
   ISBN 0 11 621062 1
5. *United Kingdom Input-Output Analyses 2001*
   ISBN 0 11 621476 7
6. *UK Environmental Accounts 1998*
   ISBN 0 11 621022 2

Economic Trends articles

Quarterly integrated economic accounts - The United Kingdom approach, Graham Jenkinson, *Economic Trends*, March 1997 (No 520)
ONS plans for the 2001 and 2002 Blue and Pink Book and Supply Use Tables, Jennie Tse, *Economic Trends*, May 2001 (No 570),
The development of the annual business inquiry, Gareth Jones, *Economic Trends*, November 2000 (No 564)
Developments in the measurement of general government output, Michael Baxter, *Economic Trends*, August 1998 (No 537)

Calendar of economic events

Calendar of economic events: 1980-2000

1980

Jan	Steel strike begins
Mar	Medium Term Financial Strategy announced
Jun	Britain becomes a net exporter of oil
May	Mount St Helens volcano erupts
Jun	Sixpence (2 1/2p) piece discontinued
Jun	Agreement to reduce UK's budget contribution to EEC
Oct	Dollar exchange rate peaks at $2.39 per £
Nov	Ronald Reagan elected US President

1981

Jan	Bottom of worst post-War slump in Britain
Feb	The Times sold to Rupert Murdoch
Mar	Budget announces windfall tax on banks
Apr	Rioting in Brixton
Apr	Social Democratic Party founded
Jul	Cuts in university spending announced
Jul	Rioting in Toxteth
Jul	Prince of Wales marries Lady Diana Spencer
Aug	Minimum Lending Rate (MLR) suspended
Dec	Heavy snow causes chaos

1982

Feb	Laker Airlines collapses
Mar	British naval task force sent to Falklands
Jun	Ceasefire in Falklands
Jul	Hire purchase controls abolished
Aug	Barclays Bank starts opening on Saturdays
Sep	Unemployment reaches 3 million
Nov	Channel 4 Television begins transmission

1983

Apr	Pound coin issued for the first time
Jun	£450m EC budget rebate granted to UK
Jul	£500m public spending cuts announced
Sep	3% target set for public sector pay
Oct	European Parliament freezes budget rebate

1984

Mar	Miners' strike begins
Jun	Robert Maxwell buys *Daily Mirror*
Jun	Fontainebleau Summit agrees permanent settlement of UK's contribution to EEC
Oct	Bank of England rescues Johnson Matthey
Nov	British Telecom plc privatised
Dec	Agreement to hand over Hong Kong to China in 1997

1985

Jan	FT Index reaches 1,000 for the first time
Mar	End of year-long miners' strike
Mar	Dollar exchange rate bottoms out at $1.05/£
Dec	NatWest, Barclays and Lloyds Banks announce 'free banking'

1986

Jan	Michael Heseltine resigns from Government over Westland Helicopters affair
Feb	Single European Act signed
Mar	Budget cuts basic rate of income tax to 29% and introduces Personal Equity Plans (PEPs)
Mar	Greater London Council abolished
Apr	Chernobyl nuclear reactor disaster
Oct	Bus services deregulated
Oct	*The Independent* newspaper founded
Nov	'Big Bang' deregulates dealing in the City
Dec	British Gas privatisation

1987

Jan	Prosecutions for insider dealing in Guinness case
Jan	British Airways privatisation
Mar	Budget reduces basic rate of tax to 27%
Oct	Hurricane strikes Britain
Oct	'Black Monday': collapse of stock market

1988

Mar	Budget reduces basic rate of tax to 25%; top rate to 40%
Mar	BL sold to BMW
Jun	Barlow-Clowes collapses
Jul	*Piper Alpha* oil rig disaster
Sep	Worst ever UK trade deficit announced
Nov	George Bush elected US President
Dec	Salmonella outbreak in Britain

1989

Mar	*Exon Valdez* oil spillage disaster in Alaska
Apr	Chinese authorities quell dissidents in Tiananmen Square
Jul	*Blue Arrow* report from DTI
Oct	Nigel Lawson resigns as Chancellor
Nov	Ford takes over Jaguar
Nov	Fall of Berlin Wall

1990

Mar	Budget introduces tax-exempt savings accounts (TESSAs)
Apr	BSE ('mad cow disease') identified
Apr	New Education Act brings in student loans
Apr	Community Charge ('poll tax') introduced
Aug	Kuwait invaded by Iraq
Oct	Official reunification of Germany
Oct	UK enters Exchange Rate Mechanism
Nov	John Major replaces Mrs Thatcher as PM
Nov	Privatisation of electricity boards

1991

Jan	NHS internal market created
Jan	Gulf War begins
Jan	Central Statistical Office (forerunner of ONS) celebrates its 50th anniversary
Feb	Gulf War ends
Mar	Air Europe collapses
Mar	Budget restricts mortgage interest relief to basic rate: Corporation Tax reduced and VAT increased
Jul	BCCI closed by Bank of England
Sep	Rioting in Cardiff, Oxford and Birmingham
Nov	Robert Maxwell drowns
Nov	Maastricht agreement signed with UK opt-outs
Dec	Mikhail Gorbachev replaced by Boris Yeltsin as President of the Soviet Union

1992

Jan	Russia agrees to join the IMF
Jan	Bill McLennan appointed as director of the Central Statistical Office and Head of the Government Statistical Service
Feb	'Delors Package' raises EC's spending limits to 1.37% of GDP to aid poorer member states
Mar	Budget raises lower rate of income tax to 20% and announces that from next year Budgets will be in the autumn
Mar	Midland Bank agrees merger with Hong Kong and Shanghai Bank
Apr	Conservatives win General Election
May	Swiss vote in a referendum to join the IMF and IBRD
May	Reform of EC Common Agricultural Policy agreed, switching from farm price support to income support
Sep	'Black Wednesday': UK leaves Exchange Rate Mechanism

Calendar of economic events

Oct	North American Free Trade Agreement (NAFTA) signed
Dec	Plan for National Lottery announced

1993

Jan	Council Tax announced as replacement for Community Charge
Jan	University status given to polytechnics
Mar	Budget imposes VAT on domestic fuel
Nov	Parliament votes to relax Sunday trading rules
Nov	First autumn Budget cuts public expenditure and increases taxes
Dec	Uruguay Round of tariff reductions approved

1994

Jan	European Economic Area formed linking EU and EFTA
Apr	Eurotunnel opens
Aug	IRA ceasefire begins
Oct	Brent Walker leisure group collapses
Nov	First draw of National Lottery
Dec	Coal industry privatised

1995

Jan	EU expanded to include Sweden, Finland and Austria
Jan	World Trade Organisation succeeds GATT
Feb	Barings Bank collapses
Aug	Hottest ever
Sep	Net Book Agreement suspended

1996

Jan	Gilt 'repo' market established
Mar	Rebates worth £1billion paid to electricity consumers after break-up of National Grid
Apr	Office for National Statistics created
May	Railtrack privatised, reducing public service borrowing requirement by £1.1 billion
Sep	Privatisation of National Power and PowerGen reduces PSBR by further £1.0 billion
Aug	CREST clearing system initiated

1997

Apr	Alliance and Leicester Building Society converts to bank
May	Labour Party wins General Election
May	Chancellor announces operational independence for the Bank of England, decisions on interest rates to be taken by a new Monetary Policy Committee
Jun	Halifax Building Society converts to a bank
Jun	Norwich Union floated on the stock market
Jun	Economic and Fiscal Strategy Report announces new format for public finances, distinguishing between current and capital spending
Jul	Gordon Brown presents his first Budget, setting inflation target of 2.5%
Jul	Woolwich Building Society converts to a bank
Jul	Bristol and West Building Society converts to a bank
Aug	Stock market falls in Far East, Hang Seng Index ending 20 per cent lower than a year earlier
Aug	Economic and financial crisis in Russia
Aug	Diana Princess of Wales dies in car accident in Paris
Dec	The first instalment of the windfall tax on utilities (£2.6 billion) is paid

1998

Apr	Sterling Exchange Rate Index hits its highest point since 1989
Apr	Mortgage payments rise as MIRAS is cut from 15% to 10%
Apr	The *New Deal* for the unemployed is introduced
June	The Bank of England's 'repo' rate is raised by 0.25% to a peak of 7.5%
June	The World Cup kicks-off in France
Aug	BP merge with Amoco to create the UK's largest company
Oct	The Working Time Directive, setting a 48-hour week, takes effect
Dec	The second instalment of the windfall tax on utilities (£2.6 billion) is paid
Dec	Ten of the eleven countries about to enter the euro harmonised interest rates at 3.0%

1999

Jan	Introduction of Euro currency
Mar	Allocation of new car registration letters switched from yearly in August to twice yearly
Mar	Budget, energy tax announced
Apr	Introduction of ISA's replaces PEP's and TESSA's
Apr	Introduction of national minimum wage
Apr	Advanced Corporation tax abolished
Jun	The Bank of England 'repo' rate reduced to low point of 5%
Nov	Jubilee Line extension completed
Dec	Pre-budget statement
Dec	Year 2000 preparations (Y2K)

2000

Jan	Confounding expectations, the millennium passed without any major problems
Feb	House price growth peaks at 15% in January and February
	Oil price rises to highest level in ten years
	The UK company Vodafone takes over the German company Mannesman for £113bn
	3rd generation mobile phone license auction raises £22.5bn for the government
May	Share prices in so-called internet companies start falling
	Competition commission finds that UK car prices high relative to EU prices
	BMW sells Rover and Ford shuts Dagenham plant
June	Inward investment in the UK hits record levels, with a large proportion made up of take-over deals
July	Hauliers and farmers stage large scale protests over the price of fuel
Aug	European banking regulators investigate £117bn of new loans made to telecommunications companies, reflecting concerns that banks have overlent to the sector
Dec	US GDP growth slows sharply, following prolonged expansion

United Kingdom National Accounts 2001, © Crown copyright 2001

Part 1

Main aggregates and summary accounts

Main aggregates and summary accounts

The National Accounts at a glance

Gross domestic product

In 2000 the output of the economy as measured by **gross domestic product** (GDP) at constant market prices was 2.9 per cent higher than in 1999, compared with a rise of 2.1 per cent in 1999 over 1998. Over the period 1980 to 2000 GDP at constant market prices has risen by an average of 2.3 per cent a year.

Money GDP (at current market prices) increased by 4.7 per cent between 1999 and 2000, compared to a 4.8 per cent increase in 1999 over 1998. Since 1980, money GDP has risen by an average of 7.8 per cent a year.

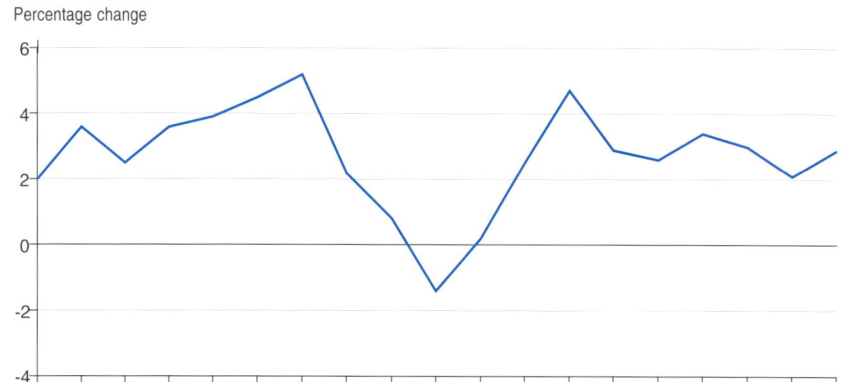

Annual changes in GDP at constant market prices

Percentage change

Gross domestic product deflator

This graph shows changes in the implied GDP deflator based on expenditure at market prices.

The annual rate of growth in the GDP expenditure deflator is 1.7 per cent in 2000 over 1999. This is the lowest annual increase since 1994 when it rose by 1.4 per cent.

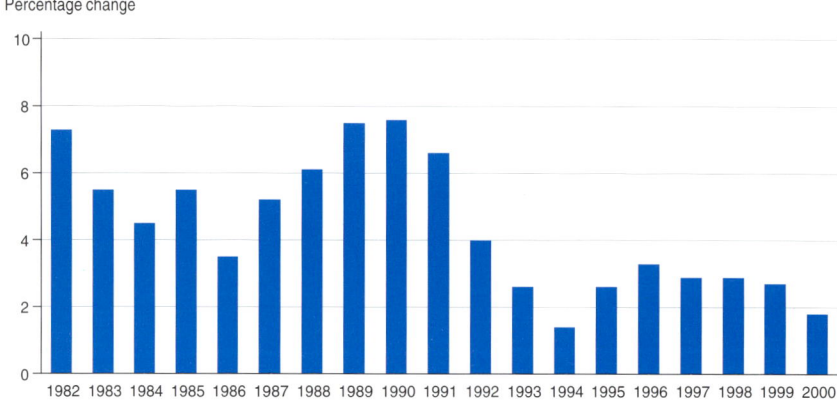

Annual changes in the GDP market prices deflator

Percentage change

GDP: contribution of expenditure components to growth in 2000.

The growth in the volume of GDP at constant market prices of 2.9 per cent in 2000 can be split amongst the various expenditure components. This table shows what effect the change in each component would have had if all other components had remained unchanged. The rise in household expenditure has been the strongest positive influence on growth. In contrast, the strongest negative influence on growth was net exports of goods and services.

Contributions to annual growth in GDP at constant market prices, 2000

Component	change in GDP £m	%
Households and NPISH final expenditure	21,340	2.7
General government final expenditure	2,383	0.3
GFCF	7,300	0.9
Change in inventories	-2,527	-0.3
Net exports	-5,281	-0.7
Other[1]	-88	0.0
Total	23,127	2.9

1 Comprises acquisition of valuables and the statistical discrepancy between the expenditure measure and the average measure of GDP

United Kingdom National Accounts 2001, © Crown copyright 2001

Main aggregates and summary accounts

Gross final expenditure: share by category of expenditure

Gross final expenditure (GFE) measures the sum of final uses of goods and services produced by the UK. In 2000, half of the total GFE was attributed to households and NPISH final consumption. Export of goods and services accounted for around a quarter and the remainder was divided equally between general government consumption and gross capital formation.

GFE at constant market prices: share by category of expenditure

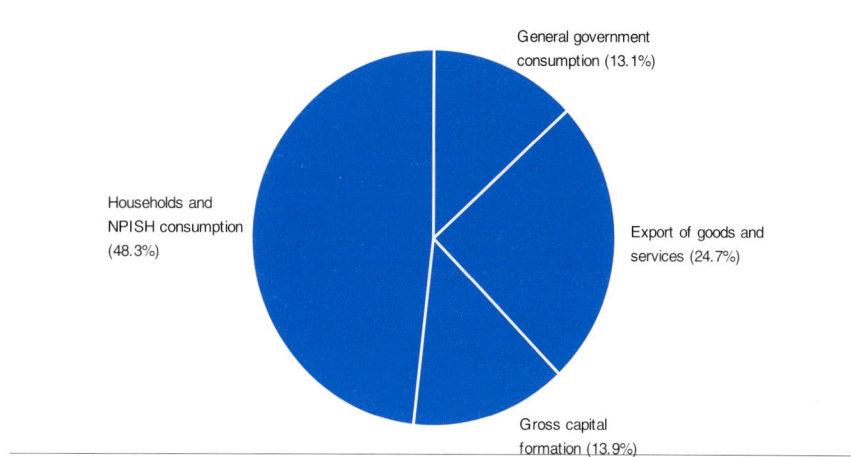

Gross Domestic Product: share by category of income

The income approach to GDP measures the income earned by individuals and corporations in the production of goods and services. In 2000, over half of GDP at current market prices was compensation of employees, which is largely comprised of wages and salaries. Total operating surplus, which includes corporations' gross trading profits accounted for over a quarter. Taxes on production and imports and subsidies, included to convert the estimate to market prices, accounted for the majority of the remainder.

GDP at current market prices: share by category of income

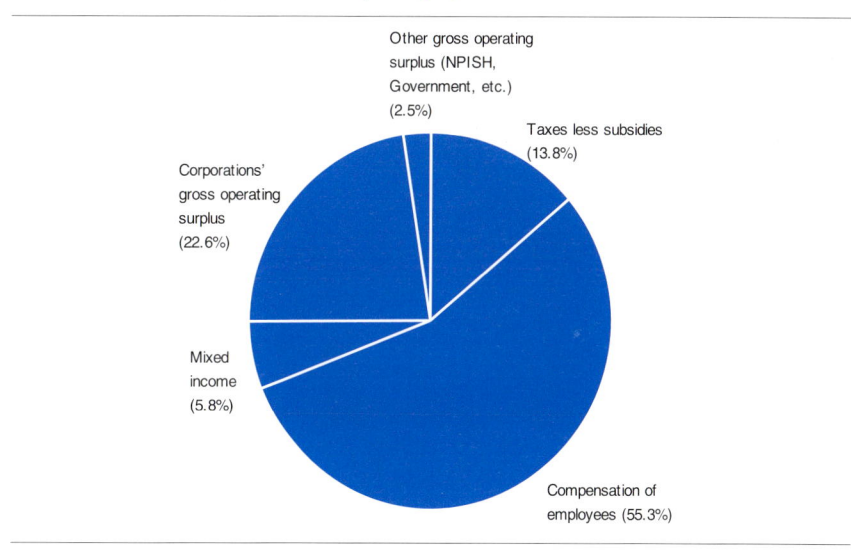

Gross value added at basic prices, by industry

In 2000 compared to 1999, growth in the output of the production sector was 1.7 per cent, while growth in the service sector was 3.4 per cent. Over the period from 1990 to 2000 the average annual increase in the output of the production sector was 1.1 per cent, whereas that for the service sector was 2.9 per cent.

GVA at basic prices, by industry

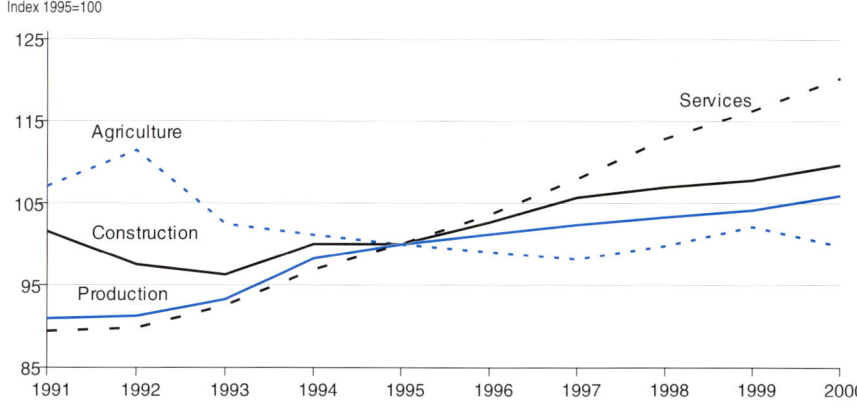

United Kingdom National Accounts 2001, © Crown copyright 2001

Main aggregates and summary accounts

Gross value added at basic prices, by industry, 1995

In 1995, the current base year, two thirds of total gross value added was from the services sector compared to a quarter from the production sector. Most of the remainder was attributed to the construction sector.

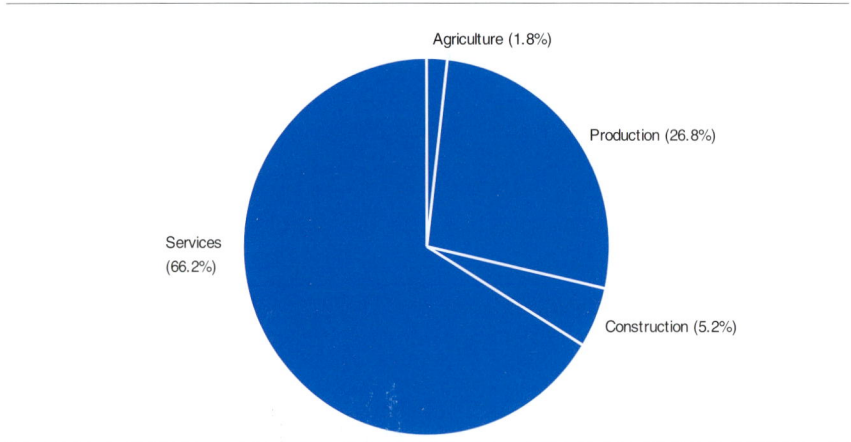

GVA at basic prices, by industry, 1995

Gross domestic product per head

GDP per head at constant market prices rose by 2.4 per cent in 2000 compared to 1.7 per cent in 1999.

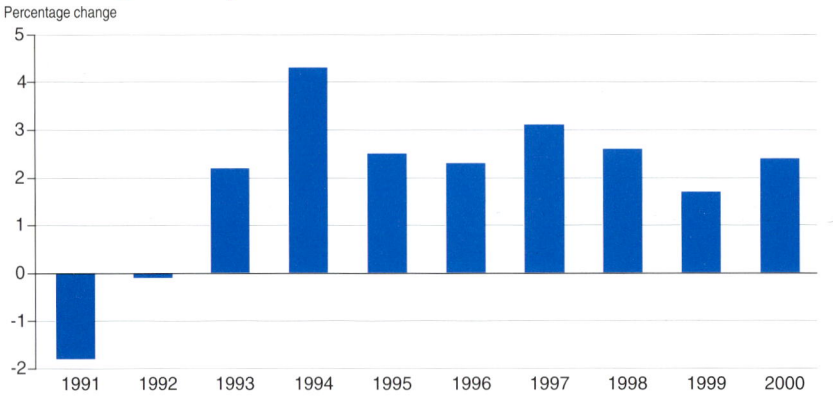

Annual changes in GDP per head

GDP and real household disposable income

Real household disposable income (RHDI) is the total resources available to the households sector after deductions.

RHDI rose strongly in 2000 by 4.4 per cent, while GDP at constant prices rose by 2.9 per cent. In the period 1990 to 2000, RHDI rose by an average of 2.7 per cent a year compared with an average increase in GDP of 2.2 per cent.

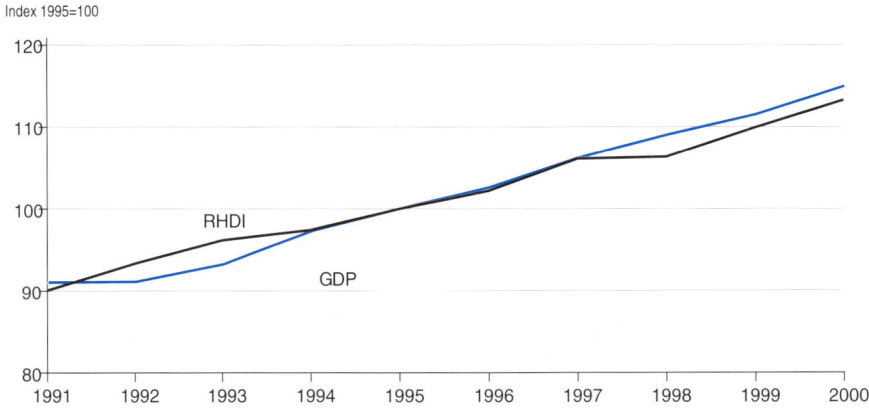

Comparison of GDP and real household disposable income

United Kingdom National Accounts 2001, © Crown copyright 2001

Part 1:
Main aggregates and summary accounts

UK GDP and national income (Tables 1.1, 1.2, 1.3, 1.4)

Gross domestic product at current prices

The three approaches and the need for balancing

An understanding of the United Kingdom system can begin with a brief discussion of gross domestic product (GDP). GDP is arguably the most important aggregate or summary indicator for purposes of economic analysis and comparisons over time. It measures total domestic activity and can be defined in three different ways:

- GDP is the sum of gross value added of the institutional sectors or the industries *plus* taxes and *less* subsidies on products (which are not allocated to sectors and industries). It is also the balancing item in the total economy production account.

- GDP is the sum of final uses of goods and services by resident institutional units (actual final consumption and gross capital formation), plus exports and minus imports of goods and services.

- GDP is the sum of uses in the total economy generation of income account (compensation of employees, taxes on production and imports less subsidies, gross operating surplus and gross mixed income of the total economy).

This is also the basis of estimating GDP. Use of three different methods which, as far as possible, use independent sources of information avoids sole reliance on one source and allows greater confidence in the overall estimation process.

The resulting estimates however, like all statistical estimates, contain errors and omissions; we obtain the best estimate of GDP (i.e. the published figure) by reconciling the estimates obtained from all three approaches. On an annual basis this reconciliation is carried out through the construction of the Input-Output Supply and Use Tables for the years for which data are available, and for subsequent periods by carrying forward the level of GDP set by the annual balancing process by using the quarterly movements in production, income and expenditure totals.

For years in which no input-output balance has been struck a statistical discrepancy exists between estimates of the total expenditure components of GDP and the total income components of GDP after the balancing process has been carried out. This statistical discrepancy is made up of two components which are shown in the accounts, namely:

the *statistical discrepancy (expenditure adjustment)*, which is the difference between the sum of the expenditure components and the definitive estimate of GDP, *plus*

the *statistical discrepancy (income adjustment)*, which is the difference between the sum of the income components and the definitive estimate of GDP *(with sign reversed)*.

As outlined in the framework above, the different approaches to the measurement of GDP provide a breakdown into different component parts and give different perspectives on the data. These approaches are described in more detail in turn below.

The income approach

The income approach provides estimates of GDP and its 'income' component parts at current market prices. The sources and methods of this approach are described in detail in Chapter 14 of *Concepts, Sources and Methods*[1].

As it suggests, the income approach adds up all income earned by resident individuals or corporations in the production of goods and services and is therefore the sum of uses in the generation of income account for the total economy (or alternatively the sum of primary incomes distributed by resident producer units).

However some types of income are not included - these are transfer payments like unemployment benefit, child benefit or state pensions. Although they do provide individuals with money to spend, the payments are made out of, for example, taxes and national insurance contributions. Transfer payments are a *redistribution* of existing incomes and do not themselves represent any addition to current economic activity. To avoid double counting, these transfer payments and other current transfers (for example taxes on income and wealth) are excluded from the calculation of GDP although they are recorded in the secondary distribution of income account.

In the UK the income measure of GDP is obtained by summing together:

> gross operating surplus,
> gross mixed income,
> compensation of employees (wages and salaries and employers' social contributions),
> taxes on production and imports
> *less* any subsidies on production.

Mixed income is effectively the operating surplus of unincorporated enterprises owned by households, which implicitly includes remuneration for work done by the owner or other members of the household. This remuneration cannot be identified separately from the return to the owner as entrepreneur.

Main aggregates and summary accounts

As most of these incomes are subject to tax the figures are usually obtained from data collected for tax purposes by the Inland Revenue. However, because there is some delay in providing good quality estimates by this method, other sources are used to provide initial estimates.

In the old UK system a 'stock appreciation adjustment' (as it was known) was required to remove the effects of holding gains on inventories resulting from revaluation; under ESA95 this adjustment is no longer shown. The operating surplus and mixed income are measures of profit that exclude any holding gains. (Holding gains result when, although no new goods or services have been produced, the value of inventories and fixed assets has increased simply as the result of an increase in the price of the item.)

National Statistics aims to cover the UK economy as comprehensively as possible. It is recognised that some income is not declared to the tax authorities, and to allow for this adjustments are routinely made to the GDP income measure. In 1999 the adjustment for undeclared income was about £14 billion, approximately one and a half per cent of GDP.

Although the income approach cannot be used to calculate constant price estimates directly (because it is not possible to separate income components into prices and quantities in the same way as for goods and services) some estimates are obtained indirectly. The expenditure-based *GDP deflator at market prices* (also known as the *index of total home costs*) is used to deflate the current market price estimates to provide a constant price version of the total income component of GDP.

Data on the income components can be found in Table 1.2.

The expenditure approach

The expenditure approach measures total expenditure on finished or final goods and services produced in the domestic economy or, alternatively, the sum of final uses of goods and services by resident institutional units *less* the value of imports of goods and services.

The total is obtained from the sum of final consumption expenditure by households, non-profit institutions serving households and government on goods and services, gross capital formation (capital expenditure on tangible and intangible fixed assets, changes in inventories and acquisitions *less* disposals of valuables) and net exports of goods and services.

This approach can be represented by the following equation:

$$GDP = C + G + I + X - M$$

Where: C = final consumption expenditure by households and NPISH sectors,
G = government consumption expenditure,
I = investment or gross capital formation,
X = exports and M = imports.

The data for these categories are estimated from a wide variety of sources including expenditure surveys, the government's internal accounting system, surveys of traders and the administrative documents used in the importing and exporting of some goods.

To avoid double counting in this approach it is important to classify consumption expenditures as either final or intermediate. *Final consumption* involves the consumption of goods purchased by or for the ultimate consumer or user. These expenditures are final because the goods are no longer part of the economic flow or being traded in the market place. *Intermediate consumption* on the other hand is consumption of goods and services which are used or consumed in the production process. Gross capital formation is treated separately from intermediate expenditure as the goods involved are not used up within the production process in an accounting period.

Exports include all sales to non-residents, and exports of both goods and services have to be regarded as final consumption expenditure, since they are final as far as the UK economy is concerned.

Imports of goods and services are deducted because although they are included directly or indirectly in final consumption expenditure they are not part of domestic production. What remains is what has been produced in the United Kingdom - gross domestic product using the expenditure approach.

Data on the current price expenditure components can be found in Table 1.2.

As well as GDP at current prices the expenditure approach is used to provide information on expenditure at constant prices. In constant price series, the transactions are revalued for all years to a fixed price level, that is, at the average prices of a selected year (known as the base year). The constant price series shows the change in GDP *after* the effects of inflation have been removed.

GDP at market prices

£ million

	At current prices	At constant 1995 prices
1991	586,149	650,085
1992	610,854	651,566
1993	642,327	667,804
1994	681,327	698,915
1995	719,176	719,176
1996	762,214	738,046
1997	811,067	763,472
1998	859,805	786,303
1999	901,269	803,019
2000	943,416	826,145

Main aggregates and summary accounts

As the constant price figures are valued at 1995 prices, 1995 is called the base year.

How do we remove the effects of inflation to obtain this constant price series? Two methods are used. For some series, price indices for particular goods and services - such as components of the retail prices index (RPI) or the producer price index (PPI) - are used to 'deflate' the current price series. For other series, constant price expenditure is assumed to be proportional to the volume of goods or services. The calculation of constant price series is explained below.

Constant price versions of GDP and its main expenditure components are found in Table 1.3.

The production approach

The production approach to the estimation of GDP, which is also referred to as the output approach, looks at the contribution to production of each economic unit; that is the value at basic prices of their total output *less* the value of the inputs used up in the production process. However, information on inputs is only available when the accounts are balanced through the Input-Output framework. The sum of this gross value added, *plus* taxes and *less* subsidies on products for all producers, is GDP at market prices: the production account balancing item. The following paragraphs give a brief overview of the methodology. It should be noted that the production approach concentrates on the basic price concept.

In theory, value added at constant prices should be estimated by double deflation; that is, deflating separately the inputs and the outputs of each economic unit (valued at constant prices) and then subtracting one from the other. But because it is hard to get reliable information from companies which would make this calculation possible on a timely basis, double deflation is only used in the estimation of output for the agriculture and electricity industries.

In practice, for the estimation of the value added of most other economic units in the economy, a simplifying assumption is made: at constant prices, changes from the base year in gross value added are assumed to be proportional to corresponding changes in the output produced. Movements in the gross value added by these industries at constant prices are then estimated by the use of output series. For industries whose outputs are goods, output can be estimated from the physical quantities of goods produced or from the value of output deflated by an index of price.

Apart from the use of output to measure value added at constant prices which accounts for around 80 per cent of the total of the production measure, a number of other kinds of indicator might be used as a proxy for the change in gross value added. For example, they may be estimated by changes in inputs, where the inputs chosen may be materials used, employment or some combination of these.

In the short term it is reasonable to assume that movements in value added can be measured this way. However, changes in the ratio of output and inputs to gross value added can be caused by many factors: new production processes, new products made and inputs used; and changes in inputs from other industries will all occur over time. Aggregated over all industries the impact of these changes will be lessened. In the longer term all indicators are under constant review, with more suitable ones being used as they become available. In addition, the ratio of the proxy series to value added is re-established every five years when the production measure is rebased.

The estimate of gross value added for all industries (the proxy for the quarterly production measure of GDP) is finally obtained by combining or 'weighting together' the estimates for each industrial sector according to its relative importance (as established in the Input-Output Supply and Use Tables) in the base year. Data can be found in Table 2.4.

Headline GDP

Gross domestic product at market prices, provides the key indicator of the state of the economy when measured at constant prices. This is sometimes called "headline" GDP. *Gross value added at constant basic prices*, another useful short-term indicator of growth in the economy is the headline measure for the production approach. It is compiled in a way which is relatively free of short-term fluctuations due to uncertainties of timing. The construction of *gross domestic product at constant factor cost* however, requires an adjustment for the relevant taxes and subsidies which can be subject to erratic changes. As a result the factor cost measure is less suitable as an indicator of short-term movements in the economy.

The figure below shows the distinction between market prices, basic prices and factor cost measures.

ESA95 code	
	Gross domestic product, at market prices
D.211	less value added taxes (VAT) on products
D.212, D.214	less other taxes on products (e.g. alcohol duty)
D.31	plus subsidies on products
	Gross value added, at basic prices
D.29	less taxes on production other than taxes on products (e.g. business rates, vehicle excise duty paid by businesses and operating licences)
	Gross value added, at factor cost

GDP at market prices includes taxes on production, whilst GDP at basic prices includes only those taxes on production, such as business rates which are not taxes on products and GDP at factor cost excludes all taxes on production. A more detailed explanation of taxes follows.

Main aggregates and summary accounts

Taxes

Taxes on production and imports including taxes on products (D.2), along with subsidies (D.3) (which can be regarded as negative taxes) make up the factor cost adjustment which represents the difference between GDP at market prices (sum of final expenditures) and GVA at factor cost (sum of incomes). This adjustment has to be added to the sum of incomes to obtain GDP at market prices. The basic price adjustment, which is the sum of *taxes on products (D.21)* less *subsidies on products (D.31)*, is the difference between GVA at basic prices and GDP at market prices. Details of the taxes which comprise *taxes on production* are included in Table 10.1.

Taxes on production and imports (D.2) are taxes paid during the production or import of goods and services. They are paid irrespective of whether profits are made. They comprise taxes on products (D.21) and other taxes on production (D.29).

Taxes on products (D.21) are taxes paid per unit of good or service consumed in the production process. They are included in the prices paid to suppliers of goods and services, so they are included in intermediate consumption at purchaser prices (except for deductible VAT). Fuel duty is an example.

Deductible VAT differs from other *taxes on products*. It is levied like other *taxes on products* but producers are reimbursed by government for the amount they pay when goods and services are bought. Intermediate consumption at *purchaser prices* is the price paid less deductible VAT refunded. *Producer prices* include the gross amount of VAT charged; there is no reduction to allow for VAT that might be reclaimed by the purchaser.

Suppliers are required to pay to government any *taxes on products* included in their prices. So the supplier's net revenue from selling the good is the selling price less the taxes on products included in the selling price. This is the *basic price*. It is the price at which market output is measured since it represents the producer's actual revenue.

Other taxes on production (D.29) are taxes which producers have to pay but they are not paid when goods and services are bought and so are not included in intermediate consumption. They are levied separately and are usually linked to the use of fixed capital or to the right to undertake certain regulated activities. Examples are non-domestic rates, vehicle excise duty, and various licence fees where the fee is much higher than the cost of administering the licence and so, in effect, is classified as taxation.

Other aggregates - Gross national disposable income

In the discussions so far we have yet to consider the measure which represents the total *disposable income* of the country's residents. Gross national income (GNI) represents the *total income* of UK residents and is the balancing item of the UK allocation of primary income account. It can also be derived from GDP by adding net employment income and net property income from the rest of the world. However there are two other areas which affect UK residents' command over resources.

First, there are flows into and out of the country which are not concerned with economic production. These are current transfers from abroad and current transfers paid abroad. They include transactions with the European Union, overseas aid and private gifts. An estimate of gross national disposable income (GNDI) is reached by adjusting GNI by the amount of net income received. GNI and GNDI are shown in Table 1.1.

Second, disposable income is affected by the terms of trade effect. Some of the expenditure by UK residents is on imported goods and services; some of the income earned by residents is from exports of goods and services. If UK export prices fell relative to the price of imports then the terms of trade effect would move against the UK; that is, residents would have to sell more exports to be able to continue to buy the same amount of imports. The purchasing power of UK residents would be diminished to this extent. Similarly, if UK export prices rose relative to prices of imports then the effect would be opposite: the purchasing power of residents would rise. An adjustment is made specifically for the terms of trade effect in calculating the constant price version of GNDI, also shown in Table 1.1.

UK GDP at constant prices (Tables 1.1, 1.3, 1.4)

When looking at the change in the economy over time, the main concern is usually whether more goods and services are actually being produced now than at some time in the past. Over time, changes in current price GDP show changes in the monetary value of the components of GDP and, as these changes in value can reflect changes in both price and volume, it is difficult to establish how much of an increase in the series is due either to increased activity in the economy or to an increase in the price level. As a result when looking at the real growth in the economy over time, it is useful to look at volume (or constant price) estimates of gross domestic product.

In constant price series, transactions are re-valued to a constant price level using the average prices of a selected year, known as the base year. In most cases the revaluation (known as deflation) is carried out by using price indices such as component series of the retail prices index or producer price index to deflate current price series at a detailed level of disaggregation.

Some constant price series are expressed as index numbers in which the constant price series are simply scaled proportionately to a value of 100 in the base year. These constant price index numbers are volume indices. They are of the 'base weighted' or 'Laspeyres' form. (see Chapter 2 of *Concepts, Sources and Methods*[1]) Aggregate price indices are of the 'Paasche' or 'current-weighted' form. They are generally calculated indirectly by dividing the current price value by the corresponding constant price value and multiplying by 100. Examples are the GDP deflator and the households' consumption deflator.

Value indices are calculated by scaling current price values proportionately to a value of 100 in the base year. By definition such a value index, if divided by the corresponding volume index and multiplied by 100, will give the corresponding price index.

In the UK economic accounts the expenditure approach is used to provide current price and volume measures of GDP. Because of the difficulties in accounting for changes in labour productivity it is not possible to obtain direct estimates of GDP at constant prices from the income data. However, an approximate aggregate measure is calculated by deflating the current price estimates using the GDP deflator derived from the expenditure measure. The production or output approach has traditionally been used to produce a constant price measure only. However, an experimental current price production measure has been developed largely independently of the constant price production measure, which is used to allocate the industry breakdown of current price output for the latest year.

In the expenditure approach all of the components are expressed in terms of the average prices prevailing in the base year, and constant price GDP is aggregated from these. The output approach involves weighting together the detailed components, expressed in index number form, according to their relative importance in the base year. The choice of base year can be very important.

The base year and the need for rebasing

Volume measures of GDP are compiled over a set time period, with reference to a given base year. For example, from the 1998 *Blue Book*, volume measures for the UK economic accounts for recent years are compiled using the base year 1995. In theory because the base year fixes the price structure used for comparison it should be selected because it most closely reflects the price structure of the period covered. In practice this is not easy and the base year is simply moved forwards, or rebased, every five years in line with international recommendations, though there is a degree of flexibility in defining the 'set time period' to which this base refers.

The 1995 price structure has been used to compile the data from 1994 onwards. This means that for these years the expenditure components of GDP will be calculated in terms of average 1995 prices, and the components of production will be indexed and weighted together using value added in 1995.

This rebasing is required because of the need to update the pricing structure used. Comparisons of the volume series over time are complicated by changes in the relative prices of different goods and services and by qualitative changes in the goods and services themselves. As time passes some goods escalate in price more rapidly than others. Others change so much that they become, in effect, different goods or services from those produced previously under the same name. Because of these changes the relative prices of goods and services in the base year become less representative of the relative values put on them in the current period and the changes in measured volume will not be representative of recent growth.

However, rebasing does not mean that the whole series of constant price estimates (some going back as far as 1948) are recalculated using the relative weights of the new base year. This would mean imposing inappropriate weights on estimates for earlier periods: as already mentioned the base year is only used to compile estimates over a set time period. So currently, although constant price and volume estimates are expressed as 'at 1995 prices', for series prior to 1994 more appropriate pricing structures will have been used and for them 1995 is only being used as a reference year.

In order to link all of the constant price estimates a process called *chain linking* is used. Each series is divided into several blocks of years, and each block of years is associated with a base year and link year. (See chain linking blocks below.)

Chain linking blocks are:

Period	Base year	Link year	
1948 to 1957	1958	1958	
1958 to 1962	1963	1963	
1963 to 1968	1963	1968	Output
1968 to 1972	1970	1973	Output
1963 to 1972	1970	1973	Expenditure and income
1973 to 1977	1975	1978	
1978 to 1983	1980	1983	
1983 to 1986	1985	1986	
1986 to 1994	1990	1994	
1994 to present	1995		

Within each of these blocks all constant price figures are calculated with reference to the same base year. In the link years, figures are calculated with reference to two consecutive base years, so that a linking factor may be obtained and the whole series, as published, may be shown with reference to the latest base year. By this process the whole period is rescaled to the same base year, but within each block the relative prices used to re-value to constant prices are those most appropriate to that period.

Reasonable comparisons can be made between the constant price values for any pair of years which fall within the same block. Otherwise comparisons between any two years which fall in different blocks give only a general indication of changes in the volume measured.

The choice of the link year is significant as it is important to find a period

Main aggregates and summary accounts

where relative prices are as stable as possible. For example, 1986 was chosen as the link year between 1985 and 1990 prices because relative prices stabilised in 1986 following the dramatic fall in oil prices in 1985. As a result it was thought more appropriate to measure growth in the period from 1983 to 1986 using 1985 prices and the period from 1986 onwards using 1990 prices.

The effects of rebasing

For most types of expenditure, rebasing has the effect of reducing the estimates of growth slightly for periods after the link year. This reflects normal behaviour by consumers who will tend, on average, to increase their consumption of the goods and services whose unit prices have fallen or grown the least, in substitution for goods and services whose unit prices have grown more. Thus when rebasing takes place the weight given to the products whose consumption has been increased will be increased, and the weight of the products whose consumption has been reduced will also be reduced. A similar principle holds for the output components. At each rebasing an article is published in *Economic Trends* evaluating its effects, most recently in June 1998[2].

At the same time as the estimates are rebased, component series are reviewed to improve coverage, sources and methods. These changes when taken along with the usual revisions to estimates normally have a bigger impact on the resulting series than rebasing itself.

The future of rebasing and the introduction of annual chain linking

The UK will be moving to annually weighted and chained estimates of volumes, as recommended in SNA93. This is because changes in relative prices can cause fixed-base indices to misrepresent volume growth.

Requirements for the delivery of chain-linked and harmonised volume estimates to Eurostat, the statistical office of the European Union, were laid down in a Commission Decision of November 1998. The UK will be introducing annually chain-linked estimates of GDP with the 2003 Blue Book. An article giving more details of the changes was published in the November 1999 edition of *Economic Trends*[3]. A further article updating this information and illustrating some of the effects on the accounts will be published in the October 2001 edition of *Economic Trends*[4].

Population, employment and GDP per head (Table 1.5)

Population and employment data are supplementary to the system of accounts. The estimated population of the UK is as at 30th June and includes all those resident in the UK, whatever their nationality. They include members of both UK and non-UK armed forces and their dependants stationed in the UK and exclude *members of H.M. armed forces* stationed in the rest of the world. This is recognised as not being in strict accord with ESA95 requirements, which are for all UK armed forces and dependants, wherever stationed, to be included and all non-UK ones to be excluded. At present, this is the most appropriate estimate available; it is used to calculate GDP per head.

The total employment data are from the UK Labour Force Survey (LFS) which is recognised as the most appropriate source for coherent national aggregate labour market estimates. The LFS is a household survey which uses definitions which are consistent with the International Labour Organisation recommendations and have been adopted by all EU member countries. The coverage of the LFS is people living in private households and, from 1992, student halls of residence and NHS accommodation; it is not precisely consistent with either the home population data or the ESA95 requirements.

The employment data in the table are estimates of people according to their economic and employment status. They are not comparable with estimates of jobs, as shown in Table 2.5, as some people have more than one job. The total employment figures include people on government sponsored training and employment programmes and, from 1992, unpaid family workers.

UK summary accounts (Tables 1.6.0 - 1.6.9)

The UK summary accounts show the full set of accounts for the UK total economy. The accounts comprise the goods and services account, the production account, the distribution and use of income account and the accumulation accounts. The structure of the accounts is explained in the introduction.

UK summary accounts by sector (Tables 1.7.1 - 1.7.9)

The framework

As can be seen in Table 1.7, the UK sector accounts can be used to show the economic accounting framework in considerable detail by elaborating the accounts in three different dimensions:
- the institutional sectors;
- the types of transaction;
- the national and sector balance sheets.

The institutional sectors

The first dimension involves the breakdown of the current account into institutional sectors grouped broadly according to their roles in the economy. Examples of these roles are: income distribution, income redistribution, private consumption, collective consumption, investment, financial intermediation, etc. Most units have more than one role but a natural classification is to distinguish between corporations, government and households. The rest of the world sector is also identified as having a role although it is obviously not part of the domestic economy.

Main aggregates and summary accounts

The types of transaction

The second dimension is that of the type of transaction which relates to the particular account within which the transaction appears. These can be grouped broadly according to purpose, whether current, capital or financial.

Summary of the UK institutional sectors	
Sectors and sub-sectors	**ESA95 code**
Non-financial corporations	S.11
Public	S.11001
National private and foreign controlled	S.11002/3
Financial corporations	S.12
Central bank	S.121
Other monetary financial institutions	S.122
Other financial intermediaries	S.123
Financial auxiliaries	S.124
Insurance corporations and pension funds	S.125
General government:	S.13
Central government	S.1311
Local government	S.1313
Households	S.14
Non-profit institutions serving	
households (NPISH)	S.15
Rest of the world	S.2

The balance sheets

To complete the full set of accounts the system includes balance sheets and a reconciliation of the changes that have brought about the change between the beginning and the end of the period. At present the UK only compiles the former.

In theory the net lending or borrowing from the capital account for each sector should equal the net borrowing or lending from the financial account. In practice, because of errors and omissions in the accounts, a balance is rarely achieved and the difference is known as the *statistical discrepancy* although, across all accounts, when an Input-Output balance is available, these sum to zero. Consolidating the current and accumulation accounts would provide a balanced account which would look like many of the presentations of commercial accounts.

Accuracy and bias

National Statistics strives to publish timely, consistent and coherent estimates of GDP which accurately represent productive activity in the economy. The basis of these estimates is strengthened by the interrelationships within the system, and the subsequent requirement that the many (and often independent) data sources are internally consistent. However, it remains very difficult to comment on the accuracy of GDP.

Estimates of GDP are built from numerous sources of information: business surveys, household and other social surveys, administrative information and survey data from the Inland Revenue and many other sources. Data are collected monthly, quarterly, annually or in some cases from ad hoc surveys. Some of the resulting estimates which feed into GDP will be firmly based whilst others may be weak.

Sampling errors can be calculated for estimates derived from random samples. At present sampling errors are calculated for several surveys which feed into GDP, though for other surveys there remain technical problems to be solved before reliable estimates of error can be estimated. A programme of work is currently underway which will lead to the publication of sampling errors for all major ONS business surveys.

In addition to sampling errors, reliability is also affected by non-sampling errors such as limitations in coverage and measurement problems. Though there is limited information about non-sampling errors it is likely that for some surveys non-sampling errors are the more important source of error. Data validation by survey statisticians, additional consistency checks performed by compilers and the inclusion of coverage adjustments where survey sources are known to have shortcomings reduce non-sampling error and improve the quality of the accounts.

Even if the reliability of individual data sources were known, the complexity of the process by which GDP is estimated is such that it would be difficult to build up an overall estimate of reliability from the component series. The process of bringing together the three approaches to GDP into one measure, which uses detailed supply and demand balances, and brings in extra information about the reliability of the raw data and consistency with other sources, adds significantly to the reliability of the overall estimate of GDP, but this reliability cannot be measured scientifically. Our current approach to measuring reliability is to use the evidence from analyses of revisions to growth rates, outlined below.

Testing for bias in the initial estimates of GDP

ONS regularly monitors the revisions to growth rates of the components of GDP, in terms of income, output and expenditure. The revision series analysed are the difference between the inital estimate of annual constant price GDP growth and the corresponding 'final' estimates published two years later when that year's growth appears in the Blue Book for the second time. The growth rates compared are year-on-year annual growth rates.

In the analysis the revisions to initial estimates of growth rates of components of GDP are tested for bias, or in statistical terminology, to discover if the mean revision is significantly different from zero. The revisions are also analysed for the effects of economic cycles; that is,

Main aggregates and summary accounts

whether the expansion or contraction phases of the economy cause any bias to emerge.

The results of the latest analysis published in Economic Trends (March 2001)[5] relate to data from 1970 to 1998 (the latest data to have been published in two Blue Books). In selecting the sample period it is necessary to balance the number of years on which the test is based (the higher the number, the more robust the test statistics) and the need to assume comparability of the annual GDP data over that period of time. The main result is that the average mean revision to real annual GDP growth is statistically biased for the period under consideration, but the mean revision is 0.2 percentage points, relatively low compared to the average annual GDP growth for the period of 2.0 per cent. Furthermore, estimation of GDP growth has improved over the past 30 years, with the average bias and volatility of the revisions to the initial estimates of GDP growth falling over this period. The 1990s has seen a fall in the mean revision to the initial estimate of GDP to an average revision of 0.1 percentage point, compared to 0.3 percentage points in the 1970s.

Of the components of GDP, research showed that only gross operating surplus and gross fixed capital formation show statistically significant bias, with mean revisions over to period of 0.9 and 0.7 percentage points respectively.

Examining the bias visually over periods of economic growth and contraction shows that in years of strong growth (defined as growth of above 3.0 per cent per annum) the average revision is 0.3 percentage points. In contrast, GDP tends to be revised downwards after a period of negative or negligible growth. However, there are too few data points to establish a statistically significant relationship between the size of the revision and GDP growth.

ONS regularly looks at bias in initial estimates and has not to date found reason to put in bias correction factors, although the information is used in the GDP balancing procedure. Regular monitoring of the revisions to estimates continues, and the results are published in Economic Trends.

Balances

Further assessment of the reliability of the consolidated economic and sector accounts can be gained by examination of the capital and financial accounts which should, in theory, show a balance between the net lending/borrowing in the capital account and financial account for each sector. However, because of errors and omissions in the accounts, such a balance is rarely achieved. The resulting *statistical discrepancy items* required to equate these accounts are shown in the *Blue Book*.

These discrepancies provide a measure of reliability as they reflect errors and omissions in the accounts. Some components of the accounts (for example, estimates for general government) provide excellent coverage and are very reliable whilst others (for example life insurance and pension funds) are less fully covered. A detailed table, which looks specifically at the reliability of components of the sector financial accounts, is published in *Financial Statistics Explanatory Handbook*. However, because of the many sources of information that feed into the economic accounts it is not possible to generalise these 'reliability measures' to the aggregate estimates.

Spurious accuracy and rounding to the nearest £million

One final point must also be made about the reliability of the statistics. In most of the published tables no attempt is made to round estimates beyond the nearest £million. In some instances this shows figures which appear to have more precision than evidence warrants.

The reasons for this presentation are as follows:

- Rounded figures can distort differences over time or between items.
- Some of the estimates in the tables are fairly precise and, if such an estimate is small, rounding would unnecessarily distort what it shows; yet if such series were not rounded to the nearest £million the major aggregates of which they are components would appear precise even though other components were heavily rounded.
- Not rounding beyond the nearest £million aids users who prepare derived statistics, by avoiding the accumulation of rounding errors which can occur when a number of rounded numbers are manipulated.

In presenting numbers to the nearest £million, the rounding is usually such that the components add to the total at current prices, so that the accounts balance. In particular the quarterly estimates, both before and after seasonal adjustment, add up to the calendar year totals. However, there are some small differences between the sum of component series and the total shown, due to rounding.

References

1. *National Accounts Concepts, Sources and Methods.* ISBN 0 11 621062 1
2. Rebasing the National Accounts, Francis Jones, Economic Trends, June 1998 (No. 535)
3. The Development of Chain-Linked and Harmonised Estimates of GDP at Constant prices, Anna Brueton, *Economic Trends*, November 1999 (Number 552)
4. The Effects of Annual Chain-linking on the Output Measure of GDP, Amanda Tuke and Geoff Reed, *Economic Trends*, October 2001 (Number 575)
5. Revisions Analysis of Initial Estimates of Annual Constant Price GDP and its Components, *Economic Trends*, March 2000 (Number 556)

Main aggregates and summary accounts

Economic Trends Articles

Annual Constant Price GDP and its Components, *Economic Trends*, March 2001 (Number 568)

Annual Coherence Adjustments in the National Accounts, Stephen Penneck and Sanjiv Mahajan, *Economic Trends*, October 1999 (Number 551)

Improvements to Economic Statistics, Tim Andrews, *Economic Trends*, February 2000 (Number 555)

Summary of methodological Changes

As explained in the Preface, this edition of the Blue Book contains a number of significant changes and data revisions that have been taken back as far as the data exists, which is 1948 for some series. These changes arise from the development of new methodology; new classifications; and new and enhanced data sources as well as a few changes to bring us in line with ESA95 recommendations. An analysis of revisions since last year's *Blue Book* is shown in table B.

This introduction does not aim to give a comprehensive description all the changes implemented this year, which are described more fully in an *Economic Trends* article published in May 2001 but rather to give users an overview of the more important changes.

The key developments and changes included this year are: the use of Annual Business Inquiry (ABI) data; estimates for personal imports and smuggling of alcohol and tobacco; expansion of the use of direct measures of government output; changes to the treatment of several taxes; resectorisation of government market activities; review of our adjustments to exclude the offshore territories from the UK; and a new treatment for interest rate swaps.

Inclusion of results for the new Annual Business Inquiry (ABI)

An *Economic Trends* article published in November 2000 describes the development of the ABI in detail. This is a new, integrated survey of employment and accounting information replacing several annual survey systems. The ABI was first conducted in respect of the year 1998 and estimates for growth for that year were, therefore, included in last year's Blue Book. However, the less restrictive revisions policy for this year's exercise means that revisions to levels have been made as far as appropriate.

Inclusion of estimates for personal imports and smuggling of alcohol and tobacco

Under the ESA95 and the SNA93, estimates for tobacco and alcohol smuggling are included within the boundary of economic activity in the National Accounts. Until now, estimates for household final consumption expenditure for alcohol and tobacco were based on the duty received by HM Customs and Excise. As a result, imports and expenditure on smuggled alcohol and tobacco were not included. Associated retail or wholesale activity and mixed income were similarly not included in output measures, or in imports. Estimates for these have been derived through a research project by the ONS with the assistance of HM Customs and Excise and are included this year.

Expansion of the use of direct measures of government output

The ONS has, over the last few years been developing improved methodology for measuring government output at constant prices. This methodology measures the output of general government directly rather than deriving it using volumes of inputs such as staff numbers or deflated intermediate consumption. It is also, therefore, able to take account of productivity and efficiency changes and is recommended by SNA93. Around fifty three per cent of the government sector is already measured in this manner and the coverage of this methodology has been expanded this year to include Local Authority Personal Social Services (LAPSS) and Fire Brigades, increasing coverage to sixty one per cent. In addition, this year sees the application of all these new measures to earlier periods.

Trade in Services

Previously, flows for the majority of financial and other business services were measured on a net exports basis. This years estimates can now be shown on a gross basis showing exports and imports separately.

Taxes and subsidies

A number of changes to taxes and subsidies are included this year. There has been a review of the allocation of taxes and subsidies between those on products and those on production. We have also extended our methodology to measure taxes and subsidies on an accrued rather than cash basis.

Resectorisation of government market activities

Following a review of the implementation of ESA95, where separate institutional accounts are available, market activities previously included in the government sector have been reclassified to the public corporations sector. These include the Local Authority Housing Revenue Account, Export Credit Guarantee Department as well as some other local authority companies and central trading bodies.

Economic territory

The methodology used to derive adjustments made in 1998 to exclude the offshore territories from the UK territorial coverage, in line with ESA95 requirements, has been reviewed. As a result, the quality of these adjustments has been improved and the changes impact mostly on investment income.

Main aggregates and summary accounts

Interest rate swaps

An article in the March 2000 edition of Economic Trends described our plans to reclassify the settlement flows on interest rate swaps and forward rate agreements. Previously they have been included in figures for portfolio investment income in line with the original version of SNA93. However SNA93 was revised at the end of 1999 and these flows have been reclassified to a special financial derivatives category within the financial account.

Changes since last year's Blue Book

An analysis of revisions since last year's Blue Book is shown in Table B. A substantial package of methodological improvements and data changes has been incorporated in this year's edition. These changes have resulted in revisions to some series back to the start of the National Accounts dataset in 1948.

A major source of the revisions has been the ONS Annual Business Inquiry (ABI). In addition, the annual inquiry data covered within the ABI has reported data for 1999 for the first time. This has led to significant upward revisions to household expenditure, changes in inventories and exports of services. However, these are partly offset by downward revisions to gross fixed capital formation. The most significant new information available relates to sales by manufacturers to final consumers and has led to upward revisions to gross value added and household expenditure back to 1986.

These estimates incorporate for the first time significant revisions made to the Producer Price Index for computers, first released in June 2001. The new index shows sharper price falls of computers from 1996 onwards and has led to higher estimates for production within manufacturing output, gross fixed capital formation and imports and exports of goods.

As usual the Blue Book exercise has taken on the latest Inland Revenue estimates used in estimating incomes of households, non-financial corporations and the self-employed. There are substantial upward revisions in 1999 from the latest Inland Revenue data for non-financial corporations' profits included within the operating surplus for that sector.

Within the income measure there have been some major reallocations of income between sectors following various methodological changes.

The ONS has reviewed the allocation of income earned by the self-employed. After consultation estimates with Inland Revenue the proportion of income allocated to partnerships within the non-financial corporations sector has been reduced, while there are substantial upward revisions to mixed income received by the household sector.

Within the household sector estimates of rental income received are now included within mixed income, they were formally included in the household operating surplus.

There are significant upward revisions to the operating surplus of insurance corporations, included within financial corporations' operating surplus, following a review of methodology.

Main aggregates and summary accounts

 Revisions since ONS Blue Book, 2000 edition

		1992	1993	1994	1995	1996	1997	1998	1999
National accounts aggregates									
At current prices									
Gross domestic product at market prices	YBHA	2 689	2 971	3 733	5 196	6 156	5 665	8 151	10 163
less Basic price adjustment	NQBU	1 742	887	713	786	565	100	2 130	2 524
Gross value added at basic prices	ABML	947	2 084	3 020	4 410	5 591	5 565	6 021	7 639
At 1995 prices									
Gross domestic product at market prices	ABMI	1 278	2 377	4 299	5 196	5 843	5 551	8 366	8 653
less Basic price adjustment	NTAQ	278	289	716	786	446	650	2 053	2 327
Gross value added at basic prices	ABMM	980	2 049	3 583	4 410	5 397	4 901	6 313	6 326
Expenditure components at current prices									
Domestic expenditure on goods and services at market prices									
Households	ABPB	2 611	2 862	3 135	4 914	5 959	5 067	5 674	3 186
Non-profit making institutions serving households	ABNV	–	–	–	–	–	–	145	134
General government	NMRK	–16	121	–119	–44	19	738	114	3 173
Gross fixed capital formation	NPQX	305	–203	924	1 088	87	243	3 468	–2 964
Changes in inventories	ABMP	–	–	–	–	–	–	–1	6 921
Acquisitions less disposals of valuables	NPJO	–19	–20	–23	–29	27	–65	–57	–116
Total exports	KTMW	800	1 562	1 741	1 097	2 788	2 296	3 327	7 071
Statistical discrepancy (expenditure)	GIXM	–	–	–	–	–	–	–	464
Total imports	KTMX	992	1 351	1 925	1 830	2 724	2 614	4 519	7 706
Expenditure components at constant 1995 prices									
Domestic expenditure on goods and services at market prices									
Households	ABPF	1 178	2 192	3 888	4 914	6 074	6 037	5 113	4 893
Non-profit making institutions serving households	ABNU	–	–	–	–	–	–	153	217
General government	NMRU								
Gross fixed capital formation	NPQR	310	–240	919	1 088	934	421	4 655	–2 806
Changes in inventories	ABMQ	–	–	–	–	–	–	–1	6 363
Acquisitions less disposals of valuables	NPJP	–	–	–25	–29	4	–66	–58	–110
Total exports	KTMZ	926	1 691	1 782	1 097	2 668	2 209	3 263	8 506
Statistical discrepancy (expenditure)	GIXS	–	–	–	–	–	–	–	414
Total imports	KTNB	1 133	1 347	1 975	1 830	3 038	4 334	6 697	10 571
Income components at current prices									
Compensation of employeees	HAEA	677	1 339	–315	1 321	948	572	1 214	2 813
Gross operating surplus									
Public non-financial corporations	NRJT	4 370	4 982	5 484	5 620	5 742	5 553	6 162	6 638
Private non-financial corporations	NRJK	–2 596	–2 171	–200	–921	–1 060	–907	–160	3 860
Financial corporations	NQNV	–2 008	–667	–2 908	–2 239	–1 835	–3 345	–690	–3 470
FISIM	-NSRV	1 911	456	3 291	2 284	2 977	3 282	–266	–408
General government	NMXV	–4 544	–4 850	–5 176	–5 123	–5 429	–5 160	–5 606	–5 334
Household sector	QWLS	–1 881	–2 127	–2 156	–1 919	–1 753	–1 947	–882	–2 861
Mixed income	HAXH	5 649	6 244	5 983	6 408	7 441	8 796	7 481	8 808
Taxes on production and imports	NZGX	1 385	–156	187	265	–426	–224	1 457	663
less subsidies	-AAXJ	–274	–79	–457	–500	–449	–955	–559	642
Statistical discrepancy (income)	GIXQ	–	–	–	–	–	–	–	–1 188
Output components index at constant 1995 basic prices									
Agriculture, forestry and fishing	GDQA	1.4	1.3	1.2	–	–2.9	–5.3	–1.9	–0.9
Mining and quarrying including oil and gas extraction	CKYX	–	–	–	–	–	–	–0.1	0.2
Manufacturing	CKYY	–	–	–	–	0.3	0.3	0.6	0.9
Electricity, gas and water supply	CKYZ	–	–	–0.1	–	–0.2	–	–0.1	0.1
Construction	GDQB	–0.8	–0.8	–0.8	–	1.2	1.0	0.9	1.4
Services	GDQS	0.1	–	0.1	–	0.3	0.2	0.6	0.7
Gross value added at basic prices	CGCE	–0.5	–0.4	–0.1	–	0.2	–	0.3	0.2

United Kingdom National Accounts 2001, © Crown copyright 2001

Main aggregates and summary accounts

1.1 UK national and domestic product
Main aggregates: index numbers and values
At current and constant 1995 prices

			1983	1984	1985	1986	1987	1988	1989	1990	1991
	INDICES (1995=100)										
	VALUES AT CURRENT PRICES										
B.1*g	Gross domestic product at current market prices ("money GDP")	YBEU	42.0	45.1	49.4	53.0	58.3	65.2	71.5	77.5	81.5
B.1g	Gross value added at current basic prices	YBEX	42.9	45.8	50.1	53.4	58.7	65.5	72.2	78.3	81.9
	VALUES AT 1995 PRICES										
B.1*g	Gross domestic product at 1995 market prices	YBEZ	73.3	75.2	77.9	81.0	84.6	89.0	90.9	91.6	90.4
B.6*g	Gross national disposable income at 1995 market prices	YBFP	74.7	76.3	78.3	81.3	84.3	88.9	90.8	91.4	91.2
B.1g	Gross value added at 1995 basic prices	CGCE	73.3	75.0	78.0	80.8	84.3	88.3	90.3	91.3	90.3
	PRICES										
	Implied deflator of GDP at market prices (expenditure based, "total home costs per unit of output")	YBGB	57.4	60.0	63.3	65.5	68.9	73.1	78.6	84.6	90.2
	VALUES AT CURRENT PRICES (£ million)										
	Gross measures, before deduction of fixed capital consumption **at current market prices**										
B.1*g	Gross domestic product at current market prices ("money GDP")	YBHA	302 512	324 227	354 952	381 317	419 631	468 386	514 168	557 300	586 149
D.1+D.4	Employment, property and entrepreneurial income from the rest of the world (receipts *less* payments)	YBGG	191	1 190	−997	1 694	917	753	−792	−2 979	−3 307
D.21-D.31	Subsidies (receipts) *less* taxes (payments) on products from/to the rest of the world	-QZOZ	−1 958	−1 934	−2 508	−3 175	−3 907	−3 168	−4 202	−5 181	−3 566
D.29-D.39	Subsidies on production	NHQR	31	18	18	47	16	18	35	43	54
B.5*g	Gross national income at current market prices	ABMX	300 776	323 501	351 465	379 883	416 656	465 985	509 209	549 183	579 330
D.5,6,7	Current transfers from the rest of the world (receipts *less* payments)	-YBGF	536	350	−434	1 034	333	−340	−267	215	2 287
B.6*g	Gross national disposable income at current market prices	NQCO	301 312	323 851	351 031	380 917	416 989	465 645	508 942	549 398	581 617
	adjustment to current basic prices										
B.1*g	Gross domestic product at current market prices	YBHA	302 512	324 227	354 952	381 317	419 631	468 386	514 168	557 300	586 149
-D.21 +D.31	Adjustment to current basic prices (*less* taxes *plus* subsidies on products)	-NQBU	−28 060	−31 331	−34 489	−39 405	−43 917	−49 199	−52 646	−55 862	−62 214
B.1g	Gross value added at current basic prices	ABML	274 452	292 896	320 463	341 912	375 713	419 183	461 522	501 438	523 935
	Net measures, after deduction of										
-K.1	fixed capital consumption	-NQAE	−40 140	−43 514	−46 668	−50 005	−54 685	−59 658	−63 901	−68 617	−74 458
B.1*n	Net domestic product at current market prices	NHRK	262 372	280 713	308 284	331 315	364 945	408 724	450 267	488 683	511 691
B.5*n	Net national income at current market prices	NSRX	261 926	281 350	306 413	332 060	361 971	406 327	445 308	480 566	504 872
B.6*n	Net national disposable income at current market prices	NQCP	261 172	280 337	304 363	331 002	362 304	405 987	445 041	480 781	507 159
	VALUES AT 1995 PRICES (£ million)										
	Gross measures, before deduction of fixed capital consumption **at 1995 market prices**										
B.1*g	Gross domestic product at 1995 market prices	ABMI	527 390	540 745	560 255	582 362	608 604	640 219	654 019	659 171	650 085
TGL	Terms of trade effect ("Trading gain or loss")	YBGJ	1 572	403	1 787	−3 598	−3 204	−1 600	563	2 234	4 330
GDI	Real gross domestic income	YBGL	528 962	541 148	562 042	578 764	605 400	638 619	654 583	661 405	654 415
D.1+ D.4	Real employment, property and entrepreneurial income from the rest of the world (receipts *less* payments)	YBGI	4 800	6 372	2 620	6 693	1 322	1 026	−1 007	−3 537	−3 696
D.3- D.2	Subsidies (receipts) *less* taxes (payments) on production from/to the rest of the world	-QZPB	−4 129	−3 849	−4 550	−5 557	−6 111	−4 506	−5 314	−5 846	−2 848
B.5*g	Gross national income at 1995 market prices	YBGM	529 633	543 671	560 112	579 900	600 611	635 139	648 262	652 022	647 871
D.5,6,7	Real current transfers from the rest of the world (receipts *less* payments)	-YBGP	3 128	584	−688	1 569	846	−477	−313	296	2 610
B.6*g	Gross national disposable income at 1995 market prices	YBGO	532 353	543 827	558 978	581 015	601 095	634 468	647 727	652 011	649 856
	adjustment to 1995 basic prices										
B.1*g	Gross domestic product at 1995 market prices	ABMI	527 390	540 745	560 255	582 362	608 604	640 219	654 019	659 171	650 085
-D.21 +D.31	Adjustment to 1995 basic prices (*less* taxes *plus* subsidies on products)	-NTAQ	−58 032	−60 667	−60 961	−65 948	−69 806	−75 667	−77 269	−75 785	−72 615
B.1g	Gross value added at 1995 basic prices	ABMM	469 442	480 302	499 301	516 728	539 251	565 345	577 556	583 902	577 678
	Net measures, after deduction of										
-K.1	fixed capital consumption at 1995 prices	-YBFX	−65 631	−68 056	−69 018	−70 172	−72 180	−73 860	−74 166	−75 026	−80 261
B.5*n	Net national income at 1995 market prices	YBET	464 241	475 810	491 380	509 659	528 769	561 370	574 859	577 723	567 764
B.6*n	Net national disposable income at 1995 market prices	YBEY	467 383	476 379	490 666	509 656	533 643	565 902	579 690	582 835	573 987

Main aggregates and summary accounts

1.1 continued
UK national and domestic product
Main aggregates: index numbers and values
At current and constant 1995 prices

			1992	1993	1994	1995	1996	1997	1998	1999	2000
	INDICES (1995=100)										
	VALUES AT CURRENT PRICES										
B.1*g	Gross domestic product at current market prices ("money GDP")	YBEU	84.9	89.3	94.8	100.0	106.0	112.8	119.6	125.3	131.2
B.1g	Gross value added at current basic prices	YBEX	85.4	89.9	95.1	100.0	106.2	112.6	119.0	124.2	129.9
	VALUES AT 1995 PRICES										
B.1*g	Gross domestic product at 1995 market prices	YBEZ	90.6	92.9	97.2	100.0	102.6	106.2	109.3	111.7	114.9
B.6*g	Gross national disposable income at 1995 market prices	YBFP	91.8	94.0	98.4	100.0	103.0	108.2	113.1	114.8	118.8
B.1g	Gross value added at 1995 basic prices	CGCE	90.6	92.8	97.3	100.0	102.7	106.0	109.4	111.6	114.8
	PRICES										
	Implied deflator of GDP at market prices (expenditure based, "total home costs per unit of output")	YBGB	93.8	96.2	97.5	100.0	103.3	106.2	109.3	112.2	114.2
	VALUES AT CURRENT PRICES (£ million)										
	Gross measures, before deduction of fixed capital consumption **at current market prices**										
B.1*g	Gross domestic product at current market prices ("money GDP")	YBHA	610 854	642 327	681 327	719 176	762 214	811 067	859 805	901 269	943 412
D.1+D.4	Employment, property and entrepreneurial income from the rest of the world (receipts *less* payments)	YBGG	128	−191	3 348	2 101	1 204	3 906	12 558	4 019	6 117
D.21-D.31	Subsidies (receipts) *less* taxes (payments) on products from/to the rest of the world	-QZOZ	−4 319	−4 725	−3 349	−5 220	−4 141	−2 811	−3 683	−3 551	−3 446
D.29-D.39	Subsidies on production	NHQR	66	215	286	293	253	206	246	370	361
B.5*g	Gross national income at current market prices	ABMX	606 729	637 626	681 612	716 350	759 530	812 368	868 926	902 107	946 448
D.5,6,7	Current transfers from the rest of the world (receipts *less* payments)	-YBGF	−1 275	−734	−2 309	−2 649	−1 902	−3 209	−4 790	−4 067	−5 377
B.6*g	Gross national disposable income at current market prices	NQCO	605 454	636 892	679 303	713 701	757 628	809 159	864 136	898 040	940 706
	adjustment to current basic prices										
B.1*g	Gross domestic product at current market prices	YBHA	610 854	642 327	681 327	719 176	762 214	811 067	859 805	901 269	943 412
-D.21 +D.31	Adjustment to current basic prices (*less* taxes *plus* subsidies on products)	-NQBU	−64 420	−66 866	−72 587	−79 268	−82 594	−90 375	−98 487	−106 244	−112 359
B.1g	Gross value added at current basic prices	ABML	546 434	575 461	608 740	639 908	679 620	720 692	761 318	795 025	831 053
	Net measures, after deduction of fixed capital consumption										
-K.1		-NQAE	−77 115	−83 522	−85 161	−86 959	−89 639	−93 531	−96 074	−100 650	−106 047
B.1*n	Net domestic product at current market prices	NHRK	533 739	558 805	596 166	632 217	672 575	717 536	763 731	800 619	837 369
B.5*n	Net national income at current market prices	NSRX	529 614	554 104	596 451	629 391	669 891	718 837	772 852	801 457	840 401
B.6*n	Net national disposable income at current market prices	NQCP	528 339	553 370	594 142	626 742	667 989	715 628	768 062	797 390	834 659
	VALUES AT 1995 PRICES (£ million)										
	Gross measures, before deduction of fixed capital consumption **at 1995 market prices**										
B.1*g	Gross domestic product at 1995 market prices	ABMI	651 566	667 804	698 915	719 176	738 046	763 472	786 303	803 019	826 144
TGL	Terms of trade effect ("Trading gain or loss")	YBGJ	7 284	7 950	4 835	–	2 610	10 677	16 671	19 559	25 105
GDI	Real gross domestic income	YBGL	658 850	675 753	703 750	719 176	740 656	774 149	802 974	822 578	851 248
D.1+ D.4	Real employment, property and entrepreneurial income from the rest of the world (receipts *less* payments)	YBGI	138	−201	3 459	2 101	1 170	3 728	11 756	3 686	5 546
D.3- D.2	Subsidies (receipts) *less* taxes (payments) on production from/to the rest of the world	-QZPB	−2 755	−3 695	−2 679	−5 220	−5 181	−2 576	−3 082	−3 364	−4 375
B.5*g	Gross national income at 1995 market prices	YBGM	656 233	671 857	704 530	716 057	736 645	775 301	811 648	822 900	852 419
D.5,6,7	Real current transfers from the rest of the world (receipts *less* payments)	-YBGP	−1 312	−545	−2 087	−2 354	−1 601	−2 864	−4 252	−3 389	−4 875
B.6*g	Gross national disposable income at 1995 market prices	YBGO	654 834	671 113	702 443	713 703	735 044	772 437	807 396	819 511	847 544
	adjustment to 1995 basic prices										
B.1*g	Gross domestic product at 1995 market prices	ABMI	651 566	667 804	698 915	719 176	738 046	763 472	786 303	803 019	826 144
-D.21 +D.31	Adjustment to 1995 basic prices (*less* taxes *plus* subsidies on products)	-NTAQ	−71 802	−73 672	−76 491	−79 268	−80 984	−85 193	−86 432	−88 734	−91 582
B.1g	Gross value added at 1995 basic prices	ABMM	579 834	594 215	622 424	639 908	657 062	678 279	699 871	714 285	734 562
	Net measures, after deduction of										
-K.1	fixed capital consumption at 1995 prices	-YBFX	−85 215	−89 925	−88 894	−86 959	−87 163	−88 968	−89 644	−91 305	−96 520
B.5*n	Net national income at 1995 market prices	YBET	570 785	581 431	615 648	629 098	649 497	686 229	721 522	730 498	755 901
B.6*n	Net national disposable income at 1995 market prices	YBEY	572 298	583 362	619 421	631 768	647 654	683 168	717 270	727 109	751 026

Main aggregates and summary accounts

1.2 UK gross domestic product and national income
Current prices

£ million

			1983	1984	1985	1986	1987	1988	1989	1990	1991
	GROSS DOMESTIC PRODUCT										
	Gross domestic product: output approach										
B.1g	Gross value added, at basic prices										
P.1	Output of goods and services, at basic prices	NQAF	..	..	..	..	..	..	930 408	1 018 467	1 048 451
-P.2	less intermediate consumption, at purchasers' prices	-NQAJ	..	..	..	..	..	..	-468 886	-517 028	-524 516
B.1g	Total	ABML	274 452	292 896	320 463	341 912	375 713	419 183	461 522	501 438	523 935
D.211	Value added taxes (VAT) on products	QYRC	16 081	19 297	20 780	22 886	25 559	29 207	31 986	33 687	38 191
D.212,4	Other taxes on products	NSUI	17 209	18 372	19 758	21 603	23 630	25 009	25 170	27 208	29 291
-D.31	less subsidies on products	-NZHC	-5 230	-6 338	-6 049	-5 084	-5 272	-5 017	-4 510	-5 033	-5 268
B.1*g	Gross domestic product at market prices	YBHA	302 512	324 227	354 952	381 317	419 631	468 386	514 168	557 300	586 149
	Gross domestic product: expenditure approach										
P.3	Final consumption expenditure										
P.41	Actual individual consumption										
P.3	Household final consumption expenditure	ABPB	176 695	189 397	206 700	228 870	251 390	283 965	311 437	337 646	359 616
P.3	Final consumption expenditure of NPISH	ABNV	4 597	5 133	5 820	6 719	7 526	8 763	9 986	11 401	11 096
P.31	Individual government final consumption expenditure	NNAQ	35 096	36 866	38 605	41 995	46 206	50 823	54 732	59 841	66 965
P.41	Total actual individual consumption	ABRE	216 388	231 396	251 125	277 584	305 122	343 551	376 155	408 888	437 677
P.32	Collective government final consumption expenditure	NNAR	31 306	33 492	35 642	37 742	39 300	41 320	45 094	50 409	54 438
P.3	Total final consumption expenditure	ABKW	247 694	264 888	286 767	315 326	344 422	384 871	421 249	459 297	492 115
P.3	Households and NPISH	NSSG	181 292	194 530	212 520	235 589	258 916	292 728	321 423	349 047	370 712
P.3	Central government	NMBJ	40 674	43 115	45 664	48 493	51 309	55 003	60 168	66 434	73 028
P.3	Local government	NMMT	25 728	27 243	28 583	31 244	34 197	37 140	39 658	43 816	48 375
P.5	Gross capital formation										
P.51	Gross fixed capital formation	NPQX	51 490	58 589	64 400	68 546	78 996	96 243	111 324	114 300	105 179
P.52	Changes in inventories	ABMP	1 465	1 296	821	682	1 228	4 333	2 677	-1 800	-4 927
P.53	Acquisitions less disposals of valuables	NPJO	–	–	–	-23	-130	42	-1	-127	-97
P.5	Total gross capital formation	NPDN	52 955	59 885	65 221	69 205	80 094	100 618	114 000	112 373	100 155
P.6	Exports of goods and services	KTMW	79 886	91 659	102 074	97 679	106 564	107 554	121 609	133 887	135 940
-P.7	less imports of goods and services	-KTMX	-77 428	-92 577	-98 723	-100 893	-111 449	-124 657	-142 690	-148 257	-142 061
B.11	External balance of goods and services	KTMY	2 458	-918	3 351	-3 214	-4 885	-17 103	-21 081	-14 370	-6 121
de	Statistical discrepancy between expenditure components and GDP	GIXM	-595	372	-387	–	–	–	–	–	–
B.1*g	Gross domestic product at market prices	YBHA	302 512	324 227	354 952	381 317	419 631	468 386	514 168	557 300	586 149
	Gross domestic product: income approach										
B.2g	Operating surplus, gross										
	Non-financial corporations										
	Public non-financial corporations	NRJT	13 335	11 634	10 843	11 699	10 399	10 962	9 851	7 655	6 102
	Private non-financial corporations	NRJK	52 559	60 032	70 147	69 177	78 940	91 360	101 542	104 903	105 722
	Financial corporations	NQNV	8 629	6 785	7 278	9 925	10 047	8 213	9 600	10 045	7 050
-P.119	Adjustment for financial services	-NSRV	-11 893	-12 487	-12 474	-14 429	-12 351	-13 117	-16 816	-17 651	-15 301
	General government	NMXV	3 863	4 008	4 270	4 541	4 842	5 379	6 190	6 565	6 448
	Households and non-profit institutions serving households	QWLS	12 161	12 788	13 867	15 040	16 396	18 438	20 763	24 586	27 968
B.2g	Total operating surplus, gross	ABNF	78 654	82 760	93 931	95 953	108 273	121 235	131 130	136 103	137 989
B.3	Mixed income	HAXH	16 873	19 092	20 727	24 066	27 149	29 932	32 512	37 123	36 580
D.1	Compensation of employees	HAEA	170 213	181 904	197 360	212 885	230 374	257 256	286 271	316 102	335 704
D.2	Taxes on production and imports	NZGX	43 355	47 271	49 728	54 609	60 124	66 103	69 991	74 309	82 373
-D.3	less subsidies	-AAXJ	-6 332	-7 420	-7 182	-6 190	-6 291	-6 149	-5 736	-6 337	-6 497
di	Statistical discrepancy between income components and GDP	GIXQ	-251	620	388	–	–	–	–	–	–
B.1*g	Gross domestic product at market prices	YBHA	302 512	324 227	354 952	381 317	419 631	468 386	514 168	557 300	586 149
	GROSS NATIONAL INCOME at market prices										
B.1*g	Gross domestic product at market prices	YBHA	302 512	324 227	354 952	381 317	419 631	468 386	514 168	557 300	586 149
D.1	Compensation of employees										
	receipts from the rest of the world	KTMN	290	323	344	369	413	445	476	543	551
	less payments to the rest of the world	-KTMO	-379	-417	-464	-525	-587	-509	-614	-653	-614
D.1	Total	KTMP	-89	-94	-120	-156	-174	-64	-138	-110	-63
-D.2	less Taxes on products paid to the rest of the world										
+D.3	plus Subsidies received from the rest of the world	-QZOZ	-1 958	-1 934	-2 508	-3 175	-3 907	-3 168	-4 202	-5 181	-3 566
	Subsidies on production	NHQR	31	18	18	47	16	18	35	43	54
D.4	Property and entrepreneurial income										
	receipts from the rest of the world	HMBN	41 632	50 629	51 011	46 431	47 079	55 444	72 604	77 663	75 073
	less payments to the rest of the world	-HMBO	-41 352	-49 345	-51 888	-44 581	-45 988	-54 627	-73 258	-80 532	-78 317
D.4	Total	HMBM	280	1 284	-877	1 850	1 091	817	-654	-2 869	-3 244
B.5*g	Gross national income at market prices	ABMX	300 776	323 501	351 465	379 883	416 656	465 985	509 209	549 183	579 330

Main aggregates and summary accounts

1.2 UK gross domestic product and national income
Current prices
continued

£ million

			1992	1993	1994	1995	1996	1997	1998	1999	2000
	GROSS DOMESTIC PRODUCT										
	Gross domestic product: output approach										
B.1g	Gross value added, at basic prices										
P.1	Output of goods and services, at basic prices	NQAF	1 100 189	1 172 054	1 270 951	1 363 534	1 455 417	1 539 896	1 631 361	1 721 728	1 818 849
-P.2	less intermediate consumption, at purchasers' prices	-NQAJ	-553 755	-596 593	-662 211	-723 626	-775 797	-819 204	-870 043	-926 703	-987 792
B.1g	Total	ABML	546 434	575 461	608 740	639 908	679 620	720 692	761 318	795 025	831 053
D.211	Value added taxes (VAT) on products	QYRC	41 485	42 429	46 117	48 424	51 389	55 454	58 521	62 475	64 906
D.212,4	Other taxes on products	NSUI	29 033	30 815	33 450	37 995	39 724	43 003	46 933	50 465	54 271
-D.31	less subsidies on products	-NZHC	-6 098	-6 378	-6 980	-7 151	-8 519	-8 082	-6 967	-6 696	-6 818
B.1*g	Gross domestic product at market prices	YBHA	610 854	642 327	681 327	719 176	762 214	811 067	859 805	901 269	943 412
	Gross domestic product: expenditure approach										
P.3	Final consumption expenditure										
P.41	Actual individual consumption										
P.3	Household final consumption expenditure	ABPB	379 758	401 970	422 397	443 367	473 800	503 374	536 525	567 555	594 782
P.3	Final consumption expenditure of NPISH	ABNV	10 806	13 981	15 287	16 481	18 385	19 602	21 117	22 671	22 866
P.31	Individual government final consumption expenditure	NNAQ	73 412	74 549	77 545	81 093	84 968	87 551	92 271	100 504	106 176
P.41	Total actual individual consumption	ABRE	463 976	490 500	515 229	540 941	577 153	610 527	649 913	690 730	723 824
P.32	Collective government final consumption expenditure	NNAR	55 783	56 985	58 710	59 938	61 811	61 596	62 610	65 790	68 615
P.3	Total final consumption expenditure	ABKW	519 759	547 485	573 939	600 879	638 964	672 123	712 523	756 520	792 439
P.3	Households and NPISH	NSSG	390 564	415 951	437 684	459 848	492 185	522 976	557 642	590 226	617 648
P.3	Central government	NMBJ	78 275	81 566	84 385	86 791	90 396	92 190	95 298	100 647	105 464
P.3	Local government	NMMT	50 920	49 968	51 870	54 240	56 383	56 957	59 583	65 647	69 327
P.5	Gross capital formation										
P.51	Gross fixed capital formation	NPQX	100 583	101 027	108 314	117 448	125 762	134 396	151 539	155 408	165 247
P.52	Changes in inventories	ABMP	-1 937	329	3 708	4 512	1 771	4 388	4 460	4 975	1 855
P.53	Acquisitions less disposals of valuables	NPJO	17	-29	113	-121	-158	-26	430	230	-3
P.5	Total gross capital formation	NPDN	98 663	101 327	112 135	121 839	127 375	138 758	156 429	160 613	167 099
P.6	Exports of goods and services	KTMW	144 091	163 640	180 508	203 509	223 091	231 622	228 801	236 720	265 305
-P.7	less imports of goods and services	-KTMX	-151 659	-170 125	-185 255	-207 051	-227 216	-231 436	-237 948	-252 584	-281 024
B.11	External balance of goods and services	KTMY	-7 568	-6 485	-4 747	-3 542	-4 125	186	-9 147	-15 864	-15 719
de	Statistical discrepancy between expenditure components and GDP	GIXM	–	–	–	–	–	–	–	–	-407
B.1*g	Gross domestic product at market prices	YBHA	610 854	642 327	681 327	719 176	762 214	811 067	859 805	901 269	943 412
	Gross domestic product: income approach										
B.2g	Operating surplus, gross										
	Non-financial corporations										
	Public non-financial corporations	NRJT	6 607	8 188	9 111	10 987	10 856	9 758	10 216	10 376	9 101
	Private non-financial corporations	NRJK	105 864	116 282	133 037	142 165	157 745	168 871	174 261	178 260	188 526
	Financial corporations	NQNV	13 649	17 726	20 708	17 838	17 135	14 806	18 436	14 701	15 548
-P.119	Adjustment for financial services	-NSRV	-19 086	-19 569	-23 119	-23 215	-22 580	-22 396	-27 998	-30 819	-37 091
	General government	NMXV	6 075	5 870	5 991	6 447	6 876	7 316	7 534	7 767	7 761
	Households and non-profit institutions serving households	QWLS	31 509	33 026	35 354	38 165	40 160	43 147	48 023	51 197	53 206
B.2g	Total operating surplus, gross	ABNF	144 618	161 523	181 082	192 387	210 192	221 502	230 472	231 482	237 051
B.3	Mixed income	HAXH	39 521	42 340	44 319	46 647	49 011	50 461	50 292	52 464	54 442
D.1	Compensation of employees	HAEA	347 713	357 662	369 645	386 718	405 469	432 960	464 258	494 186	521 443
D.2	Taxes on production and imports	NZGX	86 196	88 310	94 288	101 633	107 042	115 143	122 741	130 953	137 955
-D.3	less subsidies	-AAXJ	-7 194	-7 508	-8 007	-8 209	-9 500	-8 999	-7 958	-7 816	-7 724
di	Statistical discrepancy between income components and GDP	GIXQ	–	–	–	–	–	–	–	–	245
B.1*g	Gross domestic product at market prices	YBHA	610 854	642 327	681 327	719 176	762 214	811 067	859 805	901 269	943 412
	GROSS NATIONAL INCOME at market prices										
B.1*g	Gross domestic product at market prices	YBHA	610 854	642 327	681 327	719 176	762 214	811 067	859 805	901 269	943 412
D.1	Compensation of employees										
	receipts from the rest of the world	KTMN	551	595	681	887	911	1 007	840	960	1 014
	less payments to the rest of the world	-KTMO	-600	-560	-851	-1 183	-818	-924	-850	-759	-871
D.1	Total	KTMP	-49	35	-170	-296	93	83	-10	201	143
-D.2	less Taxes on products paid to the rest of the world										
+D.3	plus Subsidies received from the rest of the world	-QZOZ	-4 319	-4 725	-3 349	-5 220	-4 141	-2 811	-3 683	-3 551	-3 446
	Subsidies on production	NHQR	66	215	286	293	253	206	246	370	361
D.4	Property and entrepreneurial income										
	receipts from the rest of the world	HMBN	66 153	72 333	73 702	87 132	91 621	95 337	102 945	99 312	132 983
	less payments to the rest of the world	-HMBO	-65 976	-72 559	-70 184	-84 735	-90 510	-91 514	-90 377	-95 494	-127 009
D.4	Total	HMBM	177	-226	3 518	2 397	1 111	3 823	12 568	3 818	5 974
B.5*g	Gross national income at market prices	ABMX	606 729	637 626	681 612	716 350	759 530	812 368	868 926	902 107	946 448

United Kingdom National Accounts 2001, © Crown copyright 2001

Main aggregates and summary accounts

1.3 UK gross domestic product
Constant (1995) prices

£ million

			1983	1984	1985	1986	1987	1988	1989	1990	1991
	GROSS DOMESTIC PRODUCT										
	Gross domestic product: expenditure approach										
P.3	Final consumption expenditure										
P.41	Actual individual consumption										
P.3	Household final consumption expenditure	ABPF	312 888	319 296	331 084	352 689	371 301	398 851	412 276	415 557	408 865
P.3	Final consumption expenditure of non-profit institutions serving households	ABNU	8 105	8 571	9 229	9 283	9 928	10 971	11 202	12 079	12 217
P.31	Individual government final consumption expenditure	NSZK	65 843	65 111	64 700	69 966	70 260	70 776	70 924	72 225	74 763
P.41	Total actual individual consumption	YBIO	386 268	392 483	404 614	431 464	450 974	480 036	493 773	499 356	495 443
P.32	Collective government final consumption expenditure	NSZL	59 912	62 321	62 371	58 869	58 526	58 245	59 355	60 933	62 412
P.3	Total final consumption expenditure	ABKX	445 755	454 272	466 568	490 425	509 568	538 316	553 159	560 328	557 912
P.5	Gross capital formation										
P.51	Gross fixed capital formation	NPQR	79 489	86 763	90 339	92 095	100 618	115 562	122 476	119 338	109 508
P.52	Changes in inventories	ABMQ	1 890	1 510	1 143	1 384	1 907	5 883	3 123	–2 079	–5 349
P.53	Acquisitions less disposals of valuables	NPJP	–	–	–	–68	–216	38	–8	–130	–90
P.5	Total gross capital formation	NPQU	81 586	88 493	91 707	93 641	102 520	121 391	125 780	117 784	104 989
	Gross domestic final expenditure	YBIK	526 262	542 346	557 949	583 373	612 061	661 416	680 834	678 753	661 908
P.6	Exports of goods and services	KTMZ	113 489	120 963	128 158	133 617	141 734	142 596	149 058	157 166	156 961
	Gross final expenditure	ABME	638 155	662 479	686 008	716 809	753 619	803 726	829 619	835 724	818 712
-P.7 de	*less* imports of goods and services	-KTNB	–111 521	–122 582	–125 679	–134 297	–144 880	–163 417	–175 558	–176 508	–168 554
	Statistical discrepancy between expenditure components and GDP	GIXS	–1 039	618	–613	–	–	–	–	–	–
B.1*g	Gross domestic product at 1995 market prices	ABMI	527 390	540 745	560 255	582 362	608 604	640 219	654 019	659 171	650 085
B.11	*of which* External balance of goods and services	KTNC	1 968	–1 619	2 479	–680	–3 146	–20 821	–26 500	–19 342	–11 593

Main aggregates and summary accounts

1.3 UK gross domestic product
Constant (1995) prices

continued

£ million

			1992	1993	1994	1995	1996	1997	1998	1999	2000
	GROSS DOMESTIC PRODUCT										
	Gross domestic product: expenditure approach										
P.3	Final consumption expenditure										
P.41	Actual individual consumption										
P.3	Household final consumption expenditure	ABPF	411 204	422 273	435 350	443 367	460 760	478 738	496 491	517 757	538 458
P.3	Final consumption expenditure of non-profit institutions serving households	ABNU	12 445	14 723	15 900	16 481	16 691	17 055	18 265	18 769	19 408
P.31	Individual government final consumption expenditure	NSZK	77 053	78 616	78 479	81 093	83 112	84 808	86 244	88 475	90 071
P.41	Total actual individual consumption	YBIO	500 344	515 535	529 729	540 941	560 563	580 601	601 000	625 001	647 937
P.32	Collective government final consumption expenditure	NSZL	61 127	58 579	60 145	59 938	59 590	57 971	58 747	60 585	61 372
P.3	Total final consumption expenditure	ABKX	561 511	574 114	589 874	600 879	620 153	638 572	659 747	685 586	709 309
P.5	Gross capital formation										
P.51	Gross fixed capital formation	NPQR	108 556	108 887	113 961	117 448	122 976	131 667	149 092	150 466	157 766
P.52	Changes in inventories	ABMQ	−1 962	360	4 836	4 512	1 830	3 762	4 228	4 977	2 450
P.53	Acquisitions less disposals of valuables	NPJP	39	−9	115	−121	−182	−52	399	213	478
P.5	Total gross capital formation	NPQU	107 239	109 629	118 912	121 839	124 624	135 377	153 719	155 656	160 694
	Gross domestic final expenditure	YBIK	667 959	682 932	708 786	722 718	744 777	773 949	813 466	841 242	870 003
P.6	Exports of goods and services	KTMZ	163 745	170 916	186 655	203 509	220 268	238 492	245 761	258 935	285 433
	Gross final expenditure	ABME	831 594	853 767	895 441	926 227	965 045	1 012 441	1 059 227	1 100 177	1 155 436
−P.7	*less* imports of goods and services	−KTNB	−180 012	−185 954	−196 526	−207 051	−226 999	−248 969	−272 924	−297 158	−328 937
de	Statistical discrepancy between expenditure components and GDP	GIXS	−	−	−	−	−	−	−	−	−355
B.1*g	Gross domestic product at 1995 market prices	ABMI	651 566	667 804	698 915	719 176	738 046	763 472	786 303	803 019	826 144
B.11	*of which* External balance of goods and services	KTNC	−16 267	−15 038	−9 871	−3 542	−6 731	−10 477	−27 163	−38 223	−43 504

United Kingdom National Accounts 2001, © Crown copyright 2001

Main aggregates and summary accounts

1.4 Indices of value, volume, prices and costs

Indices 1995=100

			1983	1984	1985	1986	1987	1988	1989	1990	1991
	INDICES OF VALUE AT CURRENT PRICES										
	Gross measures, before deduction of fixed capital consumption										
	at current market prices										
B.1*g	Gross domestic product at current market prices ("money GDP")	YBEU	42.0	45.1	49.4	53.0	58.3	65.2	71.5	77.5	81.5
B.5*g	Gross national income at current market prices	YBEV	42.0	45.2	49.1	53.0	58.2	65.0	71.1	76.7	80.9
B.6*g	Gross national disposable income at current market prices	YBEW	42.2	45.4	49.2	53.4	58.4	65.2	71.3	77.0	81.5
	at current basic prices										
B.1g	Gross value added at current basic prices	YBEX	42.9	45.8	50.1	53.4	58.7	65.5	72.2	78.3	81.9
	INDICES OF VALUE AT 1995 PRICES ("volume", "real terms")										
	Gross measures, before deduction of fixed capital consumption										
	at 1995 market prices										
B.1*g	Gross domestic product at 1995 market prices	YBEZ	73.3	75.2	77.9	81.0	84.6	89.0	90.9	91.6	90.4
	Categories of expenditure on GDP										
P.3	Final consumption expenditure	YBFA	74.2	75.6	77.7	81.6	84.8	89.6	92.0	93.3	92.8
	by households and non-profit institutions serving households	YBFB	69.8	71.3	74.0	78.7	82.9	89.1	92.1	93.0	91.6
	by general government	YBFC	89.1	90.2	90.0	91.3	91.3	91.5	92.4	94.4	97.3
P.51	Gross fixed capital formation	YBFG	67.7	73.9	76.9	78.4	85.7	98.4	104.3	101.6	93.2
	Gross domestic final expenditure	YBFH	72.8	75.1	77.2	80.7	84.7	91.6	94.2	93.9	91.6
P.6	Exports of goods and services	YBFI	55.8	59.5	63.0	65.7	69.7	70.1	73.3	77.2	77.1
	of which, goods	YBFJ	53.3	57.7	60.8	63.5	67.2	68.7	72.7	77.3	78.1
	services	YBFK	63.8	65.1	69.9	72.6	77.4	74.6	75.0	77.1	74.2
	Gross final expenditure	YBFF	68.9	71.5	74.1	77.4	81.4	86.8	89.6	90.2	88.4
P.7	Imports of goods and services	YBFL	53.9	59.2	60.7	64.9	70.0	78.9	84.8	85.2	81.4
	of which, goods	YBFM	53.0	59.0	60.9	65.3	70.4	79.8	86.4	86.4	81.8
	services	YBFN	58.0	60.4	60.2	62.7	67.9	75.0	78.2	80.4	79.8
B.5*g	Gross national income at 1995 market prices	YBFO	74.0	75.9	78.2	81.0	83.9	88.7	90.5	91.1	90.5
B.6*g	Gross national disposable income at 1995 market prices	YBFP	74.7	76.3	78.3	81.3	84.3	88.9	90.8	91.4	91.2
	Adjustment to 1995 basic prices										
D.21-D.31	Taxes less subsidies on products	YBFQ	73.2	76.5	76.9	83.2	88.1	95.5	97.5	95.6	91.6
B.1g	Gross value added at 1995 basic prices	CGCE	73.3	75.0	78.0	80.8	84.3	88.3	90.3	91.3	90.3
	PRICE INDICES (IMPLIED DEFLATORS)[1]										
	Categories of expenditure on GDP at market prices										
P.3	Final consumption expenditure	YBGA	55.6	58.3	61.5	64.3	67.6	71.5	76.2	82.0	88.2
	by households and non-profit institutions serving households	YBFS	56.5	59.3	62.4	65.1	67.9	71.4	75.9	81.6	88.1
	by general government	YBFT	52.8	55.3	58.5	61.9	66.4	71.4	76.6	82.8	88.5
P.51	Gross fixed capital formation	YBFU	64.8	67.5	71.3	74.4	78.5	83.3	90.9	95.8	96.0
	Total domestic expenditure	YBFV	57.1	59.9	63.1	65.9	69.4	73.4	78.6	84.2	89.5
P.6	Exports of goods and services	YBFW	70.4	75.8	79.6	73.1	75.2	75.4	81.6	85.2	86.6
	of which, goods	BQNK	74.4	79.7	83.8	74.9	77.0	76.5	83.0	86.2	86.7
	services	FKNW	59.3	65.0	68.2	68.1	70.0	72.1	77.4	82.0	86.4
	Total final expenditure	YBFY	59.6	62.9	66.2	67.3	70.5	73.8	79.2	84.4	88.9
P.7	Imports of goods and services	YBFZ	69.4	75.5	78.6	75.1	76.9	76.3	81.3	84.0	84.3
	of which, goods	BQNL	71.3	77.8	81.1	76.3	78.2	77.3	82.0	84.6	84.3
	services	FHMA	61.6	66.3	68.1	70.3	71.8	72.0	78.2	81.8	84.3
B.1*g	Gross domestic product at market prices	YBGB	57.4	60.0	63.3	65.5	68.9	73.1	78.6	84.6	90.2
	HOME COSTS PER UNIT OF OUTPUT[2]										
B.1*g	Total home costs (based on expenditure components of GDP at current and 1995 market prices)	YBGC	57.8	60.6	64.1	66.0	69.5	73.8	79.5	85.6	90.5
D.1	Compensation of employees	YBGD	60.0	62.6	65.5	67.9	70.4	74.7	81.4	89.2	96.1
B.2g,B.3g	Gross operating surplus and mixed income	YBGE	54.5	56.7	61.6	62.0	66.9	71.0	75.3	79.1	80.8

1 Implied deflators are derived by dividing the estimates for each component at current market prices by the corresponding estimate at constant market prices.
2 These index numbers show how employment and operating incomes relate to the implied deflator of GDP at market prices.

Main aggregates and summary accounts

1.4 Indices of value, volume, prices and costs
continued

Indices 1995=100

			1992	1993	1994	1995	1996	1997	1998	1999	2000
	INDICES OF VALUE AT CURRENT PRICES										
	Gross measures, before deduction of fixed capital consumption										
	at current market prices										
B.1*g	Gross domestic product at current market prices ("money GDP")	YBEU	84.9	89.3	94.8	100.0	106.0	112.8	119.6	125.3	131.2
B.5*g	Gross national income at current market prices	YBEV	84.7	89.0	95.2	100.0	106.0	113.4	121.3	125.9	132.1
B.6*g	Gross national disposable income at current market prices	YBEW	84.8	89.2	95.2	100.0	106.2	113.4	121.1	125.8	131.8
	at current basic prices										
B.1g	Gross value added at current basic prices	YBEX	85.4	89.9	95.1	100.0	106.2	112.6	119.0	124.2	129.9
	INDICES OF VALUE AT 1995 PRICES ("volume", "real terms")										
	Gross measures, before deduction of fixed capital consumption										
	at 1995 market prices										
B.1*g	Gross domestic product at 1995 market prices	YBEZ	90.6	92.9	97.2	100.0	102.6	106.2	109.3	111.7	114.9
	Categories of expenditure on GDP										
P.3	Final consumption expenditure	YBFA	93.5	95.5	98.2	100.0	103.2	106.3	109.8	114.1	118.0
	by households and non-profit institutions serving households	YBFB	92.1	95.0	98.2	100.0	103.8	107.8	111.9	116.7	121.3
	by general government	YBFC	98.0	97.3	98.3	100.0	101.2	102.8	105.7	107.3	
P.51	Gross fixed capital formation	YBFG	92.4	92.7	97.0	100.0	104.7	112.1	126.9	128.1	134.3
	Gross domestic final expenditure	YBFH	92.4	94.5	98.1	100.0	103.1	107.1	112.6	116.4	120.4
P.6	Exports of goods and services	YBFI	80.4	84.0	91.7	100.0	108.2	117.2	120.8	127.2	140.3
	of which, goods	YBFJ	80.0	83.0	91.3	100.0	107.6	116.7	118.2	123.3	137.3
	services	YBFK	81.8	86.9	93.0	100.0	110.1	118.7	128.7	139.3	149.4
	Gross final expenditure	YBFF	89.8	92.2	96.7	100.0	104.2	109.3	114.3	118.8	124.7
P.7	Imports of goods and services	YBFL	86.9	89.8	94.9	100.0	109.6	120.3	131.8	143.5	158.9
	of which, goods	YBFM	87.2	90.4	94.4	100.0	109.5	120.3	131.1	141.3	158.2
	services	YBFN	86.0	87.2	96.8	100.0	110.2	120.0	134.7	152.4	161.5
B.5*g	Gross national income at 1995 market prices	YBFO	91.6	93.8	98.4	100.0	102.9	108.3	113.3	114.9	119.0
B.6*g	Gross national disposable income at 1995 market prices	YBFP	91.8	94.0	98.4	100.0	103.0	108.2	113.1	114.8	118.8
	Adjustment to 1995 basic prices										
D.21-D.31	Taxes *less* subsidies on products	YBFQ	90.6	92.9	96.5	100.0	102.2	107.5	109.0	112.0	115.5
B.1g	Gross value added at 1995 basic prices	CGCE	90.6	92.8	97.3	100.0	102.7	106.0	109.4	111.6	114.8
	PRICE INDICES (IMPLIED DEFLATORS)[1]										
	Categories of expenditure on GDP at market prices										
P.3	Final consumption expenditure	YBGA	92.6	95.4	97.3	100.0	103.0	105.3	108.0	110.3	111.7
	by households and non-profit institutions serving households	YBFS	92.2	95.2	97.0	100.0	103.1	105.5	108.3	110.0	110.7
	by general government	YBFT	93.5	95.9	98.3	100.0	102.9	104.5	106.8	111.6	115.4
P.51	Gross fixed capital formation	YBFU	92.7	92.8	95.0	100.0	102.3	102.1	101.6	103.3	104.7
	Total domestic expenditure	YBFV	92.6	95.0	96.8	100.0	102.9	104.8	106.8	109.0	110.3
P.6	Exports of goods and services	YBFW	88.0	95.7	96.7	100.0	101.3	97.1	93.1	91.4	92.9
	of which, goods	BQNK	87.8	95.8	96.4	100.0	101.2	95.9	90.4	87.7	89.0
	services	FKNW	88.7	95.5	97.7	100.0	101.7	100.7	100.7	101.4	104.1
	Total final expenditure	YBFY	91.7	95.2	96.8	100.0	102.5	103.0	103.6	104.9	106.0
P.7	Imports of goods and services	YBFZ	84.2	91.5	94.3	100.0	100.1	93.0	87.2	85.0	85.4
	of which, goods	BQNL	83.7	90.3	93.5	100.0	99.8	92.5	85.6	82.8	83.2
	services	FHMA	86.3	96.3	97.2	100.0	101.3	94.8	93.3	93.2	94.1
B.1*g	Gross domestic product at market prices	YBGB	93.8	96.2	97.5	100.0	103.3	106.2	109.3	112.2	114.2
	HOME COSTS PER UNIT OF OUTPUT[2]										
B.1*g	Total home costs (based on expenditure components of GDP at current and 1995 market prices)	YBGC	94.1	96.7	97.9	100.0	103.5	106.2	108.6	111.1	112.8
D.1	Compensation of employees	YBGD	99.3	99.6	98.4	100.0	102.2	105.4	109.8	114.4	117.4
B.2g,B.3g	Gross operating surplus and mixed income	YBGE	85.0	91.8	97.0	100.0	105.7	107.2	107.4	106.4	106.2

1 Implied deflators are derived by dividing the estimates for each component at current market prices by the corresponding estimate at constant market prices.
2 These index numbers show how employment and operating incomes relate to the implied deflator of GDP at market prices.

Main aggregates and summary accounts

1.5 Population, employment and GDP per head

			1992	1993	1994	1995	1996	1997	1998	1999	2000
	POPULATION AND EMPLOYMENT (thousands)[1]										
POP	Home population	DYAY	58 013	58 198	58 401	58 612	58 807	59 014	59 237	59 501	59 756
	Household population aged 16+										
ESE	Self-employed[2]	MGRQ	3 228	3 186	3 303	3 364	3 304	3 358	3 290	3 214	3 160
EEM	Employees[2]	MGRN	22 084	21 877	21 998	22 312	22 730	23 218	23 657	24 084	24 497
ETO	Total employment[2,3]	MGRZ	25 868	25 568	25 780	26 100	26 412	26 916	27 227	27 560	27 913
EUN	ILO Unemployed[2]	MGSC	2 831	2 997	2 798	2 518	2 394	2 087	1 822	1 795	1 661
	All economically active[2]	MGSF	28 699	28 565	28 578	28 618	28 806	29 004	29 049	29 356	29 574
	Economically inactive[2]	MGSI	16 611	16 836	16 909	17 023	17 030	17 032	17 204	17 075	17 007
	Total[2]	MGSL	45 310	45 400	45 488	45 641	45 835	46 036	46 253	46 431	46 581
	GROSS DOMESTIC PRODUCT PER HEAD £										
	At current prices										
	Gross domestic product at market prices	YBGR	10 530	11 036	11 666	12 270	12 962	13 743	14 514	15 147	15 788
	At 1995 prices										
	Gross domestic product at market prices	YBGS	11 231	11 474	11 967	12 270	12 550	12 937	13 273	13 496	13 826
	Gross value added at basic prices	YBGT	9 995	10 211	10 657	10 918	11 172	11 494	11 814	12 003	12 290

1 Components may not sum to totals due to rounding.
2 These seasonally adjusted data relate to spring (March to May) quarters in the Labour Force Survey, which does not include those resident in communal establishments except for those in student halls of residence and NHS accommodation.
3 Includes people on Government-supported training and employment programmes and, from 1992, unpaid family workers.

Main aggregates and summary accounts

1.6.0 UK summary accounts
Total economy ESA95 sector S.1

£ million

			1992	1993	1994	1995	1996	1997	1998	1999	2000
0	**GOODS AND SERVICES ACCOUNT**										
	Resources										
P.1	Output										
P.11	Market output[1]	NQAG	921 050	986 313	1 076 977	1 160 306	1 242 591	1 320 012	1 399 189	1 473 080	..
P.12	Output for own final use[1]	NQAH	39 138	40 226	42 432	45 716	47 662	51 135	56 174	59 683	..
P.13	Other non-market output[1]	NQAI	140 001	145 515	151 542	157 512	165 164	168 749	175 998	188 965	..
P.1	Total output	NQAF	1 100 189	1 172 054	1 270 951	1 363 534	1 455 417	1 539 896	1 631 361	1 721 728	1 818 849
D.21	Taxes on products	NZGW	70 518	73 244	79 567	86 419	91 113	98 457	105 454	112 940	119 177
-D.31	*less* Subsidies on products	-NZHC	−6 098	−6 378	−6 980	−7 151	−8 519	−8 082	−6 967	−6 696	−6 818
P.7	Imports of goods and services	KTMX	151 659	170 125	185 255	207 051	227 216	231 436	237 948	252 584	281 024
Total	Total resources	NQBM	1 316 268	1 409 045	1 528 793	1 649 853	1 765 227	1 861 707	1 967 796	2 080 556	2 212 232
	Uses										
P.2	Intermediate consumption	NQAJ	553 755	596 593	662 211	723 626	775 797	819 204	870 043	926 703	987 792
P.3	Final consumption expenditure										
P.31	By households	ABPB	379 758	401 970	422 397	443 367	473 800	503 374	536 525	567 555	594 782
P.31	By non-profit institutions serving households	ABNV	10 806	13 981	15 287	16 481	18 385	19 602	21 117	22 671	22 866
P.3	By government										
P.31	For individual consumption	NNAQ	73 412	74 549	77 545	81 093	84 968	87 551	92 271	100 504	106 176
P.32	For collective consumption	NNAR	55 783	56 985	58 710	59 938	61 811	61 596	62 610	65 790	68 615
P.3	Total by government	NMRK	129 195	131 534	136 255	141 031	146 779	149 147	154 881	166 294	174 791
P.3	Total final consumption expenditure[2]	ABKW	519 759	547 485	573 939	600 879	638 964	672 123	712 523	756 520	792 439
P.5	Gross capital formation										
P.51	Gross fixed capital formation	NPQX	100 583	101 027	108 314	117 448	125 762	134 396	151 539	155 408	165 247
P.52	Changes in inventories	ABMP	−1 937	329	3 708	4 512	1 771	4 388	4 460	4 975	1 855
P.53	Acquisitions less disposals of valuables	NPJO	17	−29	113	−121	−158	−26	430	230	−3
P.5	Total gross capital formation	NPDN	98 663	101 327	112 135	121 839	127 375	138 758	156 429	160 613	167 099
P.6	Exports of goods and services	KTMW	144 091	163 640	180 508	203 509	223 091	231 622	228 801	236 720	265 305
de	Statistical discrepancy between expenditure components and GDP	GIXM	–	–	–	–	–	–	–	–	−407
Total	Total uses	NQBM	1 316 268	1 409 045	1 528 793	1 649 853	1 765 227	1 861 707	1 967 796	2 080 556	2 212 232

1 These series are not available for the latest year
2 For the total economy, Total final consumption expenditure = P.4 Actual final consumption

Main aggregates and summary accounts

1.6.1 UK summary accounts
Total economy ESA95 sector S.1

£ million

			1992	1993	1994	1995	1996	1997	1998	1999
I	**PRODUCTION ACCOUNT**									
	Resources									
P.1	Output									
P.11	Market output	NQAG	921 050	986 313	1 076 977	1 160 306	1 242 591	1 320 012	1 399 189	1 473 080
P.12	Output for own final use	NQAH	39 138	40 226	42 432	45 716	47 662	51 135	56 174	59 683
P.13	Other non-market output	NQAI	140 001	145 515	151 542	157 512	165 164	168 749	175 998	188 965
P.1	Total output	NQAF	1 100 189	1 172 054	1 270 951	1 363 534	1 455 417	1 539 896	1 631 361	1 721 728
D.21-D.31	Taxes less Subsidies on products	NQBU	64 420	66 866	72 587	79 268	82 594	90 375	98 487	106 244
Total	Total resources	NQBP	1 164 609	1 238 920	1 343 538	1 442 802	1 538 011	1 630 271	1 729 848	1 827 972
	Uses									
P.2	Intermediate consumption	NQAJ	553 755	596 593	662 211	723 626	775 797	819 204	870 043	926 703
B.1*g	Gross domestic product	YBHA	610 854	642 327	681 327	719 176	762 214	811 067	859 805	901 269
Total	Total uses	NQBP	1 164 609	1 238 920	1 343 538	1 442 802	1 538 011	1 630 271	1 729 848	1 827 972
B.1*g	Gross domestic product	YBHA	610 854	642 327	681 327	719 176	762 214	811 067	859 805	901 269
-K.1	less Fixed capital consumption	-NQAE	-77 115	-83 522	-85 161	-86 959	-89 639	-93 531	-96 074	-100 650
B.1*n	Net domestic product	NHRK	533 739	558 805	596 166	632 217	672 575	717 536	763 731	800 619

1.6.2 UK summary accounts
Total economy ESA95 sector S.1

£ million

			1992	1993	1994	1995	1996	1997	1998	1999
II	**DISTRIBUTION AND USE OF INCOME ACCOUNTS**									
II.1	**PRIMARY DISTRIBUTION OF INCOME ACCOUNT**									
II.1.1	**GENERATION OF INCOME ACCOUNT**									
	Resources									
B.1*g	Total resources, gross domestic product	YBHA	610 854	642 327	681 327	719 176	762 214	811 067	859 805	901 269
	Uses									
D.1	Compensation of employees									
D.11	Wages and salaries	NQAU	303 057	311 580	322 349	337 269	352 192	376 843	402 331	428 565
D.12	Employers' social contributions	NQAV	44 656	46 082	47 296	49 449	53 277	56 117	61 927	65 621
D.1	Total	HAEA	347 713	357 662	369 645	386 718	405 469	432 960	464 258	494 186
D.2	Taxes on production and imports, paid									
D.21	Taxes on products and imports	QZPQ	70 518	73 244	79 567	86 419	91 113	98 457	105 454	112 940
D.29	Production taxes other than on products	NMYD	15 678	15 066	14 721	15 214	15 929	16 686	17 287	18 013
D.2	Total taxes on production and imports	NZGX	86 196	88 310	94 288	101 633	107 042	115 143	122 741	130 953
-D.3	less Subsidies, received									
-D.31	Subsidies on products	-NZHC	-6 098	-6 378	-6 980	-7 151	-8 519	-8 082	-6 967	-6 696
-D.39	Production subsidies other than on products	-LIUB	-1 096	-1 130	-1 027	-1 058	-981	-917	-991	-1 120
-D.3	Total subsidies on production	-AAXJ	-7 194	-7 508	-8 007	-8 209	-9 500	-8 999	-7 958	-7 816
B.2g	Operating surplus, gross	ABNF	144 618	161 523	181 082	192 387	210 192	221 502	230 472	231 482
B.3g	Mixed income, gross	HAXH	39 521	42 340	44 319	46 647	49 011	50 461	50 292	52 464
di	Statistical discrepancy between income components and GDP	GIXQ	–	–	–	–	–	–	–	–
B.1*g	Total uses	YBHA	610 854	642 327	681 327	719 176	762 214	811 067	859 805	901 269
-K.1	After deduction of fixed capital consumption	-NQAE	-77 115	-83 522	-85 161	-86 959	-89 639	-93 531	-96 074	-100 650
B.2n	Operating surplus, net	NQAR	72 952	84 083	102 284	111 760	127 451	135 819	142 747	140 214
B.3n	Mixed income, net	EAWX	34 072	36 258	37 956	40 315	42 113	42 613	41 943	43 082

1.6.3 UK summary accounts
Total economy ESA95 sector S.1

Main aggregates and summary accounts

£ million

			1992	1993	1994	1995	1996	1997	1998	1999	2000
II.1.2	**ALLOCATION OF PRIMARY INCOME ACCOUNT**										
	Resources										
B.2g	Operating surplus, gross	ABNF	144 618	161 523	181 082	192 387	210 192	221 502	230 472	231 482	237 051
B.3g	Mixed income, gross	HAXH	39 521	42 340	44 319	46 647	49 011	50 461	50 292	52 464	54 442
D.1	Compensation of employees										
D.11	Wages and salaries	HAEC	303 008	311 615	322 179	336 973	352 285	376 926	402 321	428 766	451 032
D.12	Employers' social contributions	HAED	44 656	46 082	47 296	49 449	53 277	56 117	61 927	65 621	70 554
D.1	Total	NVCK	347 664	357 697	369 475	386 422	405 562	433 043	464 248	494 387	521 586
di	Statistical discrepancy between income components and GDP	GIXQ	–	–	–	–	–	–	–	–	245
D.2	Taxes on production and imports, received										
D.21	Taxes on products										
D.211	Value added tax (VAT)	NZGF	37 426	37 958	42 996	43 579	46 918	52 057	54 293	58 664	60 702
D.212	Taxes and duties on imports excluding VAT	NMBU	–	–	–	–	–	–	–	–	–
D.2121	Import duties	NMBS	–	–	–	–	–	–	–	–	–
D.2122	Taxes on imports excluding VAT and import duties	NMBT	–	–	–	–	–	–	–	–	–
D.214	Taxes on products excluding VAT and import duties	NMBV	27 036	28 586	31 218	35 482	37 380	40 621	44 815	48 395	52 141
D.21	Total taxes on products	NVCE	64 462	66 544	74 214	79 061	84 298	92 678	99 108	107 059	112 843
D.29	Other taxes on production	NMYD	15 678	15 066	14 721	15 214	15 929	16 686	17 287	18 013	18 778
D.2	Total taxes on production and imports, received	NMYE	80 140	81 610	88 935	94 275	100 227	109 364	116 395	125 072	131 621
-D.3	*less* Subsidies, paid										
-D.31	Subsidies on products	-NMYF	–4 361	–4 403	–4 976	–5 013	–5 845	–5 114	–4 304	–4 366	–3 930
-D.39	Other subsidies on production	-NMCC	–1 030	–914	–741	–765	–725	–710	–744	–747	–538
-D.3	Total subsidies	-NMRL	–5 391	–5 318	–5 717	–5 778	–6 573	–5 825	–5 049	–5 116	–4 475
D.4	Property income, received										
D.41	Interest	NHQY	205 398	170 971	169 209	198 313	199 940	219 596	263 838	228 829	282 461
D.42	Distributed income of corporations	NHQZ	69 078	69 284	77 668	92 128	98 872	106 378	104 586	113 752	121 748
D.43	Reinvested earnings on direct foreign investment	NHSK	5 224	10 096	13 827	14 378	17 271	16 112	14 071	21 304	27 076
D.44	Property income attributed to insurance policy holders	QYNF	35 440	36 000	37 735	42 859	48 324	52 638	56 130	54 335	59 708
D.45	Rent	NHRP	883	929	891	921	1 025	972	800	684	1 436
D.4	Total property income	NHRO	316 023	287 280	299 330	348 599	365 432	395 696	439 425	418 904	492 429
Total	Total resources	NQBQ	922 575	925 132	977 424	1 062 552	1 123 851	1 204 241	1 295 783	1 317 193	1 432 903
	Uses										
D.4	Property income, paid										
D.41	Interest	NHQW	214 348	178 122	176 490	206 625	207 825	227 610	267 394	236 273	290 609
D.42	Distributed income of corporations	NHQX	64 352	67 490	76 105	89 748	98 559	103 425	99 826	114 694	116 991
D.43	Reinvested earnings on direct foreign investment	NHSJ	121	4 385	3 953	5 254	7 873	6 386	1 522	7 855	16 146
D.44	Property income attributed to insurance policy holders	NSCU	36 142	36 580	38 373	43 654	49 039	53 480	57 315	55 580	61 273
D.45	Rent	NHRN	883	929	891	921	1 025	972	800	684	1 436
D.4	Total property income	NHRL	315 846	287 506	295 812	346 202	364 321	391 873	426 857	415 086	486 455
B.5*g	National income, gross	ABMX	606 729	637 626	681 612	716 350	759 530	812 368	868 926	902 107	946 448
Total	Total uses	NQBQ	922 575	925 132	977 424	1 062 552	1 123 851	1 204 241	1 295 783	1 317 193	1 432 903
-K.1	After deduction of fixed capital consumption	-NQAE	–77 115	–83 522	–85 161	–86 959	–89 639	–93 531	–96 074	–100 650	–106 047
B.5*n	National income, net	NSRX	529 614	554 104	596 451	629 391	669 891	718 837	772 852	801 457	840 401

Main aggregates and summary accounts

1.6.4 UK summary accounts
Total economy ESA95 sector S.1

£ million

			1992	1993	1994	1995	1996	1997	1998	1999	2000
II.2	**SECONDARY DISTRIBUTION OF INCOME ACCOUNT**										
	Resources										
B.5*g	National income, gross	ABMX	606 729	637 626	681 612	716 350	759 530	812 368	868 926	902 107	946 448
D.5	Current taxes on income, wealth etc.										
D.51	Taxes on income	NMZJ	80 291	78 313	85 348	95 042	99 310	107 647	124 060	129 044	140 960
D.59	Other current taxes	NVCQ	10 299	10 551	11 140	11 937	12 795	13 820	14 993	16 263	17 102
D.5	Total	NMZL	90 590	88 864	96 488	106 979	112 105	121 467	139 053	145 307	158 062
D.61	Social contributions										
D.611	Actual social contributions										
D.6111	Employers' actual social contributions	NQDA	34 960	36 850	38 146	39 934	43 916	46 773	51 297	55 365	60 146
D.6112	Employees' social contributions	NQDE	46 593	45 493	49 707	53 842	60 008	66 997	71 281	73 322	76 166
D.6113	Social contributions by self- and non-employed persons	NQDI	1 281	1 472	1 469	1 541	1 771	1 848	1 760	1 801	1 973
D.611	Total	NQCY	82 834	83 815	89 322	95 317	105 695	115 618	124 338	130 488	138 285
D.612	Imputed social contributions	NQDK	9 696	9 232	9 150	9 515	9 361	9 344	10 630	10 256	10 408
D.61	Total	NQCX	92 530	93 047	98 472	104 832	115 056	124 962	134 968	140 744	148 693
D.62	Social benefits other than social transfers in kind	QZQP	127 663	136 084	142 229	149 151	156 612	165 695	170 931	178 050	187 235
D.7	Other current transfers										
D.71	Net non-life insurance premiums	NQBY	27 188	23 987	22 650	25 088	35 860	23 774	25 059	22 752	27 205
D.72	Non-life insurance claims	NQDX	21 288	19 741	18 505	20 095	26 102	19 356	20 898	19 099	22 836
D.73	Current transfers within general government	NQDY	54 527	55 891	57 736	58 587	59 458	59 506	60 421	64 775	66 327
D.74	Current international cooperation from institutions of the EC	NMDL	1 907	2 558	1 752	1 233	2 424	1 739	1 384	3 176	2 084
D.75	Miscellaneous current transfers	QYNA	11 538	16 033	17 847	18 677	20 984	21 503	22 123	22 769	25 424
D.7	Total other current transfers	NQDU	116 448	118 210	118 490	123 680	144 828	125 878	129 885	132 571	143 876
Total	Total resources	NQBT	1 033 960	1 073 831	1 137 291	1 200 992	1 288 131	1 350 370	1 443 763	1 498 779	1 584 314
	Uses										
D.5	Current taxes on income, wealth etc.										
D.51	Taxes on income	NQCR	80 384	78 468	85 439	95 127	99 544	107 883	123 984	129 021	140 867
D.59	Other current taxes	NQCU	10 299	10 551	11 140	11 937	12 795	13 820	14 993	16 263	17 102
D.5	Total	NQCQ	90 683	89 019	96 579	107 064	112 339	121 703	138 977	145 284	157 969
D.61	Social contributions										
D.611	Actual social contributions										
D.6111	Employers' actual social contributions	NQDB	34 960	36 850	38 146	39 934	43 916	46 773	51 297	55 365	60 146
D.6112	Employees' actual social contributions	NQDF	46 477	45 415	49 615	53 747	59 900	66 890	71 182	73 235	76 111
D.6113	Social contributions by self- and non-employed persons	NQDJ	1 281	1 472	1 469	1 541	1 771	1 848	1 760	1 801	1 973
D.611	Total actual social contributions	NQCZ	82 718	83 737	89 230	95 222	105 587	115 511	124 239	130 401	138 230
D.612	Imputed social contributions	QZQQ	9 696	9 232	9 150	9 515	9 361	9 344	10 630	10 256	10 408
D.61	Total	NQBS	92 414	92 969	98 380	104 737	114 948	124 855	134 869	140 657	148 638
D.62	Social benefits other than social transfers in kind	NQDN	128 420	136 957	143 198	150 195	157 723	166 874	172 165	179 293	188 488
D.7	Other current transfers										
D.71	Net non-life insurance premiums	NQDW	21 288	19 741	18 505	20 095	26 102	19 356	20 898	19 099	22 836
D.72	Non-life insurance claims	NQBZ	27 188	23 987	22 650	25 088	35 860	23 774	25 059	22 752	27 205
D.73	Current transfers within general government	NNAF	54 527	55 891	57 736	58 587	59 458	59 506	60 421	64 775	66 327
D.74	Current international cooperation to institutions of the EC	NMDZ	2 237	1 961	2 007	2 224	1 814	1 700	1 705	1 667	2 418
D.75	Miscellaneous current transfers	NUHK	11 749	16 414	18 933	19 301	22 259	23 443	25 533	27 212	29 727
	GNP based fourth own resource	NMFH	914	1 558	2 071	1 826	2 454	2 458	3 920	4 632	4 379
D.7	Total other current transfers	NQDV	116 989	117 994	119 831	125 295	145 493	127 779	133 616	135 505	148 513
B.6*g	Disposable income, gross	NQCO	605 454	636 892	679 303	713 701	757 628	809 159	864 136	898 040	940 706
Total	Total uses	NQBT	1 033 960	1 073 831	1 137 291	1 200 992	1 288 131	1 350 370	1 443 763	1 498 779	1 584 314
-K.1	After deduction of fixed capital consumption	-NQAE	–77 115	–83 522	–85 161	–86 959	–89 639	–93 531	–96 074	–100 650	–106 047
B.6*n	Disposable income, net	NQCP	528 339	553 370	594 142	626 742	667 989	715 628	768 062	797 390	834 659

Main aggregates and summary accounts

1.6.5 UK summary accounts
Total economy ESA95 sector S.1

£ million

			1992	1993	1994	1995	1996	1997	1998	1999	2000
II.3	**REDISTRIBUTION OF INCOME IN KIND ACCOUNT**										
	Resources										
B.6*g	Disposable income, gross	NQCO	605 454	636 892	679 303	713 701	757 628	809 159	864 136	898 040	940 706
D.63	Social transfers in kind										
D.631	Social benefits in kind										
D.6313	Social assistance benefits in kind	NRNC	–	–	–	–	–	–	–	–	–
D.632	Transfers of individual non-market goods and services	NRNE	84 218	88 530	92 832	97 574	103 353	107 153	113 388	123 175	129 042
D.63	Total social transfers in kind	NRNF	84 218	88 530	92 832	97 574	103 353	107 153	113 388	123 175	129 042
Total	Total resources	NQCB	689 672	725 422	772 135	811 275	860 981	916 312	977 524	1 021 215	1 069 748
	Uses										
D.63	Social transfers in kind										
D.631	Social benefits in kind										
D.6313	Social assistance benefits in kind	NRNI	–	–	–	–	–	–	–	–	–
D.632	Transfers of individual non-market goods and services	NRNK	84 218	88 530	92 832	97 574	103 353	107 153	113 388	123 175	129 042
D.63	Total social transfers in kind	NRNL	84 218	88 530	92 832	97 574	103 353	107 153	113 388	123 175	129 042
B.7g	Adjusted disposable income, gross	NRNM	605 454	636 892	679 303	713 701	757 628	809 159	864 136	898 040	940 706
Total	Total uses	NQCB	689 672	725 422	772 135	811 275	860 981	916 312	977 524	1 021 215	1 069 748

United Kingdom National Accounts 2001, © Crown copyright 2001

Main aggregates and summary accounts

1.6.6 UK summary accounts
Total economy ESA95 sector S.1

£ million

				1992	1993	1994	1995	1996	1997	1998	1999	2000
II.4	USE OF INCOME ACCOUNT											
II.4.1	USE OF DISPOSABLE INCOME ACCOUNT											
	Resources											
B.6g	Disposable income, gross		NQCO	605 454	636 892	679 303	713 701	757 628	809 159	864 136	898 040	940 706
D.8	Adjustment for the change in net equity of households in pension funds		NVCI	13 265	10 742	10 577	11 690	14 824	15 131	16 105	15 417	15 216
Total	Total resources		NVCW	618 719	647 634	689 880	725 391	772 452	824 290	880 241	913 457	955 922
	Uses											
P.3	Final consumption expenditure											
P.31	Individual consumption expenditure		NQEO	463 976	490 500	515 229	540 941	577 153	610 527	649 913	690 730	723 824
P.32	Collective consumption expenditure		NNAR	55 783	56 985	58 710	59 938	61 811	61 596	62 610	65 790	68 615
P.3	Total		ABKW	519 759	547 485	573 939	600 879	638 964	672 123	712 523	756 520	792 439
D.8	Adjustment for the change in net equity of households in pension funds		NQEL	13 271	10 741	10 574	11 688	14 822	15 129	16 103	15 415	15 212
B.8g	Saving, gross		NQCA	85 689	89 408	105 367	112 824	118 666	137 038	151 615	141 522	148 271
Total	Total uses		NVCW	618 719	647 634	689 880	725 391	772 452	824 290	880 241	913 457	955 922
-K.1	After deduction of fixed capital consumption		-NQAE	-77 115	-83 522	-85 161	-86 959	-89 639	-93 531	-96 074	-100 650	-106 047
B.8n	Saving, net		NQEJ	8 574	5 886	20 206	25 865	29 027	43 507	55 541	40 872	42 224
II.4.2	USE OF ADJUSTED DISPOSABLE INCOME ACCOUNT											
	Resources											
B.7g	Adjusted disposable income		NRNM	605 454	636 892	679 303	713 701	757 628	809 159	864 136	898 040	940 706
D.8	Adjustment for the change in net equity of households in pension funds		NVCI	13 265	10 742	10 577	11 690	14 824	15 131	16 105	15 417	15 216
Total	Total resources		NVCW	618 719	647 634	689 880	725 391	772 452	824 290	880 241	913 457	955 922
	Uses											
P.4	Actual final consumption											
P.41	Actual individual consumption		ABRE	463 976	490 500	515 229	540 941	577 153	610 527	649 913	690 730	723 824
P.42	Actual collective consumption		NRMZ	55 783	56 985	58 710	59 938	61 811	61 596	62 610	65 790	68 615
P.4	Total actual final consumption		NRMX	519 759	547 485	573 939	600 879	638 964	672 123	712 523	756 520	792 439
D.8	Adjustment for the change in net equity of households in pension funds		NQEL	13 271	10 741	10 574	11 688	14 822	15 129	16 103	15 415	15 212
B.8g	Saving, gross		NQCA	85 689	89 408	105 367	112 824	118 666	137 038	151 615	141 522	148 271
Total	Total uses		NVCW	618 719	647 634	689 880	725 391	772 452	824 290	880 241	913 457	955 922

Main aggregates and summary accounts

1.6.7 UK summary accounts
Total economy ESA95 sector S.1

£ million

			1992	1993	1994	1995	1996	1997	1998	1999	2000
III	**ACCUMULATION ACCOUNTS**										
III.1	**CAPITAL ACCOUNT**										
III.1.1	**CHANGE IN NET WORTH DUE TO SAVING & CAPITAL TRANSFERS**										
	Changes in liabilities and net worth										
B.8g	Saving, gross	NQET	85 689	89 408	105 367	112 824	118 666	137 038	151 615	141 522	148 271
D.9	Capital transfers receivable										
D.91	Capital taxes	NQEY	1 227	1 279	1 438	1 441	1 621	1 601	1 796	1 951	2 215
D.92	Investment grants	NQFB	10 663	11 851	10 755	10 035	10 052	9 433	8 343	9 372	9 377
D.99	Other capital transfers	NQFD	6 001	777	729	2 420	2 606	942	1 160	1 360	1 995
D.9	Total	NQEW	17 891	13 907	12 922	13 896	14 279	11 976	11 299	12 683	13 587
-D.9	*less* Capital transfers payable										
-D.91	Capital taxes	-NQCC	-1 227	-1 279	-1 438	-1 441	-1 621	-1 601	-1 796	-1 951	-2 215
-D.92	Investment grants	-NVDG	-10 302	-11 523	-10 283	-9 699	-9 545	-8 733	-8 112	-9 211	-8 531
-D.99	Other capital transfers	-NQCE	-5 941	-796	-1 168	-2 223	-2 391	-804	-870	-725	-905
-D.9	Total	-NQCF	-17 470	-13 598	-12 889	-13 363	-13 557	-11 138	-10 778	-11 887	-11 651
B.10.1g	Total change in liabilities and net worth	NQCT	86 110	89 717	105 400	113 357	119 388	137 876	152 136	142 318	150 207
	Changes in assets										
B.10.1g	Changes in net worth due to gross saving and capital transfers	NQCT	86 110	89 717	105 400	113 357	119 388	137 876	152 136	142 318	150 207
-K.1	After deduction of fixed capital consumption	-NQAE	-77 115	-83 522	-85 161	-86 959	-89 639	-93 531	-96 074	-100 650	-106 047
B.10.1n	Changes in net worth due to net saving and capital transfers	NQER	8 995	6 195	20 239	26 398	29 749	44 345	56 062	41 668	44 160
III.1.2	**ACQUISITION OF NON-FINANCIAL ASSETS ACCOUNT**										
	Changes in liabilities and net worth										
B.10.1n	Changes in net worth due to net saving and capital transfers	NQER	8 995	6 195	20 239	26 398	29 749	44 345	56 062	41 668	44 160
K.1	Consumption of fixed capital	NQAE	77 115	83 522	85 161	86 959	89 639	93 531	96 074	100 650	106 047
Total	Total change in liabilities and net worth	NQCT	86 110	89 717	105 400	113 357	119 388	137 876	152 136	142 318	150 207
	Changes in assets										
P.5	Gross capital formation										
P.51	Gross fixed capital formation	NPQX	100 583	101 027	108 314	117 448	125 762	134 396	151 539	155 408	165 247
P.52	Changes in inventories	ABMP	-1 937	329	3 708	4 512	1 771	4 388	4 460	4 975	1 855
P.53	Acquisitions less disposals of valuables	NPJO	17	-29	113	-121	-158	-26	430	230	-3
P.5	Total	NPDN	98 663	101 327	112 135	121 839	127 375	138 758	156 429	160 613	167 099
K.2	Acquisitions less disposals of non-produced non-financial assets	NQFJ	–	–	–	–	-14	34	48	-12	-37
de	Statistical discrepancy between expenditure components and GDP	RVFD	–	–	–	–	–	–	–	–	-403
B.9	Net lending(+) / net borrowing(-)	NQFH	-12 553	-11 610	-6 735	-8 482	-7 973	-916	-4 341	-18 283	-16 452
Total	Total change in assets	NQCT	86 110	89 717	105 400	113 357	119 388	137 876	152 136	142 318	150 207

Main aggregates and summary accounts

1.6.8 UK summary accounts
Total economy ESA95 sector S.1 Unconsolidated

£ million

			1992	1993	1994	1995	1996	1997	1998	1999	2000
III.2	**FINANCIAL ACCOUNT**										
F.A	**Net acquisition of financial assets**										
F.1	Monetary gold and special drawing rights (SDRs)	NQAD	−962	−462	932	−120	−54	1 199	915	−374	−956
F.2	Currency and deposits										
F.21	Currency	NYPY	1 552	1 440	1 568	1 657	442	1 861	3 065	5 331	595
F.22	Transferable deposits										
F.221	Deposits with UK monetary financial institutions	NYQC	32 918	37 151	33 798	56 769	115 551	110 381	67 728	29 594	143 685
F.229	Deposits with rest of the world monetary financial institutions	NYQK	26 756	53 172	31 115	35 705	98 524	137 522	15 859	43 040	220 886
F.29	Other deposits	NYQM	4 910	4 925	4 995	3 611	7 604	2 512	−1 497	−1 540	5 926
F.2	Total currency and deposits	NQAK	66 136	96 688	71 476	97 742	222 121	252 276	85 155	76 425	371 092
F.3	Securities other than shares										
F.331	Short term: money market instruments										
F.3311	Issued by UK central government	NYQQ	−2 464	−100	1 220	10 189	−13 259	−656	1 820	−831	−1 689
F.3312	Issued by UK local authorities	NYQY	2	−29	–	4	−6	5	−6	–	–
F.3315	Issued by UK monetary financial institutions	NYRA	−1 559	−4 531	5 528	7 020	25 110	14 310	15 194	16 319	−14 231
F.3316	Issued by other UK residents	NYRK	−3	1 160	316	350	787	84	921	943	−1 362
F.3319	Issued by the rest of the world	NYRM	690	6 242	−4 448	2 743	−2 170	8 557	2 685	13 623	−2 728
F.332	Medium (1 to 5 year) and long term (over 5 year) bonds										
F.3321	Issued by UK central government	NYRQ	21 658	35 543	18 725	23 556	25 095	19 066	−5 108	723	−11 581
F.3322	Issued by UK local authorities	NYRW	4	7	288	78	163	13	6	−2	−12
F.3325	Medium term bonds issued by UK MFIs[1]	NYRY	1 386	1 347	3 894	2 764	2 624	2 300	2 704	7 265	2 034
F.3326	Other medium & long term bonds issued by UK residents	NYSE	5 330	12 406	1 078	6 399	5 991	11 457	20 846	39 634	65 028
F.3329	Long term bonds issued by the rest of the world	NYSG	31 085	75 682	−16 770	27 828	49 021	43 825	27 448	−9 055	52 922
F.34	Financial derivatives	NYSI	−1 139	−253	−2 374	−1 650	−948	−1 122	3 098	−2 659	−1 482
F.3	Total securities other than shares	NQAL	54 990	127 474	7 457	79 281	92 408	97 839	69 608	65 960	86 899
F.4	Loans										
F.41	Short term loans										
F.411	Loans by UK monetary financial institutions, excluding loans secured on dwellings & financial leasing	NYSS	4 487	−6 533	14 676	51 722	112 543	100 472	31 892	65 499	154 783
F.42	Long term loans										
F.421	Direct investment	NYTE	4 328	5 741	5 155	9 746	3 503	8 949	33 269	27 035	34 984
F.422	Loans secured on dwellings	NYTK	18 441	16 072	19 368	15 091	19 162	24 452	25 339	37 753	41 118
F.423	Finance leasing	NYTS	−1 179	−249	−154	958	1 930	2 028	558	134	−291
F.424	Other long-term loans by UK residents	NYTU	−4 347	641	3 625	5 746	−3 638	15 450	2 845	23 280	25 282
F.4	Total loans	NQAN	21 730	15 672	42 670	83 263	133 500	151 351	93 903	153 701	255 876
F.5	Shares and other equity										
F.51	Shares and other equity, excluding mutual funds' shares										
F.514	Quoted UK shares	NYUG	−271	4 378	15 125	8 488	6 241	15 375	−3 210	−7 461	65 730
F.515	Unquoted UK shares	NYUI	−4 561	−2 904	−270	−4 958	1 181	2 486	−2 603	−12 474	−15 039
F.516	Other UK equity (including direct investment in property)	NYUK	59	158	−47	−685	4 048	36	−66	20	−24
F.519	Shares and other equity issued by the rest of the world	NYUQ	6 729	22 724	22 234	30 823	32 242	33 262	63 851	140 420	199 037
F.52	Mutual funds' shares										
F.521	UK mutual funds' shares	NYUY	−228	6 134	2 802	5 365	8 113	8 964	10 974	14 716	13 862
F.529	Rest of the world mutual funds' shares	NYVA	61	−114	730	105	241	–	–	–	–
F.5	Total shares and other equity	NQAP	1 789	30 376	40 574	39 138	52 066	60 123	68 946	135 221	263 566
F.6	Insurance technical reserves										
F.61	Net equity of households in life assurance and pension funds' reserves	NQAX	28 092	27 389	28 052	30 374	36 668	32 405	42 013	42 475	44 675
F.62	Prepayments of insurance premiums and reserves for outstanding claims	NQBD	3 349	1 382	2 200	3 918	5 286	633	−566	−939	665
F.6	Total insurance technical reserves	NQAW	31 441	28 771	30 252	34 292	41 954	33 038	41 447	41 536	45 340
F.7	Other accounts receivable	NQBK	−2 384	2 821	7 241	11 672	2 677	10 902	9 535	14 372	34 909
F.A	Total net acquisition of financial assets	NQBL	172 740	301 340	200 602	345 268	544 672	606 728	369 509	486 841	1 056 726

1 UK monetary financial institutions

Main aggregates and summary accounts

1.6.8 UK summary accounts
Total economy ESA95 sector S.1 Unconsolidated

continued

£ million

				1992	1993	1994	1995	1996	1997	1998	1999	2000
III.2	FINANCIAL ACCOUNT *continued*											
F.L	**Net acquisition of financial liabilities**											
F.2	Currency and deposits											
F.21	Currency		NYPZ	1 642	1 429	1 640	1 694	392	1 793	3 134	5 431	683
F.22	Transferable deposits											
F.221	Deposits with UK monetary financial institutions		NYQD	63 824	76 990	82 598	83 227	186 849	258 267	115 825	41 823	342 226
F.29	Other deposits		NYQN	4 722	4 946	5 945	4 095	6 998	1 753	−1 193	−847	6 454
F.2	Total currency and deposits		NQCK	70 188	83 365	90 183	89 016	194 239	261 813	117 766	46 407	349 363
F.3	Securities other than shares											
F.331	Short term: money market instruments											
F.3311	Issued by UK central government		NYQR	−4 880	−405	1 080	11 513	−13 498	−1 569	86	−409	−1 652
F.3312	Issued by UK local authorities		NYQZ	2	−29	–	4	−6	5	−6	–	–
F.3315	Issued by UK monetary financial institutions		NYRB	−12 777	−22 845	6 358	23 215	36 572	21 983	−1 218	31 203	23 953
F.3316	Issued by other UK residents		NYRL	−714	2 510	2 614	1 602	2 645	1 796	3 350	2 725	1 375
F.332	Medium (1 to 5 year) and long term (over 5 year) bonds											
F.3321	Issued by UK central government		NYRR	30 484	53 115	24 031	22 542	31 338	16 665	−3 201	−4 560	−12 718
F.3322	Issued by UK local authorities		NYRX	4	7	288	78	163	13	6	−2	−12
F.3325	Medium term bonds issued by UK MFIs[1]		NYRZ	2 756	5 268	10 313	3 937	7 894	5 196	4 140	11 911	4 751
F.3326	Other medium & long term bonds issued by UK residents[2]		NYSF	8 960	19 476	12 352	20 228	18 323	25 858	17 080	63 376	74 221
F.34	Financial derivatives		NYSJ	114	−8	−1	17	15	34	55	26	21
F.3	Total securities other than shares		NQCM	23 949	57 089	57 035	83 136	83 446	69 981	20 292	104 270	89 939
F.4	Loans											
F.41	Short term loans											
F.411	Loans by UK monetary financial institutions, excluding loans secured on dwellings & financial leasing		NYST	−752	921	18 426	39 920	73 593	69 391	30 925	48 608	100 620
F.419	Loans by rest of the world monetary financial institutions		NYTB	23 381	83 954	−57 546	39 367	83 637	52 916	11 243	49 853	79 076
F.42	Long term loans											
F.421	Direct investment		NYTF	6 305	2 871	5 439	−40	4 895	11 873	36 312	21 403	58 054
F.422	Loans secured on dwellings		NYTL	18 441	16 072	19 368	15 091	19 162	24 452	25 339	37 753	41 118
F.423	Finance leasing		NYTT	−1 179	−249	−154	958	1 930	2 028	558	134	−291
F.424	Other long-term loans by UK residents		NYTV	−4 618	348	3 795	5 672	−3 820	15 439	3 107	23 271	25 307
F.429	Other long-term loans by the rest of the world		NYTX	−173	399	−539	−234	281	−54	−254	−122	−293
F.4	Total loans		NQCN	41 405	104 316	−11 211	100 734	179 678	176 045	107 230	180 900	303 591
F.5	Shares and other equity											
F.51	Shares and other equity, excluding mutual funds' shares											
F.514	Quoted UK shares[2]		NYUH	10 184	21 649	18 811	16 579	16 049	23 823	50 113	87 829	197 164
F.515	Unquoted UK shares[2]		NYUJ	1 622	6 974	7 557	9 814	12 831	15 950	10 529	18 008	46 312
F.516	Other UK equity (including direct investment in property)		NYUL	360	618	425	−461	4 661	886	632	833	1 298
F.52	Mutual funds' shares											
F.521	UK mutual funds' shares		NYUZ	−210	6 211	2 929	5 399	8 144	8 980	10 976	14 719	13 889
F.5	Total shares and other equity		NQCS	11 956	35 452	29 722	31 331	41 685	49 639	72 250	121 389	258 663
F.6	Insurance technical reserves											
F.61	Net equity of households in life assurance and pension funds' reserves		NQCD	28 098	27 388	28 049	30 372	36 666	32 403	42 011	42 473	44 671
F.62	Prepayments of insurance premiums and reserves for outstanding claims		NQDD	4 277	1 678	2 693	4 891	12 079	897	−563	−1 601	1 767
F.6	Total insurance technical reserves		NQCV	32 375	29 066	30 742	35 263	48 745	33 300	41 448	40 872	46 438
F.7	Other accounts payable		NQDG	−2 044	3 382	6 257	10 752	2 394	10 884	10 768	14 465	35 107
F.L	**Total net acquisition of financial liabilities**		NQDH	177 829	312 670	202 728	350 232	550 187	601 662	369 754	508 303	1 083 101
B.9	**Net lending / borrowing**											
F.A	Total net acquisition of financial assets		NQBL	172 740	301 340	200 602	345 268	544 672	606 728	369 509	486 841	1 056 726
-F.L	*less* Total net acquisition of financial liabilities		-NQDH	−177 829	−312 670	−202 728	−350 232	−550 187	−601 662	−369 754	−508 303	−1 083 101
B.9f	Net lending (+) / net borrowing (-), from financial account		NQDL	−5 089	−11 330	−2 126	−4 964	−5 515	5 066	−245	−21 462	−26 375
dB.9f	Statistical discrepancy between financial and non-financial accounts		NYVK	−7 464	−280	−4 609	−3 518	−2 458	−5 982	−4 096	3 179	9 923
B.9	Net lending (+) / net borrowing (-), from capital account		NQFH	−12 553	−11 610	−6 735	−8 482	−7 973	−916	−4 341	−18 283	−16 452

United Kingdom National Accounts 2001, © Crown copyright 2001

Main aggregates and summary accounts

1.6.9 UK summary accounts
Total economy ESA95 sector S.1 Unconsolidated

£ billion

			1992	1993	1994	1995	1996	1997	1998	1999	2000
IV.3	**FINANCIAL BALANCE SHEET** at end of period										
AN	**Non-financial assets**	CGJB	2 644.6	2 851.0	2 836.7	2 845.1	3 053.4	3 238.0	3 515.7	3 847.2	4 061.4
AF.A	**Financial assets**										
AF.1	Monetary gold and special drawing rights (SDRs)	NYVN	4.4	5.1	4.8	4.9	4.2	3.5	4.3	4.0	3.1
AF.2	Currency and deposits										
AF.21	Currency	NYVV	22.4	23.8	25.4	27.0	27.4	29.2	32.1	37.3	37.9
AF.22	Transferable deposits										
AF.221	Deposits with UK monetary financial institutions institutions	NYVZ	702.8	741.0	775.9	859.0	946.9	1 080.6	1 132.3	1 150.2	1 307.9
AF.229	Deposits with rest of the world monetary financial institutions	NYWH	513.6	565.8	596.0	677.1	698.6	855.1	879.5	902.0	1 131.2
AF.29	Other deposits	NYWJ	48.8	53.4	58.7	62.4	70.0	70.8	72.5	70.5	76.2
AF.2	Total currency and deposits	NYVT	1 287.5	1 384.0	1 455.9	1 625.5	1 742.9	2 035.8	2 116.3	2 160.1	2 553.2
AF.3	Securities other than shares										
AF.331	Short term: money market instruments										
AF.3311	Issued by UK central government	NYWP	5.6	5.5	6.7	17.0	3.4	2.7	4.3	3.9	2.6
AF.3312	Issued by UK local authorities	NYWX	2.2	1.9	1.9	2.0	1.8	1.4	1.1	1.3	1.2
AF.3315	Issued by UK monetary financial institutions	NYWZ	89.2	83.6	88.7	95.8	119.3	133.4	149.1	165.8	153.3
AF.3316	Issued by other UK residents	NYXJ	7.7	11.5	11.6	13.1	13.2	16.2	15.1	25.9	30.6
AF.3319	Issued by the rest of the world	NYXL	14.3	20.4	15.5	21.9	17.5	25.4	27.3	43.1	42.5
AF.332	Medium (1 to 5 year) and long term (over 5 year) bonds										
AF.3321	Issued by UK central government	NYXP	126.6	180.0	173.4	207.1	229.0	264.2	288.4	272.9	251.5
AF.3322	Issued by UK local authorities	NYXV	0.2	0.2	0.5	0.5	0.7	0.7	0.7	0.8	0.8
AF.3325	Medium term bonds issued by UK MFIs[1]	NYXX	9.4	10.8	14.7	17.6	19.4	21.2	24.5	32.1	34.9
AF.3326	Other medium & long term bonds issued by UK residents	NYYD	63.9	83.4	73.5	84.4	95.4	120.4	150.2	186.3	239.8
AF.3329	Long term bond issued by the rest of the world	NYYF	186.3	265.4	238.4	270.8	298.2	332.3	373.1	350.6	448.5
AF.34	Financial derivatives	NYYH	–	–	–	–	–	–	–	–	–
AF.3	Total securities other than shares	NYWL	505.4	662.6	624.8	730.2	797.9	917.7	1 033.8	1 082.6	1 205.8
AF.4	Loans										
AF.41	Short term loans										
AF.411	Loans by UK monetary financial institutions, excluding loans secured on dwellings & financial leasing	NYYT	479.0	459.8	465.5	557.2	634.8	729.0	767.5	817.6	985.7
AF.42	Long term loans										
AF.421	Direct investment	NYZF	51.5	53.9	57.7	70.1	71.5	80.3	100.5	126.0	160.3
AF.422	Loans secured on dwellings	NYZL	338.2	356.5	375.1	389.7	408.8	430.0	456.0	493.8	533.7
AF.423	Finance leasing	NYZT	18.2	17.9	17.8	18.7	20.6	22.6	23.2	23.3	23.0
AF.424	Other long-term loans by UK residents	NYZV	106.8	107.7	112.8	112.2	114.0	125.0	129.7	136.6	144.9
AF.4	Total loans	NYYP	993.6	995.8	1 028.9	1 147.9	1 249.8	1 386.9	1 476.9	1 597.3	1 847.6
AF.5	Shares and other equity										
AF.51	Shares and other equity, excluding mutual funds' shares										
AF.514	Quoted UK shares	NZAJ	512.4	644.0	607.3	720.4	798.7	930.4	975.7	1 229.5	1 124.6
AF.515	Unquoted UK shares	NZAL	161.3	199.5	192.4	222.6	246.4	303.7	330.4	419.1	429.0
AF.516	Other UK equity (including direct investment in property)	NZAN	1.3	1.4	1.3	0.6	1.4	1.5	2.0	2.1	2.1
AF.519	Shares and other equity issued by the rest of the world	NZAT	285.6	358.0	352.8	405.9	437.7	504.6	588.1	787.5	997.2
AF.52	Mutual funds' shares										
AF.521	UK mutual funds' shares	NZBB	80.7	122.7	118.8	142.8	164.9	192.1	216.6	297.3	302.8
AF.529	Rest of the world mutual fund share	NZBD	1.1	1.5	2.1	2.3	2.2	1.5	1.1	2.1	1.7
AF.5	Total shares and other equity	NYZZ	1 042.4	1 327.1	1 274.7	1 494.6	1 651.3	1 933.6	2 113.9	2 737.7	2 857.4
AF.6	Insurance technical reserves										
AF.61	Net equity of households in life assurance and pension funds' reserves	NZBH	684.9	875.1	823.7	968.1	1 053.6	1 285.7	1 416.3	1 623.5	1 434.8
AF.62	Prepayments of insurance premiums and reserves for outstanding claims	NZBN	33.8	35.4	37.7	42.3	48.5	49.1	49.1	47.8	50.2
AF.6	Total insurance technical reserves	NZBF	714.6	907.8	858.3	1 006.2	1 097.6	1 329.7	1 466.7	1 685.9	1 672.7
AF.7	Other accounts receivable	NZBP	206.3	208.7	213.8	221.9	220.8	229.1	236.9	249.3	282.0
AF.A	**Total financial assets**	NZBV	4 758.4	5 493.7	5 464.4	6 235.3	6 769.0	7 841.4	8 447.4	9 502.3	10 234.0

1 UK monetary financial institutions

1.6.9 UK summary accounts
continued
Total economy ESA95 sector S.1 Unconsolidated

Main aggregates and summary accounts

£ billion

			1992	1993	1994	1995	1996	1997	1998	1999	2000
IV.3	**FINANCIAL BALANCE SHEET** continued at end of period										
AF.L	**Financial liabilities**										
AF.2	Currency and deposits										
AF.21	Currency	NYVW	22.7	24.1	25.8	27.5	27.9	29.7	32.5	37.9	38.6
AF.22	Transferable deposits										
AF.221	Deposits with UK monetary financial institutions	NYWA	1 329.7	1 403.7	1 488.5	1 659.8	1 727.9	2 034.0	2 171.1	2 183.8	2 574.0
AF.29	Other deposits	NYWK	49.0	53.7	59.9	64.1	71.0	71.1	73.1	71.8	78.0
AF.2	Total currency and deposits	NYVU	1 401.4	1 481.5	1 574.1	1 751.4	1 826.8	2 134.8	2 276.7	2 293.6	2 690.6
AF.3	Securities other than shares										
AF.331	Short term: money market instruments										
AF.3311	Issued by UK central government	NYWQ	8.1	7.3	8.5	20.2	6.4	4.6	4.9	4.3	2.7
AF.3312	Issued by UK local authorities	NYWY	2.2	1.9	1.9	2.0	1.8	1.4	1.1	1.3	1.2
AF.3315	Issued by UK monetary financial institutions	NYXA	145.0	123.1	127.3	151.3	180.5	205.3	204.4	234.4	265.3
AF.3316	Issued by other UK residents	NYXK	14.6	19.8	21.3	24.4	24.5	29.5	30.7	43.7	51.0
AF.332	Medium (1 to 5 year) and long term (over 5 year) bonds										
AF.3321	Issued by UK central government	NYXQ	163.9	238.2	230.0	265.8	293.7	328.5	359.3	334.0	314.4
AF.3322	Issued by UK local authorities	NYXW	0.2	0.2	0.5	0.5	0.7	0.7	0.7	0.8	0.8
AF.3325	Medium term bonds issued by UK MFIs[1]	NYXY	19.0	24.5	34.3	38.3	43.3	47.4	53.3	67.7	74.6
AF.3326	Other medium & long term bonds issued by UK residents	NYYE	108.9	137.9	144.5	172.0	190.2	230.4	259.4	313.4	381.2
AF.34	Financial derivatives	NYYI	–	–	–	–	–	–	–	–	–
AF.3	Total securities other than shares	NYWM	461.7	552.8	568.1	674.4	741.2	847.9	913.7	999.6	1 091.1
AF.4	Loans										
AF.41	Short term loans										
AF.411	Loans by UK monetary financial institutions, excluding loans secured on dwellings & financial leasing	NYYU	364.4	353.1	364.8	432.4	488.3	536.5	564.0	602.3	709.0
AF.419	Loans by rest of the world monetary financial institutions	NYZC	63.1	85.4	81.6	104.1	129.1	149.2	141.4	166.3	201.8
AF.42	Long term loans										
AF.421	Direct investment	NYZG	75.6	74.6	73.0	78.4	84.0	101.1	117.0	151.6	206.7
AF.422	Loans secured on dwellings	NYZM	338.2	356.5	375.1	389.7	408.8	430.0	456.0	493.8	533.7
AF.423	Finance leasing	NYZU	18.2	17.9	17.8	18.7	20.6	22.6	23.2	23.3	23.0
AF.424	Other long-term loans by UK residents	NYZW	104.3	105.0	110.2	109.9	111.6	122.7	127.7	134.8	143.3
AF.429	Other long-term loans by the rest of the world	NYZY	54.6	123.1	68.9	91.1	132.2	150.3	152.9	168.3	197.4
AF.4	Total loans	NYYQ	1 018.4	1 115.5	1 091.3	1 224.4	1 374.7	1 512.4	1 582.3	1 740.4	2 014.9
AF.5	Shares and other equity										
AF.51	Shares and other equity, excluding mutual funds' shares										
AF.514	Quoted UK shares	NZAK	600.1	771.5	726.3	864.9	963.9	1 225.2	1 370.8	1 751.1	1 756.1
AF.515	Unquoted UK shares	NZAM	248.5	292.2	284.9	335.1	367.6	437.2	489.5	624.7	717.5
AF.516	Other UK equity (including direct investment in property)	NZAO	8.4	9.0	9.8	9.3	10.7	11.6	12.9	13.9	15.1
AF.52	Mutual funds' shares										
AF.521	UK mutual funds' shares	NZBC	81.3	123.6	119.8	143.9	166.1	193.3	217.9	299.0	304.4
AF.5	Total shares and other equity	NZAA	938.4	1 196.3	1 140.8	1 353.2	1 508.2	1 867.4	2 091.1	2 688.8	2 793.1
AF.6	Insurance technical reserves										
AF.61	Net equity of households in life assurance and pension funds' reserves	NZBI	685.0	875.2	823.8	968.3	1 053.8	1 285.9	1 416.5	1 623.7	1 435.0
AF.62	Prepayments of insurance premiums and reserves for outstanding claims	NZBO	38.0	39.7	42.4	47.5	58.6	59.5	60.8	58.9	62.5
AF.6	Total insurance technical reserves	NZBG	723.0	915.0	866.2	1 015.8	1 112.4	1 345.5	1 477.3	1 682.7	1 497.5
AF.7	Other accounts payable	NZBQ	193.0	196.2	201.6	208.5	207.5	216.1	224.5	236.2	270.0
AF.L	**Total financial liabilities**	NZBW	4 735.9	5 457.3	5 442.2	6 227.7	6 770.8	7 924.0	8 565.5	9 641.2	10 357.2
BF.90	**Net financial assets / liabilities**										
AF.A	Total financial assets	NZBV	4 758.4	5 493.7	5 464.4	6 235.3	6 769.0	7 841.4	8 447.4	9 502.3	10 234.0
-AF.L	*less* Total financial liabilities	-NZBW	-4 735.9	-5 457.3	-5 442.2	-6 227.7	-6 770.8	-7 924.0	-8 565.5	-9 641.2	-10 357.2
BF.90	**Net financial assets (+) / liabilities (-)**	NQFT	22.5	36.4	22.2	7.6	-1.9	-82.6	-118.1	-138.9	-123.2
	Net worth										
AN	Non-financial assets	CGJB	2 644.6	2 851.0	2 836.7	2 845.1	3 053.4	3 238.0	3 515.7	3 847.2	4 061.4
BF.90	Net financial assets (+) / liabilities (-)	NQFT	22.5	36.4	22.2	7.6	-1.9	-82.6	-118.1	-138.9	-123.2
B.90	**Net worth**	CGDA	2 657.4	2 882.4	2 854.6	2 822.5	2 984.0	3 162.6	3 380.5	3 713.8	3 943.7

1 UK monetary financial institutions

Main aggregates and summary accounts

1.7 UK summary accounts 1997

Total economy: all sectors and the rest of the world

£ million

		RESOURCES						USES	TOTAL
		UK total economy S.1	Non-financial corporations S.11	Financial corporations S.12	General government S.13	Households & NPISH S.14+S.15	Not sector -ised S.N	Rest of the world S.2	Goods & services

Current accounts

I 0   PRODUCTION / EXTERNAL ACCOUNT OF GOODS AND SERVICES

Code	Description	S.1	S.11	S.12	S.13	S.14+S.15	S.N	S.2	Total
P.7	Imports of goods and services							231 436	231 436
P.6	Exports of goods and services							231 622	231 622
P.1	Output at basic prices	1 539 896	1 058 652	93 933	156 893	230 418			1 539 896
P.2	Intermediate consumption						819 204		819 204
D.21-D.31	Taxes less subsidies on products	90 375					90 375		90 375

II.1.1 GENERATION OF INCOME

Code	Description	S.1	S.11	S.12	S.13	S.14+S.15	S.N	S.2	Total
B.1g	Gross domestic product, value added at market prices	811 067	502 646	38 630	69 526	132 286	67 979		811 067
B.11	External balance of goods and services							−186	−186

II.1.2 ALLOCATION OF PRIMARY INCOME

Code	Description	S.1	S.11	S.12	S.13	S.14+S.15	S.N	S.2	Total
D.1	Compensation of employees	433 043				433 043		924	433 967
D.21-D.31	Taxes less subsidies on products	90 375			104 250			2 811	197 436
D.29-D.39	Other taxes less subsidies on production	15 769			15 769				15 769
B.2g	Operating surplus, gross	221 502	178 629	14 806	7 316	43 147	−22 396		221 502
B.3g	Mixed income, gross	50 461				50 461			50 461
di	Statistical discrepancy between income components and GDP	−					−		−
D.4	Property income	395 696	48 673	215 161	15 856	116 006		91 514	487 210
-P.119	Adjustment to property income for financial services (FISIM)			−22 396			22 396		

II.2 SECONDARY DISTRIBUTION OF INCOME

Code	Description	S.1	S.11	S.12	S.13	S.14+S.15	S.N	S.2	Total
B.5g	National income, balance of primary incomes, gross	812 368	112 808	6 259	92 902	600 399	−		812 368
D.5	Current taxes on income, wealth etc	121 467			121 467			638	122 105
D.61	Social contributions	124 962	3 173	61 016	60 363	410		−	124 962
D.62	Social benefits other than social transfers in kind	165 695				165 695		1 179	166 874
D.7	Other current transfers	125 878	4 747	24 587	62 062	34 482		11 395	137 273

II.3 REDISTRIBUTION OF INCOME IN KIND

Code	Description	S.1	S.11	S.12	S.13	S.14+S.15	S.N	S.2	Total
B.6g	Disposable income, gross	809 159	85 406	16 910	144 389	562 454	−		809 159
D.63	Social transfers in kind	107 153				107 153			107 153

II.4 USE OF INCOME

Code	Description	S.1	S.11	S.12	S.13	S.14+S.15	S.N	S.2	Total
B.7g	Adjusted disposable income, gross	809 159	85 406	16 910	56 838	650 005	−		809 159
B.6g	Disposable income, gross	809 159	85 406	16 910	144 389	562 454	−		809 159
P.4	Actual final consumption							672 123	672 123
P.3	Final consumption expenditure							672 123	672 123
D.8	Adjustment for change in households' net equity in pension funds	15 131				15 131		−2	15 131

Accumulation accounts

III.1.1 CHANGE IN NET WORTH DUE TO SAVING AND CAPITAL TRANSFERS

Code	Description	S.1	S.11	S.12	S.13	S.14+S.15	S.N	S.2	Total
B.8g	Saving, gross	137 038	85 406	1 781	−4 758	54 609	−		137 038
B.12	Current external balance							1 720	1 720
D.9	Capital transfers receivable	11 976	2 505	−	5 015	4 456		785	12 761
D.9	Capital transfers payable	−11 138	−188	−	−8 757	−2 193		−1 623	−12 761

III.1.2 ACQUISITION ON NON-FINANCIAL ASSETS
Changes in liabilities and net worth

Code	Description	S.1	S.11	S.12	S.13	S.14+S.15	S.N	S.2	Total
B.10.1g	Changes in net worth due to saving and capital transfers	137 876	87 723	1 781	−8 500	56 872	−	882	138 758
P.51	Gross fixed capital formation							134 396	134 396
-K.1	(Consumption of fixed capital)								
P.52	Changes in inventories							4 388	4 388
P.53	Acquisitions less disposals of valuables							−26	−26
K.2	Acquisitions less disposals of non-produced non-financial assets								
de	Statistical discrepancy between expenditure components and GDP							−	−

III.2 FINANCIAL ACCOUNT

Code	Description	S.1	S.11	S.12	S.13	S.14+S.15	S.N	S.2	Total
B.9	Net lending(+) / net borrowing(-)	−916	−2 194	−4 319	−17 723	23 320	−	916	−
	Changes in liabilities								
F.2	Currency and deposits	261 813		259 872	1 941	−		137 640	399 453
F.3	Securities other than shares	69 981	15 125	39 603	15 114	139		51 226	123 519
F.4	Loans	176 045	40 953	97 792	−1 613	38 913		40 041	216 086
F.5	Shares and other equity	49 639	31 015	18 624		−		33 262	82 901
F.6	Insurance technical reserves	33 300		33 300					33 300
F.7	Other accounts payable	10 884	1 020	4 776	2 610	2 478		41	10 925

Main aggregates and summary accounts

1.7 continued
UK summary accounts 1997
Total economy: all sectors and the rest of the world

£ million

		USES						RESOURCES		TOTAL
		UK total economy	Non-financial corporations	Financial corporations	General government	Households & NPISH	Not sector -ised	Rest of the world	Goods & services	
		S.1	S.11	S.12	S.13	S.14+S.15	S.N	S.2		

		Current accounts								
I / 0		**PRODUCTION / EXTERNAL ACCOUNT OF GOODS AND SERVICES**								
P.7	Imports of goods and services								231 436	231 436
P.6	Exports of goods and services							231 622		231 622
P.1	Output at basic prices								1 539 896	1 539 896
P.2	Intermediate consumption	819 204	556 006	55 303	87 367	98 132	22 396			819 204
D.21-D.31	Taxes less subsidies on products								90 375	90 375
B.1g	**Gross domestic product, value added at market prices**	**811 067**	**502 646**	**38 630**	**69 526**	**132 286**	**67 979**			**811 067**
B.11	External balance of goods and services							−186		−186
II.1.1		**GENERATION OF INCOME**								
D.1	Compensation of employees	432 960	311 256	22 416	60 520	38 768		1 007		433 967
D.21-D.31	Taxes less subsidies on products	90 375					90 375			197 436
D.29-D.39	Other taxes less subsidies on production	15 769	12 761	1 408	1 690	−90				15 769
B.2g	Operating surplus, gross	221 502	178 629	14 806	7 316	43 147	−22 396			221 502
B.3g	Mixed income, gross	50 461				50 461				50 461
di	Statistical discrepancy between income components and GDP	−					−			
II.1.2		**ALLOCATION OF PRIMARY INCOME**								
D.4	Property income	391 873	114 494	201 312	33 809	42 258		95 337		487 210
−P.119	Adjustment to property income for financial services (FISIM)									
B.5g	National income, balance of primary incomes, gross	812 368	112 808	6 259	92 902	600 399	−			812 368
II.2		**SECONDARY DISTRIBUTION OF INCOME**								
D.5	Current taxes on income, wealth etc	121 703	27 557	4 412		89 734		402		122 105
D.61	Social contributions	124 855				124 855		107		124 962
D.62	Social benefits other than social transfers in kind	166 874	3 173	45 887	116 934	880		615		166 874
D.7	Other current transfers	127 779	4 592	24 653	75 471	23 063		9 494		137 273
B.6g	Disposable income, gross	809 159	85 406	16 910	144 389	562 454	−			809 159
II.3		**REDISTRIBUTION OF INCOME IN KIND**								
D.63	Social transfers in kind	107 153			87 551	19 602				107 153
B.7g	Adjusted disposable income, gross	809 159	85 406	16 910	56 838	650 005	−			809 159
II.4		**USE OF INCOME ACCOUNT**								
B.6g	Disposable income, gross									
P.4	Actual final consumption	672 123			61 596	610 527				672 123
P.3	Final consumption expenditure	672 123			149 147	522 976				672 123
D.8	Adjustment for change in households' net equity in pension funds	15 129		15 129						15 129
B.8g	Saving, gross	137 038	85 406	1 781	−4 758	54 609	−			137 038
B.12	Current external balance							1 720		1 720

		Accumulation accounts								
III.1.1		**CHANGE IN NET WORTH DUE TO SAVING AND CAPITAL TRANSFERS**								
D.9	Capital transfers receivable									
D.9	Capital transfers payable									
B.10.1g	Changes in net worth due to saving and capital transfers	137 876	87 723	1 781	−8 500	56 872	−	882		138 758
III.1.2		**ACQUISITION OF NON-FINANCIAL ASSETS**								
		Changes in assets								
P.51	Gross fixed capital formation	134 396	86 052	6 208	9 455	32 681				134 396
−K.1	(Consumption of fixed capital)	−93 531	−60 356	−3 902	−7 316	−21 957				−93 531
P.52	Changes in inventories	4 388	3 730	35	140	483				4 388
P.53	Acquisitions less disposals of valuables	−26	−60	−104	−	138				−26
K.2	Acquisitions less disposals of non-produced non-financial assets	34	195	−39	−372	250		−34		−
de	Statistical discrepancy between expenditure components and GDP	−					−			−
B.9	**Net lending(+) / net borrowing(−)**	−916	−2 194	−4 319	−17 723	23 320	−	916		−
III.2		**FINANCIAL ACCOUNT: changes in assets**								
F.1	Monetary gold and SDRs	1 199			1 199			−1 199		
F.2	Currency and deposits	252 276	22 768	190 085	996	38 427		147 177		399 453
F.3	Securities other than shares	97 839	−3 971	106 202	−3 552	−840		23 368		123 519
F.4	Loans	151 351	11 856	138 582	1 269	−356		64 735		216 086
F.5	Shares and other equity	60 123	53 362	12 079	−1 770	−3 548		22 778		82 901
F.6	Insurance technical reserves	33 038	163	30	12	32 833		262		33 300
F.7	Other accounts receivable	10 902	1 585	2 017	2 574	4 726		23		10 925
dB.9f	Statistical discrepancy between non-financial and financial transactions	−5 982	156	653	−399	−6 392	−	5 982		−

57

Main aggregates and summary accounts

1.7 UK summary accounts 1998
continued

Total economy: all sectors and the rest of the world

£ million

		RESOURCES						USES	TOTAL
		UK total economy	Non-financial corporations	Financial corporations	General government	Households & NPISH	Not sector-ised	Rest of the world	Goods & services
		S.1	S.11	S.12	S.13	S.14+S.15	S.N	S.2	

		Current accounts							
I 0		**PRODUCTION / EXTERNAL ACCOUNT OF GOODS AND SERVICES**							
P.7	Imports of goods and services							237 948	237 948
P.6	Exports of goods and services								228 801	228 801
P.1	Output at basic prices	1 631 361	1 116 284	107 907	162 846	244 324			1 631 361
P.2	Intermediate consumption								870 043	870 043
D.21-D.31	Taxes less subsidies on products	98 487					98 487		98 487
II.1.1		**GENERATION OF INCOME**							
B.1g	Gross domestic product, value added at market prices	**859 805**	**533 219**	**44 382**	**70 994**	**140 721**	**70 489**		**859 805**
B.11	External balance of goods and services							9 147	9 147
II.1.2		**ALLOCATION OF PRIMARY INCOME**							
D.1	Compensation of employees	464 248				464 248		850	465 098
D.21-D.31	Taxes less subsidies on products	98 487			112 091			3 683	214 261
D.29-D.39	Other taxes less subsidies on production	16 296			16 296			246	16 296
B.2g	Operating surplus, gross	230 472	184 477	18 436	7 534	48 023	−27 998		230 472
B.3g	Mixed income, gross	50 292				50 292			50 292
di	Statistical discrepancy between income components and GDP	–					–		–
D.4	Property income	439 425	50 586	248 434	17 281	123 124		90 377	529 802
-P.119	Adjustment to property income for financial services (FISIM)			−27 998			27 998		
II.2		**SECONDARY DISTRIBUTION OF INCOME**							
B.5g	National income, balance of primary incomes, gross	868 926	120 300	13 381	101 287	633 958	–		868 926
D.5	Current taxes on income, wealth etc	139 053			139 053			454	139 507
D.61	Social contributions	134 968	3 801	65 968	64 721	478		–	134 968
D.62	Social benefits other than social transfers in kind	170 931				170 931		1 234	172 165
D.7	Other current transfers	129 885	5 444	25 385	62 686	36 370		12 706	142 591
II.3		**REDISTRIBUTION OF INCOME IN KIND**							
B.6g	Disposable income, gross	864 136	94 942	22 092	171 770	575 332	–		864 136
D.63	Social transfers in kind	113 388				113 388			113 388
II.4		**USE OF INCOME**							
B.7g	Adjusted disposable income, gross	864 136	94 942	22 092	79 499	667 603	–		864 136
B.6g	Disposable income, gross	864 136	94 942	22 092	171 770	575 332	–		864 136
P.4	Actual final consumption							712 523	712 523
P.3	Final consumption expenditure							712 523	712 523
D.8	Adjustment for change in households' net equity in pension funds	16 105				16 105		−2	16 105

		Accumulation accounts							
III.1.1		**CHANGE IN NET WORTH DUE TO SAVING AND CAPITAL TRANSFERS**							
B.8g	Saving, gross	151 615	94 942	5 989	16 889	33 795	–		151 615
B.12	Current external balance							4 814	4 814
D.9	Capital transfers receivable	11 299	2 213	–	4 642	4 444		859	12 158
D.9	Capital transfers payable	−10 778	−193	–	−8 258	−2 327		−1 380	−12 158
III.1.2		**ACQUISITION ON NON-FINANCIAL ASSETS**							
		Changes in liabilities and net worth							
B.10.1g	Changes in net worth due to saving and capital transfers	152 136	96 962	5 989	13 273	35 912	–	4 293	156 429
P.51	Gross fixed capital formation							151 539	151 539
-K.1	(Consumption of fixed capital)								
P.52	Changes in inventories							4 460	4 460
P.53	Acquisitions less disposals of valuables							430	430
K.2	Acquisitions less disposals of non-produced non-financial assets								
de	Statistical discrepancy between expenditure components and GDP							–	–
III.2		**FINANCIAL ACCOUNT**							
B.9	Net lending(+) / net borrowing(-)	−4 341	−3 649	−5 368	3 458	1 218	–	4 341	–
		Changes in liabilities							
F.2	Currency and deposits	117 766		118 792	−1 026	–		15 899	133 665
F.3	Securities other than shares	20 292	20 535	2 634	−3 115	238		33 176	47 382
F.4	Loans	107 230	52 077	10 116	1 594	43 443		33 974	141 204
F.5	Shares and other equity	72 250	52 259	19 991		–		63 851	136 101
F.6	Insurance technical reserves	41 448		41 448					41 448
F.7	Other accounts payable	10 768	4 561	2 434	671	3 102		−1 168	9 600

Main aggregates and summary accounts

1.7 continued
UK summary accounts 1998
Total economy: all sectors and the rest of the world

£ million

		USES						RESOURCES	TOTAL
		UK total economy S.1	Non-financial corporations S.11	Financial corporations S.12	General government S.13	Households & NPISH S.14+S.15	Not sector -ised S.N	Rest of the world S.2	Goods & services	

Current accounts

I 0 PRODUCTION / EXTERNAL ACCOUNT OF GOODS AND SERVICES

Code	Item	S.1	S.11	S.12	S.13	S.14+S.15	S.N	S.2	G&S	Total
P.7	Imports of goods and services								237 948	237 948
P.6	Exports of goods and services							228 801		228 801
P.1	Output at basic prices								1 631 361	1 631 361
P.2	Intermediate consumption	870 043	583 065	63 525	91 852	103 603	27 998			870 043
D.21-D.31	Taxes less subsidies on products								98 487	98 487
B.1g	**Gross domestic product, value added at market prices**	**859 805**	**533 219**	**44 382**	**70 994**	**140 721**	**70 489**			**859 805**
B.11	External balance of goods and services							9 147		9 147

II.1.1 GENERATION OF INCOME

Code	Item	S.1	S.11	S.12	S.13	S.14+S.15	S.N	S.2	G&S	Total
D.1	Compensation of employees	464 258	335 562	24 460	61 704	42 532		840		465 098
D.21-D.31	Taxes less subsidies on products	98 487					98 487			214 261
D.29-D.39	Other taxes less subsidies on production	16 296	13 925	1 486	1 756	120				16 296
B.2g	Operating surplus, gross	230 472	184 477	18 436	7 534	48 023	−27 998			230 472
B.3g	Mixed income, gross	50 292				50 292				50 292
di	Statistical discrepancy between income components and GDP	−					−			

II.1.2 ALLOCATION OF PRIMARY INCOME

Code	Item	S.1	S.11	S.12	S.13	S.14+S.15	S.N	S.2	Total
D.4	Property income	426 857	114 763	225 491	34 874	51 729		102 945	529 802
−P.119	Adjustment to property income for financial services (FISIM)								
B.5g	National income, balance of primary incomes, gross	868 926	120 300	13 381	101 287	633 958	−		868 926

II.2 SECONDARY DISTRIBUTION OF INCOME

Code	Item	S.1	S.11	S.12	S.13	S.14+S.15	S.N	S.2	Total
D.5	Current taxes on income, wealth etc	138 977	25 590	7 318		106 069		530	139 507
D.61	Social contributions	134 869				134 869		99	134 968
D.62	Social benefits other than social transfers in kind	172 165	3 801	49 865	117 549	950		783	172 165
D.7	Other current transfers	133 616	5 212	25 459	78 428	24 517		8 975	142 591
B.6g	Disposable income, gross	864 136	94 942	22 092	171 770	575 332	−		864 136

II.3 REDISTRIBUTION OF INCOME IN KIND

Code	Item	S.1	S.11	S.12	S.13	S.14+S.15	S.N	S.2	Total
D.63	Social transfers in kind	113 388			92 271	21 117			113 388
B.7g	Adjusted disposable income, gross	864 136	94 942	22 092	79 499	667 603	−		864 136

II.4 USE OF INCOME ACCOUNT

Code	Item	S.1	S.11	S.12	S.13	S.14+S.15	S.N	S.2	Total
B.6g	Disposable income, gross								
P.4	Actual final consumption	712 523			62 610	649 913			712 523
P.3	Final consumption expenditure	712 523			154 881	557 642			712 523
D.8	Adjustment for change in households' net equity in pension funds	16 103		16 103					16 103
B.8g	Saving, gross	151 615	94 942	5 989	16 889	33 795	−		151 615
B.12	Current external balance							4 814	4 814

Accumulation accounts

III.1.1 CHANGE IN NET WORTH DUE TO SAVING AND CAPITAL TRANSFERS

Code	Item	S.1	S.11	S.12	S.13	S.14+S.15	S.N	S.2	Total
D.9	Capital transfers receivable								
D.9	Capital transfers payable								
B.10.1g	Changes in net worth due to saving and capital transfers	152 136	96 962	5 989	13 273	35 912	−	4 293	156 429

III.1.2 ACQUISITION OF NON-FINANCIAL ASSETS
Changes in assets

Code	Item	S.1	S.11	S.12	S.13	S.14+S.15	S.N	S.2	Total
P.51	Gross fixed capital formation	151 539	95 385	11 277	10 661	34 216			151 539
−K.1	(Consumption of fixed capital)	−96 074	−60 844	−4 094	−7 534	−23 602			−96 074
P.52	Changes in inventories	4 460	4 196	35	107	122			4 460
P.53	Acquisitions less disposals of valuables	430	28	49	14	339			430
K.2	Acquisitions less disposals of non-produced non-financial assets	48	1 002	−4	−967	17		−48	−
de	Statistical discrepancy between expenditure components and GDP	−					−		−
B.9	**Net lending(+) / net borrowing(-)**	−4 341	−3 649	−5 368	3 458	1 218	−	4 341	−

III.2 FINANCIAL ACCOUNT: changes in assets

Code	Item	S.1	S.11	S.12	S.13	S.14+S.15	S.N	S.2	Total
F.1	Monetary gold and SDRs	915			915			−915	
F.2	Currency and deposits	85 155	5 741	48 374	−1 516	32 556		48 510	133 665
F.3	Securities other than shares	69 608	2 783	70 164	1 216	−4 555		−16 140	47 382
F.4	Loans	93 903	30 537	63 074	748	−456		47 301	141 204
F.5	Shares and other equity	68 946	78 477	14 741	78	−24 350		67 155	136 101
F.6	Insurance technical reserves	41 447	−109	−7	−11	41 574		1	41 448
F.7	Other accounts receivable	9 535	1 341	4 359	758	3 077		65	9 600
dB.9f	Statistical discrepancy between non-financial and financial transactions	−4 096	7 013	−10 658	−606	155	−	4 096	−

Main aggregates and summary accounts

1.7 UK summary accounts 1999
continued

Total economy: all sectors and the rest of the world

£ million

		RESOURCES						USES	TOTAL
		UK total economy	Non-financial corporations	Financial corporations	General government	Households & NPISH	Not sector -ised	Rest of the world	Goods & services
		S.1	S.11	S.12	S.13	S.14+S.15	S.N	S.2	
	Current accounts								
I 0	**PRODUCTION / EXTERNAL ACCOUNT OF GOODS AND SERVICES**								
P.7	Imports of goods and services							252 584	252 584
P.6	Exports of goods and services							236 720	236 720
P.1	Output at basic prices	1 721 728	1 173 096	115 947	174 874	257 811			1 721 728
P.2	Intermediate consumption							926 703	926 703
D.21-D.31	Taxes *less* subsidies on products	106 244					106 244		106 244
II.1.1	**GENERATION OF INCOME**								
B.1g	**Gross domestic product, value added at market prices**	901 269	561 218	41 855	74 126	148 645	75 425		901 269
B.11	External balance of goods and services							15 864	15 864
II.1.2	**ALLOCATION OF PRIMARY INCOME**								
D.1	Compensation of employees	494 387				494 387		759	495 146
D.21-D.31	Taxes *less* subsidies on products	106 244			106 244			3 551	230 501
D.29-D.39	Other taxes *less* subsidies on production	16 893			16 893				16 893
B.2g	Operating surplus, gross	231 482	188 636	14 701	7 767	51 197	–30 819		231 482
B.3g	Mixed income, gross	52 464				52 464			52 464
di	Statistical discrepancy between income components and GDP	–					–		–
D.4	Property income	418 904	48 754	235 337	16 274	118 539		95 494	514 398
-P.119	Adjustment to property income for financial services (FISIM)			–30 819			30 819		
II.2	**SECONDARY DISTRIBUTION OF INCOME**								
B.5g	National income, balance of primary incomes, gross	902 107	112 191	7 905	113 349	668 662	–		902 107
D.5	Current taxes on income, wealth etc	145 307			145 307			505	145 812
D.61	Social contributions	140 744	3 535	69 508	67 251	450		–	140 744
D.62	Social benefits other than social transfers in kind	178 050				178 050		1 243	179 293
D.7	Other current transfers	132 571	4 762	23 389	68 620	35 800		12 947	145 518
II.3	**REDISTRIBUTION OF INCOME IN KIND**								
B.6g	Disposable income, gross	898 040	90 792	13 062	189 643	604 543	–		898 040
D.63	Social transfers in kind	123 175				123 175			123 175
II.4	**USE OF INCOME**								
B.7g	Adjusted disposable income, gross	898 040	90 792	13 062	89 139	705 047	–		898 040
B.6g	Disposable income, gross	898 040	90 792	13 062	189 643	604 543	–		898 040
P.4	Actual final consumption							756 520	756 520
P.3	Final consumption expenditure							756 520	756 520
D.8	Adjustment for change in households' net equity in pension funds	15 417				15 417		–2	15 417
	Accumulation accounts								
III.1.1	**CHANGE IN NET WORTH DUE TO SAVING AND CAPITAL TRANSFERS**								
B.8g	Saving, gross	141 522	90 792	–2 353	23 349	29 734	–		141 522
B.12	Current external balance							19 091	19 091
D.9	Capital transfers receivable	12 683	2 492	–	5 358	4 833		680	13 363
D.9	Capital transfers payable	–11 887	–216	–	–9 221	–2 450		–1 476	–13 363
III.1.2	**ACQUISITION ON NON-FINANCIAL ASSETS** Changes in liabilities and net worth								
B.10.1g	Changes in net worth due to saving and capital transfers	142 318	93 068	–2 353	19 486	32 117	–	18 295	160 613
P.51	Gross fixed capital formation							155 408	155 408
-K.1	(Consumption of fixed capital)								
P.52	Changes in inventories							4 975	4 975
P.53	Acquisitions less disposals of valuables							230	230
K.2	Acquisitions less disposals of non-produced non-financial assets								
de	Statistical discrepancy between expenditure components and GDP							–	–
III.2	**FINANCIAL ACCOUNT**								
B.9	**Net lending(+) / net borrowing(-)**	–18 283	–12 540	–9 935	10 333	–6 141	–	18 283	–
	Changes in liabilities								
F.2	Currency and deposits	46 407		47 055	–648	–		43 021	89 428
F.3	Securities other than shares	104 270	41 816	67 447	–4 971	–22		1 883	111 523
F.4	Loans	180 900	45 058	63 767	7 460	64 615		43 935	224 835
F.5	Shares and other equity	121 389	95 529	25 860		–		140 420	261 809
F.6	Insurance technical reserves	40 872		40 872					40 872
F.7	Other accounts payable	14 465	8 095	4 173	–1 577	3 774		–228	14 237

Main aggregates and summary accounts

1.7 continued
UK summary accounts 1999
Total economy: all sectors and the rest of the world

£ million

		USES						RESOURCES		TOTAL
		UK total economy	Non-financial corporations	Financial corporations	General government	Households & NPISH	Not sector-ised	Rest of the world	Goods & services	
		S.1	S.11	S.12	S.13	S.14+S.15	S.N	S.2		

Current accounts

I / 0 PRODUCTION / EXTERNAL ACCOUNT OF GOODS AND SERVICES

Code	Item	S.1	S.11	S.12	S.13	S.14+S.15	S.N	S.2	G&S	Total
P.7	Imports of goods and services								252 584	252 584
P.6	Exports of goods and services							236 720		236 720
P.1	Output at basic prices								1 721 728	1 721 728
P.2	Intermediate consumption	926 703	611 878	74 092	100 748	109 166	30 819			926 703
D.21-D.31	Taxes less subsidies on products								106 244	106 244
B.1g	**Gross domestic product, value added at market prices**	**901 269**	**561 218**	**41 855**	**74 126**	**148 645**	**75 425**			**901 269**
B.11	External balance of goods and services							15 864		15 864

II.1.1 GENERATION OF INCOME

Code	Item	S.1	S.11	S.12	S.13	S.14+S.15	S.N	S.2		Total
D.1	Compensation of employees	494 186	358 742	25 627	64 584	45 233		960		495 146
D.21-D.31	Taxes less subsidies on products	106 244					106 244			230 501
D.29-D.39	Other taxes less subsidies on production	16 893	14 590	1 527	1 775	121				16 893
B.2g	Operating surplus, gross	231 482	188 636	14 701	7 767	51 197	–30 819			231 482
B.3g	Mixed income, gross	52 464				52 464				52 464
di	Statistical discrepancy between income components and GDP	–				–				–

II.1.2 ALLOCATION OF PRIMARY INCOME

Code	Item	S.1	S.11	S.12	S.13	S.14+S.15	S.N	S.2		Total
D.4	Property income	415 086	125 199	211 314	30 648	47 925		99 312		514 398
-P.119	Adjustment to property income for financial services (FISIM)									
B.5g	National income, balance of primary incomes, gross	902 107	112 191	7 905	113 349	668 662	–			902 107

II.2 SECONDARY DISTRIBUTION OF INCOME

Code	Item	S.1	S.11	S.12	S.13	S.14+S.15	S.N	S.2		Total
D.5	Current taxes on income, wealth etc	145 284	21 637	10 192		113 455		528		145 812
D.61	Social contributions	140 657				140 657		87		140 744
D.62	Social benefits other than social transfers in kind	179 293	3 535	54 084	120 752	922		434		179 293
D.7	Other current transfers	135 505	4 524	23 464	84 132	23 385		10 013		179 293
B.6g	Disposable income, gross	898 040	90 792	13 062	189 643	604 543	–			898 040

II.3 REDISTRIBUTION OF INCOME IN KIND

Code	Item	S.1	S.11	S.12	S.13	S.14+S.15	S.N	S.2		Total
D.63	Social transfers in kind	123 175			100 504	22 671				123 175
B.7g	Adjusted disposable income, gross	898 040	90 792	13 062	89 139	705 047	–			898 040

II.4 USE OF INCOME ACCOUNT

Code	Item	S.1	S.11	S.12	S.13	S.14+S.15	S.N	S.2		Total
B.6g	Disposable income, gross									
P.4	Actual final consumption	756 520			65 790	690 730				756 520
P.3	Final consumption expenditure	756 520			166 294	590 226				756 520
D.8	Adjustment for change in households' net equity in pension funds	15 415		15 415						15 415
B.8g	Saving, gross	141 522	90 792	–2 353	23 349	29 734	–			141 522
B.12	Current external balance							19 091		19 091

Accumulation accounts

III.1.1 CHANGE IN NET WORTH DUE TO SAVING AND CAPITAL TRANSFERS

Code	Item	S.1	S.11	S.12	S.13	S.14+S.15	S.N	S.2		Total
D.9	Capital transfers receivable									
D.9	Capital transfers payable									
B.10.1g	Changes in net worth due to saving and capital transfers	142 318	93 068	–2 353	19 486	32 117	–	18 295		160 613

III.1.2 ACQUISITION OF NON-FINANCIAL ASSETS
Changes in assets

Code	Item	S.1	S.11	S.12	S.13	S.14+S.15	S.N	S.2		Total
P.51	Gross fixed capital formation	155 408	99 947	7 537	10 107	37 817				155 408
-K.1	(Consumption of fixed capital)	–100 650	–62 981	–3 974	–7 767	–25 928				–100 650
P.52	Changes in inventories	4 975	4 984	47	–268	212				4 975
P.53	Acquisitions less disposals of valuables	230	–17	–28	10	265				230
K.2	Acquisitions less disposals of non-produced non-financial assets	–12	694	26	–696	–36		12		–
de	Statistical discrepancy between expenditure components and GDP	–				–				–
B.9	**Net lending(+) / net borrowing(-)**	**–18 283**	**–12 540**	**–9 935**	**10 333**	**–6 141**	–	**18 283**		

III.2 FINANCIAL ACCOUNT: changes in assets

Code	Item	S.1	S.11	S.12	S.13	S.14+S.15	S.N	S.2		Total
F.1	Monetary gold and SDRs	–374			–374			374		
F.2	Currency and deposits	76 425	27 292	14 109	3 029	31 995		13 003		89 428
F.3	Securities other than shares	65 960	–3 942	73 966	–3 116	–948		40 193		111 523
F.4	Loans	153 701	25 329	120 865	3 746	3 761		71 134		224 835
F.5	Shares and other equity	135 221	125 679	25 681	–225	–15 914		126 588		261 809
F.6	Insurance technical reserves	41 536	–291	–44	–29	41 900		–664		40 872
F.7	Other accounts receivable	14 372	–2 361	5 304	6 994	4 435		–135		14 237
dB.9f	Statistical discrepancy between non-financial and financial transactions	3 179	6 252	–642	572	–3 003	–	–3 179		–

61

Main aggregates and summary accounts

1.7 continued UK summary accounts 2000
Total economy: all sectors and the rest of the world
£ million

		RESOURCES						USES	TOTAL
		UK total economy S.1	Non-financial corporations S.11	Financial corporations S.12	General government S.13	Households & NPISH S.14+S.15	Not sector -ised S.N	Rest of the world S.2	Goods & services

Current accounts

I 0 PRODUCTION / EXTERNAL ACCOUNT OF GOODS AND SERVICES

P.7	Imports of goods and services							281 024	281 024
P.6	Exports of goods and services							265 305	265 305
P.1	Output at basic prices	1 818 849	..	..	..	..			1 818 849
P.2	Intermediate consumption							987 792	987 792
D.21-D.31	Taxes less subsidies on products	112 359					112 359		112 359

II.1.1 GENERATION OF INCOME

B.1g	Gross domestic product, value added at market prices	943 412	..	..	..	..	..		943 412
B.11	External balance of goods and services							15 719	15 719

II.1.2 ALLOCATION OF PRIMARY INCOME

D.1	Compensation of employees	521 586				521 586		871	522 457
D.21-D.31	Taxes less subsidies on products	112 359			127 691			3 446	243 496
D.29-D.39	Other taxes less subsidies on production	17 872			17 872				17 872
B.2g	Operating surplus, gross	237 051	197 627	15 548	7 761	53 206	−37 091		237 051
B.3g	Mixed income, gross	54 442				54 442			54 442
di	Statistical discrepancy between income components and GDP	249					249		249
D.4	Property income	492 429	61 009	283 140	17 549	130 731		127 009	619 438
-P.119	Adjustment to property income for financial services (FISIM)			−37 091			37 091		

II.2 SECONDARY DISTRIBUTION OF INCOME

B.5g	National income, balance of primary incomes, gross	946 448	125 879	−7 590	121 526	706 384	249		946 697
D.5	Current taxes on income, wealth etc	158 062			158 062			427	158 489
D.61	Social contributions	148 693	3 625	74 236	70 458	374		−	148 693
D.62	Social benefits other than social transfers in kind	187 235				187 235		1 253	188 488
D.7	Other current transfers	143 876	5 585	27 967	69 181	41 143		14 426	158 302

II.3 REDISTRIBUTION OF INCOME IN KIND

B.6g	Disposable income, gross	940 706	101 101	−1 056	205 445	634 967	249		940 706
D.63	Social transfers in kind	129 042				129 042			129 042

II.4 USE OF INCOME

B.7g	Adjusted disposable income, gross	940 706	101 101	−1 056	99 269	741 143	249		940 706
B.6g	Disposable income, gross	940 706	101 101	−1 056	205 445	634 967	249		940 706
P.4	Actual final consumption							792 439	792 439
P.3	Final consumption expenditure							792 439	792 439
D.8	Adjustment for change in households' net equity in pension funds	15 216				15 216		−4	15 216

Accumulation accounts

III.1.1 CHANGE IN NET WORTH DUE TO SAVING AND CAPITAL TRANSFERS

B.8g	Saving, gross	148 271	101 101	−16 268	30 654	32 535	249		148 271
B.12	Current external balance							18 425	18 425
D.9	Capital transfers receivable	13 587	1 448	−	6 966	5 173		708	14 295
D.9	Capital transfers payable	−11 651	−290	−	−8 685	−2 676		−2 644	−14 295

III.1.2 ACQUISITION ON NON-FINANCIAL ASSETS
Changes in liabilities and net worth

B.10.1g	Changes in net worth due to saving and capital transfers	150 207	102 259	−16 268	28 935	35 032	249	16 489	166 696
P.51	Gross fixed capital formation							165 247	165 247
-K.1	(Consumption of fixed capital)								
P.52	Changes in inventories							1 855	1 855
P.53	Acquisitions less disposals of valuables							−3	−3
K.2	Acquisitions less disposals of non-produced non-financial assets								
de	Statistical discrepancy between expenditure components and GDP							−403	−403

III.2 FINANCIAL ACCOUNT

B.9	Net lending(+) / net borrowing(-)	−16 452	−4 839	−27 943	18 367	−2 689	652	16 452	−
	Changes in liabilities								
F.2	Currency and deposits	349 363		345 587	3 776	−		220 862	570 225
F.3	Securities other than shares	89 939	41 619	62 679	−14 382	23		48 691	141 736
F.4	Loans	303 591	99 050	138 850	699	64 992		89 122	392 713
F.5	Shares and other equity	258 663	198 420	60 243		−		199 037	457 700
F.6	Insurance technical reserves	46 438		46 438					46 438
F.7	Other accounts payable	35 107	4 006	6 984	24 056	61		−288	34 819

62

1.7 continued UK summary accounts 2000

Main aggregates and summary accounts

Total economy: all sectors and the rest of the world

£ million

		USES						RESOURCES	TOTAL
		UK total economy S.1	Non-financial corporations S.11	Financial corporations S.12	General government S.13	Households & NPISH S.14+S.15	Not sector -ised S.N	Rest of the world S.2	Goods & services
	Current accounts								
I 0	**PRODUCTION / EXTERNAL ACCOUNT OF GOODS AND SERVICES**								
P.7	Imports of goods and services								281 024	281 024
P.6	Exports of goods and services							265 305		265 305
P.1	Output at basic prices								1 818 849	1 818 849
P.2	Intermediate consumption	987 792	..	..	..	..	37 091			987 792
D.21-D.31	Taxes less subsidies on products								112 359	112 359
B.1g	**Gross domestic product, value added at market prices**	**943 412**	..	..	..	..	..			**943 412**
B.11	External balance of goods and services							15 719		15 719
II.1.1	**GENERATION OF INCOME**									
D.1	Compensation of employees	521 443	..	27 110	..	..		1 014		522 457
D.21-D.31	Taxes less subsidies on products	112 359					112 359			243 496
D.29-D.39	Other taxes less subsidies on production	17 872	..	1 501	..	..				17 872
B.2g	Operating surplus, gross	237 051	197 627	15 548	7 761	53 206	−37 091			237 051
B.3g	Mixed income, gross	54 442				54 442				54 442
di	Statistical discrepancy between income components and GDP	249					249			249
II.1.2	**ALLOCATION OF PRIMARY INCOME**									
D.4	Property income	486 455	132 757	269 187	30 930	53 581		132 983		619 438
-P.119	Adjustment to property income for financial services (FISIM)									
B.5g	National income, balance of primary incomes, gross	946 448	125 879	−7 590	121 526	706 384	249			946 697
II.2	**SECONDARY DISTRIBUTION OF INCOME**									
D.5	Current taxes on income, wealth etc	157 969	25 017	8 599		124 353		520		158 489
D.61	Social contributions	148 638				148 638		55		148 693
D.62	Social benefits other than social transfers in kind	188 488	3 625	59 024	124 991	848		659		188 488
D.7	Other current transfers	148 513	5 346	28 046	88 791	26 330		9 789		158 302
B.6g	Disposable income, gross	940 706	101 101	−1 056	205 445	634 967	249			940 706
II.3	**REDISTRIBUTION OF INCOME IN KIND**									
D.63	Social transfers in kind	129 042			106 176	22 866				129 042
B.7g	Adjusted disposable income, gross	940 706	101 101	−1 056	99 269	741 143	249			940 706
II.4	**USE OF INCOME ACCOUNT**									
B.6g	Disposable income, gross									
P.4	Actual final consumption	792 439			68 615	723 824				792 439
P.3	Final consumption expenditure	792 439			174 791	617 648				792 439
D.8	Adjustment for change in households' net equity in pension funds	15 212		15 212						15 212
B.8g	Saving, gross	148 271	101 101	−16 268	30 654	32 535	249			148 271
B.12	Current external balance							18 425		18 425
	Accumulation accounts									
III.1.1	**CHANGE IN NET WORTH DUE TO SAVING AND CAPITAL TRANSFERS**									
D.9	Capital transfers receivable									
D.9	Capital transfers payable									
B.10.1g	Changes in net worth due to saving and capital transfers	150 207	102 259	−16 268	28 935	35 032	249	16 489		166 696
III.1.2	**ACQUISITION OF NON-FINANCIAL ASSETS** Changes in assets									
P.51	Gross fixed capital formation	165 247	104 676	11 737	11 349	37 485				165 247
-K.1	(Consumption of fixed capital)	−106 047	−65 927	−4 233	−7 761	−28 126				−106 047
P.52	Changes in inventories	1 855	1 912	55	−140	28				1 855
P.53	Acquisitions less disposals of valuables	−3	−74	−130	2	199				−3
K.2	Acquisitions less disposals of non-produced non-financial assets	−37	584	13	−643	9		37		−
de	Statistical discrepancy between expenditure components and GDP	−403					−403			−403
B.9	**Net lending(+) / net borrowing(-)**	−16 452	−4 839	−27 943	18 367	−2 689	652	16 452		−
III.2	**FINANCIAL ACCOUNT: changes in assets**									
F.1	Monetary gold and SDRs	−956			−956			956		
F.2	Currency and deposits	371 092	50 147	265 578	17 871	37 496		199 133		570 225
F.3	Securities other than shares	86 899	3 800	77 422	7 028	−1 351		51 731		141 736
F.4	Loans	255 876	49 470	201 505	5 216	−315		136 837		392 713
F.5	Shares and other equity	263 566	203 244	80 183	107	−19 968		194 134		457 700
F.6	Insurance technical reserves	45 340	321	49	32	44 938		1 098		46 438
F.7	Other accounts receivable	34 909	25 131	1 297	2 364	6 117		−90		34 819
dB.9f	Statistical discrepancy between non-financial and financial transactions	9 923	6 143	6 804	854	−4 530	652	−9 923		−

Main aggregates and summary accounts

1.7.1 UK summary accounts 1999
Total economy: all sectors and the rest of the world

£ million

		UK total economy S.1	Non-financial corporations S.11	Financial corporations S.12	Monetary financial institutions S.121+S.122	Other financial intermediaries & auxiliaries S.123+S.124	Insurance corporations & pension funds S.125
I	**PRODUCTION ACCOUNT**						
	Resources						
P.1	Output						
P.11	Market output*	1 473 080	1 168 703	115 249			
P.12	Output for own final use	59 683	4 393	698			
P.13	Other non-market output	188 965					
P.1	Total output	1 721 728	1 173 096	115 947			
D.21	Taxes on products	112 940					
-D.31	less Subsidies on products	–6 696					
Total	Total resources	1 827 972	1 173 096	115 947			
P.119	*of which* FISIM (financial intermediation services indirectly measured)	30 819		30 819			
	Uses						
P.2	Intermediate consumption	926 703	611 878	74 092			
B.1*g	**Gross domestic product**, gross value added	901 269	561 218	41 855	28 448	2 434	10 973
Total	Total uses	1 827 972	1 173 096	115 947			
B.1*g	Gross domestic product, gross value added	901 269	561 218	41 855	28 448	2 434	10 973
-K.1	less Fixed capital consumption	–100 650	–62 981	–3 974			
B.1*n	**Net domestic product**, net value added	800 619	498 237	37 881			

1.7.2 UK summary accounts 1999
Total economy: all sectors and the rest of the world

£ million

		UK total economy S.1	Non-financial corporations S.11	Financial corporations S.12	Monetary financial institutions S.121+S.122	Other financial intermediaries & auxiliaries S.123+S.124	Insurance corporations & pension funds S.125
II	**DISTRIBUTION AND USE OF INCOME ACCOUNTS**						
II.1	**PRIMARY DISTRIBUTION OF INCOME ACCOUNT**						
II.1.1	**GENERATION OF INCOME ACCOUNT**						
	Resources						
B.1*g	Total resources, gross domestic product, gross value added external balance of goods & services	901 269	561 218	41 855	28 448	2 434	10 973
	Uses						
D.1	Compensation of employees						
D.11	Wages and salaries	428 565	316 224	22 111	10 488	5 583	6 040
D.12	Employers' social contributions	65 621	42 518	3 516	1 671	1 175	670
D.1	Total	494 186	358 742	25 627	12 159	6 758	6 710
D.2	Taxes on production and imports, paid						
D.21	Taxes on products and imports	112 940					
D.29	Production taxes other than on products	18 013	14 590	1 527	832	444	251
D.2	Total taxes on production and imports	130 953	14 590	1 527	832	444	251
-D.3	less Subsidies, received						
-D.31	Subsidies on products	–6 696					
-D.39	Production subsidies other than on products	–1 120	–750	–	–	–	–
-D.3	Total subsidies on production	–7 816	–750	–	–	–	–
B.2g	Operating surplus, gross	231 482	188 636	14 701	15 457	–4 768	4 012
B.3g	Mixed income, gross	52 464					
di	Statistical discrepancy between income components and GDP	–					
Total	Total uses	901 269	561 218	41 855	28 448	2 434	10 973
-K.1	After deduction of fixed capital consumption	–100 650	–62 981	–3 974			
B.2n	Operating surplus, net	140 214	125 655	10 727			
B.3n	Mixed income, net	43 082					

Main aggregates and summary accounts

1.7.1 UK summary accounts 1999
continued

Total economy: all sectors and the rest of the world £ million

		General government	Central government	Local government	Households & NPISH	Not sector -ised	Rest of the world
		S.13	S.1311	S.1313	S.14+S.15	S.N	S.2
I	**PRODUCTION ACCOUNT**						
	Resources						
P.1	Output						
P.11	Market output	8 119	2 668	5 451	181 009		
P.12	Output for own final use	461	155	306	54 131		
P.13	Other non-market output	166 294	100 647	65 647	22 671		
P.1	Total output	174 874	103 470	71 404	257 811		
D.21	Taxes on products					112 940	
-D.31	*less* Subsidies on products					−6 696	
Total	Total resources	174 874	103 470	71 404	257 811	106 244	
	of which FISIM (financial intermediation services indirectly measured)						
	Uses						
P.2	Intermediate consumption	100 748	75 145	25 603	109 166	30 819	
B.1*g	**Gross domestic product**, gross value added	74 126	28 325	45 801	148 645	75 425	
Total	Total uses	174 874	103 470	71 404	257 811	106 244	
B.1*g	Gross domestic product, gross value added	74 126	28 325	45 801	148 645	75 425	
-K.1	*less* Fixed capital consumption	−7 767	−4 489	−3 278	−25 928		
B.1*n	**Net domestic product**, net value added	66 359	23 836	42 523	122 717	75 425	

1.7.2 UK summary accounts 1999
continued

Total economy: all sectors and the rest of the world £ million

		General government	Central government	Local government	Households & NPISH	Not sector -ised	Rest of the world
		S.13	S.1311	S.1313	S.14+S.15	S.N	S.2
II	**DISTRIBUTION AND USE OF INCOME ACCOUNTS**						
II.1	**PRIMARY DISTRIBUTION OF INCOME ACCOUNT**						
II.1.1	**GENERATION OF INCOME ACCOUNT**						
	Resources						
B.1*g,B.11	Total resources, gross domestic product, gross value added, external balance of goods & services	74 126	28 325	45 801	148 645	75 425	15 864
	Uses						
D.1	Compensation of employees						
D.11	Wages and salaries	51 202	19 294	31 908	39 028		960
D.12	Employers' social contributions	13 382	4 014	9 368	6 205		
D.1	Total	64 584	23 308	41 276	45 233		960
D.2	Taxes on production and imports, paid						
D.21	Taxes on products and imports					112 940	–
D.29	Production taxes other than on products	1 775	528	1 247	121		
D.2	Total taxes on production and imports	1 775	528	1 247	121		–
-D.3	*less* Subsidies, received						
-D.31	Subsidies on products					−6 696	
-D.39	Production subsidies other than on products	–	–	–	−370		
-D.3	Total subsidies on production	–	–	–	−370	−6 696	
B.2g	Operating surplus, gross	7 767	4 489	3 278	51 197	−30 819	
B.3g	Mixed income, gross				52 464		
di	Statistical discrepancy between income components and GDP					–	
Total	Total uses	74 126	28 325	45 801	148 645	75 425	
-K.1	After deduction of fixed capital consumption	−7 767	−4 489	−3 278	−25 928		
B.2n	Operating surplus, net	–	–	–	34 651	−30 819	
B.3n	Mixed income, net				43 082		

United Kingdom National Accounts 2001, © Crown copyright 2001

Main aggregates and summary accounts

1.7.3 UK summary accounts 1999
Total economy: all sectors and the rest of the world

£ million

		UK total economy S.1	Non-financial corporations S.11	Financial corporations S.12	Monetary financial institutions S.121+S.122	Other financial intermediaries & auxiliaries S.123+S.124	Insurance corporations & pension funds S.125
II.1.2	**ALLOCATION OF PRIMARY INCOME ACCOUNT**						
	Resources						
B.2g	Operating surplus, gross	231 482	188 636	14 701	15 457	−4 768	4 012
B.3g	Mixed income, gross	52 464					
D.1	Compensation of employees						
D.11	Wages and salaries	428 766					
D.12	Employers' social contributions	65 621					
D.1	Total	494 387					
di	Statistical discrepancy between income components and GDP	−					
D.2	Taxes on production and imports, received						
D.21	Taxes on products						
D.211	Value added tax (VAT)	58 664					
D.212	Taxes and duties on imports excluding VAT	−					
D.2121	Import duties	−					
D.2122	Taxes on imports excluding VAT and import duties	−					
D.214	Taxes on products excluding VAT and import duties	48 395					
D.21	Total taxes on products	107 059					
D.29	Other taxes on production	18 013					
D.2	Total taxes on production and imports, received	125 072					
-D.3	*less* Subsidies, paid						
-D.31	Subsidies on products	−4 366					
-D.39	Other subsidies on production	−747					
-D.3	Total subsidies	−5 116					
D.4	Property income, received						
D.41	Interest	228 829	10 756	184 465	140 659	20 780	23 026
D.42	Distributed income of corporations	113 752	21 440	45 602	4 562	13 666	27 374
D.43	Reinvested earnings on direct foreign investment	21 304	16 108	5 196	1 431	2 763	1 002
D.44	Property income attributed to insurance policy holders	54 335	333	45	12	9	24
D.45	Rent	684	117	29	−	−	29
D.4	Total property income	418 904	48 754	235 337	146 664	37 218	51 455
-P.119	Adjustment to property income for financial services (FISIM)			−30 819	−32 258	1 439	
Total	Total resources	1 317 193	237 390	219 219	129 863	33 889	55 467
	Uses						
D.4	Property income, paid						
D.41	Interest	236 273	32 965	124 950	100 008	23 819	1 123
D.42	Distributed income of corporations	114 694	85 645	29 049	13 020	13 037	2 992
D.43	Reinvested earnings on direct foreign investment	7 855	6 120	1 735	972	752	11
D.44	Property income attributed to insurance policy holders	55 580		55 580	−	−	55 580
D.45	Rent	684	469	−	−	−	−
D.4	Total property income	415 086	125 199	211 314	114 000	37 608	59 706
B.5*g	National income or Balance of primary income, gross	902 107	112 191	7 905	15 863	−3 719	−4 239
Total	Total uses	1 317 193	237 390	219 219	129 863	33 889	55 467
-K.1	After deduction of fixed capital consumption	−100 650	−62 981	−3 974			
B.5*n	National income or Balance of primary income, net	801 457	49 210	3 931			

66   United Kingdom National Accounts 2001, © Crown copyright 2001

1.7.3 UK summary accounts 1999
Main aggregates and summary accounts
Total economy: all sectors and the rest of the world

£ million

		General government S.13	Central government S.1311	Local government S.1313	Households & NPISH S.14+S.15	Not sector-ised S.N	Rest of the world S.2
II.1.2	**ALLOCATION OF PRIMARY INCOME ACCOUNT**						
	Resources						
B.2g	Operating surplus, gross	7 767	4 489	3 278	51 197	–30 819	
B.3g	Mixed income, gross				52 464		
D.1	Compensation of employees						
D.11	Wages and salaries				428 766		759
D.12	Employers' social contributions				65 621		
D.1	Total				494 387		759
di	Statistical discrepancy between income components and GDP					–	
D.2	Taxes on production and imports, received						
D.21	Taxes on products						
D.211	Value added tax (VAT)	58 664	58 664				3 811
D.212	Taxes and duties on imports excluding VAT						
D.2121	Import duties	–	–				2 024
D.2122	Taxes on imports excluding VAT and import duties	–	–				–
D.214	Taxes on products excluding VAT and import duties	48 395	48 395				46
D.21	Total taxes on products	107 059	107 059				5 881
D.29	Other taxes on production	18 013	17 871	142			
D.2	Total taxes on production and imports, received	125 072	124 930	142			5 881
-D.3	*less* Subsidies, paid						
-D.31	Subsidies on products	–4 366	–3 579	–787			–2 330
-D.39	Other subsidies on production	–750	–747	–3			–370
-D.3	Total subsidies	–5 116	–4 326	–790			–2 700
D.4	Property income, received						
D.41	Interest	9 328	8 502	826	24 280		67 417
D.42	Distributed income of corporations	6 484	1 398	5 086	40 226		18 977
D.43	Reinvested earnings on direct foreign investment				–		7 855
D.44	Property income attributed to insurance policy holders	29		29	53 928		1 245
D.45	Rent	433	433	–	105		
D.4	Total property income	16 274	10 333	5 941	118 539		95 494
-P.119	Adjustment to property income for financial services (FISIM)					30 819	
Total	Total resources	143 997	135 426	8 571	716 587	–	
	Uses						
D.4	Property income, paid						
D.41	Interest	30 648	26 224	4 424	47 710		59 973
D.42	Distributed income of corporations						18 035
D.43	Reinvested earnings on direct foreign investment						21 304
D.44	Property income attributed to insurance policy holders						
D.45	Rent				215		
D.4	Total property income	30 648	26 224	4 424	47 925		99 312
B.5*g	National income or Balance of primary incomes, gross	113 349	109 202	4 147	668 662	–	
Total	Total uses	143 997	135 426	8 571	716 587	–	
-K.1	After deduction of fixed capital consumption	–7 767	–4 489	–3 278	–25 928		
B.5*n	National income or Balance of primary incomes, net	105 582	104 713	869	642 734	–	

United Kingdom National Accounts 2001, © Crown copyright 2001

Main aggregates and summary accounts

1.7.4 UK summary accounts
1999
Total economy: all sectors and the rest of the world

£ million

		UK total economy S.1	Non-financial corporations S.11	Financial corporations S.12	Monetary financial institutions S.121+S.122	Other financial intermediaries & auxiliaries S.123+S.124	Insurance corporations & pension funds S.125
II.2	**SECONDARY DISTRIBUTION OF INCOME ACCOUNT**						
	Resources						
B.5*g	National income or balance of primary incomes, gross	902 107	112 191	7 905	15 863	–3 719	–4 239
D.5	Current taxes on income, wealth etc.						
D.51	Taxes on income	129 044					
D.59	Other current taxes	16 263					
D.5	Total	145 307					
D.61	Social contributions						
D.611	Actual social contributions						
D.6111	Employers' actual social contributions	55 365		22 257			22 257
D.6112	Employees' social contributions	73 322		46 803			46 803
D.6113	Social contributions by self- and non-employed persons	1 801		–			–
D.611	Total	130 488		69 060			69 060
D.612	Imputed social contributions	10 256	3 535	448	212	150	86
D.61	Total	140 744	3 535	69 508	212	150	69 146
D.62	Social benefits other than social transfers in kind	178 050					
D.7	Other current transfers						
D.71	Net non-life insurance premiums	22 752		22 752			22 752
D.72	Non-life insurance claims	19 099	4 151	637	160	136	341
D.73	Current transfers within general government	64 775					
D.74	Current international cooperation from institutions of the EC	3 176					
D.75	Miscellaneous current transfers	22 769	611	–		–	
D.7	Total, other current transfers	132 571	4 762	23 389	160	136	23 093
Total	Total resources	1 498 779	120 488	100 802	16 235	–3 433	88 000
	Uses						
D.5	Current taxes on income, wealth etc.						
D.51	Taxes on income	129 021	21 637	10 192	4 439	3 132	2 621
D.59	Other current taxes	16 263					
D.5	Total	145 284	21 637	10 192	4 439	3 132	2 621
D.61	Social contributions						
D.611	Actual social contributions						
D.6111	Employers' actual social contributions	55 365					
D.6112	Employees' actual social contributions	73 235					
D.6113	Social contributions by self- and non-employed persons	1 801					
D.611	Total actual social contributions	130 401					
D.612	Imputed social contributions	10 256					
D.61	Total	140 657					
D.62	Social benefits other than social transfers in kind	179 293	3 535	54 084	212	150	53 722
D.7	Other current transfers						
D.71	Net non-life insurance premiums	19 099	4 151	637	160	136	341
D.72	Non-life insurance claims	22 752		22 752			22 752
D.73	Current transfers within general government	64 775					
D.74	Current international cooperation to institutions of the EC	1 667					
D.75	Miscellaneous current transfers	27 212	373	75	52	23	–
	GNP based fourth own resource	4 632					
D.7	Total other current transfers	135 505	4 524	23 464	212	159	23 093
B.6*g	Disposable income, gross	898 040	90 792	13 062	11 372	–6 874	8 564
Total	Total uses	1 498 779	120 488	100 802	16 235	–3 433	88 000
-K.1	After deduction of fixed capital consumption	–100 650	–62 981	–3 974			
B.6*n	Disposable income, net	797 390	27 811	9 088			

1.7.4 UK summary accounts 1999
Main aggregates and summary accounts
continued

Total economy: all sectors and the rest of the world

£ million

		General government	Central government	Local government	Households & NPISH	Not sector-ised	Rest of the world
		S.13	S.1311	S.1313	S.14+S.15	S.N	S.2
II.2	**SECONDARY DISTRIBUTION OF INCOME ACCOUNT**						
	Resources						
B.5*g	National income or Balance of primary incomes, gross	113 349	109 202	4 147	668 662	–	
D.5	Current taxes on income, wealth etc.						
D.51	Taxes on income	129 044	129 044				505
D.59	Other current taxes	16 263	3 437	12 826			
D.5	Total	145 307	132 481	12 826			505
D.61	Social contributions						
D.611	Actual social contributions						
D.6111	Employers' actual social contributions	33 108	33 108				
D.6112	Employees' social contributions	26 519	25 939	580			
D.6113	Social contributions by self- and non-employed persons	1 801	1 801				–
D.611	Total	61 428	60 848	580			
D.612	Imputed social contributions	5 823	4 109	1 714	450		
D.61	Total	67 251	64 957	2 294	450		–
D.62	Social benefits other than social transfers in kind				178 050		1 243
D.7	Other current transfers						
D.71	Net non-life insurance premiums						10
D.72	Non-life insurance claims	410	–	410	13 901		3 663
D.73	Current transfers within general government	64 775	–	64 775			
D.74	Current international cooperation	3 176	3 176				1 667
	from institutions of the EC	3 176	3 176				
D.75	Miscellaneous current transfers	259	259		21 899		7 607
	GNP based fourth own resource						4 632
D.7	Total, other current transfers	68 620	3 435	65 185	35 800		12 947
Total	Total resources	394 527	310 075	84 452	882 962	–	
	Uses						
D.5	Current taxes on income, wealth etc.						
D.51	Taxes on income				97 192		528
D.59	Other current taxes				16 263		
D.5	Total				113 455		528
D.61	Social contributions						
D.611	Actual social contributions						
D.6111	Employers' actual social contributions				55 365		
D.6112	Employees' actual social contributions				73 235		87
D.6113	Social contributions by self- and non-employed persons				1 801		
D.611	Total actual social contributions				130 401		87
D.612	Imputed social contributions				10 256		
D.61	Total				140 657		87
D.62	Social benefits other than social transfers in kind	120 752	105 934	14 818	922		434
D.7	Other current transfers						
D.71	Net non-life insurance premiums	410	–	410	13 901		3 663
D.72	Non-life insurance claims						10
D.73	Current transfers within general government	64 775	64 775	–			
D.74	Current international cooperation	1 667	1 667				3 176
	to institutions of the EC	11	11				
D.75	Miscellaneous current transfers	17 280	17 280		9 484		3 164
	GNP based fourth own resource	4 632	4 632				
D.7	Total other current transfers	84 132	83 722	410	23 385		10 013
B.6*g	Disposable income, gross	189 643	120 419	69 224	604 543	–	
Total	Total uses	394 527	310 075	84 452	882 962	–	
-K.1	After deduction of fixed capital consumption	–7 767	–4 489	–3 278	–25 928		
B.6*n	Disposable income, net	181 876	115 930	65 946	578 615	–	

United Kingdom National Accounts 2001, © Crown copyright 2001

Main aggregates and summary accounts

1.7.5 UK summary accounts
1999
Total economy: all sectors and the rest of the world

£ million

		UK total economy S.1	Non-financial corporations S.11	Financial corporations S.12	Monetary financial institutions S.121+S.122	Other financial intermediaries & auxiliaries S.123+S.124	Insurance corporations & pension funds S.125
II.3	**REDISTRIBUTION OF INCOME IN KIND ACCOUNT**						
	Resources						
B.6*g	Disposable income, gross	898 040	90 792	13 062	11 372	–6 874	8 564
D.63	Social transfers in kind						
D.631	Social benefits in kind						
D.6313	Social assistance benefits in kind	–					
D.632	Transfers of individual non-market goods and services	123 175					
D.63	Total social transfers in kind	123 175					
Total	Total resources	1 021 215	90 792	13 062	11 372	–6 874	8 564
	Uses						
D.63	Social transfers in kind						
D.631	Social benefits in kind						
D.6313	Social assistance benefits in kind	–					
D.632	Transfers of individual non-market goods and services	123 175					
D.63	Total social transfers in kind	123 175					
B.7g	Adjusted disposable income, gross	898 040	90 792	13 062	11 372	–6 874	8 564
Total	Total uses	1 021 215	90 792	13 062	11 372	–6 874	8 564

1.7.5 UK summary accounts 1999

continued

Total economy: all sectors and the rest of the world

£ million

		General government	Central government	Local government	Households & NPISH	Not sector -ised	Rest of the world
		S.13	S.1311	S.1313	S.14+S.15	S.N	S.2
II.3	**REDISTRIBUTION OF INCOME IN KIND ACCOUNT**						
	Resources						
B.6*g	Disposable income, gross	189 643	120 419	69 224	604 543	–	
D.63	Social transfers in kind						
D.631	Social benefits in kind						
D.6313	Social assistance benefits in kind				–		
D.632	Transfers of individual non-market goods and services	100 504	56 337	44 167	123 175		
D.63	Total social transfers in kind				123 175		
Total	Total resources	189 643	120 419	69 224	727 718	–	
	Uses						
D.63	Social transfers in kind						
D.631	Social benefits in kind						
D.6313	Social assistance benefits in kind				–		
D.632	Transfers of individual non-market goods and services	100 504	56 337	44 167	22 671		
D.63	Total social transfers in kind	100 504	56 337	44 167	22 671		
B.7g	Adjusted disposable income, gross	89 139	64 082	25 057	705 047	–	
Total	Total uses	189 643	120 419	69 224	727 718	–	

Main aggregates and summary accounts

1.7.6 UK summary accounts 1999
Total economy: all sectors and the rest of the world   £ million

		UK total economy S.1	Non-financial corporations S.11	Financial corporations S.12	Monetary financial institutions S.121+S.122	Other financial intermediaries & auxiliaries S.123+S.124	Insurance corporations & pension funds S.125
II.4	**USE OF INCOME ACCOUNT**						
II.4.1	**USE OF DISPOSABLE INCOME ACCOUNT**						
	Resources						
B.6g	Disposable income, gross	898 040	90 792	13 062	11 372	−6 874	8 564
D.8	Adjustment for the change in net equity of households in pension funds	15 417					
Total	Total resources	913 457	90 792	13 062	11 372	−6 874	8 564
	Uses						
P.3	Final consumption expenditure						
P.31	Individual consumption expenditure	690 730					
P.32	Collective consumption expenditure	65 790					
P.3	Total	756 520					
D.8	Adjustment for the change in net equity of households in pension funds	15 415		15 415			15 415
B.8g	Saving, gross	141 522	90 792	−2 353	11 372	−6 874	−6 851
B.12	Current external balance						
Total	Total uses	913 457	90 792	13 062	11 372	−6 874	8 564
−K.1	After deduction of fixed capital consumption	−100 650	−62 981	−3 974			
B.8n	Saving, net	40 872	27 811	−6 327			
II.4.2	**USE OF ADJUSTED DISPOSABLE INCOME ACCOUNT**						
	Resources						
B.7g	Adjusted disposable income	898 040	90 792	13 062	11 372	−6 874	8 564
D.8	Adjustment for the change in net equity of households in pension funds	15 417					
Total	Total resources	913 457	90 792	13 062	11 372	−6 874	8 564
	Uses						
P.4	Actual final consumption						
P.41	Actual individual consumption	690 730					
P.42	Actual collective consumption	65 790					
P.4	Total actual final consumption	756 520					
D.8	Adjustment for the change in net equity of households in pension funds	15 415		15 415			
B.8g	Saving, gross	141 522	90 792	−2 353	11 372	−6 874	−6 851
Total	Total uses	913 457	90 792	13 062	11 372	−6 874	8 564

Main aggregates and summary accounts

1.7.6 UK summary accounts 1999
Total economy: all sectors and the rest of the world

£ million

		General government	Central government	Local government	Households & NPISH	Not sector-ised	Rest of the world
		S.13	S.1311	S.1313	S.14+S.15	S.N	S.2
II.4	**USE OF INCOME ACCOUNT**						
II.4.1	**USE OF DISPOSABLE INCOME ACCOUNT**						
	Resources						
B.6g	Disposable income, gross	189 643	120 419	69 224	604 543	–	
D.8	Adjustment for the change in net equity of households in pension funds				15 417		–2
Total	Total resources	189 643	120 419	69 224	619 960	–	
	Uses						
P.3	Final consumption expenditure						
P.31	Individual consumption expenditure	100 504	56 337	44 167	590 226		
P.32	Collective consumption expenditure	65 790	44 310	21 480			
P.3	Total	166 294	100 647	65 647	590 226		
D.8	Adjustment for the change in net equity of households in pension funds						
B.8g	Saving, gross	23 349	19 772	3 577	29 734	–	
B.12	Current external balance						19 091
Total	Total uses	189 643	120 419	69 224	619 960	–	
–K.1	After deduction of fixed capital consumption	–7 767	–4 489	–3 278	–25 928		
B.8n	Saving, net	15 582	15 283	299	3 806	–	
II.4.2	**USE OF ADJUSTED DISPOSABLE INCOME ACCOUNT**						
	Resources						
B.7g	Adjusted disposable income	89 139	64 082	25 057	705 047	–	
D.8	Adjustment for the change in net equity of households in pension funds				15 417		–2
Total	Total resources	89 139	64 082	25 057	720 464	–	
	Uses						
P.4	Actual final consumption						
P.41	Actual individual consumption				690 730		
P.42	Actual collective consumption	65 790	44 310	21 480			
P.4	Total actual final consumption	65 790	44 310	21 480	690 730		
D.8	Adjustment for the change in net equity of households in pension funds						
B.8g	Saving, gross	23 349	19 772	3 577	29 734	–	
Total	Total uses	89 139	64 082	25 057	720 464	–	

United Kingdom National Accounts 2001, © Crown copyright 2001

Main aggregates and summary accounts

1.7.7 UK summary accounts 1999
Total economy: all sectors and the rest of the world

£ million

		UK total economy S.1	Non-financial corporations S.11	Financial corporations S.12	Monetary financial institutions S.121+S.122	Other financial intermediaries & auxiliaries S.123+S.124	Insurance corporations & pension funds S.125
III	**ACCUMULATION ACCOUNTS**						
III.1	**CAPITAL ACCOUNT**						
III.1.1	**CHANGE IN NET WORTH DUE TO SAVING & CAPITAL TRANSFERS**						
	Changes in liabilities and net worth						
B.8g	Saving, gross	141 522	90 792	−2 353	11 372	−6 874	−6 851
B.12	Current external balance						
D.9	Capital transfers receivable						
D.91	Capital taxes	1 951					
D.92	Investment grants	9 372	2 481	−	−	−	−
D.99	Other capital transfers	1 360	11				
D.9	Total	12 683	2 492	−	−	−	−
-D.9	*less* Capital transfers payable						
-D.91	Capital taxes	−1 951	−	−	−	−	−
-D.92	Investment grants	−9 211					
-D.99	Other capital transfers	−725	−216				
-D.9	Total	−11 887	−216	−	−	−	−
B.10.1g	Total change in liabilities and net worth	142 318	93 068	−2 353	11 372	−6 874	−6 851
	Changes in assets						
B.10.1g	Changes in net worth due to gross saving and capital transfers	142 318	93 068	−2 353	11 372	−6 874	−6 851
-K.1	After deduction of fixed capital consumption	−100 650	−62 981	−3 974			
B.10.1n	Changes in net worth due to net saving and capital transfers	41 668	30 087	−6 327			
III.1.2	**ACQUISITION OF NON-FINANCIAL ASSETS ACCOUNT**						
	Changes in liabilities and net worth						
B.10.1n	Changes in net worth due to net saving and capital transfers	41 668	30 087	−6 327			
K.1	Consumption of fixed capital	100 650	62 981	3 974			
B.10.1g	Total change in liabilities and net worth	142 318	93 068	−2 353	11 372	−6 874	−6 851
	Changes in assets						
P.5	Gross capital formation						
P.51	Gross fixed capital formation	155 408	99 947	7 537	2 810	1 261	3 466
P.52	Changes in inventories	4 975	4 984	47	47	−	−
P.53	Acquisitions less disposals of valuables	230	−17	−28	−	−	−28
P.5	Total	160 613	104 914	7 556	2 857	1 261	3 438
K.2	Acquisitions less disposals of non-produced non-financial assets	−12	694	26	−	63	−37
de	Statistical discrepancy between expenditure components and GDP	−					
B.9	Net lending(+) / net borrowing(−)	−18 283	−12 540	−9 935	8 515	−8 198	−10 252
Total	Total change in assets	142 318	93 068	−2 353	11 372	−6 874	−6 851

Main aggregates and summary accounts

1.7.7 continued
UK summary accounts 1999
Total economy: all sectors and the rest of the world

£ million

		General government	Central government	Local government	Households & NPISH	Not sector-ised	Rest of the world
		S.13	S.1311	S.1313	S.14+S.15	S.N	S.2
III	**ACCUMULATION ACCOUNTS**						
III.1	**CAPITAL ACCOUNT**						
III.1.1	**CHANGE IN NET WORTH DUE TO SAVING SAVING & CAPITAL TRANSFERS**						
	Changes in liabilities and net worth						
B.8g	Saving, gross	23 349	19 772	3 577	29 734	–	
B.12	Current external balance						19 091
D.9	Capital transfers receivable						
D.91	Capital taxes	1 951	1 951				
D.92	Investment grants	3 202		3 202	3 689		171
D.99	Other capital transfers	205	–	205	1 144		509
D.9	Total	5 358	1 951	3 407	4 833		680
-D.9	*less* Capital transfers payable						
-D.91	Capital taxes				-1 951		
-D.92	Investment grants	-9 211	-8 055	-1 156			-332
-D.99	Other capital transfers	-10	-10	–	-499		-1 144
-D.9	Total	-9 221	-8 065	-1 156	-2 450		-1 476
B.10.1g	Total change in liabilities and net worth	19 486	13 658	5 828	32 117	–	18 295
	Changes in assets						
B.10.1g	Changes in net worth due to gross saving and capital transfers	19 486	13 658	5 828	32 117	–	18 295
-K.1	After deduction of fixed capital consumption	-7 767	-4 489	-3 278	-25 928		
B.10.1n	Changes in net worth due to net saving and capital transfers	11 719	9 169	2 550	6 189	–	
III.1.2	**ACQUISITION OF NON-FINANCIAL ASSETS ACCOUNT**						
	Changes in liabilities and net worth						
B.10.1n	Changes in net worth due to net saving and capital transfers	11 719	9 169	2 550	6 189	–	
K.1	Consumption of fixed capital	7 767	4 489	3 278	25 928		
Total	Total change in liabilities and net worth	19 486	13 658	5 828	32 117	–	18 295
	Changes in assets						
P.5	Gross capital formation						
P.51	Gross fixed capital formation	10 107	4 136	5 971	37 817		
P.52	Changes in inventories	-268	-268	–	212		
P.53	Acquisitions less disposals of valuables	10	10		265		
P.5	Total	9 849	3 878	5 971	38 294		
K.2	Acquisitions less disposals of non-produced non-financial assets	-696	-35	-661	-36		12
de	Statistical discrepancy between expenditure components and GDP					–	
B.9	Net lending(+) / net borrowing(-)	10 333	9 815	518	-6 141	–	18 283
Total	Total change in assets	19 486	13 658	5 828	32 117	–	18 295

Main aggregates and summary accounts

1.7.8 UK summary accounts 1999

Total economy: all sectors and the rest of the world. Unconsolidated £ million

		UK total economy S.1	Non-financial corporations S.11	Financial corporations S.12	Monetary financial institutions S.121+S.122	Other financial intermediaries & auxiliaries S.123+S.124	Insurance corporations & pension funds S.125
III.2	**FINANCIAL ACCOUNT**						
F.A	**Net acquisition of financial assets**						
F.1	Monetary gold and special drawing rights (SDRs)	−374					
F.2	Currency and deposits						
F.21	Currency	5 331	383	2 717	2 717	−	−
F.22	Transferable deposits						
F.221	Deposits with UK monetary financial institutions	29 594	8 636	−6 844	3 427	−3 804	−6 467
F.229	Deposits with rest of the world monetary financial institutions	43 040	18 450	18 245	−29 289	47 413	121
F.29	Other deposits	−1 540	−177	−9	−9	−	−
F.2	Total currency and deposits	76 425	27 292	14 109	−23 154	43 609	−6 346
F.3	Securities other than shares						
F.331	Short term: money market instruments						
F.3311	Issued by UK central government	−831	144	−1 162	36	−638	−560
F.3312	Issued by UK local authorities	−	−	−	−	−	−
F.3315	Issued by UK monetary financial institutions	16 319	−1 915	16 891	10 707	5 654	530
F.3316	Issued by other UK residents	943	−75	1 056	64	192	800
F.3319	Issued by the rest of the world	13 623	722	13 238	9 732	3 574	−68
F.332	Medium (1 to 5 year) and long term (over 5 year) bonds						
F.3321	Issued by UK central government	723	−453	3 073	−6 090	3 710	5 453
F.3322	Issued by UK local authorities	−2	−	28	−	16	12
F.3325	Medium term bonds issued by UK MFIs[1]	7 265	21	7 244	5 047	538	1 659
F.3326	Other medium & long term bonds issued by UK residents	39 634	−1 350	41 355	6 860	12 391	22 104
F.3329	Long term bonds issued by the rest of the world	−9 055	−1 062	−5 072	12 997	−27 690	9 621
F.34	Financial derivatives	−2 659	26	−2 685	−2 685	−	−
F.3	Total securities other than shares	65 960	−3 942	73 966	36 668	−2 253	39 551
F.4	Loans						
F.41	Short term loans						
F.411	Loans by UK monetary financial institutions, excluding loans secured on dwellings & financial leasing			65 499	65 499		
F.419	Loans by rest of the world monetary financial institutions						
F.42	Long term loans						
F.421	Direct investment	27 035	26 435	600	−123	1 293	−570
F.422	Loans secured on dwellings	37 753	−	37 780	32 130	6 291	−641
F.423	Finance leasing	134		134	437	−303	
F.424	Other long-term loans by UK residents	23 280	−1 106	16 852		3 068	13 784
F.429	Other long-term loans by the rest of the world						
F.4	Total loans	153 701	25 329	120 865	97 943	10 349	12 573
F.5	Shares and other equity						
F.51	Shares and other equity, excluding mutual funds' shares						
F.514	Quoted UK shares	−7 461	24 186	−3 191	208	4 537	−7 936
F.515	Unquoted UK shares	−12 474	−10 751		1 933	−3 210	−363
F.516	Other UK equity (including direct investment in property)	20		−			
F.519	Shares and other equity issued by the rest of the world	140 420	112 243	27 554	1 722	20 580	5 252
F.52	Mutual funds' shares						
F.521	UK mutual funds' shares	14 716	1	2 958	3	35	2 920
F.529	Rest of the world mutual funds' shares	−					
F.5	Total shares and other equity	135 221	125 679	25 681	3 866	21 942	−127
F.6	Insurance technical reserves						
F.61	Net equity of households in life assurance and pension funds' reserves	42 475					
F.62	Prepayments of insurance premiums and reserves for outstanding claims	−939	−291	−44	−		−24
F.6	Total insurance technical reserves	41 536	−291	−44	−		−24
F.7	Other accounts receivable	14 372	−2 361	5 304	−468	706	5 066
F.A	Total net acquisition of financial assets	486 841	171 706	239 881	114 855	74 333	50 693

1 UK monetary financial institutions

Main aggregates and summary accounts

1.7.8 UK summary accounts 1999
continued

Total economy: all sectors and the rest of the world. Unconsolidated

£ million

		General government	Central government	Local government	Households & NPISH	Rest of the world
		S.13	S.1311	S.1313	S.14+S.15	S.2
III.2	**FINANCIAL ACCOUNT**					
F.A	**Net acquisition of financial assets**					
F.1	Monetary gold and special drawing rights (SDRs)	−374	−374			374
F.2	Currency and deposits					
F.21	Currency				2 231	81
F.22	Transferable deposits					
F.221	Deposits with UK monetary financial institutions	−148	−74	−74	27 950	12 229
F.229	Deposits with rest of the world monetary financial institutions	3 177	3 177		3 168	
F.29	Other deposits	–		–	−1 354	693
F.2	Total currency and deposits	3 029	3 103	−74	31 995	13 003
F.3	Securities other than shares					
F.331	Short term: money market instruments					
F.3311	Issued by UK central government	204		204	−17	422
F.3312	Issued by UK local authorities	–	–			–
F.3315	Issued by UK monetary financial institutions	565		565	778	14 884
F.3316	Issued by other UK residents	−38		−38	–	1 782
F.3319	Issued by the rest of the world	−337	−337			
F.332	Medium (1 to 5 year) and long term (over 5 year) bonds					
F.3321	Issued by UK central government	−18		−18	−1 879	−5 283
F.3322	Issued by UK local authorities				−30	–
F.3325	Medium term bonds issued by UK MFIs[1]					4 646
F.3326	Other medium & long term bonds issued by UK residents	−387	−387		16	23 742
F.3329	Long term bonds issued by the rest of the world	−3 105	−3 105		184	
F.34	Financial derivatives	–	–	–	–	
F.3	Total securities other than shares	−3 116	−3 829	713	−948	40 193
F.4	Loans					
F.41	Short term loans					
F.411	Loans by UK monetary financial institutions, excluding loans secured on dwellings & financial leasing					
F.419	Loans by rest of the world monetary financial institutions					16 400
F.42	Long term loans					
F.421	Direct investment					21 403
F.422	Loans secured on dwellings	−27	−1	−26		
F.423	Finance leasing					
F.424	Other long-term loans by UK residents	3 773	3 700	73	3 761	
F.429	Other long-term loans by the rest of the world					−122
F.4	Total loans	3 746	3 699	47	3 761	71 134
F.5	Shares and other equity					
F.51	Shares and other equity, excluding mutual funds' shares					
F.514	Quoted UK shares	−316	−12	−304	−28 140	95 290
F.515	Unquoted UK shares	–	–	–	−83	30 482
F.516	Other UK equity (including direct investment in property)	–	–		20	813
F.519	Shares and other equity issued by the rest of the world	91	91		532	
F.52	Mutual funds' shares					
F.521	UK mutual funds' shares				11 757	3
F.529	Rest of the world mutual funds' shares				–	
F.5	Total shares and other equity	−225	79	−304	−15 914	126 588
F.6	Insurance technical reserves					
F.61	Net equity of households in life assurance and pension funds' reserves				42 475	−2
F.62	Prepayments of insurance premiums and reserves for outstanding claims	−29		−29	−575	−662
F.6	Total insurance technical reserves	−29		−29	41 900	−664
F.7	Other accounts receivable	6 994	6 899	95	4 435	−135
F.A	Total net acquisition of financial assets	10 025	9 577	448	65 229	250 493

1 UK monetary financial institutions

Main aggregates and summary accounts

1.7.8 UK summary accounts 1999
continued

Total economy: all sectors and the rest of the world. Unconsolidated

£ million

		UK total economy S.1	Non-financial corporations S.11	Financial corporations S.12	Monetary financial institutions S.121+S.122	Other financial intermediaries & auxiliaries S.123+S.124	Insurance corporations & pension funds S.125
III.2	**FINANCIAL ACCOUNT** continued						
F.L	**Net acquisition of financial liabilities**						
F.2	Currency and deposits						
F.21	Currency	5 431		5 232	5 232		
F.22	Transferable deposits						
F.221	Deposits with UK monetary financial institutions	41 823		41 823	41 823		
F.229	Deposits with rest of the world monetary financial institutions						
F.29	Other deposits	–847		–			
F.2	Total currency and deposits	46 407		47 055	47 055		
F.3	Securities other than shares						
F.331	Short term: money market instruments						
F.3311	Issued by UK central government	–409					
F.3312	Issued by UK local authorities	–					
F.3315	Issued by UK monetary financial institutions	31 203		31 203	31 203		
F.3316	Issued by other UK residents	2 725	2 716	31		31	
F.3319	Issued by the rest of the world						
F.332	Medium (1 to 5 year) and long term (over 5 year) bonds						
F.3321	Issued by UK central government	–4 560					
F.3322	Issued by UK local authorities	–2					
F.3325	Medium term bonds issued by UK MFIs[1]	11 911		11 911	11 911		
F.3326	Other medium & long term bonds issued by UK residents	63 376	39 100	24 276	5 988	17 162	1 126
F.3329	Long term bonds issued by the rest of the world						
F.34	Financial derivatives	26	–	26	26	–	–
F.3	Total securities other than shares	104 270	41 816	67 447	49 128	17 193	1 126
F.4	Loans						
F.41	Short term loans						
F.411	Loans by UK monetary financial institutions, excluding loans secured on dwellings & financial leasing	48 608	16 748	14 289		12 258	2 031
F.419	Loans by rest of the world monetary financial institutions	49 853	5 960	43 058		41 659	1 399
F.42	Long term loans						
F.421	Direct investment	21 403	19 463	1 940	9	255	1 676
F.422	Loans secured on dwellings	37 753					
F.423	Finance leasing	134	–33	–323	–168	–155	
F.424	Other long-term loans by UK residents	23 271	2 920	4 759		1 094	3 665
F.429	Other long-term loans by the rest of the world	–122	–	44		44	
F.4	Total loans	180 900	45 058	63 767	–159	55 155	8 771
F.5	Shares and other equity						
F.51	Shares and other equity, excluding mutual funds' shares						
F.514	Quoted UK shares	87 829	85 600	2 229	–519	2 355	393
F.515	Unquoted UK shares	18 008	9 096	8 912	1 097	7 804	11
F.516	Other UK equity (including direct investment in property)	833	833	–	–		
F.519	Shares and other equity issued by the rest of the world						
F.52	Mutual funds' shares						
F.521	UK mutual funds' shares	14 719		14 719		14 719	
F.529	Rest of the world mutual funds' shares						
F.5	Total shares and other equity	121 389	95 529	25 860	578	24 878	404
F.6	Insurance technical reserves						
F.61	Net equity of households in life assurance and pension funds' reserves	42 473		42 473			42 473
F.62	Prepayments of insurance premiums and reserves for outstanding claims	–1 601		–1 601			–1 601
F.6	Total insurance technical reserves	40 872		40 872			40 872
F.7	Other accounts payable	14 465	8 095	4 173	–261	–166	4 600
F.L	**Total net acquisition of financial liabilities**	508 303	190 498	249 174	96 341	97 060	55 773
B.9	**Net lending / borrowing**						
F.A	Total net acquisition of financial assets	486 841	171 706	239 881	114 855	74 333	50 693
-F.L	*less* Total net acquisition of financial liabilities	–508 303	–190 498	–249 174	–96 341	–97 060	–55 773
B.9f	**Net lending (+) / net borrowing (-), from financial account**	–21 462	–18 792	–9 293	18 514	–22 727	–5 080
dB.9f	**Statistical discrepancy between financial & non-financial accounts**	3 179	6 252	–642	–9 999	14 529	–5 172
B.9	**Net lending (+) / net borrowing (-), from capital account**	–18 283	–12 540	–9 935	8 515	–8 198	–10 252

Main aggregates and summary accounts

1.7.8 continued UK summary accounts 1999
Total economy: all sectors and the rest of the world. Unconsolidated

£ million

		General government	Central government	Local government	Households & NPISH	Not sector -ised	Rest of the world
		S.13	S.1311	S.1313	S.14+S.15	S.N	S.2
III.2	**FINANCIAL ACCOUNT** continued						
F.L	**Net acquisition of financial liabilities**						
F.2	Currency and deposits						
F.21	Currency	199	199				–19
F.22	Transferable deposits						
F.221	Deposits with UK monetary financial institutions						
F.229	Deposits with rest of the world monetary financial institutions						43 040
F.29	Other deposits	–847	–847				
F.2	Total currency and deposits	–648	–648				43 021
F.3	Securities other than shares						
F.331	Short term: money market instruments						
F.3311	Issued by UK central government	–409	–409				
F.3312	Issued by UK local authorities	–		–			
F.3315	Issued by UK monetary financial institutions						
F.3316	Issued by other UK residents				–22		
F.3319	Issued by the rest of the world						13 623
F.332	Medium (1 to 5 year) and long term (over 5 year) bonds						
F.3321	Issued by UK central government	–4 560	–4 560				
F.3322	Issued by UK local authorities	–2		–2			
F.3325	Medium term bonds issued by UK MFIs[1]						
F.3326	Other medium & long term bonds issued by UK residents				–		
F.3329	Long term bonds issued by the rest of the world						–9 055
F.34	Financial derivatives	–	–	–	–		
F.3	Total securities other than shares	–4 971	–4 969	–2	–22		1 883
F.4	Loans						
F.41	Short term loans						
F.411	Loans by UK monetary financial institutions, excluding loans secured on dwellings & financial leasing	5 312	6 128	–816	12 259		16 891
F.419	Loans by rest of the world monetary financial institutions	–45	–1	–44	880		
F.42	Long term loans						
F.421	Direct investment						27 035
F.422	Loans secured on dwellings				37 753		
F.423	Finance leasing	490	437	53			–
F.424	Other long-term loans by UK residents	1 869	–38	1 907	13 723		9
F.429	Other long-term loans by the rest of the world	–166	–105	–61			
F.4	Total loans	7 460	6 421	1 039	64 615		43 935
F.5	Shares and other equity						
F.51	Shares and other equity, excluding mutual funds' shares						
F.514	Quoted UK shares						
F.515	Unquoted UK shares						
F.516	Other UK equity (including direct investment in property)						
F.519	Shares and other equity issued by the rest of the world						140 420
F.52	Mutual funds' shares						
F.521	UK mutual funds' shares						
F.529	Rest of the world mutual funds' shares						–
F.5	Total shares and other equity						140 420
F.6	Insurance technical reserves						
F.61	Net equity of households in life assurance and pension funds' reserves						
F.62	Prepayments of insurance premiums and reserves for outstanding claims						
F.6	Total insurance technical reserves						
F.7	Other accounts payable	–1 577	–1 112	–465	3 774		–228
F.L	**Total net acquisition of financial liabilities**	264	–308	572	68 367		229 031
B.9	**Net lending / borrowing**						
F.A	Total net acquisition of financial assets	10 025	9 577	448	65 229		250 493
-F.L	*less* Total net acquisition of financial liabilities	–264	308	–572	–68 367		–229 031
B.9f	**Net lending (+) / net borrowing (-), from financial account**	9 761	9 885	–124	–3 138		21 462
dB.9f	**Statistical discrepancy between financial & non-financial accounts**	572	–70	642	–3 003	–	–3 179
B.9	**Net lending (+) / net borrowing (-), from capital account**	10 333	9 815	518	–6 141	–	18 283

Main aggregates and summary accounts

1.7.9 UK summary accounts 1999

Total economy: all sectors and the rest of the world. Unconsolidated

£ billion

		UK total economy S.1	Non-financial corporations S.11	Financial corporations S.12	Monetary financial institutions S.121+S.122	Other financial intermediaries & auxiliaries S.123+S.124	Insurance corporations & pension funds S.125
IV.3	**FINANCIAL BALANCE SHEET** at end of period						
AF.A	**Financial assets**						
AF.1	Monetary gold and special drawing rights (SDRs)	4.0					
AF.2	Currency and deposits						
AF.21	Currency	37.3	3.4	9.9	9.9	0.1	
AF.22	Transferable deposits						
AF.221	Deposits with UK monetary financial institutions	1 150.2	142.1	506.0	305.8	144.6	54.7
AF.229	Deposits with rest of the world monetary financial institutions	902.0	67.1	796.1	620.1	175.9	0.2
AF.29	Other deposits	70.5	7.3	0.1	0.1	–	–
AF.2	Total currency and deposits	2 160.1	219.9	1 312.1	935.8	321.5	54.9
AF.3	Securities other than shares						
AF.331	Short term: money market instruments						
AF.3311	Issued by UK central government	3.9	0.2	3.6	2.8	–	0.8
AF.3312	Issued by UK local authorities	1.3	0.3	0.6	0.3	0.1	0.3
AF.3315	Issued by UK monetary financial institutions	165.8	5.6	157.2	116.0	28.8	12.4
AF.3316	Issued by other UK residents	25.9	13.9	6.1	0.7	2.8	2.6
AF.3319	Issued by the rest of the world	43.1	1.9	39.4	31.7	7.5	0.2
AF.332	Medium (1 to 5 year) and long term (over 5 year) bonds						
AF.3321	Issued by UK central government	272.9	3.8	244.0	15.8	15.3	212.9
AF.3322	Issued by UK local authorities	0.8	–	0.7	–	–	0.7
AF.3325	Medium term bonds issued by UK MFIs[1]	32.1	0.2	31.8	16.6	3.8	11.4
AF.3326	Other medium & long term bonds issued by UK residents[2]	186.3	2.0	180.2	66.1	29.8	84.3
AF.3329	Long term bonds issued by the rest of the world	350.6	6.4	329.4	239.5	6.8	83.1
AF.34	Financial derivatives	–	–	–	–	–	–
AF.3	Total securities other than shares	1 082.6	34.2	993.1	489.6	94.9	408.6
AF.4	Loans						
AF.41	Short term loans						
AF.411	Loans by UK monetary financial institutions, excluding loans secured on dwellings & financial leasing	817.6		817.6	817.6		
AF.419	Loans by rest of the world monetary financial institutions						
AF.42	Long term loans						
AF.421	Direct investment	126.0	121.6	4.4	–	2.8	1.6
AF.422	Loans secured on dwellings	493.8	–	493.6	458.7	33.2	1.7
AF.423	Finance leasing	23.3		23.3	2.7	20.6	
AF.424	Other long-term loans by UK residents	136.6	9.9	39.9		9.2	30.7
AF.429	Other long-term loans by the rest of the world						
AF.4	Total loans	1 597.3	131.5	1 378.8	1 279.0	65.8	34.1
AF.5	Shares and other equity						
AF.51	Shares and other equity, excluding mutual funds' shares						
AF.514	Quoted UK shares	1 229.5	38.8	905.7	7.5	166.6	731.7
AF.515	Unquoted UK shares	419.1	64.7	110.6	40.9	64.3	5.4
AF.516	Other UK equity (including direct investment in property)	2.1					
AF.519	Shares and other equity issued by the rest of the world	787.5	343.1	423.3	23.1	155.7	244.5
AF.52	Mutual funds' shares						
AF.521	UK mutual funds' shares	297.3	0.6	141.7	1.7	3.5	136.5
AF.529	Rest of the world mutual funds' shares	2.1					
AF.5	Total shares and other equity	2 737.7	447.2	1 581.3	73.2	390.1	1 118.1
AF.6	Insurance technical reserves						
AF.61	Net equity of households in life assurance and pension funds' reserves	1 623.5					
AF.62	Prepayments of insurance premiums and reserves for outstanding claims	47.8	24.2	2.1		1.5	0.6
AF.6	Total insurance technical reserves	1 685.9	24.2	2.1		1.5	0.6
AF.7	Other accounts receivable	249.3	91.3	36.5	5.9	10.4	20.2
AF.A	**Total financial assets**	9 502.3	948.3	5 303.9	2 783.4	884.2	1 636.3

1 UK monetary financial institutions

1.7.9 UK summary accounts 1999
Main aggregates and summary accounts
continued Total economy: all sectors and the rest of the world. Unconsolidated

£ billion

		General government S.13	Central government S.1311	Local government S.1313	Households & NPISH S.14+S.15	Rest of the world S.2
IV.3	**FINANCIAL BALANCE SHEET** at end of period					
AF.A	**Financial assets**					
AF.1	Monetary gold and special drawing rights (SDRs)	4.0	4.0			
AF.2	Currency and deposits					
AF.21	Currency				24.1	1.1
AF.22	Transferable deposits					
AF.221	Deposits with UK monetary financial institutions	14.4	1.8	12.7	487.7	1 032.2
AF.229	Deposits with rest of the world monetary financial institutions	8.7	8.7		30.1	
AF.29	Other deposits	–	–	–	63.1	1.3
AF.2	Total currency and deposits	23.1	10.6	12.6	604.9	1 036.0
AF.3	Securities other than shares					
AF.331	Short term: money market instruments					
AF.3311	Issued by UK central government	0.1		0.1	–	0.4
AF.3312	Issued by UK local authorities	0.2	0.2		0.1	–
AF.3315	Issued by UK monetary financial institutions	0.1		0.1	2.9	68.7
AF.3316	Issued by other UK residents	0.1		5.7	0.2	17.8
AF.3319	Issued by the rest of the world	1.8	1.8			
AF.332	Medium (1 to 5 year) and long term (over 5 year) bonds					
AF.3321	Issued by UK central government	–	–	–	25.1	61.0
AF.3322	Issued by UK local authorities	–	–		0.1	–
AF.3325	Medium term bonds issued by UK MFIs[1]					35.7
AF.3326	Other medium & long term bonds issued by UK residents	0.2	0.2		3.9	127.1
AF.3329	Long term bonds issued by the rest of the world	7.6	7.6		7.1	
AF.34	Financial derivatives	–		–	–	–
AF.3	Total securities other than shares	15.9	9.9	6.0	39.4	310.7
AF.4	Loans					
AF.41	Short term loans					
AF.411	Loans by UK monetary financial institutions, excluding loans secured on dwellings & financial leasing					
AF.419	Loans by rest of the world monetary financial institutions					166.3
AF.42	Long term loans					
AF.421	Direct investment					161.2
AF.422	Loans secured on dwellings	0.2	0.1	0.1		
AF.423	Finance leasing					
AF.424	Other long-term loans by UK residents	80.2	79.9	0.3	6.5	
AF.429	Other long-term loans by the rest of the world					168.3
AF.4	Total loans	80.4	80.0	0.4	6.5	486.2
AF.5	Shares and other equity					
AF.51	Shares and other equity, excluding mutual funds' shares					
AF.514	Quoted UK shares	1.6	0.2	1.4	283.4	521.6
AF.515	Unquoted UK shares	0.5	0.1	0.4	243.3	205.6
AF.516	Other UK equity (including direct investment in property)				2.1	11.8
AF.519	Shares and other equity issued by the rest of the world	6.6	6.6		14.5	
AF.52	Mutual funds' shares					
AF.521	UK mutual funds' shares				155.1	1.7
AF.529	Rest of the world mutual funds' shares				2.1	
AF.5	Total shares and other equity	8.7	6.9	1.8	700.4	740.7
AF.6	Insurance technical reserves					
AF.61	Net equity of households in life assurance and pension funds' reserves				1 623.5	0.2
AF.62	Prepayments of insurance premiums and reserves for outstanding claims	0.9		0.9	20.7	11.1
AF.6	Total insurance technical reserves	0.9		0.9	1 644.3	11.3
AF.7	Other accounts receivable	47.2	45.0	2.2	74.4	4.5
AF.A	**Total financial assets**	180.2	156.3	23.8	3 070.0	2 589.4

1 See footnotes on first page of this table.

Main aggregates and summary accounts

1.7.9 UK summary accounts 1999 (continued)

Total economy: all sectors and the rest of the world. Unconsolidated

£ billion

		UK total economy S.1	Non-financial corporations S.11	Financial corporations S.12	Monetary financial institutions S.121+S.122	Other financial intermediaries & auxiliaries S.123+S.124	Insurance corporations & pension funds S.125
IV.3	**FINANCIAL BALANCE SHEET** continued at end of period						
AF.L	**Financial liabilities**						
AF.2	Currency and deposits						
AF.21	Currency	37.9		35.1	35.1		
AF.22	Transferable deposits						
AF.221	Deposits with UK monetary financial institutions	2 183.8		2 183.8	2 183.8		
AF.229	Deposits with rest of the world monetary financial institutions						
AF.29	Other deposits	71.8		–			
AF.2	Total currency and deposits	2 293.6		2 219.0	2 219.0		
AF.3	Securities other than shares						
AF.331	Short term: money market instruments						
AF.3311	Issued by UK central government	4.3					
AF.3312	Issued by UK local authorities	1.3					
AF.3315	Issued by UK monetary financial institutions	234.4		234.4	234.4		
AF.3316	Issued by other UK residents	43.7	22.5	21.2		21.2	
AF.3319	Issued by the rest of the world						
AF.332	Medium (1 to 5 year) and long term (over 5 year) bonds						
AF.3321	Issued by UK central government	334.0					
AF.3322	Issued by UK local authorities	0.8					
AF.3325	Medium term bonds issued by UK MFIs[1]	67.7		67.7	67.7		
AF.3326	Other medium & long term bonds issued by UK residents	313.4	146.5	164.1	55.3	108.8	0.1
AF.3329	Long term bonds issued by the rest of the world						
AF.34	Financial derivatives	–	–	–	–	–	–
AF.3	Total securities other than shares	999.6	169.0	487.5	357.4	130.0	0.1
AF.4	Loans						
AF.41	Short term loans						
AF.411	Loans by UK monetary financial institutions, excluding loans secured on dwellings & financial leasing	602.3	222.1	255.3	–	244.2	11.1
AF.419	Loans by rest of the world monetary financial institutions	166.3	85.4	69.4		69.4	
AF.42	Long term loans						
AF.421	Direct investment	151.6	132.3	19.3	6.6	5.0	7.6
AF.422	Loans secured on dwellings	493.8					
AF.423	Finance leasing	23.3	18.5	2.3	1.1	1.2	
AF.424	Other long-term loans by UK residents	134.8	57.5	13.9	–	13.5	0.5
AF.429	Other long-term loans by the rest of the world	168.3	0.4	166.7		166.7	
AF.4	Total loans	1 740.4	516.1	526.9	7.7	500.0	19.2
AF.5	Shares and other equity						
AF.51	Shares and other equity, excluding mutual funds' shares						
AF.514	Quoted UK shares	1 751.1	1 394.4	356.8	63.4	220.5	72.8
AF.515	Unquoted UK shares	624.7	465.0	159.7	45.5	105.8	8.3
AF.516	Other UK equity (including direct investment in property)	13.9	13.9				
AF.519	Shares and other equity issued by the rest of the world						
AF.52	Mutual funds' shares						
AF.521	UK mutual funds' shares	299.0		299.0		299.0	
AF.529	Rest of the world mutual funds' shares						
AF.5	Total shares and other equity	2 688.8	1 873.3	815.5	108.9	625.4	81.2
AF.6	Insurance technical reserves						
AF.61	Net equity of households in life assurance and pension funds' reserves	1 623.7		1 623.7			1 623.7
AF.62	Prepayments of insurance premiums and reserves for outstanding claims	58.9		58.9			58.9
AF.6	Total insurance technical reserves	1 682.7		1 682.7			1 682.7
AF.7	Other accounts payable	236.2	136.1	25.9	3.8	1.2	20.9
AF.L	**Total financial liabilities**	9 641.2	2 694.6	5 757.4	2 696.9	1 256.6	1 804.0
BF.90	**Net financial assets / liabilities**						
AF.A	Total financial assets	9 502.3	948.3	5 303.9	2 783.4	884.2	1 636.3
-AF.L	less Total financial liabilities	-9 641.2	-2 694.6	-5 757.4	-2 696.9	-1 256.6	-1 804.0
BF.90	**Net financial assets (+) / liabilities (-)**	−138.9	−1 746.3	−453.5	86.5	−372.4	−167.7

[1] See footnotes on first page of this table.

Main aggregates and summary accounts

1.7.9 continued
UK summary accounts
1999
Total economy: all sectors and the rest of the world. Unconsolidated

£ billion

		General government S.13	Central government S.1311	Local government S.1313	Households & NPISH S.14+S.15	Rest of the world S.2
IV.3	**FINANCIAL BALANCE SHEET** continued at end of period					
AF.L	**Financial liabilities**					
AF.2	Currency and deposits					
AF.21	Currency	2.8	2.8			0.5
AF.22	Transferable deposits					
AF.221	Deposits with UK monetary financial institutions					
AF.229	Deposits with rest of the world monetary financial institutions					902.0
AF.29	Other deposits	71.8	71.8			
AF.2	Total currency and deposits	74.6	74.6			902.5
AF.3	Securities other than shares					
AF.331	Short term: money market instruments					
AF.3311	Issued by UK central government	4.3	4.3			
AF.3312	Issued by UK local authorities	1.3		1.3		
AF.3315	Issued by UK monetary financial institutions					
AF.3316	Issued by other UK residents				–	
AF.3319	Issued by the rest of the world					43.1
AF.332	Medium (1 to 5 year) and long term (over 5 year) bonds					
AF.3321	Issued by UK central government	334.0	334.0			
AF.3322	Issued by UK local authorities	0.8		0.8		
AF.3325	Medium term bonds issued by UK MFIs[1]					
AF.3326	Other medium & long term bonds issued by UK residents				2.7	
AF.3329	Long term bonds issued by the rest of the world					350.6
AF.34	Financial derivatives	–	–	–	–	
AF.3	Total securities other than shares	340.3	338.3	2.0	2.8	393.7
AF.4	Loans					
AF.41	Short term loans					
AF.411	Loans by UK monetary financial institutions, excluding loans secured on dwellings & financial leasing	21.7	19.6	2.1	103.2	215.3
AF.419	Loans by rest of the world monetary financial institutions	0.2	–	0.2	11.3	
AF.42	Long term loans					
AF.421	Direct investment					134.0
AF.422	Loans secured on dwellings				493.7	
AF.423	Finance leasing	2.5	0.9	1.6		
AF.424	Other long-term loans by UK residents	48.1	–	48.1	15.3	1.8
AF.429	Other long-term loans by the rest of the world	1.2	0.4	0.9		
AF.4	Total loans	73.7	20.9	52.8	623.6	343.0
AF.5	Shares and other equity					
AF.51	Shares and other equity, excluding mutual funds' shares					
AF.514	Quoted UK shares					
AF.515	Unquoted UK shares					
AF.516	Other UK equity (including direct investment in property)					
AF.519	Shares and other equity issued by the rest of the world					787.5
AF.52	Mutual funds' shares					
AF.521	UK mutual funds' shares					
AF.529	Rest of the world mutual funds' shares					2.1
AF.5	Total shares and other equity					789.6
AF.6	Insurance technical reserves					
AF.61	Net equity of households in life assurance and pension funds' reserves					
AF.62	Prepayments of insurance premiums and reserves for outstanding claims					
AF.6	Total insurance technical reserves					
AF.7	Other accounts payable	18.4	9.1	9.3	55.8	17.6
AF.L	**Total financial liabilities**	507.1	442.9	64.1	682.1	2 446.5
BF.90	**Net financial assets / liabilities**					
AF.A	Total financial assets	180.2	156.3	23.8	3 070.0	2 589.4
-AF.L	*less* Total financial liabilities	–507.1	–442.9	–64.1	–682.1	–2 446.5
BF.90	**Net financial assets (+) / liabilities (-)**	–326.9	–286.6	–40.3	2 387.8	142.9

1 See footnotes on first page of this table.

Part 2

The industrial analyses

Industrial analyses

The industrial analyses at a glance from Table 2.1

Gross value added at basic prices by industry

An analysis of the eleven broad industrial sectors shows that in 1999, the financial intermediation and other business services sector provided the largest contribution to gross value added at current basic prices, at £220.6 billion out of a total of £795.0 billion. Also the manufacturing sector contributed £152.7 billion and the wholesaling and retailing sectors £125.6 billion.

Breakdown of gross value added at basic prices by industry for 1999
£ billion

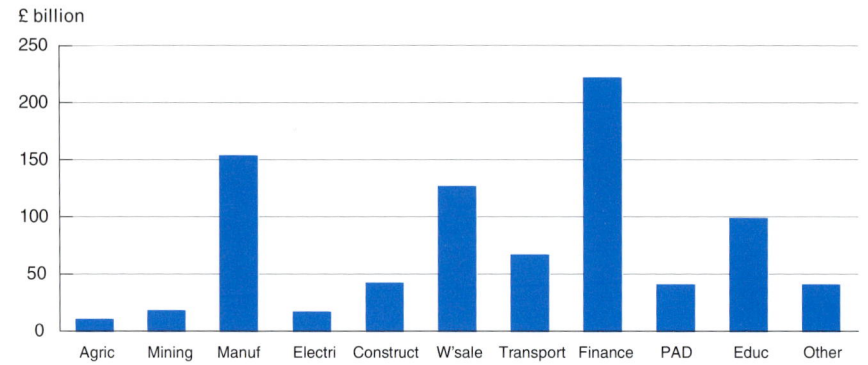

More details of the composition of gross value added for each industry group can be found in Tables 2.1, 2.2, 2.3 and the *UK Input-Output Analyses* (2001 edition).

Final demand

In 1999 just under half (49.2 per cent) of all goods and services entering into final demand were purchased by consumers. 20.5 per cent were exported. 14.4 per cent were consumed by government, both central and local. Gross capital formation by all sectors of the economy amounted to 13.9 per cent of the total.

Composition of final demand for 1999

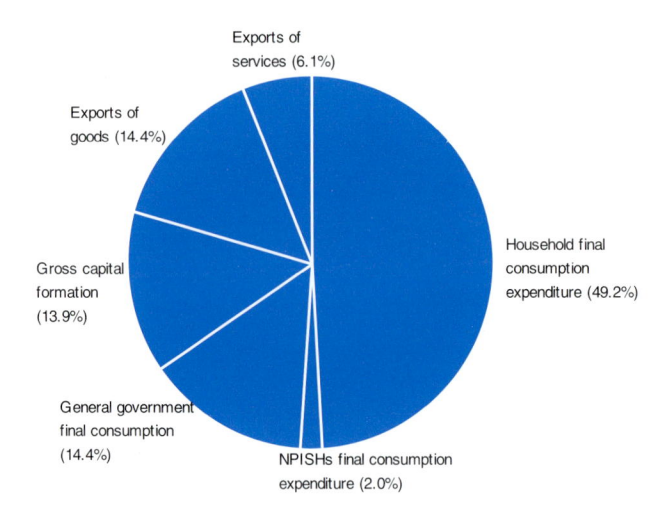

- Exports of services (6.1%)
- Exports of goods (14.4%)
- Gross capital formation (13.9%)
- General government final consumption (14.4%)
- NPISHs final consumption expenditure (2.0%)
- Household final consumption expenditure (49.2%)

A more detailed analysis of the demand for products can be found in Table 2.1 and the *UK Input-Output Analyses* (2001 edition).

Compensation of employees by industry

Manufacturing industries showed the highest level of compensation of employees in 1999 at £109.1 billion. After manufacturing, the next largest industries in terms of their contribution to total compensation of employees were financial intermediation and other business services at £94.9 billion, education and health services at £83.2 billion and wholesaling and retailing at £76.5 billion.

Compensation of employees by industry 1999
£ billion

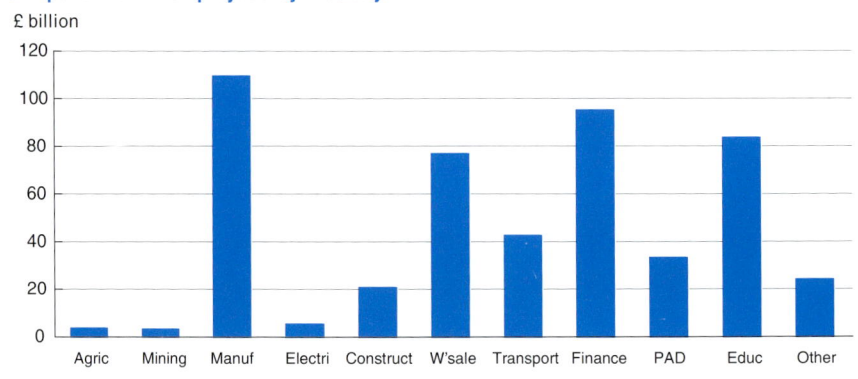

More details can be found in Tables 2.1, 2.2 and the *UK Input-Output Analyses* (2001 edition).

Part 2:
Industrial analyses

Input-Output Supply and Use Tables

The annual estimates prepared for the *Blue Book* incorporate the results of annual inquiries which become available in the first part of the year, although estimates for the latest year are still based largely on quarterly information. As new data are collected it is likely that revisions will be necessary. The process of reassessing these estimates involves the preparation of Input-Output (I-O) Supply and Use Tables. This I-O approach amalgamates all the available information on inputs, outputs, value added, income and expenditure. Similarly the production of the consolidated sector and financial accounts requires the preparation of 'top-to-bottom' sector and sub-sector accounts to identify discrepancies in the estimates relating to each sector. The thorough and detailed nature of this estimation process is time consuming and so estimates for earlier years are not normally revisited unless there are strong reasons for doing so.

GDP and the balancing of the annual accounts

As discussed in Part 1, there are three different approaches to the estimation of current price GDP in the UK: the income approach, the expenditure approach and the production approach. In theory the three different approaches should produce the same result. However, the different approaches are based on different surveys and administrative data sources and each produces estimates which, like all statistical estimates, are subject to errors and omissions. A definitive GDP estimate can only emerge after a process of balancing and adjustment. ONS believes that the most reliable 'definitive' estimate of the current price level of GDP is that derived using the annual I-O framework. Thus, for the years when I-O Supply and Use Tables are available, GDP is set at the level derived from that year's balance. For periods subsequent to the latest I-O Supply and Use Tables, the level of GDP is carried forward using movements in income, expenditure and production totals. (This quarterly balancing process is described in Chapter 11 of *Concepts, Sources and Methods*[1].)

The Input-Output framework

The accounting framework shown in Figure 1 on page 10 is mainly concerned with the composition and value of goods and services entering into final demand (for example, purchases by consumers) and the outputs and incomes generated in the production process. It does not display the inter-industry transactions which link these activities.

The UK I-O Supply and Use Tables, however, do include these intermediate transactions which form inputs into these processes, thus providing an extra dimension. The I-O analyses are constructed to show a balanced and complete picture of the flows of products in the economy and illustrate the relationships between producers and consumers of goods and services.

On an annual basis I-O Supply and Use Tables are used to achieve consistency in the economic accounts' aggregates by linking the components of value added, inputs, outputs and final demand. As the income, production and expenditure measures of GDP can all be calculated from the I-O Supply and Use Tables, a single estimate of GDP can be derived by balancing the supply and demand for goods and services and reconciling them with the corresponding value added estimates. For the years 1989 to 1999, the balancing process has been used to set the level of current price GDP and has disposed of the need for statistical discrepancies in the form of a GDP expenditure adjustment and a GDP income adjustment.

The I-O process, which produces Supply and Use Tables annually, has been speeded up considerably over the last few years and can now produce the first balance for a year around eighteen months after the end of that year. These full I-O Supply and Use Tables, consistent with the national accounts *Blue Book*, are published as separate publications at the same time as the *Blue Book*. The latest annual I-O publication[2] covers the periods 1992-1999, with summary information provided in the *Blue Book* itself.

Some background on the structure of the Supply and Use Tables

The I-O Supply and Use Tables are based on a framework which incorporates estimates of industry inputs, outputs and value added. The tables comprise of two matrices: the *Supply* matrix and the *Use* matrix, each of which breaks down and balances 123 different industries and products at purchasers' prices. Further details on the matrices are given in Chapter 13 of *Concepts, Sources and Methods*[1]. A full description of the present methodology is given in the *Input-Output Balances Methodological Guide*[4]. A new *Guide* based on the ESA95 methodology will be published within the next year. The following paragraphs summarise the methodology.

Supply table

At a very aggregate level the *Supply* table can be represented as follows:

	Output by industry	Imports of goods and services	Distributors' trading margins	Taxes *less* subsidies on products
Output by product	MAKE matrix			

The *Make* matrix shows estimates of domestic industries' output (total sales adjusted for changes in inventories of work in progress and finished goods) compiled at basic prices. Basic prices value the goods leaving the factory gate but exclude any taxes on products and include any

Industrial analyses

subsidies on products. However, for the balancing process, the estimates of supply of products are required at purchasers' prices, i.e. those actually paid by the purchasers to take delivery of the goods, excluding any deductible VAT.

To convert the estimates of domestic output valued at basic prices (from the *Make* matrix) to the total supply of products valued at purchasers' prices requires the addition of:

- the value of imports of goods and services;
- distributors' trading margins;
- taxes on products (e.g. VAT, excise duties, air passenger tax, insurance premium tax etc);

less

- subsidies on products (e.g. agricultural and transport subsidies).

Use table

The *Use* table reveals the input structure of each industry in terms of combined domestic and imported goods and services. It also shows the product composition of final demand and, for each industry, the intermediate purchases adjusted for changes in inventories of materials and fuels.

Consumption of products is represented in the rows of the balance while purchases by industries, and final demands, are represented in the columns. At a very aggregate level the *Use* table can be considered in three parts as shown below.

	Industry consumption	Final demands
Products consumed	Shows consumption by each industry to produce their own output (i.e. intermediate consumption).	Shows final demand categories (e.g. households' expenditure) and the values of products going to these categories.
Primary inputs	Shows the value added components of each industry, taxes *less* subsidies on production other than product-specific taxes and subsidies, compensation of employees and gross operating surplus.	

The body of the matrix, which represents consumption of products, is at purchasers' prices and so already includes the product-specific taxes and subsidies separately added to the *Make* matrix in the *Supply* table.

The I-O balance is effectively achieved when:

For industries:
Inputs (from the *Use* table)
equal

Outputs (from the *Supply* table)
For products:
Supply (from the *Supply* table)
equals
Demand (from the *Use* table)

That is, when the data from the income, expenditure and production approaches used to fill the matrices all produce the same estimate of current price GDP at market prices. GDP at current market prices can be derived from the balances by taking the estimate of total value added at basic prices (from the *Use* table) and adding taxes on products less subsidies on products (from the *Supply* table).

The balancing process

The balancing process is carried out over a number of months, and involves the current price I-O team as well as the compilers who feed data directly into the process from surveys or through the economic accounts compilation process.

Initial estimates

Once the initial data estimates have been gathered, estimates of the components of supply and demand for products are prepared, together with the estimates of industry outputs and inputs and thus gross value added. The resulting production-based estimates of current price gross value added are then compared with the expenditure and income measures, and the checks and analyses which follow extend the validation checks which will already have been carried out on the initial data estimates. The investigations which follow often lead to the revision and redelivery of data.

In parallel with this work alternative estimates of gross value added for each of the 123 industries are prepared using income-based data.

The coherence of these initial estimates is then assessed by:

- comparisons of gross value added for each industry using the income and production-based approaches, and

- comparisons of the components of supply and demand for each type of product (which effectively compare the production and expenditure approaches).

In addition a variety of time series (e.g. growth rates and the ratio of gross value added to total output) are compiled to aid the assessment.

At this stage the resulting income, production and expenditure aggregates will typically show different profiles over time.

Industrial analyses

Revised estimates

To obtain the revised estimates an iterative process begins, to reconcile:

- the income and production-based estimates of industry gross value added, and
- the supply and demand for each product.

These estimates are scrutinised, validated and checked for their plausibility and coherence across all industries and products. Consistency and coherence over time are also important and the impact of revisions to earlier years and the quality of the relative data sources are also taken into account. When necessary other sources (e.g. detailed National Statistics survey data and company reports and accounts) are used to inform the investigation of particular areas. Discussions follow between the current price I-O team and data compilers and any issues are resolved.

Final estimates

As final estimates are received from data compilers the steps of assessment, scrutiny, comparison and reconciliation continue. For the time-series under consideration the quality of source data, revisions performance and any specific estimation problems are taken into account. Any changes to estimates are agreed and the inconsistencies between supply and demand, and between production and income-based value added, are progressively reduced. This process continues until convergence between the aggregate totals is achieved.

The single best estimate of GDP which emerges will reflect the relative merits of the output, income and expenditure estimates at the aggregate level. It will also have been assessed after consideration of the effect on current price and constant price expenditure growth rates, the impact on the expenditure deflator and the relationship between current price and constant price value added.

Once this GDP estimate has been fine-tuned and agreed by all concerned, the industry value added estimates and the value added weights (for the base year) are fixed after a full reconciliation of the income-based components with the output-based estimate. Product supply and demand will still differ at this stage, mainly reflecting the approximations in transforming source data to I-O group level. Further adjustments are made at this stage to address these imbalances; for example, distributors' trading margins and the allocation of other services provided by manufacturers. The *Use* matrix is then fully balanced by adjusting the intermediate purchases within the predetermined column and row totals.

This final step in the balancing process is to apply the r.A.s. method to the intermediate section of the *Use* matrix. This process will adjust the intermediate purchases in line with pre-determined row and column totals, resulting in a fully-balanced table. The term r.A.s. refers to an iterative mathematical process, where A is the coefficient form of the intermediate section of the *Use* matrix. A is pre-multiplied by a diagonal matrix, with the vector r of replacement factors forming the diagonal, and post-multiplied by a diagonal matrix with the substitution vector s forming the diagonal. A single iteration applies the above process for each row and then for each column. After each iteration the replacement factors are changed appropriately and the process is repeated until the desired balance has been achieved, that is supply equalling demand for each product.

The end result is a full set of I-O Supply and Use Tables where, for each of the 123 industries, inputs equal outputs, and for each of the 123 product groups, supply equals demand.

Annual coherence adjustments in the 2001 *Blue Book* and the 2001 *I-O Annual Supply and Use Tables*

As described, the role of the I-O framework aims to present a fully consistent picture of the UK economy. In practice the data sources used in the national accounts are subject to statistical error and complete coherence between measures of economic activity is not achieved without making specific adjustments. For the periods 1989 to 1999, these adjustments are made through the current price balancing process using I-O Supply and Use Tables and its underlying framework.

An article in the October 1999 *Economic Trends*[3] describes the background to the adjustments and briefly shows how they are made. The balancing process is described in more detail in the *I-O Methodological Guide*[4]. The process of achieving coherence in the accounts by balancing I-O Supply and Use Tables can most simply be explained as a series of different types of adjustment. The three main types of adjustment described in the *Economic Trends* article are:

- Conceptual and coverage adjustments
- Quality adjustments
- Coherence adjustments

The annual current price quality and coherence adjustments agreed for the 2001 *Blue Book* dataset and the 2001 *I-O Supply and Use Tables* are shown in the table below:

Current price analyses (Tables 2.1, 2.2 and 2.3)

The analyses of gross value added and other variables by industry shown in Part 2 reflect estimates based on the Standard Industrial Classification, Revised 1992 (SIC92). Tables 2.1, 2.2 and 2.3 are based on current price data reconciled through the I-O process for 1992 to 1999. The aggregate figures for the latest year, 2000, as shown in Tables 2.2 and 2.3, are based on data reconciled through the national accounts balancing process. This process is explained in Chapter 11 of *Concepts, Sources and Methods*[1]. The industry detail for the year 2000 is based on current price output estimates from a variety of sources, both within the ONS and in other government departments. These estimates will be revised

Industrial analyses

Coherence adjustments within 1998 and 1999 annual current price GDP (£ million)

	1998	1999
Expenditure Measure		
Household final consumption	2,795	3,365
NPISHs	480	280
Central government	-300	-
Local authorities	-100	-
Gross fixed capital formation	4,771	6,459
Change in inventories	-	-
Exports of services	716	420
Imports of services	239	445
Production Measure		
Agriculture	-20	-20
Mining and quarrying	-400	1,050
Manufacturing	1,676	-374
Electricity, gas and water supply	-420	190
Construction	337	-806
Wholesale and retail trade	-2,171	-2,782
Transport and communication	648	477
Financial intermediation	-2,358	-2,782
Public administration	-	-
Education, health and social work	797	754
Other services	183	-473
Income Measure		
Private non-financial corporations' profits	-533	-413
Compensation of employees	1,173	2,088
Rental income	-250	-

when the first I-O Supply and Use balances for 2000 become available.

Estimates of total output and gross value added are valued at basic prices, the method recommended by ESA95. Thus the only taxes included in the price will be taxes paid as part of the production process (such as business rates and vehicle excise duty), and not any taxes specifically levied on the production of a unit of output (such as VAT). Any subsidies on products received will also be included in the valuation of output.

Constant (1995=100) price analyses (Table 2.4)

Table 2.4 shows constant price estimates of gross value added at basic prices by industry. The basic methodology for these estimates can be found in the Government Statistical Service methodological publications 'Gross Domestic Product: Output approach'[6,7]. A more detailed explanation is in Concepts, Sources and Methods[1].

The output approach provides the lead indicator of economic change in the short term. However in the longer term, it is required to follow reasonably closely the path indicated by the constant price expenditure measure of GDP (usually within 0.2 per cent of the average annual GDP growth). To achieve this, balancing adjustments (or coherence factors) are sometimes required to be included within the output based gross value added estimates. These can be necessary particularly in periods of rapid change in economic activity or technological or structural changes when the proportion of inputs to outputs may vary. The adoption of ESA95 has given rise to additional measurement difficulties for historical periods. The need to reduce discrepancies which arise as a result of this can also lead to the use of balancing adjustments.

An examination of the constant price gross value added and expenditure measures of GDP, shows what are considered to be excessive differences in growth for a small number of recent years:

- The output-based estimate falls by more than the expenditure measure in 1991 and falls less in 1992.

Industrial analyses

- During both 1998 and 1999 the output-based estimate increases by more than the expenditure measure.

To reduce these discrepancies, a number of balancing adjustments have been made to the constant price gross value added annual growth rates.

For years before 1995, balancing adjustments have been applied equally to all four quarters within the year. It was not considered necessary to apply the adjustments to subsequent years.

For 1991 and 1992:

The adjustments concentrate on the industrial divisions or sections in the composition of gross value added where the estimates of change are considered to be least well based. The adjustments are, as follows:

1991:

(a) An upward adjustment of 0.4 per cent has been applied to:
- construction
- hotels and restaurants
- education
- health and social work
- part of transport and storage.

(b) An upward adjustment of 1.4 per cent has been applied to part of wholesale and retail trade.

(c) An upward adjustment of 0.8 per cent has been applied to:
- financial intermediation
- parts of the real estate, renting and business activities section

The total effect of these 1991 adjustments is:

to increase the level of gross value added at constant basic prices by 0.2 per cent in 1991. This has the effect of increasing the 1990/91 growth rate by 0.2 per cent and reducing the 1991/92 growth estimate correspondingly.

1992:

(a) A downward adjustment of 0.4 per cent has been applied to:
- agriculture, forestry and fishing
- construction
- part of wholesale and retail trade
- hotels and restaurants
- transport and storage
- communication
- part of other real estate, renting and business activities
- education
- health and social work
- other social and personal services, private households with employees and extra-territorial organisations.

(b) A downward adjustment of 1.4 per cent has been applied to part of wholesale and retail trade.

(c) A downward adjustment of 0.9 per cent has been applied to part of financial intermediation and part of other real estate, renting and business activities.

The total effect of the 1992 adjustments is:

to reduce the level of gross value added at constant basic prices by 0.3 per cent in 1992. This has the effect of reducing the 1991/92 growth rate by 0.3 per cent (in addition to the effect of the 1991 adjustments) and increasing the 1992/93 growth estimate correspondingly.

For 1998 and 1999:

To help estimate how best to distribute the output adjustments across industries a commodity flow approach was used. This attempts to balance estimates of supply and demand by product and has produced more informed industry adjustments for a range of service industries. For technical and other reasons balancing adjustments are not at present made to the production industries for any years. More details on this can be found in the recently published: *Review of Short-Term Output Indicators*[8].

The balancing adjustments for 1998 in last year's *Blue Book* were larger than had been applied to a single year previously. This stimulated an improvement in the way annual balancing adjustments are distributed across the quarters within a year. In order to avoid disproportionate disruption to growth into the first quarter of the year, these 1998 adjustments were scaled in arithmetically throughout the quarters of the year. The method chosen was to apply 40 per cent of the annual adjustment in quarter one, 80 per cent in quarter two, 120 per cent in quarter three, and 160 per cent in quarter four. This method has been used for the - smaller - 1998 adjustments this year.

Where annual balancing adjustments are only applied to a year when the output growth estimate exceeds that from the expenditure approach, their omission from the succeeding year will cause an opposite revision to the quarterly growth estimates for the first quarter of that year and for the year as a whole. In years where adjustments are small, this has not been too disruptive to quarterly growths (see '**1991 and 1992**' above and earlier Blue Books). However, the large size of some recent adjustments has led to the adjustment in the fourth quarter of the year being carried forward to subsequent quarters and years - in order to avoid distorting the growth into the first quarter of the next year. This procedure avoids undue disruption to quarterly GDP growth estimates but will automatically cause a further change in the annual growth for the next year, dragging it further in the same direction as the previous year's

Industrial analyses

annual adjustment (because the adjustment carried forward is that for the fourth quarter of the previous year not the average for that year).

This automatic 'dragging' effect on the subsequent year's growth can be helpful where the estimated growth from the output approach also exceeds that from the expenditure approach for the following year - as it did for the 1998 and 1999 estimates last year (and does again this year). However for this year the largest downward adjustments are necessary to 1999's output growth: for the year 2000 the output based estimate of growth is not above that from the expenditure approach. Therefore the output based growth estimate for the year 2000 should not be revised down at all if possible. To avoid this, while still limiting the disruption to quarterly growths, a different distribution of the annual adjustment through the quarters was used for 1999. For the first quarter 50 per cent of the annual adjustment was applied, for the second, 100 per cent and for the third and fourth quarters 125 per cent of the annual adjustment was applied. Finally, the adjustment taken forward into 2000 and later is not that for the fourth quarter but that of the second quarter of 1999 to reduce the unwanted effects on the 2000 annual growth.

1998:

A downward adjustment of 0.5 percent has been applied to industrial sections for:
- Communication (part of industry Section I);
- All business activities (section K) except real estate and ownership of dwellings.

The total effect of these 1998 adjustments is:

to reduce the level of gross value added at constant basic prices by 0.1 per cent for 1998. This has the effect of reducing the 1997/1998 growth rate by 0.1 per cent.

1999:

For industries where an adjustment has been applied to 1998 the fourth quarter value represents the starting position for the 1999 adjustments. The full range of industries where adjustments are applied for 1999 is wider than that for 1998, as follows:

(a) A downward adjustment of 0.8 per cent for:
all of wholesale and retail distribution including motor trades (industry Section G).

(b) A downward adjustment of 1.6 per cent for:
- Communication (part of industry Section I);
- All business activities (Section K) except real estate and ownership of dwellings.

(c) A downward adjustment of 1.0 per cent for:

Those parts of industry Sections O and P concerned with sewage, 'other personal service' and 'private household' activities.

The total effect of these 1999 adjustments is:

to reduce the level of gross value added at constant basic prices by 0.5 per cent for 1999. This has the effect of reducing the 1998/1999 growth rate by 0.5 per cent.

The total effect of carrying forward the 1999 adjustments into 2000 as described is:

to reduce the level of gross value added at constant basic prices by 0.1 per cent for 2000. This has the effect of reducing the 1999/2000 growth rate by 0.1 per cent. These adjustments have no effect on growths for subsequent years as levels are thereafter reduced by a constant proportion.

All adjustments are thought to be within the likely error range of the data and within the level of accuracy of those results indicated generally by the Office for National Statistics.

Employment analyses (Table 2.5)

Table 2.5 breaks down employment data into six broad industry groupings. Employee jobs, the main component of the employment figures, uses an industry breakdown which is consistent with most other parts of the national accounts. This is because employee figures are obtained from surveys of businesses whose details are stored on National Statistics' Business Register. This is the same register which is used for all other business surveys collecting economic data.

The estimates of self-employment jobs come from the Labour Force Survey. This is a household survey which codes respondents according to their own view of the industry in which they work. Because of this, the industrial coding of the self-employment jobs may not be consistent with the industrial codes for employees. Note that the data do not include UK armed forces or government supported trainees, which are the other components of the Workforce Jobs series.

References:

1 *National Accounts Concepts, Sources and Methods, 1998 edition.*
Published by The Stationery Office. ISBN 0 11 621062 1

2 *United Kingdom Input-Output Analyses,* 2001 edition.
Published by The Stationery Office. ISBN 0 11 621476 7

3 *Economic Trends No. 551 October 1999*
Annual Coherence Adjustments in the National Accounts

4 *Input-Output Balances Methodological Guide 1997 edition,*
February 1997. Published by ONS. ISBN 1 85774 234 6

Industrial analyses

5   *Input-Output Tables for the United Kingdom,* 10th edition, February 1997. Published by ONS. ISBN 0 11 620664 0

6   *Gross Domestic Product: Output methodological guide.* Published by Government Statistical Service 1998. ISBN 1 85774 250 8

7   *Gross Domestic Product: Output approach (Gross Value Added) GSS Methodology Series #15:.* Published by Government Statistical Service 1998. ISBN 1 85774 318 0

8   *Review of Short-Term Output Indicators: National Statistics Quality Review Series Report No. 1: 2000.* Published by ONS. ISBN 1 85774 391 1

Industrial analyses

2.1 Supply and Use Tables for the United Kingdom: 1992

Supply Table

£ million

1992	Domestic output of products at basic prices	Imports Goods EU	Imports Goods Non-EU	Imports Services EU	Imports Services Non-EU	Distributors' trading margins	Taxes less subsidies on products	Total[1] supply of products at purchasers' prices
PRODUCTS[2]								
Agriculture	21 623	2 195	1 955	109	99	1 447	- 1 144	26 284
Mining and quarrying	18 944	742	6 439	59	115	1 551	- 483	27 368
Manufacturing	287 401	65 779	41 561	3 245	3 623	101 665	47 453	550 727
Electricity, gas and water supply	36 961	362	-	38	19	-	1 987	39 367
Construction	78 336	-	-	29	58	-	3 169	81 591
Wholesale and retail trade	146 466	-	-	2 657	2 508	- 104 663	4 899	51 868
Transport and communication	79 182	-	-	3 247	4 187	-	485	87 102
Financial intermediation	228 608	307	228	3 270	4 725	-	4 950	242 088
Public administration	64 354	-	-	34	64	-	-	64 452
Education, health and social work	99 135	-	-	405	299	-	508	100 347
Other services	39 178	525	820	1 054	902	-	2 595	45 074
Total[1]	1 100 189	69 910	51 003	14 147	16 599	-	64 420	1 316 268
of which:								
Market output	921 050							
Output for own final use	39 138							
Other non-market output	140 001							

Use Table at Purchasers' prices

1992	Agriculture	Mining and quarrying	Manufacturing	Electricity, gas and water supply	Construction	Wholesale and retail trade	Transport and communication	Financial intermediation	Public administration	Education, health and social work	Other services	Not allocated to industries
PRODUCTS[2]												
Agriculture	3 889	1	11 609	-	3	1 044	37	9	19	138	46	-
Mining and quarrying	4	1 382	8 348	6 851	1 645	121	48	9	41	50	36	-
Manufacturing	5 029	2 359	131 707	2 885	15 025	17 438	9 705	9 872	11 757	13 042	4 317	-
Electricity, gas and water supply	296	289	5 597	12 234	233	1 310	809	1 148	696	1 428	418	-
Construction	195	905	751	387	19 392	585	337	5 274	2 994	655	413	-
Wholesale and retail trade	695	77	637	91	68	3 015	1 781	2 076	287	554	327	-
Transport and communication	334	728	9 025	214	913	14 806	12 716	13 064	1 906	2 022	1 448	-
Financial intermediation	1 612	1 861	19 865	1 230	9 303	18 357	8 536	44 707	5 581	5 944	7 589	19 086 *
Public administration	13	10	73	5	19	8	95	1 252	67	3	6	-
Education, health and social work	162	15	617	71	137	431	437	1 811	1 191	10 779	498	-
Other services	358	69	1 906	69	71	467	461	1 157	919	954	4 359	-
Total consumption[1]	12 586	7 696	190 135	24 038	46 808	57 583	34 961	80 380	25 458	35 568	19 456	19 086 *
Taxes *less* subsidies on production	34	216	2 213	1 375	318	5 021	1 232	1 759	572	1 117	725	-
Compensation of employees	3 228	4 073	84 186	5 799	14 826	48 988	30 330	55 736	34 455	53 309	12 783	-
Gross operating surplus	6 656	9 129	29 492	7 754	14 876	25 597	13 546	73 632	4 183	9 811	8 549	- 19 086 *
Gross value added at basic prices[1]	9 918	13 418	115 891	14 928	30 020	79 606	45 108	131 127	39 210	64 237	22 057	- 19 086 *
Output at basic prices[1]	22 504	21 114	306 026	38 966	76 828	137 189	80 069	211 507	64 668	99 805	41 513	-
Supplementary information:												
Gross fixed capital formation	2 080	7 218	13 008	6 755	848	8 374	8 978	12 927	8 356	4 620	5 515	21 921 **
Changes in inventories	30	74	- 1 544	- 136	- 821	418	- 15	74	- 17	-	-	-
Total gross capital formation	2 110	7 292	11 464	6 619	27	8 792	8 963	13 001	8 339	4 620	5 515	21 921 **

1 Differences between totals and sums of components are due to rounding.
2 Some of the industry/product group headings have been truncated. See Table 2.2 for full titles.
3 Purchases of products by industry and by final consumption categories are valued at purchaser prices.

* This relates to FISIM.
** This includes investment in dwellings, transfer costs of land and existing buildings, and valuables.

Industrial analyses

2.1 Supply and Use Tables for the United Kingdom: 1992
continued

Gross value added at basic prices
£ billions

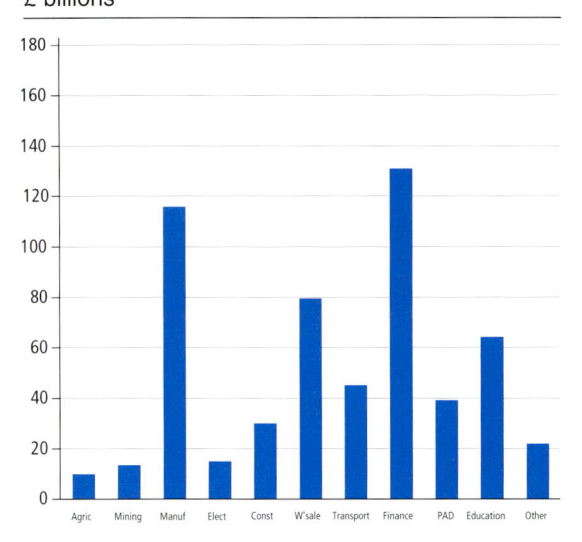

Components of final demand
Per cent

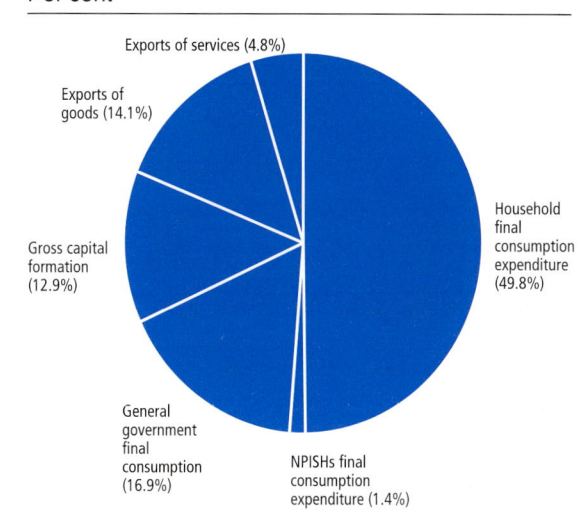

Exports of services (4.8%)
Exports of goods (14.1%)
Gross capital formation (12.9%)
General government final consumption (16.9%)
NPISHs final consumption expenditure (1.4%)
Household final consumption expenditure (49.8%)

£ million

		FINAL CONSUMPTION EXPENDITURE			GROSS CAPITAL FORMATION			EXPORTS				TOTAL[1]
								Goods		Services		
1992	Total[1] intermediate consumption	Households	NPISHs	GGFC	GFCF	Valuables	Changes in inventories	EU	Non-EU	EU	Non-EU	
PRODUCTS[2]												
Agriculture	16 794	7 080	-	-	556	-	41	1 418	316	33	46	26 284
Mining and quarrying	18 535	618	-	-	1 508	-	59	4 013	2 479	56	99	27 368
Manufacturing	223 135	186 745	-	-	41 101	- 69	- 1 010	58 737	38 948	1 301	1 839	550 727
Electricity, gas and water supply	24 458	14 973	-	-	-	-	- 107	-	-	18	25	39 367
Construction	31 887	3 832	-	-	46 694	-	- 926	-	-	25	79	81 591
Wholesale and retail trade	9 606	37 648	-	-	-	86	-	-	-	1 871	2 657	51 868
Transport and communication	57 178	20 401	-	-	962	-	-	-	-	3 064	5 497	87 102
Financial intermediation	143 671	72 163	420	-	8 217	-	6	278	137	6 493	10 703	242 088
Public administration	1 551	804	-	60 894	614	-	-	-	-	271	318	64 452
Education, health and social work	16 149	13 056	7 103	63 391	-	-	-	-	-	271	378	100 347
Other services	10 789	22 439	3 283	4 910	931	-	-	530	1 007	418	766	45 074
Total consumption[1]	553 755	379 758	10 806	129 195	100 583	17	- 1 937	64 976	42 887	13 819	22 409	1 316 268
Taxes *less* subsidies on production	14 582											
Compensation of employees	347 713											
Gross operating surplus	184 139											
Gross value added at basic prices[1]	546 434											
Output at basic prices[1]	1 100 189											
Supplementary information:												
Gross fixed capital formation	100 600 **											
Changes in inventories	- 1 937											
Total gross capital formation	98 663 **											

Notes for information:
Gross value added at basic prices plus taxes *less* subsidies on products gives GDP at market prices.
Gross operating surplus includes gross mixed income.
Changes in inventories includes materials and fuels, work-in-progress and finished goods.
Valuables include both 'transfer costs' and 'acquisitions *less* disposals'.
GFCF can be broken down by institutional sectors and assets, see Chapter 9.

FISIM represents Financial Intermediation Services Indirectly Measured.
NPISHs represents Non-Profit Institutions Serving Households.
GGFC represents General Government Final Consumption.
GFCF represents Gross Fixed Capital Formation.

Industrial analyses

2.1 Supply and Use Tables for the United Kingdom: 1993

Supply Table

£ million

1993	Domestic output of products at basic prices	Imports Goods EU	Imports Goods Non-EU	Imports Services EU	Imports Services Non-EU	Distributors' trading margins	Taxes less subsidies on products	Total[1] supply of products at purchasers' prices
PRODUCTS[2]								
Agriculture	22 454	2 151	2 142	110	104	2 235	- 1 929	27 267
Mining and quarrying	19 037	724	7 454	58	131	1 663	- 285	28 782
Manufacturing	305 280	70 702	49 983	3 503	3 995	109 660	49 267	592 389
Electricity, gas and water supply	37 016	447	-	33	20	-	1 905	39 421
Construction	77 288	-	-	29	76	-	3 713	81 107
Wholesale and retail trade	158 479	-	-	3 016	2 971	- 113 559	5 075	55 983
Transport and communication	85 269	-	-	3 596	4 890	-	789	94 544
Financial intermediation	245 369	320	299	3 599	5 673	-	5 077	260 337
Public administration	66 165	-	-	30	52	-	-	66 247
Education, health and social work	113 452	-	-	421	344	-	550	114 767
Other services	42 244	90	983	1 117	1 062	-	2 704	48 200
Total[1]	1 172 054	74 434	60 861	15 513	19 317	-	66 866	1 409 045

of which:
Market output	986 313
Output for own final use	40 226
Other non-market output	145 515

Use Table at Purchasers' prices

INTERMEDIATE CONSUMPTION BY INDUSTRY GROUP[2,3]

1993	Agriculture	Mining and quarrying	Manufac-turing	Electricity, gas and water supply	Construc-tion	Wholesale and retail trade	Transport and communi-cation	Financial intermed-iation	Public adminis-tration	Education, health and social work	Other services	Not allocated to industries
PRODUCTS[2]												
Agriculture	3 654	1	12 600	-	4	1 180	38	10	19	165	46	-
Mining and quarrying	3	1 432	8 748	6 348	1 551	118	49	9	42	44	33	-
Manufacturing	5 579	2 284	140 977	2 919	16 169	19 886	11 399	10 776	11 734	13 525	4 855	-
Electricity, gas and water supply	276	241	5 792	11 800	230	1 362	843	1 140	722	1 285	399	-
Construction	192	927	846	312	18 017	591	354	5 651	3 479	635	444	-
Wholesale and retail trade	732	86	714	97	72	3 264	1 935	2 185	317	617	346	-
Transport and communication	327	798	9 156	198	971	16 165	14 555	14 002	2 122	2 206	1 593	-
Financial intermediation	1 550	2 006	22 596	1 271	9 558	19 622	9 311	47 085	5 722	6 501	7 856	19 569 *
Public administration	2	12	86	6	20	9	106	1 477	73	5	6	-
Education, health and social work	181	21	806	79	143	473	476	1 848	1 243	19 728	533	-
Other services	327	71	2 390	74	77	534	534	1 295	1 003	958	5 159	-
Total consumption[1]	12 823	7 879	204 709	23 104	46 812	63 205	39 601	85 477	26 476	45 668	21 270	19 569 *
Taxes *less* subsidies on production	- 105	203	2 001	1 343	319	5 035	1 115	1 918	576	894	637	-
Compensation of employees	3 129	3 344	85 804	6 212	13 234	52 671	31 419	56 364	35 206	56 981	13 297	-
Gross operating surplus	7 520	9 979	33 184	8 716	15 613	26 357	13 874	83 722	4 206	10 661	9 600	- 19 569 *
Gross value added at basic prices[1]	10 544	13 526	120 989	16 271	29 166	84 063	46 408	142 004	39 988	68 536	23 535	- 19 569 *
Output at basic prices[1]	23 367	21 405	325 698	39 375	75 978	147 268	86 009	227 481	66 464	114 204	44 805	-

Supplementary information:
Gross fixed capital formation	2 337	6 088	13 005	6 380	1 019	8 643	9 511	11 956	8 734	4 440	5 443	23 442 **
Changes in inventories	30	- 73	- 1 511	- 253	- 227	2 237	- 17	167	- 24	-	-	-
Total gross capital formation	2 367	6 015	11 494	6 127	792	10 880	9 494	12 123	8 710	4 440	5 443	23 442 **

1 Differences between totals and sums of components are due to rounding.
2 Some of the industry/product group headings have been truncated. See Table 2.2 for full titles.
3 Purchases of products by industry and by final consumption categories are valued at purchaser prices.

* This relates to FISIM.
** This includes investment in dwellings, transfer costs of land and existing buildings, and valuables.

Industrial analyses

2.1 Supply and Use Tables for the United Kingdom: 1993
continued

Gross value added at basic prices
£ billions

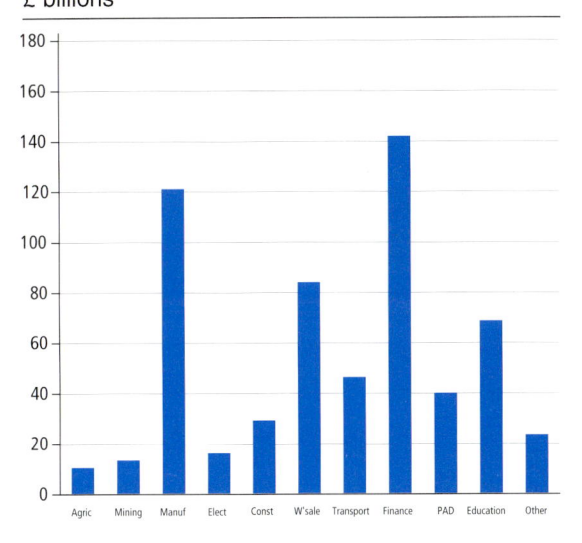

Components of final demand
Per cent

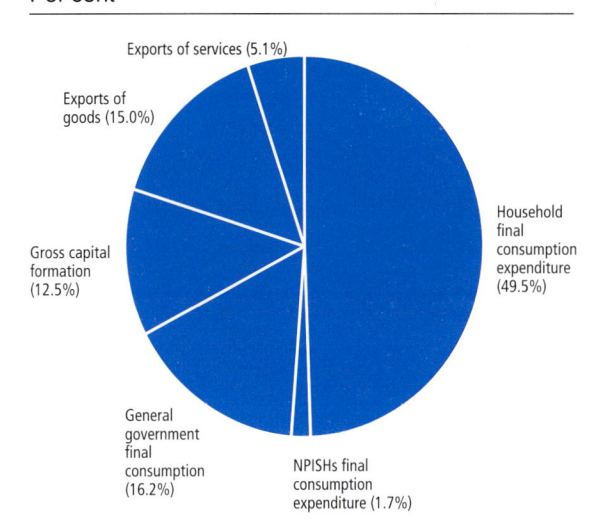

Exports of services (5.1%)
Exports of goods (15.0%)
Gross capital formation (12.5%)
General government final consumption (16.2%)
NPISHs final consumption expenditure (1.7%)
Household final consumption expenditure (49.5%)

£ million

1993	Total[1] intermediate consumption	FINAL CONSUMPTION EXPENDITURE				GROSS CAPITAL FORMATION			EXPORTS				TOTAL[1]
							Changes in inventories	Goods		Services		
		Households	NPISHs	GGFC	GFCF	Valuables		EU	Non-EU	EU	Non-EU	
PRODUCTS[2]												
Agriculture	17 716	7 280	-	-	591	-	94	1 081	415	37	54	27 267
Mining and quarrying	18 378	614	-	-	1 213	-	- 69	4 991	3 510	51	95	28 782
Manufacturing	240 103	195 373	-	-	42 227	- 82	699	62 868	47 601	1 461	2 140	592 389
Electricity, gas and water supply	24 091	15 335	-	-	-	-	- 55	-	-	21	30	39 421
Construction	31 446	3 637	-	-	46 257	-	- 351	-	-	29	88	81 107
Wholesale and retail trade	10 365	40 179	-	-	-	53	-	-	-	2 176	3 210	55 983
Transport and communication	62 092	21 943	-	-	881	-	-	-	-	3 402	6 226	94 544
Financial intermediation	152 647	78 822	467	-	8 242	-	12	351	145	7 137	12 514	260 337
Public administration	1 801	870	-	62 403	585	-	-	-	-	176	412	66 247
Education, health and social work	25 531	13 784	10 372	64 309	-	-	-	-	-	298	474	114 767
Other services	12 423	24 133	3 142	4 822	1 031	-	-	111	1 156	455	927	48 200
Total consumption[1]	596 593	401 970	13 981	131 534	101 027	- 29	329	69 402	52 827	15 242	26 169	1 409 045
Taxes less subsidies on production	13 936											
Compensation of employees	357 662											
Gross operating surplus	203 863											
Gross value added at basic prices[1]	575 461											
Output at basic prices[1]	1 172 054											
Supplementary information:												
Gross fixed capital formation	100 998	**										
Changes in inventories	329											
Total gross capital formation	101 327	**										

Notes for information:
Gross value added at basic prices plus taxes less subsidies on products gives GDP at market prices.
Gross operating surplus includes gross mixed income.
Changes in inventories includes materials and fuels, work-in-progress and finished goods.
Valuables include both 'transfer costs' and 'acquisitions less disposals'.
GFCF can be broken down by institutional sectors and assets, see Chapter 9.

FISIM represents Financial Intermediation Services Indirectly Measured.
NPISHs represents Non-Profit Institutions Serving Households.
GGFC represents General Government Final Consumption.
GFCF represents Gross Fixed Capital Formation.

Industrial analyses

2.1 Supply and Use Tables for the United Kingdom: 1994

Supply Table

£ million

1994	Domestic output of products at basic prices	Imports Goods EU	Imports Goods Non-EU	Imports Services EU	Imports Services Non-EU	Distributors' trading margins	Taxes less subsidies on products	Total[1] supply of products at purchasers' prices
PRODUCTS[2]								
Agriculture	22 640	2 343	2 273	125	108	2 324	- 1 874	27 940
Mining and quarrying	20 775	650	6 351	62	123	1 585	- 211	29 335
Manufacturing	331 234	78 518	53 742	3 927	4 149	117 539	53 104	642 213
Electricity, gas and water supply	39 002	391	-	36	21	-	2 611	42 062
Construction	83 096	-	-	32	83	-	3 875	87 087
Wholesale and retail trade	169 347	-	-	3 478	3 194	- 121 448	5 253	59 825
Transport and communication	94 833	-	-	4 064	5 279	-	422	104 598
Financial intermediation	266 224	430	302	4 221	6 655	-	5 731	283 563
Public administration	67 570	-	-	29	48	-	-	67 647
Education, health and social work	129 918	-	-	476	370	-	659	131 422
Other services	46 312	116	1 153	1 307	1 199	-	3 015	53 101
Total[1]	1 270 951	82 448	63 821	17 756	21 230	-	72 587	1 528 793

of which:
Market output	1 076 977
Output for own final use	42 432
Other non-market output	151 542

Use Table at Purchasers' prices

INTERMEDIATE CONSUMPTION BY INDUSTRY GROUP[2,3]

1994	Agriculture	Mining and quarrying	Manufacturing	Electricity, gas and water supply	Construction	Wholesale and retail trade	Transport and communication	Financial intermediation	Public administration	Education, health and social work	Other services	Not allocated to industries
PRODUCTS[2]												
Agriculture	3 578	1	13 273	-	4	1 303	42	10	22	176	49	-
Mining and quarrying	3	1 880	8 444	6 658	1 526	122	52	10	47	42	41	-
Manufacturing	5 966	2 493	153 820	3 331	17 469	21 277	12 300	10 936	11 901	14 357	5 050	-
Electricity, gas and water supply	266	269	6 758	13 238	211	1 251	771	1 071	755	1 286	362	-
Construction	192	976	894	528	19 831	708	419	6 279	3 649	742	492	-
Wholesale and retail trade	705	112	965	113	86	3 885	2 260	2 776	398	709	414	-
Transport and communication	307	774	10 184	229	991	17 964	17 619	15 343	2 338	2 428	1 712	-
Financial intermediation	1 471	2 099	24 411	1 291	9 978	21 477	11 051	51 912	6 333	7 193	8 572	23 119 *
Public administration	17	11	92	5	20	9	105	1 430	81	6	6	-
Education, health and social work	181	10	939	78	154	543	564	2 201	1 534	30 470	617	-
Other services	302	77	2 717	91	88	651	669	1 638	1 211	1 057	6 283	-
Total consumption[1]	12 989	8 702	222 500	25 562	50 359	69 190	45 851	93 606	28 269	58 466	23 598	23 119 *
Taxes *less* subsidies on production	- 169	158	1 934	1 359	322	4 890	986	1 977	754	837	646	-
Compensation of employees	3 140	3 500	89 151	6 095	13 651	54 645	32 935	58 223	34 346	59 752	14 207	-
Gross operating surplus	7 646	11 130	39 682	8 704	17 243	28 856	15 651	92 654	4 497	11 676	10 781	- 23 119 *
Gross value added at basic prices	10 617	14 788	130 767	16 158	31 216	88 391	49 572	152 854	39 597	72 265	25 634	- 23 119 *
Output at basic prices[1]	23 606	23 490	353 267	41 720	81 575	157 581	95 423	246 460	67 866	130 731	49 232	-
Supplementary information:												
Gross fixed capital formation	2 447	5 001	14 225	5 766	1 189	8 932	11 535	14 487	9 360	4 521	5 796	25 168 **
Changes in inventories	- 12	- 220	1 244	- 533	664	2 546	62	208	- 251	-	-	-
Total gross capital formation	2 435	4 781	15 469	5 233	1 853	11 478	11 597	14 695	9 109	4 521	5 796	25 168 **

1 Differences between totals and sums of components are due to rounding.
2 Some of the industry/product group headings have been truncated. See Table 2.2 for full titles.
3 Purchases of products by industry and by final consumption categories are valued at purchaser prices.

* This relates to FISIM.
** This includes investment in dwellings, transfer costs of land and existing buildings, and valuables.

Industrial analyses

2.1 Supply and Use Tables for the United Kingdom: 1994
continued

Gross value added at basic prices
£ billions

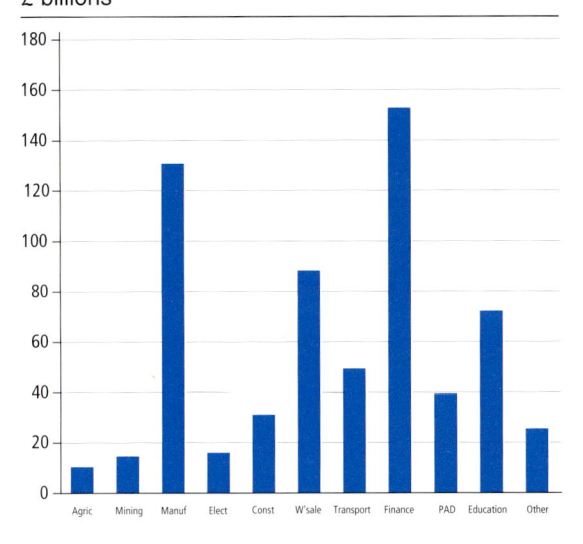

Components of final demand
Per cent

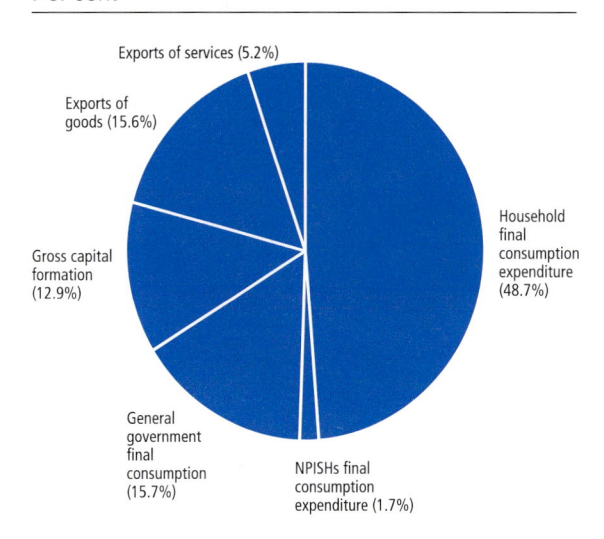

- Exports of services (5.2%)
- Exports of goods (15.6%)
- Gross capital formation (12.9%)
- General government final consumption (15.7%)
- NPISHs final consumption expenditure (1.7%)
- Household final consumption expenditure (48.7%)

£ million

1994	Total[1] intermediate consumption	FINAL CONSUMPTION EXPENDITURE Households	NPISHs	GGFC	GROSS CAPITAL FORMATION GFCF	Valuables	Changes in inventories	EXPORTS Goods EU	Non-EU	Services EU	Non-EU	TOTAL[1]
PRODUCTS≤												
Agriculture	18 458	7 554	-	-	481	-	- 169	1 163	356	40	57	27 940
Mining and quarrying	18 825	617	-	-	939	-	- 544	5 140	4 156	71	132	29 335
Manufacturing	258 901	206 028	-	-	47 301	50	3 891	70 023	52 361	1 514	2 143	642 213
Electricity, gas and water supply	26 238	15 803	-	-	-	-	- 29	-	-	21	29	42 062
Construction	34 711	3 251	-	-	48 447	-	540	-	-	40	98	87 087
Wholesale and retail trade	12 424	41 636	-	-	-	63	-	-	-	2 350	3 352	59 825
Transport and communication	69 888	23 630	-	-	775	-	-	-	-	3 608	6 697	104 598
Financial intermediation	168 906	82 640	436	-	8 618	-	19	407	200	8 190	14 147	283 563
Public administration	1 783	891	-	63 895	548	-	-	-	-	170	360	67 647
Education, health and social work	37 292	14 441	11 514	67 347	-	-	-	-	-	330	498	131 422
Other services	14 785	25 906	3 337	5 013	1 205	-	-	143	1 194	504	1 014	53 101
Total consumption[1]	662 211	422 397	15 287	136 255	108 314	113	3 708	76 876	58 267	16 838	28 527	1 528 793
Taxes *less* subsidies on production	13 694											
Compensation of employees	369 645											
Gross operating surplus	225 401											
Gross value added at basic prices	608 740											
Output at basic prices[1]	1 270 951											
Supplementary information:												
Gross fixed capital formation	108 427	**										
Changes in inventories	3 708											
Total gross capital formation	112 135	**										

Notes for information:
Gross value added at basic prices plus taxes *less* subsidies on products gives GDP at market prices.
Gross operating surplus includes gross mixed income.
Changes in inventories includes materials and fuels, work-in-progress and finished goods.
Valuables include both 'transfer costs' and 'acquisitions *less* disposals'.
GFCF can be broken down by institutional sectors and assets, see Chapter 9.

FISIM represents Financial Intermediation Services Indirectly Measured.
NPISHs represents Non-Profit Institutions Serving Households.
GGFC represents General Government Final Consumption.
GFCF represents Gross Fixed Capital Formation.

Industrial analyses

2.1 Supply and Use Tables for the United Kingdom: 1995

Supply Table

£ million

1995	Domestic output of products at basic prices	Imports Goods EU	Imports Goods Non-EU	Imports Services EU	Imports Services Non-EU	Distributors' trading margins	Taxes less subsidies on products	Total[1] supply of products at purchasers' prices
PRODUCTS[2]								
Agriculture	24 273	2 551	2 540	131	111	2 721	- 1 990	30 337
Mining and quarrying	22 720	642	6 527	62	126	1 629	221	31 927
Manufacturing	358 159	89 906	61 256	4 190	4 294	126 463	55 976	700 244
Electricity, gas and water supply	38 511	410	-	33	20	-	2 818	41 791
Construction	87 602	-	-	37	91	-	4 125	91 856
Wholesale and retail trade	181 822	-	-	3 833	3 394	- 130 813	5 315	63 552
Transport and communication	103 785	-	-	4 268	5 500	-	569	114 122
Financial intermediation	284 316	499	270	4 543	7 135	-	6 630	303 392
Public administration	70 080	-	-	32	52	-	-	70 164
Education, health and social work	141 882	-	-	522	394	-	659	143 457
Other services	50 385	51	948	1 388	1 295	-	4 944	59 011
Total[1]	1 363 534	94 059	71 541	19 039	22 412	-	79 268	1 649 853
of which:								
Market output	1 160 306							
Output for own final use	45 716							
Other non-market output	157 512							

Use Table at Purchasers' prices

INTERMEDIATE CONSUMPTION BY INDUSTRY GROUP[2,3]

1995	Agriculture	Mining and quarrying	Manufacturing	Electricity, gas and water supply	Construction	Wholesale and retail trade	Transport and communication	Financial intermediation	Public administration	Education, health and social work	Other services	Not allocated to industries
PRODUCTS[2]												
Agriculture	3 719	0	14 611	-	5	1 370	47	11	23	203	55	-
Mining and quarrying	3	2 072	8 866	7 418	1 655	135	60	12	42	33	44	-
Manufacturing	6 160	2 661	170 491	2 991	17 668	23 779	13 307	12 449	12 540	15 337	5 572	-
Electricity, gas and water supply	258	320	6 734	13 183	189	1 073	603	912	781	1 220	321	-
Construction	212	1 127	997	221	21 859	854	522	7 094	4 063	824	478	-
Wholesale and retail trade	817	133	1 082	129	96	4 276	2 368	3 226	492	814	505	-
Transport and communication	323	721	10 350	271	976	19 127	21 818	16 431	2 454	2 718	1 942	-
Financial intermediation	1 528	2 323	25 683	1 688	10 424	23 558	12 441	58 065	6 969	7 707	9 412	23 215 *
Public administration	18	11	96	7	20	11	114	1 473	85	7	7	-
Education, health and social work	199	9	1 029	102	154	606	649	2 414	1 659	36 507	725	-
Other services	299	83	2 728	92	90	709	751	1 791	1 492	1 141	7 282	-
Total consumption[1]	13 536	9 461	242 666	26 102	53 134	75 498	52 680	103 878	30 600	66 512	26 344	23 215 *
Taxes *less* subsidies on production	- 166	140	1 920	1 335	330	5 064	1 039	2 231	818	803	642	-
Compensation of employees	3 114	3 371	93 819	5 434	15 521	57 677	33 811	61 218	34 030	63 506	15 217	-
Gross operating surplus	8 818	12 858	44 050	8 817	17 154	30 124	16 490	95 692	4 908	11 950	11 388	- 23 215 *
Gross value added at basic prices[1]	11 766	16 369	139 789	15 586	33 005	92 865	51 340	159 141	39 756	76 259	27 247	- 23 215 *
Output at basic prices[1]	25 302	25 830	382 455	41 688	86 139	168 363	104 020	263 019	70 356	142 771	53 591	-
Supplementary information:												
Gross fixed capital formation	2 394	5 805	17 725	5 227	1 254	11 557	11 818	15 430	9 338	4 757	6 519	25 503 **
Changes in inventories	26	- 157	2 685	- 208	336	1 814	18	152	- 154	-	-	-
Total gross capital formation	2 420	5 648	20 410	5 019	1 590	13 371	11 836	15 582	9 184	4 757	6 519	25 503 **

1 Differences between totals and sums of components are due to rounding.
2 Some of the industry/product group headings have been truncated. See Table 2.2 for full titles.
3 Purchases of products by industry and by final consumption categories are valued at purchaser prices.

* This relates to FISIM.
** This includes investment in dwellings, transfer costs of land and existing buildings, and valuables.

# Industrial analyses

2.1 Supply and Use Tables for the United Kingdom: 1995
continued

Gross value added at basic prices
£ billions

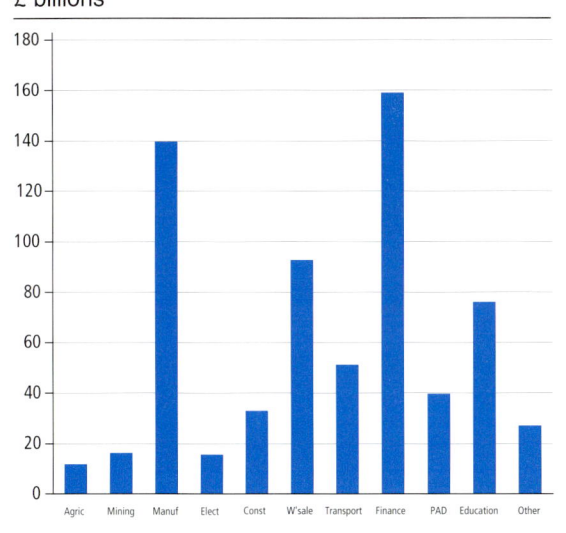

(Bar chart showing values for: Agric, Mining, Manuf, Elect, Const, W'sale, Transport, Finance, PAD, Education, Other)

Components of final demand
Per cent

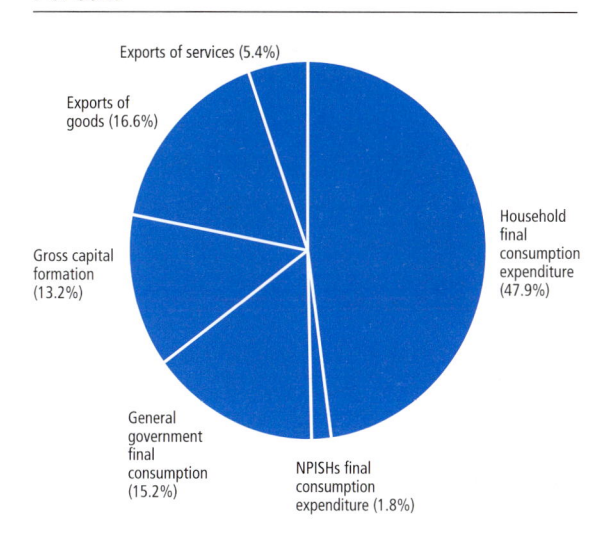

(Pie chart):
- Household final consumption expenditure (47.9%)
- NPISHs final consumption expenditure (1.8%)
- General government final consumption (15.2%)
- Gross capital formation (13.2%)
- Exports of goods (16.6%)
- Exports of services (5.4%)

£ million

1995	Total[1] intermediate consumption	FINAL CONSUMPTION EXPENDITURE Households	NPISHs	GGFC	GROSS CAPITAL FORMATION GFCF	Valuables	Changes in inventories	EXPORTS Goods EU	Non-EU	Services EU	Non-EU	TOTAL[1]
PRODUCTS[2]												
Agriculture	20 043	8 059	-	-	464	-	- 84	1 340	400	48	67	30 337
Mining and quarrying	20 340	636	-	-	1 086	-	- 179	5 840	4 056	55	93	31 927
Manufacturing	282 954	214 566	-	-	54 056	- 196	4 650	81 761	58 158	1 827	2 468	700 244
Electricity, gas and water supply	25 593	16 183	-	-	-	-	- 47	2	-	26	34	41 792
Construction	38 250	3 283	-	-	49 838	-	326	-	-	50	109	91 856
Wholesale and retail trade	13 938	42 611	-	-	-	75	-	-	-	2 934	3 993	63 552
Transport and communication	77 133	24 999	-	-	879	-	-	-	-	4 102	7 009	114 122
Financial intermediation	183 014	86 321	461	-	9 133	-	- 154	501	204	8 934	14 978	303 392
Public administration	1 850	949	-	66 091	652	-	-	-	-	205	417	70 164
Education, health and social work	44 053	15 540	12 429	70 552	-	-	-	-	-	362	521	143 457
Other services	16 456	30 221	3 591	4 388	1 340	-	-	92	1 223	584	1 116	59 011
Total consumption[1]	723 626	443 367	16 481	141 031	117 448	- 121	4 512	89 536	64 041	19 127	30 805	1 649 853
Taxes *less* subsidies on production	14 156											
Compensation of employees	386 718											
Gross operating surplus	239 034											
Gross value added at basic prices[1]	639 908											
Output at basic prices[1]	1 363 534											
Supplementary information:												
Gross fixed capital formation	117 327 **											
Changes in inventories	4 512											
Total gross capital formation	121 839 **											

Notes for information:
Gross value added at basic prices plus taxes *less* subsidies on products gives GDP at market prices.
Gross operating surplus includes gross mixed income.
Changes in inventories includes materials and fuels, work-in-progress and finished goods.
Valuables include both 'transfer costs' and 'acquisitions *less* disposals'.
GFCF can be broken down by institutional sectors and assets, see Chapter 9.

FISIM represents Financial Intermediation Services Indirectly Measured.
NPISHs represents Non-Profit Institutions Serving Households.
GGFC represents General Government Final Consumption.
GFCF represents Gross Fixed Capital Formation.

Industrial analyses

2.1 Supply and Use Tables for the United Kingdom: 1996

Supply Table

£ million

1996	Domestic output of products at basic prices	Imports Goods EU	Imports Goods Non-EU	Imports Services EU	Imports Services Non-EU	Distributors' trading margins	Taxes less subsidies on products	Total[1] supply of products at purchasers' prices
PRODUCTS[2]								
Agriculture	24 452	2 749	2 907	127	111	2 951	- 3 030	30 267
Mining and quarrying	25 611	937	7 424	10	179	1 770	231	36 162
Manufacturing	373 641	96 011	68 998	4 216	4 436	137 939	58 921	744 161
Electricity, gas and water supply	41 065	380	-	29	22	-	2 524	44 019
Construction	91 794	-	-	43	111	-	4 676	96 624
Wholesale and retail trade	197 996	-	-	4 106	3 760	- 142 660	5 745	68 948
Transport and communication	112 635	-	-	5 069	6 469	-	921	125 093
Financial intermediation	308 168	360	204	5 479	7 975	-	7 233	329 419
Public administration	70 975	-	-	27	43	-	-	71 045
Education, health and social work	153 635	-	-	604	427	-	771	155 437
Other services	55 445	191	757	1 583	1 472	-	4 602	64 050
Total[1]	1 455 417	100 628	80 290	21 292	25 006	-	82 594	1 765 227

of which:
Market output	1 242 591
Output for own final use	47 662
Other non-market output	165 164

Use Table at Purchasers' prices

INTERMEDIATE CONSUMPTION BY INDUSTRY GROUP[2,3]

1996	Agriculture	Mining and quarrying	Manufac- turing	Electricity, gas and water supply	Construc- tion	Wholesale and retail trade	Transport and communi- cation	Financial intermed- iation	Public adminis- tration	Education, health and social work	Other services	Not allocated to industries
PRODUCTS[2]												
Agriculture	3 463	0	13 353	-	5	1 462	48	13	19	243	57	-
Mining and quarrying	3	2 254	10 564	7 915	1 861	158	71	15	36	26	49	-
Manufacturing	6 351	2 715	176 131	2 667	18 366	26 105	15 245	13 616	12 910	16 459	6 006	-
Electricity, gas and water supply	303	348	7 499	12 830	221	1 377	761	1 152	756	1 343	368	-
Construction	214	997	842	685	23 245	949	1 124	7 632	4 090	883	621	-
Wholesale and retail trade	871	129	1 111	114	111	4 780	2 677	3 787	571	982	587	-
Transport and communication	356	744	10 970	295	1 043	21 766	24 012	18 525	2 491	3 240	2 219	-
Financial intermediation	1 752	2 071	27 745	1 766	10 918	26 335	14 206	65 539	7 153	8 724	10 239	22 580 *
Public administration	13	10	99	8	17	11	115	1 125	96	9	7	-
Education, health and social work	201	6	1 126	135	152	651	730	2 684	1 862	40 484	758	-
Other services	288	73	2 929	109	96	813	909	2 126	1 569	1 304	8 445	-
Total consumption[1]	13 815	9 347	252 369	26 524	56 035	84 407	59 898	116 214	31 553	73 697	29 358	22 580 *
Taxes *less* subsidies on production	- 112	160	2 241	1 118	344	5 507	1 113	2 131	845	879	722	-
Compensation of employees	3 089	2 983	96 892	5 348	16 325	61 011	34 707	66 825	33 590	68 037	16 662	-
Gross operating surplus	8 758	16 625	46 946	9 814	17 918	33 288	17 653	100 734	5 274	12 191	12 582	- 22 580 *
Gross value added at basic prices[1]	11 735	19 768	146 079	16 280	34 587	99 806	53 473	169 690	39 709	81 107	29 966	- 22 580 *
Output at basic prices[1]	25 550	29 115	398 448	42 804	90 622	184 213	113 371	285 904	71 262	154 804	59 324	-
Supplementary information:												
Gross fixed capital formation	2 622	5 976	18 464	4 499	1 156	11 787	13 934	19 562	8 217	5 359	6 992	27 036 **
Changes in inventories	36	- 33	- 152	15	- 254	1 407	- 108	694	166	-	-	-
Total gross capital formation	2 658	5 943	18 312	4 514	902	13 194	13 826	20 256	8 383	5 359	6 992	27 036 **

1 Differences between totals and sums of components are due to rounding.
2 Some of the industry/product group headings have been truncated. See Table 2.2 for full titles.
3 Purchases of products by industry and by final consumption categories are valued at purchaser prices.

* This relates to FISIM.
** This includes investment in dwellings, transfer costs of land and existing buildings, and valuables.

Industrial analyses

2.1 Supply and Use Tables for the United Kingdom: 1996
continued

Gross value added at basic prices
£ billions

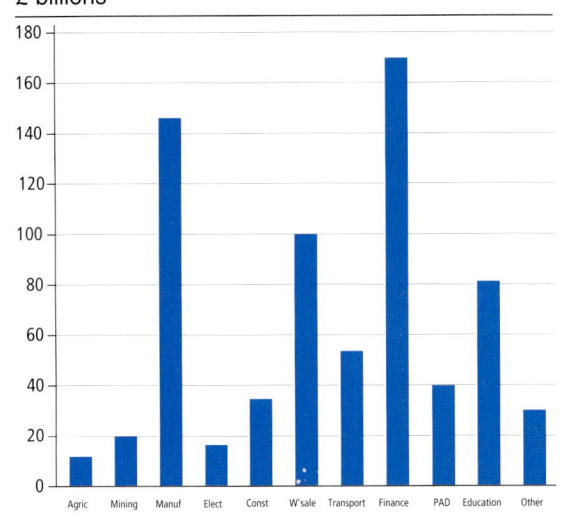

Components of final demand
Per cent

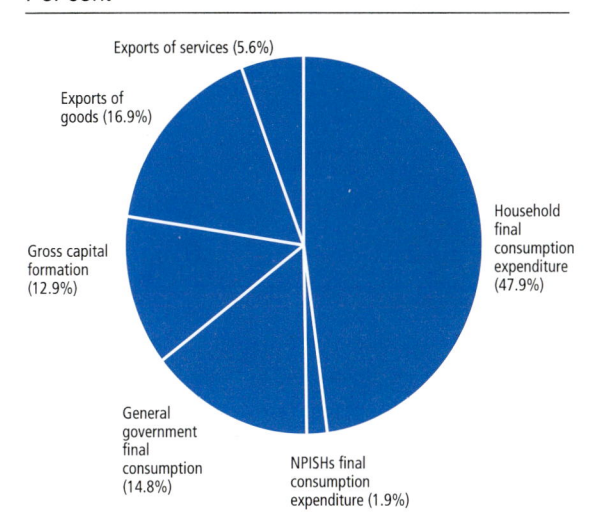

- Exports of services (5.6%)
- Exports of goods (16.9%)
- Gross capital formation (12.9%)
- General government final consumption (14.8%)
- NPISHs final consumption expenditure (1.9%)
- Household final consumption expenditure (47.9%)

£ million

	Total[1] intermediate consumption	FINAL CONSUMPTION EXPENDITURE			GROSS CAPITAL FORMATION			EXPORTS				TOTAL[1]
1996		Households	NPISHs	GGFC	GFCF	Valuables	Changes in inventories	Goods		Services		
								EU	Non-EU	EU	Non-EU	
PRODUCTS[2]												
Agriculture	18 664	8 660	-	-	561	-	450	1 320	489	52	72	30 267
Mining and quarrying	22 950	663	-	-	1 096	-	23	7 185	4 105	50	89	36 162
Manufacturing	296 572	231 040	-	-	58 773	- 279	1 485	86 607	65 510	1 895	2 559	744 161
Electricity, gas and water supply	26 959	17 021	-	-	-	-	- 24	2	-	26	35	44 019
Construction	41 282	3 266	-	-	52 175	-	- 303	-	-	60	144	96 624
Wholesale and retail trade	15 721	45 601	-	-	-	121	-	-	-	3 167	4 338	68 948
Transport and communication	85 661	26 480	-	-	924	-	-	-	-	4 497	7 532	125 093
Financial intermediation	199 027	91 272	502	-	10 036	-	140	364	147	10 294	17 638	329 419
Public administration	1 510	1 015	-	67 120	739	-	-	-	-	126	535	71 045
Education, health and social work	48 789	16 370	14 189	75 087	-	-	-	-	-	405	597	155 437
Other services	18 662	32 413	3 694	4 572	1 459	-	-	280	1 187	581	1 202	64 050
Total consumption[1]	775 797	473 800	18 385	146 779	125 762	- 158	1 771	95 758	71 438	21 154	34 741	1 765 227
Taxes *less* subsidies on production	14 948											
Compensation of employees	405 469											
Gross operating surplus	259 203											
Gross value added at basic prices[1]	679 620											
Output at basic prices[1]	1 455 417											
Supplementary information:												
Gross fixed capital formation	125 604	**										
Changes in inventories	1 771											
Total gross capital formation	127 375	**										

Notes for information:
Gross value added at basic prices plus taxes *less* subsidies on products gives GDP at market prices.
Gross operating surplus includes gross mixed income.
Changes in inventories includes materials and fuels, work-in-progress and finished goods.
Valuables include both 'transfer costs' and 'acquisitions *less* disposals'.
GFCF can be broken down by institutional sectors and assets, see Chapter 9.

FISIM represents Financial Intermediation Services Indirectly Measured.
NPISHs represents Non-Profit Institutions Serving Households.
GGFC represents General Government Final Consumption.
GFCF represents Gross Fixed Capital Formation.

Industrial analyses

2.1 Supply and Use Tables for the United Kingdom: 1997

Supply Table

£ million

1997	Domestic output of products at basic prices	Imports Goods EU	Imports Goods Non-EU	Imports Services EU	Imports Services Non-EU	Distributors' trading margins	Taxes less subsidies on products	Total[1] supply of products at purchasers' prices
PRODUCTS[2]								
Agriculture	22 306	2 781	2 656	131	111	3 124	- 2 641	28 467
Mining and quarrying	23 659	631	7 377	6	121	1 802	183	33 779
Manufacturing	384 121	96 059	72 581	4 321	4 876	150 828	62 882	775 668
Electricity, gas and water supply	41 984	395	-	28	19	-	1 762	44 189
Construction	97 983	-	-	116	86	-	5 615	103 799
Wholesale and retail trade	215 982	-	-	4 295	3 826	- 155 754	6 414	74 762
Transport and communication	122 062	-	-	5 169	6 869	-	1 296	135 396
Financial intermediation	339 435	373	185	5 178	8 046	-	8 568	361 785
Public administration	71 104	-	-	26	40	-	-	71 170
Education, health and social work	160 691	-	-	577	455	-	873	162 597
Other services	60 569	277	950	1 425	1 450	-	5 424	70 095
Total[1]	1 539 896	100 516	83 749	21 271	25 900	-	90 375	1 861 707
of which:								
Market output	1 320 012							
Output for own final use	51 135							
Other non-market output	168 749							

Use Table at Purchasers' prices

INTERMEDIATE CONSUMPTION BY INDUSTRY GROUP[2,3]

1997	Agriculture	Mining and quarrying	Manufacturing	Electricity, gas and water supply	Construction	Wholesale and retail trade	Transport and communication	Financial intermediation	Public administration	Education, health and social work	Other services	Not allocated to industries
PRODUCTS[2]												
Agriculture	2 898	0	12 049	-	6	1 276	42	10	17	209	42	-
Mining and quarrying	3	1 928	9 888	7 265	2 122	173	76	15	27	22	51	-
Manufacturing	6 278	2 432	181 606	3 103	19 052	26 484	15 129	13 613	13 669	16 732	5 632	-
Electricity, gas and water supply	277	347	7 513	13 611	262	1 446	763	1 167	714	1 285	330	-
Construction	213	1 013	1 043	785	23 493	1 030	1 175	8 082	3 673	880	473	-
Wholesale and retail trade	852	135	1 294	126	140	5 888	3 138	4 600	647	1 138	634	-
Transport and communication	357	682	11 259	413	1 207	24 929	26 257	20 599	2 507	3 467	2 128	-
Financial intermediation	1 792	2 079	27 714	2 242	13 261	31 464	16 655	76 308	6 852	9 237	10 182	22 396 *
Public administration	13	11	103	1	19	14	132	901	109	10	7	-
Education, health and social work	217	0	1 087	143	180	793	832	3 050	1 952	41 980	775	-
Other services	297	84	2 995	125	135	1 173	1 245	2 916	1 570	1 471	10 861	-
Total consumption[1]	13 198	8 712	256 551	27 814	59 877	94 669	65 443	131 261	31 737	76 431	31 115	22 396 *
Taxes *less* subsidies on production	- 53	157	2 594	1 145	421	5 612	1 178	2 232	815	866	802	-
Compensation of employees	3 126	2 878	100 690	5 204	18 663	65 117	37 325	75 440	33 198	72 091	19 228	-
Gross operating surplus	7 072	15 080	49 021	9 792	17 795	38 426	18 890	106 211	5 646	12 714	13 712	- 22 396 *
Gross value added at basic prices[1]	10 145	18 115	152 305	16 141	36 879	109 155	57 393	183 883	39 659	85 671	33 742	- 22 396 *
Output at basic prices[1]	23 343	26 827	408 856	43 955	96 756	203 824	122 836	315 144	71 396	162 102	64 857	-
Supplementary information:												
Gross fixed capital formation	2 459	5 813	20 153	5 288	1 922	14 031	17 283	16 671	6 909	5 238	8 753	29 850 **
Changes in inventories	- 23	62	- 792	70	750	3 346	- 4	839	140	-	-	-
Total gross capital formation	2 436	5 875	19 361	5 358	2 672	17 377	17 279	17 510	7 049	5 238	8 753	29 850 **

1 Differences between totals and sums of components are due to rounding.
2 Some of the industry/product group headings have been truncated. See Table 2.2 for full titles.
3 Purchases of products by industry and by final consumption categories are valued at purchaser prices.

* This relates to FISIM.
** This includes investment in dwellings, transfer costs of land and existing buildings, and valuables.

Industrial analyses

2.1 Supply and Use Tables for the United Kingdom: 1997
continued

Gross value added at basic prices
£ billions

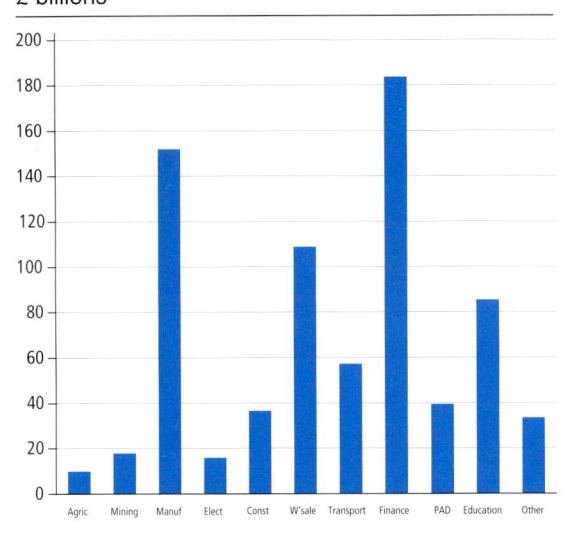

Components of final demand
Per cent

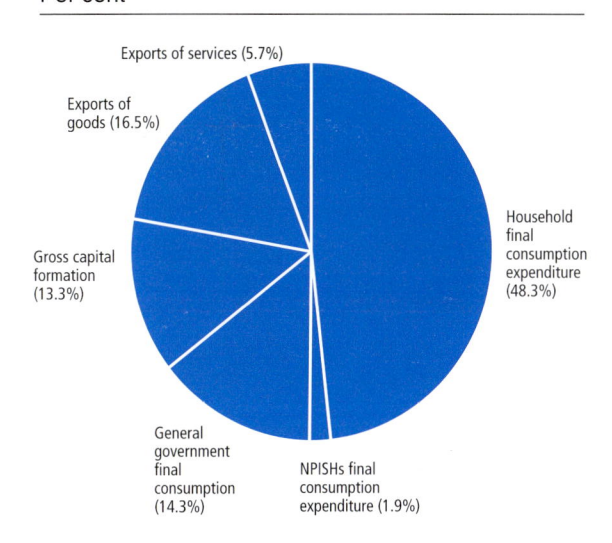

- Exports of services (5.7%)
- Exports of goods (16.5%)
- Gross capital formation (13.3%)
- General government final consumption (14.3%)
- NPISHs final consumption expenditure (1.9%)
- Household final consumption expenditure (48.3%)

£ million

1997	Total[1] intermediate consumption	FINAL CONSUMPTION EXPENDITURE			GROSS CAPITAL FORMATION			EXPORTS				TOTAL[1]
								Goods		Services		
		Households	NPISHs	GGFC	GFCF	Valuables	Changes in inventories	EU	Non-EU	EU	Non-EU	
PRODUCTS[2]												
Agriculture	16 548	9 014	-	-	636	-	538	1 129	485	46	71	28 467
Mining and quarrying	21 570	606	-	-	1 195	-	210	7 238	2 835	44	81	33 779
Manufacturing	303 732	245 943	-	-	61 491	- 233	2 246	87 063	71 015	1 751	2 660	775 668
Electricity, gas and water supply	27 715	16 425	-	-	-	-	- 10	-	-	24	35	44 189
Construction	41 860	3 579	-	-	57 249	-	813	-	-	98	201	103 799
Wholesale and retail trade	18 591	48 180	-	-	-	207	-	-	-	3 064	4 720	74 762
Transport and communication	93 804	28 734	-	-	863	-	-	-	-	4 272	7 723	135 396
Financial intermediation	220 182	98 199	512	-	10 618	-	591	305	143	11 481	19 755	361 785
Public administration	1 319	1 031	-	67 366	797	-	-	-	-	171	486	71 170
Education, health and social work	51 011	17 747	15 264	77 529	-	-	-	-	-	399	647	162 597
Other services	22 872	33 918	3 826	4 252	1 547	-	-	313	1 397	644	1 326	70 095
Total consumption[1]	819 204	503 374	19 602	149 147	134 396	- 26	4 388	96 048	75 875	21 992	37 707	1 861 707
Taxes *less* subsidies on production	15 769											
Compensation of employees	432 960											
Gross operating surplus	271 963											
Gross value added at basic prices[1]	720 692											
Output at basic	1 539 896											
Supplementary information:												
Gross fixed capital formation	134 370 **											
Changes in inventories	4 388											
Total gross capital formation	138 758 **											

Notes for information:
Gross value added at basic prices plus taxes *less* subsidies on products gives GDP at market prices.
Gross operating surplus includes gross mixed income.
Changes in inventories includes materials and fuels, work-in-progress and finished goods.
Valuables include both 'transfer costs' and 'acquisitions *less* disposals'.
GFCF can be broken down by institutional sectors and assets, see Chapter 9.

FISIM represents Financial Intermediation Services Indirectly Measured.
NPISHs represents Non-Profit Institutions Serving Households.
GGFC represents General Government Final Consumption.
GFCF represents Gross Fixed Capital Formation.

Industrial analyses

2.1 Supply and Use Tables for the United Kingdom: 1998

Supply Table

£ million

1998	Domestic output of products at basic prices	Imports Goods EU	Imports Goods Non-EU	Imports Services EU	Imports Services Non-EU	Distributors' trading margins	Taxes less subsidies on products	Total[1] supply of products at purchasers' prices
PRODUCTS[2]								
Agriculture	20 548	2 764	2 598	141	123	3 266	- 2 295	27 145
Mining and quarrying	21 266	401	5 633	68	134	1 824	142	29 467
Manufacturing	376 953	97 936	73 794	4 841	5 418	167 397	66 758	793 097
Electricity, gas and water supply	42 863	355	-	22	16	-	1 108	44 364
Construction	104 113	-	-	62	89	-	6 084	110 348
Wholesale and retail trade	236 705	-	-	4 941	4 451	- 172 488	6 648	80 257
Transport and communication	133 406	-	-	5 688	7 180	-	2 579	148 853
Financial intermediation	387 082	429	176	6 180	8 818	-	10 516	413 202
Public administration	72 141	-	-	27	36	-	-	72 204
Education, health and social work	170 934	-	-	590	485	-	1 017	173 026
Other services	65 349	376	1 407	1 371	1 398	-	5 931	75 832
Total[1]	1 631 361	102 261	83 608	23 930	28 149	-	98 487	1 967 796
of which:								
Market output	1 399 189							
Output for own final use	56 174							
Other non-market output	175 998							

Use Table at Purchasers' prices

INTERMEDIATE CONSUMPTION BY INDUSTRY GROUP[2,3]

1998	Agriculture	Mining and quarrying	Manufacturing	Electricity, gas and water supply	Construction	Wholesale and retail trade	Transport and communication	Financial intermediation	Public administration	Education, health and social work	Other services	Not allocated to industries
PRODUCTS[2]												
Agriculture	2 280	0	11 394	-	7	1 484	39	13	15	240	43	-
Mining and quarrying	3	2 669	7 677	6 967	2 829	227	114	20	22	18	61	-
Manufacturing	5 659	1 945	175 169	3 121	19 617	27 073	16 184	14 429	14 145	17 343	5 465	-
Electricity, gas and water supply	289	299	7 234	14 494	283	1 564	802	1 324	656	1 280	337	-
Construction	187	635	1 272	958	24 571	1 142	1 312	8 899	3 528	906	443	-
Wholesale and retail trade	747	63	1 212	114	150	6 128	3 224	5 115	697	1 255	636	-
Transport and communication	359	756	12 186	416	1 365	27 513	28 964	23 895	2 504	3 754	2 209	-
Financial intermediation	1 869	1 681	30 819	2 484	15 273	37 360	19 155	92 013	7 359	10 321	10 758	27 998 *
Public administration	12	10	115	1	26	18	165	737	99	12	8	-
Education, health and social work	200	0	1 237	143	185	814	863	3 285	1 968	45 158	752	-
Other services	319	64	3 176	131	147	1 266	1 369	3 367	1 644	1 657	12 053	-
Total consumption[1]	11 925	8 122	251 492	28 830	64 453	104 589	72 192	153 097	32 637	81 944	32 764	27 998 *
Taxes *less* subsidies on production	- 88	144	2 729	1 189	501	5 557	1 348	2 342	847	870	857	-
Compensation of employees	3 208	2 973	105 550	5 136	19 755	70 242	40 089	86 005	33 061	76 586	21 653	-
Gross operating surplus	6 508	12 562	44 993	9 635	18 761	41 884	20 697	119 708	5 843	13 468	14 703	- 27 998 *
Gross value added at basic prices[1]	9 628	15 679	153 272	15 960	39 017	117 683	62 134	208 055	39 751	90 924	37 213	- 27 998 *
Output at basic prices[1]	21 553	23 801	404 764	44 790	103 470	222 272	134 326	361 152	72 388	172 868	69 977	-
Supplementary information:												
Gross fixed capital formation	1 969	6 479	20 642	5 578	1 814	17 224	19 743	24 197	7 199	6 014	9 511	31 599 **
Changes in inventories	- 120	8	549	-	272	2 118	- 16	1 539	107	-	3	-
Total gross capital formation	1 849	6 487	21 191	5 578	2 086	19 342	19 727	25 736	7 306	6 014	9 514	31 599 **

1 Differences between totals and sums of components are due to rounding.
2 Some of the industry/product group headings have been truncated. See Table 2.2 for full titles.
3 Purchases of products by industry and by final consumption categories are valued at purchaser prices.

* This relates to FISIM.
** This includes investment in dwellings, transfer costs of land and existing buildings, and valuables.

Industrial analyses

2.1 Supply and Use Tables for the United Kingdom: 1998
continued

Gross value added at basic prices
£ billions

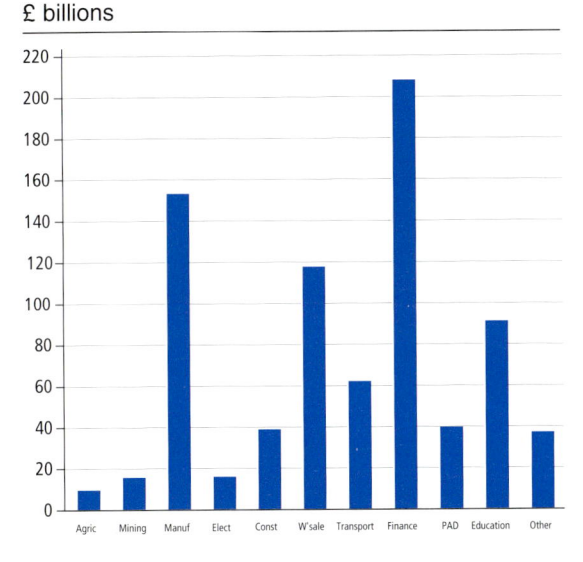

Components of final demand
Per cent

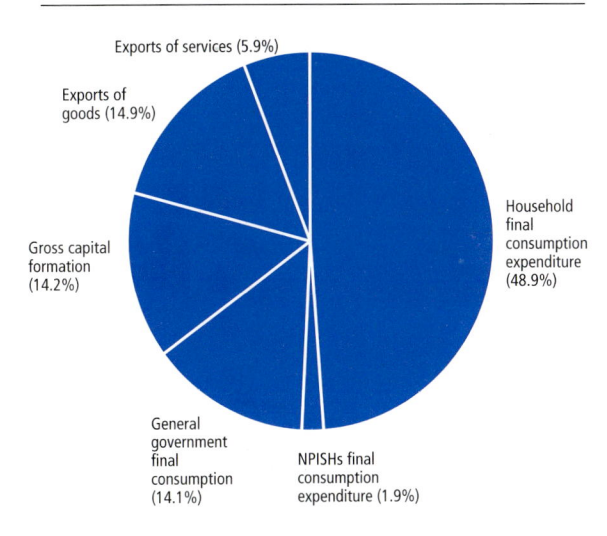

- Exports of services (5.9%)
- Exports of goods (14.9%)
- Gross capital formation (14.2%)
- General government final consumption (14.1%)
- NPISHs final consumption expenditure (1.9%)
- Household final consumption expenditure (48.9%)

£ million

	Total¹ intermediate consumption	FINAL CONSUMPTION EXPENDITURE			GROSS CAPITAL FORMATION			EXPORTS				TOTAL¹
								Goods		Services		
1998		Households	NPISHs	GGFC	GFCF	Valuables	Changes in inventories	EU	Non-EU	EU	Non-EU	
PRODUCTS²												
Agriculture	15 515	9 396	-	-	578	-	23	1 134	361	53	85	27 145
Mining and quarrying	20 607	548	-	-	762	-	56	5 226	2 100	60	107	29 467
Manufacturing	300 151	259 285	-	-	72 322	206	3 444	88 681	64 400	1 789	2 819	793 097
Electricity, gas and water supply	28 563	15 737	-	-	-	-	-	3	-	24	37	44 364
Construction	43 852	3 735	-	-	62 127	-	302	-	-	144	188	110 348
Wholesale and retail trade	19 342	52 514	-	-	-	224	-	-	-	3 156	5 021	80 257
Transport and communication	103 921	31 417	-	-	974	-	-	-	-	4 619	7 921	148 853
Financial intermediation	257 090	107 321	532	-	12 346	-	632	294	107	13 346	21 534	413 201
Public administration	1 203	1 059	-	68 497	837	-	-	-	-	158	450	72 204
Education, health and social work	54 606	18 915	16 538	81 918	-	-	-	-	-	401	649	173 026
Other services	25 192	36 597	4 047	4 466	1 593	-	3	352	1 398	832	1 352	75 832
Total consumption¹	870 043	536 525	21 117	154 881	151 539	430	4 460	95 690	68 366	24 583	40 162	1 967 796
Taxes less subsidies on production	16 296											
Compensation of employees	464 258											
Gross operating surplus	280 764											
Gross value added at basic prices¹	761 318											
Output at basic prices¹	1 631 361											
Supplementary information:												
Gross fixed capital formation	151 969 **											
Changes in inventories	4 460											
Total gross capital formation	156 429 **											

Notes for information:
Gross value added at basic prices plus taxes *less* subsidies on products gives GDP at market prices.
Gross operating surplus includes gross mixed income.
Changes in inventories includes materials and fuels, work-in-progress and finished goods.
Valuables include both 'transfer costs' and 'acquisitions less disposals'.
GFCF can be broken down by institutional sectors and assets, see Chapter 9.
No subsidies on production are recorded on an ESA95 basis in the UK.

FISIM represents Financial Intermediation Services Indirectly Measured.
NPISHs represents Non-Profit Institutions Serving Households.
GGFC represents General Government Final Consumption.
GFCF represents Gross Fixed Capital Formation.

Industrial analyses

2.1 Supply and Use Tables for the United Kingdom:

Supply Table

£ million

1999	Domestic output of products at basic prices	Imports Goods EU	Imports Goods Non-EU	Imports Services EU	Imports Services Non-EU	Distributors' trading margins	Taxes less subsidies on products	Total[1] supply of products at purchasers' prices
PRODUCTS[2]								
Agriculture	20 092	2 538	2 531	168	137	3 569	- 2 172	26 863
Mining and quarrying	22 918	487	6 506	95	137	1 803	152	32 098
Manufacturing	371 172	100 891	78 107	5 639	5 655	181 427	69 676	812 567
Electricity, gas and water supply	44 681	372	-	41	20	-	996	46 110
Construction	110 376	-	-	69	70	-	8 176	118 691
Wholesale and retail trade	254 577	-	-	5 814	4 711	- 186 800	6 999	85 302
Transport and communication	141 739	-	-	6 947	7 153	-	2 738	158 577
Financial intermediation	424 376	504	157	8 225	9 520	-	12 563	455 344
Public administration	74 027	-	-	25	31	-	-	74 083
Education, health and social work	187 869	-	-	737	504	-	1 093	190 203
Other services	69 901	321	1 308	1 675	1 489	-	6 023	80 718
Total[1]	1 721 728	105 113	88 609	29 437	29 425	-	106 244	2 080 556

of which:
Market output	1 473 080
Output for own final use	59 683
Other non-market output	188 965

Use Table at Purchasers' prices

INTERMEDIATE CONSUMPTION BY INDUSTRY GROUP[2,3]

1999	Agriculture	Mining and quarrying	Manufacturing	Electricity, gas and water supply	Construction	Wholesale and retail trade	Transport and communication	Financial intermediation	Public administration	Education, health and social work	Other services	Not allocated to industries
PRODUCTS[2]												
Agriculture	2 355	0	10 653	-	8	1 554	34	15	13	276	46	-
Mining and quarrying	3	2 244	8 761	6 594	3 086	209	118	22	16	15	60	-
Manufacturing	5 269	2 530	171 331	3 535	20 587	29 558	18 557	17 006	14 706	19 312	6 034	-
Electricity, gas and water supply	279	327	7 169	16 550	284	1 603	790	1 441	644	1 394	340	-
Construction	187	882	1 300	943	26 075	1 183	1 318	9 346	3 656	1 045	436	-
Wholesale and retail trade	755	71	1 225	127	151	6 444	3 267	5 524	773	1 457	670	-
Transport and communication	357	823	12 756	444	1 447	29 181	29 757	26 833	2 540	4 299	2 293	-
Financial intermediation	1 907	2 039	31 796	2 618	16 495	40 810	20 499	106 461	7 977	12 539	11 907	30 819 *
Public administration	12	11	111	9	24	18	153	854	120	14	8	-
Education, health and social work	192	0	1 292	151	172	772	816	3 515	2 182	50 279	722	-
Other services	327	34	3 236	132	149	1 272	1 339	3 599	1 897	1 933	12 598	-
Total consumption[1]	11 642	8 962	249 630	31 103	68 477	112 604	76 648	174 617	34 524	92 562	35 115	30 819 *
Taxes less subsidies on production	- 204	143	2 429	1 264	580	6 108	1 475	2 434	863	882	919	-
Compensation of employees	3 268	2 904	109 105	5 026	20 426	76 501	42 206	94 860	32 931	83 219	23 740	-
Gross operating surplus	6 396	14 043	41 119	9 719	20 136	43 032	22 229	123 331	5 992	13 676	15 092	- 30 819 *
Gross value added at basic prices[1]	9 460	17 090	152 653	16 009	41 142	125 641	65 910	220 625	39 786	97 777	39 751	- 30 819 *
Output at basic prices[1]	21 102	26 052	402 283	47 112	109 619	238 245	142 558	395 242	74 310	190 339	74 866	-
Supplementary information:												
Gross fixed capital formation	1 615	4 750	18 631	5 944	2 048	15 794	21 323	27 120	6 827	6 404	11 059	34 123 **
Changes in inventories	45	- 226	- 62	- 158	748	3 165	185	1 367	- 268	40	139	-
Total gross capital formation	1 660	4 524	18 569	5 786	2 796	18 959	21 508	28 487	6 559	6 444	11 198	34 123 **

1 Differences between totals and sums of components are due to rounding.
2 Some of the industry/product group headings have been truncated. See Table 2.2 for full titles.
3 Purchases of products by industry and by final consumption categories are valued at purchaser prices.

* This relates to FISIM.
** This includes investment in dwellings, transfer costs of land and existing buildings, and valuables.

Industrial analyses

2.1 Supply and Use Tables for the United Kingdom: 1999
continued

Gross value added at basic prices
£ billions

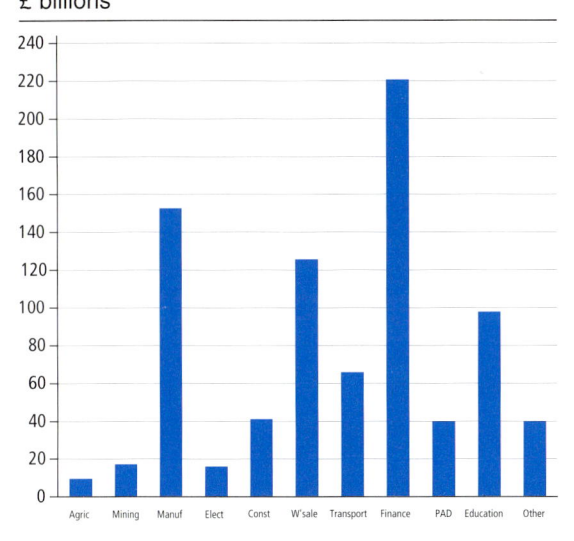

Bar chart showing values for: Agric (~10), Mining (~17), Manuf (~153), Elect (~16), Const (~42), W'sale (~126), Transport (~66), Finance (~221), PAD (~41), Education (~98), Other (~41)

Components of final demand
Per cent

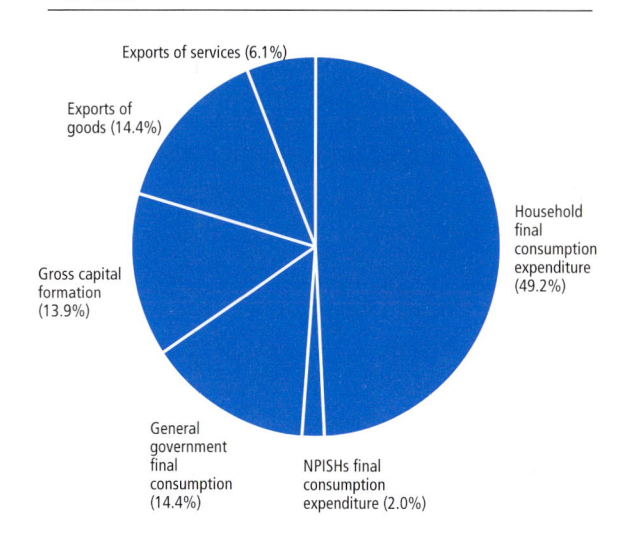

Pie chart:
- Household final consumption expenditure (49.2%)
- NPISHs final consumption expenditure (2.0%)
- General government final consumption (14.4%)
- Gross capital formation (13.9%)
- Exports of goods (14.4%)
- Exports of services (6.1%)

£ million

		FINAL CONSUMPTION EXPENDITURE			GROSS CAPITAL FORMATION			EXPORTS				TOTAL[1]
								Goods		Services		
1999	Total[1] intermediate consumption	Households	NPISHs	GGFC	GFCF	Valuables	Changes in inventories	EU	Non-EU	EU	Non-EU	
PRODUCTS[2]												
Agriculture	14 955	9 896	-	-	423	-	15	997	431	55	91	26 863
Mining and quarrying	21 129	596	-	-	458	-	- 252	6 569	3 441	60	97	32 097
Manufacturing	308 425	273 390	-	-	70 436	- 14	3 239	89 688	62 860	1 730	2 813	812 567
Electricity, gas and water supply	30 822	15 285	-	-	-	-	- 65	8	-	23	38	46 110
Construction	46 371	3 847	-	-	67 436	-	752	-	-	91	194	118 691
Wholesale and retail trade	20 463	56 490	-	-	-	244	-	-	-	3 082	5 023	85 302
Transport and communication	110 730	34 026	-	-	968	-	118	-	-	5 064	7 671	158 577
Financial intermediation	285 866	114 088	560	-	12 948	-	990	298	116	15 777	24 702	455 344
Public administration	1 332	1 117	-	70 139	976	-	-	-	-	140	379	74 083
Education, health and social work	60 094	19 918	17 791	91 235	-	-	40	-	-	421	704	190 203
Other services	26 516	38 903	4 320	4 920	1 763	-	139	244	1 546	860	1 507	80 718
Total consumption[1]	926 703	567 555	22 671	166 294	155 408	230	4 975	97 804	68 394	27 304	43 218	2 080 556
Taxes *less* subsidies on production	16 893											
Compensation of employees	494 186											
Gross operating surplus	283 946											
Gross value added at basic prices[1]	795 025											
Output at basic prices[1]	1 721 728											
Supplementary information:												
Gross fixed capital formation	155 638 **											
Changes in inventories	4 975											
Total gross capital formation	160 613 **											

Notes for information:
Gross value added at basic prices plus taxes *less* subsidies on products gives GDP at market prices.
Gross operating surplus includes gross mixed income.
Changes in inventories includes materials and fuels, work-in-progress and finished goods.
Valuables include both 'transfer costs' and 'acquisitions less disposals'.
GFCF can be broken down by institutional sectors and assets, see Chapter 9.
No subsidies on production are recorded on an ESA95 basis in the UK.

FISIM represents Financial Intermediation Services Indirectly Measured.
NPISHs represents Non-Profit Institutions Serving Households.
GGFC represents General Government Final Consumption.
GFCF represents Gross Fixed Capital Formation.

UK industrial analyses

2.2 Output and capital formation: by industry[1,2]
Gross value added at current basic prices

£ million

			1992	1993	1994	1995	1996	1997	1998	1999	2000
	Agriculture, hunting, forestry and fishing										
P.1	Output										
D.1	Compensation of employees	CFHE	3 228	3 129	3 140	3 114	3 089	3 126	3 208	3 268	..
D.29-D.39	Taxes *less* subsidies on production other than those on products	EWTZ	34	−105	−169	−166	−112	−53	−88	−204	..
B.2g/B.3g	Operating surplus/Mixed income, gross	ESMU	6 656	7 520	7 646	8 818	8 758	7 072	6 508	6 396	..
B.1g	Gross value added at basic prices	EWSH	9 918	10 544	10 617	11 766	11 735	10 145	9 628	9 460	8 912
P.2	Intermediate consumption at purchasers' prices	EWSI	12 586	12 823	12 989	13 536	13 815	13 198	11 925	11 642	..
P.1	Total output at basic prices	EWSJ	22 504	23 367	23 606	25 302	25 550	23 343	21 553	21 102	..
P.5	Gross capital formation	EWSK	2 110	2 367	2 435	2 420	2 658	2 436	1 849	1 660	..
	Mining and quarrying										
P.1	Output										
D.1	Compensation of employees	CFHF	4 073	3 344	3 500	3 371	2 983	2 878	2 973	2 904	..
D.29-D.39	Taxes *less* subsidies on production other than those on products	EWUA	216	203	158	140	160	157	144	143	..
B.2g/B.3g	Operating surplus/Mixed income, gross	ESMQ	9 129	9 979	11 130	12 858	16 625	15 080	12 562	14 043	..
B.1g	Gross value added at basic prices	EWSL	13 418	13 526	14 788	16 369	19 768	18 115	15 679	17 090	24 244
P.2	Intermediate consumption at purchasers' prices	EWSM	7 696	7 879	8 702	9 461	9 347	8 712	8 122	8 962	..
P.1	Total output at basic prices	EWSN	21 114	21 405	23 490	25 830	29 115	26 827	23 801	26 052	..
P.5	Gross capital formation	EWSO	7 292	6 015	4 781	5 648	5 943	5 875	6 487	4 524	..
	Manufacturing[3]										
P.1	Output										
D.1	Compensation of employees	CFHG	84 186	85 804	89 151	93 819	96 892	100 690	105 550	109 105	..
D.29-D.39	Taxes *less* subsidies on production other than those on products	EWUB	2 213	2 001	1 934	1 920	2 241	2 594	2 729	2 429	..
B.2g/B.g	Operating surplus/Mixed income, gross	ESMT	29 492	33 184	39 682	44 050	46 946	49 021	44 993	41 119	..
B.1g	Gross value added at basic prices	EWSP	115 891	120 989	130 767	139 789	146 079	152 305	153 272	152 653	155 531
P.2	Intermediate consumption at purchasers' prices	EWSQ	190 135	204 709	222 500	242 666	252 369	256 551	251 492	249 630	..
P.1	Total output at basic prices	EWSR	306 026	325 698	353 267	382 455	398 448	408 856	404 764	402 283	..
P.5	Gross capital formation	EWSS	11 464	11 494	15 469	20 410	18 312	19 361	21 191	18 569	..

1 The contribution of each industry to the gross domestic product before providing for consumption of fixed capital. The industrial composition in this table is consistent with the Input-Output analyses in Table 2.1, which show data from 1992 to 1999. The industrial composition for 1989-91 is based on Input-Output analyses also, but there are improvements to the underlying data from 1992. Between 1989 and 1991, the data were compiled on a different basis, which lead to step changes in 1991 and 1992.
2 Components may not sum to totals due to rounding.
3 Further detail is given in Table 2.3.

UK industrial analyses

2.2 Output and capital formation: by industry[1,2]
Gross value added at current basic prices
continued

£ million

				1992	1993	1994	1995	1996	1997	1998	1999	2000
	Electricity, gas and water supply											
P.1	Output											
D.1	Compensation of employees	CFHI		5 799	6 212	6 095	5 434	5 348	5 204	5 136	5 026	..
D.29-D.39	Taxes *less* subsidies on production other than those on products	EWUC		1 375	1 343	1 359	1 335	1 118	1 145	1 189	1 264	..
B.2g/B.3g	Operating surplus/Mixed income, gross	ESMV		7 754	8 716	8 704	8 817	9 814	9 792	9 635	9 719	..
B.1g	Gross value added at basic prices	EWST		14 928	16 271	16 158	15 586	16 280	16 141	15 960	16 009	15 677
P.2	Intermediate consumption at purchasers' prices	EWSU		24 038	23 104	25 562	26 102	26 524	27 814	28 830	31 103	..
P.1	Total output at basic prices	EWSV		38 966	39 375	41 720	41 688	42 804	43 955	44 790	47 112	..
P.5	Gross capital formation	EWSW		6 619	6 127	5 233	5 019	4 514	5 358	5 578	5 786	..
	Construction											
P.1	Output											
D.1	Compensation of employees	CFHU		14 826	13 234	13 651	15 521	16 325	18 663	19 755	20 426	..
D.29-D.39	Taxes *less* subsidies on production other than those on products	EWUD		318	319	322	330	344	421	501	580	..
B.2g/B.3g	Operating surplus/Mixed income, gross	ESMW		14 876	15 613	17 243	17 154	17 918	17 795	18 761	20 136	..
B.1g	Gross value added at basic prices	EWSX		30 020	29 166	31 216	33 005	34 587	36 879	39 017	41 142	43 287
P.2	Intermediate consumption at purchasers' prices	EWSY		46 808	46 812	50 359	53 134	56 035	59 877	64 453	68 477	..
P.1	Total output at basic prices	EWSZ		76 828	75 978	81 575	86 139	90 622	96 756	103 470	109 619	..
P.5	Gross capital formation	EWTA		27	792	1 853	1 590	902	2 672	2 086	2 796	..
	Distribution, hotels and catering											
P.1	Output											
D.1	Compensation of employees	CFIK		48 988	52 671	54 645	57 677	61 011	65 117	70 242	76 501	..
D.29-D.39	Taxes *less* subsidies on production other than those on products	EWUE		5 021	5 035	4 890	5 064	5 507	5 612	5 557	6 108	..
B.2g/B.3g	Operating surplus/Mixed income, gross	ESMX		25 597	26 357	28 856	30 124	33 288	38 426	41 884	43 032	..
B.1g	Gross value added at basic prices	EWTB		79 606	84 063	88 391	92 865	99 806	109 155	117 683	125 641	130 782
P.2	Intermediate consumption at purchasers' prices	EWTC		57 583	63 205	69 190	75 498	84 407	94 669	104 589	112 604	..
P.1	Total output at basic prices	EWTD		137 189	147 268	157 581	168 363	184 213	203 824	222 272	238 245	..
P.5	Gross capital formation	EWTE		8 792	10 880	11 478	13 371	13 194	17 377	19 342	18 959	..

See footnotes on first page of this table.

United Kingdom National Accounts 2001, © Crown copyright 2001

UK industrial analyses

2.2 Output and capital formation: by industry[1,2]
Gross value added at current basic prices
continued

£ million

			1992	1993	1994	1995	1996	1997	1998	1999	2000
	Transport, storage and communication										
P.1	Output										
D.1	Compensation of employees	CFIM	30 330	31 419	32 935	33 811	34 707	37 325	40 089	42 206	..
D.29-D.39	Taxes less subsidies on production other than those on products	EWUF	1 232	1 115	986	1 039	1 113	1 178	1 348	1 475	..
B.2g/B.3g	Operating surplus/Mixed income, gross	ESMY	13 546	13 874	15 651	16 490	17 653	18 890	20 697	22 229	..
B.1g	Gross value added at basic prices	EWTF	45 108	46 408	49 572	51 340	53 473	57 393	62 134	65 910	68 195
P.2	Intermediate consumption at purchasers' prices	EWTG	34 961	39 601	45 851	52 680	59 898	65 443	72 192	76 648	..
P.1	Total output at basic prices	EWTH	80 069	86 009	95 423	104 020	113 371	122 836	134 326	142 558	..
P.5	Gross capital formation	EWTI	8 963	9 494	11 597	11 836	13 826	17 279	19 727	21 508	..
	Business services and finance										
P.1	Output										
D.1	Compensation of employees	CFIP	55 736	56 364	58 223	61 218	66 825	75 440	86 005	94 860	..
D.29-D.39	Taxes less subsidies on production other than those on products	EWUG	1 759	1 918	1 977	2 231	2 131	2 232	2 342	2 434	..
B.2g/B.3g	Operating surplus/Mixed income, gross	ESMZ	73 632	83 722	92 654	95 692	100 734	106 211	119 708	123 331	..
B.1g	Gross value added at basic prices	EWTJ	131 127	142 004	152 854	159 141	169 690	183 883	208 055	220 625	238 510
P.2	Intermediate consumption at purchasers' prices	EWTK	80 380	85 477	93 606	103 878	116 214	131 261	153 097	174 617	..
P.1	Total output at basic prices	EWTL	211 507	227 481	246 460	263 019	285 904	315 144	361 152	395 242	..
P.5	Gross capital formation	EWTM	13 001	12 123	14 695	15 582	20 256	17 510	25 736	28 487	..
	Adjustment for financial services										
B.1g	Gross value added at basic prices	-NSRV	−19 086	−19 569	−23 119	−23 215	−22 580	−22 396	−27 998	−30 819	−37 091
P.2	Intermediate consumption at purchasers' prices	NSRV	19 086	19 569	23 119	23 215	22 580	22 396	27 998	30 819	37 091
	Public administration and defence										
P.1	Output										
D.1	Compensation of employees	CFIV	34 455	35 206	34 346	34 030	33 590	33 198	33 061	32 931	..
D.29-D.39	Taxes less subsidies on production other than those on products	EWUH	572	576	754	818	845	815	847	863	..
B.2g	Operating surplus, gross	EWUW	4 183	4 206	4 497	4 908	5 274	5 646	5 843	5 992	..
B.1g	Gross value added at basic prices	EWTN	39 210	39 988	39 597	39 756	39 709	39 659	39 751	39 786	42 091
P.2	Intermediate consumption at purchasers' prices	EWTO	25 458	26 476	28 269	30 600	31 553	31 737	32 637	34 524	..
P.1	Total output at basic prices	EWTP	64 668	66 464	67 866	70 356	71 262	71 396	72 388	74 310	..
P.5	Gross capital formation	EWTQ	8 339	8 710	9 109	9 184	8 383	7 049	7 306	6 559	..

See footnotes on first page of this table.

UK industrial analyses

2.2 Output and capital formation: by industry[1,2]
Gross value added at current basic prices
continued

£ million

			1992	1993	1994	1995	1996	1997	1998	1999	2000
	Education, health and social work										
P.1	Output										
D.1	Compensation of employees	CFIW	53 309	56 981	59 752	63 506	68 037	72 091	76 586	83 219	..
D.29-D.39	Taxes less subsidies on production other than those on products	EWUI	1 117	894	837	803	879	866	870	882	..
B.2g/B.3g	Operating surplus/Mixed income, gross	EWSF	9 811	10 661	11 676	11 950	12 191	12 714	13 468	13 676	..
B.1g	Gross value added at basic prices	EWTR	64 237	68 536	72 265	76 259	81 107	85 671	90 924	97 777	102 489
P.2	Intermediate consumption at purchasers' prices	EWTS	35 568	45 668	58 466	66 512	73 697	76 431	81 944	92 562	..
P.1	Total output at basic prices	EWTT	99 805	114 204	130 731	142 771	154 804	162 102	172 868	190 339	..
P.5	Gross capital formation	EWTU	4 620	4 440	4 521	4 757	5 359	5 238	6 014	6 444	..
	Other services										
P.1	Output										
D.1	Compensation of employees	CFIX	12 783	13 297	14 207	15 217	16 662	19 228	21 653	23 740	..
D.29-D.39	Taxes less subsidies on production other than those on products	EWUJ	725	637	646	642	722	802	857	919	..
B.2g/B.3g	Operating surplus/Mixed income, gross	EWSG	8 549	9 600	10 781	11 388	12 582	13 712	14 703	15 092	..
B.1g	Gross value added at basic prices	EWTV	22 057	23 535	25 634	27 247	29 966	33 742	37 213	39 751	42 560
P.2	Intermediate consumption at purchasers' prices	EWTW	19 456	21 270	23 598	26 344	29 358	31 115	32 764	35 115	..
P.1	Total output at basic prices	EWTX	41 513	44 805	49 232	53 591	59 324	64 857	69 977	74 866	..
P.5	Gross capital formation	EWTY	5 515	5 443	5 796	6 519	6 992	8 753	9 514	11 198	..
	Not allocated to industries										
P.5	Gross capital formation[4]	EWUV	21 921	23 442	25 168	25 503	27 036	29 850	31 599	34 123	..
	All industries including adjustment for financial services										
P.1	Output										
D.1	Compensation of employees	HAEA	347 713	357 662	369 645	386 718	405 469	432 960	464 258	494 186	521 443
D.29-D.39	Taxes less subsidies on production other than those on products	QZPC	14 582	13 936	13 694	14 156	14 948	15 769	16 296	16 893	17 872
B.2g	Operating surplus, gross	ABNF	144 618	161 523	181 082	192 387	210 192	221 502	230 472	231 482	237 051
B.3g	Mixed income, gross	HAXH	39 521	42 340	44 319	46 647	49 011	50 461	50 292	52 464	54 442
di	Statistical discrepancy between income and GDP	GIXQ	–	–	–	–	–	–	–	–	245
B.1g	Gross value added at basic prices	ABML	546 434	575 461	608 740	639 908	679 620	720 692	761 318	795 025	831 053
P.2	Intermediate consumption at purchasers' prices	NQAJ	553 755	596 593	662 211	723 626	775 797	819 204	870 043	926 703	987 792
P.1	Total output at basic prices	NQAF	1 100 189	1 172 054	1 270 951	1 363 534	1 455 417	1 539 896	1 631 361	1 721 728	1 818 849
P.5	Gross capital formation										
P.51	Gross fixed capital formation	NPQX	100 583	101 027	108 314	117 448	125 762	134 396	151 539	155 408	165 247
P.52	Changes in inventories	ABMP	−1 937	329	3 708	4 512	1 771	4 388	4 460	4 975	1 855
P.53	Acquisitions less disposals of valuables	NPJO	17	−29	113	−121	−158	−26	430	230	−3
P.5	Total gross capital formation	NPDN	98 663	101 327	112 135	121 839	127 375	138 758	156 429	160 613	167 099

See footnotes on first page of this table.

4 Includes investment in dwellings, transfer costs of land and existing buildings, and valuables.

United Kingdom National Accounts 2001, © Crown copyright 2001

UK industrial analyses

2.3 Gross value added at current basic prices: by industry[1,2]

£ million

			1992	1993	1994	1995	1996	1997	1998	1999	2000
A,B	**Agriculture, hunting, forestry and fishing**	QTOP	9 919	10 544	10 616	11 766	11 735	10 145	9 628	9 460	8 912
C,D,E	**Production**										
C	Mining and quarrying										
CA	Mining and quarrying of energy producing materials										
C10	Mining of coal	QTOQ	2 482	1 472	1 048	1 223	1 045	987	826	622	497
C11	Extraction of mineral oil and natural gas	QTOR	9 725	10 892	12 493	13 704	17 124	15 435	13 203	14 810	22 047
CB	Other mining and quarrying	QTOS	1 211	1 162	1 247	1 443	1 600	1 694	1 650	1 658	1 700
C	Total mining and quarrying	QTOT	13 418	13 526	14 788	16 369	19 768	18 115	15 678	17 091	24 244
D	Manufacturing										
DA	Food; beverages and tobacco	QTOU	17 563	18 086	18 230	18 260	19 894	20 323	20 032	20 264	20 014
DB	Textiles and textile products	QTOV	6 231	6 258	6 452	6 821	7 266	7 697	6 922	6 431	6 202
DC	Leather and leather products	QTOW	1 034	1 019	1 018	946	892	842	802	824	841
DD	Wood and wood products	QTOX	1 686	1 582	1 746	1 918	2 026	2 237	2 284	2 109	2 150
DE	Pulp, paper and paper products; publishing and printing	QTOY	14 632	15 480	16 214	17 582	18 153	18 376	18 946	20 207	20 710
DF	Coke, petroleum products and nuclear fuel	QTOZ	2 639	2 542	2 688	2 923	2 531	2 382	2 576	2 811	2 568
DG	Chemicals, chemical products and man-made fibres	QTPA	12 670	13 005	13 908	15 311	15 726	15 322	15 048	14 854	15 062
DH	Rubber and plastic products	QTPB	5 752	6 048	6 321	6 789	7 220	7 978	8 195	7 770	7 958
DI	Other non-metal mineral products	QTPC	3 675	3 892	4 697	5 158	5 189	5 181	5 003	4 859	4 729
DJ	Basic metals and fabricated metal products	QTPD	12 857	13 146	14 243	16 124	16 410	17 050	17 653	16 897	17 814
DK	Machinery and equipment not elsewhere classified	QTPE	9 425	9 813	11 052	12 273	12 469	13 364	13 552	12 600	12 620
DL	Electrical and optical equipment	QTPF	13 554	14 544	16 523	17 757	18 592	19 980	20 029	20 678	23 272
DM	Transport equipment	QTPG	10 840	11 856	13 258	13 067	14 318	15 588	15 998	16 028	15 214
DN	Manufacturing not elsewhere classified	QTPH	3 331	3 717	4 417	4 857	5 394	5 985	6 228	6 320	6 378
D	Total manufacturing	QTPI	115 891	120 989	130 767	139 789	146 078	152 304	153 268	152 653	155 531
E	Electricity, gas and water supply	QTPJ	14 928	16 271	16 157	15 585	16 280	16 141	15 960	16 008	15 677
C,D,E	Total production	QTPK	144 238	150 786	161 713	171 744	182 128	186 561	184 907	185 752	195 451
F	**Construction**	QTPL	30 020	29 166	31 216	33 006	34 587	36 878	39 017	41 142	43 287
G-Q	**Service industries**										
G	Wholesale and retail trade (including motor trade); repair of motor vehicles, personal and household goods	QTPM	64 597	68 324	71 537	74 612	79 668	86 747	93 352	100 046	104 854
H	Hotels and restaurants	QTPN	15 009	15 738	16 855	18 252	20 139	22 407	24 331	25 595	25 928
I	Transport, storage and communication										
	Transport and storage	QTPO	28 073	28 990	31 391	33 045	34 878	37 367	39 650	41 265	41 214
	Communication	QTPP	17 035	17 420	18 180	18 295	18 594	20 026	22 486	24 645	26 980
I	Total	QTPQ	45 109	46 407	49 572	51 340	53 472	57 393	62 134	65 910	68 195
J	Financial intermediation	QTPR	35 188	39 289	42 358	40 089	40 912	40 584	45 313	42 657	42 602
-P.119	Adjustment for financial services	-NSRV	–19 086	–19 569	–23 119	–23 215	–22 580	–22 396	–27 998	–30 819	–37 091
K	Real estate, renting and business activities										
	Letting of dwellings including imputed rent of owner occupiers	QTPS	37 771	40 003	42 366	45 083	46 716	50 273	55 469	58 723	60 793
	Other real estate, renting and business activities	QTPT	58 167	62 711	68 131	73 970	82 060	93 026	107 272	119 245	130 983
K	Total	QTPU	95 939	102 715	110 496	119 052	128 777	143 299	162 741	177 968	191 777
L	Public administration and defence	QTPV	39 210	39 989	39 597	39 756	39 709	39 660	39 751	39 786	42 091
M	Education	QTPW	29 910	31 428	32 771	34 208	36 540	38 799	41 356	44 743	46 176
N	Health and social work	QTPX	34 328	37 108	39 495	42 051	44 568	46 871	49 569	53 033	56 313
O,P,Q	Other social and personal services, private households with employees and extra-territorial organisations	QTPY	22 058	23 535	25 634	27 248	29 966	33 743	37 212	39 752	42 560
G-Q	Total service industries	QTPZ	362 259	384 965	405 194	423 393	451 171	487 107	527 761	558 671	583 407
B.1g	**All industries**	ABML	546 434	575 461	608 740	639 908	679 620	720 692	761 318	795 025	831 053

1 Components may not sum to totals as a result of rounding.
2 Because of differences in the annual and monthly production inquiries, estimates of current price output and value-added by industry derived from the current price input-output supply-use balances are not consistent with the equivalent measures of constant price growth given in Table 2.4. These differences do not affect GDP totals. For further information see "Experimental Constant Price Input-Output Supply-Use Balances: An approach to improving the quality of the national accounts" Nadim Ahmad, *Economic Trends*, July 1999 (No. 548).

UK industrial analyses

2.4 Gross value added at 1995 basic prices: by industry[1,2,3]
Index numbers

Indices 1995=100

		Weight per 1000[1] 1995		1992	1993	1994	1995	1996	1997	1998	1999	2000
A,B	Agriculture, hunting, forestry and fishing	18.4	GDQA	111.5	102.5	101.2	100.0	99.1	98.2	99.9	102.2	99.9
C,D,E	**Production**											
C	Mining and quarrying											
CA	Mining and quarrying of energy producing materials											
C10	Mining of coal	1.9	CKZP	181.8	142.3	94.6	100.0	95.5	90.3	76.5	69.1	59.3
C11	Extraction of mineral oil and natural gas	21.4	CKZO	68.4	77.5	96.1	100.0	105.6	104.7	107.5	112.2	110.7
CB	Other mining and quarrying	2.3	CKZQ	103.4	105.6	105.3	100.0	88.7	87.3	97.0	103.6	111.0
C	Total mining and quarrying	25.6	CKYX	78.9	84.2	96.8	100.0	103.3	102.1	104.3	108.2	106.9
D	Manufacturing											
DA	Food; beverages and tobacco	28.5	CKZA	98.9	99.2	101.7	100.0	100.9	103.2	101.5	100.8	99.6
DB	Textiles and textile products	10.7	CKZB	101.9	101.3	103.6	100.0	98.2	95.9	89.0	81.9	78.2
DC	Leather and leather products	1.5	CKZC	95.8	99.1	98.6	100.0	98.6	103.5	89.5	86.6	79.1
DD	Wood and wood products	3.0	CKZD	97.8	100.0	107.8	100.0	98.1	95.5	94.6	89.7	91.6
DE	Pulp, paper and paper products; publishing and printing	27.5	CKZE	93.0	96.0	98.5	100.0	98.0	98.2	98.9	99.1	99.0
DF	Coke, petroleum products and nuclear fuel	4.6	CKZF	88.6	89.0	89.8	100.0	91.8	93.8	88.3	79.4	82.8
DG	Chemicals, chemical products and man-made fibres	23.9	CKZG	88.5	90.4	95.1	100.0	100.6	102.4	104.0	107.4	111.8
DH	Rubber and plastic products	10.6	CKZH	85.1	88.8	97.9	100.0	98.8	98.5	101.6	100.9	100.2
DI	Other non-metallic mineral products	8.1	CKZI	94.7	99.1	102.7	100.0	96.6	99.3	96.9	95.7	95.8
DJ	Basic metals and fabricated metal products	25.2	CKZJ	96.0	95.0	97.3	100.0	99.9	101.1	99.2	95.3	95.5
DK	Machinery and equipment not elsewhere classified	19.2	CKZK	94.7	94.6	99.8	100.0	98.0	95.7	95.8	90.0	89.8
DL	Electrical and optical equipment	27.8	CKZL	79.0	83.4	93.5	100.0	104.9	108.1	114.8	126.0	144.4
DM	Transport equipment	20.4	CKZM	99.9	98.1	100.8	100.0	107.7	112.1	118.2	120.1	115.2
DN	Manufacturing not elsewhere classified	7.6	CKZN	97.2	98.6	101.7	100.0	102.0	104.0	105.3	106.6	104.5
D	Total manufacturing	218.5	CKYY	92.8	94.1	98.5	100.0	100.7	102.0	102.8	103.1	105.1
E	Electricity, gas and water supply	24.4	CKYZ	92.9	96.8	97.7	100.0	105.1	105.7	107.5	109.4	113.1
C,D,E	Total production	268.4	CKYW	91.3	93.3	98.3	100.0	101.3	102.4	103.4	104.2	106.0
F	**Construction**	51.6	GDQB	97.5	96.3	100.0	100.0	102.7	105.7	107.0	107.8	109.7
G-Q	**Service industries**											
G	Wholesale and retail trade (including motor trade); repair of motor vehicles, personal and household goods	116.6	GDQC	87.7	92.8	97.8	100.0	104.3	107.3	110.8	113.9	117.4
H	Hotels and restaurants	28.5	GDQD	96.0	98.1	100.8	100.0	102.9	103.5	104.5	104.6	101.7
I	Transport, storage and communication											
	Transport and storage	51.6	GDQF	88.1	89.9	96.9	100.0	101.1	106.6	114.5	116.7	118.7
	Communication	28.6	GDQG	79.4	83.5	90.5	100.0	112.7	128.9	139.4	158.8	179.4
I	Total	80.2	GDQH	84.9	87.6	94.6	100.0	105.2	114.6	123.4	131.7	140.3
J	Financial intermediation	65.8	GDQI	93.4	95.5	96.5	100.0	103.7	108.5	113.8	115.3	119.8
-P.119	Adjustment for financial services	−39.4	GDQJ	87.7	88.4	92.5	100.0	106.8	114.1	122.9	125.9	132.1
K	Real estate, renting and business activities											
	Letting of dwellings, including imputed rent of owner occupiers	70.5	GDQL	94.9	96.1	97.4	100.0	101.2	103.2	105.8	107.6	107.9
	Other real estate, renting and business activities	115.6	GDQK	82.0	84.1	92.8	100.0	107.4	118.7	131.6	138.3	147.5
K	Total	186.0	GDQM	86.8	88.9	94.5	100.0	105.1	112.8	121.8	126.7	132.5
L	Public administration and defence	61.0	GDQO	104.6	102.5	100.9	100.0	99.2	98.4	97.4	96.8	98.0
M	Education	55.5	GDQP	95.0	95.0	98.7	100.0	101.3	102.4	102.9	103.7	104.1
N	Health and social work	64.7	GDQQ	89.4	93.5	95.9	100.0	103.2	106.5	110.2	113.7	116.7
O,P,Q	Other social and personal services, private households with employees and extra-territorial organisations	42.6	GDQR	83.5	90.5	96.1	100.0	105.4	107.5	112.8	115.0	119.3
G-Q	Total service industries	661.6	GDQS	89.8	92.5	96.9	100.0	103.6	108.0	112.9	116.3	120.3
B.1g	**All industries**	1 000.0	CGCE	90.6	92.8	97.3	100.0	102.7	106.0	109.4	111.6	114.8

1 The weights are in proportion to total gross value added in 1995. The GVA for sections L, M, and N in this table follows the SIC(92) and differs from that shown in Table 2.3, which is based on Input-Output groups. Central government expenditure on teachers' pay is included in Education in Table 2.4 but in PAD in Table 2.3. The administration costs of the NHS are included in PAD in Table 2.4 but are included in Health and social work in Table 2.3.

2 The output analysis of gross value added is estimated in terms of change and expressed in index number form. It is therefore inappropriate to show as a statistical adjustment any divergence of an output measure of GDP derived from it from other measures of GDP. Such an adjustment does, however, exist implicitly.

3 See footnote 2 to Table 2.3.

UK industrial analyses

2.5 Employment: by industry

Thousands

			1992	1993	1994	1995	1996	1997	1998	1999	2000
A,B	**Agriculture, hunting & forestry; fishing**										
	Self-employment jobs	YEKN	282	261	283	275	267	263	246	208	204
	Employee jobs	YEKO	312	330	302	274	280	314	322	318	320
	Total employed	YEKP	595	590	585	549	547	577	569	526	524
C-E	**Production industries, including energy**										
	Self-employment jobs	YEKQ	297	302	294	275	282	276	297	268	253
	Employee jobs	YEKR	4 481	4 259	4 242	4 317	4 349	4 406	4 416	4 252	4 134
	Total employed	YEKS	4 778	4 560	4 536	4 592	4 631	4 682	4 713	4 520	4 387
F	**Construction**										
	Self-employment jobs	YEKT	800	790	805	821	823	730	676	674	660
	Employee jobs	YEKU	1 058	962	962	933	921	976	1 098	1 112	1 171
	Total employed	YEKV	1 858	1 753	1 767	1 753	1 745	1 706	1 774	1 785	1 831
G-I	**Wholesale & retail trade (including motor trade); repair of motor vehicles, personal & household goods; hotels and restaurants; transport, storage & communication**										
	Self-emloyment jobs	YEKW	984	1 003	937	950	875	939	870	875	836
	Employee jobs	YEKX	6 767	6 659	6 764	6 876	6 972	7 148	7 306	7 458	7 594
	Total employed	YEKY	7 751	7 661	7 701	7 826	7 847	8 087	8 177	8 333	8 430
J-K	**Financial intermediation; real estate, renting & business activities**										
	Self-employment jobs	YEKZ	530	515	552	564	598	614	617	660	651
	Employee jobs	YELA	3 718	3 775	3 796	3 986	4 087	4 309	4 476	4 636	4 707
	Total employed	YELB	4 247	4 290	4 348	4 551	4 685	4 922	5 093	5 296	5 358
L-Q	**Other service activities** Public administration & defence, education, health and social work, other community, social & personal services, private households with employees										
	Self-employment jobs	YEJW	542	567	673	713	765	785	777	825	816
	Employee jobs	YEJX	6 880	6 895	6 906	6 932	6 993	7 003	7 061	7 228	7 372
	Total employed	YEJY	7 422	7 462	7 578	7 644	7 758	7 788	7 838	8 053	8 189
A-Q	**All industries**										
ESE	Self-employment jobs	BCAG	3 441	3 445	3 547	3 610	3 615	3 609	3 487	3 513	3 423
EEM	Employee jobs	BCAD	23 216	22 879	22 971	23 317	23 601	24 156	24 680	25 004	25 299
ETO	Total employed	YEJZ	26 657	26 324	26 516	26 921	27 216	27 765	28 167	28 517	28 721

1 Data sources are: Labour Force Survey for self-employed; employer surveys for employees. Figures as at June of each year.

Part 3

The sector accounts

The sector accounts

The Sector Accounts at a glance

Net lending/borrowing

Net lending by general government was a record £18.4 billion in 2000 compared to £10.3 billion in 1999. The rise was due to increases in receipts, mainly from taxes on income and products out-stripping increases in expenditure. Net borrowing by non-financial corporations of £12.5 billion in 1999 fell to £4.8 billion 2000. This change was largely due to increased profits and higher net dividend income. The government and non-financial corporations net borrowing /lending figures include £0.5 billion of spectrum-use payments by 3G mobile phone companies, the remaining £22 billion from the auctions is accrued over the next two decades. Net borrowing by the households sector of £6.1 billion in 1999 fell to £2.7 billion in 2000. Net borrowing by financial corporations in 1999 of £9.9 billion grew to net borrowing of £27.9 billion in 2000. This change was due to falling trading profits, increased property income payments and higher capital investment spending. Net lending by the rest of the world of £18.3 billion in 1999 became net lending of £16.5 billion in 2000.

Net lending/borrowing, 2000
£ billion

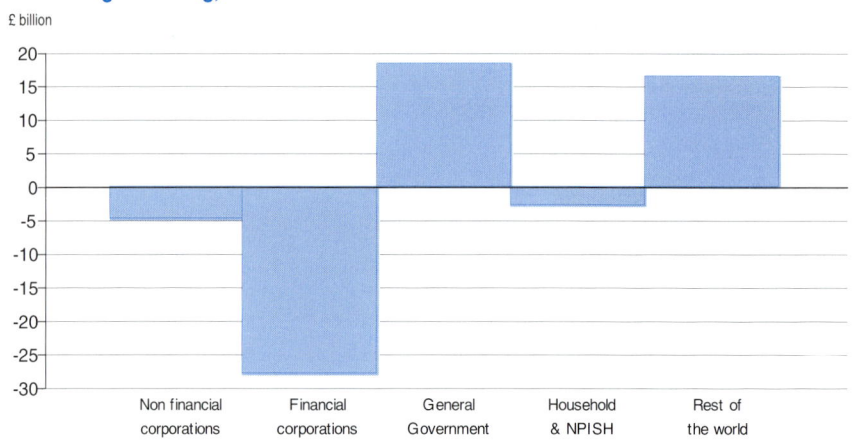

Net financial transactions

Net financial transactions by general government were £17.5 billion in 2000 compared to £9.8 billion in 1999. This is reflected in increased bank deposits, due to receipts from taxes and spectrum fees, and net redemptions of British Government securities. These were partially offset by increased liabilities in other accounts receivable/payable which included adjustments for the pre-payments of spectrum rents by 3G mobile phone companies. The financial corporations sector deficit was a record in 2000. The fall from 1999 was largely due to record movements in bank deposits transactions.

Financial balances by sector
£ billion

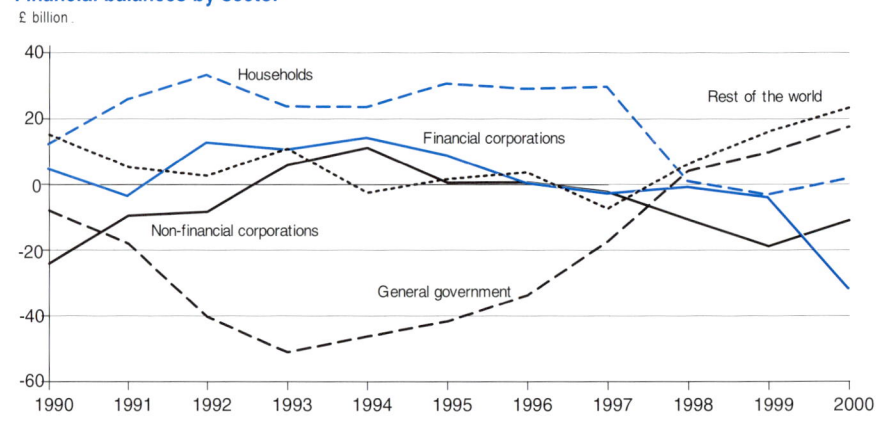

The sector accounts

Gross trading profits of Private non-financial corporations

Gross trading profits in the largest component of private non-financial corporations gross operating surplus. Profits increased by 6.0 per cent between 1999 and 2000 compared to an increase of 3.1 per cent between 1998 and 1999. This increase was due to higher profits by oil and gas extraction companies.

Gross trading profits of private non-financial corporations
£ billion

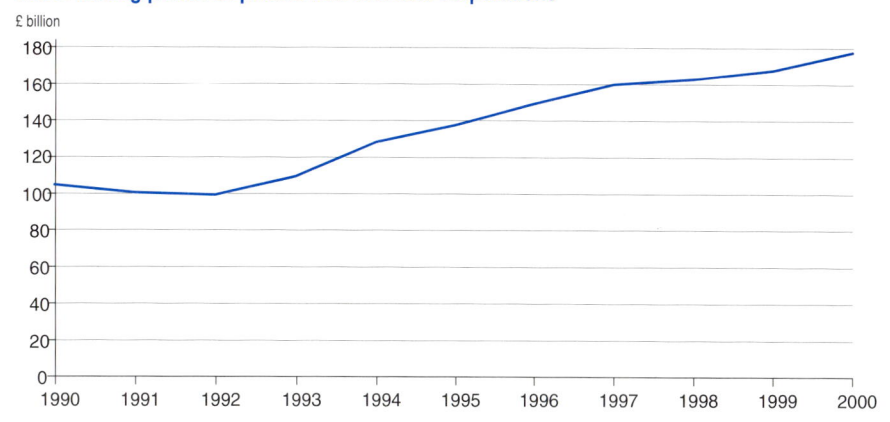

Real household disposable income

Real household disposable income (RHDI) is the amount of money in real terms the households sector has available for spending after taxes and other deductions. Between 1999 and 2000 RHDI increased by £24.0 billion compared to an increase of just £18.5 billion between 1998 and 1999. The main reason for this rise in 2000 was a lower deflator in 2000 than in 1999.

Annual changes in real household disposable income
Percentage change

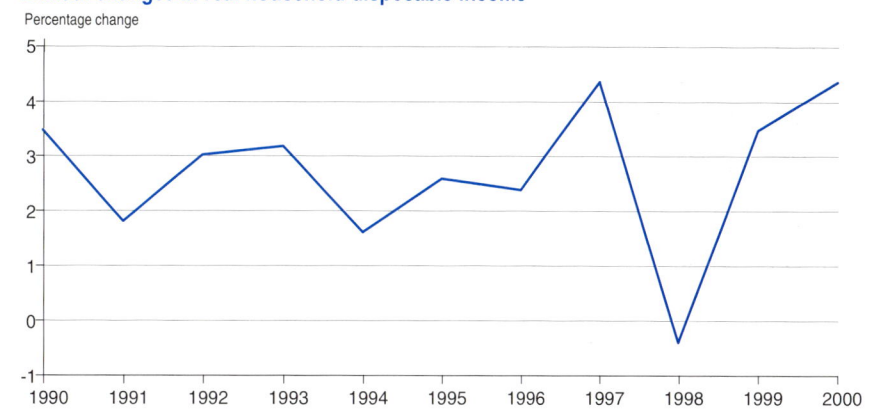

Household saving ratio

The household saving ratio reflects household gross savings as a percentage of their total available resource (the amount available to spend or save). A rise in household resources of 4.9 per cent between 1999 and 2000 was not quite matched by the 4.6 per cent increase in household and NPISH final consumption expenditure at current prices. As a consequence the household saving ratio rose to 5.0 per cent in 2000 compared to 4.8 per cent in 1999.

Household saving ratio
Percentage

United Kingdom National Accounts 2001, © Crown copyright 2001

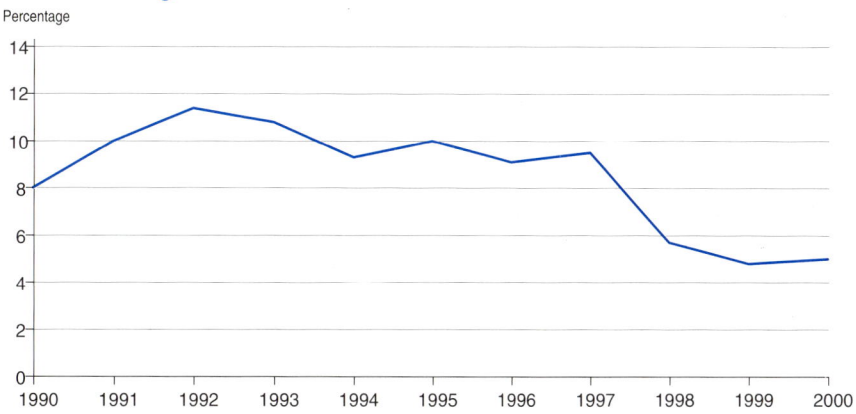

C The sector accounts: Key economic indicators

£ million

			1992	1993	1994	1995	1996	1997	1998	1999	2000
	Net lending/borrowing by:										
B.9	Non-financial corporations	EABO	−7 906	4 099	12 941	4 276	6 957	−2 194	−3 649	−12 540	−4 839
B.9	Financial corporations	NHCQ	1 975	4 202	4 473	2 814	−2 086	−4 319	−5 368	−9 935	−27 943
B.9	General government	NNBK	−39 071	−50 823	−45 835	−41 438	−33 662	−17 723	3 458	10 333	18 367
B.9	Households and NPISH's	NSSZ	32 449	30 912	21 686	25 866	20 818	23 320	1 218	−6 141	−2 689
B.9	Rest of the world	NHRB	12 553	11 610	6 735	8 482	7 973	916	4 341	18 283	16 452
	Private non-financial corporations										
	Gross trading profits										
	Continental shelf profits	CAGJ	8 457	9 375	10 776	12 124	15 702	13 978	11 696	13 663	21 436
	Others	CAED	90 930	100 167	117 450	125 151	133 508	145 693	150 975	154 077	156 291
	Rental of buildings	FCBW	8 288	9 132	8 641	9 379	9 493	9 561	10 837	12 066	12 961
	less Holding gains of inventories	−DLQZ	−1 811	−2 392	−3 830	−4 489	−958	−361	753	−1 546	−2 162
B.2g	Gross operating surplus	NRJK	105 864	116 282	133 037	142 165	157 745	168 871	174 261	178 260	188 526
	Households and NPISH										
B.6g	Household gross disposable income	QWND	427 774	455 709	471 834	499 059	526 693	562 454	575 332	604 543	634 967
	Implied deflator of household and NPISH individual consumption expenditure index 1995=100[1]	YBFS	92.2	95.2	97.0	100.0	103.1	105.5	108.3	110.0	110.7
	Real household disposable income:										
	£ million at 1995 prices	RVGK	464 011	478 766	486 458	499 059	510 926	533 219	531 086	549 540	573 509
	Index 1995=100	OSXR	93.0	95.9	97.5	100.0	102.4	106.8	106.4	110.1	114.9
B.8g	Gross saving	NSSH	50 475	50 500	44 727	50 901	49 332	54 609	33 795	29 734	32 535
	Households total resources	NSSJ	514 451	541 000	559 956	591 842	626 485	665 136	683 708	720 464	756 359
	Saving ratio, per cent	RVGL	11.4	10.8	9.3	10.0	9.1	9.5	5.7	4.8	5.0

1 Rounded to one decimal place

Part 3:
The sector accounts

The sector accounts show the relationships between different sectors of the economy and different types of transactions. They summarise the transactions of particular groups of institutions in the economy, showing how income is distributed and redistributed, and how savings are used to add to wealth through investment in physical or financial assets. This section introduces the tables in Chapters 3 to 7 which deal with individual areas and subdivisions of the accounts.

This introduction to the sector accounts has been divided into the following areas:

The framework of the accounts
The institutional sectors
The types of transactions
The sequence of accounts
The statistical adjustment items
Balance sheets

The framework of the accounts

The framework of national accounts detailed in Part 1 highlights the five main kinds of accounts; goods and services, production, distribution and use of income, capital, and financial. The production account records the activity of producing goods and services. The distribution and use of income accounts record how incomes are generated by production, distributed to institutional units with claims on the value added created by production, redistributed among institutional units, and eventually used by households, government units or non-profit institutions serving households for purposes of final consumption or saving. The capital account records the flows of non-financial assets acquired and disposed. The financial account shows how the net lending or borrowing on the capital account is financed by transactions in financial instruments.

The distribution and use of income accounts can be elaborated to form a consistent set of sector accounts. This is done in two dimensions, by sectors and types of transaction. A third dimension, related to capital and financial transactions is that of asset and liability levels, the national and sector balance sheets. The sectors and types of transaction are described below.

The institutional sectors

The system identifies two kinds of institutions: consuming units (mostly households); and production units (mainly corporations and non-profit institutions or government). Units can own goods and assets, incur liabilities and engage in economic activities and transactions with other units in their own right. All units within the country are put in one of the sectors. Also, the rest of the world is treated as a sector in respect of its dealings with the United Kingdom.

Non-financial corporations are those which exist to produce goods and non-financial services. They are, in the UK, mainly public limited companies, private companies and partnerships. They are mostly owned privately, but there are some public corporations, which are shown separately.

Financial corporations are those engaged primarily in financial activities, and are subdivided into monetary financial institutions, other financial intermediaries and financial auxiliaries, and insurance corporations and pension funds.

General government comprises central government and local government.

The Households sector contains all the resident people of the United Kingdom as receivers of income and consumers of products. It includes individuals such as prisoners as well as conventional family units. It also contains one person businesses where household and business accounts cannot be separated. This sector currently includes non-profit institutions serving households, which include productive units such as charities and universities.

The Rest of the world sector comprises those units that are not in the United Kingdom. The accounts for the rest of the world only record transactions between units in the rest of the world and units in the UK, and are equivalent to the balance of payments.

The tables in Chapters 3 to 7 are based on the sector classification detailed above. More detailed definitions of these sectors are given in the appropriate chapters of UK National Accounts Concepts, Sources and Methods and, in full detail in the *Business Monitor MA23 Sector classification for the national accounts*, available from The Stationery Office.

The types of transactions

The other dimension is that of the types of transactions. These are divided into three types.

Transactions in products are related to goods and services, and include output, intermediate and final consumption, gross capital formation and exports and imports.

Distributive transactions transfer income or wealth between units of the economy, and include property income, taxes and subsidies, social contributions and benefits, and other current or capital transfers.

Financial transactions differ from distributive transactions in that they relate to transactions in financial claims by one unit on another, whereas distributive transactions are unrequited. The main categories in the classification of financial instruments are monetary gold and special drawing rights, deposits, securities other than shares, loans, shares and other equity, insurance and pension funds reserves and other accounts receivable/payable.

The sector accounts

The sequence of accounts

The transactions can be grouped broadly according to purpose in the production, distribution and use of income, capital or financial accounts. These are described briefly below:

Production account

The production account displays the transactions involved in the generation of income by the production of goods and services. This account is produced for the UK total economy (Table 1.6.1) and for the first four sectors (Tables 3.1.1, 4.1.1 etc.); the rest of the world does not have a production account. For each of the four sectors, the balancing item *gross value added* is shown as output less intermediate consumption. Gross value added at basic prices for each sector differs from gross domestic product for the UK total economy in that taxes *less* subsidies on products are not taken into the production accounts by sector but they are included within resources for the UK total economy. The sum of gross value added and taxes less subsidies on products for the UK economy is GDP at market prices.

Distribution and use of income account

The distribution and use of income accounts exist for all the main institutional sectors. To obtain the disposable income and savings of each sector we need to take account of transfers in and out of the sector. The accounts are not consolidated, so that in the whole economy account, transfers such as social contributions and benefits appear in both uses and resources.

These accounts describe the distribution and redistribution of income and its use in the form of final consumption. The distribution and use of income are analysed in four stages, each of which is presented as a separate account:

- the generation of income account
- the allocation of primary income account
- the secondary distribution of income account
- the use of disposable income account

Generation of income account

This is the first of the distribution and use of income accounts. It shows the sectors, sub-sectors and industries which are the source, rather than the destination, of income. It shows the derivation of the 'profit' arising from production, called the operating surplus (or mixed income in the case of unincorporated businesses in the households sector). The industry dimension is shown in Part 2, Table 2.1.

This account analyses the degree to which value added covers the compensation of employees (their wages and salaries etc.) and other taxes less subsidies on production. So it gives a figure for the operating surplus: the surplus (or deficit) on production activities before distributions such as interest, rent and income tax charges have been considered. Hence the operating surplus is the income which units obtain from their own use of the production facilities.

Note that taxes on production and imports are shown as a *use* by producing sectors in this account but not as a *resource* of government. This is because they do not relate to productive activity by government, and cannot therefore contribute to its operating surplus. They become a *resource* of government in the allocation of primary income account which follows.

Allocation of primary income account

This account shows the resident units and institutional sectors as recipients rather than producers of primary income. It demonstrates the extent to which operating surpluses are distributed (for example by dividends) to the owners of the enterprises. Also recorded in this account is the property income received by an owner of a financial asset in return for providing funds to, or putting a tangible non-produced asset at the disposal of, another unit. The receipt by government of taxes on production *less* subsidies is shown in *resources*.

The resources side of the allocation of primary income accounts includes the components of the income approach to measurement of gross domestic product and this is the starting point for the quarterly sector accounts. The accounts also include property income recorded as both resources for receipts and uses for payments.

The balance of this account is the gross balance of primary income (B.5g) for each sector, and if the gross balance of primary income is aggregated across all sectors of the UK economy the result is gross national income.

Secondary distribution of income account

This account describes how the balance of primary income for each institutional sector is allocated by redistribution; through transfers such as taxes on income, social contributions and benefits and other current transfers. It excludes social transfers in kind.

The balancing item of this account is gross disposable income (B.6g) which reflects current transactions and explicitly excludes capital transfers, real holding gains and losses, and the consequences of events such as natural disasters.

Use of disposable income account

This account illustrates how disposable income is split between final consumption expenditure and saving. In the system for recording economic accounts, only the government and the households and NPISH sectors have final consumption. In addition, for households and pension funds, there is an adjustment item in the account which reflects the way that transactions between households and pension funds are recorded. (This adjustment is D.8: Adjustment for the changes in the net equity of households in pension funds reserves.)

The sector accounts

The balancing item for this account, and thus for this whole group of distribution and use of income accounts, is gross saving (B.8g).

Thus it is only in the case of non-financial corporations (public and private), that undistributed income and saving are equivalent.

Capital account

The capital account is presented in two parts.

The first part shows that saving (B.8g) – the balance between national disposable income and final consumption expenditure from the production and distribution and use of income accounts – is reduced or increased by the balance of capital transfers (D.9) to provide an amount available for financing investment (in both non-financial and financial assets).

Then in the second part, total investment in non-financial assets is the sum of gross fixed capital formation (P.51), changes in inventories (P.52), acquisitions less disposals of valuables (P.53) and acquisitions less disposals of non-financial non-produced assets (K.2). The balance on the capital account is known as net lending or borrowing. Conceptually this net lending or borrowing for all the domestic sectors represents net lending or borrowing to the rest of the world sector.

Thus, if investment is lower than the amount available for investment, the balance will be positive and is regarded as lending (if negative the balance is borrowing). Where the capital accounts relate to the individual institutional sectors, the net lending/borrowing of a particular sector represents the amounts available for lending or borrowing to other sectors. The value of net lending/borrowing is the same irrespective of whether the accounts are shown before or after deduction of fixed capital consumption (K.1), provided a consistent approach is adopted throughout.

Financial account

The financial account elaborates the acquisition and disposal of financial assets and liabilities. Examples of financial assets include: bank deposits (which are assets of the depositors and liabilities of the banks), unit trust units (assets of the holders and liabilities of unit trusts) and Treasury Bills (assets of the holders and a liability of central government). The balance of all transactions in the financial account is net lending or borrowing.

The statistical adjustment items

Although in theory the net lending/borrowing from the financial account and the net lending/borrowing from the capital account for each sector should be equal, in practice they are not. This is because of the (sometimes substantial) errors and omissions in the accounts. The difference between the two balances is known as the statistical adjustment item.

Part of the balancing process for the economic accounts statistics for years before the latest one shown (i.e., for years t-1 and earlier) involves assessing and modifying the component variables so that the estimates of net lending/borrowing made from the income and capital accounts, and from the financial accounts, are the same at the level of the whole economy, and reasonably close to each other at the sector level.

The sectoral statistical adjustment items are shown in Table D below. They provide a measure of the reliability of the accounts.

Balance sheets

A financial balance sheet for each sector has been compiled using the same financial instrument classification as that used for financial transactions. The changes in the end period levels in the financial balance sheets do not equal the financial transactions because of holding gains or losses and reclassifications of units between sectors. Non-financial balance sheets for the ESA95 sectors are now included.

Further information

In addition to the articles and publications mentioned in Part 1, further information relating to the sector accounts and in particular the financial accounts can be found in the following articles and publications:

D Table D: Sector statistical adjustment

£ million

		1992	1993	1994	1995	1996	1997	1998	1999	2000
Households sector	NZDV	−893	7 064	−1 908	−4 808	−8 254	−6 392	155	−3 003	−4 530
Private non-financial corporations	NYPM	1 344	−1 979	1 380	3 709	6 138	342	7 145	6 504	6 950
Financial corporations	NYOX	−10 801	−6 382	−9 693	−6 083	−2 467	−1 659	−4 572	−6 012	3 698
Public corporations	NYPI	−822	296	422	90	177	−186	−132	−252	−807
Central government	NZDW	351	862	−64	268	−112	–	−231	−70	64
Local government	NYPC	851	−631	508	−28	134	−399	−375	642	790
Rest of the world	NYPO	9 970	770	9 355	6 852	4 384	8 294	−1 990	2 191	−6 817
Total[1]	-RVFE	–	–	–	–	–	–	–	–	−652

1 Equals, but opposite in sign to, the residual error observed between GDP measured by the factor income approach and by the expenditure approach

United Kingdom National Accounts 2001, © Crown copyright 2001

The sector accounts

Office for National Statistics *'Financial Statistics: Explanatory Handbook 2000 edition',* 1999, The Stationery Office

Office for National Statistics *'Financial Statistics',* monthly publication, The Stationery Office

Philip Turnbull (Central Statistical Office) *'The UK Sector Accounts'* Economic Trends, September 1993, HMSO

Bank Of England *'Bank Of England Statistical Abstract', 1999,* Bank Of England

Articles relating to the Public Sector Finances

Jeff Golland, Nigel Louth, Chris Hill *'New Format For Public Finances'* Economic Trends, June 1998, The Stationery Office

Articles relating to monetary aggregates (M0, M4)

Bank of England *'The Determination of M0 and M4'* Bank of England Quarterly Bulletin pages 46 to 50, February 1994

Bank of England *'Divisia measures of money'* Bank of England Quarterly Bulletin, May 1993

Articles relating to non-financial balance sheets and capital stock

Paul West (Office for National Statistics) *'Improving the Non-financial Balance Sheets'* Economic Trends, November 1998, The Stationery Office

Paul West and Alex Clifton-Fearnside (Office for National Statistics) *'The capital stock of the United Kingdom - some new developments in coverage and methodology'* Economic Trends, March 1999, The Stationery Office

Paul West and Alex Clifton-Fearnside (Office for National Statistics) *'Improving the Non-financial Balance Sheets and Capital Stock Estimates'* Economic Trends, November 1999, The Stationery Office

Part 3

Chapter 3

Non-financial corporations

Non-financial corporations

Non-financial corporations

3.1.1 Non-financial corporations
ESA95 sector S.11

£ million

			1992	1993	1994	1995	1996	1997	1998	1999
I	**PRODUCTION ACCOUNT**									
	Resources									
P.1	Output									
P.11	Market output	FAIN	715 027	769 305	845 618	915 806	987 054	1 054 129	1 112 016	1 168 703
P.12	Output for own final use	FAIO	5 148	4 626	4 289	4 484	4 245	4 523	4 268	4 393
P.1	Total resources	FAFA	720 175	773 931	849 907	920 290	991 299	1 058 652	1 116 284	1 173 096
	Uses									
P.2	Intermediate consumption	FAIQ	368 054	398 009	440 071	483 315	522 737	556 006	583 065	611 878
B.1g	Value added, gross	FAIS	352 121	375 922	409 836	436 975	468 562	502 646	533 219	561 218
Total	Total uses	FAFA	720 175	773 931	849 907	920 290	991 299	1 058 652	1 116 284	1 173 096
B.1g	Value added, gross	FAIS	352 121	375 922	409 836	436 975	468 562	502 646	533 219	561 218
-K.1	*less* Consumption of fixed capital	-DBGF	−50 785	−55 907	−56 632	−57 527	−58 526	−60 356	−60 844	−62 981
B.1n	Value added, net	FAIT	301 336	320 015	353 204	379 448	410 036	442 290	472 375	498 237

3.1.2 Non-financial corporations
ESA95 sector S.11

£ million

			1992	1993	1994	1995	1996	1997	1998	1999
II	**DISTRIBUTION AND USE OF INCOME ACCOUNTS**									
II.1	**PRIMARY DISTRIBUTION OF INCOME ACCOUNT**									
II.1.1	**GENERATION OF INCOME ACCOUNT** before deduction of fixed capital consumption									
	Resources									
B.1g	Total resources, gross value added	FAIS	352 121	375 922	409 836	436 975	468 562	502 646	533 219	561 218
	Uses									
D.1	Compensation of employees									
D.11	Wages and salaries	FAKT	202 394	212 337	227 222	241 175	253 831	274 961	295 601	316 224
D.12	Employers' social contributions	FAKU	25 547	27 731	29 426	31 314	34 105	36 294	39 961	42 518
D.1	Total	FCFV	227 941	240 068	256 648	272 489	287 937	311 256	335 562	358 742
D.2	Taxes on production and imports, paid									
D.29	Production taxes other than on products	EACJ	12 739	12 300	11 781	12 099	12 752	13 472	13 925	14 590
-D.3	*less* Subsidies, received									
-D.39	Production subsidies other than on products	-FCZK	−1 030	−915	−741	−765	−728	−711	−745	−750
B.2g	Operating surplus, gross	NQBE	112 471	124 470	142 148	153 152	168 601	178 629	184 477	188 636
Total	Total uses	FAIS	352 121	375 922	409 836	436 975	468 562	502 646	533 219	561 218
-K.1	After deduction of fixed capital consumption	-DBGF	−50 785	−55 907	−56 632	−57 527	−58 526	−60 356	−60 844	−62 981
B.2n	Operating surplus, net	FAIR	61 686	68 563	85 516	95 625	110 075	118 273	123 633	125 655

United Kingdom National Accounts 2001, © Crown copyright 2001

Non-financial corporations

3.1.3 Non-financial corporations
ESA95 sector S.11

£ million

			1992	1993	1994	1995	1996	1997	1998	1999	2000
II.1.2	**ALLOCATION OF PRIMARY INCOME ACCOUNT** before deduction of fixed capital consumption										
	Resources										
B.2g	Operating surplus, gross	NQBE	112 471	124 470	142 148	153 152	168 601	178 629	184 477	188 636	197 627
D.4	Property income, received										
D.41	Interest	EABC	10 816	7 596	7 566	9 337	9 660	9 874	13 940	10 756	13 980
D.42	Distributed income of corporations	EABD	14 962	14 281	16 446	22 367	22 919	26 548	25 086	21 440	23 896
D.43	Reinvested earnings on direct foreign investment	HDVR	4 711	7 748	12 138	11 376	13 417	11 747	10 979	16 108	22 610
D.44	Attributed property income of insurance policy-holders	FAOF	471	470	338	395	423	386	463	333	406
D.45	Rent	FAOG	110	106	108	110	114	118	118	117	117
D.4	Total	FAKY	31 070	30 201	36 596	43 585	46 533	48 673	50 586	48 754	61 009
Total	Total resources	FBXJ	143 541	154 671	178 744	196 737	215 134	227 302	235 063	237 390	258 636
	Uses										
D.4	Property income, paid										
D.41	Interest	EABG	29 131	23 247	23 243	26 575	26 047	27 738	33 025	32 965	40 094
D.42	Distributed income of corporations	NVCS	52 394	53 461	60 304	71 532	76 136	80 813	78 037	85 645	79 151
D.43	Reinvested earnings on direct foreign investment	HDVB	62	2 004	4 310	4 662	6 117	5 187	3 117	6 120	12 291
D.45	Rent	FBXO	682	734	693	719	815	756	584	469	1 221
D.4	Total	FBXK	82 269	79 446	88 550	103 488	109 115	114 494	114 763	125 199	132 757
B.5g	Balance of primary incomes, gross	NQBG	61 272	75 225	90 194	93 249	106 019	112 808	120 300	112 191	125 879
Total	Total uses	FBXJ	143 541	154 671	178 744	196 737	215 134	227 302	235 063	237 390	258 636
-K.1	After deduction of fixed capital consumption	-DBGF	-50 785	-55 907	-56 632	-57 527	-58 526	-60 356	-60 844	-62 981	-65 927
B.5n	Balance of primary incomes, net	FBXQ	10 487	19 318	33 562	35 722	47 493	52 452	59 456	49 210	59 952

3.1.4 Non-financial corporations
ESA95 sector S.11

£ million

			1992	1993	1994	1995	1996	1997	1998	1999	2000
II.2	**SECONDARY DISTRIBUTION OF INCOME ACCOUNT**										
	Resources										
B.5g	Balance of primary incomes, gross	NQBG	61 272	75 225	90 194	93 249	106 019	112 808	120 300	112 191	125 879
D.61	Social contributions										
D.612	Imputed social contributions	NSTJ	3 316	2 966	2 884	3 329	3 209	3 173	3 801	3 535	3 625
D.7	Current transfers other than taxes, social contributions and benefits										
D.72	Non-life insurance claims	FCBP	6 689	6 044	4 031	4 716	5 508	4 190	4 849	4 151	4 963
D.75	Miscellaneous transfers	NRJY	112	256	420	494	537	557	595	611	622
D.7	Total	NRJB	6 801	6 300	4 451	5 210	6 045	4 747	5 444	4 762	5 585
Total	Total resources	FCBR	71 389	84 491	97 529	101 788	115 273	120 728	129 545	120 488	135 089
	Uses										
D.5	Current taxes on income, wealth etc.										
D.51	Taxes on income	FCBS	14 246	13 536	15 234	19 005	22 417	27 557	25 590	21 637	25 017
D.62	Social benefits other than social transfers in kind	NSTJ	3 316	2 966	2 884	3 329	3 209	3 173	3 801	3 535	3 625
D.7	Current transfers other than taxes, social contributions and benefits										
D.71	Net non-life insurance premiums	FCBY	6 689	6 044	4 031	4 716	5 508	4 190	4 849	4 151	4 963
D.75	Miscellaneous current transfers	FDBI	240	272	311	343	1 455	402	363	373	383
D.7	Total, other current transfers	FCBX	6 929	6 316	4 342	5 059	6 963	4 592	5 212	4 524	5 346
B.6g	Disposable income, gross	NRJD	46 898	61 673	75 069	74 395	82 684	85 406	94 942	90 792	101 101
Total	Total uses	FCBR	71 389	84 491	97 529	101 788	115 273	120 728	129 545	120 488	135 089
-K.1	After deduction of fixed capital consumption	-DBGF	-50 785	-55 907	-56 632	-57 527	-58 526	-60 356	-60 844	-62 981	-65 927
B.6n	Disposable income, net	FCCF	-3 887	5 766	18 437	16 868	24 158	25 050	34 098	27 811	35 174

3.1.6 Non-financial corporations
ESA95 sector S.11

£ million

			1992	1993	1994	1995	1996	1997	1998	1999	2000
II.4.1	USE OF DISPOSABLE INCOME ACCOUNT										
	Resources										
B.6g	Total resources, gross disposable income	NRJD	46 898	61 673	75 069	74 395	82 684	85 406	94 942	90 792	101 101
	Uses										
B.8g	Total uses, gross saving	NRJD	46 898	61 673	75 069	74 395	82 684	85 406	94 942	90 792	101 101
-K.1	After deduction of fixed capital consumption	-DBGF	−50 785	−55 907	−56 632	−57 527	−58 526	−60 356	−60 844	−62 981	−65 927
B.8n	Saving, net	FCCF	−3 887	5 766	18 437	16 868	24 158	25 050	34 098	27 811	35 174

3.1.7 Non-financial corporations
ESA95 sector S.11

£ million

			1992	1993	1994	1995	1996	1997	1998	1999	2000
III	ACCUMULATION ACCOUNTS										
III.1	CAPITAL ACCOUNT										
III.1.1	CHANGE IN NET WORTH DUE TO SAVING AND CAPITAL TRANSFERS										
	Changes in liabilities and net worth										
B.8g	Saving, gross	NRJD	46 898	61 673	75 069	74 395	82 684	85 406	94 942	90 792	101 101
D.9	Capital transfers receivable										
D.92	Investment grants	FCCO	3 328	3 196	3 282	3 274	3 459	2 502	2 211	2 481	1 436
D.99	Other capital transfers	NZGD	43	107	12	1 604	144	3	2	11	12
D.9	Total	FCCQ	3 371	3 303	3 294	4 878	3 603	2 505	2 213	2 492	1 448
-D.9	*less* Capital transfers payable										
-D.91	Capital taxes	-QYKB	–	–	–	–	–	–	–	–	–
-D.99	Other capital transfers	-CISB	−120	−191	−126	−144	−162	−188	−193	−216	−290
-D.9	Total	-FCFX	−120	−191	−126	−144	−162	−188	−193	−216	−290
B.10.1g	Total change in liabilities and net worth	FCCY	50 149	64 785	78 237	79 129	86 125	87 723	96 962	93 068	102 259
	Changes in assets										
B.10.1g	Changes in net worth due to gross saving and capital transfers	FCCY	50 149	64 785	78 237	79 129	86 125	87 723	96 962	93 068	102 259
-K.1	After deduction of fixed capital consumption	-DBGF	−50 785	−55 907	−56 632	−57 527	−58 526	−60 356	−60 844	−62 981	−65 927
B.10.1n	Changes in net worth due to net saving and capital transfers	FCCV	−636	8 878	21 605	21 602	27 599	27 367	36 118	30 087	36 332
III.1.2	ACQUISITION OF NON-FINANCIAL ASSETS ACCOUNT										
	Changes in liabilities and net worth										
B.10.1n	Changes in net worth due to net saving and capital transfers	FCCV	−636	8 878	21 605	21 602	27 599	27 367	36 118	30 087	36 332
K.1	Consumption of fixed capital	DBGF	50 785	55 907	56 632	57 527	58 526	60 356	60 844	62 981	65 927
B.10.1g	Total change in liabilities and net worth	FCCY	50 149	64 785	78 237	79 129	86 125	87 723	96 962	93 068	102 259
	Changes in assets										
P.5	Gross capital formation										
P.51	Gross fixed capital formation	DBGP	59 946	60 388	61 494	70 220	77 669	86 052	95 385	99 947	104 676
P.52	Changes in inventories	DBGM	−1 907	74	3 591	4 384	1 452	3 730	4 196	4 984	1 912
P.53	Acquisitions less disposals of valuables	NPOV	−25	−30	−3	−52	−70	−60	28	−17	−74
P.5	Total gross capital formation	FCCZ	58 014	60 432	65 082	74 552	79 051	89 722	99 609	104 914	106 514
K.2	Acquisitions less disposals of non-produced non-financial assets	FCFY	41	254	214	301	117	195	1 002	694	584
B.9	Net lending(+) / net borrowing(-)	EABO	−7 906	4 099	12 941	4 276	6 957	−2 194	−3 649	−12 540	−4 839
Total	Total change in assets	FCCY	50 149	64 785	78 237	79 129	86 125	87 723	96 962	93 068	102 259

Non-financial corporations

3.1.8 Non-financial corporations
ESA95 sector S.11 Unconsolidated

£ million

			1992	1993	1994	1995	1996	1997	1998	1999	2000
III.2	**FINANCIAL ACCOUNT**										
F.A	**Net acquisition of financial assets**										
F.2	Currency and deposits										
F.21	Currency	NGIJ	−86	228	198	210	112	107	190	383	295
F.22	Transferable deposits										
F.2211	Sterling deposits with UK banks	NGIM	64	6 158	5 730	7 549	8 549	7 628	5 119	6 588	10 452
F.2212	Foreign currency deposits with UK banks	NGIN	−1 278	719	1 141	−1 021	4 538	2 279	−1 149	1 895	3 138
F.2213	Sterling deposits with building societies	NGIO	955	798	549	−901	174	40	−126	153	−134
F.229	Deposits with rest of the world monetary financial institutions	NGIP	−3 729	3 181	1 745	3 489	6 141	11 784	4 505	18 450	36 305
F.29	Other deposits	NGIQ	−19	1 907	430	405	802	930	−2 798	−177	91
F.2	Total currency and deposits	NGII	−4 093	12 991	9 793	9 731	20 316	22 768	5 741	27 292	50 147
F.3	Securities other than shares										
F.331	Short term: money market instruments										
F.3311	Issued by UK central government	NGIT	22	−86	−109	65	−97	9	8	144	−78
F.3312	Issued by UK local authorities	NGIX	−	−	−	−	−	−	−	−	−
F.3315	Issued by UK monetary financial institutions	NGIY	−583	−347	907	461	1 122	−1 303	2 543	−1 915	−126
F.3316	Issued by other UK residents	NGJD	−442	1 039	130	460	−112	−755	−1 486	−75	−2 901
F.3319	Issued by the rest of the world	NGJE	−535	912	73	−2	390	279	−956	722	1 110
F.332	Medium (1 to 5 year) and long term (over 5 year) bonds										
F.3321	Issued by UK central government	NGJG	−654	637	−87	428	−270	−62	1 363	−453	230
F.3322	Issued by UK local authorities	NGJJ	−	−	−	−	−	−	−	−	−
F.3325	Medium term bonds issued by UK MFIs[1]	NGJK	−37	−24	58	39	−116	64	44	21	−280
F.3326	Other medium & long term bonds issued by UK residents	NGJN	284	1 300	816	1 451	−1 600	−344	627	−1 350	1 297
F.3329	Long term bonds issued by the rest of the world	NGJO	675	174	2 443	1 040	884	−1 893	585	−1 062	4 527
F.34	Financial derivatives	NGJP	114	−8	−1	17	15	34	55	26	21
F.3	Total securities other than shares	NGIR	−1 156	3 597	4 230	3 959	216	−3 971	2 783	−3 942	3 800
F.4	Loans										
F.42	Long term loans										
F.421	Direct investment	NGKB	4 438	5 114	4 021	8 055	3 064	8 018	32 996	26 435	34 930
F.422	Loans secured on dwellings	NGKE	3	−	−1	−3	−2	−1	−	−	−
F.424	Other long-term loans by UK residents	NGKJ	−89	−416	−100	327	−2 103	3 839	−2 459	−1 106	14 540
F.4	Total loans	NGJT	4 352	4 698	3 920	8 379	959	11 856	30 537	25 329	49 470
F.5	Shares and other equity										
F.51	Shares and other equity, excluding mutual funds' shares										
F.514	Quoted UK shares	NGKQ	2 296	1 737	3 069	17 170	15 595	26 182	23 986	24 186	58 183
F.515	Unquoted UK shares	NGKR	−3 739	−2 725	1 248	−1 811	3 713	−1 620	5 993	−10 751	−26 718
F.519	Shares and other equity issued by the rest of the world	NGKV	8 290	11 563	18 120	18 322	18 372	28 794	48 497	112 243	171 770
F.52	Mutual funds' shares										
F.521	UK mutual funds' shares	NGKZ	6	26	42	12	11	6	1	1	9
F.5	Total shares and other equity	NGKL	6 853	10 601	22 479	33 693	37 691	53 362	78 477	125 679	203 244
F.6	Insurance technical reserves										
F.62	Prepayments of insurance premiums and reserves for outstanding claims	NGLE	1 052	422	479	920	2 694	163	−109	−291	321
F.7	Other accounts receivable	NGLF	1 582	1 803	3 340	−309	−864	1 585	1 341	−2 361	25 131
F.A	**Total net acquisition of financial assets**	NRGP	8 590	34 112	44 241	56 373	61 012	85 763	118 770	171 706	332 113

1 UK monetary financial institutions

3.1.8 Non-financial corporations
ESA95 sector S.11 Unconsolidated

£ million

				1992	1993	1994	1995	1996	1997	1998	1999	2000
III.2	**FINANCIAL ACCOUNT** continued											
F.L	**Net acquisition of financial liabilities**											
F.3	Securities other than shares											
F.331	Short term: money market instruments											
F.3316	Issued by UK residents other than government or monetary financial institutions		NGMH	−961	1 761	2 408	1 273	1 817	1 361	3 435	2 716	1 366
F.332	Medium (1 to 5 year) and long term (over 5 year) bonds											
F.3326	Other medium & long term bonds issued by UK residents or monetary financial institutions		NGMR	2 928	6 255	3 523	11 977	4 867	13 764	17 100	39 100	40 253
F.34	Financial derivatives		NGMT	–	–	–	–	–	–	–	–	–
F.3	Total securities other than shares		NGLV	1 967	8 016	5 931	13 250	6 684	15 125	20 535	41 816	41 619
F.4	Loans											
F.41	Short term loans											
F.411	Loans by UK monetary financial institutions, excluding loans secured on dwellings & financial leasing		NGMZ	−2 020	−12 243	−4 375	15 275	17 832	7 617	18 055	16 748	25 593
F.419	Loans by rest of the world monetary financial institutions		NGND	2 432	7 189	575	3 628	7 470	17 351	−3 254	5 960	13 950
F.42	Long term loans											
F.421	Direct investment		NGNF	6 558	3 204	4 891	1 051	4 031	10 617	36 102	19 463	57 812
F.423	Finance leasing		NGNM	−944	−100	20	1 040	1 385	1 570	67	−33	−199
F.424	Other long-term loans by UK residents		NGNN	1 114	262	1 235	652	−2 842	4 004	1 112	2 920	1 894
F.429	Other long-term loans by the rest of the world		NGNO	−587	−73	−117	−145	−14	−206	−5	–	–
F.4	Total loans		NGMX	6 553	−1 761	2 229	21 501	27 862	40 953	52 077	45 058	99 050
F.5	Shares and other equity											
F.51	Shares and other equity, excluding mutual funds' shares											
F.514	Quoted UK shares		NGNU	8 297	16 535	12 854	13 672	14 155	22 872	45 680	85 600	179 418
F.515	Unquoted UK shares		NGNV	966	3 208	5 571	6 735	8 425	7 257	5 947	9 096	17 704
F.516	Other UK equity (including direct investment in property)		NGNW	367	562	425	−474	4 680	886	632	833	1 298
F.5	Total shares and other equity		NGNP	9 630	20 305	18 850	19 933	27 260	31 015	52 259	95 529	198 420
F.7	Other accounts payable		NGOJ	−1 132	1 770	6 092	1 212	−1 436	1 020	4 561	8 095	4 006
F.L	**Total net acquisition of financial liabilities**		NRGR	17 018	28 330	33 102	55 896	60 370	88 113	129 432	190 498	343 095
B.9	**Net lending / borrowing**											
F.A	Total net acquisition of financial assets		NRGP	8 590	34 112	44 241	56 373	61 012	85 763	118 770	171 706	332 113
-F.L	*less* Total net acquisition of financial liabilities		−NRGR	−17 018	−28 330	−33 102	−55 896	−60 370	−88 113	−129 432	−190 498	−343 095
B.9f	**Net lending (+) / net borrowing (-), from financial account**		NYNT	−8 428	5 782	11 139	477	642	−2 350	−10 662	−18 792	−10 982
dB.9f	**Statistical discrepancy**		NYPF	522	−1 683	1 802	3 799	6 315	156	7 013	6 252	6 143
B.9	**Net lending (+) / net borrowing (-), from capital account**		EABO	−7 906	4 099	12 941	4 276	6 957	−2 194	−3 649	−12 540	−4 839

United Kingdom National Accounts 2001, © Crown copyright 2001

Non-financial corporations

3.1.9 Non-financial corporations
ESA95 sector S.11 Unconsolidated

£ billion

			1992	1993	1994	1995	1996	1997	1998	1999	2000
IV.3	**FINANCIAL BALANCE SHEET** at end of period										
AN	Non-financial assets	CGES	918.9	1 076.6	1 077.1	1 077.6	1 148.3	1 199.1	1 220.9	1 286.8	1 347.5
AF.A	**Financial assets**										
AF.2	Currency and deposits										
AF.21	Currency	NNZG	2.3	2.6	2.8	3.0	3.0	3.1	3.0	3.4	3.6
AF.22	Transferable deposits										
AF.221	Deposits with UK monetary financial institutions	NNZI	85.3	95.2	101.2	107.0	120.4	129.2	132.7	142.1	156.9
AF.229	Deposits with rest of the world monetary financial institutions	NNZM	36.8	41.9	43.1	46.7	47.5	60.1	65.0	78.7	102.4
AF.29	Other deposits	NNZN	4.5	7.9	8.3	8.8	10.1	10.5	7.8	7.4	7.5
AF.2	Total currency and deposits	NNZF	128.9	147.4	155.4	165.5	181.0	202.9	208.5	231.5	270.4
AF.3	Securities other than shares										
AF.331	Short term: money market instruments										
AF.3311	Issued by UK central government	NNZQ	0.3	0.2	0.1	0.1	–	–	–	0.2	0.1
AF.3312	Issued by UK local authorities	NNZU	–	–	–	–	–	–	–	–	–
AF.3315	Issued by UK monetary financial institutions	NNZV	3.8	3.6	4.4	4.9	6.1	4.7	7.1	5.3	5.9
AF.3316	Issued by other UK residents	NOLO	4.2	7.7	7.4	8.6	8.0	10.1	6.3	13.7	16.4
AF.3319	Issued by the rest of the world	NOLP	0.8	1.7	1.7	1.7	1.8	2.1	1.2	1.9	3.0
AF.332	Medium (1 to 5 year) and long term (over 5 year) bonds										
AF.3321	Issued by UK central government	NOLR	2.0	2.6	2.5	3.0	2.7	2.7	4.2	3.8	4.0
AF.3322	Issued by UK local authorities	NOLU	–	–	–	–	–	–	–	–	–
AF.3325	Medium term bonds issued by UK MFIs[1]	NOLV	–	–	0.1	0.1	0.1	0.2	0.2	0.2	0.1
AF.3326	Other medium & long term bonds issued by UK residents	NOLY	2.8	4.0	4.4	5.7	3.6	2.8	3.5	2.0	2.3
AF.3329	Long term bonds issued by the rest of the world	NOLZ	1.8	2.0	4.4	5.5	4.4	3.4	6.3	7.1	11.8
AF.34	Financial derivatives	NOMA	–	–	–	–	–	–	–	–	–
AF.3	Total securities other than shares	NNZO	15.7	21.8	25.0	29.6	26.6	26.1	28.9	34.2	43.7
AF.4	Loans										
AF.42	Long term loans										
AF.421	Direct investment	NOMM	50.4	52.3	55.7	65.6	69.3	75.8	109.9	129.4	167.7
AF.422	Loans secured on dwellings	NOMP	–	–	–	–	–	–	–	–	–
AF.424	Other long-term loans by UK residents	NOMU	8.9	9.5	10.2	10.3	10.3	10.6	10.2	10.5	10.1
AF.4	Total loans	NOME	59.3	61.8	65.9	76.0	79.6	86.4	120.1	140.0	177.8
AF.5	Shares and other equity										
AF.51	Shares and other equity, excluding mutual funds' shares										
AF.514	Quoted UK shares	NONB	12.1	7.6	11.4	9.1	10.2	14.2	20.5	39.4	26.4
AF.515	Unquoted UK shares	NONC	24.4	30.3	28.9	33.5	37.1	44.1	49.3	64.7	63.9
AF.519	Shares and other equity issued by the rest of the world	NONG	122.2	130.8	133.3	151.2	153.0	167.6	214.0	343.4	530.5
AF.52	Mutual funds' shares										
AF.521	UK mutual funds' shares	NONK	0.2	0.3	0.3	0.4	0.4	0.4	0.4	0.6	0.5
AF.5	Total shares and other equity	NOMW	158.9	169.0	173.9	194.3	200.7	226.3	284.2	448.0	621.2
AF.6	Insurance technical reserves										
AF.62	Prepayments of insurance premiums and reserves for outstanding claims	NONP	9.3	10.0	7.5	8.9	13.1	10.7	11.8	10.8	11.4
AF.7	Other accounts receivable	NONQ	90.0	90.9	92.3	91.8	90.8	92.4	93.2	92.1	117.0
AF.A	**Total financial assets**	NNZB	462.2	501.0	520.1	566.1	591.7	644.8	746.7	956.7	1 241.6

1 UK monetary financial institutions

3.1.9 Non-financial corporations
ESA95 sector S.11 Unconsolidated

Non-financial corporations

£ billion

			1992	1993	1994	1995	1996	1997	1998	1999	2000
IV.3	**FINANCIAL BALANCE SHEET** continued at end of period										
AF.L	**Financial liabilities**										
AF.3	Securities other than shares										
AF.331	Short term: money market instruments										
AF.3316	Issued by UK residents other than government or monetary financial institutions	NOOS	8.4	10.3	12.0	14.0	13.8	15.4	18.6	22.5	24.7
AF.332	Medium (1 to 5 year) and long term (over 5 year) bonds										
AF.3326	Other medium & long term bonds issued by UK residents or monetary financial institutions	NOPC	55.0	66.3	67.5	82.5	86.4	101.5	124.9	155.0	192.8
AF.34	Financial derivatives	NOPE	–	–	–	–	–	–	–	–	–
AF.3	Total securities other than shares	NOOG	63.4	76.7	79.5	96.5	100.2	116.9	143.5	177.5	217.5
AF.4	Loans										
AF.41	Short term loans										
AF.411	Loans by UK monetary financial institutions, excluding loans secured on dwellings & financial leasing	NOPK	185.9	171.2	161.5	174.5	188.6	191.6	205.5	222.1	249.6
AF.419	Loans by rest of the world monetary financial institutions	NOPO	39.0	54.2	54.7	63.1	64.7	79.7	77.7	92.3	101.5
AF.42	Long term loans										
AF.421	Direct investment	NOPQ	71.1	69.1	66.3	71.7	79.2	91.3	128.1	145.3	206.7
AF.423	Finance leasing	NOPX	14.8	14.7	14.5	15.5	16.9	18.5	18.5	18.5	18.3
AF.424	Other long-term loans by UK residents	NOPY	43.7	46.8	51.3	48.5	49.4	52.0	57.4	70.1	69.0
AF.429	Other long-term loans by the rest of the world	NOPZ	0.6	0.5	0.7	0.6	0.6	0.4	0.4	0.4	0.4
AF.4	Total loans	NOPI	354.9	356.5	349.0	373.9	399.4	433.4	487.6	548.6	645.5
AF.5	Shares and other equity										
AF.51	Shares and other equity, excluding mutual funds' shares										
AF.514	Quoted UK shares	NOQF	522.0	649.8	620.3	719.8	797.8	948.5	1 059.5	1 394.4	1 375.4
AF.515	Unquoted UK shares	NOQG	188.0	219.2	212.9	249.9	264.0	306.2	356.3	476.3	538.3
AF.516	Other UK equity (including direct investment in property)	NOQH	8.4	9.0	9.8	10.1	10.7	11.6	12.2	13.1	14.4
AF.5	Total shares and other equity	NOQA	718.4	877.9	843.1	979.8	1 072.5	1 266.3	1 428.0	1 883.7	1 928.1
AF.7	Other accounts payable	NOQU	117.1	121.2	126.1	127.1	126.0	128.3	130.0	137.0	138.7
AF.L	**Total financial liabilities**	NONT	1 253.8	1 432.3	1 397.6	1 577.3	1 698.2	1 945.1	2 189.2	2 746.8	2 929.9
BF.90	**Net financial assets / liabilities**										
AF.A	Total financial assets	NNZB	462.2	501.0	520.1	566.1	591.7	644.8	746.7	956.7	1 241.6
-AF.L	*less* Total financial liabilities	-NONT	–1 253.8	–1 432.3	–1 397.6	–1 577.3	–1 698.2	–1 945.1	–2 189.2	–2 746.8	–2 929.9
BF.90	Net financial assets (+) / liabilities (-)	NYOM	–791.6	–931.3	–877.5	–1 011.2	–1 106.5	–1 300.2	–1 442.5	–1 790.1	–1 688.3
	Net worth										
AN	Non-financial assets	CGES	918.9	1 076.6	1 077.1	1 077.6	1 148.3	1 199.1	1 220.9	1 286.8	1 347.5
BF.90	Net financial assets(+)/ liabilities(-)	NYOM	–791.6	–931.3	–877.5	–1 011.2	–1 106.5	–1 300.2	–1 442.5	–1 790.1	–1 688.3
B.90	**Net worth**	CGRV	127.3	145.3	199.6	66.4	41.8	–101.2	–221.6	–503.4	–340.7

United Kingdom National Accounts 2001, © Crown copyright 2001

Non-financial corporations

Non-financial corporations

3.2.1 Public non-financial corporations[1]
ESA95 sector S.11001

£ million

			1992	1993	1994	1995	1996	1997	1998	1999
I	**PRODUCTION ACCOUNT**									
	Resources									
P.1	Output									
P.11	Market output	FCZI	42 440	49 349	61 929	68 858	67 068	64 120	65 571	71 329
P.12	Output for own final use	GIRZ	698	511	266	179	185	210	213	224
P.1	Total resources	FCZG	43 138	49 860	62 195	69 037	67 253	64 330	65 784	71 553
	Uses									
P.2	Intermediate consumption	QZLQ	18 242	19 838	25 982	28 338	26 425	24 426	24 606	27 344
B.1g	Value added, gross	FACW	24 896	30 022	36 213	40 699	40 828	39 904	41 178	44 209
Total	Total uses	FCZG	43 138	49 860	62 195	69 037	67 253	64 330	65 784	71 553
B.1g	Value added, gross	FACW	24 896	30 022	36 213	40 699	40 828	39 904	41 178	44 209
-K.1	less Consumption of fixed capital	-NSRM	–5 868	–6 065	–6 312	–6 516	–5 740	–5 076	–5 052	–5 060
B.1n	Value added, net	FACX	19 028	23 957	29 901	34 183	35 088	34 828	36 126	39 149

1 Public financial corporations are also included to avoid disclosure of commercial information

3.2.2 Public non-financial corporations[1]
ESA95 sector S.11001

£ million

			1992	1993	1994	1995	1996	1997	1998	1999
II	**DISTRIBUTION AND USE OF INCOME ACCOUNTS**									
II.1	**PRIMARY DISTRIBUTION OF INCOME ACCOUNT**									
II.1.1	**GENERATION OF INCOME ACCOUNT**									
	before deduction of fixed capital consumption									
	Resources									
B.1g	Total resources, gross value added	FACW	24 896	30 022	36 213	40 699	40 828	39 904	41 178	44 209
	Uses									
D.1	Compensation of employees									
D.11	Wages and salaries	FAIZ	16 338	19 314	23 652	25 852	25 959	26 138	26 734	29 199
D.12	Employers' social contributions	FAOH	2 638	3 225	3 991	4 436	4 628	4 610	4 862	5 256
D.1	Total	FDDI	18 976	22 539	27 643	30 288	30 587	30 748	31 596	34 455
D.2	Taxes on production and imports, paid									
D.29	Production taxes other than on products	FAOK	343	210	200	189	113	109	111	109
-D.3	less Subsidies, received									
-D.39	Production subsidies other than on products	-ARDD	–1 030	–915	–741	–765	–728	–711	–745	–731
B.2g	Operating surplus, gross	NRJT	6 607	8 188	9 111	10 987	10 856	9 758	10 216	10 376
Total	Total uses	FACW	24 896	30 022	36 213	40 699	40 828	39 904	41 178	44 209
-K.1	After deduction of fixed capital consumption	-NSRM	–5 868	–6 065	–6 312	–6 516	–5 740	–5 076	–5 052	–5 060
B.2n	Operating surplus, net	FAOO	739	2 123	2 799	4 471	5 116	4 682	5 164	5 316

1 Public financial corporations are also included to avoid disclosure of commercial information

Non-financial corporations

3.2.3 Public non-financial corporations[1]
ESA95 sector S.11001

£ million

			1992	1993	1994	1995	1996	1997	1998	1999	2000
II.1.2	**ALLOCATION OF PRIMARY INCOME ACCOUNT** before deduction of fixed capital consumption										
	Resources										
B.2g	Operating surplus, gross	NRJT	6 607	8 188	9 111	10 987	10 856	9 758	10 216	10 376	9 101
D.4	Property income, received										
D.41	Interest	CPBV	444	413	492	639	820	697	849	657	643
D.42	Distributed income of corporations	FACT	15	15	14	22	18	22	23	30	31
D.44	Property income attributed to insurance policy-holders	FAOT	–	–	–	–	–	–	–	–	–
D.45	Rent	FAOZ	–	–	–	–	–	–	–	–	–
D.4	Total	FAOP	459	428	506	661	838	719	872	687	674
Total	Total resources	FAOU	7 066	8 616	9 617	11 648	11 694	10 477	11 088	11 063	9 775
	Uses										
D.4	Property income, paid										
D.41	Interest	XAQZ	1 222	1 492	2 186	2 415	2 557	1 916	2 335	2 689	2 362
D.42	Distributed income of corporations	ZOYB	4 223	5 107	5 492	5 380	5 413	4 972	5 342	4 810	4 773
D.45	Rent	FAOZ	–	–	–	–	–	–	–	–	–
D.4	Total	FAOV	5 445	6 599	7 678	7 795	7 970	6 888	7 677	7 499	7 135
B.5g	Balance of primary incomes, gross	NRJX	1 621	2 017	1 939	3 853	3 724	3 589	3 411	3 564	2 640
Total	Total uses	FAOU	7 066	8 616	9 617	11 648	11 694	10 477	11 088	11 063	9 775
-K.1	After deduction of fixed capital consumption	-NSRM	–5 868	–6 065	–6 312	–6 516	–5 740	–5 076	–5 052	–5 060	–4 983
B.5n	Balance of primary incomes, net	FARX	–4 247	–4 048	–4 373	–2 663	–2 016	–1 487	–1 641	–1 496	–2 343

1 Public financial corporations are also included to avoid disclosure of commercial information

3.2.4 Public non-financial corporations[1]
ESA95 sector S.11001

£ million

			1992	1993	1994	1995	1996	1997	1998	1999	2000
II.2	**SECONDARY DISTRIBUTION OF INCOME ACCOUNT**										
	Resources										
B.5g	Balance of primary incomes, gross	NRJX	1 621	2 017	1 939	3 853	3 724	3 589	3 411	3 564	2 640
D.61	Social contributions										
D.612	Imputed social contributions	EWRS	217	261	362	341	288	266	260	259	244
D.7	Current transfers other than taxes, social contributions and benefits										
D.72	Net non-life insurance claims	FDDF	–	–	–	–	–	–	–	–	–
D.75	Miscellaneous transfers	RUDY	112	256	420	494	537	557	595	611	622
D.7	Total	FDEK	112	256	420	494	537	557	595	611	622
Total	Total resources	FDDH	1 950	2 534	2 721	4 688	4 549	4 412	4 266	4 434	3 506
	Uses										
D.5	Current taxes on income, wealth etc.										
D.51	Taxes on income	FCCS	199	162	174	299	268	374	379	340	218
D.62	Social benefits other than social transfers in kind	EWRS	217	261	362	341	288	266	260	259	244
D.7	Current transfers other than taxes, social contributions and benefits										
D.71	Net non-life insurance premiums	FDDM	–	–	–	–	–	–	–	–	–
B.6g	Disposable income, gross	NRKD	1 534	2 111	2 185	4 048	3 993	3 772	3 627	3 835	3 044
Total	Total uses	FDDH	1 950	2 534	2 721	4 688	4 549	4 412	4 266	4 434	3 506
-K.1	After deduction of fixed capital consumption	-NSRM	–5 868	–6 065	–6 312	–6 516	–5 740	–5 076	–5 052	–5 060	–4 983
B.6n	Disposable income, net	FDDP	–4 334	–3 954	–4 127	–2 468	–1 747	–1 304	–1 425	–1 225	–1 939

1 Public financial corporations are also included to avoid disclosure of commercial information

Non-financial corporations

3.2.6 Public non-financial corporations
ESA95 sector S.11001

£ million

			1992	1993	1994	1995	1996	1997	1998	1999	2000
II.4.1	USE OF DISPOSABLE INCOME ACCOUNT										
	Resources										
B.6g	Total resources, gross disposable income	NRKD	1 534	2 111	2 185	4 048	3 993	3 772	3 627	3 835	3 044
	Uses										
B.8g	Total uses, gross saving	NRKD	1 534	2 111	2 185	4 048	3 993	3 772	3 627	3 835	3 044
-K.1	After deduction of fixed capital consumption	-NSRM	–5 868	–6 065	–6 312	–6 516	–5 740	–5 076	–5 052	–5 060	–4 983
B.8n	Saving, net	FDDP	–4 334	–3 954	–4 127	–2 468	–1 747	–1 304	–1 425	–1 225	–1 939

3.2.7 Public non-financial corporations[1]
ESA95 sector S.11001

£ million

			1992	1993	1994	1995	1996	1997	1998	1999	2000
III	ACCUMULATION ACCOUNTS										
III.1	CAPITAL ACCOUNT										
III.1.1	CHANGE IN NET WORTH DUE TO SAVING AND CAPITAL TRANSFERS										
	Changes in liabilities and net worth										
B.8g	Saving, gross	NRKD	1 534	2 111	2 185	4 048	3 993	3 772	3 627	3 835	3 044
D.9	Capital transfers receivable										
D.92	Investment grants	FDBV	2 893	2 781	2 747	2 697	2 869	1 790	1 121	1 416	875
D.99	Other capital transfers	NZGD	43	107	12	1 604	144	3	2	11	12
D.9	Total	FDBU	2 936	2 888	2 759	4 301	3 013	1 793	1 123	1 427	887
B.10.1g	Total change in liabilities and net worth	FDEG	4 470	4 999	4 944	8 349	7 006	5 565	4 750	5 262	3 931
	Changes in assets										
B.10.1g	Changes in net worth due to gross saving and capital transfers	FDEG	4 470	4 999	4 944	8 349	7 006	5 565	4 750	5 262	3 931
-K.1	After deduction of fixed capital consumption	-NSRM	–5 868	–6 065	–6 312	–6 516	–5 740	–5 076	–5 052	–5 060	–4 983
B.10.1n	Changes in net worth due to net saving and capital transfers	FDED	–1 398	–1 066	–1 368	1 833	1 266	489	–302	202	–1 052
III.1.2	ACQUISITION OF NON-FINANCIAL ASSETS ACCOUNT										
	Changes in liabilities and net worth										
B.10.1n	Changes in net worth due to net saving and capital transfers	FDED	–1 398	–1 066	–1 368	1 833	1 266	489	–302	202	–1 052
K.1	Consumption of fixed capital	NSRM	5 868	6 065	6 312	6 516	5 740	5 076	5 052	5 060	4 983
B.10.1g	Total change in liabilities and net worth	FDEG	4 470	4 999	4 944	8 349	7 006	5 565	4 750	5 262	3 931
	Changes in assets										
P.5	Gross capital formation										
P.51	Gross fixed capital formation	FCCJ	5 669	5 457	5 627	5 776	5 256	4 551	4 400	4 754	4 831
P.52	Changes in inventories	DHHL	14	–164	–313	–158	–199	–1	215	–117	–208
P.5	Total	FDEH	5 683	5 293	5 314	5 618	5 057	4 550	4 615	4 637	4 623
K.2	Acquisitions less disposals of non-produced non-financial assets	FDEJ	–264	–297	–319	–139	–215	–267	–257	–184	–123
B.9g	Net lending (+) / net borrowing (-)	CPCM	–949	3	–51	2 870	2 164	1 282	392	809	–569
Total	Total change in assets	FDEG	4 470	4 999	4 944	8 349	7 006	5 565	4 750	5 262	3 931

1 Public financial corporations are also included to avoid disclosure of commercial information

Non-financial corporations

3.2.8 Public non-financial corporations
ESA95 sector S.11001 Unconsolidated

£ million

			1992	1993	1994	1995	1996	1997	1998	1999	2000
III.2	**FINANCIAL ACCOUNT**										
F.A	Net acquisition of financial assets										
F.2	Currency and deposits										
F.21	Currency	NCXV	−148	87	122	72	−8	−106	53	125	116
F.22	Transferable deposits										
F.2211	Sterling deposits with UK banks	NCXY	366	500	−155	625	−633	412	1 019	−763	−669
F.2212	Foreign currency deposits with UK banks	NCXZ	23	−29	58	3	−9	−59	−31	−5	65
F.2213	Sterling deposits with building societies	NCYA	−2	−6	158	−117	84	45	−127	−10	−92
F.229	Deposits with rest of the world monetary financial institutions	NCYB	−	−	−	−	−	−	−	−	−
F.29	Other deposits	NCYC	156	1 089	644	989	832	835	−2 778	82	311
F.2	Total currency and deposits	NCXU	395	1 641	827	1 572	266	1 127	−1 864	−571	−269
F.3	Securities other than shares										
F.331	Short term: money market instruments										
F.3311	Issued by UK central government	NCYF	30	112	−142	100	−101	−	−	140	−50
F.3312	Issued by UK local authorities	NCYJ	−	−	−	−	−	−	−	−	−
F.3315	Issued by UK monetary financial institutions	NCYK	−	−	−	−	−	−	359	−	−
F.3316	Issued by other UK residents	NCYP	−	−	−	−	−	−	288	−191	−
F.332	Medium (1 to 5 year) and long term (over 5 year) bonds										
F.3321	Issued by UK central government	NCYS	−21	43	519	410	845	326	981	358	−173
F.3326	Other medium & long term bonds issued by UK residents	NCYZ	−	−	−	−	−	−	−	−	−
F.3329	Long term bonds issued by the rest of the world	NCZA	−	−	−	−	−	−	−	−	−
F.34	Financial derivatives	NSUH	114	−8	−1	17	15	34	55	26	21
F.3	Total securities other than shares	NCYD	123	147	376	527	759	360	1 683	333	−202
F.4	Loans										
F.42	Long term loans										
F.421	Direct investment loans	CFZI	−	−	−	−	−	−	−	−	310
F.422	Loans secured on dwellings	NCZQ	3	−	−1	−3	−2	−1	−	−	−
F.424	Other long-term loans by UK residents	NCZV	17	100	209	93	−473	−20	173	91	−177
F.4	Total loans	NCZF	20	100	208	90	−475	−21	173	91	133
F.5	Shares and other equity										
F.51	Shares and other equity, excluding mutual funds' shares										
F.514	Quoted UK shares	NEBC	−	−	−	−	−	12	−8	−	−
F.515	Unquoted UK shares	NEBD	−7	−1	−2	−400	−2 310	−353	−45	−	−
F.519	Shares and other equity issued by the rest of the world	NEBH	84	210	101	64	−9	68	20	379	30
F.5	Total shares and other equity	NCZX	77	209	99	−336	−2 319	−273	−33	379	30
F.6	Insurance technical reserves										
F.62	Prepayments of insurance premiums and reserves for outstanding claims	NEBQ	−	−	−	−	−	−	−	−	−
F.7	Other accounts receivable	NEBR	17	−837	383	−722	84	269	896	963	665
F.A	**Total net acquisition of financial assets**	NCXQ	632	1 260	1 893	1 131	−1 685	1 462	855	1 195	357

Non-financial corporations

3.2.8 Public non-financial corporations
ESA95 sector S.11001 Unconsolidated

continued

£ million

			1992	1993	1994	1995	1996	1997	1998	1999	2000
III.2	**FINANCIAL ACCOUNT** continued										
F.L	**Net acquisition of financial liabilities**										
F.3	Securities other than shares										
F.332	Medium (1 to 5 year) and long term (over 5 year) bonds										
F.3326	Other medium & long term bonds issued by UK residents or monetary financial institutions	NEOF	−10	−6	−2	−7	–	–	–	–	–
F.3	Total securities other than shares	NENJ	−10	−6	−2	−7	–	–	–	–	–
F.4	Loans										
F.41	Short term loans										
F.411	Loans by UK monetary financial institutions, excluding loans secured on dwellings & financial leasing	NEON	−66	−60	−40	−11	−117	−12	97	−26	82
F.42	Long term loans										
F.423	Finance leasing	NEPA	8	1	11	−12	4	−1	16	35	23
F.424	Other long-term loans by UK residents	NEPB	1 269	1 123	713	−817	−5 954	91	−148	227	42
F.429	Other long-term loans by the rest of the world	NEPC	−430	−18	−116	−144	−14	−206	−5	–	–
F.4	Total loans	NEOL	781	1 046	568	−984	−6 081	−128	−40	236	147
F.5	Shares and other equity										
F.51	Shares and other equity, excluding mutual funds' shares										
F.515	Unquoted UK shares	NEPJ	12	16	9	10	−1	–	–	–	–
F.516	Other UK equity (including direct investment in property)	NEPK	–	–	–	–	3 283	–	–	–	–
F.5	Total shares and other equity	NEPD	12	16	9	10	3 282	–	–	–	–
F.7	Other accounts payable	NEPX	−24	497	1 791	−668	−873	122	371	−102	−28
F.L	**Total net acquisition of financial liabilities**	NEBU	759	1 553	2 366	−1 649	−3 672	−6	331	134	119
B.9	**Net lending / borrowing**										
F.A	Total net acquisition of financial assets	NCXQ	632	1 260	1 893	1 131	−1 685	1 462	855	1 195	357
-F.L	*less* Total net acquisition of financial liabilities	-NEBU	−759	−1 553	−2 366	1 649	3 672	6	−331	−134	−119
B.9f	**Net lending (+) / net borrowing (−), from financial account**	NZEC	−127	−293	−473	2 780	1 987	1 468	524	1 061	238
dB.9f	Statistical discrepancy	NYPI	−822	296	422	90	177	−186	−132	−252	−807
B.9g	**Net lending (+) / net borrowing (−), from capital account**	CPCM	−949	3	−51	2 870	2 164	1 282	392	809	−569

Non-financial corporations

3.2.9 Public non-financial corporations
ESA95 sector S.11001 Unconsolidated

£ billion

			1992	1993	1994	1995	1996	1997	1998	1999	2000
IV.3	**FINANCIAL BALANCE SHEET** at end of period										
AN	Non-financial assets	CGGN	142.6	144.3	147.8	131.9	127.8	125.5	133.5	136.6	143.3
AF.A	**Financial assets**										
AF.2	Currency and deposits										
AF.21	Currency	NKDS	0.5	0.6	0.7	0.8	0.8	0.7	0.7	0.9	1.0
AF.22	Transferable deposits										
AF.221	Deposits with UK monetary financial institutions	NKDU	2.3	2.1	2.4	2.9	2.4	2.3	3.2	2.5	1.6
AF.229	Deposits with rest of the world monetary financial institutions	NKDY	–	–	–	–	–	–	–	–	–
AF.29	Other deposits	NKDZ	1.5	2.6	3.1	4.1	4.9	5.8	3.0	2.9	3.1
AF.2	Total currency and deposits	NKDR	4.3	5.3	6.3	7.8	8.1	8.8	6.9	6.2	5.7
AF.3	Securities other than shares										
AF.331	Short term: money market instruments										
AF.3311	Issued by UK central government	NKEC	–	0.1	–	0.1	–	–	–	0.1	0.1
AF.3312	Issued by UK local authorities	NKEG	–	–	–	–	–	–	–	–	–
AF.3315	Issued by UK monetary financial institutions	NKEH	–	–	–	–	–	–	0.4	0.4	0.4
AF.3316	Issued by other UK residents	NKEM	–	–	–	–	–	–	0.3	0.1	0.1
AF.332	Medium (1 to 5 year) and long term (over 5 year) bonds										
AF.3321	Issued by UK central government	NKEP	0.2	0.2	0.7	1.1	2.0	2.3	3.3	3.7	3.5
AF.3322	Issued by UK local authorities	NKES	–	–	–	–	–	–	–	–	–
AF.3326	Other medium & long term bonds issued by UK residents	NKEW	–	–	–	–	–	–	–	–	–
AF.3	Total securities other than shares	NKEA	0.2	0.4	0.8	1.3	2.0	2.4	4.0	4.3	4.1
AF.4	Loans										
AF.42	Long term loans										
AF.421	Direct investment loans	ZYBN	–	–	–	–	–	–	–	–	0.3
AF.422	Loans secured on dwellings	NKFN	–	–	–	–	–	–	–	–	–
AF.424	Other long-term loans by UK residents	NKFS	3.0	3.3	3.5	3.6	3.2	3.1	2.5	2.6	2.2
AF.4	Total loans	NKFC	3.0	3.4	3.6	3.6	3.3	3.2	2.5	2.6	2.5
AF.5	Shares and other equity										
AF.51	Shares and other equity, excluding mutual funds' shares										
AF.514	Quoted UK shares	NKFZ	–	–	–	–	–	–	–	–	–
AF.515	Unquoted UK shares	NKGA	0.2	0.3	0.2	0.3	0.3	0.3	0.3	0.3	0.3
AF.519	Shares and other equity issued by the rest of the world	NKGE	0.4	0.6	0.7	0.8	0.7	0.8	0.8	1.1	1.3
AF.5	Total shares and other equity	NKFU	0.7	0.9	1.0	1.0	1.0	1.1	1.1	1.4	1.6
AF.6	Insurance technical reserves										
AF.62	Prepayments of insurance premiums and reserves for outstanding claims	NKGN	–	–	–	–	–	–	–	–	–
AF.7	Other accounts receivable	NKGO	4.2	3.5	3.9	2.9	2.7	2.5	2.7	2.5	3.0
AF.A	**Total financial assets**	NKFB	12.5	13.4	15.4	16.7	17.1	17.8	17.3	17.1	16.9

3.2.9 Public non-financial corporations
ESA95 sector S.11001 Unconsolidated

Non-financial corporations

£ billion

			1992	1993	1994	1995	1996	1997	1998	1999	2000
IV.3	**FINANCIAL BALANCE SHEET** continued at end of period										
AF.L	**Financial liabilities**										
AF.3	Securities other than shares										
AF.332	Medium (1 to 5 year) and long term (over 5 year) bonds										
AF.3326	Other medium & long term bonds issued by UK residents or monetary financial institutions	NKIA	1.3	0.9	0.9	0.4	0.7	0.8	1.0	1.2	1.3
AF.3	Total securities other than shares	NKHE	1.3	0.9	0.9	0.4	0.7	0.8	1.0	1.2	1.3
AF.4	Loans										
AF.41	Short term loans										
AF.411	Loans by UK monetary financial institutions, excluding loans secured on dwellings & financial leasing	NKII	0.8	0.8	0.4	0.4	0.3	0.3	0.4	0.3	0.4
AF.419	Loans by rest of the world monetary financial institutions	NKIM	–	–	–	–	–	–	–	–	–
AF.42	Long term loans										
AF.423	Finance leasing	NKIV	0.3	0.3	0.3	0.3	0.3	0.3	0.3	0.3	0.3
AF.424	Other long-term loans by UK residents	NKIW	23.5	24.9	25.6	24.8	21.9	22.0	26.5	25.7	25.9
AF.429	Other long-term loans by the rest of the world	NKIX	0.1	0.1	0.3	0.2	0.2	–	–	–	–
AF.4	Total loans	NKIG	24.7	26.0	26.5	25.5	22.6	22.6	27.2	26.4	26.6
AF.5	Shares and other equity										
AF.51	Shares and other equity, excluding mutual funds' shares										
AF.515	Unquoted UK shares	NKJE	0.4	0.4	1.1	1.1	0.4	0.3	0.4	0.4	0.4
AF.5	Total shares and other equity	NKIY	0.4	0.4	1.1	1.1	0.4	0.3	0.4	0.4	0.4
AF.7	Other accounts payable	NKJS	5.7	8.0	10.0	9.4	8.6	8.2	8.1	8.5	8.4
AF.L	**Total financial liabilities**	NKIF	32.1	35.3	38.6	36.4	32.3	31.9	36.7	36.5	36.8
BF.90	**Net financial assets / liabilities**										
AF.A	Total financial assets	NKFB	12.5	13.4	15.4	16.7	17.1	17.8	17.3	17.1	16.9
-AF.L	*less* Total financial liabilities	-NKIF	−32.1	−35.3	−38.6	−36.4	−32.3	−31.9	−36.7	−36.5	−36.8
BF.90	**Net financial assets (+) / liabilities (-)**	NYOP	−19.7	−21.9	−23.1	−19.7	−15.1	−14.0	−19.4	−19.5	−19.9
	Net worth										
AN	Non-financial assets	CGGN	142.6	144.3	147.8	131.9	127.8	125.5	133.5	136.6	143.3
BF.90	Net financial assets (+) / liabilities (-)	NYOP	−19.7	−21.9	−23.1	−19.7	−15.1	−14.0	−19.4	−19.5	−19.9
B.90	**Net worth**	CGRW	123.0	122.4	124.7	112.3	112.7	111.5	114.0	117.1	123.4

Non-financial corporations

Non-financial corporations

3.3.1 Private non-financial corporations
ESA95 sectors S.11002 National controlled and S.11003 Foreign controlled

£ million

			1992	1993	1994	1995	1996	1997	1998	1999
I	**PRODUCTION ACCOUNT**									
	Resources									
P.1	Output									
P.11	Market output	FBXS	672 587	719 956	783 689	846 948	919 986	990 009	1 046 445	1 097 374
P.12	Output for own final use	FDCG	4 450	4 115	4 023	4 305	4 060	4 313	4 055	4 169
P.1	Total resources	FBXR	677 037	724 071	787 712	851 253	924 046	994 322	1 050 500	1 101 543
	Uses									
P.2	Intermediate consumption	FARP	349 812	378 171	414 089	454 977	496 312	531 580	558 459	584 534
B.1g	Value added, gross	FARR	327 225	345 900	373 623	396 276	427 734	462 742	492 041	517 009
Total	Total uses	FBXR	677 037	724 071	787 712	851 253	924 046	994 322	1 050 500	1 101 543
B.1g	Value added, gross	FARR	327 225	345 900	373 623	396 276	427 734	462 742	492 041	517 009
-K.1	*less* Consumption of fixed capital	-NSRK	-44 917	-49 842	-50 320	-51 011	-52 786	-55 280	-55 792	-57 921
B.1n	Value added, net	FARS	282 308	296 058	323 303	345 265	374 948	407 462	436 249	459 088

3.3.2 Private non-financial corporations
ESA95 sectors S.11002 National controlled and S.11003 Foreign controlled

£ million

			1992	1993	1994	1995	1996	1997	1998	1999
II	**DISTRIBUTION AND USE OF INCOME ACCOUNTS**									
II.1	**PRIMARY DISTRIBUTION OF INCOME ACCOUNT**									
II.1.1	**GENERATION OF INCOME ACCOUNT** before deduction of fixed capital consumption									
	Resources									
B.1g	Total resources, gross value added	FARR	327 225	345 900	373 623	396 276	427 734	462 742	492 041	517 009
	Uses									
D.1	Compensation of employees									
D.11	Wages and salaries	FAAX	186 056	193 023	203 570	215 323	227 872	248 823	268 867	287 025
D.12	Employers' social contributions	FABH	22 909	24 506	25 435	26 878	29 477	31 684	35 099	37 262
D.1	Total	FBDA	208 965	217 529	229 005	242 201	257 350	280 508	303 966	324 287
D.2	Taxes on production and imports, paid									
D.29	Production taxes other than on products	FACQ	12 396	12 090	11 581	11 910	12 639	13 363	13 814	14 481
-D.39	Production subsidies other than on products	-LITS	–	–	–	–	–	–	–	-19
B.2g	Operating surplus, gross	NRJK	105 864	116 282	133 037	142 165	157 745	168 871	174 261	178 260
Total	Total uses	FARR	327 225	345 900	373 623	396 276	427 734	462 742	492 041	517 009
-K.1	After deduction of fixed capital consumption	-NSRK	-44 917	-49 842	-50 320	-51 011	-52 786	-55 280	-55 792	-57 921
B.2n	Operating surplus, net	FACU	60 947	66 440	82 717	91 154	104 959	113 591	118 469	120 339

United Kingdom National Accounts 2001, © Crown copyright 2001

Non-financial corporations

3.3.3 Private non-financial corporations
ESA95 sectors S.11002 National controlled and S.11003 Foreign controlled

£ million

			1992	1993	1994	1995	1996	1997	1998	1999	2000
II.1.2	**ALLOCATION OF PRIMARY INCOME ACCOUNT** before deduction of fixed capital consumption										
	Resources										
B.2g	Operating surplus, gross[1]	NRJK	105 864	116 282	133 037	142 165	157 745	168 871	174 261	178 260	188 526
D.4	Property income, received										
D.41	Interest	DSZR	10 372	7 183	7 074	8 698	8 840	9 177	13 091	10 099	13 337
D.42	Distributed income of corporations	DSZS	14 947	14 266	16 432	22 345	22 901	26 526	25 063	21 410	23 865
D.43	Reinvested earnings on direct foreign investment	HDVR	4 711	7 748	12 138	11 376	13 417	11 747	10 979	16 108	22 610
D.44	Property income attributed to insurance policy-holders	FCFP	471	470	338	395	423	386	463	333	406
D.45	Rent	FAOL	110	106	108	110	114	118	118	117	117
D.4	Total	FACV	30 611	29 773	36 090	42 924	45 695	47 954	49 714	48 067	60 335
Total	Total resources	FCFQ	136 475	146 055	169 127	185 089	203 440	216 825	223 975	226 327	248 861
	Uses										
D.4	Property income, paid										
D.41	Interest	DSZV	27 909	21 755	21 057	24 160	23 490	25 822	30 690	30 276	37 732
D.42	Distributed income of corporations[2]	NVDC	48 171	48 354	54 812	66 152	70 723	75 841	72 695	80 835	74 378
D.43	Reinvested earnings on direct foreign investment	HDVB	62	2 004	4 310	4 662	6 117	5 187	3 117	6 120	12 291
D.45	Rent	FCFU	682	734	693	719	815	756	584	469	1 221
D.4	Total	FCFR	76 824	72 847	80 872	95 693	101 145	107 606	107 086	117 700	125 622
B.5g	Balance of primary incomes, gross	NRJM	59 651	73 208	88 255	89 396	102 295	109 219	116 889	108 627	123 239
Total	Total uses	FCFQ	136 475	146 055	169 127	185 089	203 440	216 825	223 975	226 327	248 861
-K.1	After deduction of fixed capital consumption	-NSRK	-44 917	-49 842	-50 320	-51 011	-52 786	-55 280	-55 792	-57 921	-60 944
B.5n	Balance of primary incomes, net	FCFW	14 734	23 366	37 935	38 385	49 509	53 939	61 097	50 706	62 295

1 Companies gross trading profits and rental of buildings less holding gains of inventories, details of which are shown in the sector accounts summary table on page 108

2 *of which*:

		1992	1993	1994	1995	1996	1997	1998	1999	2000
Dividend payments	NETZ	31 728	32 250	36 365	46 218	51 609	56 250	51 686	60 772	51 900

3.3.4 Private non-financial corporations
ESA95 sectors S.11002 National controlled and S.11003 Foreign controlled

£ million

			1992	1993	1994	1995	1996	1997	1998	1999	2000
II.2	**SECONDARY DISTRIBUTION OF INCOME ACCOUNT**										
	Resources										
B.5g	Balance of primary incomes, gross	NRJM	59 651	73 208	88 255	89 396	102 295	109 219	116 889	108 627	123 239
D.61	Social contributions										
D.612	Imputed social contributions	EWRT	3 099	2 705	2 522	2 988	2 921	2 907	3 541	3 276	3 381
D.7	Current transfers other than taxes, social contributions and benefits										
D.72	Net non-life insurance claims	FDBA	6 689	6 044	4 031	4 716	5 508	4 190	4 849	4 151	4 963
Total	Total resources	FDBC	69 439	81 957	94 808	97 100	110 724	116 316	125 279	116 054	131 583
	Uses										
D.5	Current taxes on income, wealth etc.										
D.51	Taxes on income	FCCP	14 047	13 374	15 060	18 706	22 149	27 183	25 211	21 297	24 799
D.62	Social benefits other than social transfers in kind	EWRT	3 099	2 705	2 522	2 988	2 921	2 907	3 541	3 276	3 381
D.7	Current transfers other than taxes, social contributions and benefits										
D.71	Net non-life insurance premiums	FDBH	6 689	6 044	4 031	4 716	5 508	4 190	4 849	4 151	4 963
D.75	Miscellaneous current transfers	FDBI	240	272	311	343	1 455	402	363	373	383
D.7	Total	FCCN	6 929	6 316	4 342	5 059	6 963	4 592	5 212	4 524	5 346
B.6g	Disposable income, gross	NRJQ	45 364	59 562	72 884	70 347	78 691	81 634	91 315	86 957	98 057
Total	Total uses	FDBC	69 439	81 957	94 808	97 100	110 724	116 316	125 279	116 054	131 583
-K.1	After deduction of fixed capital consumption	-NSRK	-44 917	-49 842	-50 320	-51 011	-52 786	-55 280	-55 792	-57 921	-60 944
B.6n	Disposable income, net	FDBK	447	9 720	22 564	19 336	25 905	26 354	35 523	29 036	37 113

Non-financial corporations

3.3.6 Private non-financial corporations
ESA95 sectors S.11002 National controlled and S.11003 Foreign controlled

£ million

			1992	1993	1994	1995	1996	1997	1998	1999	2000
II.4.1	USE OF DISPOSABLE INCOME ACCOUNT										
	Resources										
B.6g	Total resources, gross disposable income	NRJQ	45 364	59 562	72 884	70 347	78 691	81 634	91 315	86 957	98 057
	Uses										
B.8g	Total uses, gross saving	NRJQ	45 364	59 562	72 884	70 347	78 691	81 634	91 315	86 957	98 057
-K.1	After deduction of fixed capital consumption	-NSRK	-44 917	-49 842	-50 320	-51 011	-52 786	-55 280	-55 792	-57 921	-60 944
B.8n	Saving, net	FDBK	447	9 720	22 564	19 336	25 905	26 354	35 523	29 036	37 113

3.3.7 Private non-financial corporations
ESA95 sectors S.11002 National controlled and S.11003 Foreign controlled

£ million

			1992	1993	1994	1995	1996	1997	1998	1999	2000
III	ACCUMULATION ACCOUNTS										
III.1	CAPITAL ACCOUNT										
III.1.1	CHANGE IN NET WORTH DUE TO SAVING AND CAPITAL TRANSFERS										
	Changes in liabilities and net worth										
B.8g	Saving, gross	NRJQ	45 364	59 562	72 884	70 347	78 691	81 634	91 315	86 957	98 057
D.9	Capital transfers receivable										
D.92	Investment grants	AIBR	435	415	535	577	590	712	1 090	1 065	561
-D.9	*less* Capital transfers payable										
-D.91	Capital taxes	-QYKB	–	–	–	–	–	–	–	–	–
-D.99	Other capital transfers	-CISB	-120	-191	-126	-144	-162	-188	-193	-216	-290
-D.9	Total	-FCFX	-120	-191	-126	-144	-162	-188	-193	-216	-290
B.10.1g	Total change in liabilities and net worth	NRMG	45 679	59 786	73 293	70 780	79 119	82 158	92 212	87 806	98 328
	Changes in assets										
B.10.1g	Changes in net worth due to gross saving and capital transfers	NRMG	45 679	59 786	73 293	70 780	79 119	82 158	92 212	87 806	98 328
-K.1	After deduction of fixed capital consumption	-NSRK	-44 917	-49 842	-50 320	-51 011	-52 786	-55 280	-55 792	-57 921	-60 944
B.10.1n	Changes in net worth due to net saving and capital transfers	FDCH	762	9 944	22 973	19 769	26 333	26 878	36 420	29 885	37 384
III.1.2	ACQUISITION OF NON-FINANCIAL ASSETS ACCOUNT										
	Changes in liabilities and net worth										
B.10.1n	Changes in net worth due to net saving and capital transfers	FDCH	762	9 944	22 973	19 769	26 333	26 878	36 420	29 885	37 384
K.1	Consumption of fixed capital	NSRK	44 917	49 842	50 320	51 011	52 786	55 280	55 792	57 921	60 944
B.10.1g	Total change in liabilities and net worth	NRMG	45 679	59 786	73 293	70 780	79 119	82 158	92 212	87 806	98 328
	Changes in assets										
P.5	Gross capital formation										
P.51	Gross fixed capital formation	FDBM	54 277	54 931	55 867	64 444	72 413	81 501	90 985	95 193	99 845
P.52	Changes in inventories	DLQX	-1 921	238	3 904	4 542	1 651	3 731	3 981	5 101	2 120
P.53	Acquisitions less disposals of valuables	NPOV	-25	-30	-3	-52	-70	-60	28	-17	-74
P.5	Total	FDCL	52 331	55 139	59 768	68 934	73 994	85 172	94 994	100 277	101 891
K.2	Acquisitions less disposals of non-produced non-financial assets	FDCN	305	551	533	440	332	462	1 259	878	707
B.9	Net lending (+) / net borrowing (-)	DTAL	-6 957	4 096	12 992	1 406	4 793	-3 476	-4 041	-13 349	-4 270
Total	Total change in assets	NRMG	45 679	59 786	73 293	70 780	79 119	82 158	92 212	87 806	98 328

United Kingdom National Accounts 2001, © Crown copyright 2001

Non-financial corporations

3.3.8 Private non-financial corporations
ESA95 sectors S.11002 National controlled and S.11003 Foreign controlled. Unconsolidated

£ million

			1992	1993	1994	1995	1996	1997	1998	1999	2000
III.2	**FINANCIAL ACCOUNT**										
F.A	**Net acquisition of financial assets**										
F.2	Currency and deposits										
F.21	Currency	NEQF	62	141	76	138	120	213	137	258	179
F.22	Transferable deposits										
F.2211	Sterling deposits with UK banks	NEQI	−302	5 658	5 885	6 924	9 182	7 216	4 100	7 351	11 121
F.2212	Foreign currency deposits with UK banks	NEQJ	−1 301	748	1 083	−1 024	4 547	2 338	−1 118	1 900	3 073
F.2213	Sterling deposits with building societies	NEQK	957	804	391	−784	90	−5	1	163	−42
F.229	Deposits with rest of the world monetary financial institutions	NEQL	−3 729	3 181	1 745	3 489	6 141	11 784	4 505	18 450	36 305
F.29	Other deposits	NEQM	−175	818	−214	−584	−30	95	−20	−259	−220
F.2	Total currency and deposits	NEQE	−4 488	11 350	8 966	8 159	20 050	21 641	7 605	27 863	50 416
F.3	Securities other than shares										
F.331	Short term: money market instruments										
F.3311	Issued by UK central government	NEQP	−8	−198	33	−35	4	9	8	4	−28
F.3312	Issued by UK local authorities	NEQT	−	−	−	−	−	−	−	−	−
F.3315	Issued by UK monetary financial institutions	NEQU	−583	−347	907	461	1 122	−1 303	2 184	−1 915	−126
F.3316	Issued by other UK residents	NEQZ	−442	1 039	130	460	−112	−755	−1 774	116	−2 901
F.3319	Issued by the rest of the world	NERA	−535	912	73	−2	390	279	−956	722	1 110
F.332	Medium (1 to 5 year) and long term (over 5 year) bonds										
F.3321	Issued by UK central government	NERC	−633	594	−606	18	−1 115	−388	382	−811	403
F.3325	Medium term bonds issued by UK MFIs[1]	NERG	−37	−24	58	39	−116	64	44	21	−280
F.3326	Other medium & long term bonds issued by UK residents	NERJ	284	1 300	816	1 451	−1 600	−344	627	−1 350	1 297
F.3329	Long term bonds issued by the rest of the world	NERK	675	174	2 443	1 040	884	−1 893	585	−1 062	4 527
F.34	Financial derivatives	NERL	−	−	−	−	−	−	−	−	−
F.3	Total securities other than shares	NEQN	−1 279	3 450	3 854	3 432	−543	−4 331	1 100	−4 275	4 002
F.4	Loans										
F.42	Long term loans										
F.4211	Outward direct investment	NERY	3 796	3 398	1 799	4 174	2 828	5 538	21 721	17 778	25 352
F.4212	Inward direct investment	NERZ	642	1 716	2 222	3 881	236	2 480	11 275	8 657	9 268
F.424	Other long-term loans by UK residents	NESF	−106	−516	−309	234	−1 630	3 859	−2 632	−1 197	14 717
F.4	Total loans	NERP	4 332	4 598	3 712	8 289	1 434	11 877	30 364	25 238	49 337
F.5	Shares and other equity										
F.51	Shares and other equity, excluding mutual funds' shares										
F.514	Quoted UK shares	NESM	2 296	1 737	3 069	17 170	15 595	26 170	23 994	24 186	58 183
F.515	Unquoted UK shares	NESN	−3 732	−2 724	1 250	−1 411	6 023	−1 267	6 038	−10 751	−26 718
F.519	Shares and other equity issued by the rest of the world	NESR	8 206	11 353	18 019	18 258	18 381	28 726	48 477	111 864	171 740
F.52	Mutual funds' shares										
F.521	UK mutual funds' shares	NESV	6	26	42	12	11	6	1	1	9
F.5	Total shares and other equity	NESH	6 776	10 392	22 380	34 029	40 010	53 635	78 510	125 300	203 214
F.6	Insurance technical reserves										
F.62	Prepayments of insurance premiums and reserves for outstanding claims	NETA	1 052	422	479	920	2 694	163	−109	−291	321
F.7	Other accounts receivable	NETB	1 565	2 640	2 957	413	−948	1 316	445	−3 324	24 466
F.A	**Total net acquisition of financial assets**	NEQA	7 958	32 852	42 348	55 242	62 697	84 301	117 915	170 511	331 756

1 UK monetary financial institutions

Non-financial corporations

3.3.8 Private non-financial corporations
ESA95 sectors S.11002 National controlled and S.11003 Foreign controlled. Unconsolidated

£ million

			1992	1993	1994	1995	1996	1997	1998	1999	2000
III.2	**FINANCIAL ACCOUNT** continued										
F.L	**Net acquisition of financial liabilities**										
F.3	Securities other than shares										
F.331	Short term: money market instruments										
F.3316	Issued by UK residents other than government or monetary financial institutions	NEUD	−961	1 761	2 408	1 273	1 817	1 361	3 435	2 716	1 366
F.332	Medium (1 to 5 year) and long term (over 5 year) bonds										
F.3326	Other medium & long term bonds issued by UK residents or monetary financial institutions	NEUN	2 938	6 261	3 525	11 984	4 867	13 764	17 100	39 100	40 253
F.3	Total securities other than shares	NETR	1 977	8 022	5 933	13 257	6 684	15 125	20 535	41 816	41 619
F.4	Loans										
F.41	Short term loans										
F.411	Loans by UK monetary financial institutions,										
	Sterling loans by UK banks	NEUW	−864	−6 649	−2 234	14 245	15 268	5 603	8 667	9 075	21 912
	Foreign currency loans by UK banks	NEUX	−1 605	−5 898	−1 642	283	1 707	1 212	8 157	6 080	1 997
	Sterling loans by building societies	NEUY	515	364	−459	758	974	814	1 134	1 619	1 602
F.419	Loans by rest of the world monetary financial institutions	NEUZ	2 432	7 189	575	3 628	7 470	17 351	−3 254	5 960	13 950
F.42	Long term loans										
F.4211	Outward direct investment	NEVC	3 217	470	2 378	1 366	3 381	5 671	10 483	10 760	40 953
F.4212	Inward direct investment	NEVD	3 341	2 734	2 513	−315	650	4 946	25 619	8 703	16 859
F.423	Finance leasing	NEVI	−952	−101	9	1 052	1 381	1 571	51	−68	−222
F.424	Other long-term loans by UK residents	NEVJ	−155	−861	522	1 469	3 112	3 913	1 260	2 693	1 852
F.429	Other long-term loans by the rest of the world	NEVK	−157	−55	−1	−1	–	–	–	–	–
F.4	Total loans	NEUT	5 772	−2 807	1 661	22 485	33 943	41 081	52 117	44 822	98 903
F.5	Shares and other equity										
F.51	Shares and other equity, excluding mutual funds' shares										
F.514	Quoted UK shares	NEVQ	8 297	16 535	12 854	13 672	14 155	22 872	45 680	85 600	179 418
F.515	Unquoted UK shares	NEVR	954	3 192	5 562	6 725	8 426	7 257	5 947	9 096	17 704
F.516	Other UK equity (including direct investment in property)	NEVS	367	562	425	−474	1 397	886	632	833	1 298
F.5	Total shares and other equity	NEVL	9 618	20 289	18 841	19 923	23 978	31 015	52 259	95 529	198 420
F.7	Other accounts payable	NEWF	−1 108	1 273	4 301	1 880	−563	898	4 190	8 197	4 034
F.L	**Total net acquisition of financial liabilities**	NETE	16 259	26 777	30 736	57 545	64 042	88 119	129 101	190 364	342 976
B.9	**Net lending / borrowing**										
F.A	Total net acquisition of financial assets	NEQA	7 958	32 852	42 348	55 242	62 697	84 301	117 915	170 511	331 756
−F.L	*less* Total net acquisition of financial liabilities	−NETE	−16 259	−26 777	−30 736	−57 545	−64 042	−88 119	−129 101	−190 364	−342 976
B.9f	Net lending (+) / net borrowing (−), from financial account	NYOA	−8 301	6 075	11 612	−2 303	−1 345	−3 818	−11 186	−19 853	−11 220
dB.9f	**Statistical discrepancy**	NYPM	1 344	−1 979	1 380	3 709	6 138	342	7 145	6 504	6 950
B.9	**Net lending (+) / net borrowing (−), from capital account**	DTAL	−6 957	4 096	12 992	1 406	4 793	−3 476	−4 041	−13 349	−4 270

United Kingdom National Accounts 2001, © Crown copyright 2001

Non-financial corporations

3.3.9 Private non-financial corporations
ESA95 sectors S.11002 National controlled and S.11003 Foreign controlled. Unconsolidated

£ billion

			1992	1993	1994	1995	1996	1997	1998	1999	2000
IV.3	**FINANCIAL BALANCE SHEET** at end of period										
AN	Non-financial assets	TMPL	776.3	932.3	929.3	945.6	1 020.5	1 073.5	1 087.5	1 150.2	1 204.3
AF.A	**Financial assets**										
AF.2	Currency and deposits										
AF.21	Currency	NKKA	1.8	2.0	2.0	2.2	2.3	2.4	2.3	2.5	2.6
AF.22	Transferable deposits										
AF.2211	Sterling deposits with UK banks	NKKD	67.8	76.3	80.7	87.5	98.6	106.5	109.7	117.6	129.0
AF.2212	Foreign currency deposits with UK banks	NKKE	11.2	12.1	13.0	12.6	15.4	18.4	17.4	19.5	24.1
AF.2213	Sterling deposits with building societies	NKKF	3.9	4.7	5.1	4.0	3.9	1.9	2.4	2.5	2.2
AF.229	Deposits with rest of the world monetary financial institutions	NKKG	36.8	41.9	43.1	46.7	47.5	60.1	65.0	78.7	102.4
AF.29	Other deposits	NKKH	3.0	5.3	5.2	4.6	5.2	4.7	4.8	4.5	4.3
AF.2	Total currency and deposits	NKJZ	124.6	142.1	149.1	157.7	172.9	194.1	201.6	225.3	264.7
AF.3	Securities other than shares										
AF.331	Short term: money market instruments										
AF.3311	Issued by UK central government	NKKK	0.2	–	0.1	–	–	–	–	–	–
AF.3312	Issued by UK local authorities	NKKO	–	–	–	–	–	–	–	–	–
AF.3315	Issued by UK monetary financial institutions	NKKP	3.7	3.6	4.4	4.9	6.0	4.7	6.8	4.9	5.6
AF.3316	Issued by other UK residents	NKKU	4.2	7.7	7.4	8.6	8.0	10.1	6.0	13.6	16.3
AF.3319	Issued by the rest of the world	NKKV	0.8	1.7	1.7	1.7	1.8	2.1	1.2	1.9	3.0
AF.332	Medium (1 to 5 year) and long term (over 5 year) bonds										
AF.3321	Issued by UK central government	NKKX	1.8	2.4	1.8	1.8	0.7	0.4	0.9	0.1	0.5
AF.3322	Issued by UK local authorities	NKLA	–	–	–	–	–	–	–	–	–
AF.3325	Medium term bonds issued by UK MFIs[1]	NKLB	–	–	0.1	0.1	0.1	0.2	0.2	0.2	0.1
AF.3326	Other medium & long term bonds issued by UK residents	NKLE	2.8	4.0	4.4	5.7	3.6	2.8	3.5	1.9	2.3
AF.3329	Long term bonds issued by the rest of the world	NKLF	1.8	2.0	4.4	5.5	4.4	3.4	6.3	7.1	11.8
AF.34	Financial derivatives	NKWU	–	–	–	–	–	–	–	–	–
AF.3	Total securities other than shares	NKKI	15.5	21.4	24.3	28.3	24.6	23.7	24.9	29.9	39.6
AF.4	Loans										
AF.42	Long term loans										
AF.4211	Outward direct investment	NKXH	36.9	41.0	41.5	48.3	47.3	50.7	73.0	82.3	111.0
AF.4212	Inward direct investment	NKXI	13.5	11.3	14.1	17.3	21.9	25.1	36.9	47.2	56.4
AF.424	Other long-term loans by UK residents	NKXO	5.9	6.1	6.7	6.7	7.0	7.4	7.7	8.0	7.9
AF.4	Total loans	NKWY	56.3	58.5	62.4	72.4	76.3	83.3	117.6	137.4	175.3
AF.5	Shares and other equity										
AF.51	Shares and other equity, excluding mutual funds' shares										
AF.514	Quoted UK shares	NKXV	12.1	7.6	11.4	9.1	10.2	14.2	20.5	39.4	26.4
AF.515	Unquoted UK shares	NKXW	24.1	30.0	28.7	33.3	36.9	43.8	48.9	64.4	63.5
AF.519	Shares and other equity issued by the rest of the world	NKYA	121.8	130.2	132.5	150.5	152.2	166.8	213.2	342.3	529.2
AF.52	Mutual funds' shares										
AF.521	UK mutual funds' shares	NKYE	0.2	0.3	0.3	0.4	0.4	0.4	0.4	0.6	0.5
AF.5	Total shares and other equity	NKXQ	158.2	168.1	173.0	193.2	199.7	225.2	283.0	446.6	619.7
AF.6	Insurance technical reserves										
AF.62	Prepayments of insurance premiums and reserves for outstanding claims	NKYJ	9.3	10.0	7.5	8.9	13.1	10.7	11.8	10.8	11.4
AF.7	Other accounts receivable	NKYK	85.8	87.4	88.4	88.8	88.0	90.0	90.5	89.6	114.0
AF.A	**Total financial assets**	NKWX	449.8	487.5	504.7	549.3	574.6	627.0	729.4	939.6	1 224.7

1 UK monetary financial institutions

3.3.9 Private non-financial corporations

ESA95 sectors S.11002 National controlled and S.11003 Foreign controlled. Unconsolidated

continued

£ billion

			1992	1993	1994	1995	1996	1997	1998	1999	2000
IV.3	**FINANCIAL BALANCE SHEET** continued at end of period										
AF.L	**Financial liabilities**										
AF.3	Securities other than shares										
AF.331	Short term: money market instruments										
AF.3316	Issued by UK residents other than government or monetary financial institutions	NKZM	8.4	10.3	12.0	14.0	13.8	15.4	18.6	22.5	24.7
AF.332	Medium (1 to 5 year) and long term (over 5 year) bonds										
AF.3326	Other medium & long term bonds issued by UK residents or monetary financial institutions	NKZW	53.8	65.4	66.6	82.1	85.7	100.7	123.9	153.7	191.5
AF.34	Financial derivatives	NKZY	–	–	–	–	–	–	–	–	–
AF.3	Total securities other than shares	NKZA	62.1	75.8	78.6	96.1	99.6	116.2	142.5	176.2	216.2
AF.4	Loans										
AF.41	Short term loans										
AF.4111	Sterling deposits with UK banks	NLBF	144.8	136.0	129.1	140.0	155.5	159.8	166.5	176.2	197.7
AF.4112	Foreign currency deposits with UK banks	NLBG	37.1	30.9	28.7	30.1	28.1	27.9	36.3	41.8	45.9
AF.4113	Sterling deposits with building societies loans secured on dwellings & financial leasing	NLBH	3.2	3.5	3.3	4.0	4.7	3.5	2.3	3.8	5.6
AF.419	Loans by rest of the world monetary financial institutions	NLBI	39.0	54.2	54.7	63.1	64.7	79.7	77.7	92.3	101.5
AF.42	Long term loans										
AF.4211	Outward direct investment	NLBL	24.5	26.5	26.6	31.4	34.4	39.0	50.9	60.3	104.8
AF.4212	Inward direct investment	NLBM	46.5	42.6	39.7	40.3	44.8	52.3	77.2	85.0	101.9
AF.423	Finance leasing	NLBR	14.5	14.4	14.2	15.3	16.7	18.2	18.3	18.2	18.0
AF.424	Other long-term loans by UK residents	NLBS	20.1	21.9	25.8	23.7	27.5	30.0	30.9	44.3	43.1
AF.429	Other long-term loans by the rest of the world	NLBT	0.4	0.4	0.4	0.5	0.4	0.4	0.4	0.4	0.4
AF.4	Total loans	NLBC	330.2	330.5	322.4	348.3	376.8	410.9	460.5	522.3	618.9
AF.5	Shares and other equity										
AF.51	Shares and other equity, excluding mutual funds' shares										
AF.514	Quoted UK shares	NLBZ	522.0	649.8	620.3	719.8	797.8	948.5	1 059.5	1 394.4	1 375.4
AF.515	Unquoted UK shares	NLCA	187.5	218.8	211.8	248.8	263.6	305.8	355.8	475.8	537.9
AF.516	Other UK equity (including direct investment in property)	NLCB	8.4	9.0	9.8	10.1	10.7	11.6	12.2	13.1	14.4
AF.5	Total shares and other equity	NLBU	718.0	877.5	841.9	978.7	1 072.1	1 266.0	1 427.6	1 883.3	1 927.7
AF.7	Other accounts payable	NLCO	111.4	113.2	116.1	117.7	117.5	120.1	121.9	128.5	130.3
AF.L	**Total financial liabilities**	NLBB	1 221.7	1 397.0	1 359.0	1 540.8	1 665.9	1 913.2	2 152.5	2 710.3	2 893.0
BF.90	**Net financial assets / liabilities**										
AF.A	Total financial assets	NKWX	449.8	487.5	504.7	549.3	574.6	627.0	729.4	939.6	1 224.7
-AF.L	*less* Total financial liabilities	-NLBB	–1 221.7	–1 397.0	–1 359.0	–1 540.8	–1 665.9	–1 913.2	–2 152.5	–2 710.3	–2 893.0
BF.90	**Net financial assets (+) / liabilities (-)**	NYOT	–771.9	–909.5	–854.4	–991.5	–1 091.3	–1 286.2	–1 423.1	–1 770.7	–1 668.3
	Net worth										
AN	Non-financial assets	TMPM	–771.9	–909.5	–854.4	–991.5	–1 091.3	–1 286.2	–1 423.1	–1 770.7	–1 668.3
BF.90	Net financial assets(+)/liabilities(-)	NYOT	–771.9	–909.5	–854.4	–991.5	–1 091.3	–1 286.2	–1 423.1	–1 770.7	–1 668.3
BF.90	**Net worth**	TMPN	4.4	22.8	74.9	–46.1	–71.9	–214.1	–335.4	–622.5	–463.0

Part 3

Chapter 4

Financial corporations

Financial corporations

Financial corporations

4.1.1 Financial corporations
ESA95 sector S.12

£ million

			1992	1993	1994	1995	1996	1997	1998	1999
I	**PRODUCTION ACCOUNT**									
	Resources									
P.1	Output									
P.11	Market output*	NHCV	75 009	78 955	84 229	84 543	87 919	93 509	107 271	115 249
P.12	Output for own final use	NHCW	386	404	421	432	446	424	636	698
P.1	Total resources	NHCT	75 395	79 359	84 650	84 975	88 365	93 933	107 907	115 947
P.119	*of which*, FISIM (financial intermediation services indirectly measured)	NSRV	19 086	19 569	23 119	23 215	22 580	22 396	27 998	30 819
	Uses									
P.2	Intermediate consumption	NHCX	39 441	40 205	43 021	46 588	49 197	55 303	63 525	74 092
B.1g	Value added, gross	NHDB	35 954	39 154	41 629	38 387	39 168	38 630	44 382	41 855
Total	Total uses	NHCT	75 395	79 359	84 650	84 975	88 365	93 933	107 907	115 947
B.1g	Value added, gross	NHDB	35 954	39 154	41 629	38 387	39 168	38 630	44 382	41 855
-K.1	*less* Consumption of fixed capital	-NHCE	–4 019	–4 602	–4 489	–4 063	–3 982	–3 902	–4 094	–3 974
B.1n	Value added, net of fixed capital consumption	NHDC	31 935	34 552	37 140	34 324	35 186	34 728	40 288	37 881

4.1.2 Financial corporations
ESA95 sector S.12

£ million

			1992	1993	1994	1995	1996	1997	1998	1999
II	**DISTRIBUTION AND USE OF INCOME ACCOUNTS**									
II.1	**PRIMARY DISTRIBUTION OF INCOME ACCOUNT**									
II.1.1	**GENERATION OF INCOME ACCOUNT**									
	Resources									
B.1g	Total resources, gross value added	NHDB	35 954	39 154	41 629	38 387	39 168	38 630	44 382	41 855
	Uses									
D.1	Compensation of employees									
D.11	Wages and salaries	NHCC	18 456	17 609	17 176	16 676	17 868	19 403	21 121	22 111
D.12	Employers' social contributions	NHCD	2 794	2 706	2 592	2 543	2 818	3 013	3 339	3 516
D.1	Total	NHCR	21 250	20 315	19 768	19 219	20 686	22 416	24 460	25 627
D.2	Taxes on production and imports, paid									
D.29	Production taxes other than on products	NHCS	1 055	1 113	1 153	1 330	1 347	1 408	1 486	1 527
-D.3	*less* Subsidies, received									
-D.39	Production subsidies other than on products	-NHCA	–	–	–	–	–	–	–	–
B.2g	Operating surplus, gross	NQNV	13 649	17 726	20 708	17 838	17 135	14 806	18 436	14 701
B.1g	Total uses	NHDB	35 954	39 154	41 629	38 387	39 168	38 630	44 382	41 855
-K.1	After deduction of fixed capital consumption	-NHCE	–4 019	–4 602	–4 489	–4 063	–3 982	–3 902	–4 094	–3 974
B.2n	Operating surplus, net	NHDA	9 630	13 124	16 219	13 775	13 153	10 904	14 342	10 727

Financial corporations

4.1.3 Financial corporations
ESA95 sector S.12

£ million

			1992	1993	1994	1995	1996	1997	1998	1999	2000
II.1.2	**ALLOCATION OF PRIMARY INCOME ACCOUNT**										
	Resources										
B.2g	Operating surplus, gross	NQNV	13 649	17 726	20 708	17 838	17 135	14 806	18 436	14 701	15 548
D.4	Property income, received										
D.41	Interest	NHCK	153 301	131 876	131 018	153 969	157 423	174 562	210 581	184 465	230 449
D.42	Distributed income of corporations	NHCL	22 083	23 177	25 886	30 302	35 294	36 131	34 699	45 602	48 131
D.43	Reinvested earnings on direct foreign investment	NHEM	513	2 348	1 689	3 002	3 854	4 365	3 092	5 196	4 466
D.44	Attributed property income of insurance policy-holders	NHDG	66	65	66	74	66	75	32	45	65
D.45	Rent	NHDH	28	28	28	28	28	28	30	29	29
D.4	Total	NHDF	175 991	157 494	158 687	187 375	196 665	215 161	248 434	235 337	283 140
-P.119	Adjustment to property income for financial services (FISIM)	-NSRV	-19 086	-19 569	-23 119	-23 215	-22 580	-22 396	-27 998	-30 819	-37 091
Total	Total resources	NQNW	170 554	155 651	156 276	181 998	191 220	207 571	238 872	219 219	261 597
	Uses										
D.4	Property income, paid										
D.41	Interest	NHCM	116 077	94 584	89 478	109 685	111 431	124 021	147 982	124 950	166 219
D.42	Distributed income of corporations	NHCN	11 958	14 029	15 801	18 216	22 423	22 612	21 789	29 049	37 840
D.43	Reinvested earnings on direct foreign investment	NHEO	59	2 381	-357	592	1 756	1 199	-1 595	1 735	3 855
D.44	Attributed property income of insurance policy-holders	NSCU	36 142	36 580	38 373	43 654	49 039	53 480	57 315	55 580	61 273
D.45	Rent	NHDK	–	–	–	–	–	–	–	–	–
D.4	Total	NHDI	164 236	147 574	143 295	172 147	184 649	201 312	225 491	211 314	269 187
B.5g	Balance of primary incomes, gross	NQNY	6 318	8 077	12 981	9 851	6 571	6 259	13 381	7 905	-7 590
Total	Total uses	NQNW	170 554	155 651	156 276	181 998	191 220	207 571	238 872	219 219	261 597
-K.1	After deduction of fixed capital consumption	-NHCE	-4 019	-4 602	-4 489	-4 063	-3 982	-3 902	-4 094	-3 974	-4 233
B.5n	Balance of primary incomes, net	NHDL	2 299	3 475	8 492	5 788	2 589	2 357	9 287	3 931	-11 823

4.1.4 Financial corporations
ESA95 sector S.12

£ million

			1992	1993	1994	1995	1996	1997	1998	1999	2000
II.2	**SECONDARY DISTRIBUTION OF INCOME ACCOUNT**										
	Resources										
B.5g	Balance of primary incomes, gross	NQNY	6 318	8 077	12 981	9 851	6 571	6 259	13 381	7 905	-7 590
D.61	Social contributions										
D.611	Actual social contributions										
D.6111	Employers' actual social contributions	NQOB	11 771	12 180	13 233	14 017	16 572	17 735	19 906	22 257	24 893
D.6112	Employees' social contributions	NQOC	30 068	28 258	30 058	32 751	38 308	42 876	45 591	46 803	48 853
D.6113	Social contributions by self-employed persons	NQOD	–	–	–	–	–	–	–	–	–
D.611	Total	NQOA	41 839	40 438	43 291	46 768	54 880	60 611	65 497	69 060	73 746
D.612	Imputed social contributions	NHDR	475	432	422	452	424	405	471	448	490
D.61	Total	NQNZ	42 314	40 870	43 713	47 220	55 304	61 016	65 968	69 508	74 236
D.7	Other current transfers										
D.71	Net non-life insurance premiums	NQOF	27 188	23 987	22 650	25 088	35 860	23 774	25 059	22 752	27 205
D.72	Non-life insurance claims	NHDN	952	840	839	879	863	813	326	637	762
D.75	Miscellaneous current transfers	NQOG	–	–	–	–	–	–	–	–	–
D.7	Total	NQOE	28 140	24 827	23 489	25 967	36 723	24 587	25 385	23 389	27 967
Total	Total resources	NQOH	76 772	73 774	80 183	83 038	98 598	91 862	104 734	100 802	94 613
	Uses										
D.5	Current taxes on income and wealth										
D.51	Taxes on income	NHDO	-1 205	-221	675	1 532	1 990	4 412	7 318	10 192	8 599
D.62	Social benefits other than social transfers in kind	NHDQ	28 954	30 129	33 139	35 532	40 491	45 887	49 865	54 084	59 024
D.7	Other current transfers										
D.71	Net non-life insurance premiums	NHDU	952	840	839	879	863	813	326	637	762
D.72	Non-life insurance claims	NQOI	27 188	23 987	22 650	25 088	35 860	23 774	25 059	22 752	27 205
D.75	Miscellaneous current transfers	NHEK	48	57	74	65	65	66	74	75	79
D.7	Total	NHDT	28 188	24 884	23 563	26 032	36 788	24 653	25 459	23 464	28 046
B.6g	Disposable income, gross	NQOJ	20 835	18 982	22 806	19 942	19 329	16 910	22 092	13 062	-1 056
Total	Total uses	NQOH	76 772	73 774	80 183	83 038	98 598	91 862	104 734	100 802	94 613
-K.1	After deduction of fixed capital consumption	-NHCE	-4 019	-4 602	-4 489	-4 063	-3 982	-3 902	-4 094	-3 974	-4 233
B.6n	Disposable income, net	NHDV	16 816	14 380	18 317	15 879	15 347	13 008	17 998	9 088	-5 289

Financial corporations

4.1.6 Financial corporations
ESA95 sector S.12

£ million

			1992	1993	1994	1995	1996	1997	1998	1999	2000
II.4.1	**USE OF DISPOSABLE INCOME ACCOUNT**										
	Resources										
B.6g	Total resources, gross disposable income	NQOJ	20 835	18 982	22 806	19 942	19 329	16 910	22 092	13 062	−1 056
	Uses										
D.8	Adjustment for the change in net equity of households in pension funds	NQOK	13 271	10 741	10 574	11 688	14 822	15 129	16 103	15 415	15 212
B.8g	Saving, gross	NQOL	7 564	8 241	12 232	8 254	4 507	1 781	5 989	−2 353	−16 268
Total	Total uses	NQOJ	20 835	18 982	22 806	19 942	19 329	16 910	22 092	13 062	−1 056
−K.1	After deduction of fixed capital consumption	−NHCE	−4 019	−4 602	−4 489	−4 063	−3 982	−3 902	−4 094	−3 974	−4 233
B.8n	Saving, net	NQOM	3 545	3 639	7 743	4 191	525	−2 121	1 895	−6 327	−20 501

4.1.7 Financial corporations
ESA95 sector S.12

£ million

			1992	1993	1994	1995	1996	1997	1998	1999	2000
III	**ACCUMULATION ACCOUNTS**										
III.1	**CAPITAL ACCOUNT**										
III.1.1	**CHANGE IN NET WORTH DUE TO SAVING & CAPITAL TRANSFERS**										
	Changes in liabilities and net worth										
B.8g	Saving, gross	NQOL	7 564	8 241	12 232	8 254	4 507	1 781	5 989	−2 353	−16 268
D.9	Capital transfers receivable										
D.92	Investment grants	NHEA	−	−	−	−	−	−	−	−	−
D.99	Other capital transfers	NHEB	86	−	−	−	−	−	−	−	−
D.9	Total	NHDZ	86	−	−	−	−	−	−	−	−
−D.9	*less* Capital transfers payable										
−D.91	Capital taxes	−NHBW	−	−	−	−	−	−	−	−	−
−D.99	Other capital transfers	−NHCB	−86	−88	−518	−	−	−	−	−	−
−D.9	Total	−NHEC	−86	−88	−518	−	−	−	−	−	−
B.10.1g	Total change in liabilities and net worth	NQON	7 564	8 153	11 714	8 254	4 507	1 781	5 989	−2 353	−16 268
	Changes in assets										
B.10.1g	Changes in net worth due to gross saving and capital transfers	NQON	7 564	8 153	11 714	8 254	4 507	1 781	5 989	−2 353	−16 268
−K.1	After deduction of fixed capital consumption	−NHCE	−4 019	−4 602	−4 489	−4 063	−3 982	−3 902	−4 094	−3 974	−4 233
B.10.1n	Changes in net worth due to net saving and capital transfers	NHEF	3 545	3 551	7 225	4 191	525	−2 121	1 895	−6 327	−20 501
III.1.2	**ACQUISITION OF NON-FINANCIAL ASSETS ACCOUNT**										
	Changes in liabilities and net worth										
B.10.1n	Changes in net worth due to net saving and capital transfers	NHEF	3 545	3 551	7 225	4 191	525	−2 121	1 895	−6 327	−20 501
K.1	Consumption of fixed capital	NHCE	4 019	4 602	4 489	4 063	3 982	3 902	4 094	3 974	4 233
Total	Total change in liabilities and net worth	NQON	7 564	8 153	11 714	8 254	4 507	1 781	5 989	−2 353	−16 268
	Changes in assets										
P.5	Gross capital formation										
P.51	Gross fixed capital formation	NHCJ	5 683	4 204	7 160	5 590	6 696	6 208	11 277	7 537	11 737
P.52	Changes in inventories	NHCI	−	−	−	20	20	35	35	47	55
P.53	Acquisitions less disposals of valuables	NHEH	−45	−50	−5	−93	−122	−104	49	−28	−130
P.5	Total	NHEG	5 638	4 154	7 155	5 517	6 594	6 139	11 361	7 556	11 662
K.2	Acquisitions less disposals of non-produced non-financial assets	NHEI	−49	−203	86	−77	−1	−39	−4	26	13
B.9	Net lending(+) / net borrowing(−)	NHCQ	1 975	4 202	4 473	2 814	−2 086	−4 319	−5 368	−9 935	−27 943
Total	Total change in assets	NQON	7 564	8 153	11 714	8 254	4 507	1 781	5 989	−2 353	−16 268

United Kingdom National Accounts 2001, © Crown copyright 2001

Financial corporations

4.1.8 Financial corporations
ESA95 sector S.12 Unconsolidated

£ million

				1992	1993	1994	1995	1996	1997	1998	1999	2000
III.2	**FINANCIAL ACCOUNT**											
F.A	**Net acquisition of financial assets**											
F.2	Currency and deposits											
F.21	Currency		NFCV	632	297	293	314	–437	232	1 494	2 717	–1 413
F.22	Transferable deposits											
F.221	Deposits with UK monetary financial institutions		NFCX	16 613	13 597	21 620	24 056	79 287	66 445	36 568	–6 844	83 632
F.229	Deposits with rest of the world monetary financial institutions		NFDB	29 808	49 917	29 421	30 000	89 255	123 413	10 322	18 245	180 674
F.29	Other deposits		NFDC	–93	–19	–44	–24	–69	–5	–10	–9	2 685
F.2	Total currency and deposits		NFCU	46 960	63 792	51 290	54 346	168 036	190 085	48 374	14 109	265 578
F.3	Securities other than shares											
F.331	Short term: money market instruments											
F.3311	Issued by UK central government		NFDF	–2 479	–23	1 320	10 152	–13 209	–657	1 691	–1 162	–1 400
F.3312	Issued by UK local authorities		NFDJ	2	–29	–	4	–6	5	–6	–	–
F.3315	Issued by UK monetary financial institutions		NFDK	–824	–4 096	4 261	6 586	23 612	14 323	12 143	16 891	–15 453
F.3316	Issued by other UK residents		NFDP	638	–277	–29	–300	359	846	2 395	1 056	1 512
F.3319	Issued by the rest of the world		NFDQ	1 225	5 330	–4 521	2 745	–2 064	9 055	2 702	13 238	–4 082
F.332	Medium (1 to 5 year) and long term (over 5 year) bonds											
F.3321	Issued by UK central government		NFDS	22 635	29 196	16 342	19 471	27 238	21 078	–1 555	3 073	–10 491
F.3322	Issued by UK local authorities		NFDV	26	203	342	31	119	124	–39	28	69
F.3325	Medium term bonds issued by UK MFIs[1]		NFDW	1 423	1 371	3 836	2 725	2 740	2 236	2 660	7 244	2 314
F.3326	Other medium & long term bonds issued by UK residents		NFDZ	5 426	11 894	2 299	4 781	9 265	11 880	20 237	41 355	63 713
F.3329	Long term bonds issued by the rest of the world		NFEA	30 986	74 269	–19 223	28 044	50 830	48 468	26 893	–5 072	42 793
F.34	Financial derivatives		NFEB	–1 253	–245	–2 373	–1 667	–963	–1 156	3 043	–2 685	–1 553
F.3	Total securities other than shares		NFDD	57 805	117 593	2 254	72 572	97 921	106 202	70 164	73 966	77 422
F.4	Loans											
F.41	Short term loans											
F.411	Loans by UK monetary financial institutions, excluding loans secured on dwellings & financial leasing		NFEH	4 487	–6 533	14 676	51 722	112 543	100 472	31 892	65 499	154 783
F.42	Long term loans											
F.421	Direct investment		NFEN	–110	627	1 134	1 691	439	931	273	600	54
F.422	Loans secured on dwellings		NFEQ	18 900	16 412	19 554	15 250	19 308	25 812	25 493	37 780	41 106
F.423	Finance leasing		NFEU	–1 179	–249	–154	958	1 930	2 028	558	134	–291
F.424	Other long-term loans by UK residents		NFEV	–387	1 044	2 895	3 805	3 061	9 339	4 858	16 852	5 853
F.4	Total loans		NFEF	21 711	11 301	38 105	73 426	137 281	138 582	63 074	120 865	201 505
F.5	Shares and other equity											
F.51	Shares and other equity, excluding mutual funds' shares											
F.514	Quoted UK shares		NFFC	1 893	13 390	12 935	1 492	1 682	–312	–1 261	–3 191	27 028
F.515	Unquoted UK shares		NFFD	629	1 292	1 119	887	3 272	4 177	–1 779	–1 640	18 312
F.519	Shares and other equity issued by the rest of the world		NFFH	–1 665	11 050	3 906	12 334	13 652	4 298	15 355	27 554	28 066
F.52	Mutual funds' shares											
F.521	UK mutual funds' shares		NFFL	1 167	4 214	4 062	4 370	3 531	3 916	2 426	2 958	6 777
F.5	Total shares and other equity		NFEX	2 024	29 946	22 022	19 083	22 137	12 079	14 741	25 681	80 183
F.6	Insurance technical reserves											
F.62	Prepayments of insurance premiums and reserves for outstanding claims		NFFQ	151	59	100	171	423	30	–7	–44	49
F.7	Other accounts receivable		NFFR	–987	–21	2 001	7 783	3 591	2 017	4 359	5 304	1 297
F.A	Total net acquisition of financial assets		NFCQ	127 664	222 670	115 772	227 381	429 389	448 995	200 705	239 881	626 034

1 UK monetary financial institutions

4.1.8 Financial corporations
ESA95 sector S.12 Unconsolidated

£ million

			1992	1993	1994	1995	1996	1997	1998	1999	2000
III.2	**FINANCIAL ACCOUNT** continued										
F.L	**Net acquisition of financial liabilities**										
F.2	Currency and deposits										
F.21	Currency	NFFZ	1 614	1 322	1 530	1 620	251	1 605	2 967	5 232	448
F.22	Transferable deposits										
F.221	Deposits with UK monetary financial institutions	NFGB	63 824	76 990	82 598	83 227	186 849	258 267	115 825	41 823	342 226
F.29	Other deposits	NFGG	–	–	–	–	–	–	–	–	2 913
F.2	Total currency and deposits	NFFY	65 438	78 312	84 128	84 847	187 100	259 872	118 792	47 055	345 587
F.3	Securities other than shares										
F.331	Short term: money market instruments										
F.3315	Issued by UK monetary financial institutions	NFGO	–12 777	–22 845	6 358	23 215	36 572	21 983	–1 218	31 203	23 953
F.3316	Issued by other non-government UK residents	NFGT	216	760	228	312	864	392	–93	31	–14
F.332	Medium (1 to 5 year) and long term (over 5 year) bonds										
F.3325	Medium term bonds issued by UK MFIs[1]	NFHA	2 756	5 268	10 313	3 937	7 894	5 196	4 140	11 911	4 751
F.3326	Other medium & long term bonds issued by UK residents	NFHD	5 949	12 931	8 698	7 904	13 363	11 998	–250	24 276	33 968
F.34	Financial derivatives	NFHF	114	–8	–1	17	15	34	55	26	21
F.3	Total securities other than shares	NFGH	–3 742	–3 894	25 596	35 385	58 708	39 603	2 634	67 447	62 679
F.4	Loans										
F.41	Short term loans										
F.411	Loans by UK monetary financial institutions, excluding loans secured on dwellings & financial leasing	NFHL	1 896	15 024	11 688	17 087	47 744	56 679	–102	14 289	59 420
F.419	Loans by rest of the world monetary financial institutions	NFHP	19 486	78 979	–58 022	35 361	75 327	33 690	14 568	43 058	63 028
F.42	Long term loans										
F.421	Direct investment	NFHR	–253	–333	548	–1 091	864	1 256	210	1 940	242
F.423	Finance leasing	NFHY	–136	–143	–197	–83	527	458	56	–323	–127
F.424	Other long-term loans by UK residents	NFHZ	79	29	760	276	–3 990	5 476	–4 501	4 759	16 317
F.429	Other long-term loans by the rest of the world	NFIA	433	404	–337	–30	302	233	–115	44	–30
F.4	Total loans	NFHJ	21 505	93 960	–45 560	51 520	120 774	97 792	10 116	63 767	138 850
F.5	Shares and other equity										
F.51	Shares and other equity, excluding mutual funds' shares										
F.514	Quoted UK shares	NFIG	1 887	5 114	5 957	2 907	1 894	951	4 433	2 229	17 746
F.515	Unquoted UK shares	NFIH	656	3 766	1 986	3 079	4 406	8 693	4 582	8 912	28 608
F.516	Other UK equity (including direct investment in property)	NFII	–7	56	–	13	–19	–	–	–	–
F.52	Mutual funds' shares										
F.521	UK mutual funds' shares	NFIP	–210	6 211	2 929	5 399	8 144	8 980	10 976	14 719	13 889
F.5	Total shares and other equity	NFIB	2 326	15 147	10 872	11 398	14 425	18 624	19 991	25 860	60 243
F.6	Insurance technical reserves										
F.61	Net equity of households in life assurance and pension funds' reserves	NFIR	28 098	27 388	28 049	30 372	36 666	32 403	42 011	42 473	44 671
F.62	Prepayments of insurance premiums and reserves for outstanding claims	NFIU	4 277	1 678	2 693	4 891	12 079	897	–563	–1 601	1 767
F.6	Total insurance technical reserves	NPWS	32 375	29 066	30 742	35 263	48 745	33 300	41 448	40 872	46 438
F.7	Other accounts payable	NFIV	–508	–15	574	3 405	1 182	4 776	2 434	4 173	6 984
F.L	**Total net acquisition of financial liabilities**	NFFU	117 394	212 576	106 352	221 818	430 934	453 967	195 415	249 174	660 781
B.9	**Net lending / borrowing**										
F.A	Total net acquisition of financial assets	NFCQ	127 664	222 670	115 772	227 381	429 389	448 995	200 705	239 881	626 034
-F.L	*less* Total net acquisition of financial liabilities	-NFFU	–117 394	–212 576	–106 352	–221 818	–430 934	–453 967	–195 415	–249 174	–660 781
B.9f	**Net lending (+) / net borrowing (-), from financial account**	NYNL	10 270	10 094	9 420	5 563	–1 545	–4 972	5 290	–9 293	–34 747
dB.9f	**Statistical discrepancy**	NYOX	–8 295	–5 892	–4 947	–2 749	–541	653	–10 658	–642	6 804
B.9	**Net lending (+) / net borrowing (-), from capital account**	NHCQ	1 975	4 202	4 473	2 814	–2 086	–4 319	–5 368	–9 935	–27 943

1 UK monetary financial institutions

Financial corporations

4.1.9 Financial corporations
ESA95 sector S.12 Unconsolidated

£ billion

			1992	1993	1994	1995	1996	1997	1998	1999	2000
IV.3	**FINANCIAL BALANCE SHEET** at end of period										
AN	Non-financial assets	CGDB	95.0	97.8	101.4	98.0	99.9	111.0	112.0	123.6	124.7
AF.A	**Financial assets**										
AF.2	Currency and deposits										
AF.21	Currency	NLJE	5.0	5.3	5.6	5.9	5.5	5.7	7.2	9.9	8.5
AF.22	Transferable deposits										
AF.221	Deposits with UK monetary financial institutions	NLJG	273.7	286.4	310.1	360.5	415.5	502.5	525.0	506.0	600.8
AF.229	Deposits with rest of the world monetary financial institutions	NLJK	453.7	500.7	529.1	597.4	615.3	770.3	790.1	790.1	997.4
AF.29	Other deposits	NLJL	0.3	0.2	0.2	0.2	0.1	0.1	0.1	0.1	2.8
AF.2	Total currency and deposits	NLJD	732.7	792.7	845.0	963.9	1 036.4	1 278.6	1 322.4	1 306.0	1 609.4
AF.3	Securities other than shares										
AF.331	Short term: money market instruments										
AF.3311	Issued by UK central government	NLJO	5.4	5.3	6.7	16.9	3.3	2.7	4.1	3.4	2.3
AF.3312	Issued by UK local authorities	NLJS	–	–	–	–	–	–	–	–	–
AF.3315	Issued by UK monetary financial institutions	NLJT	84.6	79.2	83.1	89.7	111.6	125.6	138.5	154.5	141.0
AF.3316	Issued by other UK residents	NLJY	1.4	1.2	1.4	1.5	1.6	2.2	4.4	6.2	7.4
AF.3319	Issued by the rest of the world	NLJZ	13.5	18.7	13.8	17.5	13.9	22.3	24.2	39.8	39.0
AF.332	Medium (1 to 5 year) and long term (over 5 year) bonds										
AF.3321	Issued by UK central government	NLKB	106.6	158.2	151.7	178.8	195.3	228.7	247.9	241.2	232.1
AF.3322	Issued by UK local authorities	NLKE	0.1	0.1	0.4	0.5	0.5	0.4	0.6	0.6	0.7
AF.3325	Medium term bonds issued by UK MFIs[1]	NLKF	9.3	10.8	14.6	17.5	19.3	20.9	24.3	31.8	34.9
AF.3326	Other medium & long term bonds issued by UK residents	NLKI	48.5	68.2	60.9	68.0	83.2	107.7	141.9	181.9	234.5
AF.3329	Long term bonds issued by the rest of the world	NLKJ	163.0	243.0	214.2	248.7	284.9	336.9	368.6	353.9	417.5
AF.34	Financial derivatives	NLKK	–	–	–	–	–	–	–	–	–
AF.3	Total securities other than shares	NLJM	432.3	584.6	546.7	639.0	713.6	847.4	954.4	1 013.4	1 109.3
AF.4	Loans										
AF.41	Short term loans										
AF.411	Loans by UK monetary financial institutions, excluding loans secured on dwellings & financial leasing	NLKQ	479.8	466.7	474.8	557.9	635.3	729.0	767.0	817.9	986.4
AF.42	Long term loans										
AF.421	Direct investment	NLKW	2.9	3.3	3.9	6.5	5.1	6.3	6.0	4.6	5.0
AF.422	Loans secured on dwellings	NLKZ	335.7	354.3	373.1	387.9	407.2	429.4	455.5	493.3	534.3
AF.423	Finance leasing	NLLD	18.2	17.9	17.8	18.7	20.6	22.6	23.2	23.3	23.0
AF.424	Other long-term loans by UK residents	NLLE	22.0	22.7	27.1	24.9	27.8	33.3	34.6	49.4	47.3
AF.4	Total loans	NLKO	858.6	865.0	896.6	995.8	1 096.0	1 220.6	1 286.3	1 388.5	1 596.1
AF.5	Shares and other equity										
AF.51	Shares and other equity, excluding mutual funds' shares										
AF.514	Quoted UK shares	NLLL	364.4	475.6	434.0	535.6	593.2	668.1	733.6	904.4	846.0
AF.515	Unquoted UK shares	NLLM	38.5	47.3	54.3	60.9	67.8	80.8	95.3	110.0	137.6
AF.519	Shares and other equity issued by the rest of the world	NLLQ	154.6	217.0	209.0	243.0	265.8	318.1	350.9	435.4	460.0
AF.52	Mutual funds' shares										
AF.521	UK mutual funds' shares	NLLU	49.9	69.7	61.9	71.4	84.0	92.4	116.6	142.3	137.6
AF.5	Total shares and other equity	NLLG	607.4	809.7	759.2	910.9	1 010.8	1 159.4	1 296.4	1 592.1	1 581.2
AF.6	Insurance technical reserves										
AF.62	Prepayments of insurance premiums and reserves for outstanding claims	NLLZ	1.3	1.4	1.6	1.7	2.1	2.1	0.8	1.7	1.8
AF.7	Other accounts receivable	NLMA	17.1	17.5	18.9	24.5	24.8	28.6	31.5	31.6	30.0
AF.A	**Total financial assets**	NLIZ	2 649.5	3 070.8	3 068.0	3 535.8	3 883.7	4 536.7	4 891.7	5 333.3	5 927.7

1 UK monetary financial institutions

Financial corporations

4.1.9 Financial corporations
ESA95 sector S.12 Unconsolidated
continued

£ billion

				1992	1993	1994	1995	1996	1997	1998	1999	2000
IV.3		**FINANCIAL BALANCE SHEET** continued at end of period										
AF.L		**Financial liabilities**										
AF.2		Currency and deposits										
AF.21		Currency	NLMI	20.6	21.9	23.5	25.1	25.3	26.9	29.9	35.1	35.6
AF.22		Transferable deposits										
AF.221		Deposits with UK monetary financial institutions	NLMK	1 330.1	1 404.0	1 488.5	1 659.8	1 727.9	2 034.1	2 171.0	2 182.5	2 573.0
AF.29		Other deposits	NLMP	–	–	–	–	–	–	–	–	2.9
AF.2		Total currency and deposits	NLMH	1 350.7	1 426.0	1 512.0	1 684.9	1 753.2	2 061.0	2 200.9	2 217.7	2 611.5
AF.3		Securities other than shares										
AF.331		Short term: money market instruments										
AF.3315		Issued by UK monetary financial institutions	NLMX	145.0	123.1	127.3	151.3	180.5	205.3	204.4	234.4	265.9
AF.3316		Issued by other non-government UK residents	NLNC	6.1	9.4	9.1	10.2	10.6	10.5	8.1	15.6	21.4
AF.332		Medium (1 to 5 year) and long term (over 5 year) bonds										
AF.3325		Medium term bonds issued by UK MFIs[1]	NLNJ	19.0	24.5	34.3	38.3	43.3	47.4	53.3	67.7	74.6
AF.3326		Other medium & long term bonds issued by UK residents	NLNM	48.0	65.6	72.3	82.0	99.6	122.3	148.2	172.4	213.9
AF.34		Financial derivatives	NLNO	–	–	–	–	–	–	–	–	–
AF.3		Total securities other than shares	NLMQ	218.1	222.4	243.0	281.8	334.0	385.4	413.9	490.1	575.8
AF.4		Loans										
AF.41		Short term loans										
AF.411		Loans by UK monetary financial institutions, excluding loans secured on dwellings & financial leasing	NLNU	100.8	115.8	128.4	167.6	204.8	244.3	249.1	255.3	315.8
AF.419		Loans by rest of the world monetary financial institutions	NLNY	66.6	143.1	86.9	123.3	187.7	216.0	209.5	259.7	308.3
AF.42		Long term loans										
AF.421		Direct investment	NLOA	9.5	10.0	11.0	10.7	11.7	17.5	15.3	15.9	13.9
AF.423		Finance leasing	NLOH	2.0	1.9	1.7	1.6	2.1	2.6	2.6	2.3	2.2
AF.424		Other long-term loans by UK residents	NLOI	6.0	6.6	7.5	7.7	9.3	11.3	11.6	13.9	15.1
AF.429		Other long-term loans by the rest of the world	NLOJ	1.7	1.9	1.7	0.8	0.9	0.8	0.7	0.5	0.5
AF.4		Total loans	NLNS	186.6	279.2	237.2	311.6	416.5	492.4	488.9	547.5	655.7
AF.5		Shares and other equity										
AF.51		Shares and other equity, excluding mutual funds' shares										
AF.514		Quoted UK shares	NLOP	78.1	121.7	106.0	140.1	159.6	276.7	312.5	356.7	380.7
AF.515		Unquoted UK shares	NLOQ	64.4	76.9	75.8	90.2	101.8	131.6	139.4	159.8	194.0
AF.52		Mutual funds' shares										
AF.521		UK mutual funds' shares	NLOY	81.3	123.6	119.8	143.9	166.1	193.3	217.9	299.0	304.4
AF.5		Total shares and other equity	NLOK	223.8	322.3	301.6	374.2	427.5	601.6	669.7	815.6	879.1
AF.6		Insurance technical reserves										
AF.61		Net equity of households in life assurance and pension funds' reserves	NLPA	685.0	875.2	823.8	968.3	1 053.8	1 285.9	1 421.1	1 640.8	1 625.6
AF.62		Prepayments of insurance premiums and reserves for outstanding claims	NLPD	38.0	39.7	42.4	47.5	58.6	59.5	60.8	59.5	62.9
AF.6		Total insurance technical reserves	NPYI	723.0	915.0	866.2	1 015.8	1 112.4	1 345.5	1 481.9	1 700.3	1 688.5
AF.7		Other accounts payable	NLPE	11.5	11.4	11.4	14.0	14.3	16.1	18.6	22.6	27.9
AF.L		**Total financial liabilities**	NLMD	2 713.8	3 176.2	3 171.4	3 682.3	4 058.0	4 902.1	5 274.1	5 793.8	6 438.6
BF.90		**Net financial assets / liabilities**										
AF.A		Total financial assets	NLIZ	2 649.5	3 070.8	3 068.0	3 535.8	3 883.7	4 536.7	4 891.7	5 333.3	5 927.7
-AF.L		*less* Total financial liabilities	-NLMD	–2 713.8	–3 176.2	–3 171.4	–3 682.3	–4 058.0	–4 902.1	–5 274.1	–5 793.8	–6 438.6
BF.90		**Net financial assets (+) / liabilities (-)**	NYOE	–64.3	–105.4	–103.4	–146.5	–174.4	–365.4	–382.3	–460.5	–510.8
		Net worth										
AN		Non-financial assets	CGDB	95.0	97.8	101.4	98.0	99.9	111.0	112.0	123.6	124.7
BF.90		Net financial assets (+) / liabilities (-)	NYOE	–64.3	–105.4	–103.4	–146.5	–174.4	–365.4	–382.3	–460.5	–510.8
BF.90		**Net worth**	CGRU	30.7	–7.6	–2.0	–48.6	–74.4	–254.4	–270.3	–336.9	–386.2

1 UK monetary financial institutions

United Kingdom National Accounts 2001, © Crown copyright 2001

Financial corporations

Financial corporations

4.2.2 Monetary financial institutions
ESA95 sectors S.121 Central bank & S.122 Other monetary financial institutions

£ million

			1992	1993	1994	1995	1996	1997	1998	1999
II	**DISTRIBUTION AND USE OF INCOME ACCOUNTS**									
II.1	**PRIMARY DISTRIBUTION OF INCOME ACCOUNT**									
II.1.1	**GENERATION OF INCOME ACCOUNT** before deduction of fixed capital consumption									
	Resources									
B.1g	Total resources, gross value added	NHJN	22 410	21 920	25 040	23 101	23 074	25 756	35 560	28 448
	Uses									
D.1	Compensation of employees									
D.11	Wages and salaries	NHDJ	8 440	8 076	7 626	7 247	7 896	8 947	10 019	10 488
D.12	Employers' social contributions	NHDM	1 317	1 281	1 206	1 167	1 258	1 437	1 587	1 671
D.1	Total	NHFL	9 757	9 357	8 832	8 414	9 154	10 384	11 606	12 159
D.2	Taxes on production and imports, paid									
D.29	Production taxes other than on products	NHJE	619	670	646	707	741	766	781	832
-D.3	less Subsidies, received									
-D.39	Production subsidies other than on products	-NHET	–	–	–	–	–	–	–	–
B.2g	Operating surplus, gross	NHBX	12 034	11 893	15 562	13 980	13 179	14 606	23 173	15 457
B.1g	Total uses	NHJN	22 410	21 920	25 040	23 101	23 074	25 756	35 560	28 448

4.2.3 Monetary financial institutions
ESA95 sectors S.121 Central bank & S.122 Other monetary financial institutions

£ million

			1992	1993	1994	1995	1996	1997	1998	1999	2000
II.1.2	**ALLOCATION OF PRIMARY INCOME ACCOUNT**										
	Resources										
B.2g	Operating surplus, gross	NHBX	12 034	11 893	15 562	13 980	13 179	14 606	23 173	15 457	15 800
D.4	Property income, received										
D.41	Interest	NHFE	124 538	102 936	102 497	121 905	122 653	133 903	161 713	140 659	177 822
D.42	Distributed income of corporations	NHFF	1 614	951	1 870	2 109	2 869	2 979	1 958	4 562	6 039
D.43	Reinvested earnings on direct foreign investment	NHKY	118	388	721	36	783	670	747	1 431	1 679
D.44	Property income attributed to insurance policy-holders	NHJS	38	37	38	42	38	43	8	12	16
D.45	Rent	NHJT	–	–	–	–	–	–	–	–	–
D.4	Total	NHJR	126 308	104 312	105 126	124 092	126 343	137 595	164 426	146 664	185 556
-P.119	Adjustment to property income for financial services (FISIM)	-QTFB	–19 445	–19 928	–24 888	–24 191	–24 683	–27 396	–35 737	–32 258	–35 346
Total	Total resources	NRKH	118 897	96 277	95 800	113 881	114 839	124 805	151 862	129 863	166 010
	Uses										
D.4	Property income, paid										
D.41	Interest	NHFG	102 779	81 138	76 073	94 743	95 017	102 537	120 220	100 008	132 151
D.42	Distributed income of corporations	NHFH	3 584	4 957	4 354	6 657	6 735	6 802	4 811	13 020	17 416
D.43	Reinvested earnings on direct foreign investment	NHLB	4	1 202	231	456	840	444	–320	972	1 953
D.45	Rent	NHJW	–	–	–	–	–	–	–	–	–
D.4	Total	NHJU	106 367	87 297	80 658	101 856	102 592	109 783	124 711	114 000	151 520
B.5g	Balance of primary incomes, gross	NRKI	12 530	8 980	15 142	12 025	12 247	15 022	27 151	15 863	14 490
Total	Total uses	NRKH	118 897	96 277	95 800	113 881	114 839	124 805	151 862	129 863	166 010

Financial corporations

4.2.4 Monetary financial institutions
ESA95 sectors S.121 Central bank & S.122 Other monetary financial institutions

£ million

			1992	1993	1994	1995	1996	1997	1998	1999	2000
II.2	**SECONDARY DISTRIBUTION OF INCOME ACCOUNT**										
	Resources										
B.5g	Balance of primary incomes, gross	NRKI	12 530	8 980	15 142	12 025	12 247	15 022	27 151	15 863	14 490
D.61	Social contributions										
D.612	Imputed social contributions	NHKD	218	199	188	199	187	187	222	212	241
D.7	Other current transfers										
D.72	Non-life insurance claims	NHJZ	544	480	476	502	493	465	75	160	190
Total	Total resources	NRKP	13 292	9 659	15 806	12 726	12 927	15 674	27 448	16 235	14 921
	Uses										
D.5	Current taxes on income, wealth etc.										
D.51	Taxes on income	NHKA	921	903	1 255	1 750	2 330	2 580	2 761	4 439	4 390
D.62	Social benefits other than social transfers in kind	NHKC	218	199	188	199	187	187	222	212	241
D.7	Other current transfers										
D.71	Net non-life insurance premiums	NHKG	544	480	476	502	493	465	75	160	190
D.75	Miscellaneous current transfers	NHKW	32	41	52	45	45	46	52	52	55
D.7	Total	NHKF	576	521	528	547	538	511	127	212	245
B.6g	Disposable income, gross	NRKQ	11 577	8 036	13 835	10 230	9 872	12 396	24 338	11 372	10 045
Total	Total uses	NRKP	13 292	9 659	15 806	12 726	12 927	15 674	27 448	16 235	14 921

4.2.6 Monetary financial institutions
ESA95 sectors S.121 Central bank & S.122 Other monetary financial institutions

£ million

			1992	1993	1994	1995	1996	1997	1998	1999	2000
II.4.1	**USE OF DISPOSABLE INCOME ACCOUNT**										
	Resources										
B.6g	Total resources, gross disposable income	NRKQ	11 577	8 036	13 835	10 230	9 872	12 396	24 338	11 372	10 045
	Uses										
B.8g	Total uses, gross saving	NRKT	11 577	8 036	13 835	10 230	9 872	12 396	24 338	11 372	10 045

# Financial corporations

4.2.7 Monetary financial institutions
ESA95 sectors S.121 Central bank & S.122 Other monetary financial institutions

£ million

			1992	1993	1994	1995	1996	1997	1998	1999	2000
III	**ACCUMULATION ACCOUNTS**										
III.1	**CAPITAL ACCOUNT**										
III.1.1	**CHANGE IN NET WORTH DUE TO SAVING & CAPITAL TRANSFERS ACCOUNT**										
	Changes in liabilities and net worth										
B.8g	Saving, gross	NRKT	11 577	8 036	13 835	10 230	9 872	12 396	24 338	11 372	10 045
D.9	Capital transfers receivable										
D.92	Investment grants	NHKM	–	–	–	–	–	–	–	–	–
D.99	Other capital transfers	NHKN	–	–	–	–	–	–	–	–	–
D.9	Total	NHKL	–	–	–	–	–	–	–	–	–
-D.9	*less* Capital transfers payable										
-D.91	Capital taxes	-NHEQ	–	–	–	–	–	–	–	–	–
-D.99	Other capital transfers	-NHEV	–	–88	–518	–	–	–	–	–	–
-D.9	Total	-NHKP	–	–88	–518	–	–	–	–	–	–
B.10.1g	Total change in liabilities and net worth	NRMH	11 577	7 948	13 317	10 230	9 872	12 396	24 338	11 372	10 045
	Changes in assets										
B.10.1g	Changes in net worth due to saving and capital transfers before deduction of fixed capital consumption	NRMH	11 577	7 948	13 317	10 230	9 872	12 396	24 338	11 372	10 045
III.1.2	**ACQUISITION OF NON-FINANCIAL ASSETS ACCOUNT**										
B.10.1g	**Total changes in liabilities and net worth** due to saving & capital transfers	NRMH	11 577	7 948	13 317	10 230	9 872	12 396	24 338	11 372	10 045
	Changes in assets										
P.5	Gross capital formation										
P.51	Gross fixed capital formation	NHFD	1 737	1 711	2 579	2 685	2 542	2 631	3 839	2 810	3 124
P.52	Changes in inventories	NHFC	–	–	–	20	20	35	35	47	55
P.53	Acquisitions less disposals of valuables	NHKT	–	–	–	–	–	–	–	–	–
P.5	Total	NHKS	1 737	1 711	2 579	2 705	2 562	2 666	3 874	2 857	3 179
K.2	Acquisitions less disposals of non-produced non-financial assets	NHKU	–	–	–	–	–	–	–	–	–
B.9	Net lending (+) / net borrowing (-)	NHFK	9 840	6 237	10 738	7 525	7 310	9 730	20 464	8 515	6 866
B.10.1g	Total change in assets	NRMH	11 577	7 948	13 317	10 230	9 872	12 396	24 338	11 372	10 045

United Kingdom National Accounts 2001, © Crown copyright 2001

Financial corporations

4.2.8 Monetary financial institutions
ESA95 sectors S.121 Central bank and S.122 Other monetary financial institutions Unconsolidated

£ million

				1992	1993	1994	1995	1996	1997	1998	1999	2000
III.2	FINANCIAL ACCOUNT											
F.A	Net acquisition of financial assets											
F.2	Currency and deposits											
F.21	Currency		NGCB	629	295	291	312	−437	232	1 494	2 717	−1 413
F.22	Transferable deposits											
F.221	Deposits with UK monetary financial institutions		NGCD	12 036	1 396	17 316	−3 984	42 388	23 665	21 233	3 427	39 117
F.229	Deposits with rest of the world monetary financial institutions		NGCH	13 614	2 846	50 776	10 164	26 470	114 944	16 860	−29 289	133 314
F.29	Other deposits		NGCI	−96	−9	−44	−24	−69	−5	−10	−9	−6
F.2	Total currency and deposits		NGCA	26 183	4 528	68 339	6 468	68 352	138 836	39 577	−23 154	171 012
F.3	Securities other than shares											
F.331	Short term: money market instruments											
F.3311	Issued by UK central government		NGCL	−1 930	−3	1 250	8 762	−12 113	−611	1 124	36	−1 222
F.3312	Issued by UK local authorities		NGCP	−6	25	−43	–	–	–	–	–	–
F.3315	Issued by UK monetary financial institutions		NGCQ	−242	−3 274	−706	7 748	18 901	9 853	3 576	10 707	−19 213
F.3316	Issued by other UK residents		NGCV	346	93	90	−111	−94	90	164	64	847
F.3319	Issued by the rest of the world		NGCW	2 424	3 174	−4 328	1 869	−3 531	7 818	4 248	9 732	331
F.332	Medium (1 to 5 year) and long term (over 5 year) bonds											
F.3321	Issued by UK central government		NGCY	4 515	9 739	−66	1 287	6 566	−12	−8 490	−6 090	−7 553
F.3322	Issued by UK local authorities		NGDB	−11	97	36	−16	−1	2	−2	–	–
F.3325	Medium term bonds issued by UK MFIs[1]		NGDC	593	943	1 801	467	639	749	1 606	5 047	3 973
F.3326	Other medium & long term bonds issued by UK residents		NGDF	2 368	6 717	3 073	3 602	4 597	−1 084	1 243	6 860	18 507
F.3329	Long term bonds issued by the rest of the world		NGDG	13 625	35 087	12 829	24 168	19 101	18 133	44 059	12 997	32 255
F.34	Financial derivatives		NGDH	−1 253	−245	−2 373	−1 667	−963	−1 156	3 043	−2 685	−1 553
F.3	Total securities other than shares		NGCJ	20 429	52 353	11 563	46 109	33 102	33 782	50 571	36 668	26 372
F.4	Loans											
F.41	Short term loans											
F.411	Loans by UK monetary financial institutions, excluding loans secured on dwellings & financial leasing		NGDN	4 487	−6 533	14 676	51 722	112 543	100 472	31 892	65 499	154 783
F.42	Long term loans											
F.421	Direct investment		NGDT	16	–	–	76	22	−782	−115	−123	−222
F.422	Loans secured on dwellings		NGDW	20 215	19 320	20 325	16 858	19 505	23 177	22 984	32 130	28 420
F.423	Finance leasing		NGEA	43	86	237	224	199	228	431	437	−40
F.4	Total loans		NGDL	24 761	12 873	35 238	68 880	132 269	123 095	55 192	97 943	182 941
F.5	Shares and other equity											
F.51	Shares and other equity, excluding mutual funds' shares											
F.514	Quoted UK shares		NGEI	36	−62	40	191	145	−25	472	208	635
F.515	Unquoted UK shares		NGEJ	557	1 084	1 418	1 760	3 639	4 544	985	1 933	8 926
F.519	Shares and other equity issued by the rest of the world		NGEN	218	1 181	4 313	989	5 321	−2 822	5 294	1 722	9 868
F.52	Mutual funds' shares											
F.521	UK mutual funds' shares		NGER	18	77	127	34	31	16	2	3	27
F.5	Total shares and other equity		NGED	829	2 280	5 898	2 974	9 136	1 713	6 753	3 866	19 456
F.7	Other accounts receivable		NGEX	−842	−498	317	1 167	−651	643	−12	−468	−1 286
F.A	Total net acquisition of financial assets		NGBW	71 360	71 536	121 355	125 598	242 208	298 069	152 081	114 855	398 495

1 UK monetary financial institutions

Financial corporations

4.2.8 Monetary financial institutions
ESA95 sectors S.121 Central bank and S.122 Other monetary financial institutions Unconsolidated
continued

£ million

				1992	1993	1994	1995	1996	1997	1998	1999	2000
III.2	**FINANCIAL ACCOUNT** continued											
F.L	**Net acquisition of financial liabilities**											
F.2	Currency and deposits											
F.21	Currency		NGFF	1 614	1 322	1 530	1 620	251	1 605	2 967	5 232	448
F.22	Transferable deposits											
F.221	Deposits with UK monetary financial institutions		NGFH	63 824	76 990	82 598	83 227	186 849	258 267	115 825	41 823	342 226
F.2	Total currency and deposits		NGFE	65 438	78 312	84 128	84 847	187 100	259 872	118 792	47 055	342 674
F.3	Securities other than shares											
F.331	Short term: money market instruments											
F.3315	Issued by UK monetary financial institutions		NGFU	−12 777	−22 845	6 358	23 215	36 572	21 983	−1 218	31 203	23 953
F.332	Medium (1 to 5 year) and long term (over 5 year) bonds											
F.3325	Medium term bonds issued by UK MFIs[1]		NGGG	2 756	5 268	10 313	3 937	7 894	5 196	4 140	11 911	4 751
F.3326	Other medium & long term bonds issued by UK residents		NGGJ	3 273	5 325	−8	1 879	4 877	4 245	−3 049	5 988	11 005
F.34	Financial derivatives		NGGL	114	−8	−1	17	15	34	55	26	21
F.3	Total securities other than shares		NGFN	−6 634	−12 260	16 662	29 048	49 358	31 458	−72	49 128	39 730
F.4	Loans											
F.42	Long term loans											
F.421	Direct investment		NGGX	−544	−348	412	−992	−693	147	−31	9	1
F.423	Finance leasing		NGHE	−66	−72	−99	−40	262	225	21	−168	−61
F.4	Total loans		NGGP	−610	−420	313	−1 032	−431	372	−10	−159	−60
F.5	Shares and other equity											
F.51	Shares and other equity, excluding mutual funds' shares											
F.514	Quoted UK shares		NGHM	578	1 074	560	966	924	1 241	−1 868	−519	2 410
F.515	Unquoted UK shares		NGHN	−748	475	−268	−568	−79	87	−266	1 097	10 904
F.516	Other UK equity (including direct investment in property)		NGHO	−7	56	–	13	−19	–	–	–	–
F.5	Total shares and other equity		NGHH	−177	1 605	292	411	826	1 328	−2 134	578	13 314
F.7	Other accounts payable		NGIB	−383	−792	188	858	−853	919	896	−261	1 461
F.L	**Total net acquisition of financial liabilities**		NGFA	57 634	66 445	101 583	114 132	236 000	293 949	117 472	96 341	397 119
B.9	**Net lending / borrowing**											
F.A	Total net acquisition of financial assets		NGBW	71 360	71 536	121 355	125 598	242 208	298 069	152 081	114 855	398 495
-F.L	*less* Total net acquisition of financial liabilities		-NGFA	−57 634	−66 445	−101 583	−114 132	−236 000	−293 949	−117 472	−96 341	−397 119
B.9f	**Net lending (+) / net borrowing (-), from financial account**		NYNS	13 726	5 091	19 772	11 466	6 208	4 120	34 609	18 514	1 376
dB.9f	**Statistical discrepancy**		NYPE	−3 886	1 146	−9 034	−3 941	1 102	5 610	−14 145	−9 999	5 490
B.9	**Net lending (+) / net borrowing (-), from capital account**		NHFK	9 840	6 237	10 738	7 525	7 310	9 730	20 464	8 515	6 866

1 UK monetary financial institutions

Financial corporations

4.2.9 Monetary financial institutions
ESA95 sectors S.121 Central bank and S.122 Other monetary financial institutions Unconsolidated

£ billion

			1992	1993	1994	1995	1996	1997	1998	1999	2000
IV.3	**FINANCIAL BALANCE SHEET** at end of period										
AF.A	**Financial assets**										
AF.2	Currency and deposits										
AF.21	Currency	NNSY	5.0	5.2	5.5	5.8	5.4	5.6	7.1	9.9	8.4
AF.22	Transferable deposits										
AF.221	Deposits with UK monetary financial institutions	NNTA	185.6	186.5	203.9	215.4	242.2	302.0	308.5	305.8	352.3
AF.229	Deposits with rest of the world monetary financial institutions	NNTE	407.6	412.1	460.6	507.3	474.7	628.3	666.5	622.6	773.8
AF.29	Other deposits	NNTF	0.2	0.2	0.2	0.2	0.1	0.1	0.1	0.1	0.1
AF.2	Total currency and deposits	NNSX	598.4	604.1	670.2	728.6	722.3	936.0	982.3	938.3	1 134.6
AF.3	Securities other than shares										
AF.331	Short term: money market instruments										
AF.3311	Issued by UK central government	NNTI	5.1	5.0	6.3	15.1	2.4	1.7	3.0	2.8	1.5
AF.3312	Issued by UK local authorities	NNTM	–	–	–	–	–	–	–	–	–
AF.3315	Issued by UK monetary financial institutions	NNTN	74.4	71.0	69.8	77.7	95.3	105.6	104.6	114.5	97.0
AF.3316	Issued by other UK residents	NNTS	0.4	0.5	0.6	0.5	0.4	0.5	0.7	0.7	1.9
AF.3319	Issued by the rest of the world	NNTT	12.3	15.4	10.5	13.3	8.7	16.9	21.6	31.7	34.9
AF.332	Medium (1 to 5 year) and long term (over 5 year) bonds										
AF.3321	Issued by UK central government	NNTV	16.6	27.1	28.0	26.7	30.0	30.5	21.6	15.8	8.4
AF.3322	Issued by UK local authorities	NNTY	–	–	–	–	–	–	–	–	–
AF.3325	Medium term bonds issued by UK MFIs[1]	NNTZ	5.0	5.9	7.8	8.4	9.3	9.6	11.7	16.6	21.0
AF.3326	Other medium & long term bonds issued by UK residents	NNUC	17.6	21.5	22.6	25.1	35.6	44.8	52.2	66.1	75.8
AF.3329	Long term bonds issued by the rest of the world	NNUD	72.1	110.6	120.5	146.5	156.4	183.5	228.7	239.5	288.3
AF.34	Financial derivatives	NNUE	–	–	–	–	–	–	–	–	–
AF.3	Total securities other than shares	NNTG	203.5	257.0	266.1	313.3	338.0	393.1	444.0	487.8	528.9
AF.4	Loans										
AF.41	Short term loans										
AF.411	Loans by UK monetary financial institutions, excluding loans secured on dwellings & financial leasing	NNUK	479.8	466.7	474.8	557.9	635.3	729.0	767.0	817.9	986.4
AF.42	Long term loans										
AF.421	Direct investment	NNUQ	–	–	–	–	–	–	–	–	–
AF.422	Loans secured on dwellings	NNUT	307.8	328.1	347.1	363.1	382.6	403.3	427.1	458.7	493.5
AF.423	Finance leasing	NNUX	0.9	1.0	1.2	1.4	1.6	1.8	2.3	2.7	2.7
AF.4	Total loans	NNUI	788.5	795.8	823.1	922.4	1 019.6	1 134.1	1 196.3	1 279.2	1 482.6
AF.5	Shares and other equity										
AF.51	Shares and other equity, excluding mutual funds' shares										
AF.514	Quoted UK shares	NNVF	1.5	1.6	2.5	3.6	3.8	5.1	5.8	7.5	8.8
AF.515	Unquoted UK shares	NNVG	11.1	13.7	17.0	21.7	22.4	29.0	32.4	40.9	48.1
AF.519	Shares and other equity issued by the rest of the world	NNVK	11.7	10.7	14.8	15.9	14.8	12.5	22.9	22.2	39.6
AF.52	Mutual funds' shares										
AF.521	UK mutual funds' shares	NNVO	0.6	1.0	1.0	1.1	1.2	1.3	1.3	1.7	1.6
AF.5	Total shares and other equity	NNVA	24.9	26.9	35.3	42.2	42.2	47.9	62.4	72.2	98.1
AF.7	Other accounts receivable	NNVU	5.5	5.0	5.1	6.4	5.3	5.8	6.0	5.9	4.8
AF.A	**Total financial assets**	NNST	1 620.8	1 688.8	1 799.8	2 012.9	2 127.4	2 516.9	2 691.1	2 783.4	3 248.9

1 UK monetary financial institutions

Financial corporations

4.2.9 Monetary financial institutions
continued
ESA95 sectors S.121 Central bank and S.122 Other monetary financial institutions   Unconsolidated

£ billion

			1992	1993	1994	1995	1996	1997	1998	1999	2000
IV.3	**FINANCIAL BALANCE SHEET** continued at end of period										
AF.L	**Financial liabilities**										
AF.2	Currency and deposits										
AF.21	Currency	NNWC	20.6	21.9	23.5	25.1	25.3	26.9	29.9	35.1	35.6
AF.22	Transferable deposits										
AF.221	Deposits with UK monetary financial institutions	NNWE	1 330.1	1 404.0	1 488.5	1 659.8	1 727.9	2 034.1	2 171.0	2 182.5	2 573.0
AF.2	Total currency and deposits	NNWB	1 350.7	1 426.0	1 512.0	1 684.9	1 753.2	2 061.0	2 200.9	2 217.7	2 608.6
AF.3	Securities other than shares										
AF.331	Short term: money market instruments										
AF.3315	Issued by UK monetary financial institutions	NNWR	145.0	123.1	127.3	151.3	180.5	205.3	204.4	234.4	265.9
AF.332	Medium (1 to 5 year) and long term (over 5 year) bonds										
AF.3325	Medium term bonds issued by UK MFIs[1]	NNXD	19.0	24.5	34.3	38.3	43.3	47.4	53.3	67.7	74.6
AF.3326	Other medium & long term bonds issued by UK residents	NNXG	25.3	33.1	32.8	34.3	34.5	45.1	52.5	55.3	69.3
AF.34	Financial derivatives	NNXI	–	–	–	–	–	–	–	–	–
AF.3	Total securities other than shares	NNWK	189.3	180.6	194.4	223.8	258.3	297.8	310.3	357.4	409.8
AF.4	Loans										
AF.41	Short term loans										
AF.411	Loans by UK monetary financial institutions, excluding loans secured on dwellings & financial leasing	NNXO	0.1	0.1	–	–	–	–	–	–	–
AF.42	Long term loans										
AF.421	Direct investment	NNXU	5.1	4.8	5.1	5.2	4.5	6.6	4.1	2.6	0.3
AF.423	Finance leasing	NNYB	1.0	0.9	0.8	0.8	1.1	1.3	1.3	1.1	1.1
AF.424	Other long-term loans by UK residents	NNYC	–	–	–	–	–	–	–	–	–
AF.4	Total loans	NNXM	6.2	5.8	5.9	6.0	5.6	7.9	5.4	3.7	1.3
AF.5	Shares and other equity										
AF.51	Shares and other equity, excluding mutual funds' shares										
AF.514	Quoted UK shares	NNYJ	21.3	31.0	28.7	25.8	27.5	73.5	84.6	63.4	41.0
AF.515	Unquoted UK shares	NNYK	33.0	35.9	36.7	39.3	42.0	46.6	45.7	45.4	53.7
AF.5	Total shares and other equity	NNYE	54.3	67.0	65.5	65.1	69.5	120.1	130.3	108.8	94.7
AF.7	Other accounts payable	NNYY	6.8	6.0	6.2	6.7	5.8	3.7	4.4	3.9	4.8
AF.L	**Total financial liabilities**	NNVX	1 607.4	1 685.4	1 784.0	1 986.5	2 092.4	2 490.4	2 651.4	2 691.5	3 119.3
BF.90	**Net financial assets / liabilities**										
AF.A	Total financial assets	NNST	1 620.8	1 688.8	1 799.8	2 012.9	2 127.4	2 516.9	2 691.1	2 783.4	3 248.9
-AF.L	*less* Total financial liabilities	-NNVX	–1 607.4	–1 685.4	–1 784.0	–1 986.5	–2 092.4	–2 490.4	–2 651.4	–2 691.5	–3 119.3
BF.90	**Net financial assets (+) / liabilities (-)**	NYOL	13.5	3.3	15.8	26.4	35.0	26.5	39.7	91.9	129.6

1 UK monetary financial institutions

United Kingdom National Accounts 2001, © Crown copyright 2001

Financial corporations

Financial corporations

4.3.2 Other financial intermediaries and financial auxiliaries
ESA95 sectors S.123 Other financial intermediaries & S.124 Financial auxiliaries

£ million

			1992	1993	1994	1995	1996	1997	1998	1999
II	**DISTRIBUTION AND USE OF INCOME ACCOUNTS**									
II.1	**PRIMARY DISTRIBUTION OF INCOME ACCOUNT**									
II.1.1	**GENERATION OF INCOME ACCOUNT** before deduction of fixed capital consumption									
	Resources									
B.1g	Total resources, gross value added	NHMH	5 064	5 050	3 936	4 813	3 989	717	−1 344	2 434
	Uses									
D.1	Compensation of employees									
D.11	Wages and salaries	NHED	4 103	4 312	4 536	4 621	5 033	5 091	5 228	5 583
D.12	Employers' social contributions	NHEE	855	829	770	747	885	955	1 118	1 175
D.1	Total	NHLX	4 958	5 141	5 306	5 368	5 918	6 046	6 346	6 758
D.2	Taxes on production and imports, paid									
D.29	Production taxes other than on products	NHLY	268	279	330	424	398	422	475	444
-D.3	*less* Subsidies, received									
-D.39	Production subsidies other than on products	-NHLF	–	–	–	–	–	–	–	–
B.2g	Operating surplus, gross	NHBY	−162	−370	−1 700	−979	−2 327	−5 751	−8 165	−4 768
B.1g	Total uses	NHMH	5 064	5 050	3 936	4 813	3 989	717	−1 344	2 434

4.3.3 Other financial intermediaries and financial auxiliaries
ESA95 sectors S.123 Other financial intermediaries & S.124 Financial auxiliaries

£ million

			1992	1993	1994	1995	1996	1997	1998	1999	2000
II.1.2	**ALLOCATION OF PRIMARY INCOME ACCOUNT**										
	Resources										
B.2g	Operating surplus, gross	NHBY	−162	−370	−1 700	−979	−2 327	−5 751	−8 165	−4 768	−4 050
D.4	Property income, received										
D.41	Interest	NHLQ	13 663	14 528	13 797	14 881	16 371	19 270	23 034	20 780	25 820
D.42	Distributed income of corporations	NHLR	4 418	4 491	5 661	6 354	7 924	7 085	6 513	13 666	22 895
D.43	Reinvested earnings on direct foreign investment	NHNS	449	1 414	1 391	1 761	2 381	2 445	1 810	2 763	2 740
D.44	Property income attributed to insurance policy-holders	NHMM	9	9	9	10	9	11	8	9	14
D.45	Rent	NHMN	–	–	–	–	–	–	–	–	–
D.4	Total	NHML	18 539	20 442	20 858	23 006	26 685	28 811	31 365	37 218	51 469
-P.119	Adjustment to property income for financial services (FISIM)	-QTFD	359	359	1 769	976	2 103	5 000	7 739	1 439	−1 745
Total	Total resources	NRKX	18 736	20 431	20 927	23 003	26 461	28 060	30 939	33 889	45 674
	Uses										
D.4	Property income										
D.41	Interest	NHLS	12 689	12 970	12 768	14 235	15 669	20 591	26 547	23 819	32 443
D.42	Distributed income of corporations	NHLT	6 509	6 774	9 214	8 871	11 556	11 536	12 261	13 037	15 359
D.43	Reinvested earnings on direct foreign investment	NHNU	196	1 056	−948	−146	573	391	−1 570	752	1 447
D.45	Rent	NHMQ	–	–	–	–	–	–	–	–	–
D.4	Total	NHMO	19 394	20 800	21 034	22 960	27 798	32 518	37 238	37 608	49 249
B.5g	Balance of primary incomes, gross	NRKZ	−658	−369	−107	43	−1 337	−4 458	−6 299	−3 719	−3 575
Total	Total uses	NRKX	18 736	20 431	20 927	23 003	26 461	28 060	30 939	33 889	45 674

United Kingdom National Accounts 2001, © Crown copyright 2001

Financial corporations

4.3.4 Other financial intermediaries and financial auxiliaries
ESA95 sectors S.123 Other financial intermediaries & S.124 Financial auxiliaries

£ million

			1992	1993	1994	1995	1996	1997	1998	1999	2000
II.2	SECONDARY DISTRIBUTION OF INCOME ACCOUNT										
	Resources										
B.5g	Balance of primary incomes, gross	NRKZ	−658	−369	−107	43	−1 337	−4 458	−6 299	−3 719	−3 575
D.61	Social contributions										
D.612	Imputed social contributions	NHMX	151	136	133	144	136	135	158	150	170
D.7	Other current transfers										
D.72	Non-life insurance claims	NHMT	136	121	113	126	123	116	75	136	163
D.75	Miscellaneous current transfers	NRLD	–	–	–	–	–	–	–	–	–
D.7	Total	NRLE	136	121	113	126	123	116	75	136	163
Total	Total resources	NRLF	−371	−112	139	313	−1 078	−4 207	−6 066	−3 433	−3 242
	Uses										
D.5	Current taxes on income, wealth etc.										
D.51	Taxes on income	NHMU	588	144	371	438	833	583	1 222	3 132	2 293
D.62	Social benefits other than social transfers in kind	NHMW	151	136	133	144	136	135	158	150	170
D.7	Other current transfers										
D.71	Net non-life insurance premiums	NHNA	136	121	113	126	123	116	75	136	163
D.75	Miscellaneous current transfers	NHNQ	16	16	22	20	20	20	22	23	24
D.7	Total	NHMZ	152	137	135	146	143	136	97	159	187
B.6g	Disposable income, gross	NRLG	−1 262	−529	−500	−415	−2 190	−5 061	−7 543	−6 874	−5 892
Total	Total uses	NRLF	−371	−112	139	313	−1 078	−4 207	−6 066	−3 433	−3 242

4.3.6 Other financial intermediaries and financial auxiliaries
ESA95 sectors S.123 Other financial intermediaries & S.124 Financial auxiliaries

£ million

			1992	1993	1994	1995	1996	1997	1998	1999	2000
II.4.1	USE OF DISPOSABLE INCOME ACCOUNT										
	Resources										
B.6g	Total resources, gross disposable income	NRLG	−1 262	−529	−500	−415	−2 190	−5 061	−7 543	−6 874	−5 892
	Uses										
B.8g	Total uses, gross saving	NRLJ	−1 262	−529	−500	−415	−2 190	−5 061	−7 543	−6 874	−5 892

Financial corporations

4.3.7 Other financial intermediaries and financial auxiliaries
ESA95 sectors S.123 Other financial intermediaries & S.124 Financial auxiliaries

£ million

			1992	1993	1994	1995	1996	1997	1998	1999	2000
III	**ACCUMULATION ACCOUNTS**										
III.1	**CAPITAL ACCOUNT**										
III.1.1	**CHANGE IN NET WORTH DUE TO SAVING & CAPITAL TRANSFERS ACCOUNT**										
	Changes in liabilities and net worth										
B.8g	Saving, gross	NRLJ	−1 262	−529	−500	−415	−2 190	−5 061	−7 543	−6 874	−5 892
D.9	Capital transfers receivable										
D.92	Investment grants	NHNG	−	−	−	−	−	−	−	−	−
D.99	Other capital transfers	NHNH	−	−	−	−	−	−	−	−	−
D.9	Total	NHNF	−	−	−	−	−	−	−	−	−
-D.9	*less* Capital transfers payable										
-D.91	Capital taxes	-NRXX	−	−	−	−	−	−	−	−	−
-D.99	Other capital transfers	-NHLH	−	−	−	−	−	−	−	−	−
-D.9	Total	-NHNI	−	−	−	−	−	−	−	−	−
B.10.1g	Total change in liabilities and net worth	NRMI	−1 262	−529	−500	−415	−2 190	−5 061	−7 543	−6 874	−5 892
	Changes in assets										
B.10.1g	Change in net worth due to saving and capital transfers before deduction of fixed capital consumption	NRMI	−1 262	−529	−500	−415	−2 190	−5 061	−7 543	−6 874	−5 892
III.1.2	**ACQUISITION OF NON-FINANCIAL ASSETS ACCOUNT**										
B.10.1g	**Total changes in liabilities and net worth** due to saving and capital transfers	NRMI	−1 262	−529	−500	−415	−2 190	−5 061	−7 543	−6 874	−5 892
	Changes in assets										
P.5	Gross capital formation										
P.51	Gross fixed capital formation	NHLP	1 884	1 658	1 794	2 138	3 739	1 698	2 563	1 261	1 970
P.52	Changes in inventories	NHLO	−	−	−	−	−	−	−	−	−
P.53	Acquisitions less disposals of valuables	NHNN	−	−	−	−	−	−	−	−	−
P.5	Total	NHNM	1 884	1 658	1 794	2 138	3 739	1 698	2 563	1 261	1 970
K.2	Acquisitions less disposals of non-produced non-financial assets	NHNO	−79	−179	118	−62	62	−2	33	63	52
B.9	Net lending (+) / net borrowing (-)	NHLW	−3 067	−2 008	−2 412	−2 491	−5 991	−6 757	−10 139	−8 198	−7 914
Total	Total change in assets	NRMI	−1 262	−529	−500	−415	−2 190	−5 061	−7 543	−6 874	−5 892

United Kingdom National Accounts 2001, © Crown copyright 2001

Financial corporations

4.3.8 Other financial intermediaries and financial auxiliaries
ESA95 sectors S.123 and S.124   Unconsolidated

£ million

			1992	1993	1994	1995	1996	1997	1998	1999	2000
III.2	**FINANCIAL ACCOUNT**										
F.A	**Net acquisition of financial assets**										
F.2	Currency and deposits										
F.21	Currency	NFJD	3	2	2	2	–	–	–	–	–
F.22	Transferable deposits										
F.2211	Sterling deposits with UK banks	NFJG	−3 449	7 430	−1 360	10 663	5 154	22 814	12 736	−6 841	12 640
F.2212	Foreign currency deposits with UK banks	NFJH	5 302	2 181	4 266	7 001	17 895	14 672	−2 240	2 583	20 592
F.2213	Sterling deposits with UK building societies	NFJI	73	752	161	179	255	574	300	454	141
F.229	Deposits with rest of the world monetary financial institutions	NFJJ	15 815	45 965	−21 282	19 144	61 531	7 317	−6 378	47 413	47 047
F.29	Other deposits	NFJK	3	−10	–	–	–	–	–	–	2 691
F.2	Total currency and deposits	NFJC	17 747	56 320	−18 213	36 989	84 835	45 377	4 418	43 609	83 111
F.3	Securities other than shares										
F.331	Short term: money market instruments										
F.3311	Issued by UK central government	NFJN	−509	−75	2	572	−792	−164	282	−638	−356
F.3312	Issued by UK local authorities	NFJR	8	−54	43	4	−6	5	−6	–	–
F.3315	Issued by UK monetary financial institutions	NFJS	−1 623	651	4 310	−1 989	1 265	−715	7 851	5 654	1 378
F.3316	Issued by other UK residents	NFJX	135	−188	−90	−75	295	173	1 316	192	632
F.3319	Issued by the rest of the world	NFJY	−1 264	2 105	−212	698	1 175	620	−372	3 574	−4 144
F.332	Medium (1 to 5 year) and long term (over 5 year) bonds										
F.3321	Issued by UK central government	NFKA	2 561	5 288	−2 634	2 772	2 006	1 062	3 039	3 710	8 371
F.3322	Issued by UK local authorities	NFKD	−1	7	14	−16	91	118	25	16	28
F.3325	Medium term bonds issued by UK MFIs[1]	NFKE	207	107	510	1 060	619	118	298	538	−413
F.3326	Other medium & long term bonds issued by UK residents	NFKH	415	2 676	−2 308	−464	4 311	5 720	4 899	12 391	15 460
F.3329	Long term bonds issued by the rest of the world	NFKI	13 561	40 055	−32 717	2 884	26 901	22 558	−32 320	−27 690	−904
F.34	Financial derivatives	NFKJ	–	–	–	–	–	–	–	–	–
F.3	Total securities other than shares	NFJL	13 490	50 572	−33 082	5 446	35 865	29 495	−14 988	−2 253	20 052
F.4	Loans										
F.42	Long term loans										
F.421	Direct investment	NFKV	−172	49	422	710	574	1 622	322	1 293	346
F.422	Loans secured on dwellings	NFKY	−1 430	−2 284	−71	−1 231	−31	2 693	2 395	6 291	12 669
F.423	Finance leasing	NFLC	−1 222	−335	−391	734	1 731	1 800	127	−303	−251
F.424	Other long-term loans by UK residents	NFLD	−2 565	−28	2 886	2 255	3 680	2 615	2 479	3 068	83
F.4	Total loans	NFKN	−5 389	−2 598	2 846	2 468	5 954	8 730	5 323	10 349	12 847
F.5	Shares and other equity										
F.51	Shares and other equity, excluding mutual funds' shares										
F.514	Quoted UK shares	NFLK	−229	6 604	5 316	4 224	3 835	9 952	7 421	4 537	3 395
F.515	Unquoted UK shares	NFLL	105	−42	−146	−453	−56	−376	−3 001	−3 210	10 933
F.519	Shares and other equity issued by the rest of the world	NFLP	−246	3 152	1 517	7 953	1 446	5 683	6 314	20 580	33 250
F.52	Mutual funds' shares										
F.521	UK mutual funds' shares	NFLT	87	23	262	128	140	54	−6	35	76
F.5	Total shares and other equity	NFLF	−283	9 737	6 949	11 852	5 365	15 313	10 728	21 942	47 654
F.6	Insurance technical reserves										
F.62	Prepayments of insurance premiums and reserves for outstanding claims	NFLY	108	42	70	122	303	22	−4	−20	23
F.7	Other accounts receivable	NFLZ	371	661	877	659	674	643	638	706	657
F.A	Total net acquisition of financial assets	NFIY	26 044	114 734	−40 553	57 536	132 996	99 580	6 115	74 333	164 344

1 UK monetary financial institutions

Financial corporations

4.3.8 Other financial intermediaries and financial auxiliaries
ESA95 sectors S.123 and S.124 Unconsolidated

continued £ million

			1992	1993	1994	1995	1996	1997	1998	1999	2000
III.2	**FINANCIAL ACCOUNT** continued										
F.L	**Net acquisition of financial liabilities**										
F.2	Currency and deposits	NFMG	–	–	–	–	–	–	–	–	2 913
F.3	Securities other than shares										
F.331	Short term: money market instruments										
F.3316	Issued by UK residents other than monetary financial institutions and government	NFNB	216	760	228	312	864	392	–93	31	–14
F.332	Medium (1 to 5 year) and long term (over 5 year) bonds										
F.3326	Other medium & long term bonds issued by UK residents institutions and government	NFNL	2 274	6 813	8 464	5 752	7 946	7 904	2 349	17 162	22 744
F.34	Financial derivatives	NFNN	–	–	–	–	–	–	–	–	–
F.3	Total securities other than shares	NFMP	2 490	7 573	8 692	6 064	8 810	8 296	2 256	17 193	22 730
F.4	Loans										
F.41	Short term loans										
F.4111	Sterling loans by UK banks	NFNU	3 273	2 995	2 513	6 456	6 270	18 961	21 781	13 891	22 546
F.4112	Foreign currency loans by the UK banks	NFNV	–661	11 501	6 877	4 719	39 295	31 970	–22 794	–3 601	31 953
F.4113	Sterling loans by building societies	NFNW	412	182	1 314	5 387	1 841	1 976	1 890	1 968	2 216
F.419	Loans by rest of the world monetary financial institutions	NFNX	18 873	79 414	–58 129	35 031	74 685	34 987	14 237	41 659	63 882
F.42	Long term loans										
F.421	Direct investment	NFNZ	186	50	90	16	424	618	909	255	–11
F.423	Finance leasing	NFOG	–70	–71	–98	–43	265	233	35	–155	–66
F.424	Other long-term loans by UK residents	NFOH	64	73	58	386	–4 871	5 822	–3 310	1 094	16 009
F.429	Other long-term loans by the rest of the world	NFOI	433	404	–337	–30	302	233	–115	44	–30
F.4	Total loans	NFNR	22 510	94 548	–47 712	51 922	118 211	94 800	12 633	55 155	136 499
F.5	Shares and other equity										
F.51	Shares and other equity, excluding mutual funds' shares										
F.514	Quoted UK shares	NFOO	1 247	2 725	4 992	1 741	566	–2 185	6 274	2 355	6 750
F.515	Unquoted UK shares	NFOP	1 545	3 158	1 894	3 295	4 065	8 242	4 488	7 804	17 249
F.52	Mutual funds' shares										
F.521	UK mutual funds' shares	NFOX	–210	6 211	2 929	5 399	8 144	8 980	10 976	14 719	13 889
F.5	Total shares and other equity	NFOJ	2 582	12 094	9 815	10 435	12 775	15 037	21 738	24 878	37 888
F.7	Other accounts payable	NFPD	–8	14	5	12	303	–3	–157	–166	–144
F.L	**Total net acquisition of financial liabilities**	NFMC	27 574	114 229	–29 200	68 433	140 099	118 130	36 470	97 060	199 886
B.9	**Net lending / borrowing**										
F.A	Total net acquisition of financial assets	NFIY	26 044	114 734	–40 553	57 536	132 996	99 580	6 115	74 333	164 344
-F.L	*less* Total net acquisition of financial liabilities	-NFMC	–27 574	–114 229	29 200	–68 433	–140 099	–118 130	–36 470	–97 060	–199 886
B.9f	Net lending (+) / net borrowing (-), from financial account	NYNM	–1 530	505	–11 353	–10 897	–7 103	–18 550	–30 355	–22 727	–35 542
dB.9f	**Statistical discrepancy**	NYOY	–1 537	–2 513	8 941	8 406	1 112	11 793	20 216	14 529	27 628
B.9	**Net lending (+) / net borrowing (-), from capital account**	NHLW	–3 067	–2 008	–2 412	–2 491	–5 991	–6 757	–10 139	–8 198	–7 914

Financial corporations

4.3.9 Other financial intermediaries and financial auxiliaries
ESA95 sectors S.123 and S.124 Unconsolidated

£ billion

			1992	1993	1994	1995	1996	1997	1998	1999	2000
IV.3	**FINANCIAL BALANCE SHEET** at end of period										
AF.A	**Financial assets**										
AF.2	Currency and deposits										
AF.21	Currency	NLPM	0.1	0.1	0.1	0.1	0.1	0.1	0.1	0.1	0.1
AF.22	Transferable deposits										
AF.2211	Sterling deposits with UK banks	NLPP	32.1	39.2	39.0	53.4	57.6	73.0	86.6	79.2	94.4
AF.2212	Foreign currency deposits with UK banks	NLPQ	23.0	24.9	30.2	45.2	55.5	65.8	66.4	64.1	87.6
AF.2213	Sterling deposits with UK building societies	NLPR	1.4	2.3	2.3	1.9	2.3	0.8	1.1	1.4	0.8
AF.229	Deposits with rest of the world monetary financial institutions	NLPS	45.4	87.9	67.8	89.2	139.5	140.3	123.0	167.0	223.4
AF.29	Other deposits	NLPT	–	–	–	–	–	–	–	–	2.7
AF.2	Total currency and deposits	NLPL	102.0	154.4	139.3	189.7	254.9	280.1	277.3	311.7	409.0
AF.3	Securities other than shares										
AF.331	Short term: money market instruments										
AF.3311	Issued by UK central government	NLPW	0.2	0.1	0.1	0.7	0.2	0.1	–	–	–
AF.3312	Issued by UK local authorities	NLQA	–	–	–	–	–	–	–	–	–
AF.3315	Issued by UK monetary financial institutions	NLQB	6.2	5.6	10.1	8.0	8.8	7.3	20.5	26.2	27.8
AF.3316	Issued by other UK residents	NLQG	0.4	0.4	0.5	0.8	0.9	0.8	2.0	2.9	2.9
AF.3319	Issued by the rest of the world	NLQH	0.4	2.4	2.3	3.1	3.8	3.5	1.9	7.5	3.8
AF.332	Medium (1 to 5 year) and long term (over 5 year) bonds										
AF.3321	Issued by UK central government	NLQJ	5.3	12.5	9.6	13.7	13.5	12.1	16.6	19.3	27.0
AF.3322	Issued by UK local authorities	NLQM	–	–	–	–	0.1	–	–	–	–
AF.3325	Medium term bonds issued by UK MFIs[1]	NLQN	1.1	1.2	1.7	2.8	3.1	3.2	3.5	3.8	3.2
AF.3326	Other medium & long term bonds issued by UK residents	NLQQ	7.7	12.1	10.7	8.1	10.7	13.1	18.9	29.2	40.3
AF.3329	Long term bonds issued by the rest of the world	NLQR	56.2	96.9	61.4	65.6	83.5	107.1	72.8	45.8	46.1
AF.34	Financial derivatives	NLQS	–	–	–	–	–	–	–	–	–
AF.3	Total securities other than shares	NLPU	77.5	131.2	96.4	102.9	124.6	147.0	136.3	134.8	151.1
AF.4	Loans										
AF.42	Long term loans										
AF.421	Direct investment	NLRE	0.9	0.8	1.0	2.2	1.5	2.5	1.7	3.0	3.3
AF.422	Loans secured on dwellings	NLRH	24.3	23.3	23.7	22.9	22.8	24.4	26.7	33.5	39.7
AF.423	Finance leasing	NLRL	17.3	17.0	16.6	17.3	19.0	20.8	20.9	20.6	20.4
AF.424	Other long-term loans by UK residents	NLRM	6.3	6.5	8.2	6.5	7.4	9.4	8.8	6.4	7.6
AF.4	Total loans	NLQW	48.8	47.4	49.5	48.9	50.7	57.2	58.2	63.6	70.9
AF.5	Shares and other equity										
AF.51	Shares and other equity, excluding mutual funds' shares										
AF.514	Quoted UK shares	NLRT	45.2	65.5	61.3	79.5	94.9	106.0	109.5	166.6	146.2
AF.515	Unquoted UK shares	NLRU	24.8	30.2	34.4	36.1	41.4	47.8	58.3	64.4	86.5
AF.519	Shares and other equity issued by the rest of the world	NLRY	37.3	61.7	61.7	70.6	89.8	108.8	122.7	155.6	186.5
AF.52	Mutual funds' shares										
AF.521	UK mutual funds' shares	NLSC	1.2	1.9	2.0	3.6	3.5	3.6	3.6	4.7	4.4
AF.5	Total shares and other equity	NLRO	108.5	159.3	159.4	189.9	229.5	266.3	294.2	391.3	423.6
AF.6	Insurance technical reserves										
AF.62	Prepayments of insurance premiums and reserves for outstanding claims	NLSH	0.9	1.0	1.1	1.2	1.5	1.5	0.4	0.8	0.8
AF.7	Other accounts receivable	NLSI	4.1	4.7	5.9	6.8	7.5	7.8	9.0	10.4	11.1
AF.A	**Total financial assets**	NLPH	341.8	498.0	451.6	539.4	668.8	759.9	775.3	912.5	1 066.4

1 UK monetary financial institutions

… **Financial corporations**

4.3.9 Other financial intermediaries and financial auxiliaries
ESA95 sectors S.123 and S.124 Unconsolidated
continued

£ billion

			1992	1993	1994	1995	1996	1997	1998	1999	2000
IV.3	**FINANCIAL BALANCE SHEET** continued at end of period										
AF.L	**Financial liabilities**										
AF.2	Currency and deposits	NLSP	–	–	–	–	–	–	–	–	2.9
AF.3	Securities other than shares										
AF.331	Short term: money market instruments										
AF.3316	Issued by UK residents other than monetary financial institutions and government	NLTK	6.1	9.4	9.1	10.2	10.6	10.5	8.1	15.6	21.4
AF.332	Medium (1 to 5 year) and long term (over 5 year) bonds										
AF.3326	Other medium & long term bonds issued by UK residents institutions and government	NLTU	22.7	32.5	39.0	47.7	64.8	76.8	95.5	117.0	144.5
AF.34	Financial derivatives	NLTW	–	–	–	–	–	–	–	–	–
AF.3	Total securities other than shares	NLSY	28.9	41.8	48.2	57.9	75.4	87.3	103.6	132.6	165.9
AF.4	Loans										
AF.41	Short term loans										
AF.4111	Sterling loans by UK banks	NLUD	70.5	73.4	75.8	85.4	93.0	122.2	141.8	155.6	174.1
AF.4112	Foreign currency loans by UK banks	NLUE	27.2	38.8	45.6	69.4	96.4	106.2	89.2	81.0	121.3
AF.4113	Sterling loans by UK building societies	NLUF	1.3	1.5	4.0	9.3	11.5	8.2	11.3	9.8	8.8
AF.419	Loans by rest of the world monetary financial institutions	NLUG	66.6	143.1	86.9	123.3	187.7	216.0	209.5	259.7	308.3
AF.42	Long term loans										
AF.421	Direct investment	NLUI	1.7	2.7	3.5	2.9	2.5	4.8	5.1	5.6	5.6
AF.423	Finance leasing	NLUP	1.0	0.9	0.8	0.8	1.1	1.3	1.3	1.2	1.1
AF.424	Other long-term loans by UK residents	NLUQ	6.0	6.4	7.4	7.5	9.2	11.2	10.9	13.5	14.6
AF.429	Other long-term loans by the rest of the world	NLUR	1.7	1.9	1.7	0.8	0.9	0.8	0.7	0.5	0.5
AF.4	Total loans	NLUA	176.1	268.7	225.7	299.4	402.4	470.8	469.9	526.9	634.3
AF.5	Shares and other equity										
AF.51	Shares and other equity, excluding mutual funds' shares										
AF.514	Quoted UK shares	NLUX	30.9	58.6	50.9	78.8	94.1	140.0	155.5	220.5	270.6
AF.515	Unquoted UK shares	NLUY	27.7	37.1	36.2	47.2	55.3	79.6	87.3	106.1	129.5
AF.52	Mutual funds' shares										
AF.521	UK mutual funds' shares	NLVG	81.3	123.6	119.8	143.9	166.1	193.3	217.9	299.0	304.4
AF.5	Total shares and other equity	NLUS	139.9	219.3	206.9	269.8	315.5	412.9	460.6	625.6	704.6
AF.7	Other accounts payable	NLVM	0.5	0.5	0.5	0.5	0.9	0.9	0.9	0.7	0.6
AF.L	**Total financial liabilities**	NLSL	345.3	530.3	481.3	627.6	794.1	971.8	1 035.0	1 285.9	1 508.3
BF.90	**Net financial assets / liabilities**										
AF.A	Total financial assets	NLPH	341.8	498.0	451.6	539.4	668.8	759.9	775.3	912.5	1 066.4
-AF.L	*less* Total financial liabilities	-NLSL	–345.3	–530.3	–481.3	–627.6	–794.1	–971.8	–1 035.0	–1 285.9	–1 508.3
BF.90	**Net financial assets (+) / liabilities (-)**	NYOF	–3.6	–32.3	–29.7	–88.2	–125.4	–211.9	–259.7	–373.4	–441.9

Financial corporations

Financial corporations

4.4.2 Insurance corporations and pension funds
ESA95 sector S.125

£ million

			1992	1993	1994	1995	1996	1997	1998	1999
II		DISTRIBUTION AND USE OF INCOME ACCOUNTS								
II.1		PRIMARY DISTRIBUTION OF INCOME ACCOUNT								
II.1.1		GENERATION OF INCOME ACCOUNT								
		Resources								
B.1g		Total resources, gross value added	NRHH	8 480	12 184	12 653	10 473	12 105	12 157	10 166	10 973
		Uses								
D.1		Compensation of employees								
D.11		Wages and salaries	NHEJ	5 913	5 221	5 014	4 808	4 939	5 365	5 874	6 040
D.12		Employers' social contributions	NHEL	622	596	616	629	675	621	634	670
D.1		Total	NSCV	6 535	5 817	5 630	5 437	5 614	5 986	6 508	6 710
D.2		Taxes on production and imports, paid								
D.29		Production taxes other than on products	NHOS	168	164	177	199	208	220	230	251
-D.3		*less* Subsidies, received								
-D.39		Production subsidies other than on products	-NHNZ	–	–	–	–	–	–	–	–
B.2g		Operating surplus, gross	NHBZ	1 777	6 203	6 846	4 837	6 283	5 951	3 428	4 012
Total		Total uses	NRHH	8 480	12 184	12 653	10 473	12 105	12 157	10 166	10 973

4.4.3 Insurance corporations and pension funds
ESA95 sector S.125

£ million

			1992	1993	1994	1995	1996	1997	1998	1999	2000
II.1.2		ALLOCATION OF PRIMARY INCOME ACCOUNT									
		Resources									
B.2g		Operating surplus, gross	NHBZ	1 777	6 203	6 846	4 837	6 283	5 951	3 428	4 012	3 798
D.4		Property income, received									
D.41		Interest	NHOK	15 100	14 412	14 724	17 183	18 399	21 389	25 834	23 026	26 807
D.42		Distributed income of corporations	NHOL	16 051	17 735	18 355	21 839	24 501	26 067	26 228	27 374	19 197
D.43		Reinvested earnings on direct foreign investment	NHQM	-54	546	-423	1 205	690	1 250	535	1 002	47
D.44		Property income attributed to insurance policy-holders	NHPG	19	19	19	22	19	21	16	24	35
D.45		Rent	NHPH	28	28	28	28	28	28	30	29	29
D.4		Total	NHPF	31 144	32 740	32 703	40 277	43 637	48 755	52 643	51 455	46 115
Total		Total resources	NRMN	32 921	38 943	39 549	45 114	49 920	54 706	56 071	55 467	49 913
		Uses									
D.4		Property income									
D.41		Interest	NHOM	609	476	637	707	745	893	1 215	1 123	1 625
D.42		Distributed income of corporations	NHON	1 865	2 298	2 233	2 688	4 132	4 274	4 717	2 992	5 065
D.43		Reinvested earnings on direct foreign investment	NHQO	-141	123	360	282	343	364	295	11	455
D.44		Property income attributed to insurance policy-holders	NSCU	36 142	36 580	38 373	43 654	49 039	53 480	57 315	55 580	61 273
D.45		Rent	NHPK	–	–	–	–	–	–	–	–	–
D.4		Total	NHPI	38 475	39 477	41 603	47 331	54 259	59 011	63 542	59 706	68 418
B.5g		Balance of primary incomes, gross	NRMO	-5 554	-534	-2 054	-2 217	-4 339	-4 305	-7 471	-4 239	-18 505
Total		Total uses	NRMN	32 921	38 943	39 549	45 114	49 920	54 706	56 071	55 467	49 913

United Kingdom National Accounts 2001, © Crown copyright 2001

Financial corporations

4.4.4 Insurance corporations and pension funds
ESA95 sector S.125

£ million

			1992	1993	1994	1995	1996	1997	1998	1999	2000
II.2	**SECONDARY DISTRIBUTION OF INCOME ACCOUNT**										
	Resources										
B.5g	Balance of primary incomes, gross	NRMO	−5 554	−534	−2 054	−2 217	−4 339	−4 305	−7 471	−4 239	−18 505
D.61	Social contributions										
D.611	Actual social contributions										
D.6111	Employers' actual contributions	NSAR	11 771	12 180	13 233	14 017	16 572	17 735	19 906	22 257	24 893
D.6112	Employees social contributions	NSAS	30 068	28 258	30 058	32 751	38 308	42 876	45 591	46 803	48 853
D.6113	Social contributions by the self-employed	NSAT	–	–	–	–	–	–	–	–	–
D.611	Total	NSCN	41 839	40 438	43 291	46 768	54 880	60 611	65 497	69 060	73 746
D.612	Imputed social contributions	NHPR	106	97	101	109	101	83	91	86	79
D.61	Total	NRMP	41 945	40 535	43 392	46 877	54 981	60 694	65 588	69 146	73 825
D.7	Other current transfers										
D.71	Net non-life insurance premiums	NSCT	27 188	23 987	22 650	25 088	35 860	23 774	25 059	22 752	27 205
D.72	Non-life insurance claims	NHPN	272	239	250	251	247	232	176	341	409
D.7	Total	NRMR	27 460	24 226	22 900	25 339	36 107	24 006	25 235	23 093	27 614
Total	Total resources	NRMS	63 851	64 227	64 238	69 999	86 749	80 395	83 352	88 000	82 934
	Uses										
D.5	Current taxes on income, wealth etc.										
D.51	Taxes on income	NHPO	−2 714	−1 268	−951	−656	−1 173	1 249	3 335	2 621	1 916
D.62	Social benefits other than social transfers in kind										
D.622	Private funded social benefits	SBDW	28 479	29 697	32 717	35 080	40 067	45 482	49 394	53 636	58 534
D.623	Unfunded employee social benefits	NHPR	106	97	101	109	101	83	91	86	79
D.62	Total	NHPQ	28 585	29 794	32 818	35 189	40 168	45 565	49 485	53 722	58 613
D.7	Other current transfers										
D.71	Net non-life insurance premiums	NHPU	272	239	250	251	247	232	176	341	409
D.72	Non-life insurance claims	NSCS	27 188	23 987	22 650	25 088	35 860	23 774	25 059	22 752	27 205
D.75	Miscellaneous current transfers	NHQK	–	–	–	–	–	–	–	–	–
D.7	Total	NHPT	27 460	24 226	22 900	25 339	36 107	24 006	25 235	23 093	27 614
B.6g	Disposable income, gross	NRMT	10 520	11 475	9 471	10 127	11 647	9 575	5 297	8 564	−5 209
Total	Total uses	NRMS	63 851	64 227	64 238	69 999	86 749	80 395	83 352	88 000	82 934

4.4.6 Insurance corporations and pension funds
ESA95 sector S.125

£ million

			1992	1993	1994	1995	1996	1997	1998	1999	2000
II.4.1	**USE OF DISPOSABLE INCOME ACCOUNT**										
	Resources										
B.6g	Total resources, gross disposable income	NRMT	10 520	11 475	9 471	10 127	11 647	9 575	5 297	8 564	−5 209
	Uses										
D.8	Adjustment for the change in net equity of households in pension funds	NRYH	13 271	10 741	10 574	11 688	14 822	15 129	16 103	15 415	15 212
B.8g	Saving, gross	NRMV	−2 751	734	−1 103	−1 561	−3 175	−5 554	−10 806	−6 851	−20 421
Total	Total uses	NRMT	10 520	11 475	9 471	10 127	11 647	9 575	5 297	8 564	−5 209

Financial corporations

4.4.7 Insurance corporations and pension funds
ESA95 sector S.125

£ million

			1992	1993	1994	1995	1996	1997	1998	1999	2000
III	**ACCUMULATION ACCOUNTS**										
III.1	**CAPITAL ACCOUNT**										
III.1.1	**CHANGE IN NET WORTH DUE TO SAVING & CAPITAL TRANSFERS**										
	Changes in liabilities and net worth										
B.8g	Saving, gross	NRMV	−2 751	734	−1 103	−1 561	−3 175	−5 554	−10 806	−6 851	−20 421
D.9	Capital transfers receivable										
D.92	Investment grants	NHQA	–	–	–	–	–	–	–	–	–
D.99	Other capital transfers	NHQB	86	–	–	–	–	–	–	–	–
D.9	Total	NHPZ	86	–	–	–	–	–	–	–	–
-D.9	*less* Capital transfers payable										
-D.91	Capital taxes	-NHNW	–	–	–	–	–	–	–	–	–
-D.99	Other capital transfers	-NHOB	−86	–	–	–	–	–	–	–	–
-D.9	Total	-NHQD	−86	–	–	–	–	–	–	–	–
B.10.1g	Total change in liabilities and net worth	NRYI	−2 751	734	−1 103	−1 561	−3 175	−5 554	−10 806	−6 851	−20 421
	Changes in assets										
B.10.1g	Change in net worth due to saving and capital transfers before deduction of fixed capital consumption	NRYI	−2 751	734	−1 103	−1 561	−3 175	−5 554	−10 806	−6 851	−20 421
III.1.2	**ACQUISITION OF NON-FINANCIAL ASSETS ACCOUNT**										
B.10.1g	**Total changes in liabilities and net worth due to saving and capital transfers**	NRYI	−2 751	734	−1 103	−1 561	−3 175	−5 554	−10 806	−6 851	−20 421
	Changes in assets										
P.5	Gross capital formation										
P.51	Gross fixed capital formation	NHOJ	2 062	835	2 787	767	415	1 879	4 875	3 466	6 643
P.52	Changes in inventories	NHOI	–	–	–	–	–	–	–	–	–
P.53	Acquisitions less disposals of valuables	NHQH	−45	−50	−5	−93	−122	−104	49	−28	−130
P.5	Total	NHQG	2 017	785	2 782	674	293	1 775	4 924	3 438	6 513
K.2	Acquisitions less disposals of non-produced non-financial assets	NHQI	30	−24	−32	−15	−63	−37	−37	−37	−39
B.9	Net lending (+) / net borrowing (-)	NHOQ	−4 798	−27	−3 853	−2 220	−3 405	−7 292	−15 693	−10 252	−26 895
Total	Total change in assets	NRYI	−2 751	734	−1 103	−1 561	−3 175	−5 554	−10 806	−6 851	−20 421

United Kingdom National Accounts 2001, © Crown copyright 2001

Financial corporations

4.4.8 Insurance corporations and pension funds
ESA95 sector S.125 Unconsolidated

£ million

			1992	1993	1994	1995	1996	1997	1998	1999	2000
III.2	**FINANCIAL ACCOUNT**										
F.A	Net acquisition of financial assets										
F.2	Currency and deposits										
F.22	Transferable deposits										
F.2211	Sterling deposits with UK banks	NBSK	1 437	2 060	536	9 522	12 313	4 818	4 851	−7 183	11 218
F.2213	Sterling deposits with UK building societies	NBSM	1 214	−222	701	675	1 282	−98	−312	716	−76
F.229	Deposits with rest of the world monetary financial institutions	NBSN	379	1 106	−73	692	1 254	1 152	−160	121	313
F.29	Other deposits	NBSO	–	–	–	–	–	–	–	–	–
F.2	Total currency and deposits	NBSG	3 030	2 944	1 164	10 889	14 849	5 872	4 379	−6 346	11 455
F.3	Securities other than shares										
F.331	Short term: money market instruments										
F.3311	Issued by UK central government	NBSR	−40	55	68	818	−304	118	285	−560	178
F.3312	Issued by UK local authorities	NBSV	–	–	–	–	–	–	–	–	–
F.3315	Issued by UK monetary financial institutions	NBSW	1 041	−1 473	657	827	3 446	5 185	716	530	2 382
F.3316	Issued by other UK residents	NBTB	157	−182	−29	−114	158	583	915	800	33
F.3319	Issued by the rest of the world	NBTC	65	51	19	178	292	617	−1 174	−68	−269
F.332	Medium (1 to 5 year) and long term (over 5 year) bonds										
F.3321	Issued by UK central government	NBTE	15 559	14 169	19 042	15 412	18 666	20 028	3 896	5 453	−11 309
F.3322	Issued by UK local authorities	NBTH	38	99	292	63	29	4	−62	12	41
F.33251	Medium term bonds issued by UK banks	NBTJ	165	712	1 609	680	1 038	1 344	618	1 246	−1 234
F.33252	Medium term bonds issued by UK building societies	NBTK	458	−391	−84	518	444	25	138	413	−12
F.3326	Other medium & long term bonds issued by UK residents	NBTL	2 643	2 501	1 534	1 643	357	7 244	14 095	22 104	29 746
F.3329	Long term bonds issued by the rest of the world	NBTM	3 800	−873	665	992	4 828	7 777	15 154	9 621	11 442
F.34	Financial derivatives	NBTN	–	–	–	–	–	–	–	–	–
F.3	Total securities other than shares	NBSP	23 886	14 668	23 773	21 017	28 954	42 925	34 581	39 551	30 998
F.4	Loans										
F.42	Long term loans										
F.421	Direct investment	NBTZ	46	578	712	905	−157	91	66	−570	−70
F.422	Loans secured on dwellings	NBUC	115	−624	−700	−377	−166	−58	114	−641	17
F.424	Other long-term loans by UK residents	NBUH	2 178	1 072	9	1 550	−619	6 724	2 379	13 784	5 770
F.4	Total loans	NBTR	2 339	1 026	21	2 078	−942	6 757	2 559	12 573	5 717
F.5	Shares and other equity										
F.51	Shares and other equity, excluding mutual funds' shares										
F.514	Quoted UK shares	NBUO	2 086	6 848	7 579	−2 923	−2 298	−10 239	−9 154	−7 936	22 998
F.515	Unquoted UK shares	NBUP	−33	250	−153	−420	−311	9	237	−363	−1 547
F.519	Shares and other equity issued by the rest of the world	NBUT	−1 637	6 717	−1 924	3 392	6 885	1 437	3 747	5 252	−15 052
F.52	Mutual funds' shares										
F.521	UK mutual funds' shares	NBUX	1 062	4 114	3 673	4 208	3 360	3 846	2 430	2 920	6 674
F.5	Total shares and other equity	NBUJ	1 478	17 929	9 175	4 257	7 636	−4 947	−2 740	−127	13 073
F.6	Insurance technical reserves										
F.62	Prepayments of insurance premiums and reserves for outstanding claims	NBVC	43	17	30	49	120	8	−3	−24	26
F.7	Other accounts receivable	NBVD	−516	−184	807	5 957	3 568	731	3 733	5 066	1 926
F.A	Total net acquisition of financial assets	NBSC	30 260	36 400	34 970	44 247	54 185	51 346	42 509	50 693	63 195

Financial corporations

4.4.8 Insurance corporations and pension funds
ESA95 sector S.125 Unconsolidated
continued

£ million

			1992	1993	1994	1995	1996	1997	1998	1999	2000
III.2	**FINANCIAL ACCOUNT** continued										
F.L	**Net acquisition of financial liabilities**										
F.3	Securities other than shares										
F.332	Medium (1 to 5 year) and long term (over 5 year) bonds										
F.3326	Other medium & long term bonds issued by UK residents institutions and government	NBWP	402	793	242	273	540	−151	450	1 126	219
F.34	Financial derivatives	NBWR	–	–	–	–	–	–	–	–	–
F.3	Total securities other than shares	NBVT	402	793	242	273	540	−151	450	1 126	219
F.4	Loans										
F.41	Short term loans										
F.411	Loans by UK monetary financial institutions, excluding loans secured on dwellings & financial leasing	NBWX	−1 128	346	984	525	338	3 772	−979	2 031	2 705
F.419	Loans by rest of the world monetary financial institutions	NBXB	613	−435	107	330	642	−1 297	331	1 399	−854
F.42	Long term loans										
F.421	Direct investment	NBXD	105	−35	46	−115	1 133	491	−668	1 676	252
F.424	Other long-term loans by UK residents	NBXL	15	−44	702	−110	881	−346	−1 191	3 665	308
F.4	Total loans	NBWV	−395	−168	1 839	630	2 994	2 620	−2 507	8 771	2 411
F.5	Shares and other equity										
F.51	Shares and other equity, excluding mutual funds' shares										
F.514	Quoted UK shares	NBXS	62	1 315	405	200	404	1 895	27	393	8 586
F.515	Unquoted UK shares	NBXT	−141	133	360	352	420	364	360	11	455
F.5	Total shares and other equity	NBXN	−79	1 448	765	552	824	2 259	387	404	9 041
F.6	Insurance technical reserves										
F.61	Net equity of households in life assurance and pension funds' reserves	NBYD	28 098	27 388	28 049	30 372	36 666	32 403	42 011	42 473	44 671
F.62	Prepayments of insurance premiums and reserves for outstanding claims	NBYG	4 277	1 678	2 693	4 891	12 079	897	−563	−1 601	1 767
F.6	Total insurance technical reserves	NPWC	32 375	29 066	30 742	35 263	48 745	33 300	41 448	40 872	46 438
F.7	Other accounts payable	NBYH	−117	763	381	2 535	1 732	3 860	1 695	4 600	5 667
F.L	**Total net acquisition of financial liabilities**	NBVG	32 186	31 902	33 969	39 253	54 835	41 888	41 473	55 773	63 776
B.9	**Net lending / borrowing**										
F.A	Total net acquisition of financial assets	NBSC	30 260	36 400	34 970	44 247	54 185	51 346	42 509	50 693	63 195
−F.L	*less* Total net acquisition of financial liabilities	−NBVG	−32 186	−31 902	33 969	−39 253	−54 835	−41 888	−41 473	−55 773	−63 776
B.9f	**Net lending (+) / net borrowing (-), from financial account**	NYNN	−1 926	4 498	1 001	4 994	−650	9 458	1 036	−5 080	−581
dB.9f	**Statistical discrepancy**	NYPB	−2 872	−4 525	−4 854	−7 214	−2 755	−16 750	−16 729	−5 172	−26 314
B.9	**Net lending (+) / net borrowing (-), from capital account**	NHOQ	−4 798	−27	−3 853	−2 220	−3 405	−7 292	−15 693	−10 252	−26 895

United Kingdom National Accounts 2001, © Crown copyright 2001

Financial corporations

4.4.9 Insurance corporations and pension funds
ESA95 sector S.125 Unconsolidated

£ billion

			1992	1993	1994	1995	1996	1997	1998	1999	2000
IV.3	**FINANCIAL BALANCE SHEET** at end of period										
AF.A	**Financial assets**										
AF.2	Currency and deposits										
AF.22	Transferable deposits										
AF.2211	Sterling deposits with UK banks	NIYH	27.3	29.4	29.9	39.5	51.8	57.3	59.0	51.8	63.0
AF.2213	Sterling deposits with UK building societies	NIYJ	4.3	4.1	4.8	5.2	6.2	3.6	3.4	3.8	2.7
AF.229	Deposits with rest of the world monetary financial institutions	NIYK	0.7	0.7	0.8	0.9	1.2	1.7	0.6	0.4	0.2
AF.29	Other deposits	NIYL	–	–	–	–	–	–	–	–	–
AF.2	Total currency and deposits	NIYD	32.3	34.2	35.5	45.6	59.2	62.6	62.9	56.0	65.8
AF.3	Securities other than shares										
AF.331	Short term: money market instruments										
AF.3311	Issued by UK central government	NIYO	0.1	0.2	0.2	1.1	0.8	0.9	1.1	0.6	0.7
AF.3312	Issued by UK local authorities	NIYS	–	–	–	–	–	–	–	–	–
AF.3315	Issued by UK monetary financial institutions	NIYT	4.0	2.5	3.2	4.0	7.5	12.6	13.3	13.9	16.2
AF.3316	Issued by other UK residents	NIYY	0.5	0.3	0.3	0.1	0.3	0.9	1.8	2.6	2.6
AF.3319	Issued by the rest of the world	NIYZ	0.8	0.9	0.9	1.1	1.4	2.0	0.6	0.5	0.3
AF.332	Medium (1 to 5 year) and long term (over 5 year) bonds										
AF.3321	Issued by UK central government	NIZB	84.7	118.6	114.2	138.4	151.7	186.1	209.7	206.1	196.7
AF.3322	Issued by UK local authorities	NIZE	0.1	0.1	0.4	0.5	0.4	0.4	0.6	0.5	0.6
AF.3325	Medium term bonds issued by UK MFIs[1]	NIZF	3.2	3.6	5.2	6.3	7.0	8.2	9.1	11.4	10.6
AF.3326	Other medium & long term bonds issued by UK residents	NIZI	23.3	34.6	27.5	34.7	36.9	49.8	70.7	86.6	118.5
AF.3329	Long term bonds issued by the rest of the world	NIZJ	34.7	35.5	32.4	36.6	45.1	46.4	67.1	68.6	83.1
AF.34	Financial derivatives	NIZK	–	–	–	–	–	–	–	–	–
AF.3	Total securities other than shares	NIYM	151.3	196.3	184.2	222.8	251.0	307.3	374.0	390.8	429.4
AF.4	Loans										
AF.42	Long term loans										
AF.421	Direct investment	NIZW	2.1	2.6	2.9	4.2	3.6	3.7	4.2	1.6	1.7
AF.422	Loans secured on dwellings	NIZZ	3.6	3.0	2.3	1.9	1.7	1.7	1.8	1.1	1.1
AF.424	Other long-term loans by UK residents	NJAE	15.7	16.2	18.9	18.4	20.4	23.9	25.8	43.0	39.8
AF.4	Total loans	NIZO	21.3	21.8	24.1	24.5	25.7	29.3	31.8	45.7	42.6
AF.5	Shares and other equity										
AF.51	Shares and other equity, excluding mutual funds' shares										
AF.514	Quoted UK shares	NJAL	317.7	408.6	370.3	452.5	494.5	557.0	618.2	730.4	691.1
AF.515	Unquoted UK shares	NJAM	2.6	3.5	2.8	3.1	4.0	4.0	4.5	4.8	3.0
AF.519	Shares and other equity issued by the rest of the world	NJAQ	105.6	144.6	132.5	156.4	161.2	196.8	205.3	257.6	233.8
AF.52	Mutual funds' shares										
AF.521	UK mutual funds' shares	NJAU	48.0	66.8	58.9	66.7	79.3	87.5	111.7	135.9	131.5
AF.5	Total shares and other equity	NJAG	473.9	623.5	564.4	678.8	739.0	845.2	939.8	1 128.6	1 059.4
AF.6	Insurance technical reserves										
AF.62	Prepayments of insurance premiums and reserves for outstanding claims	NJAZ	0.4	0.4	0.5	0.5	0.6	0.6	0.4	0.9	0.9
AF.7	Other accounts receivable	NJBA	7.6	7.8	8.0	11.3	12.1	14.9	16.5	15.4	14.2
AF.A	**Total financial assets**	NIZN	686.9	884.0	816.6	983.5	1 087.5	1 259.9	1 425.4	1 637.4	1 612.4

1 UK monetary financial institutions

Financial corporations

4.4.9 Insurance corporations and pension funds
ESA95 sector S.125 Unconsolidated
continued

£ billion

			1992	1993	1994	1995	1996	1997	1998	1999	2000
IV.3	**FINANCIAL BALANCE SHEET** continued at end of period										
AF.L	**Financial liabilities**										
AF.3	Securities other than shares										
AF.332	Medium (1 to 5 year) and long term (over 5 year) bonds										
AF.3326	Other medium & long term bonds issued by UK residents institutions and government	NJCM	–	–	0.5	0.1	0.4	0.4	0.1	0.1	0.1
AF.34	Financial derivatives	NJCO	–	–	–	–	–	–	–	–	–
AF.3	Total securities other than shares	NJBQ	–	–	0.5	0.1	0.4	0.4	0.1	0.1	0.1
AF.4	Loans										
AF.41	Short term loans										
AF.411	Loans by UK monetary financial institutions, excluding loans secured on dwellings & financial leasing	NJCU	1.7	2.0	3.0	3.5	3.9	7.6	6.8	8.9	11.6
AF.42	Long term loans										
AF.421	Direct investment	NJDA	2.6	2.5	2.4	2.6	4.6	6.0	6.1	7.6	8.0
AF.424	Other long-term loans by UK residents	NJDI	0.1	0.2	0.1	0.1	–	–	0.7	0.5	0.5
AF.4	Total loans	NJCS	4.3	4.6	5.5	6.2	8.5	13.7	13.6	17.0	20.1
AF.5	Shares and other equity										
AF.51	Shares and other equity, excluding mutual funds' shares										
AF.514	Quoted UK shares	NJDP	25.9	32.2	26.3	35.6	38.0	63.2	72.5	72.8	69.0
AF.515	Unquoted UK shares	NJDQ	3.6	3.8	2.9	3.7	4.4	5.4	6.3	8.3	10.8
AF.5	Total shares and other equity	NJDK	29.5	36.0	29.2	39.3	42.5	68.7	78.8	81.2	79.8
AF.6	Insurance technical reserves										
AF.61	Net equity of households in life assurance and pension funds' reserves	NJEA	685.0	875.2	823.8	968.3	1 053.8	1 285.9	1 421.1	1 640.8	1 625.6
AF.62	Prepayments of insurance premiums and reserves for outstanding claims	NJED	38.0	39.7	42.4	47.5	58.6	59.5	60.8	59.5	62.9
AF.6	Total insurance technical reserves	NPXS	723.0	915.0	866.2	1 015.8	1 112.4	1 345.5	1 481.9	1 700.3	1 688.5
AF.7	Other accounts payable	NJEE	4.2	4.9	4.7	6.8	7.6	11.5	13.3	18.0	22.4
AF.L	**Total financial liabilities**	NJCR	761.1	960.5	906.1	1 068.2	1 171.5	1 439.8	1 587.7	1 816.4	1 810.9
BF.90	**Net financial assets / liabilities**										
AF.A	Total financial assets	NIZN	686.9	884.0	816.6	983.5	1 087.5	1 259.9	1 425.4	1 637.4	1 612.4
-AF.L	*less* Total financial liabilities	-NJCR	–761.1	–960.5	–906.1	–1 068.2	–1 171.5	–1 439.8	–1 587.7	–1 816.4	–1 810.9
BF.90	**Net financial assets (+) / liabilities (-)**	NYOI	–74.2	–76.5	–89.5	–84.8	–84.0	–179.9	–162.3	–179.0	–198.5

United Kingdom National Accounts 2001, © Crown copyright 2001

Financial corporations

4.5 Financial derivatives: Gross positions of UK banks and securities dealers by counterparty[1]

£ million

	MFIs[1] Sterling	MFIs[1] Other currencies	Other Financial[2] Sterling	Other Financial[2] Other currencies	Other UK[3] Sterling	Other UK[3] Other currencies	Rest of World Sterling	Rest of World Other currencies	Total
1998									
FINANCIAL BALANCE SHEET									
Assets									
UK banks[4]	31 838	102 792	9 546	99 940	6 622	2 404	27 863	370 482	651 487
Securities dealers[5]	5 657	83 867	2 710	8 898	241	179	2 838	42 383	146 773
Total	37 495	186 659	12 256	108 838	6 863	2 583	30 701	412 865	798 260
Liabilities									
UK banks[4]	29 961	100 088	13 200	102 512	4 252	2 792	34 660	362 217	649 682
Securities dealers[5]	7 018	81 580	2 431	8 895	220	117	3 077	40 346	143 684
Total	36 979	181 668	15 631	111 407	4 472	2 909	37 737	402 563	793 366

Source: ONS and Bank of England

KEY:
1. These data are not included in the aggregates shown in the main tables
2. MFIs = Monetary financial institutions covers banks and building societies
3. Other Financial = Other financial institutions and insurance and pension funds
4. Other UK = Government, private and public non-financial corporations and households
5. UK banks = Within the MFI sector, the only data available on financial derivatives relate to gross positions of UK banks, and collected by the Bank of England.
6. Securities dealers = Within the the other financial institutions sector, the only data available on financial derivatives relate to gross positions of securities dealers, and collected by ONS.

Further information about the data on financial derivatives collected by ONS can be obtained from an article in the September 2001 edition of Economic Trends

Financial corporations

4.5 Financial derivatives: Gross positions of UK banks and securities dealers by counterparty[1]
continued

£ million

	MFIs[1] Sterling	MFIs[1] Other currencies	Other Financial[2] Sterling	Other Financial[2] Other currencies	Other UK[3] Sterling	Other UK[3] Other currencies	Rest of World Sterling	Rest of World Other currencies	Total
1999									
FINANCIAL BALANCE SHEET									
Assets									
UK banks[4]	25 884	88 550	8 713	100 354	5 438	3 372	29 360	360 847	622 518
Securities dealers[5]	9 602	65 577	2 202	3 227	1 347	372	4 611	58 004	144 942
Total	35 486	154 127	10 915	103 581	6 785	3 744	33 971	418 851	767 460
Liabilities									
UK banks[4]	26 689	85 503	10 981	104 378	4 214	3 627	36 101	351 865	623 358
Securities dealers[5]	16 666	60 025	2 759	9 634	933	292	5 279	51 864	147 452
Total	43 355	145 528	13 740	114 012	5 147	3 919	41 380	403 729	770 810

Source: ONS and Bank of England

KEY:

1 MFIs = Monetary financial institutions covers banks and building societies
2 Other Financial = Other financial institutions and insurance and pension funds
3 Other UK = Government, private and public non-financial corporations and households
4 UK banks = Within the MFI sector, the only data available on financial derivatives relate to gross positions of UK banks, and collected by the Bank of England.
5 Securities dealers = Within the the other financial institutions sector, the only data available on financial derivatives relate to gross positions of securities dealers, and collected by ONS.

Further information about the data on financial derivatives collected by ONS can be obtained from an article in the September 2001 edition of Economic Trends

Financial corporations

4.5 Financial derivatives: Gross positions of UK banks and securities dealers by counterparty[1]
continued

£ million

	MFIs[1] Sterling	MFIs[1] Other currencies	Other Financial[2] Sterling	Other Financial[2] Other currencies	Other UK[3] Sterling	Other UK[3] Other currencies	Rest of World Sterling	Rest of World Other currencies	Total
2000									
FINANCIAL BALANCE SHEET									
Assets									
UK banks[4]	27 593	92 072	10 182	100 899	4 368	3 751	49 883	340 492	629 240
Securities dealers[5]	8 313	79 770	1 948	2 530	1 406	328	3 198	52 551	150 044
Total	35 906	171 842	12 130	103 429	5 774	4 079	53 081	393 043	779 284
Liabilities									
UK banks[4]	30 677	81 510	16 311	106 149	4 443	3 782	49 855	352 819	645 546
Securities dealers[5]	16 330	72 350	2 821	8 082	1 183	385	4 315	46 548	152 014
Total	47 007	153 860	19 132	114 231	5 626	4 167	54 170	399 367	797 560

Source: ONS and Bank of England

KEY:

1 MFIs = Monetary financial institutions covers banks and building societies
2 Other Financial = Other financial institutions and insurance and pension funds
3 Other UK = Government, private and public non-financial corporations and households
4 UK banks = Within the MFI sector, the only data available on financial derivatives relate to gross positions of UK banks, and collected by the Bank of England.
5 Securities dealers = Within the the other financial institutions sector, the only data available on financial derivatives relate to gross positions of securities dealers, and collected by ONS.

Further information about the data on financial derivatives collected by ONS can be obtained from an article in the September 2001 edition of Economic Trends

Part 3

Chapter 5

General government

General government

General government

5.1.1 General government
ESA95 sector S.13

£ million

			1992	1993	1994	1995	1996	1997	1998	1999
I	**PRODUCTION ACCOUNT**									
	Resources									
P.1	Output									
P.11	Market output	NMXJ	7 191	6 726	6 885	7 697	7 393	7 361	7 552	8 119
P.12	Output for own final use	NMXK	399	390	384	369	381	385	413	461
P.13	Other non-market output	NMYK	129 195	131 534	136 255	141 031	146 779	149 147	154 881	166 294
P.1	Total resources	NMXL	136 785	138 650	143 524	149 097	154 553	156 893	162 846	174 874
	Uses									
P.2	Intermediate consumption	NMXM	57 045	63 556	75 088	81 127	85 975	87 367	91 852	100 748
B.1g	Value added, gross	NMXN	79 740	75 094	68 436	67 970	68 578	69 526	70 994	74 126
Total	Total uses	NMXL	136 785	138 650	143 524	149 097	154 553	156 893	162 846	174 874
B.1g	Value added, gross	NMXN	79 740	75 094	68 436	67 970	68 578	69 526	70 994	74 126
K.1	less Consumption of fixed capital	-NMXO	–6 075	–5 870	–5 991	–6 447	–6 876	–7 316	–7 534	–7 767
B.1n	Value added, net of fixed capital consumption	NMXP	73 665	69 224	62 445	61 523	61 702	62 210	63 460	66 359

5.1.2 General government
ESA95 sector S.13

£ million

			1992	1993	1994	1995	1996	1997	1998	1999
II	**DISTRIBUTION AND USE OF INCOME ACCOUNTS**									
II.1	**PRIMARY DISTRIBUTION OF INCOME ACCOUNT**									
II.1.1	**GENERATION OF INCOME ACCOUNT**									
	Resources									
B.1g	Total resources, gross value added	NMXN	79 740	75 094	68 436	67 970	68 578	69 526	70 994	74 126
	Uses									
D.1	Compensation of employees									
D.11	Wages and salaries	NMXQ	59 061	55 960	49 733	48 901	48 649	48 920	48 896	51 202
D.12	Employers' social contributions	NMXR	12 807	11 700	11 017	10 938	11 334	11 600	12 808	13 382
D.1	Total	NMXS	71 868	67 660	60 750	59 839	59 983	60 520	61 704	64 584
D.2	Taxes on production and imports, paid									
D.29	Production taxes other than on products	NMXT	1 797	1 564	1 695	1 684	1 719	1 690	1 756	1 775
D.3	less Subsidies, received									
D.39	Production subsidies other than on products	-NMXU	–	–	–	–	–	–	–	–
B.2g	Operating surplus, gross	NMXV	6 075	5 870	5 991	6 447	6 876	7 316	7 534	7 767
B.1g	Total uses	NMXN	79 740	75 094	68 436	67 970	68 578	69 526	70 994	74 126
K.1	After deduction of fixed capital consumption	-NMXO	–6 075	–5 870	–5 991	–6 447	–6 876	–7 316	–7 534	–7 767
B.2n	Operating surplus, net	NMXW	–	–	–	–	–	–	–	–

United Kingdom National Accounts 2001, © Crown copyright 2001

General government

5.1.3 General government
ESA95 sector S.13

£ million

			1992	1993	1994	1995	1996	1997	1998	1999	2000
II.1.2	**ALLOCATION OF PRIMARY INCOME ACCOUNT**										
	Resources										
B.2g	Operating surplus, gross	NMXV	6 075	5 870	5 991	6 447	6 876	7 316	7 534	7 767	7 761
D.2	Taxes on production and imports, received										
D.21	Taxes on products										
D.211	Value added tax (VAT)	NZGF	37 426	37 958	42 996	43 579	46 918	52 057	54 293	58 664	60 702
D.212	Taxes and duties on imports excluding VAT										
D.2121	Import duties	NMBS	–	–	–	–	–	–	–	–	–
D.2122	Taxes on imports excluding VAT and import duties	NMBT	–	–	–	–	–	–	–	–	–
D.214	Taxes on products excluding VAT and import duties	NMBV	27 036	28 586	31 218	35 482	37 380	40 621	44 815	48 395	52 141
D.21	Total taxes on products	NVCC	64 462	66 544	74 214	79 061	84 298	92 678	99 108	107 059	112 843
D.29	Other taxes on production	NMYD	15 678	15 066	14 721	15 214	15 929	16 686	17 287	18 013	18 778
D.2	Total taxes on production and imports, received	NMYE	80 140	81 610	88 935	94 275	100 227	109 364	116 395	125 072	131 621
-D.3	*less* Subsidies, paid										
-D.31	Subsidies on products	-NMYF	-4 361	-4 403	-4 976	-5 013	-5 845	-5 114	-4 304	-4 366	-3 930
-D.39	Other subsidies on production	-LIUF	-1 030	-915	-741	-765	-728	-711	-745	-750	-545
-D.3	Total	-NMRL	-5 391	-5 318	-5 717	-5 778	-6 573	-5 825	-5 049	-5 116	-4 475
D.4	Property income, received										
D.41	Total Interest	NMYL	8 649	7 996	8 385	8 553	9 031	8 575	9 236	9 328	9 578
D.42	Distributed income of corporations	NMYM	6 330	6 601	6 754	6 915	6 882	6 527	7 450	6 484	6 746
D.44	Property income attributed to insurance policy holders	NMYO	29	28	30	32	28	33	48	29	40
D.45	Rent										
	from sectors other than general government	NMYR	647	699	658	684	780	721	547	433	1 185
D.4	Total	NMYU	15 655	15 324	15 827	16 184	16 721	15 856	17 281	16 274	17 549
Total	Total resources	NMYV	96 479	97 486	105 036	111 128	117 251	126 711	136 161	143 997	152 456
	Uses										
D.4	Property income, paid										
D.41	Total interest	NRKB	23 392	24 056	26 804	30 077	31 905	33 809	34 874	30 648	30 930
D.4	Total	NMYY	23 392	24 056	26 804	30 077	31 905	33 809	34 874	30 648	30 930
B.5g	Balance of primary incomes, gross	NMZH	73 087	73 430	78 232	81 051	85 346	92 902	101 287	113 349	121 526
Total	Total uses	NMYV	96 479	97 486	105 036	111 128	117 251	126 711	136 161	143 997	152 456
K.1	After deduction of fixed capital consumption	-NMXO	-6 075	-5 870	-5 991	-6 447	-6 876	-7 316	-7 534	-7 767	-7 761
B.5n	Balance of primary incomes, net	NMZI	67 012	67 560	72 241	74 604	78 470	85 586	93 753	105 582	113 765

5.1.4 General government
ESA95 sector S.13

General government

£ million

II.2 SECONDARY DISTRIBUTION OF INCOME ACCOUNT

			1992	1993	1994	1995	1996	1997	1998	1999	2000
	Resources										
B.5g	Balance of primary incomes, gross	NMZH	73 087	73 430	78 232	81 051	85 346	92 902	101 287	113 349	121 526
D.5	Current taxes on income, wealth etc.										
D.51	Taxes on income	NMZJ	80 291	78 313	85 348	95 042	99 310	107 647	124 060	129 044	140 960
D.59	Other current taxes	NVCM	10 299	10 551	11 140	11 937	12 795	13 820	14 993	16 263	17 102
D.5	Total	NMZL	90 590	88 864	96 488	106 979	112 105	121 467	139 053	145 307	158 062
D.61	Social contributions										
D.611	Actual social contributions										
D.6111	Employers' actual social contributions	NMZM	23 189	24 670	24 913	25 917	27 344	29 038	31 391	33 108	35 253
D.6112	Employees' social contributions	NMZN	16 525	17 235	19 649	21 091	21 700	24 121	25 690	26 519	27 313
D.6113	Social contributions by self- and non-employed persons	NMZO	1 281	1 472	1 469	1 541	1 771	1 848	1 760	1 801	1 973
D.611	Total	NMZP	40 995	43 377	46 031	48 549	50 815	55 007	58 841	61 428	64 539
D.612	Imputed social contributions	NMZQ	5 425	5 396	5 419	5 279	5 299	5 356	5 880	5 823	5 919
D.61	Total	NMZR	46 420	48 773	51 450	53 828	56 114	60 363	64 721	67 251	70 458
D.7	Other current transfers										
D.72	Non-life insurance claims	NMZS	408	361	363	377	371	349	499	410	490
D.73	Current transfers within general government	NMZT	54 527	55 891	57 736	58 587	59 458	59 506	60 421	64 775	66 327
D.74	Current international cooperation	NMZU	1 907	2 558	1 752	1 233	2 424	1 739	1 384	3 176	2 084
	from institutions of the EC	NMEX	1 898	2 558	1 752	1 233	2 424	1 739	1 384	3 176	2 084
D.75	Miscellaneous current transfers										
	from sectors other than general government	NMZX	178	296	414	461	420	468	382	259	280
D.7	Total, other current transfers										
	from general government	NMZY	54 527	55 891	57 736	58 587	59 458	59 506	60 421	64 775	66 327
	from other sectors	NMZZ	2 493	3 215	2 529	2 071	3 215	2 556	2 265	3 845	2 854
D.7	Total	NNAA	57 020	59 106	60 265	60 658	62 673	62 062	62 686	68 620	69 181
Total	Total resources	NNAB	267 117	270 173	286 435	302 516	316 238	336 794	367 747	394 527	419 227
	Uses										
D.62	Social benefits other than social transfers in kind	NNAD	95 339	102 965	106 295	110 409	113 124	116 934	117 549	120 752	124 991
D.7	Other current transfers										
D.71	Net non-life insurance premiums	NNAE	408	361	363	377	371	349	499	410	490
D.73	Current transfers within general government	NNAF	54 527	55 891	57 736	58 587	59 458	59 506	60 421	64 775	66 327
D.74	Current international cooperation	NNAG	2 237	1 961	2 007	2 224	1 814	1 700	1 705	1 667	2 418
	to institutions of the EC	NMFA	–	2	7	8	8	31	–1	11	6
D.75	Miscellaneous current transfers										
	to sectors other than general government	NNAI	4 659	8 467	10 440	10 614	12 549	13 916	15 803	17 280	19 556
	GNP based fourth own resource	NMFH	914	1 558	2 071	1 826	2 454	2 458	3 920	4 632	4 379
D.7	Total other current transfers										
	to general government	NNAL	54 527	55 891	57 736	58 587	59 458	59 506	60 421	64 775	66 327
	to other sectors	NNAM	7 304	10 789	12 810	13 215	14 734	15 965	18 007	19 357	22 464
D.7	Total	NNAN	61 831	66 680	70 546	71 802	74 192	75 471	78 428	84 132	88 791
B.6g	Disposable income, gross	NNAO	109 947	100 528	109 594	120 305	128 922	144 389	171 770	189 643	205 445
Total	Total uses	NNAB	267 117	270 173	286 435	302 516	316 238	336 794	367 747	394 527	419 227
K.1	After deduction of fixed capital consumption	-NMXO	–6 075	–5 870	–5 991	–6 447	–6 876	–7 316	–7 534	–7 767	–7 761
B.6n	Disposable income, net	NNAP	103 872	94 658	103 603	113 858	122 046	137 073	164 236	181 876	197 684

General government

5.1.5 General government
ESA95 sector S.13

£ million

			1992	1993	1994	1995	1996	1997	1998	1999	2000
II.3	**REDISTRIBUTION OF INCOME IN KIND ACCOUNT**										
	Resources										
B.6g	Total resources, gross disposable income	NNAO	109 947	100 528	109 594	120 305	128 922	144 389	171 770	189 643	205 445
	Uses										
D.63	Social transfers in kind										
D.632	Transfers of individual non-market goods and services	NSZE	73 412	74 549	77 545	81 093	84 968	87 551	92 271	100 504	106 176
B.7g	Adjusted disposable income, gross	NSZI	36 535	25 979	32 049	39 212	43 954	56 838	79 499	89 139	99 269
Total	Total uses	NNAO	109 947	100 528	109 594	120 305	128 922	144 389	171 770	189 643	205 445

5.1.6 General government
ESA95 sector S.13

£ million

			1992	1993	1994	1995	1996	1997	1998	1999	2000
II.4	**USE OF INCOME ACCOUNT**										
II.4.1	**USE OF DISPOSABLE INCOME ACCOUNT**										
	Resources										
B.6g	Total resources, gross disposable income	NNAO	109 947	100 528	109 594	120 305	128 922	144 389	171 770	189 643	205 445
	Uses										
P.3	Final consumption expenditure										
P.31	Individual consumption expenditure	NNAQ	73 412	74 549	77 545	81 093	84 968	87 551	92 271	100 504	106 176
P.32	Collective consumption expenditure	NNAR	55 783	56 985	58 710	59 938	61 811	61 596	62 610	65 790	68 615
P.3	Total	NMRK	129 195	131 534	136 255	141 031	146 779	149 147	154 881	166 294	174 791
B.8g	Saving, gross	NNAU	–19 248	–31 006	–26 661	–20 726	–17 857	–4 758	16 889	23 349	30 654
Total	Total uses	NNAO	109 947	100 528	109 594	120 305	128 922	144 389	171 770	189 643	205 445
-K.1	After deduction of fixed capital consumption	-NMXO	–6 075	–5 870	–5 991	–6 447	–6 876	–7 316	–7 534	–7 767	–7 761
B.8n	Saving, net	NNAV	–25 323	–36 876	–32 652	–27 173	–24 733	–12 074	9 355	15 582	22 893
II.4.2	**USE OF ADJUSTED DISPOSABLE INCOME ACCOUNT**										
	Resources										
B.7g	Total resources, adjusted disposable income, gross	NSZI	36 535	25 979	32 049	39 212	43 954	56 838	79 499	89 139	99 269
	Uses										
P.4	Actual final consumption										
P.42	Actual collective consumption	NRMZ	55 783	56 985	58 710	59 938	61 811	61 596	62 610	65 790	68 615
B.8g	Saving, gross	NNAU	–19 248	–31 006	–26 661	–20 726	–17 857	–4 758	16 889	23 349	30 654
Total	Total uses	NSZI	36 535	25 979	32 049	39 212	43 954	56 838	79 499	89 139	99 269

5.1.7 General government
ESA95 sector S.13

General government

£ million

			1992	1993	1994	1995	1996	1997	1998	1999	2000
III	**ACCUMULATION ACCOUNTS**										
III.1	**CAPITAL ACCOUNT**										
III.1.1	**CHANGE IN NET WORTH DUE TO SAVING & CAPITAL TRANSFERS**										
	Changes in liabilities and net worth										
B.8g	Saving, gross	NNAU	−19 248	−31 006	−26 661	−20 726	−17 857	−4 758	16 889	23 349	30 654
D.9	Capital transfers receivable										
D.91	Capital taxes										
	from sectors other than general government	NMGI	1 227	1 279	1 438	1 441	1 621	1 601	1 796	1 951	2 215
D.92	Investment grants										
	from general government	NSZM	2 714	3 055	2 624	2 574	2 719	2 822	2 476	3 059	3 846
	from other sectors	NSZN	276	213	305	219	310	407	179	143	495
D.92	Total	NSZF	2 990	3 268	2 929	2 793	3 029	3 229	2 655	3 202	4 341
D.99	Other capital transfers										
	from general government	NSZO	5 100	−	−	−	1 600	−	−	−	132
	from other sectors	NSZP	84	86	114	138	159	185	191	205	278
D.99	Total	NNAX	5 184	86	114	138	1 759	185	191	205	410
D.9	Total capital transfers receivable										
	from general government	NSZQ	7 814	3 055	2 624	2 574	4 319	2 822	2 476	3 059	3 978
	from other sectors	NSZR	1 587	1 578	1 857	1 798	2 090	2 193	2 166	2 299	2 988
D.9	Total	NNAY	9 401	4 633	4 481	4 372	6 409	5 015	4 642	5 358	6 966
−D.9	*less* Capital transfers payable										
−D.92	Investment grants										
	to general government	−NSZS	−2 714	−3 055	−2 624	−2 574	−2 719	−2 822	−2 476	−3 059	−3 846
	to other sectors	−NSZT	−7 588	−8 468	−7 659	−7 125	−6 826	−5 911	−5 636	−6 152	−4 685
−D.92	Total	−NNAW	−10 302	−11 523	−10 283	−9 699	−9 545	−8 733	−8 112	−9 211	−8 531
−D.99	Other capital transfers										
	to general government	−NSZU	−5 100	−	−	−	−1 600	−	−	−	−132
	to other sectors	−NSZV	−106	−21	−24	−1 626	−164	−24	−146	−10	−22
−D.99	Total	−NNBB	−5 206	−21	−24	−1 626	−1 764	−24	−146	−10	−154
−D.9	Total capital transfers payable										
	to general government	−NSZW	−7 814	−3 055	−2 624	−2 574	−4 319	−2 822	−2 476	−3 059	−3 978
	to other sectors	−NSZX	−7 694	−8 489	−7 683	−8 751	−6 990	−5 935	−5 782	−6 162	−4 707
−D.9	Total	−NNBC	−15 508	−11 544	−10 307	−11 325	−11 309	−8 757	−8 258	−9 221	−8 685
B.10.1g	Total change in liabilities and net worth	NMWG	−25 355	−37 917	−32 487	−27 679	−22 757	−8 500	13 273	19 486	28 935
	Changes in assets										
B.10.1g	Changes in net worth due to gross saving and capital transfers	NMWG	−25 355	−37 917	−32 487	−27 679	−22 757	−8 500	13 273	19 486	28 935
K.1	After deduction of fixed capital consumption	−NMXO	−6 075	−5 870	−5 991	−6 447	−6 876	−7 316	−7 534	−7 767	−7 761
B.10.1n	Changes in net worth due to net saving and capital transfers	NNBD	−31 430	−43 787	−38 478	−34 126	−29 633	−15 816	5 739	11 719	21 174
III.1.2	**ACQUISITION OF NON-FINANCIAL ASSETS ACCOUNT**										
	Changes in liabilities and net worth										
B.10.1n	Changes in net worth due to net saving and capital transfers	NNBD	−31 430	−43 787	−38 478	−34 126	−29 633	−15 816	5 739	11 719	21 174
K.1	Consumption of fixed capital	NMXO	6 075	5 870	5 991	6 447	6 876	7 316	7 534	7 767	7 761
B.10.1g	Total change in liabilities and net worth	NMWG	−25 355	−37 917	−32 487	−27 679	−22 757	−8 500	13 273	19 486	28 935
	Changes in assets										
P.5	Gross capital formation										
P.51	Gross fixed capital formation	NNBF	14 045	13 427	14 084	14 056	11 206	9 455	10 661	10 107	11 349
P.52	Changes in inventories	NNBG	−17	−24	−251	−154	166	140	107	−268	−140
P.53	Acquisitions less disposals of valuables	NPOZ	−	−	−	−	−	−	14	10	2
P.5	Total	NNBI	14 028	13 403	13 833	13 902	11 372	9 595	10 782	9 849	11 211
K.2	Acquisitions less disposals of non-produced non-financial assets	NNBJ	−312	−497	−485	−143	−467	−372	−967	−696	−643
B.9g	Net lending(+) / net borrowing(-)	NNBK	−39 071	−50 823	−45 835	−41 438	−33 662	−17 723	3 458	10 333	18 367
Total	Total change in assets	NMWG	−25 355	−37 917	−32 487	−27 679	−22 757	−8 500	13 273	19 486	28 935

General government

5.1.8 General government
ESA95 sector S.13 Unconsolidated

£ million

			1992	1993	1994	1995	1996	1997	1998	1999	2000
III.2	**FINANCIAL ACCOUNT**										
F.A	**Net acquisition of financial assets**										
F.1	Monetary gold and special drawing rights (SDRs)	NWXM	−962	−462	932	−120	−54	1 199	915	−374	−956
F.2	Currency and deposits										
F.22	Transferable deposits with monetary financial institutions										
F.221	UK institutions	NFPN	1 207	6 012	−3 976	1 647	587	861	288	−148	15 798
F.229	Rest of the world institutions[1]	NFPR	274	−138	27	622	1 148	135	−1 804	3 177	−840
F.29	Other deposits	NFPS	–	–	–	–	–	–	–	–	2 913
F.2	Total currency and deposits	NFPK	1 481	5 874	−3 949	2 269	1 735	996	−1 516	3 029	17 871
F.3	Securities other than shares										
F.331	Short term: money market instruments										
F.3311	Issued by UK central government	NFPV	−5	13	11	−24	–	31	106	204	−218
F.3312	Issued by UK local authorities	NFPZ	–	–	–	–	–	–	–	–	–
F.3315	Issued by UK monetary financial institutions	NFQA	−49	−5	3	−5	−2	269	232	565	1 850
F.3316	Issued by other UK residents	NFQF	85	419	215	147	491	29	58	−38	27
F.3319	Issued by the rest of the world[1]	NFQG	–	–	–	–	−496	−777	939	−337	244
F.332	Medium (1 to 5 year) and long term (over 5 year) bonds										
F.3321	Issued by UK central government	NFQI	2	27	28	15	−2	70	95	−18	−194
F.3326	Other medium & long term bonds issued by UK residents	NFQP	−596	−946	−2 276	–	−1 745	−238	–	−387	−149
F.3329	Long term bonds issued by the rest of the world	NFQQ	−716	1 298	87	−700	−1 107	−2 936	−214	−3 105	5 418
F.34	Financial derivatives	NFQR	–	–	–	–	–	–	–	–	50
F.3	Total securities other than shares	NFPT	−1 279	806	−1 932	−567	−2 861	−3 552	1 216	−3 116	7 028
F.4	Loans										
F.42	Long term loans										
F.422	Loans secured on dwellings	NFRG	−462	−340	−185	−156	−144	−1 359	−154	−27	12
F.424	Other long-term loans by UK residents	NFRL	−4 480	−43	112	1 603	−4 541	2 628	902	3 773	5 204
F.4	Total loans	NFQV	−4 942	−383	−73	1 447	−4 685	1 269	748	3 746	5 216
F.5	Shares and other equity										
F.51	Shares and other equity, excluding mutual funds' shares										
F.514	Quoted UK shares	NFRS	−6 929	−4 471	−3 646	−2 367	−4 287	−1 803	51	−316	54
F.515	Unquoted UK shares	NFRT	−60	16	−715	−100	−18	−30	−40	–	–
F.516	Other UK equity (including direct investment in property)	NFRU	−7	56	–	13	3 264	–	–	–	–
F.519	Shares and other equity issued by the rest of the world	NFRX	68	79	90	85	81	63	67	91	53
F.5	Total shares and other equity	NFRN	−6 928	−4 320	−4 271	−2 369	−960	−1 770	78	−225	107
F.6	Insurance technical reserves										
F.62	Prepayments of insurance premiums and reserves for outstanding claims	NFSG	65	25	42	73	181	12	−11	−29	32
F.7	Other accounts receivable	NFSH	−2 346	1 556	534	1 173	−807	2 574	758	6 994	2 364
F.A	Total net acquisition of financial assets	NFPG	−14 911	3 096	−8 717	1 906	−7 451	728	2 188	10 025	31 662

es
General government

5.1.8 General government
ESA95 sector S.13 Unconsolidated
continued

£ million

			1992	1993	1994	1995	1996	1997	1998	1999	2000
III.2	**FINANCIAL ACCOUNT** continued										
F.L	**Net acquisition of financial liabilities**										
F.2	Currency and deposits										
F.21	Currency	NFSP	28	107	110	74	141	188	167	199	235
F.29	Non-transferable deposits	NFSW	4 722	4 946	5 945	4 095	6 998	1 753	−1 193	−847	3 541
F.2	Total currency and deposits	NFSO	4 750	5 053	6 055	4 169	7 139	1 941	−1 026	−648	3 776
F.3	Securities other than shares										
F.331	Short term: money market instruments										
F.3311	Issued by UK central government	NFSZ	−4 880	−405	1 080	11 513	−13 498	−1 569	86	−409	−1 652
F.3312	Issued by UK local authorities	NFTD	2	−29	–	4	−6	5	−6	–	–
F.332	Medium (1 to 5 year) and long term (over 5 year) bonds										
F.3321	Issued by UK central government	NFTM	30 484	53 115	24 031	22 542	31 338	16 665	−3 201	−4 560	−12 718
F.3322	Issued by UK local authorities	NFTP	4	7	288	78	163	13	6	−2	−12
F.34	Financial derivatives	NFTV	–	–	–	–	–	–	–	–	–
F.3	Total securities other than shares	NFSX	25 610	52 688	25 399	34 137	17 997	15 114	−3 115	−4 971	−14 382
F.4	Loans										
F.41	Short term loans										
F.411	Loans by UK monetary financial institutions, excluding loans secured on dwellings & financial leasing	NFUB	−841	−1 143	7 383	1 752	1 180	−2 550	529	5 312	−453
F.419	Loans by rest of the world monetary financial institutions	NFUF	1 210	−2 931	−122	−95	−82	−226	−44	−45	−39
F.42	Long term loans										
F.423	Finance leasing	NFUO	−99	−6	23	1	18	–	435	490	35
F.424	Other long-term loans by UK residents	NFUP	−5 840	−1 627	−497	2 046	156	1 244	808	1 869	1 419
F.429	Other long-term loans by the rest of the world	NFUQ	−19	68	−85	−59	−7	−81	−134	−166	−263
F.4	Total loans	NFTZ	−5 589	−5 639	6 702	3 645	1 265	−1 613	1 594	7 460	699
F.7	Other accounts payable	NFVL	591	2 048	−594	1 633	−168	2 610	671	−1 577	24 056
F.L	**Total net acquisition of financial liabilities**	NFSK	25 362	54 150	37 562	43 584	26 233	18 052	−1 876	264	14 149
B.9	**Net lending / borrowing**										
F.A	Total net acquisition of financial assets	NFPG	−14 911	3 096	−8 717	1 906	−7 451	728	2 188	10 025	31 662
-F.L	*less* Total net acquisition of financial liabilities	-NFSK	−25 362	−54 150	−37 562	−43 584	−26 233	−18 052	1 876	−264	−14 149
B.9f	**Net lending (+) / net borrowing (-), from financial account**	NYNO	−40 273	−51 054	−46 279	−41 678	−33 684	−17 324	4 064	9 761	17 513
dB.9f	Statistical discrepancy	NYOZ	1 202	231	444	240	22	−399	−606	572	854
B.9g	**Net lending (+) / net borrowing (-), from capital account**	NNBK	−39 071	−50 823	−45 835	−41 438	−33 662	−17 723	3 458	10 333	18 367

General government

5.1.9 General government ESA95 S.13 Unconsolidated

£ billion

			1992	1993	1994	1995	1996	1997	1998	1999	2000
IV.3	**FINANCIAL BALANCE SHEET** at end of period										
AN	Non-financial assets	CGIX	273.8	272.1	284.7	300.6	309.7	318.9	342.9	347.7	383.5
AF.A	**Financial assets**										
AF.1	Monetary gold and special drawing rights (SDRs)	NIFC	4.4	5.1	4.8	4.9	4.2	3.5	4.3	4.0	3.1
AF.2	Currency and deposits										
AF.22	Transferable deposits										
AF.221	Deposits with UK monetary financial institutions	NLVW	9.4	15.4	11.5	13.0	13.6	15.4	14.8	14.5	32.2
AF.229	Deposits with rest of the world monetary financial institutions	NLWA	1.3	1.3	1.3	7.3	7.3	7.7	6.1	8.7	6.6
AF.29	Other deposits	NLWB	–	–	–	–	–	–	–	–	2.9
AF.2	Total currency and deposits	NLUT	10.7	16.7	12.8	20.4	20.9	23.2	20.9	23.2	41.7
AF.3	Securities other than shares										
AF.331	Short term: money market instruments										
AF.3311	Issued by UK central government	NLWE	–	–	–	–	–	0.1	0.2	0.5	0.2
AF.3312	Issued by UK local authorities	NLWI	–	–	–	–	–	–	–	–	–
AF.3315	Issued by UK monetary financial institutions	NLWJ	0.1	0.1	0.1	0.1	0.1	2.2	2.4	3.0	5.4
AF.3316	Issued by other UK residents	NLWO	2.0	2.4	2.6	2.8	3.2	0.1	0.1	0.1	0.2
AF.3319	Issued by the rest of the world	NLWP	–	–	–	2.6	1.7	1.0	2.1	1.8	2.3
AF.332	Medium (1 to 5 year) and long term (over 5 year) bonds										
AF.3321	Issued by UK central government	NLWR	0.1	0.1	0.1	0.2	0.1	0.7	0.8	0.7	0.5
AF.3322	Issued by UK local authorities	NLWU	–	–	–	–	–	–	–	–	–
AF.3326	Other medium & long term bonds issued by UK residents	NLWY	4.4	3.2	1.4	1.4	0.8	0.6	0.6	0.2	0.1
AF.3329	Long term bonds issued by the rest of the world	NLWZ	22.5	23.4	24.6	17.0	14.1	10.6	10.9	7.6	16.7
AF.34	Financial derivatives	NLXA	–	–	–	–	–	–	–	–	0.1
AF.3	Total securities other than shares	NLWC	29.1	29.3	28.9	24.0	20.1	15.3	17.2	13.9	25.4
AF.4	Loans										
AF.42	Long term loans										
AF.422	Loans secured on dwellings	NLXP	2.5	2.1	2.0	1.8	1.6	0.3	0.5	0.3	0.2
AF.424	Other long-term loans by UK residents	NLXU	72.0	73.4	73.5	75.1	73.5	76.1	81.6	84.1	89.3
AF.4	Total loans	NLXE	74.5	75.5	75.4	76.9	75.1	76.4	82.1	84.4	89.5
AF.5	Shares and other equity										
AF.51	Shares and other equity, excluding mutual funds' shares										
AF.514	Quoted UK shares	NLYB	11.0	9.8	5.7	3.2	0.7	1.3	1.0	2.5	1.4
AF.515	Unquoted UK shares	NLYC	0.5	0.5	1.2	1.2	0.5	0.4	0.5	0.5	0.5
AF.519	Shares and other equity issued by the rest of the world	NLYG	1.3	1.3	1.4	1.5	1.6	1.7	1.7	1.8	1.9
AF.5	Total shares and other equity	NLXW	12.8	11.6	8.4	5.9	2.8	3.3	3.2	4.8	3.8
AF.6	Insurance technical reserves										
AF.62	Prepayments of insurance premiums and reserves for outstanding claims	NLYP	0.6	0.6	0.7	0.7	0.9	0.9	1.2	1.1	1.1
AF.7	Other accounts receivable	NLYQ	29.7	31.7	32.7	34.3	34.1	36.7	37.7	44.2	45.4
AF.A	**Total financial assets**	NPUP	161.9	170.5	163.6	167.0	158.1	159.3	166.7	175.6	210.1

5.1.9 General government
ESA95 S.13 Unconsolidated
continued

General government

£ billion

			1992	1993	1994	1995	1996	1997	1998	1999	2000
IV.3	**FINANCIAL BALANCE SHEET** continued at end of period										
AF.L	**Financial liabilities**										
AF.2	Currency and deposits										
AF.21	Currency	NLYY	2.1	2.2	2.3	2.3	2.4	2.5	2.6	2.8	3.0
AF.29	Non-transferable deposits	NLZF	49.0	55.4	61.4	65.5	72.5	74.2	73.1	71.9	75.3
AF.2	Total currency and deposits	NLYX	51.1	57.6	63.7	67.8	74.9	76.7	75.8	74.7	78.3
AF.3	Securities other than shares										
AF.331	Short term: money market instruments										
AF.3311	Issued by UK central government	NLZI	8.1	7.4	8.6	20.2	6.4	4.6	4.9	4.3	2.7
AF.3312	Issued by UK local authorities	NLZM	–	–	–	–	–	–	–	–	–
AF.332	Medium (1 to 5 year) and long term (over 5 year) bonds										
AF.3321	Issued by UK central government	NLZV	163.9	238.2	230.0	265.8	293.7	328.5	359.3	334.0	325.8
AF.3322	Issued by UK local authorities	NLZY	0.2	0.2	0.5	0.5	0.7	0.7	0.8	0.8	0.8
AF.34	Financial derivatives	NNKS	–	–	–	–	–	–	–	–	–
AF.3	Total securities other than shares	NLZG	172.3	245.8	239.0	286.6	300.8	333.9	364.9	339.1	329.3
AF.4	Loans										
AF.41	Short term loans										
AF.411	Loans by UK monetary financial institutions, excluding loans secured on dwellings & financial leasing	NNKY	8.9	7.7	15.5	17.4	19.1	16.7	16.6	22.0	26.0
AF.419	Loans by rest of the world monetary financial institutions	NNLC	3.7	0.8	0.7	0.6	0.5	0.3	0.2	0.2	0.1
AF.42	Long term loans										
AF.423	Finance leasing	NNLL	1.4	1.4	1.6	1.6	1.6	1.6	2.0	2.5	2.6
AF.424	Other long-term loans by UK residents	NNLM	45.9	44.2	43.6	45.9	45.8	46.9	47.8	49.1	50.6
AF.429	Other long-term loans by the rest of the world	NNLN	1.7	1.7	1.6	1.6	1.5	1.4	1.4	1.2	1.3
AF.4	Total loans	NNKW	61.5	55.9	62.9	67.0	68.5	66.9	68.0	75.1	80.5
AF.7	Other accounts payable	NNMI	11.7	13.2	13.2	14.1	13.6	16.3	16.9	15.8	40.1
AF.L	**Total financial liabilities**	NPVQ	296.5	372.4	378.8	435.5	457.8	493.8	525.6	504.7	528.2
BF.90	**Net financial assets / liabilities**										
AN	Non-financial assets	CGIX	273.8	272.1	284.7	300.6	309.7	318.9	342.9	347.7	383.5
AF.A	Total financial assets	NPUP	161.9	170.5	163.6	167.0	158.1	159.3	166.7	175.6	210.1
-AF.L	*less* Total financial liabilities	-NPVQ	–296.5	–372.4	–378.8	–435.5	–457.8	–493.8	–525.6	–504.7	–528.2
BF.90	**Net financial assets (+) / liabilities (-)**	NYOG	–134.6	–202.0	–215.2	–268.5	–299.7	–334.5	–359.0	–329.1	–318.1
	Net worth										
AN	Non-financial assets	CGIX	273.8	272.1	284.7	300.6	309.7	318.9	342.9	347.7	383.5
BF.90	Net financial assets (+) / liabilities (-)	NYOG	–134.6	–202.0	–215.2	–268.5	–299.7	–334.5	–359.0	–329.1	–318.1
BF.90	**Net worth**	CGRX	139.1	70.2	69.6	32.1	10.1	–15.6	–16.1	18.6	65.4

General government

5.2.1 Central government
ESA95 sector S.1311

£ million

			1992	1993	1994	1995	1996	1997	1998	1999
I	**PRODUCTION ACCOUNT**									
	Resources									
P.1	Output									
P.11	Market output	NMIW	2 657	2 501	2 625	3 129	2 749	2 669	2 546	2 668
P.12	Output for own final use	QYJV	142	123	127	126	130	121	151	155
P.13	Other non-market output	NMBJ	78 275	81 566	84 385	86 791	90 396	92 190	95 298	100 647
P.1	Total resources	NMAE	81 074	84 190	87 137	90 046	93 275	94 980	97 995	103 470
	Uses									
P.2	Intermediate consumption	NMAF	40 842	47 321	55 918	60 166	63 860	65 910	69 319	75 145
B.1g	Value added, gross	NMBR	40 232	36 869	31 219	29 880	29 415	29 070	28 676	28 325
Total	Total uses	NMAE	81 074	84 190	87 137	90 046	93 275	94 980	97 995	103 470
B.1g	Value added, gross	NMBR	40 232	36 869	31 219	29 880	29 415	29 070	28 676	28 325
-K.1	*less* Consumption of fixed capital	-NSRN	–3 749	–3 551	–3 541	–3 773	–4 010	–4 277	–4 419	–4 489
B.1n	Value added, net of fixed capital consumption	NMAH	36 483	33 318	27 678	26 107	25 405	24 793	24 257	23 836

5.2.2 Central government
ESA95 sector S.1311

£ million

			1992	1993	1994	1995	1996	1997	1998	1999
II	**DISTRIBUTION AND USE OF INCOME ACCOUNTS**									
II.1	**PRIMARY DISTRIBUTION OF INCOME ACCOUNT**									
II.1.1	**GENERATION OF INCOME ACCOUNT**									
	Resources									
B.1g	Total resources, gross value added	NMBR	40 232	36 869	31 219	29 880	29 415	29 070	28 676	28 325
	Uses									
D.1	Compensation of employees									
D.11	Wages and salaries	NMAI	29 467	27 055	22 298	21 112	20 569	19 948	19 581	19 294
D.12	Employers' social contributions	NMAL	6 452	5 752	4 856	4 477	4 331	4 342	4 160	4 014
D.1	Total	NMBG	35 919	32 807	27 154	25 589	24 900	24 290	23 741	23 308
D.2	Taxes on production and imports, paid									
D.29	Production taxes other than on products	NMAN	564	511	524	518	505	503	516	528
-D.3	*less* Subsidies, received	-NMAO	–	–	–	–	–	–	–	–
-D.39	Production subsidies other than on products									
B.2g	Operating surplus, gross	NRLN	3 749	3 551	3 541	3 773	4 010	4 277	4 419	4 489
B.1g	Total uses	NMBR	40 232	36 869	31 219	29 880	29 415	29 070	28 676	28 325
-K.1	After deduction of fixed capital consumption	-NSRN	–3 749	–3 551	–3 541	–3 773	–4 010	–4 277	–4 419	–4 489
B.2n	Operating surplus, net	NMAP	–	–	–	–	–	–	–	–

5.2.3 Central government
ESA95 sector S.1311

General government

£ million

			1992	1993	1994	1995	1996	1997	1998	1999	2000
II.1.2	**ALLOCATION OF PRIMARY INCOME ACCOUNT**										
	Resources										
B.2g	Operating surplus, gross	NRLN	3 749	3 551	3 541	3 773	4 010	4 277	4 419	4 489	4 341
D.2	Taxes on production and imports, received										
D.21	Taxes on products										
D.211	Value added tax (VAT)	NZGF	37 426	37 958	42 996	43 579	46 918	52 057	54 293	58 664	60 702
D.212	Taxes and duties on imports excluding VAT										
D.2121	Import duties	NMBS	–	–	–	–	–	–	–	–	–
D.2122	Taxes on imports excluding VAT and import duties	NMBT	–	–	–	–	–	–	–	–	–
D.214	Taxes on products excluding VAT and import duties	NMBV	27 036	28 586	31 218	35 482	37 380	40 621	44 815	48 395	52 141
D.21	Total taxes on products	NMYC	64 462	66 544	74 214	79 061	84 298	92 678	99 108	107 059	112 843
D.29	Other taxes on production	NMBX	15 613	14 980	14 630	15 115	15 820	16 564	17 159	17 871	18 629
D.2	Total taxes on production and imports, received	NMBY	80 075	81 524	88 844	94 176	100 118	109 242	116 267	124 930	131 472
-D.3	*less* Subsidies, paid										
-D.31	Subsidies on products	-NMCB	–3 757	–3 800	–4 271	–4 226	–5 152	–4 181	–3 488	–3 579	–3 109
-D.39	Other subsidies on production	-NMCC	–1 030	–914	–741	–765	–725	–710	–744	–747	–538
-D.3	Total	-NMCD	–4 787	–4 714	–5 012	–4 991	–5 877	–4 891	–4 232	–4 326	–3 647
D.4	Property income										
D.41	Total Interest	NMCE	7 878	7 460	7 825	7 859	8 386	7 650	8 134	8 502	8 632
D.42	Distributed income of corporations	NMCH	1 880	1 929	1 873	1 936	1 957	1 971	2 227	1 398	1 737
D.45	Rent from sectors other than general government	NMCK	647	699	658	684	780	721	547	433	1 185
D.4	Total	NMCL	10 405	10 088	10 356	10 479	11 123	10 342	10 908	10 333	11 554
Total	Total resources	NMCM	89 442	90 449	97 729	103 437	109 374	118 970	127 362	135 426	143 720
	Uses										
D.4	Property income										
D.41	Total Interest	RVFK	18 209	19 511	22 409	25 750	27 401	29 432	30 325	26 224	26 687
D.4	Total property income	NUHA	18 209	19 511	22 409	25 750	27 401	29 432	30 325	26 224	26 687
B.5g	Balance of primary incomes, gross	NRLP	71 233	70 938	75 320	77 687	81 973	89 538	97 037	109 202	117 033
Total	Total uses	NMCM	89 442	90 449	97 729	103 437	109 374	118 970	127 362	135 426	143 720
-K.1	After deduction of fixed capital consumption	-NSRN	–3 749	–3 551	–3 541	–3 773	–4 010	–4 277	–4 419	–4 489	–4 341
B.5n	Balance of primary incomes, net	NMCT	67 484	67 387	71 779	73 914	77 963	85 261	92 618	104 713	112 692

General government

5.2.4 Central government
ESA95 sector S.1311

£ million

			1992	1993	1994	1995	1996	1997	1998	1999	2000
II.2	**SECONDARY DISTRIBUTION OF INCOME ACCOUNT**										
	Resources										
B.5g	Balance of primary incomes, gross	NRLP	71 233	70 938	75 320	77 687	81 973	89 538	97 037	109 202	117 033
D.5	Current taxes on income, wealth etc.										
D.51	Taxes on income	NMCU	80 291	78 313	85 348	95 042	99 310	107 647	124 060	129 044	140 960
D.59	Other current taxes	NMCV	2 024	2 382	2 633	2 728	2 872	3 067	3 245	3 437	3 307
D.5	Total	NMCP	82 315	80 695	87 981	97 770	102 182	110 714	127 305	132 481	144 267
D.61	Social contributions										
D.611	Actual social contributions										
D.6111	Employers' actual social contributions	NMCY	23 189	24 670	24 913	25 917	27 344	29 038	31 391	33 108	35 253
D.6112	Employees' social contributions	NMDB	16 064	16 764	19 171	20 598	21 190	23 603	25 139	25 939	26 728
D.6113	Social contributions by self- and non-employed persons	NMDE	1 281	1 472	1 469	1 541	1 771	1 848	1 760	1 801	1 973
D.611	Total	NMCX	40 534	42 906	45 553	48 056	50 305	54 489	58 290	60 848	63 954
D.612	Imputed social contributions	QYJS	4 287	4 148	4 065	3 941	3 929	3 881	4 227	4 109	4 200
D.61	Total	NMCW	44 821	47 054	49 618	51 997	54 234	58 370	62 517	64 957	68 154
D.7	Other current transfers										
D.72	Non-life insurance claims	NMDJ	–	–	–	–	–	–	–	–	–
D.73	Current transfers within general government	NMDK	–	–	–	–	–	–	–	–	–
D.74	Current international cooperation	NMDL	1 907	2 558	1 752	1 233	2 424	1 739	1 384	3 176	2 084
	from institutions of the EC	NMEX	1 898	2 558	1 752	1 233	2 424	1 739	1 384	3 176	2 084
D.75	Miscellaneous current transfers										
	from sectors other than general government	NMEZ	178	296	414	461	420	468	382	259	280
D.7	Total, other current transfers										
	from general government	NMDK	–	–	–	–	–	–	–	–	–
	from other sectors	NMEW	2 085	2 854	2 166	1 694	2 844	2 207	1 766	3 435	2 364
D.7	Total	NMDI	2 085	2 854	2 166	1 694	2 844	2 207	1 766	3 435	2 364
Total	Total resources	NMDN	200 454	201 541	215 085	229 148	241 233	260 829	288 625	310 075	331 818
	Uses										
D.62	Social benefits other than social transfers in kind	NMDR	83 728	89 223	91 258	94 859	97 995	100 996	102 040	105 934	110 674
D.7	Other current transfers										
D.71	Net non-life insurance premiums	NMDX	–	–	–	–	–	–	–	–	–
D.73	Current transfers within general government	QYJR	54 527	55 891	57 736	58 587	59 458	59 506	60 421	64 775	66 327
D.74	Current international cooperation	NMDZ	2 237	1 961	2 007	2 224	1 814	1 700	1 705	1 667	2 418
	to institutions of the EC	NMFA	–	2	7	8	8	31	–1	11	6
D.75	Miscellaneous current transfers										
	to sectors other than general government										
	GNP based fourth own resource	NMFH	914	1 558	2 071	1 826	2 454	2 458	3 920	4 632	4 379
	Grants to higher education institutions	CJTH	2 177	3 013	3 388	3 721	4 132	4 723	4 718	5 249	4 435
	Grants to further education colleges	CJTG	155	2 016	2 536	2 710	3 684	3 615	3 661	3 923	3 872
	Other grants to non profit institutions	GDXH	1 301	1 624	2 025	1 863	1 742	2 563	2 909	2 865	6 248
	Grants to fund NHS pension increases	RUDY	112	256	420	494	537	557	595	611	622
D.75	Total	NMFC	4 659	8 467	10 440	10 614	12 549	13 916	15 803	17 280	19 556
D.7	Total other current transfers										
	to general government	QYJR	54 527	55 891	57 736	58 587	59 458	59 506	60 421	64 775	66 327
	to other sectors	NMDP	6 896	10 428	12 447	12 838	14 363	15 616	17 508	18 947	21 974
D.7	Total	NMDW	61 423	66 319	70 183	71 425	73 821	75 122	77 929	83 722	88 301
B.6g	Disposable income, gross	NRLR	55 303	45 999	53 644	62 864	69 417	84 711	108 656	120 419	132 843
Total	Total uses	NMDN	200 454	201 541	215 085	229 148	241 233	260 829	288 625	310 075	331 818
-K.1	After deduction of fixed capital consumption	-NSRN	–3 749	–3 551	–3 541	–3 773	–4 010	–4 277	–4 419	–4 489	–4 341
B.6n	Disposable income, net	NMEB	51 554	42 448	50 103	59 091	65 407	80 434	104 237	115 930	128 502

General government

5.24S Central government
Social contributions and benefits
ESA95 sector S.1311

£ million

Part			1992	1993	1994	1995	1996	1997	1998	1999	2000
	SECONDARY DISTRIBUTION OF INCOME (further detail of certain items)										
	Resources										
D.61	Social contributions										
	National Insurance Contributions (NICs)										
D.611	Actual social contributions										
D.61111	Employers' NICs	CEAN	21 621	23 038	23 240	24 210	25 553	27 200	29 529	31 248	33 180
D.61121	Employees' NICs	GCSE	14 104	14 748	17 357	18 646	19 175	21 558	22 984	23 549	23 972
D.61131	Self- and non-employed persons' NICs	NMDE	1 281	1 472	1 469	1 541	1 771	1 848	1 760	1 801	1 973
D.61	Total national insurance contributions	AIIH	37 006	39 258	42 066	44 397	46 499	50 606	54 273	56 598	59 125
	Notionally funded pension schemes[1]										
D.611	Actual social contributions										
D.61112	Employers' contributions	GCMP	1 568	1 632	1 673	1 707	1 791	1 838	1 862	1 860	2 073
D.61122	Employees' contributions	GITB	1 763	1 816	1 603	1 756	1 804	1 836	1 946	2 176	2 540
D.612	Imputed social contributions[2]	GCSG	1 305	1 376	1 421	1 427	1 519	1 627	1 750	1 749	1 769
D.61	Total notionally funded schemes	GCSZ	4 636	4 824	4 697	4 890	5 114	5 301	5 558	5 785	6 382
	Unfunded pension schemes[3]										
D.611	Actual social contributions										
D.61122	Employees' voluntary contributions	GVFJ	197	200	211	196	211	209	209	214	216
D.612	Imputed social contributions	GCSH	2 982	2 772	2 644	2 514	2 410	2 254	2 477	2 360	2 431
D.61	Total unfunded schemes	GCTA	3 180	2 972	2 855	2 710	2 622	2 462	2 686	2 575	2 647
D.61	Total social contributions	NMCW	44 821	47 054	49 618	51 997	54 234	58 370	62 517	64 957	68 154
	Uses										
D.62	Social benefits										
D.621	Social security benefits in cash										
	National insurance fund										
	Retirement pensions	CSDG	27 082	28 473	28 971	29 995	31 820	33 535	35 452	37 362	39 130
	Widows' and guardians' allowances	CSDH	1 020	1 026	1 043	1 018	988	988	979	970	984
	Unemployment benefit	CSDI	1 749	1 685	1 360	1 120	874	–2	–	–1	–1
	Jobseeker's allowance	CJTJ	–	–	–	–	188	625	500	473	436
	Sickness benefit	CSDJ	348	308	390	123	–	–	–	–	–
	Invalidity benefit	CSDK	6 078	6 854	7 798	2 329	–	–	–	–	–
	Incapacity benefit	CUNL	–	–	–	5 739	7 711	7 580	7 320	6 925	6 705
	Maternity benefit	CSDL	42	34	16	30	31	35	39	40	42
	Death grant	CSDM	–	–	–	–	–	–	–	–	–
	Statutory sick pay	CSDQ	694	688	190	24	27	28	28	28	31
	Statutory maternity pay	GTKZ	411	434	481	487	489	512	543	591	634
	Payment in lieu of benefits foregone	GTKV	–	–	–	–	–	–	–	–	–
	Total national insurance fund benefits	ACHH	37 424	39 502	40 249	40 865	42 128	43 301	44 861	46 388	47 961
	Redundancy fund benefit	GTKN	308	165	180	151	113	93	106	137	159
	Maternity fund benefit	GTKO	–	–	–	–	–	–	–	–	–
	Social fund benefit	GTLQ	154	193	185	216	207	164	356	995	1 857
	Benefits paid to overseas residents	FJVZ	619	772	843	910	963	1 031	1 091	1 123	1 161
D.621	Total social security benefits in cash	QYRJ	38 505	40 632	41 457	42 142	43 411	44 589	46 414	48 643	51 138
D.623	Unfunded employee social benefits										
	Unfunded pensions paid	GCSJ	3 878	4 240	4 267	4 291	4 564	4 691	4 898	4 942	4 960
	Other unfunded employee benefits	EWRO	491	462	415	327	264	254	219	214	187
	Notionally funded pensions paid	GCRW	4 959	5 249	5 032	5 980	6 362	7 190	6 294	6 176	7 179
D.623	Total unfunded social benefits	QYJT	9 328	9 951	9 714	10 598	11 190	12 135	11 411	11 332	12 326
D.624	Social assistance benefits in cash										
	War pensions and allowances	CSDD	947	940	1 023	1 195	1 356	1 311	1 260	1 255	1 214
	Family benefits	CSDB	7 035	7 619	7 994	8 302	8 906	9 339	9 709	10 366	8 631
	Income support	CSDE	15 022	16 676	16 511	16 623	15 636	12 050	11 778	12 068	12 830
	Other social security benefits	CSDC	5 264	6 689	8 214	9 764	11 856	15 396	15 422	15 773	16 002
	Other grants to households	NZGI	2 430	2 701	2 877	3 278	3 168	3 601	3 861	4 568	3 980
	Income tax credits and reliefs	RYCQ	5 155	3 963	3 412	2 895	2 406	2 504	2 114	1 869	4 496
	Benefits paid to overseas residents	RNNF	42	52	56	62	66	71	71	60	57
D.624	Total social assistance benefits in cash	NZGO	35 895	38 640	40 087	42 119	43 394	44 272	44 215	45 959	47 210
D.62	Total social benefits	NMDR	83 728	89 223	91 258	94 859	97 995	100 996	102 040	105 934	110 674

1 Mainly teachers' and NHS pension schemes
2 Pension increase payments to compensate for inflation, funded by central government
3 Mainly civil service and armed forces' schemes

United Kingdom National Accounts 2001, © Crown copyright 2001

General government

5.2.5 Central government
ESA95 sector S.1311

£ million

			1992	1993	1994	1995	1996	1997	1998	1999	2000
II.3	**REDISTRIBUTION OF INCOME IN KIND ACCOUNT**										
	Resources										
B.6g	Total resources, gross disposable income	NRLR	55 303	45 999	53 644	62 864	69 417	84 711	108 656	120 419	132 843
	Uses										
D.63	Social transfers in kind										
D.631	Social benefits in kind										
D.632	Transfers of individual non-market goods and services	NMED	39 140	41 987	44 431	46 504	48 678	50 207	52 837	56 337	59 783
B.7g	Adjusted disposable income, gross	NSVS	16 163	4 012	9 213	16 360	20 739	34 504	55 819	64 082	73 060
Total	Total uses	NRLR	55 303	45 999	53 644	62 864	69 417	84 711	108 656	120 419	132 843

5.2.6 Central government
ESA95 sector S.1311

£ million

			1992	1993	1994	1995	1996	1997	1998	1999	2000
II.4	**USE OF INCOME ACCOUNT**										
II.4.1	**USE OF DISPOSABLE INCOME ACCOUNT**										
	Resources										
B.6g	Total resources, gross disposable income	NRLR	55 303	45 999	53 644	62 864	69 417	84 711	108 656	120 419	132 843
	Uses										
P.3	Final consumption expenditure										
P.31	Individual consumption expenditure	NMED	39 140	41 987	44 431	46 504	48 678	50 207	52 837	56 337	59 783
P.32	Collective consumption expenditure	NMEE	39 135	39 579	39 954	40 287	41 718	41 983	42 461	44 310	45 681
P.3	Total	NMBJ	78 275	81 566	84 385	86 791	90 396	92 190	95 298	100 647	105 464
B.8g	Saving, gross	NRLS	−22 972	−35 567	−30 741	−23 927	−20 979	−7 479	13 358	19 772	27 379
Total	Total uses	NRLR	55 303	45 999	53 644	62 864	69 417	84 711	108 656	120 419	132 843
−K.1	After deduction of fixed capital consumption	−NSRN	−3 749	−3 551	−3 541	−3 773	−4 010	−4 277	−4 419	−4 489	−4 341
B.8n	Saving, net	NMEG	−26 721	−39 118	−34 282	−27 700	−24 989	−11 756	8 939	15 283	23 038
II.4.2	**USE OF ADJUSTED DISPOSABLE INCOME ACCOUNT**										
	Resources										
B.7g	Total resources, adjusted disposable income, gross	NSVS	16 163	4 012	9 213	16 360	20 739	34 504	55 819	64 082	73 060
	Uses										
P.4	Actual final consumption										
P.42	Actual collective consumption	NMEE	39 135	39 579	39 954	40 287	41 718	41 983	42 461	44 310	45 681
B.8g	Saving, gross	NRLS	−22 972	−35 567	−30 741	−23 927	−20 979	−7 479	13 358	19 772	27 379
Total	Total uses	NSVS	16 163	4 012	9 213	16 360	20 739	34 504	55 819	64 082	73 060

5.2.7 Central government
ESA95 sector S.1311

General government

£ million

			1992	1993	1994	1995	1996	1997	1998	1999	2000
III	**ACCUMULATION ACCOUNTS**										
III.1	**CAPITAL ACCOUNT**										
III.1.1	**CHANGE IN NET WORTH DUE TO SAVINGS AND CAPITAL TRANSFERS**										
	Changes in liabilities and net worth										
B.8g	Saving, gross	NRLS	−22 972	−35 567	−30 741	−23 927	−20 979	−7 479	13 358	19 772	27 379
D.9	Capital transfers receivable										
D.91	Capital taxes from sectors other than general government	NMGI	1 227	1 279	1 438	1 441	1 621	1 601	1 796	1 951	2 215
D.92	Investment grants from general government	GCMT	−	−	−	−	−	−	−	−	−
D.99	Other capital transfers from general government	NMGL	−	−	−	−	−	−	−	−	−
	from other sectors	NMGM	−	−	−	−	−	−	−	−	−
D.99	Total	NMEK	−	−	−	−	−	−	−	−	−
D.9	Total capital transfers receivable from general government	QYQP	−	−	−	−	−	−	−	−	−
	from other sectors	NMGG	1 227	1 279	1 438	1 441	1 621	1 601	1 796	1 951	2 215
D.9	Total	NMEH	1 227	1 279	1 438	1 441	1 621	1 601	1 796	1 951	2 215
-D.9	*less* Capital transfers payable										
-D.92	Investment grants to general government	-QYQO	−2 714	−3 055	−2 624	−2 574	−2 719	−2 822	−2 476	−3 059	−3 846
	to other sectors	-NMGS	−6 349	−7 252	−6 432	−6 212	−5 872	−4 842	−4 354	−4 996	−3 473
-D.92	Total	-NMEN	−9 063	−10 307	−9 056	−8 786	−8 591	−7 664	−6 830	−8 055	−7 319
-D.99	Other capital transfers to general government	-NMGT	−5 100	−	−	−	−1 600	−	−	−	−132
	to other sectors	-NMGU	−106	−21	−24	−1 626	−164	−24	−146	−10	−22
-D.99	Total	-NMEO	−5 206	−21	−24	−1 626	−1 764	−24	−146	−10	−154
-D.9	Total capital transfers payable to general government	-QYQR	−7 814	−3 055	−2 624	−2 574	−4 319	−2 822	−2 476	−3 059	−3 978
	to other sectors	-NMGO	−6 455	−7 273	−6 456	−7 838	−6 036	−4 866	−4 500	−5 006	−3 495
-D.9	Total	-NMEL	−14 269	−10 328	−9 080	−10 412	−10 355	−7 688	−6 976	−8 065	−7 473
B.10.1g	Total change in liabilities and net worth	NMEP	−36 014	−44 616	−38 383	−32 898	−29 713	−13 566	8 178	13 658	22 121
	Changes in assets										
B.10.1g	Changes in net worth due to gross saving and capital transfers	NMEP	−36 014	−44 616	−38 383	−32 898	−29 713	−13 566	8 178	13 658	22 121
-K.1	After deduction of fixed capital consumption	-NSRN	−3 749	−3 551	−3 541	−3 773	−4 010	−4 277	−4 419	−4 489	−4 341
B.10.1n	Changes in net worth due to net saving and capital transfers	NMEQ	−39 763	−48 167	−41 924	−36 671	−33 723	−17 843	3 759	9 169	17 780
III.1.2	**ACQUISITION OF NON-FINANCIAL ASSETS ACCOUNT**										
	Changes in liabilities and net worth										
B.10.1n	Changes in net worth due to saving and capital transfers	NMEQ	−39 763	−48 167	−41 924	−36 671	−33 723	−17 843	3 759	9 169	17 780
K.1	Consumption of fixed capital	NSRN	3 749	3 551	3 541	3 773	4 010	4 277	4 419	4 489	4 341
B.10.1g	Total changes in liabilities and net worth	NMEP	−36 014	−44 616	−38 383	−32 898	−29 713	−13 566	8 178	13 658	22 121
	Changes in assets										
P.5	Gross capital formation										
P.51	Gross fixed capital formation	NMES	7 840	7 312	7 272	6 932	5 293	4 022	4 557	4 136	4 557
P.52	Changes in inventories	NMFE	−17	−24	−251	−154	166	140	107	−268	−140
P.53	Acquisitions less disposals of valuables	NPPD	−	−	−	−	−	−	14	10	2
P.5	Total	NMER	7 823	7 288	7 021	6 778	5 459	4 162	4 678	3 878	4 419
K.2	Acquisitions less disposals of non-produced non-financial assets	NMFG	−15	−25	−24	−8	−24	−18	−314	−35	−33
B.9g	Net lending(+) / net borrowing(-)	NMFJ	−43 822	−51 879	−45 380	−39 668	−35 148	−17 710	3 814	9 815	17 735
Total	Total change in assets	NMEP	−36 014	−44 616	−38 383	−32 898	−29 713	−13 566	8 178	13 658	22 121

United Kingdom National Accounts 2001, © Crown copyright 2001

General government
5.2.8 Central government
ESA95 sector S.1311 Unconsolidated

£ million

			1992	1993	1994	1995	1996	1997	1998	1999	2000
III.2	**FINANCIAL ACCOUNT**										
F.A	Net acquisition of financial assets										
F.1	Monetary gold and special drawing rights (SDRs)	NWXM	−962	−462	932	−120	−54	1 199	915	−374	−956
F.2	Currency and deposits										
F.22	Transferable deposits										
F.2211	Sterling deposits with UK banks	NAUB	223	3 867	−3 645	166	−118	−4	−314	−79	15 062
F.2212	Foreign currency deposits with UK banks	NARV	57	−26	−54	188	152	−305	−21	9	120
F.2213	Sterling deposits with UK building societies	NARW	−	−	14	−30	11	−8	−2	−4	11
F.229	Deposits with rest of the world monetary financial institutions	NARX	274	−138	27	622	1 148	135	−1 804	3 177	−840
F.29	Other deposits national savings & tax	RYWO	−	−	−	−	−	−	−	−	2 913
F.2	Total currency and deposits	NARQ	554	3 703	−3 658	946	1 193	−182	−2 141	3 103	17 266
F.3	Securities other than shares										
F.331	Short term: money market instruments										
F.3312	Issued by UK local authorities	NASF	−	−	−	−	−	−	−	−	−
F.3315	Issued by UK MFI's	NSUN	−	−	−	−	−	−	−	−	1 435
F.3319	Issued by the rest of the world	NASM	−	−	−	−	−496	−777	939	−337	244
F.332	Medium (1 to 5 year) and long term (over 5 year) bonds										
F.3326	Other medium & long term bonds issued by UK residents	NASV	−596	−946	−2 276	−	−1 745	−238	−	−387	−149
F.3329	Long term bonds issued by the rest of the world	NASW	−716	1 298	87	−700	−1 107	−2 936	−214	−3 105	5 418
F.34	Financial derivatives	NASX	−	−	−	−	−	−	−	−	50
F.3	Total securities other than shares	NARZ	−1 312	352	−2 189	−700	−3 348	−3 951	725	−3 829	6 998
F.4	Loans										
F.42	Long term loans										
F.422	Loans secured on dwellings	NATM	−104	−74	−37	−20	−21	−1 226	−1	−1	−1
F.424	Other long-term loans by UK residents	NATR	−4 497	−51	96	1 634	−4 557	2 578	852	3 700	5 147
F.4	Total loans	NATB	−4 601	−125	59	1 614	−4 578	1 352	851	3 699	5 146
F.5	Shares and other equity										
F.51	Shares and other equity, excluding mutual funds' shares										
F.514	Quoted UK shares	NATY	−6 912	−4 454	−3 654	−2 374	−4 321	−1 743	−21	−12	−103
F.515	Unquoted UK shares	NATZ	−72	−	−724	−110	−17	−30	−	−	−
F.516	Other UK equity (including direct investment in property)	NAUA	−7	56	−	13	3 264	−	−	−	−
F.519	Shares and other equity issued by the rest of the world	NAUD	68	79	90	85	81	63	67	91	53
F.5	Total shares and other equity	NATT	−6 923	−4 319	−4 288	−2 386	−993	−1 710	46	79	−50
F.7	Other accounts receivable	NAUN	−839	2 320	1 186	2 341	−563	2 838	1 045	6 899	2 324
F.A	Total net acquisition of financial assets	NARM	−14 083	1 469	−7 958	1 695	−8 343	−454	1 441	9 577	30 728

5.2.8 Central government
ESA95 sector S.1311 Unconsolidated

General government

£ million

			1992	1993	1994	1995	1996	1997	1998	1999	2000
III.2	**FINANCIAL ACCOUNT** continued										
F.L	**Net acquisition of financial liabilities**										
F.2	Currency and deposits										
F.21	Currency	NAUV	28	107	110	74	141	188	167	199	235
F.29	Non-transferable deposits	NAVC	4 722	4 946	5 945	4 095	6 998	1 753	−1 193	−847	3 541
F.2	Total currency and deposits	NAUU	4 750	5 053	6 055	4 169	7 139	1 941	−1 026	−648	3 776
F.3	Securities other than shares										
F.331	Short term: money market instruments										
F.3311	Issued by UK central government	NAVF	−4 880	−405	1 080	11 513	−13 498	−1 569	86	−409	−1 652
F.332	Medium (1 to 5 year) and long term (over 5 year) bonds										
F.33211	British government securities	NAVT	24 925	51 557	22 133	22 477	31 285	18 857	−3 250	−4 504	−12 702
F.33212	Other central government bonds	NAVU	5 559	1 558	1 898	65	53	−2 192	49	−56	−16
F.34	Financial derivatives	NAWB	−	−	−	−	−	−	−	−	−
F.3	Total securities other than shares	NAVD	25 604	52 710	25 111	34 055	17 840	15 096	−3 115	−4 969	−14 370
F.4	Loans										
F.41	Short term loans										
F.411	Loans by UK monetary financial institutions, excluding loans secured on dwellings & financial leasing	NAWH	−2 046	−2 389	7 000	2 078	1 813	−1 910	1 066	6 128	−171
F.419	Loans by rest of the world monetary financial institutions	NAWL	1 284	−2 855	−38	−11	−15	−166	−2	−1	−
F.42	Long term loans										
F.423	Finance leasing	NAWU	−12	−9	4	−6	6	−3	407	437	15
F.424	Other long-term loans by UK residents	NAWV	−52	−45	−24	−51	172	14	−51	−38	−25
F.429	Other long-term loans by the rest of the world	NAWW	−99	−95	−93	−94	−89	−90	−91	−105	−114
F.4	Total loans	NAWF	−925	−5 393	6 849	1 916	1 887	−2 155	1 329	6 421	−295
F.7	Other accounts payable	NAXR	661	1 840	−657	1 491	−173	2 374	208	−1 112	23 946
F.L	**Total net acquisition of financial liabilities**	NAUQ	30 090	54 210	37 358	41 631	26 693	17 256	−2 604	−308	13 057
B.9	**Net lending / borrowing**										
F.A	Total net acquisition of financial assets	NARM	−14 083	1 469	−7 958	1 695	−8 343	−454	1 441	9 577	30 728
-F.L	*less* Total net acquisition of financial liabilities	-NAUQ	−30 090	−54 210	−37 358	−41 631	−26 693	−17 256	2 604	308	−13 057
B.9f	**Net lending (+) / net borrowing (-), from financial account**	NZDX	−44 173	−52 741	−45 316	−39 936	−35 036	−17 710	4 045	9 885	17 671
dB.9f	**Statistical discrepancy**	NZDW	351	862	−64	268	−112	−	−231	−70	64
B.9g	**Net lending (+) / net borrowing (-), from capital account**	NMFJ	−43 822	−51 879	−45 380	−39 668	−35 148	−17 710	3 814	9 815	17 735

United Kingdom National Accounts 2001, © Crown copyright 2001

General government

5.2.9 Central government
ESA95 sector S.1311 Unconsolidated

£ billion

			1992	1993	1994	1995	1996	1997	1998	1999	2000
IV.3	**FINANCIAL BALANCE SHEET** at end of period										
AN	Non-financial assets	CGIY	123.1	117.9	124.3	133.0	139.1	140.3	146.3	148.5	174.2
AF.A	**Financial assets**										
AF.1	Monetary gold and special drawing rights (SDRs)	NIFC	4.4	5.1	4.8	4.9	4.2	3.5	4.3	4.0	3.1
AF.2	Currency and deposits										
AF.22	Transferable deposits										
AF.221	Deposits with UK monetary financial institutions	NIFI	2.1	6.0	2.3	2.6	2.6	2.3	1.9	1.8	18.9
AF.229	Deposits with rest of the world monetary financial institutions	NIFM	1.3	1.3	1.3	7.3	7.3	7.7	6.1	8.7	6.6
AF.29	Other deposits	NIFN	–	–	–	–	–	–	–	–	2.9
AF.2	Total currency and deposits	NIFF	3.5	7.2	3.6	10.0	10.0	10.0	8.0	10.6	28.5
AF.3	Securities other than shares										
AF.331	Short term: money market instruments										
AF.3312	Issued by UK local authorities	NIFU	–	–	–	–	–	–	–	–	–
AF.3319	Issued by the rest of the world	NIGB	–	–	–	2.6	1.7	1.0	2.1	1.8	2.3
AF.3315	Issued by UK MFI's	NSUO	–	–	–	–	–	–	–	–	2.0
AF.332	Medium (1 to 5 year) and long term (over 5 year) bonds										
AF.3322	Issued by UK local authorities	NIGG	–	–	–	–	–	–	–	–	–
AF.3326	Other medium & long term bonds issued by UK residents	NIGK	4.4	3.2	1.4	1.4	0.8	0.6	0.6	0.2	0.1
AF.3329	Long term bonds issued by the rest of the world	NIGL	22.5	23.4	24.6	17.0	14.1	10.6	10.9	7.6	16.7
AF.34	Financial derivatives	ZYBQ	–	–	–	–	–	–	–	–	0.1
AF.3	Total securities other than shares	NIFO	27.0	26.6	26.0	20.9	16.6	12.2	13.6	9.7	21.2
AF.4	Loans										
AF.42	Long term loans										
AF.422	Loans secured on dwellings	NIHB	1.5	1.4	1.4	1.3	1.3	0.1	0.1	0.1	0.1
AF.424	Other long-term loans by UK residents	NIHG	71.9	73.2	73.3	75.0	73.3	75.9	81.3	83.8	89.0
AF.4	Total loans	NIGQ	73.3	74.6	74.7	76.3	74.7	76.0	81.4	83.9	89.1
AF.5	Shares and other equity										
AF.51	Shares and other equity, excluding mutual funds' shares										
AF.514	Quoted UK shares	NIHN	10.7	9.4	5.3	2.7	0.2	0.2	0.2	0.2	0.1
AF.515	Unquoted UK shares	NIHO	0.1	0.1	0.8	0.8	0.1	0.1	0.1	0.1	0.1
AF.519	Shares and other equity issued by the rest of the world	NIHS	1.3	1.3	1.4	1.5	1.6	1.7	1.7	1.8	1.9
AF.5	Total shares and other equity	NIHI	12.0	10.8	7.6	5.0	1.9	2.0	2.0	2.2	2.0
AF.7	Other accounts receivable	NIIC	25.5	28.3	29.9	32.7	32.7	35.6	36.5	43.2	44.3
AF.A	**Total financial assets**	NIGP	145.8	152.7	146.5	149.8	140.1	139.3	145.8	153.4	188.1

General government

5.2.9 Central government
ESA95 sector S.1311 Unconsolidated
continued

£ billion

			1992	1993	1994	1995	1996	1997	1998	1999	2000
IV.3	**FINANCIAL BALANCE SHEET** continued at end of period										
AF.L	**Financial liabilities**										
AF.2	Currency and deposits										
AF.21	Currency	NIIK	2.1	2.2	2.3	2.3	2.4	2.5	2.6	2.8	3.0
AF.29	Non-transferable deposits	NIIR	49.0	55.4	61.4	65.5	72.5	74.2	73.1	71.9	75.3
AF.2	Total currency and deposits	NIIJ	51.1	57.6	63.7	67.8	74.9	76.7	75.8	74.7	78.3
AF.3	Securities other than shares										
AF.331	Short term: money market instruments										
AF.33111	Sterling Treasury bills	NIIV	5.7	4.8	5.9	17.4	3.9	2.3	2.4	4.3	2.7
AF.33112	ECU Treasury bills	NIIW	2.5	2.6	2.7	2.8	2.5	2.3	2.4	–	–
AF.332	Medium (1 to 5 year) and long term (over 5 year) bonds										
AF.33211	British government securities	NIJI	153.7	226.6	216.3	251.6	281.0	318.5	349.0	324.3	315.5
AF.33212	Other central government bonds	NIJJ	10.2	11.7	13.7	14.3	12.7	10.0	10.3	9.7	10.4
AF.34	Financial derivatives	NIJQ	–	–	–	–	–	–	–	–	–
AF.3	Total securities other than shares	NIIS	172.1	245.6	238.5	286.0	300.1	333.2	364.1	338.3	328.5
AF.4	Loans										
AF.41	Short term loans										
AF.411	Loans by UK monetary financial institutions, excluding loans secured on dwellings & financial leasing	NIJW	5.9	3.4	10.5	12.5	14.3	12.4	13.5	19.6	24.3
AF.419	Loans by rest of the world monetary financial institutions	NIKA	3.1	0.3	0.2	0.2	0.2	–	–	–	–
AF.42	Long term loans										
AF.423	Finance leasing	NIKJ	0.1	0.1	0.1	0.1	0.1	0.1	0.5	0.9	1.0
AF.424	Other long-term loans by UK residents	NIKK	–	–	–	–	0.2	0.2	0.2	0.2	0.2
AF.429	Other long-term loans by the rest of the world	NIKL	1.1	1.0	0.9	0.8	0.6	0.5	0.4	0.4	0.5
AF.4	Total loans	NIJU	10.1	4.8	11.6	13.6	15.4	13.3	14.6	21.1	26.0
AF.7	Other accounts payable	NILG	3.3	4.7	4.7	5.6	5.1	7.6	7.9	7.3	31.4
AF.L	**Total financial liabilities**	NIJT	236.6	312.7	318.6	373.1	395.6	430.8	462.5	441.4	464.2
BF.90	Net financial assets / liabilities										
AF.A	Total financial assets	NIGP	145.8	152.7	146.5	149.8	140.1	139.3	145.8	153.4	188.1
-AF.L	*less* Total financial liabilities	-NIJT	−236.6	−312.7	−318.6	−373.1	−395.6	−430.8	−462.5	−441.4	−464.2
BF.90	**Net financial assets (+) / liabilities (−)**	NZDZ	−90.8	−160.0	−172.1	−223.3	−255.5	−291.4	−316.7	−287.9	−276.1
	Net worth										
AN	Non-financial assets	CGIY	123.1	117.9	124.3	133.0	139.1	140.3	146.3	148.5	174.2
BF.90	Net financial assets (+) / liabilities (−)	NZDZ	−90.8	−160.0	−172.1	−223.3	−255.5	−291.4	−316.7	−287.9	−276.1
BF.90	**Net worth**	CGRY	32.3	−42.1	−47.8	−90.3	−116.4	−151.1	−170.4	−139.4	−101.9

General government

5.3.1 Local government
ESA95 sector S.1313

£ million

			1992	1993	1994	1995	1996	1997	1998	1999
I	**PRODUCTION ACCOUNT**									
	Resources									
P.1	Output									
P.11	Market output	NMIX	4 534	4 225	4 260	4 568	4 644	4 692	5 006	5 451
P.12	Output for own final use	QYJW	257	267	257	243	251	264	262	306
P.13	Other non-market output	NMMT	50 920	49 968	51 870	54 240	56 383	56 957	59 583	65 647
P.1	Total resources	NMIZ	55 711	54 460	56 387	59 051	61 278	61 913	64 851	71 404
	Uses									
P.2	Intermediate consumption	NMJA	16 203	16 235	19 170	20 961	22 115	21 457	22 533	25 603
B.1g	Value added, gross	NMJB	39 508	38 225	37 217	38 090	39 163	40 456	42 318	45 801
Total	Total uses	NMIZ	55 711	54 460	56 387	59 051	61 278	61 913	64 851	71 404
B.1g	Value added, gross	NMJB	39 508	38 225	37 217	38 090	39 163	40 456	42 318	45 801
-K.1	less Consumption of fixed capital	-NSRO	−2 326	−2 319	−2 450	−2 674	−2 866	−3 039	−3 115	−3 278
B.1n	Value added, net of fixed capital consumption	NMJD	37 182	35 906	34 767	35 416	36 297	37 417	39 203	42 523

5.3.2 Local government
ESA95 sector S.1313

£ million

			1992	1993	1994	1995	1996	1997	1998	1999
II	**DISTRIBUTION AND USE OF INCOME ACCOUNTS**									
II.1	**PRIMARY DISTRIBUTION OF INCOME ACCOUNT**									
II.1.1	**GENERATION OF INCOME ACCOUNT**									
	Resources									
B.1g	Total resources, gross value added	NMJB	39 508	38 225	37 217	38 090	39 163	40 456	42 318	45 801
	Uses									
D.1	Compensation of employees									
D.11	Wages and salaries	NMJF	29 594	28 905	27 435	27 789	28 080	28 972	29 315	31 908
D.12	Employers' social contributions	NMJG	6 355	5 948	6 161	6 461	7 003	7 258	8 648	9 368
D.1	Total	NMJE	35 949	34 853	33 596	34 250	35 083	36 230	37 963	41 276
D.2	Taxes on production and imports, paid									
D.29	Production taxes other than on products	NMHY	1 233	1 053	1 171	1 166	1 214	1 187	1 240	1 247
-D.3	less Subsidies, received									
-D.39	Production subsidies other than on products	-NMJL	–	–	–	–	–	–	–	–
B.2g	Operating surplus, gross	NRLT	2 326	2 319	2 450	2 674	2 866	3 039	3 115	3 278
B.1g	Total uses	NMJB	39 508	38 225	37 217	38 090	39 163	40 456	42 318	45 801
-K.1	After deduction of fixed capital consumption	-NSRO	−2 326	−2 319	−2 450	−2 674	−2 866	−3 039	−3 115	−3 278
B.2n	Operating surplus, net	NMJM	–	–	–	–	–	–	–	–

General government

5.3.3 Local government
ESA95 sector S.1313

£ million

			1992	1993	1994	1995	1996	1997	1998	1999	2000
II.1.2	**ALLOCATION OF PRIMARY INCOME ACCOUNT**										
	Resources										
B.2g	Operating surplus, gross	NRLT	2 326	2 319	2 450	2 674	2 866	3 039	3 115	3 278	3 420
D.2	Taxes on production and imports, received										
D.29	Taxes on production other than on products	NMYH	65	86	91	99	109	122	128	142	149
-D.3	*less* Subsidies, paid										
-D.31	Subsidies on products	-ADAK	−604	−604	−705	−787	−696	−934	−817	−790	−828
-D.39	Other subsidies on production	-LIUC	–	−1	–	–	−3	−1	−1	−3	−7
D.4	Property income										
D.41	Total Interest	NMKB	771	536	560	694	645	925	1 102	826	946
D.42	Distributed income of corporations	FDDA	4 450	4 672	4 881	4 979	4 925	4 556	5 223	5 086	5 009
D.44	Property income attributed to insurance policy holders	NMKK	29	28	30	32	28	33	48	29	40
D.45	Rent										
	from sectors other than general government	NMKM	–	–	–	–	–	–	–	–	–
D.4	Total property income	NMJZ	5 250	5 236	5 471	5 705	5 598	5 514	6 373	5 941	5 995
Total	Total resources	NMKN	7 037	7 037	7 307	7 691	7 877	7 741	8 799	8 571	8 736
	Uses										
D.4	Property income										
D.41	Total Interest	NCBW	5 183	4 545	4 395	4 327	4 504	4 377	4 549	4 424	4 243
D.4	Total property income	NUHI	5 183	4 545	4 395	4 327	4 504	4 377	4 549	4 424	4 243
B.5g	Balance of primary incomes, gross	NRLU	1 854	2 492	2 912	3 364	3 373	3 364	4 250	4 147	4 493
Total	Total uses	NMKN	7 037	7 037	7 307	7 691	7 877	7 741	8 799	8 571	8 736
-K.1	After deduction of fixed capital consumption	-NSRO	−2 326	−2 319	−2 450	−2 674	−2 866	−3 039	−3 115	−3 278	−3 420
B.5n	Balance of primary incomes, net	NMKZ	−472	173	462	690	507	325	1 135	869	1 073

United Kingdom National Accounts 2001, © Crown copyright 2001

General government

5.3.4 Local government
ESA95 sector S.1313

£ million

			1992	1993	1994	1995	1996	1997	1998	1999	2000
II.2	**SECONDARY DISTRIBUTION OF INCOME ACCOUNT**										
	Resources										
B.5g	Balance of primary incomes, gross	NRLU	1 854	2 492	2 912	3 364	3 373	3 364	4 250	4 147	4 493
D.5	Current taxes on income, wealth etc.										
D.59	Current taxes other than on income	NMIS	8 275	8 169	8 507	9 209	9 923	10 753	11 748	12 826	13 795
D.61	Social contributions										
D.611	Actual social contributions										
D.6112	Employees' social contributions	NMWM	461	471	478	493	510	518	551	580	585
D.612	Imputed social contributions	GCMN	1 138	1 248	1 354	1 338	1 370	1 475	1 653	1 714	1 719
D.61	Total	NSMM	1 599	1 719	1 832	1 831	1 880	1 993	2 204	2 294	2 304
D.7	Other current transfers										
D.72	Non-life insurance claims	NMLR	408	361	363	377	371	349	499	410	490
D.73	Current transfers within general government	QYJR	54 527	55 891	57 736	58 587	59 458	59 506	60 421	64 775	66 327
D.7	Total, other current transfers										
	from general government	QYJR	54 527	55 891	57 736	58 587	59 458	59 506	60 421	64 775	66 327
	from other sectors	NMLR	408	361	363	377	371	349	499	410	490
D.7	Total	NMLO	54 935	56 252	58 099	58 964	59 829	59 855	60 920	65 185	66 817
Total	Total resources	NMLX	66 663	68 632	71 350	73 368	75 005	75 965	79 122	84 452	87 409
	Uses										
D.62	Social benefits other than social transfers in kind	NSMN	11 611	13 742	15 037	15 550	15 129	15 938	15 509	14 818	14 317
D.7	Other current transfers										
D.71	Net non-life insurance premiums	NMMI	408	361	363	377	371	349	499	410	490
D.73	Current transfers within general government	NMDK	–	–	–	–	–	–	–	–	–
D.7	Total other current transfers										
	to general government	NMDK	–	–	–	–	–	–	–	–	–
	to other sectors	NMMI	408	361	363	377	371	349	499	410	490
D.7	Total	NMMF	408	361	363	377	371	349	499	410	490
B.6g	Disposable income, gross	NRLW	54 644	54 529	55 950	57 441	59 505	59 678	63 114	69 224	72 602
Total	Total uses	NMLX	66 663	68 632	71 350	73 368	75 005	75 965	79 122	84 452	87 409
-K.1	After deduction of fixed capital consumption	-NSRO	-2 326	-2 319	-2 450	-2 674	-2 866	-3 039	-3 115	-3 278	-3 420
B.6n	Disposable income, net	NMMQ	52 318	52 210	53 500	54 767	56 639	56 639	59 999	65 946	69 182

5.34S Local government
Social contributions and benefits
ESA95 sector S.1313

General government

£ million

Part			1992	1993	1994	1995	1996	1997	1998	1999	2000
	SECONDARY DISTRIBUTION OF INCOME (further detail of certain items)										
	Resources										
D.61	Social contributions										
	Unfunded pension schemes[1]										
D.611	Actual social contributions										
D.61122	Employees' voluntary contributions	NMWM	461	471	478	493	510	518	551	580	585
D.612	Imputed social contributions										
D.612	Employers' contributions	GCMN	1 138	1 248	1 354	1 338	1 370	1 475	1 653	1 714	1 719
D.61	Total social contributions	NSMM	1 599	1 719	1 832	1 831	1 880	1 993	2 204	2 294	2 304
	Uses										
D.62	Social benefits										
D.623	Unfunded employee social benefits										
	Unfunded pensions paid[1]	NMWK	1 081	1 201	1 288	1 364	1 482	1 603	1 749	1 860	1 966
	Other unfunded employee benefits	EWRN	518	518	544	467	398	390	455	434	338
D.623	Total unfunded social benefits	GCMO	1 599	1 719	1 832	1 831	1 880	1 993	2 204	2 294	2 304
D.624	Social assistance benefits in cash										
	Student grants	GCSI	2 804	3 293	3 178	2 956	2 175	2 594	2 201	1 377	779
	Rent rebates	CTML	4 193	4 799	5 272	5 350	5 428	5 485	5 372	5 353	5 331
	Rent allowances	GCSR	3 015	3 931	4 755	5 413	5 646	5 866	5 696	5 776	5 896
	Total other transfers	ZXHZ	–	–	–	–	–	–	36	18	7
D.624	Total social assistance benefits in cash	ADAL	10 012	12 023	13 205	13 719	13 249	13 945	13 305	12 524	12 013
D.62	Total social benefits	NSMN	11 611	13 742	15 037	15 550	15 129	15 938	15 509	14 818	14 317

1 Mainly police and firefighters' schemes

General government

5.3.5 Local government
ESA95 sector S.1313

£ million

			1992	1993	1994	1995	1996	1997	1998	1999	2000
II.3	**REDISTRIBUTION OF INCOME IN KIND ACCOUNT**										
	Resources										
B.6g	Total resources, gross disposable income	NRLW	54 644	54 529	55 950	57 441	59 505	59 678	63 114	69 224	72 602
	Uses										
D.63	Social transfers in kind										
D.631	Social benefits in kind										
D.632	Transfers of individual non-market goods and services	NMMU	34 272	32 562	33 114	34 589	36 290	37 344	39 434	44 167	46 393
B.7g	Adjusted disposable income, gross	NSXL	20 372	21 967	22 836	22 852	23 215	22 334	23 680	25 057	26 209
Total	Total uses	NRLW	54 644	54 529	55 950	57 441	59 505	59 678	63 114	69 224	72 602

5.3.6 Local government
ESA95 sector S.1313

£ million

			1992	1993	1994	1995	1996	1997	1998	1999	2000
II.4	**USE OF INCOME ACCOUNT**										
II.4.1	**USE OF DISPOSABLE INCOME ACCOUNT**										
	Resources										
B.6g	Total resources, gross disposable income	NRLW	54 644	54 529	55 950	57 441	59 505	59 678	63 114	69 224	72 602
	Uses										
P.3	Final consumption expenditure										
P.31	Individual consumption expenditure	NMMU	34 272	32 562	33 114	34 589	36 290	37 344	39 434	44 167	46 393
P.32	Collective consumption expenditure	NMMV	16 648	17 406	18 756	19 651	20 093	19 613	20 149	21 480	22 934
P.3	Total	NMMT	50 920	49 968	51 870	54 240	56 383	56 957	59 583	65 647	69 327
B.8g	Saving, gross	NRLX	3 724	4 561	4 080	3 201	3 122	2 721	3 531	3 577	3 275
Total	Total uses	NRLW	54 644	54 529	55 950	57 441	59 505	59 678	63 114	69 224	72 602
-K.1	After deduction of fixed capital consumption	-NSRO	-2 326	-2 319	-2 450	-2 674	-2 866	-3 039	-3 115	-3 278	-3 420
B.8n	Saving, net	NMMX	1 398	2 242	1 630	527	256	-318	416	299	-145
II.4.2	**USE OF ADJUSTED DISPOSABLE INCOME ACCOUNT**										
	Resources										
B.7g	Total resources, adjusted disposable income, gross	NSXL	20 372	21 967	22 836	22 852	23 215	22 334	23 680	25 057	26 209
	Uses										
P.4	Actual final consumption										
P.42	Actual collective consumption	NMMV	16 648	17 406	18 756	19 651	20 093	19 613	20 149	21 480	22 934
B.8g	Saving, gross	NRLX	3 724	4 561	4 080	3 201	3 122	2 721	3 531	3 577	3 275
Total	Total uses	NSXL	20 372	21 967	22 836	22 852	23 215	22 334	23 680	25 057	26 209

General government

5.3.7 Local government
ESA95 sector S.1313

£ million

			1992	1993	1994	1995	1996	1997	1998	1999	2000
III	**ACCUMULATION ACCOUNTS**										
III.1	**CAPITAL ACCOUNT**										
III.1.1	**CHANGE IN NET WORTH DUE TO SAVINGS AND CAPITAL TRANSFERS**										
	Changes in liabilities and net worth										
B.8g	Saving, gross	NRLX	3 724	4 561	4 080	3 201	3 122	2 721	3 531	3 577	3 275
D.9	Capital transfers receivable										
D.92	Investment grants										
	from general government	NMGR	2 714	3 055	2 624	2 574	2 719	2 822	2 476	3 059	3 846
	from other sectors	NMNG	276	213	305	219	310	407	179	143	495
D.92	Total	NMNE	2 990	3 268	2 929	2 793	3 029	3 229	2 655	3 202	4 341
D.99	Other capital transfers										
	from general government	NMGT	5 100	–	–	–	1 600	–	–	–	132
	from other sectors	NMNJ	84	86	114	138	159	185	191	205	278
D.99	Total	NMNH	5 184	86	114	138	1 759	185	191	205	410
D.9	Total capital transfers receivable										
	from general government	NMGN	7 814	3 055	2 624	2 574	4 319	2 822	2 476	3 059	3 978
	from other sectors	NMNA	360	299	419	357	469	592	370	348	773
D.9	Total	NMMY	8 174	3 354	3 043	2 931	4 788	3 414	2 846	3 407	4 751
-D.9	*less* Capital transfers payable										
-D.92	Investment grants										
	to general government	-NMGJ	–	–	–	–	–	–	–	–	–
	to other sectors	-NMNT	−1 239	−1 216	−1 227	−913	−954	−1 069	−1 282	−1 156	−1 212
-D.92	Total	-NMNR	−1 239	−1 216	−1 227	−913	−954	−1 069	−1 282	−1 156	−1 212
-D.99	Other capital transfers										
	to general government	-NMGL	–	–	–	–	–	–	–	–	–
	to other sectors	-NMNW	–	–	–	–	–	–	–	–	–
-D.99	Total	-NMNU	–	–	–	–	–	–	–	–	–
-D.9	Total capital transfers payable										
	to general government	-NMGF	–	–	–	–	–	–	–	–	–
	to other sectors	-NMNN	−1 239	−1 216	−1 227	−913	−954	−1 069	−1 282	−1 156	−1 212
-D.9	Total	-NMNL	−1 239	−1 216	−1 227	−913	−954	−1 069	−1 282	−1 156	−1 212
B.10.1g	Total change in liabilities and net worth	NRMJ	10 659	6 699	5 896	5 219	6 956	5 066	5 095	5 828	6 814
	Changes in assets										
B.10.1g	Changes in net worth due to gross saving and capital transfers	NRMJ	10 659	6 699	5 896	5 219	6 956	5 066	5 095	5 828	6 814
-K.1	After deduction of fixed capital consumption	-NSRO	−2 326	−2 319	−2 450	−2 674	−2 866	−3 039	−3 115	−3 278	−3 420
B.10.1n	Changes in net worth due to net saving and capital transfers	NMNX	8 333	4 380	3 446	2 545	4 090	2 027	1 980	2 550	3 394
III.1.2	**ACQUISITION OF NON-FINANCIAL ASSETS ACCOUNT**										
	Changes in liabilities and net worth										
B.10.1n	Changes in net worth due to saving and capital transfers	NMNX	8 333	4 380	3 446	2 545	4 090	2 027	1 980	2 550	3 394
K.1	Consumption of fixed capital	NSRO	2 326	2 319	2 450	2 674	2 866	3 039	3 115	3 278	3 420
B.10.1g	Total changes in liabilities and net worth	NRMJ	10 659	6 699	5 896	5 219	6 956	5 066	5 095	5 828	6 814
	Changes in assets										
P.5	Gross capital formation										
P.51	Gross fixed capital formation	NMOA	6 205	6 115	6 812	7 124	5 913	5 433	6 104	5 971	6 792
P.52	Changes in inventories	NMOB	–	–	–	–	–	–	–	–	–
P.5	Total	NMNZ	6 205	6 115	6 812	7 124	5 913	5 433	6 104	5 971	6 792
K.2	Acquisitions less disposals of non-produced non-financial assets	NMOD	−297	−472	−461	−135	−443	−354	−653	−661	−610
B.9g	Net lending(+) / net borrowing(-)	NMOE	4 751	1 056	−455	−1 770	1 486	−13	−356	518	632
Total	Total change in assets	NRMJ	10 659	6 699	5 896	5 219	6 956	5 066	5 095	5 828	6 814

United Kingdom National Accounts 2001, © Crown copyright 2001

General government

5.3.8 Local government
ESA95 sector S.1313 Unconsolidated

£ million

				1992	1993	1994	1995	1996	1997	1998	1999	2000
III.2	**FINANCIAL ACCOUNT**											
F.A	Net acquisition of financial assets											
F.2	Currency and deposits											
F.22	Transferable deposits											
F.2211	Sterling deposits with UK banks	NBYS		186	1 755	–765	1 276	–316	1 120	–91	–726	207
F.2212	Foreign currency deposits with UK banks	NBYT		20	–1	–2	28	–14	–25	21	–27	14
F.2213	Sterling deposits with building societies	NBYU		721	417	476	19	872	83	695	679	384
F.29	Other deposits	NBYW		–	–	–	–	–	–	–	–	–
F.2	Total currency and deposits	NBYO		927	2 171	–291	1 323	542	1 178	625	–74	605
F.3	Securities other than shares											
F.331	Short term: money market instruments											
F.3311	Issued by UK central government	NBYZ		–5	13	11	–24	–	31	106	204	–218
F.3315	Issued by UK monetary financial institutions	NBZE		–49	–5	3	–5	–2	269	232	565	415
F.3316	Issued by other UK residents	NBZJ		85	419	215	147	491	29	58	–38	27
F.332	Medium (1 to 5 year) and long term (over 5 year) bonds											
F.3321	Issued by UK central government	NBZM		2	27	28	15	–2	70	95	–18	–194
F.34	Financial derivatives	NBZV		–	–	–	–	–	–	–	–	–
F.3	Total securities other than shares	NBYX		33	454	257	133	487	399	491	713	30
F.4	Loans											
F.42	Long term loans											
F.422	Loans secured on dwellings	NCAK		–358	–266	–148	–136	–123	–133	–153	–26	13
F.424	Other long-term loans by UK residents	NCAP		17	8	16	–31	16	50	50	73	57
F.4	Total loans	NBZZ		–341	–258	–132	–167	–107	–83	–103	47	70
F.5	Shares and other equity											
F.51	Shares and other equity, excluding mutual funds' shares											
F.514	Quoted UK shares	NCAW		–17	–17	8	7	34	–60	72	–304	157
F.515	Unquoted UK shares	NCAX		12	16	9	10	–1	–	–40	–	–
F.5	Total shares and other equity	NCAR		–5	–1	17	17	33	–60	32	–304	157
F.6	Insurance technical reserves											
F.62	Prepayments of insurance premiums and reserves for outstanding claims	NCBK		65	25	42	73	181	12	–11	–29	32
F.7	Other accounts receivable	NCBL		–1 507	–764	–652	–1 168	–244	–264	–287	95	40
F.A	Total net acquisition of financial assets	NBYK		–828	1 627	–759	211	892	1 182	747	448	934

5.3.8 Local government
ESA95 sector S.1313 Unconsolidated

continued

General government

£ million

			1992	1993	1994	1995	1996	1997	1998	1999	2000
III.2	**FINANCIAL ACCOUNT** continued										
F.L	**Net acquisition of financial liabilities**										
F.3	Securities other than shares										
F.331	Short term: money market instruments										
F.3312	Issued by UK local authorities	NCCH	2	−29	–	4	−6	5	−6	–	–
F.332	Medium (1 to 5 year) and long term (over 5 year) bonds										
F.3322	Issued by UK local authorities	NCCT	4	7	288	78	163	13	6	−2	−12
F.34	Financial derivatives	NCCZ	–	–	–	–	–	–	–	–	–
F.3	Total securities other than shares	NCCB	6	−22	288	82	157	18	–	−2	−12
F.4	Loans										
F.41	Short term loans										
F.411	Loans by UK monetary financial institutions, excluding loans secured on dwellings & financial leasing	NCDF	1 205	1 246	383	−326	−633	−640	−537	−816	−282
F.419	Loans by rest of the world monetary financial institutions	NCDJ	−74	−76	−84	−84	−67	−60	−42	−44	−39
F.42	Long term loans										
F.423	Finance leasing	NCDS	−87	3	19	7	12	3	28	53	20
F.424	Other long-term loans by UK residents	NCDT	−5 788	−1 582	−473	2 097	−16	1 230	859	1 907	1 444
F.429	Other long-term loans by the rest of the world	NCDU	80	163	8	35	82	9	−43	−61	−149
F.4	Total loans	NCDD	−4 664	−246	−147	1 729	−622	542	265	1 039	994
F.7	Other accounts payable	NCEP	−70	208	63	142	5	236	463	−465	110
F.L	**Total net acquisition of financial liabilities**	NCBO	−4 728	−60	204	1 953	−460	796	728	572	1 092
B.9	**Net lending / borrowing**										
F.A	Total net acquisition of financial assets	NBYK	−828	1 627	−759	211	892	1 182	747	448	934
-F.L	*less* Total net acquisition of financial liabilities	-NCBO	4 728	60	−204	−1 953	460	−796	−728	−572	−1 092
B.9f	**Net lending (+) / net borrowing (-), from financial account**	NYNQ	3 900	1 687	−963	−1 742	1 352	386	19	−124	−158
dB.9f	Statistical discrepancy	NYPC	851	−631	508	−28	134	−399	−375	642	790
B.9g	**Net lending (+) / net borrowing (-), from capital account**	NMOE	4 751	1 056	−455	−1 770	1 486	−13	−356	518	632

United Kingdom National Accounts 2001, © Crown copyright 2001

General government
5.3.9 Local government
ESA95 sector S.1313 Unconsolidated

£ billion

			1992	1993	1994	1995	1996	1997	1998	1999	2000
IV.3	**FINANCIAL BALANCE SHEET** at end of period										
AN	Non-financial assets	CGIZ	150.6	154.2	160.5	167.6	170.7	178.6	196.6	199.2	209.3
AF.A	**Financial assets**										
AF.2	Currency and deposits										
AF.22	Transferable deposits										
AF.2211	Sterling deposits with UK banks	NJEP	3.6	5.3	4.6	6.2	6.1	9.0	8.7	8.3	8.7
AF.2212	Foreign currency deposits with UK banks	NJEQ	–	–	–	0.1	–	–	–	–	–
AF.2213	Sterling deposits with UK building societies	NJER	3.6	4.1	4.5	4.2	4.8	4.1	4.1	4.4	4.6
AF.29	Other deposits	NJET	–	–	–	–	–	–	–	–	–
AF.2	Total currency and deposits	NJEL	7.2	9.4	9.2	10.4	11.0	13.1	12.9	12.7	13.3
AF.3	Securities other than shares										
AF.331	Short term: money market instruments										
AF.3311	Issued by UK central government	NJEW	–	–	–	–	–	0.1	0.2	0.5	0.2
AF.3315	Issued by UK monetary financial institutions	NJFB	0.1	0.1	0.1	0.1	0.1	2.2	2.4	3.0	3.4
AF.3316	Issued by other UK residents	NJFG	2.0	2.4	2.6	2.8	3.2	0.1	0.1	0.1	0.2
AF.332	Medium (1 to 5 year) and long term (over 5 year) bonds										
AF.3321	Issued by UK central government	NJFJ	0.1	0.1	0.1	0.2	0.1	0.7	0.8	0.7	0.5
AF.34	Financial derivatives	NJFS	–	–	–	–	–	–	–	–	–
AF.3	Total securities other than shares	NJEU	2.2	2.6	2.9	3.0	3.5	3.1	3.6	4.2	4.3
AF.4	Loans										
AF.42	Long term loans										
AF.422	Loans secured on dwellings	NJGH	1.0	0.7	0.6	0.5	0.3	0.2	0.4	0.3	0.1
AF.424	Other long-term loans by UK residents	NJGM	0.2	0.2	0.2	0.1	0.1	0.2	0.3	0.3	0.3
AF.4	Total loans	NJFW	1.2	0.9	0.8	0.6	0.5	0.4	0.7	0.6	0.4
AF.5	Shares and other equity										
AF.51	Shares and other equity, excluding mutual funds' shares										
AF.514	Quoted UK shares	NJGT	0.3	0.4	0.4	0.5	0.5	1.1	0.8	2.2	1.4
AF.515	Unquoted UK shares	NJGU	0.4	0.4	0.4	0.4	0.4	0.3	0.4	0.4	0.4
AF.5	Total shares and other equity	NJGO	0.7	0.8	0.8	0.8	0.9	1.3	1.2	2.6	1.8
AF.6	Insurance technical reserves										
AF.62	Prepayments of insurance premiums and reserves for outstanding claims	NJHH	0.6	0.6	0.7	0.7	0.9	0.9	1.2	1.1	1.1
AF.7	Other accounts receivable	NJHI	4.2	3.4	2.8	1.6	1.4	1.1	1.3	1.0	1.1
AF.A	**Total financial assets**	NJFV	16.1	17.8	17.1	17.2	18.1	20.0	20.9	22.2	22.0

General government

5.3.9 Local government
ESA95 sector S.1313 Unconsolidated
continued

£ billion

			1992	1993	1994	1995	1996	1997	1998	1999	2000
IV.3	**FINANCIAL BALANCE SHEET** continued at end of period										
AF.L	**Financial liabilities**										
AF.3	Securities other than shares										
AF.331	Short term: money market instruments										
AF.3312	Issued by UK local authorities	NJIE	–	–	–	–	–	–	–	–	–
AF.332	Medium (1 to 5 year) and long term (over 5 year) bonds										
AF.3322	Issued by UK local authorities	NJIQ	0.2	0.2	0.5	0.5	0.7	0.7	0.8	0.8	0.8
AF.34	Financial derivatives	NJIW	–	–	–	–	–	–	–	–	–
AF.3	Total securities other than shares	NJHY	0.2	0.2	0.5	0.5	0.7	0.7	0.8	0.8	0.8
AF.4	Loans										
AF.41	Short term loans										
AF.411	Loans by UK monetary financial institutions, excluding loans secured on dwellings & financial leasing	NJJC	3.0	4.3	5.0	4.8	4.8	4.3	3.1	2.4	1.7
AF.419	Loans by rest of the world monetary financial institutions	NJJG	0.6	0.5	0.5	0.4	0.3	0.3	0.2	0.2	0.1
AF.42	Long term loans										
AF.423	Finance leasing	NJJP	1.3	1.3	1.5	1.5	1.5	1.5	1.5	1.6	1.6
AF.424	Other long-term loans by UK residents	NJJQ	45.9	44.2	43.6	45.9	45.6	46.7	47.6	49.0	50.4
AF.429	Other long-term loans by the rest of the world	NJJR	0.6	0.7	0.7	0.8	0.9	0.9	0.9	0.9	0.7
AF.4	Total loans	NJJA	51.3	51.1	51.3	53.4	53.1	53.6	53.4	54.0	54.5
AF.7	Other accounts payable	NJKM	8.4	8.5	8.5	8.5	8.5	8.7	9.0	8.6	8.7
AF.L	**Total financial liabilities**	NJIZ	59.9	59.8	60.2	62.4	62.2	63.1	63.2	63.3	63.9
BF.90	**Net financial assets / liabilities**										
AF.A	Total financial assets	NJFV	16.1	17.8	17.1	17.2	18.1	20.0	20.9	22.2	22.0
-AF.L	*less* Total financial liabilities	-NJIZ	–59.9	–59.8	–60.2	–62.4	–62.2	–63.1	–63.2	–63.3	–63.9
BF.90	**Net financial assets (+) / liabilities (-)**	NYOJ	–43.8	–42.0	–43.1	–45.2	–44.2	–43.1	–42.3	–41.1	–42.0
	Net worth										
AN	Non-financial assets	CGIZ	150.6	154.2	160.5	167.6	170.7	178.6	196.6	199.2	209.3
BF.90	Net financial assets (+) / liabilities (-)	NYOJ	–43.8	–42.0	–43.1	–45.2	–44.2	–43.1	–42.3	–41.1	–42.0
BF.90	**Net worth**	CGRZ	106.8	112.2	117.4	122.4	126.5	135.5	154.3	158.0	167.3

United Kingdom National Accounts 2001, © Crown copyright 2001

Part 3

Chapter 6

Households and Non-profit institutions serving households (NPISH)

Households and NPISH

6.1.1 Households and non-profit institutions serving households
ESA95 sectors S.14 and S.15

£ million

			1992	1993	1994	1995	1996	1997	1998	1999
I	**PRODUCTION ACCOUNT**									
	Resources									
P.1	Output									
P.11	Market output	QWLF	123 823	131 326	140 245	152 260	160 225	165 013	172 350	181 009
P.12	Output for own final use	QWLG	33 205	34 806	37 338	40 431	42 590	45 803	50 857	54 131
P.13	Other non-market output	QWLH	10 806	13 981	15 287	16 481	18 385	19 602	21 117	22 671
P.1	Total resources	QWLI	167 834	180 113	192 870	209 172	221 200	230 418	244 324	257 811
	Uses									
P.2	Intermediate consumption	QWLJ	70 129	75 254	80 912	89 381	95 308	98 132	103 603	109 166
B.1g	Value added, gross	QWLK	97 705	104 859	111 958	119 791	125 892	132 286	140 721	148 645
Total	Total uses	QWLI	167 834	180 113	192 870	209 172	221 200	230 418	244 324	257 811
B.1g	Value added, gross	QWLK	97 705	104 859	111 958	119 791	125 892	132 286	140 721	148 645
-K.1	less Consumption of fixed capital	-QWLL	–16 236	–17 143	–18 049	–18 922	–20 255	–21 957	–23 602	–25 928
B.1n	Value added, net	QWLM	81 469	87 716	93 909	100 869	105 637	110 329	117 119	122 717

6.1.2 Households and non-profit institutions serving households
ESA95 sectors S.14 and S.15

£ million

			1992	1993	1994	1995	1996	1997	1998	1999
II	**DISTRIBUTION AND USE OF INCOME ACCOUNTS**									
II.1	**PRIMARY DISTRIBUTION OF INCOME ACCOUNT**									
II.1.1	**GENERATION OF INCOME ACCOUNT** before deduction of fixed capital consumption									
	Resources									
B.1g	Total resources, gross value added	QWLK	97 705	104 859	111 958	119 791	125 892	132 286	140 721	148 645
	Uses									
D.1	Compensation of employees									
D.11	Wages and salaries	QWLN	23 146	25 674	28 218	30 517	31 844	33 559	36 713	39 028
D.12	Employers' social contributions	QWLO	3 508	3 945	4 261	4 654	5 019	5 209	5 819	6 205
D.1	Total	QWLP	26 654	29 619	32 479	35 171	36 863	38 768	42 532	45 233
D.2	Taxes on production and imports, paid									
D.29	Production taxes other than on products	QWLQ	87	89	92	101	111	116	120	121
-D.3	less Subsidies received									
-D.39	Production subsidies other than on products	QWLR	66	215	286	293	253	206	246	370
B.2g	Operating surplus, gross	QWLS	31 509	33 026	35 354	38 165	40 160	43 147	48 023	51 197
B.3g	Mixed income, gross	QWLT	39 521	42 340	44 319	46 647	49 011	50 461	50 292	52 464
Total	Total uses	QWLK	97 705	104 859	111 958	119 791	125 892	132 286	140 721	148 645
-K.1	After deduction of fixed capital consumption	-QWLL	–16 236	–17 143	–18 049	–18 922	–20 255	–21 957	–23 602	–25 928
B.2n	Operating surplus, net	QWLU	20 722	21 965	23 668	25 575	26 803	29 038	32 770	34 651
B.3n	Mixed income, net	QWLV	34 072	36 258	37 956	40 315	42 113	42 613	41 943	43 082

Households and NPISH

6.1.3 Households and non-profit institutions serving households
ESA95 sectors S.14 and S.15

£ million

			1992	1993	1994	1995	1996	1997	1998	1999	2000
II.1.2	**ALLOCATION OF PRIMARY INCOME ACCOUNT** before deduction of fixed capital consumption										
	Resources										
B.2g	Operating surplus, gross	QWLS	31 509	33 026	35 354	38 165	40 160	43 147	48 023	51 197	53 206
B.3g	Mixed income, gross	QWLT	39 521	42 340	44 319	46 647	49 011	50 461	50 292	52 464	54 442
D.1	Compensation of employees										
D.11	Wages and salaries	QWLW	303 008	311 615	322 179	336 973	352 285	376 926	402 321	428 766	451 032
D.12	Employers' social contributions	QWLX	44 656	46 082	47 296	49 449	53 277	56 117	61 927	65 621	70 554
D.1	Total	QWLY	347 664	357 697	369 475	386 422	405 562	433 043	464 248	494 387	521 586
D.4	Property income										
D.41	Interest	QWLZ	32 632	23 503	22 240	26 454	23 826	26 585	30 081	24 280	28 454
D.42	Distributed income of corporations	QWMA	25 703	25 225	28 582	32 544	33 777	37 172	37 351	40 226	42 975
D.43	Reinvested earnings on direct foreign investments	QWMB	–	–	–	–	–	–	–	–	–
D.44	Attributed property income of insurance policy holders	QWMC	34 874	35 437	37 301	42 358	47 807	52 144	55 587	53 928	59 197
D.45	Rent	QWMD	98	96	97	99	103	105	105	105	105
D.4	Total	QWME	93 307	84 261	88 220	101 455	105 513	116 006	123 124	118 539	130 731
Total	Total resources	QWMF	512 001	517 324	537 368	572 689	600 246	642 657	685 687	716 587	759 965
	Uses										
D.4	Property income										
D.41	Interest	QWMG	45 748	36 235	36 965	40 288	38 442	42 042	51 513	47 710	53 366
D.45	Rent	QWMH	201	195	198	202	210	216	216	215	215
D.4	Total	QWMI	45 949	36 430	37 163	40 490	38 652	42 258	51 729	47 925	53 581
B.5g	Balance of primary incomes, gross	QWMJ	466 052	480 894	500 205	532 199	561 594	600 399	633 958	668 662	706 384
Total	Total uses	QWMF	512 001	517 324	537 368	572 689	600 246	642 657	685 687	716 587	759 965
-K.1	After deduction of fixed capital consumption	-QWLL	–16 236	–17 143	–18 049	–18 922	–20 255	–21 957	–23 602	–25 928	–28 126
B.5n	Balance of primary incomes, net	QWMK	449 816	463 751	482 156	513 277	541 339	578 442	610 356	642 734	678 258

Households and NPISH

6.1.4 Households and non-profit institutions serving households
ESA95 sectors S.14 and S.15

£ million

			1992	1993	1994	1995	1996	1997	1998	1999	2000
II.2	**SECONDARY DISTRIBUTION OF INCOME ACCOUNT**										
	Resources										
B.5g	Balance of primary incomes, gross	QWMJ	466 052	480 894	500 205	532 199	561 594	600 399	633 958	668 662	706 384
D.612	Imputed social contributions	RVFH	480	438	425	455	429	410	478	450	374
D.62	Social benefits other than social transfers in kind	QWML	127 663	136 084	142 229	149 151	156 612	165 695	170 931	178 050	187 235
D.7	Other current transfers										
D.72	Non-life insurance claims	QWMM	13 239	12 496	13 272	14 123	19 360	14 004	15 224	13 901	16 621
D.75	Miscellaneous current transfers	QWMN	11 248	15 481	17 013	17 722	20 027	20 478	21 146	21 899	24 522
D.7	Total	QWMO	24 487	27 977	30 285	31 845	39 387	34 482	36 370	35 800	41 143
	Total resources	QWMP	618 682	645 393	673 144	713 650	758 022	800 986	841 737	882 962	935 136
	Uses										
D.5	Current taxes on income, wealth etc										
D.51	Taxes on income	QWMQ	67 343	65 153	69 530	74 590	75 137	75 914	91 076	97 192	107 251
D.59	Other current taxes	NVCO	10 299	10 551	11 140	11 937	12 795	13 820	14 993	16 263	17 102
D.5	Total	QWMS	77 642	75 704	80 670	86 527	87 932	89 734	106 069	113 455	124 353
D.61	Social contributions										
D.611	Actual social contributions										
D.6111	Employers' actual social contributions	QWMT	34 960	36 850	38 146	39 934	43 916	46 773	51 297	55 365	60 146
D.6112	Employees' social contributions	QWMU	46 477	45 415	49 615	53 747	59 900	66 890	71 182	73 235	76 111
D.6113	Social contributions by self and non-employed	QWMV	1 281	1 472	1 469	1 541	1 771	1 848	1 760	1 801	1 973
D.611	Total	QWMW	82 718	83 737	89 230	95 222	105 587	115 511	124 239	130 401	138 230
D.612	Imputed social contributions	QWMX	9 696	9 232	9 150	9 515	9 361	9 344	10 630	10 256	10 408
D.61	Total	QWMY	92 414	92 969	98 380	104 737	114 948	124 855	134 869	140 657	148 638
D.62	Social benefits other than social transfers in kind	QWMZ	811	897	880	925	899	880	950	922	848
D.7	Other current transfers										
D.71	Net non-life insurance premiums	QWNA	13 239	12 496	13 272	14 123	19 360	14 004	15 224	13 901	16 621
D.75	Miscellaneous current transfers	QWNB	6 802	7 618	8 108	8 279	8 190	9 059	9 293	9 484	9 709
D.7	Total	QWNC	20 041	20 114	21 380	22 402	27 550	23 063	24 517	23 385	26 330
B.6g	Disposable income, gross[1]	QWND	427 774	455 709	471 834	499 059	526 693	562 454	575 332	604 543	634 967
	Total uses	QWMP	618 682	645 393	673 144	713 650	758 022	800 986	841 737	882 962	935 136
-K.1	After deduction of fixed capital consumption	-QWLL	-16 236	-17 143	-18 049	-18 922	-20 255	-21 957	-23 602	-25 928	-28 126
B.6n	Disposable income, net	QWNE	411 538	438 566	453 785	480 137	506 438	540 497	551 730	578 615	606 841

1 Gross household disposable income revalued by the implied households and NPISH's final consumption expenditure deflator is as follows:

		1992	1993	1994	1995	1996	1997	1998	1999	2000
Real household disposable income:										
£ million at 1995 prices	RVGK	464 011	478 766	486 458	499 059	510 926	533 219	531 086	549 540	573 509
Index 1995 = 100	OSXR	93.0	95.9	97.5	100.0	102.4	106.8	106.4	110.1	114.9

Households and NPISH

6.14S Households and non-profit institutions serving households
Social benefits and contributions
ESA 95 sectors S.14 and S.15

Part			1992	1993	1994	1995	1996	1997	1998	1999	2000
	SECONDARY DISTRIBUTION OF INCOME (further detail of certain items)										
	Benefits										
	Resources										
D.62	Social benefits										
D.621	Social security benefits in cash										
	National insurance fund benefits[1]	ACHH	37 424	39 502	40 249	40 865	42 128	43 301	44 861	46 388	47 961
	Redundancy fund benefit	GTKN	308	165	180	151	113	93	106	137	159
	Social fund benefit	GTLQ	154	193	185	216	207	164	356	995	1 857
	Maternity fund benefits	GTKO	–	–	–	–	–	–	–	–	–
D.621	Total social security benefits in cash	HAYQ	37 886	39 860	40 614	41 232	42 448	43 558	45 323	47 520	49 977
D.622	Private funded social benefits										
	Private pensions	NSBP	17 410	19 050	21 066	21 786	23 124	24 508	25 591	27 808	29 378
	Pensions by life companies	QZBU	10 419	10 035	10 996	12 839	16 495	20 493	23 327	25 399	28 749
	Employee benefits from employers' liability insurance	NRXD	554	563	585	383	366	404	404	369	372
D.622	Total private funded social benefits	HAYR	28 383	29 648	32 647	35 008	39 985	45 405	49 322	53 576	58 499
D.623	Unfunded employee social benefits										
	Unfunded central government pensions paid[2]	GCSJ	3 878	4 240	4 267	4 291	4 564	4 691	4 898	4 942	4 960
	Unfunded local authorities pensions paid[3]	NMWK	1 081	1 201	1 288	1 364	1 482	1 603	1 749	1 860	1 966
	Other unfunded employee benefits[4]	EWRM	5 280	4 816	4 690	5 030	4 724	4 632	5 424	5 081	5 014
	Notionally funded pensions paid[5]	GCRW	4 959	5 249	5 032	5 980	6 362	7 190	6 294	6 176	7 179
D.623	Total unfunded social benefits	RVFF	15 198	15 506	15 277	16 665	17 132	18 116	18 365	18 059	19 119
D.624	Social assistance benefits in cash										
	Received from central government[1]	NZGO	35 895	38 640	40 087	42 119	43 394	44 272	44 215	45 959	47 210
	Received from local authorities	ADAL	10 012	12 023	13 205	13 719	13 249	13 945	13 305	12 524	12 013
	Received from NPISHs	HABJ	331	459	455	470	470	470	472	472	474
	Payment to the Rest of the World	-RNNF	−42	−52	−56	−62	−66	−71	−71	−60	−57
D.624	Total social assistance benefits in cash	HAYU	46 196	51 070	53 691	56 246	57 047	58 616	57 921	58 895	59 640
D.62	Total social benefits	QWML	127 663	136 084	142 229	149 151	156 612	165 695	170 931	178 050	187 235
	Uses										
D.62	Social benefits	QWMZ	811	897	880	925	899	880	950	922	848
	Contributions										
	Resources										
D.612	Imputed social contributions	RVFH	480	438	425	455	429	410	478	450	374
	Uses										
D.6111	Employers' actual social contributions										
	National Insurance contributions	CEAN	21 621	23 038	23 240	24 210	25 553	27 200	29 529	31 248	33 180
	Notionally funded pension schemes	GCMP	1 568	1 632	1 673	1 707	1 791	1 838	1 862	1 860	2 073
	Funded pension schemes	RIUO	11 771	12 180	13 233	14 017	16 572	17 735	19 906	22 257	24 893
D.6111	Total employers' actual social contributions	QWMT	34 960	36 850	38 146	39 934	43 916	46 773	51 297	55 365	60 146
D.6112	Employees' actual social contributions										
	National Insurance contributions	GCSE	14 104	14 748	17 357	18 646	19 175	21 558	22 984	23 549	23 972
	Notionally funded pension schemes	GITB	1 763	1 816	1 603	1 756	1 804	1 836	1 946	2 176	2 540
	Unfunded central government pension schemes	RUDP	183	170	186	171	183	177	180	185	192
	Unfunded local authorities pension schemes	NMWM	461	471	478	493	510	518	551	580	585
	Funded pension schemes	GCRR	29 966	28 210	29 991	32 681	38 228	42 801	45 521	46 745	48 822
D.6112	Total employees' actual social contributions	QWMU	46 477	45 415	49 615	53 747	59 900	66 890	71 182	73 235	76 111
D.6113	Social contributions by self and non-employed	QWMV	1 281	1 472	1 469	1 541	1 771	1 848	1 760	1 801	1 973
D.611	Total social contributions	QWMW	82 718	83 737	89 230	95 222	105 587	115 511	124 239	130 401	138 230
D.612	Imputed social contributions										
	Pension increase payments to notionally funded schemes	GCSG	1 305	1 376	1 421	1 427	1 519	1 627	1 750	1 749	1 769
	Employers imputed contributions to unfunded central government pension schemes	RFBJ	2 491	2 310	2 229	2 187	2 146	2 000	2 258	2 146	2 244
	Employers imputed contributions to unfunded local authorities pension schemes	NMWL	620	730	810	871	972	1 085	1 198	1 280	1 381
	Other imputed unfunded employees' contributions	EWRM	5 280	4 816	4 690	5 030	4 724	4 632	5 424	5 081	5 014
D.612	Total imputed social contributions	QWMX	9 696	9 232	9 150	9 515	9 361	9 344	10 630	10 256	10 408
D.61	Total social contributions	QWMY	92 414	92 969	98 380	104 737	114 948	124 855	134 869	140 657	148 638

1 For a more detailed analysis see table 5.24S
2 Mainly civil service and armed forces
3 Mainly police and fire fighters
4 Such as payments whilst absent from work due to illness
5 Mainly teachers and NHS staff

United Kingdom National Accounts 2001, © Crown copyright 2001

Households and NPISH

6.1.5 Households and non-profit institutions serving households
ESA95 sectors S.14 and S.15

£ million

			1992	1993	1994	1995	1996	1997	1998	1999	2000
II.3	**REDISTRIBUTION OF INCOME IN KIND ACCOUNT**										
	Resources										
B.6g	Disposable income, gross	QWND	427 774	455 709	471 834	499 059	526 693	562 454	575 332	604 543	634 967
D.63	Social transfers in kind										
D.631	Social benefits in kind										
D.6313	Social assistance benefits in kind	QWNH	–	–	–	–	–	–	–	–	–
D.632	Transfers of individual non-market goods and services	NSSA	84 218	88 530	92 832	97 574	103 353	107 153	113 388	123 175	129 042
D.63	Total social transfers in kind	NSSB	84 218	88 530	92 832	97 574	103 353	107 153	113 388	123 175	129 042
Total	Total resources	NSSC	511 992	544 239	564 666	596 633	630 046	669 607	688 720	727 718	764 009
	Uses										
D.63	Social transfers in kind										
D.631	Social benefits in kind										
D.6313	Social assistance benefits in kind	HAEJ	–	–	–	–	–	–	–	–	–
D.632	Transfers of individual non-market goods and services	HABK	10 806	13 981	15 287	16 481	18 385	19 602	21 117	22 671	22 866
D.63	Total social transfers in kind	HAEK	10 806	13 981	15 287	16 481	18 385	19 602	21 117	22 671	22 866
B.7g	Adjusted disposable income, gross	NSSD	501 186	530 258	549 379	580 152	611 661	650 005	667 603	705 047	741 143
Total	Total uses	NSSC	511 992	544 239	564 666	596 633	630 046	669 607	688 720	727 718	764 009

6.1.6 Households and non-profit institutions serving households
ESA95 sectors S.14 and S.15

£ million

			1992	1993	1994	1995	1996	1997	1998	1999	2000
II.4	**USE OF INCOME ACCOUNT**										
II.4.1	**USE OF DISPOSABLE INCOME ACCOUNT**										
	Resources										
B.6g	Disposable income, gross	QWND	427 774	455 709	471 834	499 059	526 693	562 454	575 332	604 543	634 967
D.8	Adjustment for the change in net equity of households in pension funds	NSSE	13 265	10 742	10 577	11 690	14 824	15 131	16 105	15 417	15 216
Total	Total resources	NSSF	441 039	466 451	482 411	510 749	541 517	577 585	591 437	619 960	650 183
	Uses										
P.3	Final consumption expenditure										
P.31	Individual consumption expenditure	NSSG	390 564	415 951	437 684	459 848	492 185	522 976	557 642	590 226	617 648
B.8g	Saving, gross	NSSH	50 475	50 500	44 727	50 901	49 332	54 609	33 795	29 734	32 535
Total	Total uses	NSSF	441 039	466 451	482 411	510 749	541 517	577 585	591 437	619 960	650 183
-K.1	After deduction of fixed capital consumption	-QWLL	–16 236	–17 143	–18 049	–18 922	–20 255	–21 957	–23 602	–25 928	–28 126
B.8n	Saving, net	NSSI	34 239	33 357	26 678	31 979	29 077	32 652	10 193	3 806	4 409
II.4.2	**USE OF ADJUSTED DISPOSABLE INCOME ACCOUNT**										
	Resources										
B.7g	Adjusted disposable income, gross	NSSD	501 186	530 258	549 379	580 152	611 661	650 005	667 603	705 047	741 143
D.8	Adjustment for the change in net equity of households in pension funds	NSSE	13 265	10 742	10 577	11 690	14 824	15 131	16 105	15 417	15 216
Total	Total resources	NSSJ	514 451	541 000	559 956	591 842	626 485	665 136	683 708	720 464	756 359
	Uses										
P.4	Actual final consumption										
P.41	Actual individual consumption	ABRE	463 976	490 500	515 229	540 941	577 153	610 527	649 913	690 730	723 824
B.8g	Saving, gross[1]	NSSH	50 475	50 500	44 727	50 901	49 332	54 609	33 795	29 734	32 535
Total	Total uses	NSSJ	514 451	541 000	559 956	591 842	626 485	665 136	683 708	720 464	756 359

1 Households' saving as a percentage of total available households' resources is as follows:

		1992	1993	1994	1995	1996	1997	1998	1999	2000
Households' saving ratio (per cent)	RVGL	11.4	10.8	9.3	10.0	9.1	9.5	5.7	4.8	5.0

Households and NPISH

6.1.7 Households and non-profit institutions serving households
ESA95 sectors S.14 and S.15

£ million

			1992	1993	1994	1995	1996	1997	1998	1999	2000
III	**ACCUMULATION ACCOUNTS**										
III.1	**CAPITAL ACCOUNT**										
III.1.1	**CHANGE IN NET WORTH DUE TO SAVING & CAPITAL TRANSFERS ACCOUNT**										
	Changes in liabilities and net worth										
B.8g	Saving, gross	NSSH	50 475	50 500	44 727	50 901	49 332	54 609	33 795	29 734	32 535
D.9	Capital transfers receivable										
D.92	Investment grants	NSSL	4 345	5 387	4 544	3 968	3 564	3 702	3 477	3 689	3 600
D.99	Other capital transfers	NSSM	688	584	603	678	703	754	967	1 144	1 573
D.9	Total	NSSN	5 033	5 971	5 147	4 646	4 267	4 456	4 444	4 833	5 173
-D.9	*less* Capital transfers payable										
-D.91	Capital taxes	-NSSO	-1 227	-1 279	-1 438	-1 441	-1 621	-1 601	-1 796	-1 951	-2 215
-D.99	Other capital transfers										
	to general government	-NSSP	–	–	–	–	–	–	–	–	–
	to other sectors	-NSTA	-529	-496	-500	-453	-465	-592	-531	-499	-461
-D.99	Total	-NSSQ	-529	-496	-500	-453	-465	-592	-531	-499	-461
-D.9	Total	-NSSR	-1 756	-1 775	-1 938	-1 894	-2 086	-2 193	-2 327	-2 450	-2 676
B.10.1g	Total change in liabilities and net worth	NSSS	53 752	54 696	47 936	53 653	51 513	56 872	35 912	32 117	35 032
	Changes in assets										
B.10.1g	Changes in net worth due to gross saving and capital transfers	NSSS	53 752	54 696	47 936	53 653	51 513	56 872	35 912	32 117	35 032
-K.1	After deduction of fixed capital consumption	-QWLL	-16 236	-17 143	-18 049	-18 922	-20 255	-21 957	-23 602	-25 928	-28 126
B.10.1n	Changes in net worth due to saving and capital transfers	NSST	37 516	37 553	29 887	34 731	31 258	34 915	12 310	6 189	6 906
III.1.2	**ACQUISITION OF NON-FINANCIAL ASSETS ACCOUNT**										
	Changes in liabilities and net worth										
B.10.1n	Changes in net worth due to saving and capital transfers	NSST	37 516	37 553	29 887	34 731	31 258	34 915	12 310	6 189	6 906
K.1	Consumption of fixed capital	QWLL	16 236	17 143	18 049	18 922	20 255	21 957	23 602	25 928	28 126
B.10.1g	Total change in liabilities and net worth	NSSS	53 752	54 696	47 936	53 653	51 513	56 872	35 912	32 117	35 032
	Changes in assets										
P.5	Gross capital formation										
P.51	Gross fixed capital formation	NSSU	20 909	23 008	25 576	27 582	30 191	32 681	34 216	37 817	37 485
P.52	Changes in inventories	NSSV	-13	279	368	262	133	483	122	212	28
P.53	Acquisitions less disposals of valuables	NSSW	87	51	121	24	34	138	339	265	199
P.5	Total gross capital formation	NSSX	20 983	23 338	26 065	27 868	30 358	33 302	34 677	38 294	37 712
K.2	Acquisitions less disposals of non-produced non-financial assets	NSSY	320	446	185	-81	337	250	17	-36	9
B.9	Net lending (+) / net borrowing (-)	NSSZ	32 449	30 912	21 686	25 866	20 818	23 320	1 218	-6 141	-2 689
Total	Total change in assets	NSSS	53 752	54 696	47 936	53 653	51 513	56 872	35 912	32 117	35 032

Households and NPISH

6.1.8 Households and non-profit institutions serving households
ESA95 sectors S.14 and S.15 Unconsolidated

£ million

			1992	1993	1994	1995	1996	1997	1998	1999	2000
III.2	**FINANCIAL ACCOUNT**										
F.A	**Net acquisition of financial assets**										
F.2	Currency and deposits										
F.21	Currency	NFVT	1 006	915	1 077	1 133	767	1 522	1 381	2 231	1 713
F.22	Transferable deposits										
F.2211	Sterling deposits with UK banks	NFVW	5 353	978	1 450	11 461	11 539	15 229	16 926	16 404	18 558
F.2212	Foreign currency deposits with UK banks	NFVX	8	−74	−13	−83	752	39	−409	336	724
F.2213	Sterling deposits with UK building societies	NFVY	9 996	8 963	7 297	14 061	10 125	17 860	10 511	11 210	11 517
F.229	Deposits with rest of the world monetary financial institutions	NFVZ	403	212	−78	1 594	1 980	2 190	2 836	3 168	4 747
F.29	Other deposits	NFWA	5 022	3 037	4 609	3 230	6 871	1 587	1 311	−1 354	237
F.2	Total currency and deposits	NFVS	21 788	14 031	14 342	31 396	32 034	38 427	32 556	31 995	37 496
F.3	Securities other than shares										
F.331	Short term: money market instruments										
F.3311	Issued by UK central government	NFWD	−2	−4	−2	−4	47	−39	15	−17	7
F.3312	Issued by UK local authorities	NFWH	−	−	−	−	−	−	−	−	−
F.3315	Issued by UK monetary financial institutions	NFWI	−103	−83	357	−22	378	1 021	276	778	−502
F.3316	Issued by other UK residents	NFWN	−284	−21	−	43	49	−36	−46	−	−
F.332	Medium (1 to 5 year) and long term (over 5 year) bonds										
F.3321	Issued by UK central government	NFWQ	−325	5 683	2 442	3 642	−1 871	−2 020	−5 011	−1 879	−1 126
F.3322	Issued by UK local authorities	NFWT	−22	−196	−54	47	44	−111	45	−30	−81
F.3326	Other medium & long term bonds issued by UK residents	NFWX	216	158	239	167	71	159	−18	16	167
F.3329	Long term bonds issued by the rest of the world	NFWY	140	−59	−77	−556	−1 586	186	184	184	184
F.34	Financial derivatives	NFWZ	−	−	−	−	−	−	−	−	−
F.3	Total securities other than shares	NFWB	−380	5 478	2 905	3 317	−2 868	−840	−4 555	−948	−1 351
F.4	Loans										
F.42	Long term loans										
F.424	Other long-term loans by UK residents	NFXT	609	56	718	11	−55	−356	−456	3 761	−315
F.4	Total loans	NFXD	609	56	718	11	−55	−356	−456	3 761	−315
F.5	Shares and other equity										
F.51	Shares and other equity, excluding mutual funds' shares										
F.514	Quoted UK shares	NFYA	2 469	−6 278	2 767	−7 807	−6 749	−8 692	−25 986	−28 140	−19 535
F.515	Unquoted UK shares	NFYB	−1 391	−1 487	−1 922	−3 934	−5 786	−41	−6 777	−83	−6 633
F.516	Other UK equity (including direct investment in property)	NFYC	66	102	−47	−698	784	36	−66	20	−24
F.519	Shares and other equity issued by the rest of the world	NFYF	36	32	118	82	137	107	−68	532	−852
F.52	Mutual funds' shares										
F.521	UK mutual funds' shares	NFYJ	−1 401	1 894	−1 302	983	4 571	5 042	8 547	11 757	7 076
F.529	Rest of the world mutual funds' shares	NFYK	61	−114	730	105	241	−	−	−	−
F.5	Total shares and other equity	NFXV	−160	−5 851	344	−11 269	−6 802	−3 548	−24 350	−15 914	−19 968
F.6	Insurance technical reserves										
F.61	Net equity of households in life assurance and pension funds' reserves	NFYL	28 092	27 389	28 052	30 374	36 668	32 405	42 013	42 475	44 675
F.62	Prepayments of insurance premiums and reserves for outstanding claims	NFYO	2 081	876	1 579	2 754	1 988	428	−439	−575	263
F.6	Total insurance technical reserves	NPWX	30 173	28 265	29 631	33 128	38 656	32 833	41 574	41 900	44 938
F.7	Other accounts receivable	NFYP	−633	−517	1 366	3 025	757	4 726	3 077	4 435	6 117
F.A	Total net acquisition of financial assets	NFVO	51 397	41 462	49 306	59 608	61 722	71 242	47 846	65 229	66 917

Households and NPISH

6.1.8 Households and non-profit institutions serving households
ESA95 sectors S.14 and S.15 Unconsolidated
continued

£ million

			1992	1993	1994	1995	1996	1997	1998	1999	2000
III.2	**FINANCIAL ACCOUNT** continued										
F.L	**Net acquisition of financial liabilities**										
F.3	Securities other than shares										
F.331	Short term: money market instruments										
F.3316	Issued by UK residents other than monetary financial institutions and general government	NFZR	31	−11	−22	17	−36	43	8	−22	23
F.332	Medium (1 to 5 year) and long term (over 5 year) bonds										
F.3326	Other medium & long term bonds issued by UK residents institutions and general government	NGAB	83	290	131	347	93	96	230	–	–
F.34	Financial derivatives	NGAD	–	–	–	–	–	–	–	–	–
F.3	Total securities other than shares	NFZF	114	279	109	364	57	139	238	−22	23
F.4	Loans										
F.41	Short term loans										
F.4111	Sterling loans by UK banks	NGAK	664	−421	3 324	5 300	6 258	7 832	12 360	12 458	15 868
F.4112	Foreign currency loans by UK banks	NGAL	−327	−524	112	20	−73	−334	−53	–	–
F.4113	Sterling loans by UK building societies	NGAM	−124	228	294	486	652	147	136	−199	192
F.419	Loans by rest of the world monetary financial institutions	NGAN	253	717	23	473	922	2 101	−27	880	2 137
F.42	Long term loans										
F.4221	Loans secured on dwellings by banks	NGAT	6 519	9 767	7 845	7 689	6 651	11 899	15 116	21 492	19 482
F.4222	Loans secured on dwellings by building societies	NGAU	13 696	9 553	12 480	9 169	12 854	11 278	7 868	10 638	8 938
F.4229	Loans secured on dwellings by others	NGAV	−1 774	−3 248	−957	−1 767	−343	1 275	2 355	5 623	12 698
F.424	Other long-term loans by UK residents	NGAX	29	1 684	2 297	2 698	2 856	4 715	5 688	13 723	5 677
F.4	Total loans	NGAH	18 936	17 756	25 418	24 068	29 777	38 913	43 443	64 615	64 992
F.7	Other accounts payable	NGBT	−995	−421	185	4 502	2 816	2 478	3 102	3 774	61
F.L	**Total net acquisition of financial liabilities**	NFYS	18 055	17 614	25 712	28 934	32 650	41 530	46 783	68 367	65 076
B.9	**Net lending / borrowing**										
F.A	Total net acquisition of financial assets	NFVO	51 397	41 462	49 306	59 608	61 722	71 242	47 846	65 229	66 917
-F.L	*less* Total net acquisition of financial liabilities	-NFYS	−18 055	−17 614	−25 712	−28 934	−32 650	−41 530	−46 783	−68 367	−65 076
B.9f	Net lending (+) / net borrowing (-), from financial account	NZDY	33 342	23 848	23 594	30 674	29 072	29 712	1 063	−3 138	1 841
dB.9f	Statistical discrepancy	NZDV	−893	7 064	−1 908	−4 808	−8 254	−6 392	155	−3 003	−4 530
B.9	Net lending (+) / net borrowing (-), from capital account	NSSZ	32 449	30 912	21 686	25 866	20 818	23 320	1 218	−6 141	−2 689

Households and NPISH

6.1.9 Households and non-profit institutions serving households
ESA95 sectors S.14 and S.15 Unconsolidated

£ billion

			1992	1993	1994	1995	1996	1997	1998	1999	2000
IV.3	**FINANCIAL BALANCE SHEET** at end of period										
AN.2	**Non-financial assets**	CGCZ	1 356.9	1 404.5	1 373.5	1 369.0	1 495.4	1 609.0	1 839.9	2 089.1	2 205.7
AF.A	**Financial assets**										
AF.2	Currency and deposits										
AF.21	Currency	NNMQ	15.0	15.9	17.0	18.0	18.8	20.2	21.8	24.1	25.8
AF.22	Transferable deposits										
AF.2211	Sterling deposits with UK banks	NNMT	146.4	147.2	147.6	172.4	190.3	334.8	351.3	373.5	405.4
AF.2212	Foreign currency deposits with UK banks	NNMU	2.4	2.3	2.3	2.2	2.6	3.2	2.9	3.0	3.9
AF.2213	Sterling deposits with UK building societies	NNMV	185.9	194.8	203.4	203.8	204.6	95.6	105.5	111.2	109.2
AF.229	Deposits with rest of the world monetary financial institutions	NNMW	15.3	15.6	15.5	17.8	19.2	21.5	24.3	30.4	34.0
AF.29	Other deposits	NNMX	44.0	47.0	51.7	54.9	61.2	63.3	64.7	63.1	63.3
AF.2	Total currency and deposits	NNMP	409.0	422.9	437.4	469.2	496.7	538.6	570.5	605.2	641.7
AF.3	Securities other than shares										
AF.331	Short term: money market instruments										
AF.3311	Issued by UK central government	NNNA	–	–	–	–	0.1	–	–	–	–
AF.3312	Issued by UK local authorities	NNNE	–	–	–	–	–	–	–	–	–
AF.3315	Issued by UK monetary financial institutions	NNNF	0.7	0.7	1.1	1.0	1.5	1.7	2.0	2.6	2.2
AF.3316	Issued by other UK residents	NNNK	0.2	0.2	0.2	0.2	0.3	0.3	0.2	0.2	0.5
AF.332	Medium (1 to 5 year) and long term (over 5 year) bonds										
AF.3321	Issued by UK central government	NNNN	18.0	19.1	19.0	25.0	32.1	32.1	32.4	27.2	27.7
AF.3322	Issued by UK local authorities	NNNQ	0.1	–	0.1	–	0.2	0.3	0.2	0.2	0.1
AF.3326	Other medium & long term bonds issued by UK residents	NNNU	2.3	2.5	2.7	2.9	3.1	3.4	3.6	3.9	4.1
AF.3329	Long term bonds issued by the rest of the world	NNNV	9.3	10.4	10.7	11.9	6.4	6.7	7.1	7.1	7.1
AF.34	Financial derivatives	NNNW	–	–	–	–	–	–	–	–	–
AF.3	Total securities other than shares	NNMY	30.6	33.0	33.7	41.1	43.6	44.5	45.5	41.4	41.8
AF.4	Loans										
AF.42	Long term loans										
AF.424	Other long-term loans by UK residents	NNOQ	5.2	5.3	5.3	5.4	6.3	6.4	6.8	6.6	6.7
AF.4	Total loans	NNOA	5.2	5.3	5.3	5.4	6.3	6.4	6.8	6.6	6.7
AF.5	Shares and other equity										
AF.51	Shares and other equity, excluding mutual funds' shares										
AF.514	Quoted UK shares	NNOX	124.8	151.0	156.1	147.8	136.5	251.0	232.9	308.8	300.1
AF.515	Unquoted UK shares	NNOY	98.0	121.4	108.0	127.0	141.0	178.4	184.9	243.9	227.0
AF.516	Other UK equity (including direct investment in property)	NNOZ	1.3	1.4	1.3	1.4	1.4	1.5	1.4	1.4	1.4
AF.519	Shares and other equity issued by the rest of the world	NNPC	6.0	7.2	7.2	8.4	8.3	9.4	11.4	14.5	13.7
AF.52	Mutual funds' shares										
AF.521	UK mutual funds' shares	NNPG	30.6	52.6	56.6	71.0	80.5	99.2	99.6	154.5	164.7
AF.529	Rest of the world mutual funds' shares	NNPH	1.1	1.5	2.1	2.3	2.2	1.5	1.1	2.1	1.7
AF.5	Total shares and other equity	NNOS	261.7	335.1	331.3	357.8	369.9	541.0	531.1	725.2	708.5
AF.6	Insurance technical reserves										
AF.61	Net equity of households in life assurance and pension funds' reserves	NNPI	684.9	875.1	823.7	968.1	1 053.6	1 285.7	1 420.9	1 640.6	1 625.4
AF.62	Prepayments of insurance premiums and reserves for outstanding claims	NNPL	18.5	20.7	24.8	26.7	28.0	30.3	32.0	31.8	33.0
AF.6	Total insurance technical reserves	NPYL	703.4	895.8	848.5	994.9	1 081.6	1 316.1	1 452.9	1 672.4	1 658.4
AF.7	Other accounts receivable	NNPM	61.2	62.7	64.8	67.0	66.6	68.8	71.2	75.8	80.1
AF.A	**Total financial assets**	NNML	1 471.2	1 754.8	1 721.0	1 935.4	2 064.7	2 515.4	2 678.0	3 126.6	3 137.3

Households and NPISH

6.1.9 Households and non-profit institutions serving households
ESA95 sectors S.14 and S.15   Unconsolidated

£ billion

			1992	1993	1994	1995	1996	1997	1998	1999	2000
IV.3	**FINANCIAL BALANCE SHEET** continued at end of period										
AF.L	**Financial liabilities**										
AF.3	Securities other than shares										
AF.331	Short term: money market instruments										
AF.3316	Issued by other UK residents	NNQO	0.1	–	–	–	–	–	–	–	0.1
AF.332	Medium (1 to 5 year) and long term (over 5 year) bonds										
AF.3326	Other medium & long term bonds issued by UK residents	NNQY	0.5	1.2	1.2	1.7	1.9	2.0	2.3	2.7	2.8
AF.34	Financial derivatives	NNRA	–	–	–	–	–	–	–	–	–
AF.3	Total securities other than shares	NNQC	0.6	1.2	1.2	1.7	1.9	2.1	2.3	2.8	2.9
AF.4	Loans										
AF.41	Short term loans										
AF.411	Loans by UK monetary financial institutions, excluding loans secured on dwellings & financial leasing	NNRG	69.7	65.4	68.7	73.7	76.3	83.8	92.3	103.2	118.2
AF.419	Loans by rest of the world monetary financial institutions	NNRK	4.4	6.2	6.3	7.3	7.5	9.4	9.4	10.9	12.2
AF.42	Long term loans										
AF.4221	Loans secured on dwellings by banks	NNRQ	96.5	108.6	115.9	139.9	158.2	305.7	320.6	345.0	386.3
AF.4222	Loans secured on dwellings by building societies	NNRR	211.4	219.6	231.2	223.2	224.4	97.6	106.5	113.6	107.2
AF.4229	Loans secured on dwellings by others	NNRS	30.4	28.4	28.0	26.6	26.2	26.4	29.0	35.0	41.0
AF.424	Other long-term loans by UK residents	NNRU	10.1	10.5	11.0	11.5	11.0	13.8	14.5	15.6	17.1
AF.4	Total loans	NNRE	422.4	438.6	461.1	482.1	503.6	536.7	572.3	623.4	682.1
AF.7	Other accounts payable	NNSQ	45.0	44.9	44.7	47.9	48.1	51.9	54.8	54.2	52.7
AF.L	**Total financial liabilities**	NNPP	468.0	484.7	507.0	531.7	553.5	590.7	629.4	680.3	737.7
BF.90	**Net financial assets / liabilities**										
AF.A	Total financial assets	NNML	1 471.2	1 754.8	1 721.0	1 935.4	2 064.7	2 515.4	2 678.0	3 126.6	3 137.3
-AF.L	*less* Total financial liabilities	-NNPP	–468.0	–484.7	–507.0	–531.7	–553.5	–590.7	–629.4	–680.3	–737.7
BF.90	**Net financial assets (+) / liabilities (-)**	NZEA	1 003.3	1 270.1	1 213.9	1 403.6	1 511.1	1 924.7	2 048.6	2 446.3	2 399.6
	Total net worth										
AN	Non-financial assets	CGCZ	1 356.9	1 404.5	1 373.5	1 369.0	1 495.4	1 609.0	1 839.9	2 089.1	2 205.7
BF.90	Net financial assets (+) / liabilities (-)	NZEA	1 003.3	1 270.1	1 213.9	1 403.6	1 511.1	1 924.7	2 048.6	2 446.3	2 399.6
BF.90	**Net worth**	CGRC	2 360.2	2 674.6	2 587.4	2 772.6	3 006.5	3 533.7	3 888.5	4 535.4	4 605.2

Households and NPISH

6.2 Household final consumption expenditure: classified by commodity
At current market prices

£ million

		1992	1993	1994	1995	1996	1997	1998	1999	2000
Durable goods:										
Cars, motorcycles and other vehicles	CCDT	16 824	17 808	19 685	20 787	23 757	26 759	28 375	29 209	28 055
Other durable goods	ABZB	16 942	17 985	19 010	19 879	21 495	23 581	24 771	26 027	27 849
Total durable goods	AEIT	33 766	35 793	38 695	40 666	45 252	50 340	53 146	55 236	55 904
Non-durable goods:										
Food (household expenditure)	CCDW	45 683	47 171	47 855	49 790	53 025	53 832	55 192	56 886	58 252
Alchohol and tobacco	CDFH	34 266	35 538	37 139	38 174	40 907	42 991	45 142	48 226	49 652
Clothing and footwear	CDDE	23 009	24 321	26 324	27 431	28 899	30 298	31 478	32 828	33 554
Energy products	CCEC	25 403	26 142	26 856	27 189	28 867	29 085	28 734	29 002	31 234
Other goods	ABZN	45 794	48 023	51 231	54 584	58 949	63 864	68 853	73 245	77 690
Total non-durable goods	ABZR	174 155	181 195	189 405	197 168	210 647	220 070	229 399	240 187	250 382
Services:										
Rental and water charges	ABRG	48 637	52 405	55 990	59 633	62 848	66 975	73 399	77 995	81 954
Catering	CDEY	32 435	35 209	36 340	37 472	40 083	41 477	44 799	47 347	49 178
Transport and communication	ABOZ	34 621	37 876	39 789	41 766	43 881	47 427	51 201	54 827	57 822
Financial services	CEGK	14 437	15 778	15 761	16 053	18 026	20 446	22 587	24 176	26 863
Other services	AEJC	40 178	42 571	44 519	50 156	52 724	55 734	59 625	62 417	65 722
Total services	AELL	170 308	183 839	192 399	205 080	217 562	232 059	251 611	266 762	281 539
Total household final expenditure in the UK by resident and non-resident households (domestic concept)	ABQI	378 229	400 827	420 499	442 914	473 461	502 469	534 156	562 185	587 825
P.33 Final consumption expenditure outside the UK by UK resident households	ABTA	10 605	11 890	13 058	13 721	14 377	14 942	16 913	19 682	21 630
Less Final consumption expenditure in the UK by households resident in the rest of the world	CDFD	−9 076	−10 747	−11 160	−13 268	−14 038	−14 037	−14 544	−14 312	−14 673
P.31 **Final consumption expenditure by UK resident households in the UK and abroad (national concept)**	ABPB	379 758	401 970	422 397	443 367	473 800	503 374	536 525	567 555	594 782

This commodity classification of expenditure is being superseded by the Classification Of Individual Consumption by Purpose (COICOP) shown in tables 6.4 and 6.5, following. The new presentation, with additional detail, will be used in future for *Consumer Trends* and table A7 of *UK Economic Accounts*, available from the ONS website. Individual data series, annual and quarterly, are also available from ONS Databank and Timezone.

Households and NPISH

6.3 Household final consumption expenditure: classified by commodity
At 1995 market prices

£ million

		1992	1993	1994	1995	1996	1997	1998	1999	2000
Durable goods:										
Cars, motorcycles and other vehicles	CCBJ	17 772	18 796	20 232	20 787	22 990	24 824	26 147	27 092	26 370
Other durable goods	ABZD	16 811	17 772	19 109	19 879	21 429	23 896	26 026	28 928	32 794
Total durable goods	AEIV	34 585	36 569	39 341	40 666	44 419	48 720	52 173	56 020	59 164
Non-durable goods:										
Food (household expenditure)	CCBM	48 268	49 263	49 744	49 790	51 405	52 347	52 983	54 334	56 123
Alchohol and tobacco	FCCA	39 131	38 583	38 963	38 174	39 396	39 736	39 752	40 459	40 718
Clothing and footwear	FCCB	23 287	24 416	26 355	27 431	29 100	30 252	31 637	33 929	36 130
Energy products	CCBS	27 983	28 181	27 805	27 189	28 305	27 929	27 648	26 909	27 400
Other goods	ABZP	48 289	49 644	52 413	54 584	57 293	61 099	64 736	69 035	74 128
Total non-durable goods	ABZT	186 406	189 824	195 280	197 168	205 499	211 363	216 756	224 666	234 499
Services:										
Rental and water charges	ABRI	57 194	58 018	58 796	59 633	60 392	61 186	62 019	62 736	63 932
Catering	CCHS	35 832	37 150	37 215	37 472	38 977	39 027	40 656	41 477	41 451
Transport and communication	ABPD	35 699	38 468	40 397	41 766	42 804	44 797	47 393	51 057	53 742
Financial services	CEGM	15 513	16 429	15 903	16 053	17 246	18 729	19 334	20 109	21 230
Other services	AEJZ	44 894	45 694	46 385	50 156	51 004	51 797	52 631	52 606	53 077
Total services	AELN	188 681	195 684	198 696	205 080	210 423	215 536	222 033	227 985	233 432
Total household final expenditure in the UK by resident and non-resident households (domestic concept)	ABQJ	409 371	421 707	433 317	442 914	460 341	475 619	490 962	508 671	527 095
P.33 Final consumption expenditure outside the UK by UK resident households	ABTC	11 953	12 093	13 490	13 721	14 077	16 357	18 813	21 837	24 090
Less Final consumption expenditure in the UK by households resident in the rest of the world	CCHX	−10 086	−11 524	−11 457	−13 268	−13 658	−13 238	−13 284	−12 751	−12 727
P.31 **Final consumption expenditure by UK resident households in the UK and abroad (national concept)**	ABPF	411 204	422 273	435 350	443 367	460 760	478 738	496 491	517 757	538 458

This commodity classification of expenditure is being superseded by the Classification Of Individual Consumption by Purpose (COICOP) shown in tables 6.4 and 6.5, following. The new presentation, with additional detail, will be used in future for *Consumer Trends* and table A7 of *UK Economic Accounts*, available from the ONS website. Individual data series, annual and quarterly, are also available from ONS Databank and Timezone.

United Kingdom National Accounts 2001, © Crown copyright 2001

Households and NPISH

6.4 Individual consumption expenditure at current market prices by households, non-profit institutions serving households and general government
Classified by function (COICOP/COPNI/COFOG)[1]

£ million

			1992	1993	1994	1995	1996	1997	1998	1999	2000
P.31	**FINAL CONSUMPTION EXPENDITURE OF HOUSEHOLDS**										
01.	**Food and non-alcoholic beverages**	ABZV	45 683	47 171	47 855	49 790	53 025	53 832	55 192	56 886	58 252
01.1	Food	ABZW	40 720	42 133	42 665	44 324	47 323	47 996	49 134	50 537	51 550
01.2	Non-alcoholic beverages	ADFK	4 963	5 038	5 190	5 466	5 702	5 836	6 058	6 349	6 702
02.	**Alcoholic beverages and tobacco**	ADFL	16 996	17 697	18 359	18 776	20 227	21 187	22 004	23 890	24 566
02.1	Alcoholic beverages	ADFM	6 716	6 938	7 426	7 257	7 962	8 539	8 641	9 349	9 420
02.2	Tobacco	ADFN	10 280	10 759	10 933	11 519	12 265	12 648	13 363	14 541	15 146
03.	**Clothing and footwear**	ADFP	23 598	24 887	26 861	28 030	29 548	30 972	32 357	33 826	34 571
03.1	Clothing	ADFQ	19 654	20 853	22 587	23 711	25 211	26 562	27 902	29 377	30 301
03.2	Footwear	ADFR	3 944	4 034	4 274	4 319	4 337	4 410	4 455	4 449	4 270
04.	**Housing, water, electricity, gas and other fuels**	ADFS	69 862	73 890	77 378	81 412	85 975	90 265	96 273	100 658	106 269
04.1	Actual rentals for housing	ADFT	14 235	16 222	17 379	17 906	18 784	19 821	21 155	22 320	24 446
04.2	Imputed rentals for housing	ADFU	31 102	32 546	34 591	37 479	39 548	42 426	47 336	50 517	52 649
04.3	Maintenance and repair of the dwelling	ADFV	6 820	6 836	6 458	6 526	6 958	7 939	8 431	8 721	9 625
04.4	Water supply and miscellaneous dwelling services	ADFW	3 328	3 667	4 051	4 290	4 567	4 785	4 979	5 247	4 960
04.5	Electricity, gas and other fuels	ADFX	14 377	14 619	14 899	15 211	16 118	15 294	14 372	13 853	14 589
05.	**Furnishings, household equipment and routine maintenance of the house**	ADFY	22 372	23 809	25 179	26 287	28 013	29 996	31 558	33 562	36 489
05.1	Furniture, furnishings, carpets and other floor coverings	ADFZ	7 853	8 459	9 287	9 843	10 726	11 503	12 147	13 012	14 302
05.2	Household textiles	ADGG	2 592	2 802	2 843	3 020	3 233	3 412	3 692	4 003	4 376
05.3	Household appliances	ADGL	3 974	4 177	4 195	4 405	4 615	5 005	5 102	5 130	5 235
05.4	Glassware, tableware and household utensils	ADGM	2 421	2 554	2 751	2 767	2 893	3 168	3 423	3 750	4 127
05.5	Tools and equipment for house and garden	ADGN	1 686	1 773	1 889	1 911	2 001	2 184	2 339	2 533	2 762
05.6	Goods and services for routine household maintenance	ADGO	3 846	4 044	4 214	4 341	4 545	4 724	4 855	5 134	5 687
06.	**Health**	ADGP	5 807	5 987	6 668	6 835	7 260	7 583	8 112	8 563	8 955
06.1	Medical products, appliances and equipment	ADGQ	3 156	3 348	3 794	3 919	4 207	4 388	4 711	4 995	5 371
06.2	Out-patient services	ADGR	1 632	1 586	1 754	1 781	1 829	1 897	2 012	2 116	2 115
06.3	Hospital services	ADGS	1 019	1 053	1 120	1 135	1 224	1 298	1 389	1 452	1 469
07.	**Transport**	ADGT	53 612	56 671	59 970	62 733	68 520	75 546	80 437	84 342	86 827
07.1	Purchase of vehicles	ADGU	19 940	20 847	22 657	23 588	26 469	29 445	30 854	31 605	30 313
07.2	Operation of personal transport equipment	ADGV	21 142	22 362	22 977	23 861	25 581	28 081	29 886	31 619	33 870
07.3	Transport services	ADGW	12 530	13 462	14 336	15 284	16 470	18 020	19 697	21 118	22 644
08.	**Communications**	ADGX									
08.1	Communications	ADGX	7 355	7 873	8 643	9 067	9 358	10 015	11 050	12 107	12 771
09.	**Recreation and culture**	ADGY	40 107	42 677	45 552	51 075	55 400	59 975	65 306	69 867	73 929
09.1	Audio-visual, photographic and information processing equipment	ADGZ	9 090	9 633	9 620	10 862	11 994	13 531	15 086	16 014	17 425
09.2	Other major durables for recreation and culture	ADHL	1 421	1 617	1 818	2 133	2 553	2 862	3 101	3 669	4 176
09.3	Other recreational items and equipment; flowers, garden and pets	ADHZ	9 211	9 710	10 646	11 284	12 694	14 414	16 160	17 478	18 624
09.4	Recreational and cultural services	ADIA	13 463	14 265	15 251	18 241	19 272	20 037	21 412	22 516	22 901
09.5	Newspapers, books and stationery	ADIC	6 922	7 452	8 217	8 555	8 887	9 131	9 547	10 190	10 803
09.6	Package holidays[2]	ADID	–	–	–	–	–	–	–	–	–
10.	**Education**										
10.1	Educational services	ADIE	4 787	5 182	5 487	6 197	6 405	7 440	7 813	8 161	8 127
11.	**Restaurants and hotels**	ADIF	43 006	46 170	48 394	50 383	54 072	56 454	60 701	63 660	65 463
11.1	Catering services	ADIG	36 793	39 327	41 040	42 182	45 424	47 498	51 530	54 419	56 005
11.2	Accommodation services	ADIH	6 213	6 843	7 354	8 201	8 648	8 956	9 171	9 241	9 458
12.	**Miscellaneous goods and services**	ADII	45 044	48 813	50 153	52 329	55 658	59 204	63 353	66 663	71 606
12.1	Personal care	ADIJ	8 113	8 526	9 353	10 378	11 375	11 905	12 610	13 288	13 965
12.3	Personal effects n.e.c.	ADIK	3 560	3 615	3 657	3 898	4 028	4 296	4 444	4 644	4 862
12.4	Social protection	ADIL	8 108	8 430	8 413	8 187	8 236	8 259	8 363	8 537	9 106
12.5	Insurance	ADIM	14 677	16 477	16 408	16 306	16 532	17 853	19 534	19 796	20 820
12.6	Financial services n.e.c.	ADIN	4 584	5 326	5 705	5 853	6 980	7 953	8 615	9 906	11 766
12.7	Other services n.e.c.	ADIO	6 002	6 439	6 617	7 707	8 507	8 938	9 787	10 492	11 087
Total	Final consumption expenditure in the UK by resident and non-resident households (domestic concept)	ABQI	378 229	400 827	420 499	442 914	473 461	502 469	534 156	562 185	587 825
P.33	Final consumption expenditure outside the UK by UK resident households	ABTA	10 605	11 890	13 058	13 721	14 377	14 942	16 913	19 682	21 630
-P.34	less Final consumption expenditure in the UK by households resident in the rest of the world	CDFD	–9 076	–10 747	–11 160	–13 268	–14 038	–14 037	–14 544	–14 312	–14 673
P.31	**Final consumption expenditure by UK resident households in the UK and abroad (national concept)**	ABPB	379 758	401 970	422 397	443 367	473 800	503 374	536 525	567 555	594 782

1 Package holidays data are dispersed between components (transport etc)

Households and NPISH

6.4 continued
Individual consumption expenditure at current market prices by households, non-profit institutions serving households and general government
Classified by function (COICOP/COPNI/COFOG)[1]

£ million

			1992	1993	1994	1995	1996	1997	1998	1999	2000
P.31	**CONSUMPTION EXPENDITURE OF UK RESIDENT HOUSEHOLDS**										
P.31	Final consumption expenditure of UK resident households in the UK and abroad	ABPB	379 758	401 970	422 397	443 367	473 800	503 374	536 525	567 555	594 782
13.	**FINAL INDIVIDUAL CONSUMPTION EXPENDITURE OF NPISH**										
P.31	Final individual consumption expenditure of NPISH	ABNV	10 806	13 981	15 287	16 481	18 385	19 602	21 117	22 671	22 866
14.	**FINAL INDIVIDUAL CONSUMPTION EXPENDITURE OF OF GENERAL GOVERNMENT**										
14.1	Health	QYOT	33 236	35 441	37 272	38 981	41 466	42 657	45 391	50 097	53 837
14.2	Recreation and culture	QYSU	3 366	3 547	3 246	3 172	3 173	3 089	3 486	3 777	3 903
14.3	Education	QYSE	25 511	23 487	24 202	25 291	25 798	26 692	27 960	30 103	31 168
14.4	Social protection	QYSP	11 299	12 074	12 825	13 649	14 531	15 113	15 434	16 527	17 268
14.5	Housing	QYXO	–	–	–	–	–	–	–	–	–
P.31	Final individual consumption expenditure of of general government	NNAQ	73 412	74 549	77 545	81 093	84 968	87 551	92 271	100 504	106 176
P.31	Total, individual consumption expenditure/	NQEO	463 976	490 500	515 229	540 941	577 153	610 527	649 913	690 730	723 824
P.41	actual individual consumption	ABRE	463 976	490 500	515 229	540 941	577 153	610 527	649 913	690 730	723 824

1 "Purpose" or "function" classifications are designed to indicate the "socio-economic objectives" that institutional units aim to achieve through various kinds of outlays. COICOP is the Classification of Individual Consumption by Purpose and applies to households. COPNI is the Classification of the Purposes of Non-profit Institutions Serving Households and COFOG the Classification of the Functions of Government. The introduction of ESA95 coincides with the redefinition of these classifications and data will be available on a consistent basis for all European Union member states.

Households and NPISH

6.5 Individual consumption expenditure at 1995 market prices by households, non-profit institutions serving households and general government
Classified by function (COICOP/COPNI/COFOG)[1]

£ million at 1995 prices

			1992	1993	1994	1995	1996	1997	1998	1999	2000
P.31	**FINAL CONSUMPTION EXPENDITURE OF HOUSEHOLDS**										
01.	**Food and non-alcoholic beverages**	ADIP	48 268	49 262	49 744	49 790	51 405	52 347	52 983	54 334	56 123
01.1	Food	ADIQ	43 385	44 178	44 339	44 324	45 939	46 859	47 469	48 726	49 970
01.2	Non-alcoholic beverages	ADIR	4 908	5 102	5 405	5 466	5 466	5 488	5 514	5 608	6 153
02.	**Alcoholic beverages and tobacco**	ADIS	19 539	19 255	19 268	18 776	19 299	19 459	19 193	19 863	19 959
02.1	Alcoholic beverages	ADIT	6 970	7 066	7 600	7 257	7 778	8 272	8 160	8 727	8 775
02.2	Tobacco	ADIU	12 803	12 357	11 668	11 519	11 521	11 187	11 033	11 136	11 184
03.	**Clothing and footwear**	ADIW	23 644	24 923	26 884	28 030	29 729	30 920	32 360	34 694	36 819
03.1	Clothing	ADIX	19 623	20 859	22 593	23 711	25 307	26 299	27 632	29 910	32 178
03.2	Footwear	ADIY	4 031	4 068	4 291	4 319	4 422	4 621	4 728	4 784	4 641
04.	**Housing, water, electricity, gas and other fuels**	ADIZ	79 432	80 872	80 742	81 412	83 212	84 230	84 902	85 241	87 745
04.1	Actual rentals for housing	ADJA	16 890	17 685	18 177	17 906	18 070	18 122	18 070	18 049	19 095
04.2	Imputed rentals for housing	ADJB	36 171	36 186	36 359	37 479	38 084	38 766	39 722	40 442	40 576
04.3	Maintenance and repair of the dwelling	ADJC	7 107	7 098	6 642	6 526	6 666	7 238	7 368	7 480	7 985
04.4	Water supply and miscellaneous dwelling services	ADJD	4 081	4 162	4 292	4 290	4 339	4 358	4 273	4 303	4 320
04.5	Electricity, gas and other fuels	ADJE	14 994	15 526	15 272	15 211	16 053	15 746	15 469	14 967	15 769
05.	**Furnishings, household equipment and routine maintenance of the house**	ADJF	22 974	24 426	25 898	26 287	27 271	28 892	29 921	31 627	34 572
05.1	Furniture, furnishings, carpets and other floor coverings	ADJG	8 262	8 910	9 767	9 843	10 202	10 633	10 988	11 629	12 771
05.2	Household textiles	ADJH	2 586	2 848	2 882	3 020	3 167	3 329	3 559	3 876	4 381
05.3	Household appliances	ADJI	3 896	4 089	4 210	4 405	4 638	5 110	5 236	5 335	5 624
05.4	Glassware, tableware and household utensils	ADJJ	2 487	2 641	2 827	2 767	2 834	3 083	3 294	3 610	4 018
05.5	Tools and equipment for house and garden	ADJK	1 714	1 764	1 883	1 911	1 990	2 156	2 314	2 534	2 789
05.6	Goods and services for routine household maintenance	ADJL	4 020	4 148	4 329	4 341	4 440	4 581	4 530	4 643	4 989
06.	**Health**	ADJM	6 824	6 678	7 096	6 835	6 879	6 818	6 847	6 790	6 693
06.1	Medical products, appliances and equipment	ADJN	3 757	3 801	4 083	3 919	3 959	3 884	3 885	3 866	3 891
06.2	Out-patient services	ADJO	1 884	1 777	1 863	1 781	1 729	1 698	1 655	1 606	1 519
06.3	Hospital services	ADJP	1 183	1 100	1 150	1 135	1 191	1 236	1 307	1 318	1 283
07.	**Transport**	ADJQ	58 211	59 690	61 583	62 733	66 136	69 581	72 375	74 557	74 261
07.1	Purchase of vehicles	ADJR	20 832	21 878	23 192	23 588	25 665	27 496	28 850	30 165	29 894
07.2	Operation of personal transport equipment	ADJS	23 860	23 736	23 645	23 861	24 526	25 234	25 774	25 892	25 205
07.3	Transport services	ADJT	13 648	14 147	14 746	15 284	15 945	16 851	17 751	18 500	19 162
08.	**Communications**										
08.1	Communications	ADJU	6 760	7 181	8 305	9 067	9 545	10 478	11 738	13 276	14 567
09.	**Recreation and culture**	ADJV	41 550	43 583	46 379	51 075	54 118	57 878	63 413	69 889	76 475
09.1	Audio-visual, photographic and information processing equipment	ADJW	8 530	9 028	9 306	10 862	12 108	13 936	16 954	20 699	25 272
09.2	Other major durables for recreation and culture	ADJX	1 572	1 740	1 910	2 133	2 414	2 612	2 765	3 171	3 565
09.3	Other recreational items and equipment; flowers, gardens and pets	ADJY	9 328	9 808	10 740	11 284	12 462	14 015	15 669	17 271	18 754
09.4	Recreational and cultural services	ADJZ	14 553	15 158	15 827	18 241	18 731	18 876	19 502	19 919	19 769
09.5	Newspapers, books and stationery	ADKM	7 538	7 790	8 596	8 555	8 403	8 439	8 523	8 829	9 115
09.6	Package holidays[2]	ADMI	–	–	–	–	–	–	–	–	–
10.	**Education**										
10.1	Educational services	ADMJ	5 730	5 856	5 763	6 197	6 147	6 791	6 758	6 675	6 289
11.	**Restaurants and Hotels**	ADMK	47 663	49 267	50 211	50 383	52 314	52 688	54 111	54 635	53 807
11.1	Catering services	ADML	41 209	42 272	42 727	42 182	43 842	44 217	45 828	46 580	46 023
11.2	Accommodation services	ADMM	6 526	7 033	7 484	8 201	8 472	8 471	8 283	8 055	7 784
12.	**Miscellaneous goods and services**	ADMN	50 309	51 726	51 444	52 329	54 286	55 537	56 361	57 090	59 785
12.1	Personal care	ADMO	8 891	9 080	9 805	10 378	10 949	11 026	11 044	11 309	11 927
12.3	Personal effects n.e.c.	ADMP	3 878	3 761	3 685	3 898	3 983	4 224	4 278	4 321	4 530
12.4	Social protection	ADMQ	9 737	9 433	8 822	8 187	7 865	7 499	7 229	6 991	6 976
12.5	Insurance	ADMR	15 772	16 725	16 270	16 306	16 601	17 170	17 758	17 255	17 039
12.6	Financial services n.e.c.	ADMS	5 162	5 637	5 818	5 853	6 686	7 278	7 376	8 314	10 388
12.7	Other services n.e.c.	ADMT	7 015	7 177	7 044	7 707	8 202	8 340	8 676	8 900	8 925
Total	Final consumption expenditure in the UK by resident and non-resident households (domestic concept)	ABQJ	409 371	421 707	433 317	442 914	460 341	475 619	490 962	508 671	527 095
P.33	Final consumption expenditure outside the UK by UK resident households	ABTC	11 953	12 093	13 490	13 721	14 077	16 357	18 813	21 837	24 090
-P.34	less Final consumption expenditure in the UK by households resident in the rest of the world	CCHX	–10 086	–11 524	–11 457	–13 268	–13 658	–13 238	–13 284	–12 751	–12 727
P.31	Final consumption expenditure by UK resident households in the UK and abroad (national concept)	ABPF	411 204	422 273	435 350	443 367	460 760	478 738	496 491	517 757	538 458

Households and NPISH

6.5 continued
Individual consumption expenditure at 1995 market prices by households, non-profit institutions serving households and general government
Classified by function (COICOP/COPNI/COFOG)[1]

£ million at 1995 prices

			1992	1993	1994	1995	1996	1997	1998	1999	2000
P.31	**CONSUMPTION EXPENDITURE OF UK RESIDENT HOUSEHOLDS**										
P.31	Final consumption expenditure of UK resident households in the UK and abroad	ABPF	411 204	422 273	435 350	443 367	460 760	478 738	496 491	517 757	538 458
13.	**FINAL INDIVIDUAL CONSUMPTION EXPENDITURE OF NPISH**										
P.31	Final individual consumption expenditure of NPISH	ABNU	12 445	14 723	15 900	16 481	16 691	17 055	18 265	18 769	19 408
14.	**FINAL INDIVIDUAL CONSUMPTION EXPENDITURE OF GENERAL GOVERNMENT**										
14.1	Health	EMOA	34 803	36 360	37 372	38 981	40 172	41 069	42 171	43 856	44 873
14.2	Recreation and culture	EMOB	26 627	25 201	24 986	25 291	25 565	25 811	26 037	26 238	26 430
14.3	Education	EMOB	26 627	25 201	24 986	25 291	25 565	25 811	26 037	26 238	26 430
14.4	Social protection	QYXM	12 289	13 068	12 788	13 649	14 175	14 641	14 830	14 974	15 335
14.5	Housing	QYXN	–	–	–	–	–	–	–	–	–
P.31	Final individual consumption expenditure of general government	NSZK	77 053	78 616	78 479	81 093	83 112	84 808	86 244	88 475	90 071
P.31 P.41	Total, individual consumption expenditure/ actual individual consumption	YBIO	500 344	515 535	529 729	540 941	560 563	580 601	601 000	625 001	647 937

1 "Purpose" or "function" classifications are designed to indicate the "socio-economic objectives" that institutional units aim to achieve through various kinds of outlays. COICOP is the Classification of Individual Consumption by Purpose and applies to households. COPNI is the Classification of the Purposes of Non-profit Institutions Serving Households and COFOG the Classification of the Functions of Government. The introduction of ESA95 coincides with the redefinition of these classifications and data will be available on a consistent basis for all European Union member states.

2 Package holidays data are dispersed between components (transport etc)

United Kingdom National Accounts 2001, © Crown copyright 2001

Part 3

Chapter 7

Rest of the world

Rest of the world

7.1.0 Rest of the world
ESA95 sector S.2

£ million

			1992	1993	1994	1995	1996	1997	1998	1999	2000
V.I	**EXTERNAL ACCOUNT OF GOODS AND SERVICES**										
	Resources										
P.7	Imports of goods and services										
P.71	Imports of goods	LQBL	120 913	135 295	146 269	165 600	180 918	184 265	185 869	193 722	218 036
P.72	Imports of services	KTMR	30 746	34 830	38 986	41 451	46 298	47 171	52 079	58 862	62 988
P.7	Total resources, total imports	KTMX	151 659	170 125	185 255	207 051	227 216	231 436	237 948	252 584	281 024
	Uses										
P.6	Exports of goods and services										
P.61	Exports of goods	LQAD	107 863	122 229	135 143	153 577	167 196	171 923	164 056	166 198	187 656
P.62	Exports of services	KTMQ	36 228	41 411	45 365	49 932	55 895	59 699	64 745	70 522	77 649
P.6	Total exports	KTMW	144 091	163 640	180 508	203 509	223 091	231 622	228 801	236 720	265 305
B.11	External balance of goods and services	-KTMY	7 568	6 485	4 747	3 542	4 125	−186	9 147	15 864	15 719
P.7	Total uses	KTMX	151 659	170 125	185 255	207 051	227 216	231 436	237 948	252 584	281 024

United Kingdom National Accounts 2001, © Crown copyright 2001

Rest of the world

7.1.2 Rest of the world
ESA95 sector S.2

£ million

			1992	1993	1994	1995	1996	1997	1998	1999	2000
V.II	**EXTERNAL ACCOUNT OF PRIMARY INCOMES AND CURRENT TRANSFERS**										
	Resources										
B.11	External balance of goods and services	-KTMY	7 568	6 485	4 747	3 542	4 125	−186	9 147	15 864	15 719
D.1	Compensation of employees										
D.11	Wages and salaries	KTMO	600	560	851	1 183	818	924	850	759	871
D.2	Taxes on production and imports, received										
D.21	Taxes on products										
D.211	Value added type taxes (VAT)	FJKM	4 059	4 471	3 121	4 845	4 471	3 397	4 228	3 811	4 204
D.212	Taxes and duties on imports excluding VAT										
D.2121	Import duties	FJWE	1 943	2 172	2 134	2 458	2 318	2 291	2 076	2 024	2 086
D.2122	Taxes on imports excluding VAT and duties	FJWF	–	–	–	–	–	–	–	–	–
D.214	Taxes on products excluding VAT and import duties	FJWG	54	57	98	55	26	91	42	46	44
D.2	Total taxes on production and imports, received	FJWB	6 056	6 700	5 353	7 358	6 815	5 779	6 346	5 881	6 334
-D.3	*less* Subsidies, paid										
-D.31	Subsidies on products	-FJWJ	−1 737	−1 975	−2 004	−2 138	−2 674	−2 968	−2 663	−2 330	−2 888
-D.39	Other subsidies on production	-NHQR	−66	−215	−286	−293	−253	−206	−246	−370	−361
-D.3	Total	-FJWI	−1 803	−2 190	−2 290	−2 431	−2 927	−3 174	−2 909	−2 700	−3 249
D.4	Property income, received										
D.41	Interest	QYNG	58 036	58 012	55 047	66 376	66 918	68 518	72 894	67 417	89 854
D.42	Distributed income of corporations	QYNH	7 117	9 582	10 546	12 310	15 004	15 768	14 776	18 977	19 444
D.43	Reinvested earnings on direct foreign investment	QYNI	121	4 385	3 953	5 254	7 873	6 386	1 522	7 855	16 146
D.44	Property income attributed to insurance policy-holders	NHRM	702	580	638	795	715	842	1 185	1 245	1 565
D.4	Total	HMBO	65 976	72 559	70 184	84 735	90 510	91 514	90 377	95 494	127 009
D.5	Current taxes on income, wealth etc										
D.51	Taxes on income	FJWM	352	393	452	557	610	638	454	505	427
D.61	Social contributions										
D.611	Actual social contributions										
D.6112	Employees' social contributions	FJWQ	–	–	–	–	–	–	–	–	–
D.62	Social benefits other than social transfers in kind										
D.621	Social security benefits in cash	FJVZ	619	772	843	910	963	1 031	1 091	1 123	1 161
D.622	Private funded social benefits	QZEM	96	49	70	72	82	77	72	60	35
D.624	Social assistance benefits in cash	RNNF	42	52	56	62	66	71	71	60	57
D.62	Total	FJKO	757	873	969	1 044	1 111	1 179	1 234	1 243	1 253
D.7	Other current transfers										
D.71	Net non-life insurance premiums	FJKS	–	–	–	–	5	5	7	10	12
D.72	Non-life insurance claims	NHRR	5 900	4 246	4 145	4 993	9 763	4 423	4 168	3 663	4 381
D.74	Current international cooperation	FJWT	2 237	1 961	2 007	2 224	1 814	1 700	1 705	1 667	2 418
D.75	Miscellaneous current transfers	FJWU	2 803	3 510	4 105	3 951	4 668	5 267	6 826	7 607	7 615
	of which GNP based fourth own resource	NMFH	914	1 558	2 071	1 826	2 454	2 458	3 920	4 632	4 379
D.7	Total	FJWR	10 940	9 717	10 257	11 168	16 250	11 395	12 706	12 947	14 426
D.8	Adjustment for the change in net equity of households in pension funds	QZEP	6	−1	−3	−2	−2	−2	−2	−2	−4
Total	Total resources	NSUK	90 452	95 096	90 520	107 154	117 310	108 067	118 203	129 991	162 786

7.1.2 Rest of the world
ESA95 sector S.2
continued

£ million

			1992	1993	1994	1995	1996	1997	1998	1999	2000
V.II	**EXTERNAL ACCOUNT OF PRIMARY INCOMES AND CURRENT TRANSFERS** *continued*										
	Uses										
D.1	Compensation of employees										
D.11	Wages and salaries	KTMN	551	595	681	887	911	1 007	840	960	1 014
D.2	Taxes on production and imports, paid										
D.21	Taxes on products										
D.212	Taxes and duties on imports excluding VAT										
D.2121	Import duties	FJVQ	–	–	–	–	–	–	–	–	–
D.2122	Taxes on imports excluding VAT and duties	FJVR	–	–	–	–	–	–	–	–	–
D.214	Taxes on products excluding VAT and import duties	FJVS	–	–	–	–	–	–	–	–	–
D.21	Total taxes on products	FJVN	–	–	–	–	–	–	–	–	–
D.2	Total taxes on production and imports, paid	FJVM	–	–	–	–	–	–	–	–	–
D.4	Property income, paid										
D.41	Interest	QYNJ	49 086	50 861	47 766	58 064	59 033	60 504	69 338	59 973	81 706
D.42	Distributed income of corporations	QYNK	11 843	11 376	12 109	14 690	15 317	18 721	19 536	18 035	24 201
D.43	Reinvested earnings on direct foreign investment	QYNL	5 224	10 096	13 827	14 378	17 271	16 112	14 071	21 304	27 076
D.44	Property income attributed to insurance policy-holders										
D.4	Total	HMBN	66 153	72 333	73 702	87 132	91 621	95 337	102 945	99 312	132 983
D.5	Current taxes on income, wealth etc										
D.51	Taxes on income	NHRS	259	238	361	472	376	402	530	528	520
D.61	Social contributions										
D.6112	Employee's social contributions	FKAA	116	78	92	95	108	107	99	87	55
D.7	Other current transfers										
D.71	Net non-life insurance premiums	NHRX	5 900	4 246	4 145	4 993	9 763	4 423	4 168	3 663	4 381
D.72	Non-life insurance claims	FJTT	–	–	–	–	5	5	7	10	12
D.74	Current international cooperation	FJWA	1 907	2 558	1 752	1 233	2 424	1 739	1 384	3 176	2 084
D.75	Miscellaneous current transfers	NHSI	2 592	3 129	3 019	3 327	3 393	3 327	3 416	3 164	3 312
D.7	Total	NHRW	10 399	9 933	8 916	9 553	15 585	9 494	8 975	10 013	9 789
B.12	Current external balance	-HBOG	12 974	11 919	6 768	9 015	8 709	1 720	4 814	19 091	18 425
Total	Total uses	NSUK	90 452	95 096	90 520	107 154	117 310	108 067	118 203	129 991	162 786

Rest of the world

7.1.7 Rest of the World
ESA95 sector S.2

Rest of the world

			1992	1993	1994	1995	1996	1997	1998	1999	2000
V.III	**ACCUMULATION ACCOUNTS**										
V.III.1	**CAPITAL ACCOUNT**										
	Changes in liabilities and net worth										
B.12	Current external balance	-HBOG	12 974	11 919	6 768	9 015	8 709	1 720	4 814	19 091	18 425
D.9	Capital transfers receivable										
D.92	Investment grants	NHSA	261	201	188	149	143	169	182	171	225
D.99	Other capital transfers	NHSB	542	603	1 042	481	488	616	677	509	483
D.9	Total	NHRZ	803	804	1 230	630	631	785	859	680	708
-D.9	*less* Capital transfers payable										
-D.92	Investment grants	-NHQQ	−622	−529	−660	−485	−650	−869	−413	−332	−1 071
-D.99	Other capital transfers	-NHQS	−602	−584	−603	−678	−703	−754	−967	−1 144	−1 573
-D.9	Total	-NHSC	−1 224	−1 113	−1 263	−1 163	−1 353	−1 623	−1 380	−1 476	−2 644
B.10.1	Total, change in net worth due to saving (current external balance) and capital transfers	NHSD	12 553	11 610	6 735	8 482	7 987	882	4 293	18 295	16 489
	Changes in assets										
K.2	Acquisitions less disposals of non-produced non-financial assets	NHSG	–	–	–	–	14	−34	−48	12	37
B.9	Net lending(+)/net borrowing(-)	NHRB	12 553	11 610	6 735	8 482	7 973	916	4 341	18 283	16 452
Total	Total change in assets	NHSD	12 553	11 610	6 735	8 482	7 987	882	4 293	18 295	16 489

Rest of the world

7.1.8 Rest of the world
ESA95 sector S.2 Unconsolidated

£ million

			1992	1993	1994	1995	1996	1997	1998	1999	2000
III.2	**FINANCIAL ACCOUNT**										
F.A	**Net acquisition of financial assets**										
F.1	Monetary gold and special drawing rights	-NQAD	962	462	-932	120	54	-1 199	-915	374	956
F.2	Currency and deposits										
F.21	Currency	NEWN	59	71	95	66	35	50	109	81	64
F.22	Transferable deposits										
F.2211	Sterling deposits with UK banks	NWXP	4 670	-1 401	6 550	10 248	-431	16 549	13 792	19 427	32 499
F.2212	Foreign currency deposits with UK banks	NFAS	25 313	39 616	40 805	15 766	70 488	131 502	33 421	-7 754	165 475
F.2213	Sterling deposits with UK building societies	NEWS	923	1 624	1 445	444	1 241	-165	884	556	567
F.29	Other deposits	NEWU	-188	21	950	484	-606	-759	304	693	528
F.2	Total currency and deposits	NEWM	30 777	39 931	49 845	27 008	70 727	147 177	48 510	13 003	199 133
F.3	Securities other than shares										
F.331	Short term: money market instruments										
F.3311	Issued by UK central government	NEWX	-2 416	-305	-140	1 324	-239	-913	-1 734	422	37
F.3312	Issued by UK local authorities	NEXB	–	–	–	–	–	–	–	–	–
F.3315	Issued by UK monetary financial institutions	NEXC	-11 218	-18 314	830	16 195	11 462	7 673	-16 412	14 884	38 184
F.3316	Issued by other UK residents	NEXH	-711	1 350	2 298	1 252	1 858	1 712	2 429	1 782	2 737
F.332	Medium (1 to 5 year) and long term (over 5 year) bonds										
F.3321	Issued by UK central government	NEXK	8 826	17 572	5 306	-1 014	6 243	-2 401	1 907	-5 283	-1 137
F.3322	Issued by UK local authorities	NEXN	–	–	–	–	–	–	–	–	–
F.33251	Medium term bonds issued by UK banks	NEXP	1 034	3 037	4 353	1 572	5 585	3 012	1 575	4 395	903
F.33252	Medium term bonds issued by building societies	NEXQ	336	884	2 066	-399	-315	-116	-139	251	1 814
F.3326	Other medium & long term bonds issued by UK residents	NEXR	3 630	7 070	11 274	13 829	12 332	14 401	-3 766	23 742	9 193
F.3	Total securities other than shares	NEWV	-519	11 294	25 987	32 759	36 926	23 368	-16 140	40 193	51 731
F.4	Loans										
F.41	Short term loans										
F.4191	Loans by rest of the world monetary financial institutions	NEYD	4 222	12 250	-1 836	15 441	33 889	25 836	-13 299	16 400	33 652
F.4192	Other Short-term loans by Rest of the World	ZMDZ	19 159	71 704	-55 710	23 926	49 748	27 080	24 542	33 453	45 424
F.42	Long term loans										
F.4211	Outward direct investment	NEYG	3 008	127	2 921	233	2 868	5 673	10 220	13 091	40 884
F.4212	Inward direct investment	NEYH	3 297	2 744	2 518	-273	2 027	6 200	26 092	8 312	17 170
F.429	Other long-term loans by the rest of the world	QYLT	-173	399	-539	-234	281	-54	-254	-122	-293
F.4	Total loans	NEXX	29 513	87 224	-52 646	39 093	88 813	64 735	47 301	71 134	136 837
F.5	Shares and other equity										
F.51	Shares and other equity, excluding mutual funds' shares										
F.514	Quoted UK shares	NEYU	10 455	17 271	3 686	8 091	9 808	8 448	53 323	95 290	131 434
F.515	Unquoted UK shares	NEYV	6 183	9 878	7 827	14 772	11 650	13 464	13 132	30 482	61 351
F.516	Other UK equity (including direct investment in property)	NEYW	301	460	472	224	613	850	698	813	1 322
F.52	Mutual funds' shares										
F.521	UK mutual funds' shares	NEZD	18	77	127	34	31	16	2	3	27
F.5	Total shares and other equity	NEYP	16 957	27 686	12 112	23 121	22 102	22 778	67 155	126 588	194 134
F.6	Insurance technical reserves										
F.61	Net equity of households in life assurance and pension funds' reserves	NEZF	6	-1	-3	-2	-2	-2	-2	-2	-4
F.62	Prepayments of insurance premiums and reserves for outstanding claims	NEZI	928	296	493	973	6 793	264	3	-662	1 102
F.6	Total insurance technical reserves	NPWP	934	295	490	971	6 791	262	1	-664	1 098
F.7	Other accounts receivable	NEZJ	99	581	-569	297	1 077	23	65	-135	-90
F.A	Total net acquisition of financial assets	NEWI	78 723	167 473	34 287	123 369	226 490	257 144	145 977	250 493	583 799

7.1.8 Rest of the world
ESA95 sector S.2 Unconsolidated
continued

Rest of the world

£ million

			1992	1993	1994	1995	1996	1997	1998	1999	2000
III.2	**FINANCIAL ACCOUNT** continued										
F.L	**Net acquisition of financial liabilities**										
F.2	Currency and deposits										
F.21	Currency	NEZR	−31	82	23	29	85	118	40	−19	−24
F.22	Transferable deposits										
F.229	Deposits with rest of the world monetary financial institutions[1]	NEZX	26 756	53 172	31 115	35 705	98 524	137 522	15 859	43 040	220 886
F.2	Total currency and deposits	NEZQ	26 725	53 254	31 138	35 734	98 609	137 640	15 899	43 021	220 862
F.3	Securities other than shares										
F.331	Short term: money market instruments										
F.3319	Issued by the rest of the world[1]	NFAM	690	6 242	−4 448	2 743	−2 170	8 557	2 685	13 623	−2 728
F.332	Medium (1 to 5 year) and long term (over 5 year) bonds										
F.3329	Long term bonds issued by the rest of the world	NFAW	31 085	75 682	−16 770	27 828	49 021	43 825	27 448	−9 055	52 922
F.34	Financial derivatives	NSUL	−1 253	−245	−2 373	−1 667	−963	−1 156	3 043	−2 685	−1 503
F.3	Total securities other than shares	NEZZ	30 522	81 679	−23 591	28 904	45 888	51 226	33 176	1 883	48 691
F.4	Loans										
F.41	Short term loans										
F.4111	Sterling loans by UK banks	NFBE	1 602	−456	−945	619	4 802	3 340	−613	2 619	1 869
F.4112	Foreign currency loans by UK banks	NFBF	3 637	−7 002	−2 810	11 183	34 157	27 741	1 580	14 272	52 294
F.4113	Sterling loans by UK building societies	NFBG	–	4	5	–	−9	–	–	–	–
F.42	Long term loans										
F.4211	Outward direct investment	NFBK	3 590	3 724	2 314	5 300	3 006	6 093	22 214	18 354	25 647
F.4212	Inward direct investment	NFBL	738	2 017	2 841	4 446	497	2 856	11 055	8 681	9 337
F.423	Finance leasing	NFBQ	–	–	–	–	–	–	–	–	–
F.424	Other long-term loans by UK residents	NSRT	271	293	−170	74	182	11	−262	9	−25
F.4	Total loans	NFBB	9 838	−1 420	1 235	21 622	42 635	40 041	33 974	43 935	89 122
F.5	Shares and other equity										
F.51	Shares and other equity, excluding mutual funds' shares										
F.519	Shares and other equity issued by the rest of the world	NFCD	6 729	22 724	22 234	30 823	32 242	33 262	63 851	140 420	199 037
F.52	Mutual funds' shares										
F.529	Rest of the world mutual funds' shares	NFCG	61	−114	730	105	241	–	–	–	–
F.5	Total shares and other equity	NFBT	6 790	22 610	22 964	30 928	32 483	33 262	63 851	140 420	199 037
F.7	Other accounts payable	NFCN	−241	20	415	1 217	1 360	41	−1 168	−228	−288
F.L	**Total net acquisition of financial liabilities**	NEZM	73 634	156 143	32 161	118 405	220 975	262 210	145 732	229 031	557 424
B.9	**Net lending / borrowing**										
F.A	Total net acquisition of financial assets	NEWI	78 723	167 473	34 287	123 369	226 490	257 144	145 977	250 493	583 799
-F.L	*less* Total net acquisition of financial liabilities	-NEZM	−73 634	−156 143	−32 161	−118 405	−220 975	−262 210	−145 732	−229 031	−557 424
B.9f	**Net lending (+) / net borrowing (-), from financial account**	NYOD	5 089	11 330	2 126	4 964	5 515	−5 066	245	21 462	26 375
dB.9f	**Statistical discrepancy**	NYPO	7 464	280	4 609	3 518	2 458	5 982	4 096	−3 179	−9 923
B.9	**Net lending (+) / net borrowing (-), from capital account**	NHRB	12 553	11 610	6 735	8 482	7 973	916	4 341	18 283	16 452

1 There is a discontinuity in this series between 1995 and 1996 because an instrument breakdown of offical reserves is not available prior to 1996

Rest of the world

7.1.9 Rest of the world
ESA95 sector S.2 Unconsolidated

£ billion

			1992	1993	1994	1995	1996	1997	1998	1999	2000
IV.3	**FINANCIAL BALANCE SHEET** at end of period										
AF.A	**Financial assets**										
AF.2	Currency and deposits										
AF.21	Currency	NLCW	0.6	0.6	0.7	0.8	0.8	0.9	1.0	1.1	1.1
AF.22	Transferable deposits										
AF.2211	Sterling deposits with UK banks	NLCZ	87.3	86.2	92.8	103.7	106.5	134.4	147.2	167.4	200.4
AF.2212	Foreign curency deposits with UK banks	NLDA	534.2	569.5	611.3	688.2	664.6	814.9	886.7	859.6	1 060.0
AF.2213	Sterling deposits with UK building societies	NLDB	5.4	7.0	8.5	8.9	9.9	4.0	4.9	5.2	4.1
AF.29	Other deposits	NLDD	0.2	0.2	1.2	1.7	1.1	0.3	0.6	1.3	1.8
AF.2	Total currency and deposits	NLCV	627.7	663.6	714.5	803.3	782.9	954.6	1 040.4	1 034.6	1 267.5
AF.3	Securities other than shares										
AF.331	Short term: money market instruments										
AF.3311	Issued by UK central government	NLDG	2.5	1.9	1.8	3.2	3.0	1.8	0.4	0.2	–
AF.3312	Issued by UK local authorities	NLDK	–	–	–	–	–	–	–	–	–
AF.3315	Issued by UK monetary financial institutions	NLDL	55.8	39.4	38.5	55.5	61.2	71.1	54.4	69.0	111.4
AF.3316	Issued by other UK residents	NLDQ	6.8	8.2	9.6	11.2	11.3	13.4	15.6	17.8	21.7
AF.332	Medium (1 to 5 year) and long term (over 5 year) bonds										
AF.3321	Issued by UK central government	NLDT	37.3	58.2	56.6	58.9	63.5	64.4	73.9	61.0	61.5
AF.3322	Issued by UK local authorities	NLDW	–	–	–	–	–	–	–	–	–
AF.33251	Medium term bonds issued by UK banks	NLDY	7.0	10.2	13.9	15.5	19.6	24.9	27.7	34.3	37.0
AF.33252	Medium term bonds issued by UK building societies	NLDZ	2.6	3.5	5.6	5.1	4.4	1.3	1.1	1.4	2.6
AF.3326	Other medium & long term bonds issued by UK residents	NLEA	45.5	55.1	71.6	88.2	97.2	111.2	125.8	142.0	168.4
AF.3	Total securities other than shares	NLDE	157.5	176.5	197.7	237.8	260.2	288.1	299.0	325.8	402.7
AF.4	Loans										
AF.41	Short term loans										
AF.4191	Loans by rest of the world monetary financial institutions	NLEM	63.1	85.4	83.6	106.1	131.1	153.2	138.9	162.3	192.3
AF.4192	Other short-term loans by rest of the World	ZMEA	50.6	118.9	64.9	88.2	129.2	152.2	158.1	200.8	229.8
AF.42	Long term loans										
AF.4211	Outward direct investment	NLEP	32.7	33.7	35.0	39.1	41.3	48.0	56.9	67.0	109.1
AF.4212	Inward direct investment	NLEQ	47.8	45.5	42.3	43.3	49.6	60.8	86.5	94.2	111.5
AF.429	Other long-term loans by the rest of the world	NLEX	4.0	4.2	4.0	3.0	3.0	2.6	2.5	2.1	2.1
AF.4	Total loans	NLEG	198.2	287.6	229.8	279.7	354.3	416.8	442.9	526.3	644.8
AF.5	Shares and other equity										
AF.51	Shares and other equity, excluding mutual funds' shares										
AF.514	Quoted UK shares	NLFD	87.7	127.5	119.0	164.3	216.7	290.6	384.1	496.1	582.2
AF.515	Unquoted UK shares	NLFE	91.0	96.6	96.4	117.5	119.4	134.1	165.6	217.0	303.4
AF.516	Other UK equity (including direct investment in property)	NLFF	7.2	7.6	8.5	8.7	9.3	10.2	10.9	11.7	13.0
AF.52	Mutual funds' shares										
AF.521	UK mutual funds' shares	NLFM	0.6	1.0	1.0	1.1	1.2	1.3	1.3	1.7	1.6
AF.5	Total shares and other equity	NLEY	186.5	232.6	224.9	291.6	346.7	436.1	561.9	726.5	900.2
AF.6	Insurance technical reserves										
AF.61	Net equity of households in life assurance and pension funds' reserves	NLFO	0.2	0.2	0.2	0.2	0.2	0.2	0.2	0.2	0.2
AF.62	Prepayments of insurance premiums and reserves for outstanding claims	NLFR	8.2	7.0	7.8	9.5	14.7	15.5	15.0	14.1	15.5
AF.6	Total insurance technical reserves	NPYF	8.4	7.2	7.9	9.6	14.8	15.7	15.2	14.3	15.8
AF.7	Other accounts receivable	NLFS	2.5	3.1	2.5	2.8	3.8	3.8	4.0	3.9	3.8
AF.A	**Total financial assets**	NLEF	1 180.7	1 370.6	1 377.3	1 624.8	1 762.7	2 115.1	2 363.3	2 631.3	3 234.9

7.1.9 Rest of the world
ESA95 sector S.2 Unconsolidated
continued

£ billion

			1992	1993	1994	1995	1996	1997	1998	1999	2000
IV.3	**FINANCIAL BALANCE SHEET** continued at end of period										
AF.L	**Financial liabilities**										
AF.2	Currency and deposits										
AF.21	Currency	NLGA	0.2	0.3	0.3	0.4	0.4	0.5	0.5	0.5	0.5
AF.22	Transferable deposits										
AF.229	Deposits with rest of the world monetary financial institutions[1]	NLGG	507.2	559.4	589.0	669.3	689.4	859.6	885.4	907.9	1 140.4
AF.2	Total currency and deposits	NLFZ	507.4	559.7	589.3	669.6	689.8	860.1	885.9	908.3	1 140.9
AF.3	Securities other than shares										
AF.331	Short term: money market instruments										
AF.3319	Issued by the rest of the world[1]	NLGV	14.3	20.3	15.4	21.8	17.4	25.4	27.4	43.4	44.3
AF.332	Medium (1 to 5 year) and long term (over 5 year) bonds										
AF.3329	Long term bonds issued by the rest of the world	NLHF	196.6	278.8	253.9	283.1	309.7	357.7	392.8	375.8	453.1
AF.34	Financial Derivatives	NLEC	–	–	–	–	–	–	–	–	0.1
AF.3	Total securities other than shares	NLGI	210.9	299.2	269.3	304.9	327.1	383.2	420.2	419.2	497.5
AF.4	Loans										
AF.41	Short term loans										
AF.4111	Sterling loans by UK banks	NLHN	14.8	14.3	13.2	13.9	18.7	23.9	23.4	26.1	27.6
AF.4112	Foreign currency loans by UK banks	NLHO	99.8	92.4	87.5	110.9	127.8	168.6	180.1	189.1	249.1
AF.4113	Sterling loans by UK building societies	NLHP	–	–	–	–	–	–	–	–	–
AF.42	Long term loans										
AF.4211	Outward direct investment	NLHT	39.5	43.8	44.6	51.9	50.5	54.1	76.5	86.2	115.2
AF.4212	Inward direct investment	NLHU	13.9	11.8	15.0	20.2	23.9	28.0	39.4	47.8	57.5
AF.423	Finance leasing	NLHZ	–	–	–	–	–	–	–	–	–
AF.424	Other long-term loans by UK residents	NROS	2.4	2.8	2.6	2.3	2.4	2.3	1.9	1.9	1.6
AF.4	Total loans	NLHK	170.4	165.1	162.9	199.1	223.3	277.0	321.3	351.2	451.0
AF.5	Shares and other equity										
AF.51	Shares and other equity, excluding mutual funds' shares										
AF.519	Shares and other equity issued by the rest of the world	NLIM	284.0	356.3	350.9	404.1	428.6	496.8	578.0	795.1	1 006.0
AF.52	Mutual funds' shares										
AF.529	Rest of the world mutual funds' shares	NLIR	1.1	1.5	2.1	2.3	2.2	1.5	1.1	2.1	1.7
AF.5	Total shares and other equity	NLIC	285.1	357.8	353.0	406.4	430.8	498.2	579.1	797.2	1 007.7
AF.7	Other accounts payable	NLIW	15.4	15.2	15.8	17.2	18.1	17.7	17.2	18.0	17.0
AF.L	**Total financial liabilities**	NLHJ	1 189.1	1 396.9	1 390.4	1 597.3	1 689.1	2 036.2	2 223.8	2 493.9	3 114.1
BF.90	Net financial assets / liabilities										
AF.A	Total financial assets	NLEF	1 180.7	1 370.6	1 377.3	1 624.8	1 762.7	2 115.1	2 363.3	2 631.3	3 234.9
-AF.L	less Total financial liabilities	-NLHJ	–1 189.1	–1 396.9	–1 390.4	–1 597.3	–1 689.1	–2 036.2	–2 223.8	–2 493.9	–3 114.1
BF.90	**Net financial assets (+) / liabilities (-)**	NLFK	–8.3	–26.3	–13.1	27.5	73.6	79.0	139.5	137.4	120.7

1 There is a discontinuity in this series between 1995 and 1996 because an instrument breakdown of official reserves is not available prior to 1996

Part 4

Other analyses and derived statistics

Part 4

Chapter 8

Percentage distributions and growth rates

Percentage distributions and growth rates

8.1 Composition of UK gross domestic product at market prices by category of expenditure[1]
Current prices

Percentage

		Average 1981-1990	1992	1993	1994	1995	1996	1997	1998	1999	2000
	Gross domestic product: expenditure approach										
P.3	Final consumption expenditure										
P.41	Actual individual consumption										
P.3	Household final consumption expenditure	59.4	62.2	62.6	62.0	61.6	62.2	62.1	62.4	63.0	63.0
P.3	Final consumption expenditure of NPISH	1.7	1.8	2.2	2.2	2.3	2.4	2.4	2.5	2.5	2.4
P.31	Individual government final consumption expenditure	11.1	12.0	11.6	11.4	11.3	11.1	10.8	10.7	11.2	11.3
P.41	Total actual individual consumption	72.2	76.0	76.4	75.6	75.2	75.7	75.3	75.6	76.6	76.7
P.32	Collective government final consumption expenditure	9.7	9.1	8.9	8.6	8.3	8.1	7.6	7.3	7.3	7.3
P.3	Total final consumption expenditure	81.9	85.1	85.2	84.2	83.6	83.8	82.9	82.9	83.9	84.0
P.3	Households and NPISH	61.2	63.9	64.8	64.2	63.9	64.6	64.5	64.9	65.5	65.5
P.3	Central government	12.6	12.8	12.7	12.4	12.1	11.9	11.4	11.1	11.2	11.2
P.3	Local government	8.2	8.3	7.8	7.6	7.5	7.4	7.0	6.9	7.3	7.3
P.5	Gross capital formation										
P.51	Gross fixed capital formation	18.9	16.5	15.7	15.9	16.3	16.5	16.6	17.6	17.2	17.5
P.52	Changes in inventories	0.3	–0.3	0.1	0.5	0.6	0.2	0.5	0.5	0.6	0.2
P.53	Acquisitions less disposals of valuables	–	–	–	–	–	–	–	0.1	–	–
P.5	Total gross capital formation	19.1	16.2	15.8	16.5	16.9	16.7	17.1	18.2	17.8	17.7
P.6	Exports of goods and services	25.7	23.6	25.5	26.5	28.3	29.3	28.6	26.6	26.3	28.1
-P.7	*less* imports of goods and services	–26.7	–24.8	–26.5	–27.2	–28.8	–29.8	–28.5	–27.7	–28.0	–29.8
B.11	External balance of goods and services	–1.0	–1.2	–1.0	–0.7	–0.5	–0.5	–	–1.1	–1.8	–1.7
de	Statistical discrepancy between expenditure components and GDP	–	–	–	–	–	–	–	–	–	–
B.1*g	Gross domestic product at market prices	100.0	100.0	100.0	100.0	100.0	100.0	100.0	100.0	100.0	100.0

1 Based on table 1.2

8.2 Composition of UK gross domestic product at market prices by category of income[1,2]

Percentage

		Average 1981-1990	1992	1993	1994	1995	1996	1997	1998	1999	2000
B.2g	Total gross operating surplus										
	Public non-financial corporations	3.0	1.1	1.3	1.3	1.5	1.4	1.2	1.2	1.2	1.0
	Private non-financial corporations	18.5	17.3	18.1	19.5	19.8	20.7	20.8	20.3	19.8	20.0
	Financial corporations	2.2	2.2	2.8	3.0	2.5	2.2	1.8	2.1	1.6	1.6
-P.119	FISIM	–3.5	–3.1	–3.0	–3.4	–3.2	–3.0	–2.8	–3.3	–3.4	–3.9
	Central government	0.7	0.6	0.6	0.5	0.5	0.5	0.5	0.5	0.5	0.5
	Local government	0.5	0.4	0.4	0.4	0.4	0.4	0.4	0.4	0.4	0.4
	Households and NPISH	4.0	5.2	5.1	5.2	5.3	5.3	5.3	5.6	5.7	5.6
B.2g	Total gross operating surplus	25.5	23.7	25.1	26.6	26.8	27.6	27.3	26.8	25.7	25.1
B.3	Mixed income	6.1	6.5	6.6	6.5	6.5	6.4	6.2	5.8	5.8	5.8
D.1	Compensation of employees	55.9	56.9	55.7	54.3	53.8	53.2	53.4	54.0	54.8	55.3
D.2	Taxes on production and imports[2]	14.2	14.1	13.7	13.8	14.1	14.0	14.2	14.3	14.5	14.6
-D.3	Subsidies on products	–1.7	–1.2	–1.2	–1.2	–1.1	–1.2	–1.1	–0.9	–0.9	–0.8
di	Statistical discrepancy between income components and GDP	–	–	–	–	–	–	–	–	–	–
B.1*g	Gross domestic product	100.0	100.0	100.0	100.0	100.0	100.0	100.0	100.0	100.0	100.0

1 Based on table 1.2
2 Includes taxes on products

Percentage distributions and growth rates

8.3 Value added at current basic prices analysed by industry[1,2,3]

Percentage

	1992	1993	1994	1995	1996	1997	1998	1999	2000
Agriculture, hunting, forestry and fishing	1.8	1.8	1.7	1.8	1.7	1.4	1.3	1.2	1.1
Mining and quarrying	2.5	2.4	2.4	2.6	2.9	2.5	2.1	2.1	2.9
Manufacturing	21.2	21.0	21.5	21.8	21.5	21.1	20.1	19.2	18.7
Electricity, gas and water supply	2.7	2.8	2.7	2.4	2.4	2.2	2.1	2.0	1.9
Construction	5.5	5.1	5.1	5.2	5.1	5.1	5.1	5.2	5.2
Wholesale and retail trade; repairs; hotels and restaurants	14.6	14.6	14.5	14.5	14.7	15.1	15.5	15.8	15.7
Transport, storage and communication	8.3	8.1	8.1	8.0	7.9	8.0	8.2	8.3	8.2
Financial intermediation, real estate, renting and business activities	24.0	24.7	25.1	24.9	25.0	25.5	27.3	27.8	28.7
Public administration, national defence and compulsory social security	7.2	6.9	6.5	6.2	5.8	5.5	5.2	5.0	5.1
Education, health and social work	11.8	11.9	11.9	11.9	11.9	11.9	11.9	12.3	12.3
Other services[4]	4.0	4.1	4.2	4.3	4.4	4.7	4.9	5.0	5.1
FISIM	−3.5	−3.4	−3.8	−3.6	−3.3	−3.1	−3.7	−3.9	−4.5
Gross value added at basic prices	100.0	100.0	100.0	100.0	100.0	100.0	100.0	100.0	100.0

1 Based on Table 2.2.
2 Before providing for consumption of fixed capital.
3 See footnote 2 to Table 2.3.
4 Comprising sections O,P, Q of the SIC(92).

8.4 Annual increases in categories of expenditure at 1995 prices

Percentage increase over previous year

		1992	1993	1994	1995	1996	1997	1998	1999	2000
P.3	Household final consumption expenditure	0.6	2.7	3.1	1.8	3.9	3.9	3.7	4.3	4.0
P.3	NPISH final consumption expenditure	1.9	18.3	8.0	3.7	1.3	2.2	7.1	2.8	3.4
P.3	General government final consumption	0.7	−0.7	1.0	1.7	1.2	0.1	1.5	2.8	1.6
P.5	Gross fixed capital formation:									
	Private sector	−6.7	1.6	7.9	10.2	12.0	10.1	13.4	3.0	6.1
	Public non-financial corporations	28.5	−3.7	3.1	2.6	−9.0	−13.4	−3.3	8.0	1.6
	General government	−0.2	−4.4	4.9	−0.2	−20.3	−15.6	12.8	−5.2	12.3
	Total	−0.9	0.3	4.7	3.1	4.7	7.1	13.2	0.9	4.9
P.6	Exports of goods and services	4.3	4.4	9.2	9.0	8.2	8.3	3.0	5.4	10.2
P.7	Imports of goods and services	6.8	3.3	5.7	5.4	9.6	9.7	9.6	8.9	10.7
B.1*g	Gross domestic product at market prices	0.2	2.5	4.7	2.9	2.6	3.4	3.0	2.1	2.9

8.5 Some aggregates related to the gross national income[1]

Percentage of gross national income

		1992	1993	1994	1995	1996	1997	1998	1999	2000
D.2	Taxes on production and imports[2]	14.2	13.8	13.8	14.2	14.1	14.2	14.1	14.5	14.6
D.5	Current taxes on income wealth etc	14.9	13.9	14.2	14.9	14.8	15.0	16.0	16.1	16.7
D.61	Compulsory social contributions[3]	6.1	6.2	6.2	6.2	6.1	6.2	6.2	6.3	6.2
D.91	Capital taxes	0.2	0.2	0.2	0.2	0.2	0.2	0.2	0.2	0.2
	Paid to central government	33.1	31.8	32.3	33.2	33.0	33.5	34.5	35.0	35.6
	Paid to local government	1.4	1.3	1.3	1.3	1.3	1.3	1.4	1.4	1.5
	Paid to institutions of the European Union	1.0	1.1	0.8	1.0	0.9	0.7	0.7	0.7	0.7
	Total taxes	35.4	34.1	34.4	35.5	35.2	35.6	36.6	37.1	37.8
D.3	Subsidies	1.2	1.2	1.2	1.1	1.3	1.1	0.9	0.9	0.8
	Total investment at home and abroad	15.4	14.1	16.1	16.3	16.0	17.7	18.0	15.4	14.9

1 Based on tables 1.2, 10.1 and 7.1.8.
2 Including National Insurance surcharge.
3 Including employers', employees', self employed and non-employed persons contributions

Percentage distributions and growth rates

8.6 Rates of change of gross domestic product at current market prices[1] ('money GDP')

Initial year	Terminal year																				
	1959	1960	1961	1962	1963	1964	1965	1966	1967	1968	1969	1970	1971	1972	1973	1974	1975	1976	1977	1978	1979
1958	5.7	6.2	6.1	5.8	5.9	6.5	6.7	6.7	6.5	6.7	6.8	7.0	7.4	7.7	8.2	8.5	9.5	9.9	10.3	10.5	10.8
1959		6.8	6.3	5.8	6.0	6.6	6.9	6.8	6.6	6.8	6.9	7.2	7.5	7.9	8.4	8.7	9.7	10.2	10.5	10.8	11.1
1960			5.8	5.3	5.7	6.6	6.9	6.8	6.6	6.8	6.9	7.2	7.6	8.0	8.5	8.8	9.9	10.4	10.7	11.0	11.3
1961				4.8	5.7	6.9	7.2	7.0	6.7	7.0	7.0	7.4	7.8	8.2	8.7	9.1	10.2	10.7	11.1	11.3	11.6
1962					6.5	7.9	8.0	7.6	7.1	7.3	7.4	7.7	8.1	8.5	9.1	9.4	10.6	11.2	11.5	11.7	12.1
1963						9.3	8.7	7.9	7.3	7.5	7.5	7.9	8.3	8.7	9.3	9.7	11.0	11.5	11.9	12.1	12.4
1964							8.1	7.2	6.6	7.0	7.2	7.6	8.2	8.6	9.3	9.7	11.1	11.7	12.1	12.3	12.6
1965								6.4	5.9	6.7	6.9	7.5	8.2	8.7	9.5	9.9	11.4	12.0	12.4	12.6	13.0
1966									5.3	6.8	7.1	7.8	8.5	9.1	9.9	10.3	12.0	12.6	13.0	13.2	13.5
1967										8.3	8.0	8.6	9.4	9.9	10.7	11.1	12.9	13.5	13.8	13.9	14.2
1968											7.7	8.8	9.7	10.3	11.2	11.5	13.5	14.1	14.4	14.5	14.7
1969												10.0	10.8	11.2	12.1	12.3	14.5	15.1	15.2	15.2	15.5
1970													11.6	11.8	12.8	12.9	15.5	16.0	16.0	15.9	16.1
1971														12.0	13.5	13.4	16.5	16.9	16.8	16.6	16.7
1972															15.0	14.1	18.0	18.1	17.7	17.3	17.4
1973																13.2	19.5	19.1	18.4	17.8	17.8
1974																	26.2	22.2	20.2	19.0	18.7
1975																		18.4	17.4	16.7	16.9
1976																			16.3	15.8	16.4
1977																				15.3	16.4
1978																					17.5

Initial year	Terminal year																				
	1980	1981	1982	1983	1984	1985	1986	1987	1988	1989	1990	1991	1992	1993	1994	1995	1996	1997	1998	1999	2000
1958	11.1	11.0	11.0	10.9	10.8	10.7	10.6	10.6	10.6	10.6	10.5	10.3	10.2	10.0	9.9	9.8	9.7	9.6	9.5	9.4	9.3
1959	11.4	11.3	11.2	11.1	11.0	10.9	10.8	10.8	10.8	10.7	10.7	10.5	10.3	10.1	10.0	9.9	9.8	9.7	9.6	9.5	9.4
1960	11.6	11.5	11.4	11.3	11.1	11.1	10.9	10.9	10.9	10.9	10.8	10.6	10.4	10.2	10.1	10.0	9.9	9.8	9.7	9.6	9.4
1961	11.9	11.8	11.7	11.6	11.4	11.3	11.1	11.1	11.1	11.1	11.0	10.8	10.6	10.4	10.3	10.1	10.0	9.9	9.8	9.7	9.5
1962	12.3	12.2	12.0	11.9	11.7	11.6	11.4	11.4	11.4	11.3	11.2	11.0	10.8	10.6	10.4	10.3	10.2	10.0	9.9	9.8	9.6
1963	12.7	12.5	12.3	12.2	11.9	11.8	11.6	11.6	11.6	11.5	11.4	11.2	10.9	10.7	10.6	10.4	10.3	10.1	10.0	9.9	9.7
1964	12.9	12.7	12.5	12.3	12.1	12.0	11.7	11.7	11.7	11.6	11.5	11.2	11.0	10.8	10.6	10.4	10.3	10.2	10.0	9.9	9.7
1965	13.2	13.0	12.8	12.6	12.3	12.1	11.9	11.8	11.8	11.7	11.6	11.3	11.1	10.9	10.7	10.5	10.4	10.2	10.1	9.9	9.8
1966	13.7	13.4	13.2	13.0	12.6	12.5	12.2	12.1	12.1	12.0	11.8	11.5	11.3	11.0	10.8	10.7	10.5	10.4	10.2	10.1	9.9
1967	14.4	14.0	13.7	13.5	13.1	12.9	12.6	12.4	12.4	12.3	12.1	11.8	11.5	11.3	11.1	10.9	10.7	10.5	10.4	10.2	10.0
1968	14.9	14.5	14.1	13.8	13.4	13.1	12.8	12.7	12.6	12.5	12.3	12.0	11.6	11.4	11.2	10.9	10.8	10.6	10.5	10.3	10.1
1969	15.6	15.1	14.7	14.3	13.8	13.5	13.1	13.0	12.9	12.7	12.5	12.2	11.8	11.5	11.3	11.1	10.9	10.7	10.6	10.4	10.2
1970	16.2	15.6	15.1	14.6	14.0	13.7	13.3	13.1	13.0	12.9	12.6	12.3	11.9	11.6	11.4	11.1	10.9	10.7	10.6	10.4	10.2
1971	16.7	16.0	15.4	14.8	14.2	13.9	13.4	13.2	13.1	12.9	12.7	12.3	11.9	11.6	11.4	11.1	10.9	10.7	10.5	10.3	10.1
1972	17.3	16.4	15.7	15.1	14.4	14.0	13.5	13.3	13.2	13.0	12.7	12.3	11.9	11.6	11.3	11.1	10.8	10.7	10.5	10.3	10.1
1973	17.6	16.6	15.8	15.1	14.4	14.0	13.4	13.2	13.1	12.9	12.6	12.2	11.7	11.4	11.1	10.9	10.7	10.5	10.3	10.1	9.9
1974	18.4	17.1	16.1	15.3	14.5	14.0	13.5	13.2	13.1	12.9	12.6	12.1	11.7	11.3	11.0	10.8	10.6	10.4	10.2	10.0	9.8
1975	16.9	15.6	14.7	14.0	13.3	12.9	12.4	12.2	12.1	11.9	11.7	11.3	10.9	10.5	10.3	10.1	9.9	9.7	9.5	9.3	9.1
1976	16.5	15.1	14.2	13.4	12.6	12.3	11.8	11.6	11.6	11.5	11.3	10.8	10.4	10.1	9.9	9.6	9.5	9.3	9.2	9.0	8.8
1977	16.6	14.8	13.7	13.0	12.1	11.8	11.3	11.2	11.2	11.1	10.9	10.5	10.0	9.7	9.5	9.3	9.1	9.0	8.8	8.6	8.5
1978	17.2	14.6	13.3	12.5	11.6	11.3	10.8	10.7	10.8	10.7	10.5	10.1	9.7	9.4	9.1	8.9	8.8	8.6	8.5	8.3	8.2
1979	16.9	13.2	12.0	11.3	10.4	10.3	9.9	9.9	10.1	10.0	9.9	9.5	9.1	8.8	8.6	8.4	8.3	8.2	8.1	7.9	7.7
1980		9.6	9.6	9.5	8.9	9.0	8.7	8.9	9.3	9.3	9.2	8.8	8.5	8.2	8.0	7.9	7.8	7.7	7.6	7.4	7.3
1981			9.5	9.4	8.6	8.8	8.6	8.8	9.2	9.3	9.2	8.8	8.3	8.1	7.9	7.7	7.6	7.6	7.5	7.3	7.2
1982				9.2	8.2	8.6	8.3	8.7	9.1	9.2	9.1	8.7	8.2	7.9	7.8	7.6	7.5	7.4	7.3	7.2	7.0
1983					7.2	8.3	8.0	8.5	9.1	9.2	9.1	8.6	8.1	7.8	7.7	7.5	7.4	7.3	7.2	7.1	6.9
1984						9.5	8.4	9.0	9.6	9.7	9.4	8.8	8.2	7.9	7.7	7.5	7.4	7.3	7.2	7.1	6.9
1985							7.4	8.7	9.7	9.7	9.4	8.7	8.1	7.7	7.5	7.3	7.2	7.1	7.0	6.9	6.7
1986								10.0	10.8	10.5	10.0	9.0	8.2	7.7	7.5	7.3	7.2	7.1	7.0	6.8	6.7
1987									11.6	10.7	9.9	8.7	7.8	7.4	7.2	7.0	6.9	6.8	6.7	6.6	6.4
1988										9.8	9.1	7.8	6.9	6.5	6.4	6.3	6.3	6.3	6.3	6.1	6.0
1989											8.4	6.8	5.9	5.7	5.8	5.8	5.8	5.9	5.9	5.8	5.7
1990												5.2	4.7	4.8	5.2	5.2	5.4	5.5	5.6	5.5	5.4
1991													4.2	4.7	5.1	5.2	5.4	5.6	5.6	5.5	5.4
1992														5.2	5.6	5.6	5.7	5.8	5.9	5.7	5.6
1993															6.1	5.8	5.9	6.0	6.0	5.8	5.6
1994																5.6	5.8	6.0	6.0	5.8	5.6
1995																	6.0	6.2	6.1	5.8	5.6
1996																		6.4	6.2	5.7	5.5
1997																			6.0	5.4	5.2
1998																				4.8	4.7
1999																					4.7

Percentage distributions and growth rates

8.7 Rates of change of gross domestic product at constant (1995) market prices

Percentage change, at annual rate

Initial year	Terminal year 1959	1960	1961	1962	1963	1964	1965	1966	1967	1968	1969	1970	1971	1972	1973	1974	1975	1976	1977	1978	1979
1958	4.4	4.9	4.1	3.4	3.7	4.0	3.7	3.5	3.4	3.5	3.3	3.2	3.1	3.2	3.4	3.1	2.9	2.9	2.9	2.9	2.9
1959		5.4	3.9	3.0	3.5	3.9	3.6	3.4	3.3	3.4	3.2	3.1	3.0	3.1	3.4	3.0	2.8	2.8	2.8	2.8	2.8
1960			2.5	1.9	2.9	3.5	3.3	3.1	3.0	3.1	3.0	2.9	2.8	2.9	3.2	2.9	2.6	2.7	2.6	2.7	2.7
1961				1.3	3.1	3.9	3.5	3.2	3.0	3.2	3.0	3.0	2.9	2.9	3.3	2.9	2.7	2.7	2.6	2.7	2.7
1962					5.0	5.2	4.2	3.7	3.4	3.5	3.3	3.2	3.0	3.1	3.5	3.0	2.8	2.8	2.7	2.8	2.8
1963						5.4	3.9	3.2	3.0	3.2	3.0	2.9	2.8	2.9	3.3	2.9	2.6	2.6	2.6	2.6	2.6
1964							2.4	2.1	2.2	2.7	2.5	2.5	2.4	2.6	3.1	2.6	2.3	2.4	2.4	2.4	2.4
1965								1.9	2.1	2.8	2.6	2.5	2.5	2.6	3.2	2.6	2.3	2.4	2.4	2.4	2.4
1966									2.3	3.2	2.8	2.7	2.6	2.7	3.4	2.7	2.4	2.4	2.4	2.5	2.5
1967										4.1	3.1	2.8	2.6	2.8	3.6	2.8	2.4	2.4	2.4	2.5	2.5
1968											2.0	2.2	2.1	2.5	3.4	2.6	2.1	2.2	2.2	2.3	2.4
1969												2.3	2.2	2.7	3.8	2.7	2.1	2.2	2.2	2.4	2.4
1970													2.1	2.8	4.3	2.8	2.1	2.2	2.2	2.4	2.4
1971														3.6	5.4	3.0	2.1	2.3	2.3	2.4	2.4
1972															7.2	2.7	1.6	1.9	2.0	2.2	2.3
1973																-1.6	-1.1	0.2	0.7	1.2	1.5
1974																	-0.6	1.1	1.5	2.0	2.1
1975																		2.8	2.5	2.8	2.8
1976																			2.3	2.8	2.7
1977																				3.3	3.0
1978																					2.6

Initial year	Terminal year 1980	1981	1982	1983	1984	1985	1986	1987	1988	1989	1990	1991	1992	1993	1994	1995	1996	1997	1998	1999	2000
1958	2.6	2.5	2.4	2.5	2.5	2.5	2.6	2.6	2.7	2.7	2.7	2.5	2.5	2.5	2.5	2.5	2.5	2.6	2.6	2.6	2.6
1959	2.6	2.4	2.4	2.4	2.4	2.5	2.5	2.6	2.7	2.7	2.6	2.5	2.4	2.4	2.5	2.5	2.5	2.5	2.5	2.5	2.5
1960	2.4	2.2	2.2	2.3	2.3	2.3	2.4	2.5	2.6	2.6	2.5	2.4	2.3	2.3	2.4	2.4	2.4	2.4	2.4	2.4	2.5
1961	2.4	2.2	2.2	2.3	2.3	2.3	2.4	2.5	2.6	2.6	2.5	2.4	2.3	2.3	2.4	2.4	2.4	2.4	2.4	2.4	2.4
1962	2.5	2.3	2.3	2.3	2.3	2.4	2.5	2.5	2.6	2.6	2.5	2.4	2.3	2.3	2.4	2.4	2.4	2.5	2.5	2.5	2.5
1963	2.3	2.1	2.1	2.2	2.2	2.3	2.3	2.4	2.5	2.5	2.5	2.3	2.2	2.3	2.3	2.4	2.4	2.4	2.4	2.4	2.4
1964	2.1	1.9	1.9	2.0	2.0	2.1	2.2	2.3	2.4	2.4	2.3	2.2	2.1	2.1	2.2	2.3	2.3	2.3	2.3	2.3	2.3
1965	2.1	1.9	1.9	2.0	2.0	2.1	2.2	2.3	2.4	2.4	2.3	2.2	2.1	2.1	2.2	2.2	2.3	2.3	2.3	2.3	2.3
1966	2.1	1.9	1.9	2.0	2.0	2.1	2.2	2.3	2.4	2.4	2.4	2.2	2.1	2.1	2.2	2.3	2.3	2.3	2.3	2.3	2.3
1967	2.1	1.9	1.9	2.0	2.0	2.1	2.2	2.3	2.5	2.4	2.4	2.2	2.1	2.1	2.2	2.3	2.3	2.3	2.3	2.3	2.3
1968	2.0	1.7	1.7	1.9	1.9	2.0	2.1	2.2	2.4	2.4	2.3	2.1	2.0	2.1	2.2	2.2	2.2	2.2	2.3	2.3	2.3
1969	2.0	1.7	1.7	1.8	1.9	2.0	2.1	2.2	2.4	2.4	2.3	2.1	2.1	2.1	2.2	2.2	2.2	2.3	2.3	2.3	2.3
1970	1.9	1.6	1.7	1.8	1.9	2.0	2.1	2.2	2.4	2.4	2.3	2.1	2.0	2.1	2.2	2.2	2.2	2.3	2.3	2.3	2.3
1971	1.9	1.6	1.6	1.8	1.8	2.0	2.1	2.2	2.4	2.4	2.3	2.1	2.0	2.1	2.2	2.2	2.2	2.3	2.3	2.3	2.3
1972	1.7	1.4	1.4	1.6	1.7	1.8	2.0	2.2	2.3	2.3	2.2	2.0	2.0	2.0	2.1	2.1	2.2	2.2	2.2	2.2	2.3
1973	0.9	0.6	0.8	1.1	1.2	1.4	1.6	1.8	2.0	2.0	2.0	1.8	1.7	1.7	1.9	1.9	1.9	2.0	2.0	2.0	2.1
1974	1.4	1.0	1.1	1.4	1.5	1.7	1.9	2.1	2.3	2.3	2.2	2.0	1.9	1.9	2.0	2.1	2.1	2.2	2.2	2.2	2.2
1975	1.8	1.2	1.3	1.6	1.7	1.9	2.1	2.3	2.5	2.5	2.4	2.1	2.0	2.0	2.2	2.2	2.2	2.3	2.3	2.3	2.3
1976	1.5	0.9	1.1	1.4	1.6	1.8	2.0	2.2	2.5	2.5	2.3	2.1	2.0	2.0	2.1	2.2	2.2	2.3	2.3	2.3	2.3
1977	1.3	0.6	0.9	1.3	1.5	1.7	2.0	2.2	2.5	2.5	2.3	2.1	1.9	2.0	2.1	2.2	2.2	2.3	2.3	2.3	2.3
1978	0.2	-0.3	0.2	0.9	1.2	1.5	1.8	2.1	2.4	2.4	2.3	2.0	1.8	1.9	2.1	2.1	2.1	2.2	2.2	2.2	2.3
1979	-2.1	-1.8	-0.5	0.5	0.9	1.3	1.7	2.1	2.4	2.4	2.2	1.9	1.8	1.8	2.0	2.1	2.1	2.2	2.2	2.2	2.3
1980		-1.5	0.2	1.4	1.7	2.0	2.4	2.7	3.0	2.9	2.7	2.3	2.1	2.1	2.3	2.4	2.4	2.4	2.5	2.5	2.5
1981			2.0	2.8	2.7	2.9	3.1	3.4	3.6	3.4	3.1	2.7	2.5	2.5	2.6	2.6	2.6	2.7	2.7	2.7	2.7
1982				3.6	3.1	3.3	3.4	3.6	3.9	3.6	3.3	2.8	2.5	2.5	2.7	2.7	2.7	2.7	2.8	2.7	2.7
1983					2.5	3.1	3.4	3.6	4.0	3.7	3.2	2.6	2.4	2.4	2.6	2.6	2.6	2.7	2.7	2.7	2.7
1984						3.6	3.8	4.0	4.3	3.9	3.4	2.7	2.4	2.4	2.6	2.6	2.6	2.7	2.7	2.7	2.7
1985							3.9	4.2	4.5	3.9	3.3	2.5	2.2	2.2	2.5	2.5	2.5	2.6	2.6	2.6	2.6
1986								4.5	4.8	3.9	3.1	2.2	1.9	2.0	2.3	2.4	2.4	2.5	2.5	2.5	2.5
1987									5.2	3.7	2.7	1.7	1.4	1.6	2.0	2.1	2.2	2.3	2.4	2.3	2.4
1988										2.2	1.5	0.5	0.4	0.8	1.5	1.7	1.8	2.0	2.1	2.1	2.1
1989											0.8	-0.3	-0.1	0.5	1.3	1.6	1.7	2.0	2.1	2.1	2.1
1990												-1.4	-0.6	0.4	1.5	1.8	1.9	2.1	2.2	2.2	2.3
1991													0.2	1.4	2.4	2.6	2.6	2.7	2.8	2.7	2.7
1992														2.5	3.6	3.3	3.2	3.2	3.2	3.0	3.0
1993															4.7	3.8	3.4	3.4	3.3	3.1	3.1
1994																2.9	2.8	3.0	3.0	2.8	2.8
1995																	2.6	3.0	3.0	2.8	2.8
1996																		3.4	3.2	2.9	2.9
1997																			3.0	2.6	2.7
1998																				2.1	2.5
1999																					2.9

United Kingdom National Accounts 2001, © Crown copyright 2001

Percentage distributions and growth rates

8.8 Rates of change of GDP at market prices (current prices) Per capita

Percentage change, at annual rate

Initial year	Terminal year 1980	1981	1982	1983	1984	1985	1986	1987	1988	1989	1990	1991	1992	1993	1994	1995	1996	1997	1998	1999	2000
1979	16.8	13.1	11.9	11.2	10.3	10.1	9.7	9.7	9.9	9.8	9.7	9.2	8.8	8.5	8.3	8.1	8.0	7.9	7.8	7.6	7.4
1980		9.6	9.6	9.4	8.8	8.9	8.6	8.7	9.1	9.1	9.0	8.6	8.2	7.9	7.8	7.6	7.5	7.4	7.3	7.1	7.0
1981			9.6	9.3	8.5	8.7	8.4	8.6	9.0	9.0	8.9	8.5	8.1	7.8	7.6	7.4	7.3	7.2	7.1	7.0	6.8
1982				9.1	8.0	8.4	8.1	8.4	8.9	8.9	8.8	8.4	7.9	7.6	7.5	7.3	7.2	7.1	7.0	6.8	6.7
1983					6.9	8.0	7.7	8.2	8.8	8.9	8.8	8.3	7.8	7.5	7.3	7.1	7.0	6.9	6.9	6.7	6.6
1984						9.1	8.1	8.7	9.3	9.3	9.1	8.5	7.9	7.5	7.4	7.2	7.0	7.0	6.9	6.7	6.5
1985							7.1	8.4	9.4	9.4	9.1	8.4	7.7	7.3	7.2	7.0	6.8	6.8	6.7	6.5	6.4
1986								9.8	10.5	10.2	9.6	8.6	7.8	7.4	7.2	6.9	6.8	6.7	6.6	6.5	6.3
1987									11.3	10.4	9.6	8.3	7.4	7.0	6.8	6.6	6.5	6.4	6.4	6.2	6.0
1988										9.4	8.7	7.4	6.5	6.1	6.1	5.9	5.9	5.9	5.9	5.7	5.6
1989											8.0	6.4	5.5	5.3	5.4	5.4	5.4	5.5	5.5	5.4	5.3
1990												4.7	4.3	4.5	4.8	4.9	5.0	5.1	5.2	5.1	5.0
1991													3.9	4.3	4.8	4.9	5.0	5.2	5.3	5.1	5.0
1992														4.8	5.3	5.2	5.3	5.5	5.5	5.3	5.2
1993															5.7	5.4	5.5	5.6	5.6	5.4	5.2
1994																5.2	5.4	5.6	5.6	5.4	5.2
1995																	5.6	5.8	5.8	5.4	5.2
1996																		6.0	5.8	5.3	5.1
1997																			5.6	5.0	4.7
1998																				4.4	4.3
1999																					4.2

8.9 Rates of change of GDP at market prices (1995 prices) Per capita

Percentage change, at annual rate

Initial year	Terminal year 1980	1981	1982	1983	1984	1985	1986	1987	1988	1989	1990	1991	1992	1993	1994	1995	1996	1997	1998	1999	2000
1979	-2.3	-1.9	-0.6	0.4	0.8	1.2	1.5	1.9	2.2	2.2	2.0	1.7	1.5	1.6	1.8	1.8	1.8	1.9	1.9	1.9	2.0
1980		-1.5	0.2	1.3	1.6	1.9	2.2	2.5	2.8	2.7	2.4	2.1	1.9	1.9	2.1	2.1	2.1	2.2	2.2	2.2	2.2
1981			2.0	2.8	2.6	2.8	3.0	3.2	3.4	3.2	2.9	2.4	2.2	2.2	2.3	2.4	2.4	2.4	2.4	2.4	2.4
1982				3.5	2.9	3.0	3.2	3.4	3.6	3.4	3.0	2.5	2.2	2.2	2.4	2.4	2.4	2.4	2.4	2.4	2.4
1983					2.3	2.8	3.1	3.4	3.7	3.4	2.9	2.3	2.1	2.1	2.3	2.3	2.3	2.3	2.4	2.3	2.3
1984						3.3	3.5	3.7	4.0	3.6	3.0	2.3	2.0	2.0	2.3	2.3	2.3	2.3	2.4	2.3	2.3
1985							3.6	3.9	4.3	3.6	3.0	2.2	1.8	1.9	2.1	2.2	2.2	2.3	2.3	2.3	2.3
1986								4.2	4.6	3.6	2.8	1.9	1.5	1.6	2.0	2.0	2.1	2.1	2.2	2.1	2.2
1987									4.9	3.3	2.4	1.3	1.0	1.2	1.6	1.8	1.8	1.9	2.0	2.0	2.0
1988										1.8	1.1	0.1	0.1	0.5	1.1	1.3	1.4	1.6	1.7	1.7	1.8
1989											0.4	-0.7	-0.5	0.2	1.0	1.2	1.4	1.6	1.7	1.7	1.8
1990												-1.8	-1.0	0.1	1.1	1.4	1.5	1.8	1.9	1.8	1.9
1991													-0.1	1.0	2.1	2.2	2.2	2.4	2.4	2.3	2.3
1992														2.2	3.2	3.0	2.8	2.9	2.8	2.7	2.6
1993															4.3	3.4	3.0	3.0	3.0	2.7	2.7
1994																2.5	2.4	2.6	2.6	2.4	2.4
1995																	2.3	2.7	2.7	2.4	2.4
1996																		3.1	2.8	2.5	2.5
1997																			2.6	2.1	2.2
1998																				1.7	2.1
1999																					2.4

Percentage distributions and growth rates

8.10 Rates of change of household disposable income at constant prices
Total

Percentage change, at annual rate

Initial year	Terminal year 1959	1960	1961	1962	1963	1964	1965	1966	1967	1968	1969	1970	1971	1972	1973	1974	1975	1976	1977	1978	1979
1958	5.2	5.9	5.3	4.3	4.3	4.3	4.0	3.7	3.5	3.3	3.1	3.1	3.0	3.4	3.6	3.3	3.1	2.9	2.7	2.9	3.0
1959		6.7	5.4	4.0	4.1	4.1	3.7	3.5	3.3	3.1	2.9	3.0	2.8	3.2	3.5	3.1	3.0	2.8	2.5	2.8	2.9
1960			4.2	2.7	3.2	3.5	3.2	3.0	2.8	2.7	2.5	2.6	2.5	2.9	3.2	2.9	2.8	2.6	2.3	2.6	2.7
1961				1.2	2.7	3.2	2.9	2.8	2.6	2.5	2.3	2.4	2.3	2.8	3.1	2.8	2.7	2.5	2.2	2.5	2.6
1962					4.3	4.3	3.5	3.2	2.8	2.7	2.4	2.6	2.4	3.0	3.3	2.9	2.8	2.5	2.2	2.5	2.7
1963						4.3	3.1	2.8	2.5	2.3	2.1	2.3	2.2	2.9	3.2	2.8	2.7	2.4	2.1	2.4	2.6
1964							2.0	2.1	1.9	1.9	1.7	2.0	1.9	2.7	3.1	2.7	2.5	2.3	1.9	2.3	2.5
1965								2.3	1.9	1.8	1.6	2.0	1.9	2.8	3.2	2.8	2.6	2.3	1.9	2.3	2.6
1966									1.4	1.6	1.4	2.0	1.8	2.9	3.4	2.8	2.6	2.3	1.9	2.3	2.6
1967										1.8	1.3	2.1	1.9	3.2	3.7	3.0	2.7	2.4	1.9	2.4	2.7
1968											0.9	2.3	1.9	3.5	4.1	3.2	2.9	2.5	2.0	2.5	2.8
1969												3.7	2.4	4.4	4.9	3.7	3.2	2.7	2.1	2.7	3.0
1970													1.2	4.7	5.3	3.7	3.1	2.5	1.9	2.5	2.9
1971														8.4	7.4	4.5	3.6	2.8	2.0	2.7	3.1
1972															6.4	2.6	2.0	1.4	0.7	1.8	2.3
1973																-1.0	-0.1	-0.2	-0.7	0.9	1.7
1974																	0.9	0.2	-0.5	1.4	2.2
1975																		-0.4	-1.2	1.6	2.6
1976																			-2.0	2.6	3.6
1977																				7.4	6.5
1978																					5.7

Initial year	Terminal year 1980	1981	1982	1983	1984	1985	1986	1987	1988	1989	1990	1991	1992	1993	1994	1995	1996	1997	1998	1999	2000
1958	3.0	2.8	2.7	2.7	2.7	2.7	2.8	2.8	2.9	2.9	3.0	2.9	2.9	2.9	2.9	2.9	2.9	2.9	2.8	2.8	2.9
1959	2.9	2.7	2.6	2.6	2.6	2.6	2.7	2.7	2.8	2.9	2.9	2.9	2.9	2.9	2.8	2.8	2.8	2.9	2.8	2.8	2.8
1960	2.7	2.5	2.4	2.4	2.4	2.5	2.5	2.6	2.7	2.7	2.8	2.7	2.7	2.8	2.7	2.7	2.7	2.8	2.7	2.7	2.7
1961	2.6	2.4	2.3	2.3	2.4	2.4	2.5	2.5	2.6	2.7	2.7	2.7	2.7	2.7	2.7	2.7	2.7	2.7	2.6	2.7	2.7
1962	2.7	2.5	2.4	2.4	2.4	2.5	2.5	2.6	2.7	2.7	2.8	2.7	2.7	2.8	2.7	2.7	2.7	2.8	2.7	2.7	2.7
1963	2.6	2.4	2.3	2.3	2.3	2.4	2.5	2.5	2.6	2.7	2.7	2.7	2.7	2.7	2.7	2.7	2.7	2.7	2.6	2.6	2.7
1964	2.5	2.3	2.2	2.2	2.2	2.3	2.4	2.4	2.5	2.6	2.7	2.6	2.6	2.7	2.6	2.6	2.6	2.7	2.6	2.6	2.6
1965	2.5	2.3	2.2	2.2	2.3	2.3	2.4	2.4	2.6	2.7	2.7	2.7	2.7	2.7	2.6	2.6	2.6	2.7	2.6	2.6	2.7
1966	2.5	2.3	2.2	2.2	2.2	2.3	2.4	2.5	2.6	2.7	2.7	2.7	2.7	2.7	2.7	2.7	2.6	2.7	2.6	2.6	2.7
1967	2.6	2.4	2.2	2.2	2.3	2.4	2.4	2.5	2.6	2.7	2.8	2.7	2.7	2.7	2.7	2.7	2.7	2.7	2.6	2.7	2.7
1968	2.7	2.4	2.2	2.2	2.3	2.4	2.5	2.5	2.7	2.8	2.8	2.8	2.8	2.8	2.7	2.7	2.7	2.8	2.7	2.7	2.7
1969	2.8	2.5	2.3	2.3	2.4	2.5	2.6	2.6	2.8	2.9	2.9	2.8	2.8	2.9	2.8	2.8	2.8	2.8	2.7	2.8	2.8
1970	2.7	2.4	2.2	2.2	2.3	2.4	2.5	2.6	2.7	2.8	2.9	2.8	2.8	2.8	2.8	2.8	2.8	2.8	2.7	2.7	2.8
1971	2.9	2.6	2.3	2.3	2.4	2.5	2.6	2.7	2.8	2.9	2.9	2.9	2.9	2.9	2.8	2.8	2.8	2.9	2.8	2.8	2.8
1972	2.3	1.9	1.7	1.8	1.9	2.0	2.2	2.3	2.5	2.6	2.6	2.6	2.6	2.6	2.6	2.6	2.6	2.7	2.5	2.6	2.6
1973	1.7	1.4	1.2	1.3	1.5	1.7	1.9	2.0	2.2	2.4	2.4	2.4	2.4	2.5	2.4	2.4	2.4	2.5	2.4	2.4	2.5
1974	2.1	1.7	1.5	1.6	1.8	1.9	2.1	2.2	2.4	2.6	2.6	2.6	2.6	2.6	2.6	2.6	2.6	2.7	2.5	2.6	2.6
1975	2.4	1.9	1.6	1.7	1.9	2.1	2.2	2.3	2.6	2.7	2.8	2.7	2.7	2.7	2.7	2.7	2.7	2.7	2.6	2.6	2.7
1976	3.1	2.4	1.9	2.0	2.2	2.3	2.5	2.6	2.8	3.0	3.0	2.9	2.9	2.9	2.9	2.8	2.8	2.9	2.7	2.8	2.8
1977	4.8	3.5	2.7	2.7	2.8	2.9	3.0	3.1	3.3	3.4	3.4	3.3	3.3	3.3	3.2	3.1	3.1	3.2	3.0	3.0	3.1
1978	3.6	2.2	1.6	1.8	2.1	2.3	2.5	2.6	2.9	3.0	3.1	3.0	3.0	3.0	2.9	2.9	2.9	2.9	2.8	2.8	2.9
1979	1.6	0.5	0.3	0.8	1.4	1.7	2.0	2.2	2.6	2.8	2.8	2.7	2.8	2.8	2.7	2.7	2.7	2.8	2.6	2.7	2.7
1980		-0.5	-0.3	0.6	1.3	1.7	2.1	2.3	2.7	2.9	3.0	2.9	2.9	2.9	2.8	2.8	2.8	2.9	2.7	2.7	2.8
1981			-0.2	1.1	1.9	2.3	2.7	2.8	3.2	3.3	3.4	3.2	3.2	3.2	3.1	3.0	3.0	3.1	2.9	2.9	3.0
1982				2.4	3.0	3.1	3.4	3.4	3.7	3.9	3.8	3.6	3.5	3.5	3.3	3.3	3.2	3.3	3.1	3.1	3.2
1983					3.7	3.5	3.7	3.7	4.0	4.1	4.0	3.7	3.7	3.6	3.4	3.4	3.3	3.4	3.1	3.1	3.2
1984						3.4	3.8	3.7	4.1	4.2	4.1	3.7	3.7	3.6	3.4	3.3	3.2	3.3	3.1	3.1	3.2
1985							4.1	3.8	4.3	4.4	4.2	3.8	3.7	3.6	3.4	3.3	3.2	3.3	3.0	3.1	3.2
1986								3.5	4.4	4.5	4.2	3.7	3.6	3.6	3.3	3.2	3.1	3.3	2.9	3.0	3.1
1987									5.3	5.0	4.5	3.8	3.6	3.6	3.3	3.2	3.1	3.2	2.9	2.9	3.0
1988										4.6	4.0	3.3	3.2	3.2	2.9	2.9	2.8	3.0	2.7	2.7	2.9
1989											3.5	2.6	2.8	2.9	2.6	2.6	2.6	2.8	2.4	2.5	2.7
1990												1.8	2.4	2.7	2.4	2.4	2.4	2.7	2.3	2.4	2.6
1991													3.0	3.1	2.6	2.6	2.6	2.9	2.4	2.5	2.7
1992														3.2	2.4	2.5	2.4	2.8	2.3	2.4	2.7
1993															1.6	2.1	2.2	2.7	2.1	2.3	2.6
1994																2.6	2.5	3.1	2.2	2.5	2.8
1995																	2.4	3.4	2.1	2.4	2.8
1996																		4.4	2.0	2.5	2.9
1997																			-0.4	1.5	2.5
1998																				3.5	3.9
1999																					4.4

United Kingdom National Accounts 2001, © Crown copyright 2001

Percentage distributions and growth rates

8.11 Rates of change of household disposable income at constant prices
Per capita

Percentage change, at annual rate

Initial year	Terminal year 1959	1960	1961	1962	1963	1964	1965	1966	1967	1968	1969	1970	1971	1972	1973	1974	1975	1976	1977	1978	1979
1958	4.6	5.2	4.6	3.5	3.5	3.5	3.2	3.0	2.8	2.6	2.4	2.5	2.4	2.8	3.0	2.7	2.6	2.5	2.2	2.5	2.6
1959		5.8	4.6	3.1	3.2	3.3	3.0	2.8	2.6	2.4	2.2	2.3	2.2	2.6	2.9	2.6	2.5	2.3	2.1	2.4	2.5
1960			3.4	1.8	2.4	2.7	2.4	2.3	2.1	2.0	1.8	2.0	1.9	2.4	2.7	2.4	2.3	2.1	1.9	2.2	2.3
1961				0.3	1.9	2.5	2.2	2.1	1.9	1.8	1.6	1.8	1.7	2.3	2.6	2.3	2.2	2.0	1.8	2.1	2.3
1962					3.6	3.6	2.8	2.6	2.2	2.1	1.8	2.0	1.9	2.5	2.8	2.5	2.4	2.2	1.9	2.2	2.4
1963						3.6	2.5	2.2	1.9	1.8	1.5	1.8	1.7	2.4	2.7	2.4	2.3	2.0	1.8	2.1	2.3
1964							1.4	1.6	1.3	1.3	1.1	1.5	1.4	2.2	2.6	2.3	2.1	1.9	1.6	2.0	2.3
1965								1.8	1.3	1.3	1.1	1.5	1.4	2.3	2.8	2.4	2.2	2.0	1.6	2.1	2.3
1966									0.8	1.1	0.9	1.5	1.3	2.4	3.0	2.5	2.3	2.0	1.6	2.1	2.4
1967										1.4	0.9	1.7	1.5	2.7	3.3	2.7	2.4	2.1	1.7	2.2	2.5
1968											0.4	1.9	1.5	3.1	3.7	2.9	2.6	2.2	1.7	2.3	2.6
1969												3.4	2.0	4.0	4.5	3.4	3.0	2.5	1.9	2.5	2.8
1970													0.7	4.3	4.9	3.4	2.9	2.3	1.7	2.4	2.7
1971														8.1	7.1	4.4	3.4	2.7	1.9	2.6	3.0
1972															6.2	2.5	1.9	1.4	0.7	1.8	2.3
1973																-1.0	-0.1	-0.2	-0.7	0.9	1.7
1974																	0.8	0.2	-0.6	1.4	2.2
1975																		-0.4	-1.2	1.6	2.6
1976																			-2.0	2.6	3.6
1977																				7.4	6.5
1978																					5.5

Initial year	Terminal year 1980	1981	1982	1983	1984	1985	1986	1987	1988	1989	1990	1991	1992	1993	1994	1995	1996	1997	1998	1999	2000
1958	2.6	2.4	2.3	2.3	2.4	2.4	2.4	2.5	2.6	2.6	2.6	2.6	2.6	2.6	2.6	2.6	2.6	2.6	2.5	2.5	2.5
1959	2.5	2.3	2.2	2.2	2.3	2.3	2.4	2.4	2.5	2.6	2.6	2.5	2.5	2.6	2.5	2.5	2.5	2.5	2.4	2.5	2.5
1960	2.3	2.2	2.1	2.1	2.1	2.2	2.2	2.3	2.4	2.5	2.5	2.4	2.4	2.5	2.4	2.4	2.4	2.4	2.4	2.5	2.5
1961	2.2	2.1	2.0	2.0	2.1	2.1	2.2	2.3	2.4	2.4	2.4	2.4	2.4	2.4	2.4	2.4	2.4	2.4	2.3	2.4	2.4
1962	2.4	2.2	2.1	2.1	2.1	2.2	2.3	2.3	2.4	2.5	2.5	2.5	2.5	2.5	2.5	2.5	2.4	2.5	2.4	2.4	2.4
1963	2.3	2.1	2.0	2.0	2.1	2.1	2.2	2.3	2.4	2.5	2.5	2.4	2.5	2.5	2.4	2.4	2.4	2.5	2.4	2.4	2.4
1964	2.2	2.0	1.9	1.9	2.0	2.1	2.1	2.2	2.3	2.4	2.4	2.4	2.4	2.4	2.4	2.4	2.4	2.4	2.3	2.3	2.4
1965	2.3	2.1	1.9	2.0	2.0	2.1	2.2	2.3	2.4	2.5	2.5	2.4	2.4	2.5	2.4	2.4	2.4	2.5	2.4	2.4	2.4
1966	2.3	2.1	2.0	2.0	2.1	2.1	2.2	2.3	2.4	2.5	2.5	2.5	2.5	2.5	2.4	2.4	2.4	2.5	2.4	2.4	2.4
1967	2.4	2.2	2.0	2.1	2.1	2.2	2.3	2.4	2.5	2.6	2.6	2.5	2.5	2.6	2.5	2.5	2.5	2.5	2.4	2.4	2.5
1968	2.5	2.3	2.1	2.1	2.2	2.2	2.3	2.4	2.5	2.6	2.6	2.6	2.6	2.6	2.5	2.5	2.5	2.5	2.4	2.4	2.5
1969	2.7	2.4	2.2	2.2	2.3	2.3	2.4	2.5	2.7	2.7	2.8	2.7	2.7	2.7	2.6	2.6	2.6	2.6	2.5	2.5	2.6
1970	2.6	2.3	2.1	2.1	2.2	2.3	2.4	2.5	2.6	2.7	2.7	2.7	2.7	2.7	2.6	2.6	2.6	2.6	2.5	2.5	2.6
1971	2.8	2.5	2.2	2.3	2.3	2.4	2.5	2.6	2.7	2.8	2.8	2.8	2.8	2.8	2.7	2.7	2.6	2.7	2.6	2.6	2.6
1972	2.2	1.9	1.7	1.7	1.9	2.0	2.1	2.2	2.4	2.5	2.5	2.5	2.5	2.5	2.5	2.4	2.5	2.4	2.4	2.4	2.4
1973	1.6	1.4	1.2	1.3	1.5	1.6	1.8	2.0	2.2	2.3	2.3	2.3	2.3	2.3	2.3	2.3	2.3	2.3	2.2	2.2	2.3
1974	2.1	1.7	1.5	1.6	1.7	1.9	2.0	2.2	2.4	2.5	2.5	2.5	2.5	2.5	2.4	2.4	2.4	2.5	2.3	2.4	2.4
1975	2.4	1.9	1.6	1.7	1.8	2.0	2.2	2.3	2.5	2.6	2.7	2.6	2.6	2.6	2.5	2.5	2.5	2.6	2.4	2.4	2.5
1976	3.1	2.3	1.9	2.0	2.1	2.2	2.4	2.6	2.8	2.9	2.9	2.8	2.8	2.8	2.7	2.7	2.6	2.7	2.5	2.6	2.6
1977	4.8	3.4	2.7	2.6	2.7	2.8	2.9	3.0	3.2	3.3	3.3	3.1	3.1	3.1	3.0	2.9	2.9	2.9	2.8	2.8	2.8
1978	3.5	2.1	1.5	1.7	2.0	2.1	2.4	2.5	2.8	2.9	2.9	2.8	2.8	2.8	2.7	2.7	2.6	2.7	2.5	2.6	2.6
1979	1.5	0.5	0.2	0.8	1.3	1.6	1.9	2.2	2.5	2.7	2.7	2.6	2.6	2.6	2.5	2.5	2.5	2.6	2.4	2.4	2.5
1980		-0.5	-0.4	0.5	1.2	1.6	2.0	2.3	2.6	2.8	2.8	2.7	2.7	2.7	2.6	2.6	2.5	2.6	2.4	2.5	2.5
1981			-0.2	1.0	1.8	2.1	2.5	2.7	3.1	3.2	3.2	3.0	3.0	3.0	2.8	2.8	2.7	2.8	2.6	2.6	2.7
1982				2.3	2.8	2.9	3.2	3.3	3.6	3.7	3.6	3.4	3.3	3.3	3.1	3.0	3.0	3.0	2.8	2.8	2.9
1983					3.4	3.2	3.5	3.6	3.9	3.9	3.8	3.5	3.4	3.4	3.2	3.1	3.0	3.1	2.8	2.8	2.9
1984						3.1	3.6	3.7	4.0	4.1	3.9	3.5	3.4	3.4	3.2	3.1	3.0	3.1	2.8	2.8	2.9
1985							4.0	4.0	4.3	4.3	4.1	3.6	3.5	3.4	3.2	3.1	3.0	3.1	2.8	2.8	2.8
1986								3.9	4.5	4.4	4.1	3.5	3.4	3.3	3.1	3.0	2.9	3.0	2.7	2.7	2.8
1987									5.0	4.6	4.1	3.4	3.3	3.2	2.9	2.8	2.7	2.9	2.5	2.6	2.7
1988										4.3	3.7	2.9	2.8	2.8	2.6	2.5	2.5	2.6	2.3	2.4	2.5
1989											3.1	2.2	2.4	2.5	2.2	2.2	2.2	2.4	2.1	2.2	2.3
1990												1.4	2.0	2.3	2.0	2.1	2.1	2.3	1.9	2.1	2.2
1991													2.7	2.8	2.3	2.2	2.2	2.5	2.0	2.1	2.3
1992														2.9	2.1	2.1	2.1	2.5	1.9	2.1	2.3
1993															1.3	1.7	1.8	2.4	1.7	1.9	2.2
1994																2.2	2.1	2.7	1.9	2.1	2.4
1995																	2.0	3.0	1.7	2.1	2.4
1996																		4.0	1.6	2.1	2.5
1997																			-0.8	1.1	2.0
1998																				3.0	3.5
1999																					3.9

Part 4

Chapter 9

Fixed capital formation supplementary tables

Fixed capital formation supplementary tables

9.1 Gross fixed capital formation at current purchasers' prices
Analysis by type of asset and sector
Total economy

£ million

		1992	1993	1994	1995	1996	1997	1998	1999	2000
New dwellings, excluding land										
Public non-financial corporations	DEER	172	150	139	162	151	123	49	11	5
Private non-financial corporations	DLWG	192	206	211	217	231	253	269	280	304
Financial corporations	DFIX	–	–	–	–	–	–	–	–	–
Central government	DFIZ	218	368	320	221	314	289	273	250	369
Local government	DKQC	2 189	2 250	2 489	2 421	1 834	1 499	1 583	1 551	1 709
Households and NPISH	DLWK	16 054	16 918	18 074	18 643	19 918	21 765	23 052	23 920	25 436
Total	DFDK	18 825	19 892	21 233	21 664	22 448	23 929	25 226	26 012	27 823
Other buildings and structures										
Public non-financial corporations	DEES	3 332	3 416	3 492	3 781	3 397	2 671	2 465	2 662	2 857
Private non-financial corporations	DLWN	15 922	13 721	13 942	15 279	17 766	20 958	23 196	26 726	28 779
Financial corporations	GGBT	1 503	1 512	1 390	1 470	1 235	1 923	2 745	2 604	1 967
Central government	DLWP	5 143	4 550	4 853	4 575	3 948	2 954	3 057	2 518	2 723
Local government	DJYS	4 682	5 207	5 265	5 464	4 745	4 602	5 084	5 521	6 577
Households and NPISH	DLWR	957	1 019	1 098	1 274	1 751	2 343	2 476	2 734	2 409
Total	DLWS	31 539	29 425	30 040	31 843	32 842	35 451	39 023	42 765	45 312
Transport equipment										
Public non-financial corporations	DEEP	678	516	512	354	225	190	171	130	152
Private non-financial corporations	DLWU	5 635	6 863	8 539	8 343	8 406	11 251	13 417	13 124	14 625
Financial corporations	GGBR	716	328	613	967	2 066	252	851	516	414
Central government	DLWW	525	505	542	482	501	491	546	384	346
Local government	DKPN	205	179	229	235	171	184	212	227	236
Households and NPISH	DLWY	661	924	960	914	844	817	1 098	956	973
Total	DLWZ	8 420	9 315	11 395	11 295	12 213	13 185	16 295	15 337	16 746
Other machinery and equipment and cultivated assets										
Public non-financial corporations	DEEQ	873	720	761	857	765	705	758	945	740
Private non-financial corporations	DLXD	27 924	28 335	30 331	36 280	40 139	43 288	50 558	49 924	51 794
Financial corporations	DLXE	2 370	1 999	2 968	3 009	3 609	2 821	4 034	2 677	3 603
Central government	DLXF	1 692	1 653	1 349	1 456	1 432	1 090	887	1 051	930
Local government	DLXG	493	502	530	542	420	362	391	424	429
Households and NPISH	DLXH	1 719	2 107	2 287	2 868	3 362	3 678	3 746	3 943	4 329
Total	DLXI	35 071	35 316	38 226	45 012	49 727	51 944	60 374	58 964	61 827
Intangible fixed assets										
Public non-financial corporations	DLXJ	256	279	374	496	585	595	605	625	640
Private non-financial corporations	DLXK	2 759	2 566	2 403	2 585	2 664	2 811	2 684	2 535	2 680
Financial corporations	DLXL	413	432	450	462	477	454	678	743	818
Central government	DLXM	118	124	129	132	137	130	194	213	234
Local government	DLXN	118	123	128	132	136	129	193	212	233
Households and NPISH	DLXO	118	124	129	132	137	130	193	212	234
Total	DLXP	3 782	3 648	3 613	3 939	4 136	4 249	4 547	4 540	4 839
Costs associated with the transfer of ownership of non-produced assets										
Public non-financial corporations	DLXQ	358	376	349	126	133	267	352	381	432
Private non-financial corporations	DLXR	1 844	3 241	441	1 740	3 206	2 938	858	2 603	1 665
Financial corporations	DLXS	681	–67	1 739	–317	–691	758	2 969	997	4 935
Central government	DLXT	144	112	79	66	–1 039	–932	–400	–280	–45
Local government	DLXU	–1 482	–2 146	–1 829	–1 670	–1 393	–1 343	–1 359	–1 964	–2 389
Households and NPISH	DLXV	1 401	1 915	3 028	3 750	4 180	3 950	3 654	6 053	4 102
Total	DFBH	2 946	3 431	3 807	3 695	4 396	5 638	6 074	7 790	8 700

				1992	1993	1994	1995	1996	1997	1998	1999	2000
P.51		**Gross fixed capital formation**										
S.11001		Public non-financial corporations	FCCJ	5 669	5 457	5 627	5 776	5 256	4 551	4 400	4 754	4 831
S.11002		Private non-financial corporations	FDBM	54 277	54 931	55 867	64 444	72 413	81 501	90 985	95 193	99 845
S.12		Financial corporations	NHCJ	5 683	4 204	7 160	5 590	6 696	6 208	11 277	7 537	11 737
S.1311		Central government	NMES	7 840	7 312	7 272	6 932	5 293	4 022	4 557	4 136	4 557
S.1313		Local government	NMOA	6 205	6 115	6 812	7 124	5 913	5 433	6 104	5 971	6 792
S.14+S.15		Households and NPISH	NSSU	20 909	23 008	25 576	27 582	30 191	32 681	34 216	37 817	37 485
S.1, P.51		Total gross fixed capital formation	NPQX	100 583	101 027	108 314	117 448	125 762	134 396	151 539	155 408	165 247

1 Components may not sum to totals due to rounding.

Fixed capital formation supplementary tables

9.2 Gross fixed capital formation at current purchasers' prices
Analysis by broad sector and type of asset
Total economy
£ million

			1992	1993	1994	1995	1996	1997	1998	1999	2000
	Private sector										
	New dwellings, excluding land	EQBT	16 246	17 124	18 285	18 860	20 149	22 018	23 321	24 200	25 740
	Other buildings and structures	EQBU	18 382	16 252	16 430	18 023	20 752	25 224	28 417	32 064	33 155
	Transport equipment	EQBV	7 012	8 115	10 112	10 224	11 316	12 320	15 366	14 596	16 012
	Other machinery and equipment and cultivated assets	EQBW	32 013	32 441	35 586	42 157	47 110	49 787	58 338	56 544	59 726
	Intangible fixed assets	EQBX	3 290	3 122	2 982	3 179	3 278	3 395	3 555	3 490	3 732
	Costs associated with the transfer of ownership of non-produced assets	EQBY	3 926	5 089	5 208	5 173	6 695	7 646	7 481	9 653	10 702
P.51	Total	EQBZ	80 869	82 143	88 603	97 616	109 300	120 390	136 478	140 547	149 067
S.11001	**Public non-financial corporations**										
	New dwellings, excluding land	DEER	172	150	139	162	151	123	49	11	5
	Other buildings and structures	DEES	3 332	3 416	3 492	3 781	3 397	2 671	2 465	2 662	2 857
	Transport equipment	DEEP	678	516	512	354	225	190	171	130	152
	Other machinery and equipment and cultivated assets	DEEQ	873	720	761	857	765	705	758	945	740
	Intangible fixed assets	DLXJ	256	279	374	496	585	595	605	625	640
	Costs associated with the transfer of ownership of non-produced assets	DLXQ	358	376	349	126	133	267	352	381	432
P.51	Total	FCCJ	5 669	5 457	5 627	5 776	5 256	4 551	4 400	4 754	4 831
S.13	**General government**										
	New dwellings, excluding land	DFHW	2 407	2 618	2 809	2 642	2 148	1 788	1 856	1 801	2 078
	Other buildings and structures	EQCH	9 825	9 757	10 118	10 039	8 693	7 556	8 141	8 039	9 299
	Transport equipment	EQCI	730	684	771	717	672	675	758	611	580
	Other machinery and equipment and cultivated assets	EQCJ	2 185	2 155	1 879	1 998	1 852	1 452	1 278	1 475	1 359
	Intangible fixed assets	EQCK	236	247	257	264	273	259	387	425	467
	Costs associated with the transfer of ownership of non-produced assets	EQCL	−1 338	−2 034	−1 750	−1 604	−2 432	−2 275	−1 759	−2 244	−2 434
P.51	Total	NNBF	14 045	13 427	14 084	14 056	11 206	9 455	10 661	10 107	11 349
P.51	Total gross fixed capital formation	NPQX	100 583	101 027	108 314	117 448	125 762	134 396	151 539	155 408	165 247

1 Components may not sum to totals due to rounding.

9.3 Gross fixed capital formation at current purchasers' prices
Analysis by type of asset
Total economy
£ million

		1992	1993	1994	1995	1996	1997	1998	1999	2000
Tangible fixed assets										
New dwellings, excluding land	DFDK	18 825	19 892	21 233	21 664	22 448	23 929	25 226	26 012	27 823
Other buildings and structures	DLWS	31 539	29 425	30 040	31 843	32 842	35 451	39 023	42 765	45 312
Transport equipment	DLWZ	8 420	9 315	11 395	11 295	12 213	13 185	16 295	15 337	16 746
Other machinery and equipment and cultivated assets	DLXI	35 071	35 316	38 226	45 012	49 727	51 944	60 374	58 964	61 827
Total	EQCQ	93 855	93 948	100 894	109 814	117 230	124 509	140 918	143 078	151 708
Intangible fixed assets	DLXP	3 782	3 648	3 613	3 939	4 136	4 249	4 547	4 540	4 839
Costs associated with the transfer of ownership of non-produced assets	DFBH	2 946	3 431	3 807	3 695	4 396	5 638	6 074	7 790	8 700
P.51 Total gross fixed capital formation	NPQX	100 583	101 027	108 314	117 448	125 762	134 396	151 539	155 408	165 247

1 Components may not sum to totals due to rounding.

United Kingdom National Accounts 2001, © Crown copyright 2001

Fixed capital formation supplementary tables

9.4 Gross fixed capital formation at 1995 purchasers' prices[1]
Analysis by broad sector and type of asset
Total economy

£ million at 1995 prices

			1992	1993	1994	1995	1996	1997	1998	1999	2000
	Private sector										
	New dwellings, excluding land	DFDP	17 311	18 353	19 076	18 860	19 607	20 824	20 967	20 472	21 001
	Other buildings and structures	EQCU	19 288	18 018	18 018	18 023	19 776	23 802	25 731	27 748	27 524
	Transport equipment	EQCV	7 722	8 978	10 666	10 224	10 951	11 921	15 178	13 739	15 021
	Other machinery and equipment and cultivated assets	EQCW	35 179	33 758	36 169	42 157	47 089	51 542	64 472	65 639	70 541
	Intangible fixed assets	EQCX	3 417	3 154	2 997	3 179	3 298	3 288	3 249	3 078	3 174
	Costs associated with the transfer of ownership of non-produced assets	EQCY	5 045	5 821	5 705	5 173	6 094	6 199	5 530	5 693	5 374
P.51	Total	EQCZ	82 917	82 261	92 631	97 616	106 815	117 576	135 127	136 369	142 635
S.11001	**Public non-financial corporations**										
	New dwellings, excluding land [2]	DEEW	185	169	150	162	147	119	46	10	5
	Other buildings and structures [2]	DEEX	3 993	4 391	3 847	3 781	3 154	2 508	2 225	2 317	2 427
	Transport equipment [2]	DEEU	621	459	529	354	223	180	159	118	143
	Other machinery and equipment and cultivated assets [2]	DEEV	823	639	766	857	768	731	801	1 006	790
	Intangible fixed assets	EQDE	274	294	387	496	571	553	554	553	548
	Costs associated with the transfer of ownership of non-produced assets	EQDF	351	368	355	126	151	288	363	385	434
P.51	Total	EQDG	5 863	5 932	6 031	5 776	5 014	4 379	4 148	4 389	4 348
S.13	**General government**										
	New dwellings, excluding land	DFID	2 568	2 932	3 041	2 642	2 114	1 728	1 733	1 587	1 750
	Other buildings and structures	EQDI	10 192	10 963	11 287	10 039	8 431	7 391	7 239	6 977	7 854
	Transport equipment	EQDJ	786	745	804	717	659	693	696	556	540
	Other machinery and equipment and cultivated assets	EQDK	2 297	2 184	1 857	1 998	1 834	1 464	1 338	1 578	1 460
	Intangible fixed assets	EQDL	226	231	247	264	293	262	353	373	393
	Costs associated with the transfer of ownership of non-produced assets	EQDM	−1 756	−2 344	−1 937	−1 604	−2 184	−1 826	−1 542	−1 363	−1 214
P.51	Total	EQDN	14 233	14 721	15 300	14 056	11 147	9 712	9 817	9 708	10 783
P.51	Total gross fixed capital formation	NPQR	108 556	108 887	113 961	117 448	122 976	131 667	149 092	150 466	157 766

1 For the years before 1994, totals differ from the sum of their components.
2 Data not available for years before 1994.
3 Components may not sum to totals due to rounding.

9.5 Gross fixed capital formation at 1995 purchasers' prices[1]
Analysis by type of asset
Total economy

£ million at 1995 prices

		1992	1993	1994	1995	1996	1997	1998	1999	2000
Tangible fixed assets										
New dwellings, excluding land	DFDV	20 041	21 492	22 267	21 664	21 868	22 671	22 746	22 069	22 756
Other buildings and structures	EQDP	32 881	32 779	33 151	31 843	31 361	33 701	35 195	37 042	37 805
Transport equipment	DLWJ	9 279	10 281	11 998	11 295	11 833	12 794	16 033	14 413	15 704
Other machinery and equipment and cultivated assets	DLWM	38 429	36 679	38 791	45 012	49 691	53 737	66 611	68 223	72 792
Total	EQDS	101 028	101 456	106 207	109 814	114 753	122 903	140 585	141 747	149 057
Intangible fixed assets	EQDT	3 917	3 679	3 631	3 939	4 162	4 103	4 156	4 004	4 115
Costs associated with the transfer of ownership of non-produced assets	DFDW	3 715	3 889	4 123	3 695	4 061	4 661	4 351	4 715	4 594
P.51 Total gross fixed capital formation	NPQR	108 556	108 887	113 961	117 448	122 976	131 667	149 092	150 466	157 766

1 For the years before 1994, totals differ from the sum of their components.
2 Components may not sum to totals due to rounding.

Fixed capital formation supplementary tables

9.6 Consumption of fixed capital analysis by industry at current prices[1]

£ million

		1992	1993	1994	1995	1996	1997	1998	1999	2000
Agriculture, hunting, forestry and fishing	CIGG	1 739	1 820	1 911	2 025	2 148	2 161	2 124	2 125	2 001
Mining and quarrying	CIGH	6 001	6 144	6 038	6 181	6 219	6 173	6 123	5 945	5 616
Manufacturing	CIGI	16 268	18 354	17 815	17 426	16 828	16 790	16 031	16 057	16 097
Electricity, gas and water supply	CIGJ	4 239	4 442	4 736	5 135	5 405	5 618	5 711	5 766	5 681
Construction	CIGK	1 251	1 379	1 329	1 284	1 236	1 285	1 301	1 402	1 420
Wholesale and retail trade; repairs; hotels and restaurants	CIGL	6 022	6 719	6 584	6 750	6 791	6 745	6 807	6 947	7 496
Transport and storage	CIGM	3 441	3 608	3 969	4 097	4 462	4 882	4 749	5 192	5 431
Post and telecommunications	CIGN	3 486	3 772	4 002	4 228	4 424	4 847	4 913	5 326	5 770
Financial intermediation, real estate, renting and business activities	CIGO	10 061	11 616	11 725	11 272	11 463	11 816	12 415	12 686	14 715
Dwellings	EXCT	12 149	12 330	12 991	13 968	14 745	15 485	16 761	18 205	19 580
Other services[2]	CIGP	9 512	9 907	10 254	10 898	11 522	12 091	12 569	13 209	13 540
Transfer costs of land and buildings	EXCU	2 946	3 431	3 807	3 695	4 396	5 638	6 570	7 790	8 700
Total	NQAE	77 115	83 522	85 161	86 959	89 639	93 531	96 074	100 650	106 047

9.7 Consumption of fixed capital analysis by industry at 1995 prices[1]

£ million at 1995 prices

		1992	1993	1994	1995	1996	1997	1998	1999	2000
Agriculture, hunting, forestry and fishing	CIGQ	2 022	2 016	2 022	2 025	2 051	2 055	2 022	1 992	1 913
Mining and quarrying	CIGR	6 694	6 715	6 423	6 181	5 932	5 719	5 553	5 253	5 016
Manufacturing	CIGS	18 696	19 773	18 498	17 426	16 350	16 492	15 993	16 138	16 421
Electricity, gas and water supply	CIGT	4 685	4 818	4 998	5 135	5 245	5 391	5 470	5 574	5 660
Construction	CIGU	1 438	1 533	1 418	1 284	1 206	1 222	1 213	1 255	1 262
Wholesale and retail trade; repairs; hotels and restaurants	CIGV	6 675	7 222	6 844	6 750	6 644	6 653	6 730	6 815	7 294
Transport and storage	CIGW	3 967	4 059	4 184	4 097	4 325	4 511	4 409	4 804	5 111
Post and telecommunications	CIGX	3 837	3 930	4 063	4 228	4 411	4 601	4 990	5 293	5 951
Financial intermediation, real estate, renting and business activities	CIGY	10 526	12 006	11 878	11 272	11 484	11 793	12 815	13 148	15 117
Dwellings	EXDG	12 901	13 258	13 626	13 968	14 346	14 728	15 084	15 452	15 822
Other services[2]	CIGZ	10 159	10 752	10 813	10 898	11 083	11 247	11 501	11 949	12 361
Transfer costs of land and buildings	EXDH	3 607	3 831	4 115	3 695	4 071	4 660	4 346	4 729	4 592
Total	CIHA	85 207	89 913	88 882	86 959	87 148	89 072	90 126	92 402	96 520

1 Differences between totals and sums of components are due to rounding.
2 Comprising sections L, M, N, O, P and Q of the SIC(92).

Fixed capital formation supplementary tables

9.8 Consumption of fixed capital analysis by sector at current prices[1]

£ million

		1992	1993	1994	1995	1996	1997	1998	1999	2000
Dwellings:										
Public non-financial corporations	CIHD	1 756	1 687	1 637	1 596	1 545	1 497	1 525	1 573	1 514
of which Local authority housing	EXFC	1 568	1 506	1 446	1 389	1 332	1 279	1 229	1 197	1 263
Private non-financial corporations[2]	CIHC	340	356	475	638	729	818	937	1 077	1 111
Financial corporations	BGUS	–	–	–	–	–	–	–	–	–
Central government	EXFB	53	55	59	66	72	75	77	88	97
Local government[5]	BHGY	..	..	..	..	..	..	..	..	..
Households & NPISHs[3]	CIHB	10 000	10 232	10 820	11 668	12 399	13 095	14 222	15 467	16 858
Total	EXCT	12 149	12 330	12 991	13 968	14 745	15 485	16 761	18 205	19 580
Other tangible assets[4]:										
Public non-financial corporations	CIHH	3 987	4 232	4 512	4 728	3 969	3 305	3 202	3 104	3 049
Private non-financial corporations[2]	CIHF	41 810	46 630	47 001	47 532	49 202	51 541	51 796	53 735	56 693
Financial corporations	CIHG	3 619	4 176	4 066	3 647	3 579	3 457	3 571	3 383	3 564
Central government	CIHI	3 582	3 374	3 361	3 588	3 822	4 074	4 200	4 230	4 051
Local government	CIHJ	2 238	2 228	2 357	2 581	2 777	2 937	3 009	3 149	3 267
Households & NPISHs[3]	CIHE	6 117	6 781	7 103	7 131	7 734	8 733	9 233	10 288	11 075
Total	CIHK	61 353	67 421	68 400	69 207	71 083	74 047	75 011	77 889	81 699
Intangible assets:										
Public non-financial corporations	BGTZ	125	146	163	192	226	274	325	383	420
Private non-financial corporations[2]	BGTX	2 767	2 856	2 844	2 841	2 855	2 921	3 059	3 109	3 140
Financial corporations	BGTY	400	426	423	416	403	445	523	591	669
Central government	BGUA	114	122	121	119	116	128	142	171	193
Local government	BGUB	88	91	93	93	89	102	106	129	153
Households & NPISHs[3]	BGTW	119	130	126	123	122	129	147	173	193
Total	BGUC	3 613	3 771	3 770	3 784	3 811	3 999	4 302	4 556	4 768
All assets:										
Public non-financial corporations	NSRM	5 868	6 065	6 312	6 516	5 740	5 076	5 052	5 060	4 983
Private non-financial corporations[2]	NSRK	44 917	49 842	50 320	51 011	52 786	55 280	55 792	57 921	60 944
Financial corporations	NHCE	4 019	4 602	4 489	4 063	3 982	3 902	4 094	3 974	4 233
Central government	NSRN	3 749	3 551	3 541	3 773	4 010	4 277	4 419	4 489	4 341
Local government	NSRO	2 326	2 319	2 450	2 674	2 866	3 039	3 115	3 278	3 420
Households & NPISHs[3]	QWLL	16 236	17 143	18 049	18 922	20 255	21 957	23 602	25 928	28 126
Total	NQAE	77 115	83 522	85 161	86 959	89 639	93 531	96 074	100 650	106 047

1 Differences between totals and sums of components are due to rounding.
2 Including quasi-corporations.
3 Non-profit institutions serving households.
4 Including transfer costs of land and buildings. They are wholly written off in the year incurred.
5 Figures for council housing have been transferred from the Local Government Sector to Public non-financial corporations.

Fixed capital formation supplementary tables

9.9 Net capital stock analysis by sector and type of asset at current prices[1]

£ billion

		1992	1993	1994	1995	1996	1997	1998	1999	2000
New dwellings:										
Public non-financial corporations	CIWY	96.5	95.4	92.4	87.1	82.6	81.2	81.5	79.3	79.4
of which Local authority housing	EXHA	82.3	81.2	77.4	71.5	66.7	64.7	64.0	61.5	60.8
Private non-financial corporations[2]	CIWW	13.4	14.4	20.6	27.9	32.1	36.7	42.6	46.1	51.0
Financial corporations	CIWX	–	–	–	–	–	–	–	–	–
Central government	EXGZ	4.1	4.4	4.9	5.3	5.6	6.1	6.7	7.1	7.8
Local government[4]	ZLCT	–	–	–	–	–	–	–	–	–
Households & NPISHs[3]	CIWV	479.0	487.9	515.5	545.3	570.3	614.3	676.3	718.8	784.8
Total	CIWZ	593.0	602.1	633.4	665.6	690.6	738.3	807.1	851.3	923.0
Other buildings and structures:										
Public non-financial corporations	CIXD	39.9	40.8	45.7	52.0	34.8	37.1	39.6	41.8	45.5
Private non-financial corporations[2]	CIXB	227.4	231.0	252.6	282.9	327.1	348.2	373.7	393.4	427.5
Financial corporations	CIXC	33.8	33.7	36.6	40.6	42.4	44.9	49.3	53.3	57.9
Central government	CIXE	104.9	105.0	115.1	129.0	138.9	144.8	149.6	149.8	153.1
Local government	EXHH	102.6	102.5	112.3	126.8	135.6	140.9	147.2	152.8	165.4
Households & NPISHs[3]	CIXA	29.3	29.3	32.5	35.7	38.0	41.8	45.6	49.5	55.0
Total	CIXF	537.9	542.3	594.8	667.0	716.8	757.7	805.0	840.6	904.4
Transport equipment:										
Public non-financial corporations	CIWM	4.8	5.2	5.7	5.9	2.8	2.7	2.6	2.5	2.5
Private non-financial corporations[2]	CIWK	35.8	36.2	38.7	40.4	44.9	47.9	52.9	56.7	63.1
Financial corporations	CIWL	6.9	6.4	5.9	5.7	6.5	5.8	5.2	4.3	3.7
Central government	CIWN	2.6	2.7	3.0	3.0	3.0	2.9	2.8	2.7	2.4
Local government	EXGM	1.3	1.2	1.2	1.1	1.0	0.9	0.9	0.8	1.0
Households & NPISHs[3]	BGUU	7.6	7.5	7.7	7.8	7.5	7.1	7.2	7.1	7.2
Total	BGUV	59.0	59.2	62.2	63.9	65.7	67.3	71.6	74.1	79.9
Other machinery and equipment:										
Public non-financial corporations	CIWR	23.3	22.8	21.9	21.0	10.2	9.3	8.7	8.3	7.9
Private non-financial corporations[2]	CIWP	279.3	288.9	294.9	304.5	322.9	327.9	339.3	353.0	372.6
Financial corporations	CIWQ	14.2	14.0	13.7	13.3	13.7	12.3	12.6	14.6	17.6
Central government	CIWS	11.2	11.2	11.5	11.5	11.9	11.6	10.9	10.5	10.0
Local government	CIWT	4.9	4.7	4.7	4.6	4.4	4.3	4.0	3.8	3.5
Households & NPISHs[3]	CIWO	17.1	17.9	18.8	20.0	21.6	23.0	24.5	26.4	28.6
Total	CIWU	350.0	359.5	365.5	374.9	384.7	388.4	400.0	416.6	440.2
Intangible assets:										
Public non-financial corporations	BGUN	1.0	1.2	1.5	1.8	2.3	2.7	3.1	3.5	3.9
Private non-financial corporations[2]	BGUL	15.3	15.4	15.2	15.3	15.5	16.0	16.2	16.1	16.3
Financial corporations	BGUM	1.1	1.1	1.1	1.0	1.1	1.2	1.5	1.7	1.9
Central government	BGUO	0.3	0.3	0.3	0.3	0.3	0.4	0.4	0.5	0.5
Local government	BGUP	0.4	0.4	0.4	0.4	0.4	0.5	0.5	0.6	0.7
Households & NPISHs[3]	BGUK	0.3	0.3	0.3	0.3	0.3	0.4	0.4	0.5	0.5
Total	BGUQ	18.4	18.7	18.8	19.1	19.9	21.2	22.1	22.9	23.8
All assets:										
Public non-financial corporations	CIXJ	165.5	165.4	167.2	167.8	132.7	133.0	135.5	135.4	139.2
Private non-financial corporations[2]	CIXH	571.2	585.9	622.0	671.0	742.5	776.7	824.7	865.3	930.5
Financial corporations	CIXI	56.0	55.2	57.3	60.6	63.7	64.2	68.6	73.9	81.1
Central government	CIXK	123.1	123.6	134.8	149.1	159.7	165.8	170.4	170.6	173.8
Local government	CIXL	109.2	108.8	118.6	132.9	141.4	146.6	152.6	158.0	170.6
Households & NPISHs[3]	CIXG	533.3	542.9	574.8	609.1	637.7	686.6	754.0	802.3	876.1
Total	CIXM	1 558.3	1 581.8	1 674.7	1 790.5	1 877.7	1 972.9	2 105.8	2 205.5	2 371.3

1 Differences between totals and sums of the components are due to rounding.
2 Including quasi-corporations.
3 Non-profit instituions serving households.
4 Figures for council housing have been transferred from the Local Government sector to Public non-financial corporations.
5 Constant price data by industry is now available by request

United Kingdom National Accounts 2001, © Crown copyright 2001

Fixed capital formation supplementary tables

9.10 Gross capital stock analysis by industry at 1995 prices[1]

£ billion at 1995 prices

		1992	1993	1994	1995	1996	1997	1998	1999	2000
Agriculture, hunting, forestry and fishing	CIXN	45.3	45.6	46.0	46.3	46.6	46.6	46.1	45.4	44.6
Mining and quarrying	CIXO	89.6	88.9	86.8	85.3	83.9	82.5	81.8	79.6	76.7
Manufacturing	CIXP	388.3	379.1	372.8	371.0	371.2	373.2	377.0	378.8	380.2
Electricity, gas and water supply	CIXQ	178.9	182.6	185.4	187.1	187.9	189.2	190.7	192.3	193.0
Construction	CIXR	23.9	23.4	23.2	23.2	23.2	23.9	24.4	24.9	25.4
Wholesale and retail trade; repairs; hotels and restaurants	CIXS	157.8	161.3	165.2	171.5	177.6	186.3	198.7	209.7	221.2
Transport and storage	CIXT	99.4	101.5	105.0	106.0	106.1	109.9	114.0	118.9	124.9
Post and telecommunications	CIXU	70.3	71.2	71.4	73.0	77.5	81.0	87.4	95.0	104.9
Financial intermediation, real estate, renting, and business activities	CIXV	219.6	225.7	234.5	244.3	258.4	268.6	287.4	307.8	331.7
Dwellings	EXEO	957.1	975.1	993.9	1 012.0	1 030.2	1 049.1	1 067.3	1 084.7	1 102.7
Other services[2]	CIXW	441.4	452.6	464.4	475.4	485.1	494.6	505.3	516.3	527.2
Total	CIXX	2 671.8	2 707.3	2 748.7	2 795.4	2 848.1	2 905.1	2 980.4	3 053.7	3 132.5

1 Differences between totals and sums of components are due to rounding.
2 Comprising sections L,M,N,O,P+Q of SIC(92)
3 Current price data by industry is now available by request

9.11 Gross capital stock analysis by type of asset at 1995 prices[1]

£ billion at 1995 prices

		1992	1993	1994	1995	1996	1997	1998	1999	2000
New dwellings	EXEO	957.1	975.1	993.9	1 012.0	1 030.2	1 049.1	1 067.3	1 084.7	1 102.7
Other buildings and structures	CIYA	882.5	906.8	930.5	951.9	972.4	994.6	1 018.7	1 044.7	1 072.7
Road vehicles	CIXY	106.3	106.1	106.1	106.0	104.5	100.9	100.7	99.6	101.2
Railway rolling stock, ships and aircraft	EXER	16.1	16.7	17.6	16.7	16.7	18.3	20.2	22.1	24.0
Other machinery and equipment	CIXZ	673.5	666.0	664.1	672.0	687.0	704.3	734.9	763.8	792.9
Intangible assets	BGUR	36.3	36.6	36.5	36.8	37.3	37.9	38.6	38.8	39.0
Total	CIXX	2 671.8	2 707.3	2 748.7	2 795.4	2 848.1	2 905.1	2 980.4	3 053.7	3 132.5

1 Differences between totals and sums of components are due to rounding.

Part 4

Chapter 10

Non-financial balance sheets

Chapter 10:
Non-financial balance sheets

The non-financial balance sheets show the market value of the assets of the nation at the end of each year. These assets include tangible assets such as land and buildings, vehicles and plant and machinery, as well as intangible assets such as computer software and mineral exploration.

The non-financial balance sheets have been improved and the methodologies and data sources updated, with the main steps explained in the articles in the references below. Tangible assets now include, in accordance with ESA 1995, certain types of farming stock (mainly dairy cattle and orchards) and military equipment whose use is not solely destructive. Intangible assets have also been added and currently include the value of computer software, mineral exploration and artistic originals. In addition our data sources have been reviewed. One of the largest recent changes has been for the public sector, where data collected directly from government departments by the Treasury and from local authorities by the Chartered Institute of Public Finance and Accounting (CIPFA) are now used.

There are two changes to the tables this year.

Table 10.8 (Central Government) now includes a new component - the electro-magnetic spectrum. This is to take account of the money made by the Government for granting the rights to mobile phone companies to use the spectrum. It has been decided to treat the spectrum as a tangible non-produced asset and the payments made by mobile phone companies as rent. The value of the asset is equivalent to the rents paid. This change impacts in the same way on tables 10.1, 10.2, 10.7 and 10.11.

Local authority housing has been reclassified from the local government sector and is now shown in the public corporations sector. This is consistent with new methodology that shows government-owned market activities always carried out by public corporations, either in their own right or via quasi-corporations. The market housing activity of local authorities is now treated as public quasi-corporate activity and hence the housing stock has been reclassified accordingly.

Research is continuing in a number of areas, particularly on non-produced intangible assets, including patents, purchased goodwill, and transferable leases and contracts. Further improvements will be introduced as results emerge.

References

1. Paul West: Improving the Non-Financial Balance Sheets: Economic Trends November 1998

2. Paul West and Alex Clifton-Fearnside: Improving the Non-Financial Balance Sheets and Capital Stocks: Economic Trends November 1999

3. Andrew Holder: Developing the Public Sector Balance Sheet: Economic Trends November 1998

Non-financial balance sheets

10.1 National balance sheet
Sector totals: summary of net worth

£ billion at end year

			1992	1993	1994	1995	1996	1997	1998	1999	2000
	Non-financial corporations[2]										
S.11001	Public[4]	CGRW	123.0	122.4	124.7	112.3	112.7	111.5	114.0	117.1	123.4
S.11002	Private[2]	TMPN	4.4	22.8	74.9	−46.1	−71.9	−214.1	−335.4	−622.5	−463.0
S.11	Total	CGRV	127.3	145.3	199.6	66.4	41.8	−101.2	−221.6	−503.4	−340.7
S.12	Financial corporations	CGRU	30.7	−7.6	−2.0	−48.6	−74.4	−254.4	−270.3	−336.9	−386.2
	General government[4]										
S.1311	Central government	CGRY	32.3	−42.1	−47.8	−90.3	−116.4	−151.1	−170.4	−139.4	−101.9
S.1313	Local government	CGRZ	106.8	112.2	117.4	122.4	126.5	135.5	154.3	158.0	167.3
S.13	Total	CGRX	139.1	70.2	69.6	32.1	10.1	−15.6	−16.1	18.6	65.4
S.14+S.15	Households and NPISH[3]	CGRC	2 360.2	2 674.6	2 587.4	2 772.6	3 006.5	3 533.7	3 888.5	4 535.4	4 605.2
S.1	Total net worth	CGDA	2 657.4	2 882.4	2 854.6	2 822.5	2 984.0	3 162.6	3 380.5	3 713.8	3 943.7

1 See footnotes in tables 10.2-10.11 for changes to allocations of assets between sectors.
2 Including quasi-corporations.
3 Non-profit institutions serving households
4 Public sector (General government plus public non-financial corporations) is as follows:-

		1992	1993	1994	1995	1996	1997	1998	1999	2000
Public sector	CGTY	262.1	192.6	194.2	144.3	122.7	95.9	97.9	135.8	188.7

10.2 National balance sheet
Asset totals

£ billion at end year

		1992	1993	1994	1995	1996	1997	1998	1999	2000
Non-financial assets										
Tangible assets:										
Residential buildings	CGLK	1 201.1	1 220.4	1 206.4	1 205.0	1 318.9	1 420.8	1 628.2	1 855.0	1 984.7
Agricultural assets	CGMP	33.4	38.6	41.4	48.5	50.0	51.7	51.2	54.0	54.6
Commercial, industrial and other buildings	CGMU	449.8	550.2	498.8	470.2	504.3	540.9	533.4	582.2	625.2
Civil engineering works	CGQZ	249.9	299.7	359.2	378.4	400.9	413.6	437.2	444.4	449.4
Plant and machinery	CGRA	359.7	368.5	374.7	383.8	401.1	423.0	448.4	468.1	489.5
Vehicles, including ships, aircraft, etc	CGRB	39.4	42.1	47.2	47.1	48.6	52.1	53.0	56.5	61.1
Stocks and work in progress	CGRD	121.8	124.6	133.1	142.5	145.9	149.7	152.2	157.6	160.4
Spectrum[2]	ZLDX	–	–	–	–	–	–	–	–	22.2
Total tangible assets	CGRE	2 455.0	2 644.2	2 660.9	2 675.6	2 869.7	3 051.8	3 303.7	3 617.6	3 847.1
Intangible assets:										
Non-marketable tenancy rights	CGRF	171.4	188.4	157.3	150.6	164.0	165.4	190.2	206.8	192.6
Other intangible assets	CGRG	18.2	18.4	18.6	19.0	19.8	20.8	21.8	22.7	21.7
Total intangible assets	CGRH	189.6	206.8	175.8	169.6	183.8	186.2	212.1	229.5	214.3
Total non-financial assets	CGJB	2 644.6	2 851.0	2 836.7	2 845.1	3 053.4	3 238.0	3 515.7	3 847.2	4 061.4
Total net financial assets/liabilities	NQFT	12.8	31.4	17.9	−22.6	−69.4	−75.5	−135.2	−133.4	−117.7
Total net worth[1]	CGDA	2 657.4	2 882.4	2 854.6	2 822.5	2 984.0	3 162.6	3 380.5	3 713.8	3 943.7

1 Net worth was previously defined as *net wealth*.
2 Following the grant of licences to mobile phone companies, the electro- magnetic spectrum is included as an asset for the first time in 2000.

United Kingdom National Accounts 2001, © Crown copyright 2001

Non-financial balance sheets

10.3 Non-financial corporations

£ billion at end year

		1992	1993	1994	1995	1996	1997	1998	1999	2000
Non-financial assets										
Tangible assets:										
Residential buildings[2]	CGUT	117.5	116.1	109.0	111.5	118.3	116.4	120.1	122.0	126.2
of which Local Authority housing	CGVF	80.8	80.0	72.0	71.6	77.8	73.4	75.0	74.3	75.0
Agricultural assets	CGUU	3.0	3.3	3.4	4.3	4.7	4.8	4.7	4.6	4.6
Commercial, industrial and other buildings	CGUV	239.9	340.0	284.6	261.8	289.4	309.6	295.6	327.8	365.4
Civil engineering works	CGUW	133.0	177.3	224.1	226.6	242.9	248.1	253.3	259.9	256.1
Plant and machinery	CGUX	293.7	301.9	305.5	312.5	326.8	345.1	367.0	382.9	400.0
Vehicles, including ships, aircraft, etc	CGUY	24.9	28.5	33.9	34.7	36.7	41.3	43.2	47.2	51.0
Stocks and work in progress	CGUZ	90.7	93.0	100.0	109.0	111.9	115.3	117.8	122.8	125.9
Total tangible assets	CGVA	902.7	1 060.1	1 060.5	1 060.5	1 130.6	1 180.6	1 201.8	1 267.2	1 329.4
Intangible non-financial assets										
Non-marketable tenancy rights	CGVB	–	–	–	–	–	–	–	–	–
Other intangible assets	CGVC	16.3	16.5	16.6	17.1	17.7	18.5	19.1	19.6	18.1
Total intangible assets	CGVE	16.3	16.5	16.6	17.1	17.7	18.5	19.1	19.6	18.1
Total non-financial assets	CGES	918.9	1 076.6	1 077.1	1 077.6	1 148.3	1 199.1	1 220.9	1 286.8	1 347.5
Total net financial assets/liabilities	NYOM	–791.6	–931.3	–877.5	–1 011.2	–1 106.5	–1 300.2	–1 442.5	–1 790.1	–1 688.3
Total net worth[1]	CGRV	127.3	145.3	199.6	66.4	41.8	–101.2	–221.6	–503.4	–340.7

1 Net worth was previously defined as *net wealth*.
2 Residential buildings in this table now include both council housing and housing association properties. The latter were formally included in table 10.10 (Non-profit institutions serving households).

10.4 Public non-financial corporations

£ billion at end year

		1992	1993	1994	1995	1996	1997	1998	1999	2000
Non-financial assets										
Tangible assets:										
Residential buildings[2]	CGVF	80.8	80.0	72.0	71.6	77.8	73.4	75.0	74.3	75.0
of which Local authority housing	CGWM	76.1	75.2	67.1	66.5	73.9	69.4	71.0	70.0	71.0
Agricultural assets	CGVG	0.5	0.6	0.6	1.1	1.3	1.3	1.2	1.0	0.9
Commercial, industrial and other buildings	CGVH	21.3	23.3	27.1	21.4	22.0	24.0	29.6	33.4	39.3
Civil engineering works	CGVI	11.4	12.0	19.8	9.7	7.4	7.7	8.3	8.6	8.5
Plant and machinery	CGVJ	17.4	16.8	16.0	15.4	10.3	9.9	9.4	8.9	9.0
Vehicles, including ships, aircraft, etc	CGVK	4.2	4.6	5.3	5.5	1.6	1.5	1.8	1.8	1.8
Stocks and work in progress	CGVL	6.0	5.8	5.5	5.3	5.1	5.2	5.1	5.1	5.0
Total tangible assets	CGVM	141.6	143.1	146.4	130.1	125.5	122.8	130.3	133.1	139.4
Intangible non-financial assets										
Non-marketable tenancy rights	CGVN	–	–	–	–	–	–	–	–	–
Other intangible assets	CGVO	1.0	1.2	1.5	1.8	2.3	2.7	3.1	3.5	3.9
Total intangible assets	CGVP	1.0	1.2	1.5	1.8	2.3	2.7	3.1	3.5	3.9
Total non-financial assets	CGGN	142.6	144.3	147.8	131.9	127.8	125.5	133.5	136.6	143.3
Total net financial assets/liabilities	NYOP	–19.7	–21.9	–23.1	–19.7	–15.1	–14.0	–19.4	–19.5	–19.9
Total net worth[1]	CGRW	123.0	122.4	124.7	112.3	112.7	111.5	114.0	117.1	123.4

1 Net worth was previously defined as *net wealth*.
2 Residential buildings in this table now include council housing.

Non-financial balance sheets

10.5 Private non-financial corporations

£ billion at end year

		1992	1993	1994	1995	1996	1997	1998	1999	2000
Non-financial assets										
Tangible assets:										
Residential buildings[2]	TMPB	36.7	36.1	37.0	39.9	40.5	43.0	45.2	47.7	51.2
Agricultural assets	TMPC	2.5	2.7	2.8	3.2	3.4	3.5	3.4	3.6	3.7
Commercial, industrial and other buildings	TMPD	218.5	316.6	257.4	240.4	267.5	285.7	266.0	294.4	326.2
Civil engineering works	TMPE	121.6	165.3	204.2	216.9	235.5	240.4	245.0	251.3	247.7
Plant and machinery	TMPF	276.3	285.1	289.5	297.1	316.4	335.2	357.7	374.0	391.0
Vehicles, including ships, aircraft, etc	TMPO	20.7	23.9	28.6	29.2	35.1	39.8	41.5	45.4	49.3
Stocks and work in progress	TMPG	84.7	87.3	94.6	103.7	106.7	110.2	112.7	117.7	121.0
Total tangible assets	TMPH	761.0	917.0	914.1	930.4	1 005.1	1 057.8	1 071.5	1 134.1	1 190.0
Intangible non-financial assets										
Non-marketable tenancy rights	TMPI	–	–	–	–	–	–	–	–	–
Other intangible assets	TMPJ	15.2	15.3	15.1	15.2	15.4	15.8	16.0	16.1	14.3
Total intangible assets	TMPK	15.2	15.3	15.1	15.2	15.4	15.8	16.0	16.1	14.3
Total non-financial assets	TMPL	776.3	932.3	929.3	945.6	1 020.5	1 073.5	1 087.5	1 150.2	1 204.3
Total net financial assets/liabilities	TMPM	−771.9	−909.5	−854.4	−991.5	−1 091.3	−1 286.2	−1 423.1	−1 770.7	−1 668.3
Total net worth[1]	TMPN	4.4	22.8	74.9	−46.1	−71.9	−214.1	−335.4	−622.5	−463.0

1 Net worth was previously defined as *net wealth*.
2 Residential buildings now include Housing Association properties. These were formally included in table 10.10 (Non profit institutions serving households).

10.6 Financial corporations

£ billion at end year

		1992	1993	1994	1995	1996	1997	1998	1999	2000
Non-financial assets										
Tangible assets:										
Residential buildings	CGUD	6.1	4.0	1.9	1.8	1.1	1.1	1.1	1.2	1.2
Agricultural assets	CGUE	0.5	0.6	0.7	0.8	0.8	0.8	0.8	0.9	0.9
Commercial, industrial and other buildings	CGUF	66.9	72.0	77.2	73.5	74.2	84.4	85.4	97.3	97.3
Civil engineering works	CGUG	–	–	–	–	–	–	–	–	–
Plant and machinery	CGUH	14.7	15.5	16.8	18.0	19.5	20.7	21.1	21.2	21.2
Vehicles, including ships, aircraft, etc	CGUI	5.7	4.7	3.7	2.9	3.2	2.7	2.1	1.4	2.2
Stocks and work in progress	CGUO	–	–	–	–	–	–	–	–	–
Total tangible assets	CGUP	93.9	96.7	100.3	96.9	98.8	109.8	110.5	121.9	122.8
Intangible non-financial assets										
Non-marketable tenancy rights	CGUQ	–	–	–	–	–	–	–	–	–
Other intangible assets	CGUR	1.1	1.1	1.1	1.0	1.1	1.2	1.5	1.7	1.9
Total intangible assets	CGUS	1.1	1.1	1.1	1.0	1.1	1.2	1.5	1.7	1.9
Total non-financial assets	CGDB	95.0	97.8	101.4	98.0	99.9	111.0	112.0	123.6	124.7
Totat financial assets/liabilities	NYOE	−64.3	−105.4	−103.4	−146.5	−174.4	−365.4	−382.3	−460.5	−510.8
Total net worth[1]	CGRU	30.7	−7.6	−2.0	−48.6	−74.4	−254.4	−270.3	−336.9	−386.2

1 Net worth was previously defined as *net wealth*.

Non-financial balance sheets

10.7 General government

£ billion at end year

		1992	1993	1994	1995	1996	1997	1998	1999	2000
Non-financial assets										
Tangible assets:										
Residential buildings[2]	CGVQ	3.0	3.1	3.2	3.2	3.2	1.8	2.0	1.6	1.4
Agricultural assets	CGVR	1.3	1.5	1.6	1.8	1.9	1.9	1.9	2.0	2.1
Commercial, industrial and other buildings	CGVS	106.8	100.2	99.5	99.2	102.8	105.8	110.4	113.3	116.8
Civil engineering works	CGVT	115.4	121.0	133.8	150.2	156.4	164.0	182.4	182.9	191.1
Plant and machinery	CGVU	35.3	34.0	34.4	34.1	33.6	33.6	34.2	36.0	38.1
Vehicles, including ships, aircraft, etc	CGVV	3.6	3.9	4.1	4.0	3.6	3.5	3.4	3.3	3.3
Stocks and work in progress	CGVW	7.8	7.8	7.6	7.4	7.6	7.7	7.8	7.5	7.4
Spectrum[3]	ZLDB	–	–	–	–	–	–	–	–	22.2
Total tangible assets	CGVX	273.1	271.5	284.1	300.0	309.1	318.2	342.1	346.7	382.4
Intangible non-financial assets										
Non-marketable tenancy rights	CGVY	–	–	–	–	–	–	–	–	–
Other intangible assets	CGVZ	0.6	0.6	0.6	0.6	0.6	0.7	0.9	1.0	1.1
Total intangible assets	CGWA	0.6	0.6	0.6	0.6	0.6	0.7	0.9	1.0	1.1
Total non-financial assets	CGIX	273.8	272.1	284.7	300.6	309.7	318.9	342.9	347.7	383.5
Total net financial assets/liabilities	NYOG	−134.6	−202.0	−215.2	−268.5	−299.7	−334.5	−359.0	−329.1	−318.1
Total net worth[1]	CGRX	139.1	70.2	69.6	32.1	10.1	−15.6	−16.1	18.6	65.4

1 Net worth was previously defined as *net wealth*.
2 Council housing has now been transferred from General Government to the Public non-financial corporations sector.
3 Following the grant of licences to mobile phone companies, the electro-magnetic spectrum is included as an asset for the first time in 2000.

10.8 Central government[1]

£ billion at end year

		1992	1993	1994	1995	1996	1997	1998	1999	2000
Non-financial assets										
Tangible assets:										
Residential buildings	CGWB	3.0	3.1	3.2	3.2	3.2	1.8	2.0	1.6	1.4
Agricultural assets	CGWC	0.1	0.1	0.1	0.1	0.1	0.1	0.1	0.1	0.1
Commercial, industrial and other buildings	CGWD	38.9	33.8	33.9	35.3	36.0	36.2	36.6	35.9	35.3
Civil engineering works	CGWE	40.2	41.2	47.0	54.7	59.4	61.7	66.3	68.1	70.5
Plant and machinery	CGWF	30.0	28.6	29.2	29.0	29.7	29.7	30.3	32.2	34.3
Vehicles, including ships, aircraft, etc	CGWG	2.8	2.9	3.0	2.9	2.8	2.8	2.7	2.6	2.5
Stocks and work in progress	CGWH	7.8	7.8	7.6	7.4	7.6	7.7	7.8	7.5	7.4
Spectrum[3]	ZLDA	–	–	–	–	–	–	–	–	22.2
Total tangible assets	CGWI	122.8	117.6	124.0	132.7	138.7	139.9	145.9	148.1	173.7
Intangible non-financial assets										
Non-marketable tenancy rights	CGWJ	–	–	–	–	–	–	–	–	–
Other intangible assets	CGWK	0.3	0.3	0.3	0.3	0.3	0.4	0.4	0.5	0.5
Total intangible assets	CGWL	0.3	0.3	0.3	0.3	0.3	0.4	0.4	0.5	0.5
Total non-financial assets	CGIY	123.1	117.9	124.3	133.0	139.1	140.3	146.3	148.5	174.2
Total net financial assets/liabilities	NZDZ	−90.8	−160.0	−172.1	−223.3	−255.5	−291.4	−316.7	−287.9	−276.1
Total net worth[2]	CGRY	32.3	−42.1	−47.8	−90.3	−116.4	−151.1	−170.4	−139.4	−101.9

1 UK national accounts classification excludes fighting equipment from tangible assets.
2 Net worth was previously defined as *net wealth*.
3 Following the grant of licences to mobile phone companies, the electro-magnetic spectrum is included as an asset for the first time in 2000.

Non-financial balance sheets

10.9 Local government

£ billion at end year

		1992	1993	1994	1995	1996	1997	1998	1999	2000
Non-financial assets										
Tangible assets:										
Local Authority housing[2]	ZLCS	–	–	–	–	–	–	–	–	–
Agricultural assets	CGWN	1.2	1.4	1.5	1.7	1.8	1.8	1.8	1.9	2.0
Commercial, industrial and other buildings	CGWO	67.8	66.4	65.6	63.9	66.8	69.6	73.8	77.4	81.5
Civil engineering works	CGWP	75.2	79.8	86.8	95.5	97.0	102.2	116.0	114.8	120.6
Plant and machinery	CGWQ	5.3	5.3	5.3	5.1	4.0	3.9	3.9	3.8	3.8
Vehicles, including ships, aircraft, etc	CGWR	0.8	1.0	1.1	1.1	0.8	0.7	0.6	0.7	0.8
Stocks and work in progress	CGWS	–	–	–	–	–	–	–	–	–
Total tangible assets	CGWT	150.3	153.9	160.2	167.3	170.4	178.2	196.2	198.7	208.7
Intangible non-financial assets										
Non-marketable tenancy rights	CGWU	–	–	–	–	–	–	–	–	–
Other intangible assets	CGWV	0.3	0.3	0.3	0.3	0.3	0.4	0.4	0.5	0.6
Total intangible assets	CGWW	0.3	0.3	0.3	0.3	0.3	0.4	0.4	0.5	0.6
Total non-financial assets	CGIZ	150.6	154.2	160.5	167.6	170.7	178.6	196.6	199.2	209.3
Total net financial assets/liabilities	NYOJ	–43.8	–42.0	–43.1	–45.2	–44.2	–43.1	–42.3	–41.1	–42.0
Total net worth[1]	CGRZ	106.8	112.2	117.4	122.4	126.5	135.5	154.3	158.0	167.3

1 Net worth was previously defined as *net wealth*.
2 The value of council housing is now shown in table 10.4 (Public non-financial corporations).

10.10 Households & non-profit institutions serving households (NPISH)

£ billion at end year

		1992	1993	1994	1995	1996	1997	1998	1999	2000
Non-financial assets										
Tangible assets:										
Residential buildings[2]	CGRI	1 074.4	1 097.2	1 092.3	1 088.5	1 196.3	1 301.4	1 504.9	1 730.2	1 855.8
Agricultural assets	CGRJ	28.7	33.2	35.7	41.6	42.7	44.2	43.8	46.4	47.0
Commercial, industrial and other buildings	CGRK	36.2	38.1	37.6	35.7	37.8	41.1	41.9	43.8	45.7
Civil engineering works	CGRL	1.4	1.5	1.4	1.6	1.6	1.6	1.6	1.6	2.2
Plant and machinery	CGRM	16.0	17.0	17.9	19.2	21.2	23.7	26.0	28.0	30.2
Vehicles, including ships, aircraft, etc	CGRN	5.2	5.0	5.5	5.5	5.1	4.6	4.3	4.6	4.6
Stocks and work in progress	CGRO	23.3	23.7	25.5	26.1	26.5	26.7	26.6	27.2	27.1
Total tangible assets	CGRP	1 185.2	1 215.8	1 215.9	1 218.1	1 331.1	1 443.2	1 649.2	1 881.8	2 012.5
Intangible non-financial assets										
Non-marketable tenancy rights	CGRQ	171.4	188.4	157.3	150.6	164.0	165.4	190.2	206.8	192.6
Other intangible assets	CGRS	0.3	0.3	0.3	0.3	0.3	0.4	0.4	0.5	0.5
Total intangible assets	CGRT	171.7	188.7	157.6	150.9	164.3	165.8	190.6	207.3	193.1
Total non-financial assets	CGCZ	1 356.9	1 404.5	1 373.5	1 369.0	1 495.4	1 609.0	1 839.9	2 089.1	2 205.7
Total net financial assets/liabilities	NZEA	1 003.3	1 270.1	1 213.9	1 403.6	1 511.1	1 924.7	2 048.6	2 446.3	2 399.6
Total net worth[1]	CGRC	2 360.2	2 674.6	2 587.4	2 772.6	3 006.5	3 533.7	3 888.5	4 535.4	4 605.2

1 Net worth was previously defined as *net wealth*.
2 Figures for Housing association properties are now included in table 10.5 (Private non-financial corporations).

Non-financial balance sheets

10.11 Public sector

£ billion at end year

		1992	1993	1994	1995	1996	1997	1998	1999	2000
Non-financial assets										
Tangible assets:										
Residential buildings	CGWX	83.8	83.1	75.2	74.8	81.0	75.2	77.0	75.9	76.4
Agricultural assets	CGWY	1.7	2.0	2.2	2.9	3.2	3.2	3.1	3.1	3.0
Commercial, industrial and other buildings	CGWZ	128.1	123.6	126.6	120.6	124.8	129.7	140.0	146.7	156.0
Civil engineering works	CGXA	126.8	133.0	153.6	159.9	163.8	171.6	190.7	191.5	199.6
Plant and machinery	CGXB	52.7	50.8	50.5	49.5	44.0	43.4	43.5	44.9	47.1
Vehicles, including ships, aircraft, etc	CGXC	7.8	8.6	9.4	9.6	5.2	5.0	5.1	5.1	5.0
Stocks and work in progress	CGXD	13.8	13.6	13.0	12.7	12.7	12.9	12.9	12.6	12.4
Spectrum[2]	ZLDC	–	–	–	–	–	–	–	–	22.2
Total tangible assets	CGXE	414.8	414.6	430.5	430.1	434.6	441.0	472.4	479.8	521.8
Intangible non-financial assets										
Non-marketable tenancy rights	CGXF	–	–	–	–	–	–	–	–	–
Other intangible assets	CGXG	1.6	1.8	2.1	2.4	2.9	3.4	4.0	4.5	5.0
Total intangible assets	CGXH	1.6	1.8	2.1	2.4	2.9	3.4	4.0	4.5	5.0
Total non-financial assets	CGJA	416.4	416.4	432.5	432.5	437.5	444.4	476.4	484.3	526.8
Total net financial assets/liabilities	CGSA	−154.3	−223.8	−238.3	−288.2	−314.8	−348.5	−378.4	−348.5	−338.0
Total net worth[1]	CGTY	262.1	192.6	194.2	144.3	122.7	95.9	97.9	135.8	188.7

1 Net worth was previously defined as *net wealth*.
2 Following the grant of licences to mobile phone companies, the electro-magnetic spectrum is included as an asset for the first time in 2000.

Part 4

Chapter 11

General government suplementary tables

Chapter 11: Public sector supplementary tables

Taxes paid by UK residents (Table 11.1)

This table shows the taxes and national insurance contributions paid to central government, local government, and to the institutions of the European Union.

Taxes on production are included in GDP at market prices. Taxes on products are taxes levied on the sale of goods and services. Other taxes on production include taxes levied on inputs to production (for example non-domestic rates) and some compulsory unrequited levies that producers have to pay.

Taxes on income and wealth include income tax and corporation tax. Also included are some charges paid by households (for example local government taxes and motor vehicle duty), which are classified as taxes on production when paid by businesses. The totals are measured gross of any tax credits and reliefs recorded as expenditure in national accounts such as mortgage interest relief at source.

ESA95 has a category called compulsory social contributions. For simplicity in UK accounts this category includes only, and all, national insurance contributions. Details of total social contributions and benefits are shown in Tables 5.24S and 5.34S of Chapter 5.

Some UK taxes are recorded as the resources of the European Union. These include taxes on imports and an amount calculated as the hypothetical yield from VAT at a standard rate on a harmonised base across the EU.

Public expenditure

Public expenditure can be defined in various ways. The *Blue Book* shows three of the most commonly used measures of public expenditure.

Expenditure of general government (EGG) (Table 11.2)

This is the definition used by Eurostat. It is the sum of a selection of consolidated general government uses from the allocation and distribution of income accounts, and capital accounts, plus subsidies paid (recorded in ESA95 as a negative resource), in national accounts. It is shown broken down by the Classification of the Functions of Government. The definition includes some double counting: for example civil service pensions are included both as an accruing cost in final consumption and as a social benefit.

Total managed expenditure (TME) (Part of Table 11.3)

TME is the current and capital expenditure of the public sector. It is the present government's main measure of public expenditure. It represents the consolidated current and capital expenditure of general government and excludes capital grants to public corporations and adds in certain expenditure (mostly capital) by public corporations.

In terms of the present government's control measures for public expenditure, TME is the sum of Annually Managed Expenditure (AME) and Departmental Expenditure Limits (DEL).

Public sector key fiscal measures (Table 11.3)

The Chancellor's Economic and Fiscal Strategy Report in June 1998 established a number of public sector fiscal balances to be monitored. Two of these are drawn directly from national accounts:

the surplus on current budget: this is net saving plus capital taxes (B.8n+D.91 uses). This balance measures achievement against the Golden Rule, which states that over an economic cycle government should only borrow to finance investment.

net borrowing (B.9 from the capital account). General government net borrowing is often called the "government deficit" in the context of the Maastricht Treaty, which requires governments to keep their deficits below 3 per cent of GDP.

A summary derivation of these balances is show in Table 11.3 using a presentation that is consistent with how H M Treasury show public finances in the Financial Statement and Budget Report.

Table 11.3 also shows public sector net debt. This balance is related to the sustainable investment rule, which states that public sector net debt as a proportion of GDP will be held at a stable and prudent level over the economic cycle.

Reconciliation of financial transactions and balance sheets (Tables 11.4 - 11.6)

Tables 11.4, 11.5 and 11.6 reconcile financial transactions with movements in financial balance sheets for the general government sector and the central and local government sub-sectors. Movements in financial balance sheets not attributable to financial transactions consist of changes in classifications and structure (K.12), nominal holding gains / losses (K.11) and other volume changes (K.10). Changes in classification and structure (K.12) include the reclassification of a body from one sector to another and changes in balance sheets in connection with privatisations. Nominal holding gains / losses (K.11) consist of changes in balance sheets due to changes in prices; this includes both price changes due to the effect of exchange rate movements on the value of

Public sector supplementary tables

financial assets denominated in foreign currencies and changes in the market prices of marketable financial instruments. Other volume changes (K.10) include exceptional losses of currency or securities and writing-off or writing-down of bad debts by creditors (but not debt forgiveness). K.10 also includes statistical discrepancies between financial transactions and balance sheets; the ONS is taking steps to improve the quality of balance sheet data to remove these discrepancies from the accounts.

Public sector supplementary tables

11.1 Taxes paid by UK residents to general government and the European Union
Total economy sector S.1

£ million

Part			1992	1993	1994	1995	1996	1997	1998	1999	2000
	GENERATION OF INCOME										
	Uses										
D.2	Taxes on production and imports										
D.21	Taxes on products and imports										
D.211	Value added tax (VAT)										
	Paid to central government	NZGF	37 426	37 958	42 996	43 579	46 918	52 057	54 293	58 664	60 702
	Paid to the European Union	FJKM	4 059	4 471	3 121	4 845	4 471	3 397	4 228	3 811	4 204
D.211	Total	QYRC	41 485	42 429	46 117	48 424	51 389	55 454	58 521	62 475	64 906
D.212	Taxes and duties on imports excluding VAT										
D.2121	Paid to CG: import duties[1]	NMBS	–	–	–	–	–	–	–	–	–
D.2121	Paid to EU: import duties	FJWE	1 943	2 172	2 134	2 458	2 318	2 291	2 076	2 024	2 086
D.212	Total	QYRB	1 943	2 172	2 134	2 458	2 318	2 291	2 076	2 024	2 086
D.214	Taxes on products excluding VAT and import duties										
	Paid to central government										
	Customs & excise revenue										
	Beer	GTAM	2 394	2 497	2 560	2 585	2 625	2 714	2 718	2 792	2 813
	Wines, cider, perry & spirits	GTAN	2 759	2 914	3 074	2 891	3 003	3 079	3 183	3 595	3 751
	Tobacco	GTAO	6 055	6 359	6 839	7 331	7 651	7 716	7 590	7 637	7 879
	Hydrocarbon oils	GTAP	11 281	12 497	13 984	15 360	16 895	18 357	20 996	22 391	23 027
	Car tax	GTAT	603	–4	–	–	–	–	–	–	–
	Betting, gaming & lottery	CJQY	1 056	1 094	1 151	1 567	1 465	1 522	1 538	1 521	1 522
	Air passenger duty	CWAA	–	–	33	339	353	442	823	884	940
	Insurance premium tax	CWAD	–	–	116	635	671	1 044	1 245	1 423	1 707
	Landfill tax	BKOF	–	–	–	–	5	378	333	439	461
	Other	ACDN	12	–	–	–	–	–	–	–	–
	Fossil fuel levy	CIQY	1 344	1 331	1 355	1 306	978	418	181	104	84
	Gas levy	GTAZ	288	240	153	161	198	181	32	–	–
	Stamp duties	GTBC	1 224	1 635	1 831	1 920	2 209	3 226	4 451	6 000	8 325
	Levies on exports (Third country trade)	CUDF	–	1	–	–	–	–	–	–	–
	Camelot payments to National Lottery										
	Distribution Fund	LIYH	–	–	98	1 360	1 297	1 512	1 693	1 574	1 590
	Purchase Tax	EBDB	–	–	–	–	–	–	–	–	–
	Hydro-benefit	LITN	20	22	24	27	30	32	32	35	42
	Other taxes and levies	GCSP	–	–	–	–	–	–	–	–	–
	Total paid to central government	NMBV	27 036	28 586	31 218	35 482	37 380	40 621	44 815	48 395	52 141
	Paid to the European Union										
	Sugar levy	GTBA	47	56	98	55	26	91	42	46	44
	European Coal & Steel Community levy	GTBB	7	1	–	–	–	–	–	–	–
	Total paid to the European Union	FJWG	54	57	98	55	26	91	42	46	44
D.214	Total taxes on products excluding VAT & import duties	QYRA	27 090	28 643	31 316	35 537	37 406	40 712	44 857	48 441	52 185
D.21	Total taxes on products and imports	NZGW	70 518	73 244	79 567	86 419	91 113	98 457	105 454	112 940	119 177
D.29	Production taxes other than on products										
	Paid to central government										
	Consumer Credit Act fees	CUDB	162	159	148	174	120	136	187	145	105
	National non-domestic rates	CUKY	14 004	13 339	12 861	13 307	13 995	14 685	15 115	15 809	16 641
	Old style non-domestic rates	NSEZ	59	110	120	127	139	167	129	126	128
	Levies paid to CG levy-funded bodies	LITK	119	128	132	134	142	157	159	166	196
	Selective employment tax	CSAH	–	–	–	–	–	–	–	–	–
	National insurance surcharge	GTAY	–	–	–	–	–	–	–	–	–
	London regional transport levy	GTBE	–	–	–	–	–	–	–	–	–
	IBA levy	GTAL	72	–	–	–	–	–	–	–	–
	Motor vehicle duties paid by businesses	EKED	1 150	1 181	1 302	1 313	1 367	1 362	1 509	1 559	1 487
	Regulator fees	GCSQ	47	63	67	60	57	57	60	66	72
	Total	NMBX	15 613	14 980	14 630	15 115	15 820	16 564	17 159	17 871	18 629
	Paid to local government										
	Old style non-domestic rates	NMYH	65	86	91	99	109	122	128	142	149
D.29	Total production taxes other than on products	NMYD	15 678	15 066	14 721	15 214	15 929	16 686	17 287	18 013	18 778
D.2	Total taxes on production and imports, paid										
	Paid to central government	NMBY	80 075	81 524	88 844	94 176	100 118	109 242	116 267	124 930	131 472
	Paid to local government	NMYH	65	86	91	99	109	122	128	142	149
	Paid to the European Union	FJWB	6 056	6 700	5 353	7 358	6 815	5 779	6 346	5 881	6 334
D.2	Total	NZGX	86 196	88 310	94 288	101 633	107 042	115 143	122 741	130 953	137 955

1 These taxes existed before the UK's entry into the EEC in 1973

Public sector supplementary tables

11.1 continued
Taxes paid by UK residents to general government and the European Union
Total economy sector S.1

£ million

			1992	1993	1994	1995	1996	1997	1998	1999	2000
Part	**SECONDARY DISTRIBUTION OF INCOME**										
	Uses										
D.5	Current taxes on income, wealth etc										
D.51	Taxes on income										
	Paid to central government										
	Household income taxes	DRWH	68 426	66 071	70 558	75 945	76 667	78 236	90 295	96 061	105 701
	Petroleum revenue tax	DBHA	7	381	820	832	1 356	1 467	662	472	1 545
	Windfall tax	EYNK	–	–	–	–	–	2 610	2 614	–	–
	Other corporate taxes	BMNX	11 858	11 861	13 970	18 265	21 287	25 334	30 489	32 511	33 714
D.51	Total	NMCU	80 291	78 313	85 348	95 042	99 310	107 647	124 060	129 044	140 960
D.59	Other current taxes										
	Paid to central government										
	Motor vehicle duty paid by households	CDDZ	1 963	2 301	2 546	2 641	2 782	2 972	3 122	3 314	3 191
	Old style domestic rates	NSFA	56	73	78	77	79	85	115	115	112
	Licences	NSNP	5	8	9	10	11	10	8	8	4
	Total	NMCV	2 024	2 382	2 633	2 728	2 872	3 067	3 245	3 437	3 307
	Paid to local government										
	Old style domestic rates	NMHK	68	56	57	58	62	63	62	67	73
	Community charge	NMHL	8 207	2 122	–	–	–	–	–	–	–
	Council tax	NMHM	–	5 991	8 450	9 151	9 861	10 690	11 686	12 759	13 722
	Total	NMIS	8 275	8 169	8 507	9 209	9 923	10 753	11 748	12 826	13 795
D.59	Total	NVCM	10 299	10 551	11 140	11 937	12 795	13 820	14 993	16 263	17 102
D.5	Total current taxes on income, wealth etc										
	Paid to central government	NMCP	82 315	80 695	87 981	97 770	102 182	110 714	127 305	132 481	144 267
	Paid to local government	NMIS	8 275	8 169	8 507	9 209	9 923	10 753	11 748	12 826	13 795
D.5	Total	NMZL	90 590	88 864	96 488	106 979	112 105	121 467	139 053	145 307	158 062
D.61	Social contributions										
D.611	Actual social contributions										
	Paid to central government (National Insurance Contributions)										
D.61111	Employers' compulsory contributions	CEAN	21 621	23 038	23 240	24 210	25 553	27 200	29 529	31 248	33 180
D.61121	Employees' compulsory contributions	GCSE	14 104	14 748	17 357	18 646	19 175	21 558	22 984	23 549	23 972
D.61131	Self- and non-employed persons' compulsory contributions	NMDE	1 281	1 472	1 469	1 541	1 771	1 848	1 760	1 801	1 973
D.611	Total	AIIH	37 006	39 258	42 066	44 397	46 499	50 606	54 273	56 598	59 125
Part	**CAPITAL ACCOUNT**										
	Changes in liabilities and net worth										
D.91	Other capital taxes										
	Paid to central government										
	Inheritance tax	GILF	1 183	1 247	1 411	1 411	1 578	1 568	1 753	1 920	2 152
	Tax on other capital transfers	GILG	44	32	27	30	43	33	43	31	63
	Development land tax and other	GCSV	–	–	–	–	–	–	–	–	–
D.91	Total	NMGI	1 227	1 279	1 438	1 441	1 621	1 601	1 796	1 951	2 215
	TOTAL TAXES AND COMPULSORY SOCIAL CONTRIBUTIONS										
	Paid to central government	GCSS	200 623	202 756	220 329	237 784	250 420	272 163	299 641	315 960	337 079
	Paid to local government	GCST	8 340	8 255	8 598	9 308	10 032	10 875	11 876	12 968	13 944
	Paid to the European Union	FJWB	6 056	6 700	5 353	7 358	6 815	5 779	6 346	5 881	6 334
	Total	GCSU	215 019	217 711	234 280	254 450	267 267	288 817	317 863	334 809	357 357
	Total taxes and social contributions as percentage of GDP	GDWM	35.2	33.9	34.4	35.4	35.1	35.6	37.0	37.2	37.9

2 Now applies only in Northern Ireland.

Public sector supplementary tables

11.2 General government: analysis of total outlays by classification of function of government (COFOG)
Current prices

£ million

				1992	1993	1994	1995	1996	1997	1998	1999	2000
10		**General public services**										
P.3		Final consumption expenditure										
D.1		Compensation of employees	QYRL	7 760	8 018	6 964	7 077	7 016	6 205	6 198	6 444	7 626
		Net intermediate consumption plus taxes less subsidies	QYRM	−2 236	−2 064	272	2 406	1 452	1 049	1 616	2 140	1 311
K.1		Non-market capital consumption	QYRO	198	241	329	385	415	500	421	574	589
P.3		Total final consumption expenditure	QYRY	5 722	6 195	7 565	9 868	8 883	7 754	8 235	9 158	9 526
D.7		Other current transfers	QZNS	3 328	3 563	4 503	4 169	4 339	4 359	5 611	6 481	6 917
P.5		Gross capital formation	QYVA	1 023	941	1 016	1 052	996	737	1 345	1 508	1 830
K.2		Non-produced non-financial assets	QYWJ	–	–	–	–	–	–	–	–	–
D.9		Capital transfers	QZKH	341	305	273	253	238	210	375	228	292
Total		Total outlays	QYWW	10 414	11 004	13 357	15 342	14 456	13 060	15 566	17 375	18 565
20		**Defence**										
P.3		Final consumption expenditure										
D.1		Compensation of employees	QYRP	10 462	10 295	9 925	9 172	9 561	9 308	8 920	9 272	9 562
		Net intermediate consumption plus taxes less subsidies	QYRQ	11 540	11 489	11 156	10 769	11 352	12 932	12 979	12 729	14 062
K.1		Non-market capital consumption	QYRS	1 502	1 406	1 486	1 571	1 627	1 763	1 815	1 811	1 644
P.3		Total final consumption expenditure	QYRZ	23 504	23 190	22 567	21 512	22 540	24 003	23 714	23 812	25 268
D.7		Other current transfers	QZMO	10	9	20	13	4	18	4	11	9
P.5		Gross capital formation	QYVB	1 840	1 773	2 074	2 003	919	857	1 584	1 416	1 509
K.2		Non-produced non-financial assets	QYWK	−9	−14	−13	−5	−13	−10	−158	−18	−17
D.9		Capital transfers	QZIK	5	6	3	27	34	28	2	5	4
Total		Total outlays	QYWX	25 350	24 964	24 651	23 550	23 484	24 896	25 146	25 226	26 773
30		**Public order and safety**										
P.3		Final consumption expenditure										
D.1		Compensation of employees	QYRT	9 385	9 635	9 892	10 147	10 440	11 111	11 632	12 009	12 483
		Net intermediate consumption plus taxes less subsidies	QYRU	3 282	3 392	3 646	3 611	4 044	4 141	4 082	4 386	4 020
K.1		Non-market capital consumption	QYRW	193	233	244	269	275	299	314	365	382
P.3		Total final consumption expenditure	QYRX	12 860	13 260	13 782	14 027	14 759	15 551	16 028	16 760	16 885
D.7		Other current transfers	QZNT	161	159	165	179	145	129	242	268	277
P.5		Gross capital formation	QYVC	951	989	1 022	1 058	816	838	1 094	1 093	1 221
K.2		Non-produced non-financial assets	QYWL	–	–	–	–	–	–	–	–	–
D.9		Capital transfers	QZKI	–	–	–	–	–	–	–	–	–
Total		Total outlays	QYWY	13 972	14 408	14 969	15 264	15 720	16 518	17 364	18 121	18 383
40		**Economic affairs**										
P.3		Final consumption expenditure										
D.1		Compensation of employees	GVEL	2 544	2 971	2 759	2 498	2 242	2 290	2 072	2 083	2 222
		Net intermediate consumption plus taxes less subsidies	GVEN	4 782	5 023	6 005	5 707	6 694	4 420	4 488	5 458	5 909
K.1		Non-market capital consumption	GVEM	1 980	1 978	2 076	2 313	2 580	2 696	2 847	2 907	2 911
P.3		Total final consumption expenditure	GVEK	9 306	9 972	10 840	10 518	11 516	9 406	9 407	10 448	11 042
D.3		Subsidies	GVEO	3 707	3 649	4 154	3 984	4 788	3 976	3 443	3 496	2 596
D.7		Other current transfers	GVEP	1 017	1 244	983	1 675	1 314	1 693	1 924	1 501	4 262
P.5		Gross capital formation	GVEQ	4 587	4 355	4 716	4 712	4 461	3 723	3 463	2 954	3 331
K.2		Non-produced non-financial assets	QYWT	−81	−129	−128	−38	−122	−96	−319	−184	−170
D.9		Capital transfers	GVES	2 671	2 594	3 036	4 686	3 433	2 687	2 528	3 326	1 622
Total		Total outlays	GVEU	21 207	21 685	23 601	25 537	25 390	21 389	20 446	21 541	22 683
50		**Environment protection**										
P.3		Final consumption expenditure										
D.1		Compensation of employees	QYXQ	497	469	441	470	408	386	429	485	609
		Net intermediate consumption plus taxes less subsidies	EQJM	1 741	1 847	1 601	1 477	1 878	2 292	2 412	2 690	2 722
K.1		Non-market capital consumption	EQJO	55	50	104	112	121	154	155	130	164
P.3		Total final consumption expenditure	QYJU	2 293	2 366	2 146	2 059	2 407	2 832	2 996	3 305	3 495
D.3		Subsidies	QYWU	–	–	–	–	–	–	–	–	–
D.7		Other current transfers	GVFR	64	73	43	46	56	46	61	49	52
P.5		Gross capital formation	QYVI	236	250	214	249	219	282	501	551	664
K.2		Non-produced non-financial assets	QYWR	–	–	–	–	–	–	–	–	–
D.9		Capital transfers	QYWV	28	33	70	36	35	107	130	149	175
Total		Total outlays	QYXE	2 621	2 722	2 473	2 390	2 717	3 267	3 688	4 054	4 386

Public sector supplementary tables

11.2 continued
General government: analysis of total outlays by classification of function of government (COFOG)
Current prices

£ million

				1992	1993	1994	1995	1996	1997	1998	1999	2000
60		**Housing and community amenities**										
P.3		Final consumption expenditure										
D.1		Compensation of employees	QYSV	729	809	944	935	884	901	954	1 013	1 076
		Net intermediate consumption plus taxes less subsidies	QYSW	1 079	913	576	711	487	815	885	918	930
K.1		Non-market capital consumption	QYSY	290	280	290	308	335	334	391	376	393
P.3		Total final consumption expenditure	QYSZ	2 098	2 002	1 810	1 954	1 706	2 050	2 230	2 307	2 399
D.3		Subsidies	QYVP	1 434	1 335	1 143	1 232	1 183	1 223	967	900	1 057
D.7		Other current transfers	QZNY	69	54	24	21	42	22	46	30	39
P.5		Gross capital formation	QYVH	1 299	1 412	1 774	2 035	922	917	−67	−622	−650
K.2		Non-produced non-financial assets	QYWQ	–	–	–	–	–	–	–	–	–
D.9		Capital transfers	GVFX	4 129	4 755	3 495	2 835	2 704	2 453	2 291	2 105	2 218
Total		Total outlays	QYXD	9 029	9 558	8 246	8 077	6 557	6 665	5 467	4 720	5 063
70		**Health**										
P.3		Final consumption expenditure										
D.1		Compensation of employees	QWWQ	14 016	10 604	5 112	3 419	2 841	2 680	2 676	2 865	2 799
		Net intermediate consumption plus taxes less subsidies	QTLP	18 616	24 457	32 015	35 470	38 539	39 895	42 632	47 149	50 921
K.1		Non-market capital consumption	QYOB	604	380	145	92	86	82	83	83	117
P.3		Total final consumption expenditure	QYOT	33 236	35 441	37 272	38 981	41 466	42 657	45 391	50 097	53 837
D.3		Subsidies	CBRA	55	117	198	311	339	345	353	405	454
D.7		Other current transfers	QZMR	150	298	466	539	644	657	736	756	769
P.5		Gross capital formation	QYVE	1 650	1 059	500	361	356	59	78	38	8
K.2		Non-produced non-financial assets	QYWN	–	–	–	–	–	–	–	–	–
D.9		Capital transfers	QZIM	4	7	28	25	21	65	74	65	71
Total		Total outlays	QYXA	35 095	36 922	38 464	40 217	42 826	43 783	46 632	51 361	55 139
80		**Recreation, culture and religion**										
P.3		Final consumption expenditure										
D.1		Compensation of employees	QYSQ	1 228	1 284	1 212	1 336	1 182	1 254	1 307	1 380	1 468
		Net intermediate consumption plus taxes less subsidies	QYSR	2 003	2 086	1 877	1 653	1 811	1 639	1 974	2 201	2 255
K.1		Non-market capital consumption	QYST	135	177	157	183	180	196	205	196	180
P.3		Total final consumption expenditure	QYSU	3 366	3 547	3 246	3 172	3 173	3 089	3 486	3 777	3 903
D.3		Subsidies	GTBY	195	217	222	251	263	281	286	315	368
D.7		Other current transfers	QZNX	209	174	190	169	161	117	169	148	156
P.5		Gross capital formation	QYVG	747	925	875	790	936	769	729	734	781
K.2		Non-produced non-financial assets	QYWP	−147	−236	−227	−65	−221	−178	−327	−327	−302
D.9		Capital transfers	QZKL	10	10	29	15	13	29	22	15	20
Total		Total outlays	QYXC	4 380	4 637	4 335	4 332	4 325	4 107	4 365	4 662	4 926
90		**Education**										
P.3		Final consumption expenditure										
D.1		Compensation of employees	QYSA	18 898	17 109	16 909	17 834	18 223	18 938	19 837	21 121	21 482
		Net intermediate consumption plus plus taxes less subsidies	QYSB	5 635	5 422	6 301	6 391	6 464	6 616	6 981	7 814	8 469
K.1		Non-market capital consumption	QYSD	978	956	992	1 066	1 111	1 138	1 142	1 168	1 217
P.3		Total final consumption expenditure	QYSE	25 511	23 487	24 202	25 291	25 798	26 692	27 960	30 103	31 168
D.7		Other current transfers	QZNU	2 205	5 059	6 317	6 290	7 910	8 800	9 003	9 837	8 868
P.5		Gross capital formation	QYVD	1 175	1 136	1 053	1 116	1 268	1 104	1 628	1 726	1 987
K.2		Non-produced non-financial assets	QYWM	−75	−118	−117	−35	−111	−88	−163	−167	−154
D.9		Capital transfers	QZKJ	505	776	745	874	509	356	352	269	305
Total		Total outlays	QYWZ	29 321	30 340	32 200	33 536	35 374	36 864	38 780	41 768	42 174
100		**Social protection**										
P.3		Final consumption expenditure										
D.1		Compensation of employees	QYSL	6 122	6 256	6 395	6 774	7 003	7 251	7 549	7 761	8 075
		Net intermediate consumption plus taxes less subsidies	QYSM	5 037	5 649	6 262	6 727	7 382	7 708	7 724	8 609	9 029
K.1		Non-market capital consumption	QYSO	140	169	168	148	146	154	161	157	164
P.3		Total final consumption expenditure	QYSP	11 299	12 074	12 825	13 649	14 531	15 113	15 434	16 527	17 268
D.62		Social benefits other than social transfers in kind	NNAD	95 339	102 965	106 295	110 409	113 124	116 934	117 549	120 752	124 991
D.7		Other current transfers	QZNV	91	156	99	114	119	124	211	276	1 115
P.5		Gross capital formation	QYVF	520	563	589	526	479	309	427	451	530
K.2		Non-produced non-financial assets	QYWO	–	–	–	–	–	–	–	–	–
D.9		Capital transfers	QZKK	1	3	4	–	3	–	8	–	–
Total		Total outlays	QYXB	107 250	115 761	119 812	124 698	128 256	132 480	133 629	138 006	143 904

Public sector supplementary tables

11.2 continued General government: analysis of total outlays by classification of function of government (COFOG)
Current prices

£ million

			1992	1993	1994	1995	1996	1997	1998	1999	2000
110	**Expenditure not classified by division**										
D.4	Property income	NMYX	18 786	20 001	22 938	26 310	28 004	29 759	30 765	26 537	27 005
Total	Total outlays	NMYX	18 786	20 001	22 938	26 310	28 004	29 759	30 765	26 537	27 005
TCG	**Total**										
P.3	Final consumption expenditure										
D.1	Compensation of employees	QYTP	71 641	67 450	60 553	59 662	59 800	60 324	61 574	64 433	67 402
	Net intermediate consumption[1] plus taxes less subsidies	QYTQ	51 479	58 214	69 711	74 922	80 103	81 507	85 773	94 094	99 628
K.1	Non-market capital consumption	QYXP	6 075	5 870	5 991	6 447	6 876	7 316	7 534	7 767	7 761
P.3	Total final consumption expenditure	NMRK	129 195	131 534	136 255	141 031	146 779	149 147	154 881	166 294	174 791
D.3	Subsidies	NMRL	5 391	5 318	5 717	5 778	6 573	5 825	5 049	5 116	4 475
D.4	Property income	NMYX	18 786	20 001	22 938	26 310	28 004	29 759	30 765	26 537	27 005
D.62	Social benefits other than social transfers in kind	NNAD	95 339	102 965	106 295	110 409	113 124	116 934	117 549	120 752	124 991
D.7	Other current transfers	NNAM	7 304	10 789	12 810	13 215	14 734	15 965	18 007	19 357	22 464
P.5	Gross capital formation	NNBI	14 028	13 403	13 833	13 902	11 372	9 595	10 782	9 849	11 211
K.2	Non-produced non-financial assets	NNBJ	−312	−497	−485	−143	−467	−372	−967	−696	−643
D.9	Capital transfers	NSZX	7 694	8 489	7 683	8 751	6 990	5 935	5 782	6 162	4 707
Total	Total outlays	QYXI	277 425	292 002	305 046	319 253	327 109	332 788	341 848	353 371	369 001

1 Net intermediate consumption is net of sales.

Public sector supplementary tables

11.3 Public sector expenditure and key fiscal balances

£ million

		1992	1993	1994	1995	1996	1997	1998	1999	2000
PUBLIC SECTOR FISCAL BALANCES										
A. Current receipts										
Taxes on income and wealth	ANSO	80 092	78 151	85 174	94 743	99 042	107 273	123 681	128 704	140 742
Taxes on production	NMYE	80 140	81 610	88 935	94 275	100 227	109 364	116 395	125 072	131 621
Other current taxes	NVCM	10 299	10 551	11 140	11 937	12 795	13 820	14 993	16 263	17 102
Taxes on capital	NMGI	1 227	1 279	1 438	1 441	1 621	1 601	1 796	1 951	2 215
Compulsory social contributions	ANBO	37 006	39 258	42 066	44 397	46 499	50 606	54 273	56 598	59 125
Operating surplus	ANBP	12 682	14 058	15 102	17 434	17 732	17 074	17 750	18 143	16 862
Interest/dividends from private sector and RoW	ANBQ	4 904	4 209	3 514	3 343	3 568	3 427	4 051	3 582	4 598
Rent and other current transfers	ANBS	937	1 251	1 492	1 639	1 737	1 746	1 524	1 303	2 087
Total current receipts	ANBT	227 731	230 541	249 457	270 281	284 111	305 959	335 434	352 377	375 146
B. Current expenditure										
Current expenditure on goods and services	GZSN	129 166	131 506	136 225	140 999	146 751	149 114	154 833	166 265	174 751
Subsidies	NMRL	5 391	5 318	5 717	5 778	6 573	5 825	5 049	5 116	4 475
Net social benefits	ANLY	85 925	93 450	96 911	100 978	103 509	107 177	107 101	110 099	113 658
Net current grants abroad	GZSI	330	−597	255	991	−610	−39	321	−1 509	334
Other current grants	NNAI	4 659	8 467	10 440	10 614	12 549	13 916	15 803	17 280	19 556
Interest paid to private sectors and RoW	ANLO	18 747	20 013	22 947	26 158	27 582	29 351	30 015	25 991	26 459
Total current expenditure	ANLT	244 218	258 157	272 495	285 518	296 354	305 344	313 122	323 242	339 233
C. Saving, gross plus capital taxes (A-B)	ANSP	−16 487	−27 616	−23 038	−15 237	−12 243	615	22 312	29 135	35 913
D. Depreciation	ANNZ	11 943	11 935	12 303	12 963	12 616	12 392	12 586	12 827	12 744
E. Surplus on current budget (C-D)	ANMU	−28 430	−39 551	−35 341	−28 200	−24 859	−11 777	9 726	16 308	23 169
F. Net investment										
Gross capital formation	ANSQ	19 138	18 090	18 907	19 550	15 780	13 367	13 837	13 981	15 414
Depreciation	-ANNZ	−11 943	−11 935	−12 303	−12 963	−12 616	−12 392	−12 586	−12 827	−12 744
Increase in inventories and valuable	ANSR	−3	−188	−564	−312	−33	139	336	−375	−346
Capital grants to private sector and RoW	ANSS	4 801	5 708	4 936	4 456	3 980	4 145	4 661	4 746	3 832
Capital grants from private sector and RoW	-ANST	−403	−406	−431	−363	−472	−595	−372	−359	−785
Total net investment	-ANNW	11 590	11 269	10 545	10 368	6 639	4 664	5 876	5 166	5 371
G. Net borrowing (F-E)	-ANNX	40 020	50 820	45 886	38 568	31 498	16 441	−3 850	−11 142	−17 798
NET DEBT										
Net debt (£ billion)[1]	RUTN	..	235.3	278.3	313.5	342.8	357.6	353.8	352.7	316.8
Net debt as a percentage of GDP[2]	RUTO	..	35.7	39.9	42.7	44.0	43.1	40.7	38.5	33.1
ANALYSIS OF EXPENDITURE										
Total Managed Expenditure (B+D+F)	EBFT	267 751	281 361	295 343	308 849	315 609	322 400	331 584	341 235	357 348
Expenditure in real terms (1995 prices)										
Total Managed Expenditure real terms (1995 Prices)	EBFU	285 612	292 567	302 978	308 862	305 644	303 533	303 234	304 027	312 900
of which										
Current expenditure real terms	EBFV	260 483	268 401	279 534	285 508	286 945	287 443	286 328	287 972	297 031
Net investment real terms	EBFW	12 388	11 756	10 824	10 393	6 479	4 423	5 394	4 626	4 709
Expenditure as a percentage of GDP										
Total Managed Expenditure % of GDP	EBFX	43.8	43.8	43.3	42.9	41.4	39.8	38.6	37.9	37.9
of which										
Current expenditure % of GDP	EBFY	40.0	40.2	40.0	39.7	38.9	37.7	36.4	35.8	36.0
Net investment % of GDP	EBFZ	1.9	1.8	1.6	1.5	0.9	0.6	0.7	0.6	0.6

1 Net debt at the end of the year
2 Gross domestic product at market prices for 12 months centred at the end of the year

Public sector supplementary tables

11.4 General government: Reconciliation of financial balance sheets and transactions
ESA95 sector S.13 Unconsolidated

£ million

			1995	1996	1997	1998	1999	2000
	Assets							
	Financial assets at beginning of period (balance sheet)		163 626	166 992	158 131	159 322	166 651	175 604
F.A	Net acquisition of financial assets (transactions)	NFPG	1 906	−7 451	728	2 188	10 025	31 662
K.12	Changes in classifications and structure	MDQJ	–	1 125	–	–	2 250	3 522
K.11	Nominal holding gains /losses	YEPT	1 168	−2 127	−305	612	−431	4 526
K.10	Other volume changes	YEPS	292	−408	768	4 529	−2 891	−5 258
AF.A	Financial assets at end of period (balance sheet)	NPUP	166 992	158 131	159 322	166 651	175 604	210 056
	Liabilities							
	Financial liabilities at beginning of period (balance sheet)		378 818	435 512	457 806	493 828	525 640	504 665
F.L	Net acquisition of financial liabilities (transactions)	NFSK	43 584	26 233	18 052	−1 876	264	14 149
K.11	Nominal holding gains / losses	YEPW	13 507	−3 857	17 933	34 061	−20 853	9 285
K.10	Other volume changes	YEPV	−397	−82	37	−373	−386	74
AF.L	Financial liabilities at end of period (balance sheet)	NPVQ	435 512	457 806	493 828	525 640	504 665	528 173
	Net							
	Net financial balance sheet at beginning of period		−215 192	−268 520	−299 675	−334 506	−358 989	−329 061
B.9f	Net acquisition of financial assets and liabilities (transactions)	NYNO	−41 678	−33 684	−17 324	4 064	9 761	17 513
K.12	Changes in classifications and structure	MDQJ	–	1 125	–	–	2 250	3 522
K.11	Nominal holding gains / losses	YEPZ	−12 339	1 730	−18 238	−33 449	20 422	−4 759
K.10	Other volume changes	YEPY	689	−326	731	4 902	−2 505	−5 332
BF.90	Net financial balance sheet at end of period	NYOG	−268 520	−299 675	−334 506	−358 989	−329 061	−318 117

11.5 Central government: Reconciliation of financial balance sheets and transactions
ESA95 sector S.1311 Unconsolidated

£ million

			1995	1996	1997	1998	1999	2000
	Assets							
	Financial assets at beginning of period (balance sheet)		146 487	149 782	140 057	139 341	145 785	153 425
F.A	Net acquisition of financial assets (transactions)	NARM	1 695	−8 343	−454	1 441	9 577	30 728
K.12	Changes in classifications and structure	YEQA	–	1 125	–	–	–	–
K.11	Nominal holding gains /losses	YENX	1 165	−2 119	−305	613	−432	4 525
K.10	Other volume changes	YENW	435	−388	43	4 390	−1 505	−573
AF.A	Financial assets at end of period (balance sheet)	NIGP	149 782	140 057	139 341	145 785	153 425	188 105
	Liabilities							
	Financial liabilities at beginning of period (balance sheet)		318 587	373 123	395 557	430 763	462 455	441 359
F.L	Net acquisition of financial liabilities (transactions)	NAUQ	41 631	26 693	17 256	−2 604	−308	13 057
K.11	Nominal holding gains / losses	YEON	13 467	−3 840	17 949	34 058	−20 846	9 352
K.10	Other volume changes	YEOM	−562	−419	1	238	58	468
AF.L	Financial liabilities at end of period (balance sheet)	NIJT	373 123	395 557	430 763	462 455	441 359	464 236
	Net							
	Net financial balance sheet at beginning of period		−172 100	−223 341	−255 500	−291 422	−316 670	−287 934
B.9f	Net acquisition of financial assets and liabilities (transactions)	NZDX	−39 936	−35 036	−17 710	4 045	9 885	17 671
K.12	Changes in classifications and structure	YEQA	–	1 125	–	–	–	–
K.11	Nominal holding gains / losses	YEOR	−12 302	1 721	−18 254	−33 445	20 414	−4 827
K.10	Other volume changes	YEOQ	997	31	42	4 152	−1 563	−1 041
BF.90	Net financial balance sheet at end of period	NZDZ	−223 341	−255 500	−291 422	−316 670	−287 934	−276 131

Public sector supplementary tables

11.6 Local government: Reconciliation of financial balance sheets and transactions
ESA95 sector S.1313 Unconsolidated

£ million

			1995	1996	1997	1998	1999	2000
	Assets							
	Financial assets at beginning of period (balance sheet)		17 139	17 210	18 074	19 981	20 866	22 179
F.A	Net acquisition of financial assets (transactions)	NBYK	211	892	1 182	747	448	934
K.12	Changes in classifications and structure	MDQI	–	–	–	–	2 250	3 522
K.11	Nominal holding gains /losses	YEOT	3	–8	–	–1	1	1
K.10	Other volume changes	YEPD	–143	–20	725	139	–1 386	–4 685
AF.A	Financial assets at end of period (balance sheet)	NJFV	17 210	18 074	19 981	20 866	22 179	21 951
	Liabilities							
	Financial liabilities at beginning of period (balance sheet)		60 231	62 389	62 249	63 065	63 185	63 306
F.L	Net acquisition of financial liabilities (transactions)	NCBO	1 953	–460	796	728	572	1 092
K.11	Nominal holding gains / losses	YEPO	40	–17	–16	3	–7	–67
K.10	Other volume changes	YEPN	165	337	36	–611	–444	–394
AF.L	Financial liabilities at end of period (balance sheet)	NJIZ	62 389	62 249	63 065	63 185	63 306	63 937
	Net							
	Net financial balance sheet at beginning of period		–43 092	–45 179	–44 175	–43 084	–42 319	–41 127
B.9f	Net acquisition of financial assets and liabilities (transactions)	NYNQ	–1 742	1 352	386	19	–124	–158
K.12	Changes in classifications and structure	MDQI	–	–	–	–	2 250	3 522
K.11	Nominal holding gains / losses	YEPQ	–37	9	16	–4	8	68
K.10	Other volume changes	YEPP	–308	–357	689	750	–942	–4 291
BF.90	Net financial balance sheet at end of period	NYOJ	–45 179	–44 175	–43 084	–42 319	–41 127	–41 986

11.7 Housing Operating Account [1]

£ million

			1992	1993	1994	1995	1996	1997	1998	1999	2000
	Resources										
P.11	Market output	CTMQ	8 769	9 137	9 247	9 633	9 723	9 424	10 144	10 016	9 890
	of which:										
	paid by tenants	CTMK	2 934	2 792	2 619	2 927	2 984	2 645	3 305	3 253	3 075
	rent rebates	CTML	4 193	4 799	5 272	5 350	5 428	5 485	5 372	5 353	5 331
	rent on other properties	CTMM	212	229	222	219	215	209	216	218	205
	subsidies:										
	Central government	CTMN	1 030	914	741	765	725	710	744	728	506
	Local authorities	CTMO	–	1	–	–	3	1	1	3	7
	other income	CTMP	400	402	393	372	368	374	506	461	766
	Uses[2]										
	Supervision and management	CTMR	1 855	1 975	2 010	2 134	2 156	2 196	2 218	2 263	2 309
	Repairs	CTMS	2 491	2 586	2 540	2 737	2 755	2 761	2 771	2 706	2 616
	Other current expenditure	CTMT	413	383	316	270	238	226	242	267	242
B.2g	Operating surplus, gross	ADAE	4 010	4 193	4 381	4 492	4 574	4 241	4 913	4 780	4 723

1 Part of the public corporations account
2 Includes compensation of employees (D.1), intermediate consumption (P2) and taxes on production (D.29)

Part 4

Chapter 12

Statistics for European Union purposes

Statistics for European Union purposes

Chapter 12: Statistics for European Union purposes

The European Union uses national accounts data for a number of administrative and economic purposes. In the 1998 *Blue Book* the UK introduced the European System of Accounts 1995 (ESA95) for its national accounts. Most UK statistical information to the EU is supplied on this basis. However, for setting a ceiling on the European Community (EC) budget and calculating part of Member States' contributions to the budget, Gross National Product (GNP) on the basis of the European System of Accounts 1979 (ESA79) is used.

The convergence criteria for Economic and Monetary Union (EMU) set out in the 1992 Treaty on European Union (The Maastricht Treaty)[1] also include EU requirements for national accounts data on general government net borrowing and gross debt as a percentage of GDP.

The new system of accounts, the ESA95, differs from the ESA79 in a number of ways such as, for example, the recording of interest payments. Adjustments are made for these in deriving ESA79 net borrowing for general government from the UK National Accounts. Other examples of differences in treatments which have to be accounted for are in gross fixed capital formation on software and consumption of fixed capital formation on roads and bridges[2].

Data supplied for EU budgetary purposes

Until EU legislation is changed to take account of the introduction of ESA95 in all Member States, the European Commission will continue to require data based on the ESA79 for GNP for the purpose of calculating the EC budget.

This GNP measure is one component in the calculation of Member States' contributions to the EC Budget. Table 12.1 shows the GNP data provided to the EU for this purpose under the GNP Directive[3]. This is calculated using ESA95 data and then adjusting to provide ESA79 figures.

UK transactions with the institutions of the EU

Table 12.2 shows the UK's contributions to the EC budget under the four categories of revenue raising (community "own resources"), and also payments flowing back to the UK in the form of EU expenditure and the UK's budgetary rebate. UK GNP on ESA79 forms the basis of the "Fourth Resource" contributions.

Data to monitor government deficit and debt

The Maastricht Treaty requires Member States to avoid excessive government deficits defined as general government net borrowing as a percentage of GDP. Member States report their planned and actual deficits and the levels of their debt to the European Commission. Data to monitor excessive deficits are supplied in accordance with EU legislation[4].

From February 2000, data for this purpose have been supplied on an ESA95 basis.

The Treaty does not determine what constitutes an excessive deficit. That is a matter for the Economic and Finance Council (ECOFIN) to decide. However, a Protocol to the Treaty does provide a reference value of 3% of GDP for net borrowing and 60% of GDP for gross debt.

The United Kingdom submitted the estimates in the following table to the European Commission in August 2001.

	1997	1998	1999	2000
General Government net borrowing (£bn)[5]	16.3	-3.8	-11.4	-18.5
as a percentage of GDP	2.0	-0.4	-1.3	-2.0
General government gross debt at nominal value (£bn)[6]	411.7	409.5	407.4	400.1
as a percentage of GDP	51.1	48.1	45.7	42.8

References

1 Treaty on European Union (Luxembourg, Office for Official Publications of the European Communities, 1992)
2 Commission Decision 97/178/EC sets down 23 change mechanisms for deriving ESA79 GNP figures from ESA95, for the purpose of the EC budget
3 Council Directive 89/130/EEC (13 February 1989)
4 Council Regulation (EC) No. 3605/93 (22 November 1993)
5 Previously known as general government financial deficit (GGFD)
6 At end year

12.1 UK gross domestic and national product
ESA79 compiled for EU budgetary purposes

£ million

			1995	1996	1997	1998	1999	2000
	Gross domestic product: output approach (ESA95)							
P.1	Output of goods and services (at basic prices excluding VAT)	NQAF	1 363 534	1 455 417	1 539 896	1 631 361	1 721 728	1 818 849
-P.2	less Intermediate consumption (at purchasers prices)	-NQAJ	–723 626	–775 797	–819 204	–870 043	–926 703	–987 792
B.1g	Gross value added basic prices	ABML	639 908	679 620	720 692	761 318	795 025	831 053
D.211	Value added taxes on products	QYRC	48 424	51 389	55 454	58 521	62 475	64 906
D.212,4	Taxes on products	NSUI	37 995	39 724	43 003	46 933	50 465	54 271
-D.31	less Subsidies on products	-NZHC	–7 151	–8 519	–8 082	–6 967	–6 696	–6 818
B.1*g	Gross domestic product at market prices	YBHA	719 176	762 214	811 067	859 805	901 269	943 412
	Gross domestic product: expenditure approach (ESA95)							
	Total final consumption expenditure							
P.3	Household final consumption expenditure	ABPB	443 367	473 800	503 374	536 525	567 555	594 782
P.3	NPISH final consumption expenditure	ABNV	16 481	18 385	19 602	21 117	22 671	22 866
P.3	General government final consumption expenditure	NMRK	141 031	146 779	149 147	154 881	166 294	174 791
	Total final consumption expenditure	ABKW	600 879	638 964	672 123	712 523	756 520	792 439
	Gross capital formation							
P.51	Gross fixed capital formation	NPQX	117 448	125 762	134 396	151 539	155 408	165 247
P.52	Changes in inventories	ABMP	4 512	1 771	4 388	4 460	4 975	1 855
P.53	Acquisitions less disposals of valuables	NPJO	–121	–158	–26	430	230	–3
	Total gross capital formation	NPDN	121 839	127 375	138 758	156 429	160 613	167 099
P.6	Exports of goods and services	KTMW	203 509	223 091	231 622	228 801	236 720	265 305
-P.7	less Imports of goods and services	-KTMX	–207 051	–227 216	–231 436	–237 948	–252 584	–281 024
B.11	External balance of goods and services	KTMY	–3 542	–4 125	186	–9 147	–15 864	–15 719
de	Statistical discrepancy attributable to the expenditure analysis	GIXM	–	–	–	–	–	–407
B.1*g	Gross domestic product at market prices	YBHA	719 176	762 214	811 067	859 805	901 269	943 412
	Gross domestic product: income approach (ESA95)							
B.2g,B.3	Gross operating surplus and mixed income	BKUP	239 034	259 203	271 963	280 764	283 946	291 493
D.1	Compensation of employees	HAEA	386 718	405 469	432 960	464 258	494 186	521 443
D.2	Taxes on production and imports	NZGX	101 633	107 042	115 143	122 741	130 953	137 955
-D.3	less Subsidies	-AAXJ	–8 209	–9 500	–8 999	–7 958	–7 816	–7 724
di	Statistical discrepancy attributable to the income analysis	GIXQ	–	–	–	–	–	245
B.1*g	Gross domestic product at market prices	YBHA	719 176	762 214	811 067	859 805	901 269	943 412
	GROSS NATIONAL PRODUCT, ESA79 basis at market prices							
B.1*g	Gross domestic product at market prices (ESA95)	YBHA	719 176	762 214	811 067	859 805	901 269	943 412
D.1	Compensation of employees received from the ROW							
	receipts from the rest of the world	KTMN	887	911	1 007	840	960	1 014
	less payments to the rest of the world	-KTMO	–1 183	–818	–924	–850	–759	–871
D.4	Property and entrepreneurial income							
	receipts from the rest of the world	HMBN	87 132	91 621	95 337	102 945	99 312	132 983
	less payments to the rest of the world	-HMBO	–84 735	–90 510	–91 514	–90 377	–95 494	–127 009
	Total impact of differences between GDP and GNP [1]	-EWVY	–16 793	–17 358	–18 248	–16 999	–23 725	–20 686
	GROSS NATIONAL PRODUCT AT MARKET PRICES	GIZV	704 484	746 060	796 725	855 364	881 563	928 847

[1] Estimates have been calculated directly under the ESA95 and then converted to ESA79 by means of the transition mechanism set out in the Commission Decision of February 10 1997 (97/178/EC, Euratom) and subsequenly discussed at the July 1999 GNP Committee (CPNB/270). This is the total effect of the transition series.

12.2 UK official transactions with institutions of the EU
UK transactions with ESA95 sector S.212

£ million

			1992	1993	1994	1995	1996	1997	1998	1999	2000
	UK resources										
P.62	Exports of services										
	UK charge for collecting duties and levies(net)[1,2]	QWUE	200	223	223	251	235	240	212	208	217
D.31	Subsidies on products, paid (negative resources)										
	Agricultural guarantee fund	EBGL	1 742	2 153	2 245	2 392	2 898	3 160	2 900	2 700	3 249
	European Coal & Steel Community grants	FJKP	61	37	45	39	29	5	1	–	–
D.75	Social assistance										
	European Social Fund	HDIZ	437	588	320	755	804	615	783	434	659
D.74	Current international co-operation										
	Fontainebleau abatement[2]	FKKL	1 881	2 540	1 726	1 208	2 411	1 733	1 377	3 171	2 084
	Grants to research councils and miscellaneous[2]	GCSD	17	18	26	25	13	6	7	5	–
D.92	Capital transfers, payable										
	Agricultural guidance fund	FJXL	71	104	52	48	30	57	56	47	82
	European regional development fund	HBZA	551	425	608	437	620	812	357	285	989
D.99	Foot and mouth[5]	EBGO	–	–	–	–	–	–	–	–	202
	Total identified UK resources	GCSL	4 960	6 088	5 245	5 155	7 040	6 637	5 701	6 850	7 482
	UK uses										
D.21	Taxes on products										
	EU traditional own resources										
D.212	Import duties	FJWD	1 943	2 172	2 134	2 458	2 318	2 291	2 076	2 024	2 086
D.214	Sugar levy	GTBA	47	56	98	55	26	91	42	46	44
D.214	European Coal & Steel Community levy	GTBB	7	1	–	–	–	–	–	–	–
	Third own resource contribution										
D.211	VAT contribution	HCML	4 356	4 964	4 189	4 635	4 441	3 646	3 758	3 920	4 104
D.211	Adjustment to VAT contribution	FSVL	–297	–493	–1 068	210	30	–249	470	–109	100
D.75	Miscellaneous current transfers										
	Fourth own resource contribution[3]										
	GNP fourth resource	HCSO	934	1 608	2 340	1 639	2 488	2 655	3 516	4 403	4 243
	GNP adjustment	HCSM	–20	–50	–269	187	–34	–197	404	229	136
	Total GNP based fourth own resource	NMFH	914	1 558	2 071	1 826	2 454	2 458	3 920	4 632	4 379
D.74	Other current transfers										
	JET contributions and miscellaneous[3]	GVEG	–	2	7	8	8	31	–1	11	6
	Inter-government agreements[3]	HCBW	–	–	–	–	–	–	–	–	–
	EU non-budget (miscellaneous)[3]	HRTM	–	–	–	–	–	–	–	–	–
	Total identified UK uses	GCSM	6 970	8 260	7 431	9 192	9 277	8 268	10 265	10 524	10 719
	Balance, UK net contribution to the EU[4]	BLZS	–2 010	–2 172	–2 186	–4 037	–2 237	–1 631	–4 564	–3 674	–3 237

1 Before 1989 this is netted off the VAT contribution but cannot be identified separately.
2 UK central government resources.
3 UK central government uses.
4 As defined in pre-ESA95 Blue Books.
5 Before 2000 these have been included in Agricultural guarentee fund payments.

Part 5

UK Environmental Accounts

UK Environmental Accounts

The Environmental Accounts at a glance

Oil reserves

Only a small proportion of the estimated remaining recoverable reserves of oil and gas is known with any degree of certainty. Reserves of oil were estimated to total up to 3.8 billion tonnes at the end of 2000, but of these only 0.6 billion tonnes were proven (having a more than 90% chance of being produced under current technical and economic conditions). The total includes an estimate of between 0.2 and 2.3 billion tonnes of reserves which have yet to be discovered, but which may exist in areas of the UK continental shelf. Estimates of the life expectancy of remaining UK oil reserves are therefore uncertain, but they do show an overall decline between 1990 and 2000 (as would be expected given the extraction of reserves over the period).

Gas reserves

Estimates of gas reserves are made on the same basis as oil and are similarly uncertain, totalling up to 3,100 billion cubic metres at the end of 2000 (of which only 735 billion cubic metres were proven reserves). The life expectancy of gas reserves also shows an overall decline over the period, down to below 15 years at current rates of extraction by the end of 2000.

Energy consumption

Energy consumption by the non-domestic sectors of the UK economy increased by 4 per cent between 1990 and 1999, while output (Gross Domestic Product) rose by 20 per cent in real terms. Hence energy intensity (energy consumed per unit of output) decreased by 13 per cent over the period.

Estimated remaining recoverable oil reserves at end of year, 1990-2000 (million tonnes)

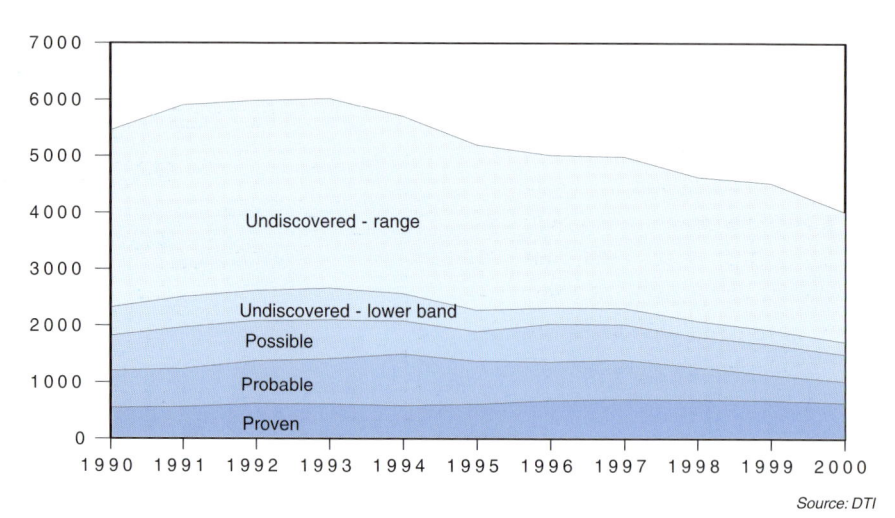

Source: DTI

Estimated remaining recoverable gas reserves at end of year, 1990-2000 (billion cubic metres)

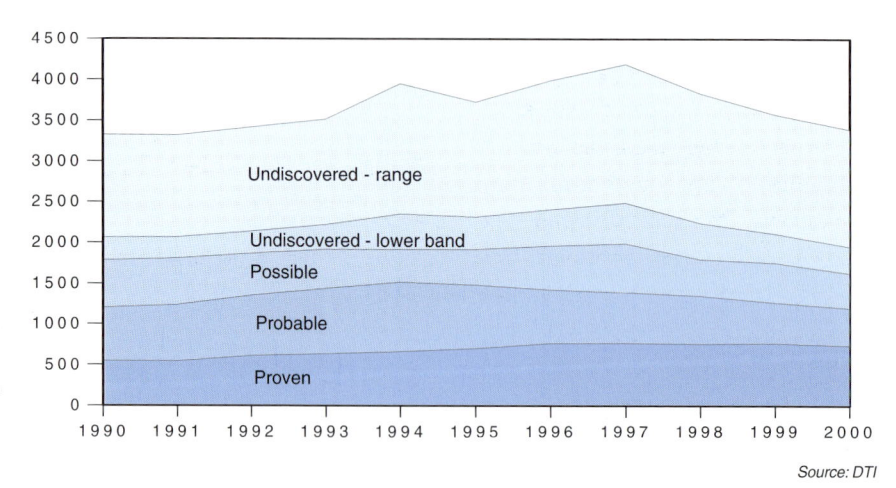

Source: DTI

Non-domestic energy consumption and output (Gross Domestic Product at constant prices) 1990-1999

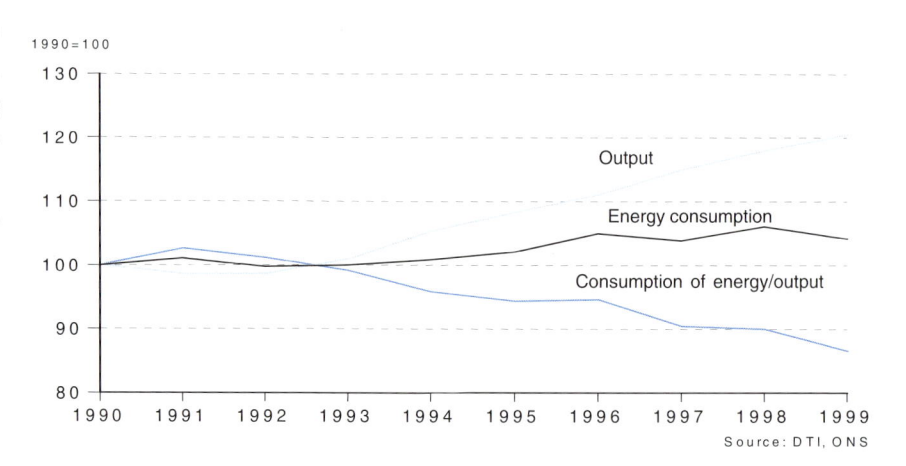

Source: DTI, ONS

UK Environmental Accounts

Atmospheric emissions

On a national accounts basis, UK non-domestic greenhouse gas and acid rain precursor emissions fell between 1990 and 1999, by 16.5 per cent and 53 per cent respectively.

The electricity, gas and water supply sector shows large reductions but remains the biggest contributor to these emissions. Its share of UK totals over the period has fallen from 28% to 23% for greenhouse gases, and from 50% to 32% for acid rain precursors. The main reason is a shift away from the use of coal and oil in power stations.

All sectors show reductions in acid rain precursor emissions since 1990, due partly to reduced emissions of nitrogen oxides from road transport, reflecting increased use of catalytic converters and low sulphur DERV.

In terms of greenhouse gas emissions per unit of output (i.e. gross value added at constant prices), most sectors show substantial improvements. The exception is the transport and retail sector where greenhouse gas emissions per unit of output in 1999 were roughly at the 1990 level.

Material flow accounting

The UK's Total Material Requirement (TMR), consisting of the mass of used domestic extraction (such as fossil fuels), imports, unused material from domestic extraction (such as quarrying overburden) and indirect flows relating to the production of imports, increased from 33.5 tonnes per person in 1970 to a peak of 38.8 tonnes per person in 1989, before declining to 35.6 tonnes per person in 1999. The main changes have been increases in crude oil and natural gas extraction and in the flows of resources associated with imports, partly offset by reductions in coal production and in sand and gravel extraction.

Atmospheric emissions of greenhouse gases and acid rain precursors, percentage change 1990-1999

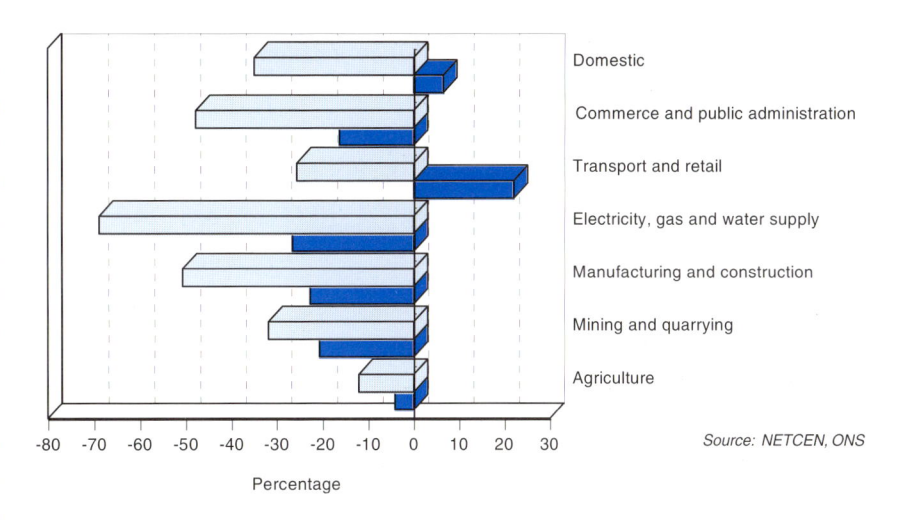

Source: NETCEN, ONS

Greenhouse gas emissions per unit of output (Gross Value Added at constant prices) 1990-1999

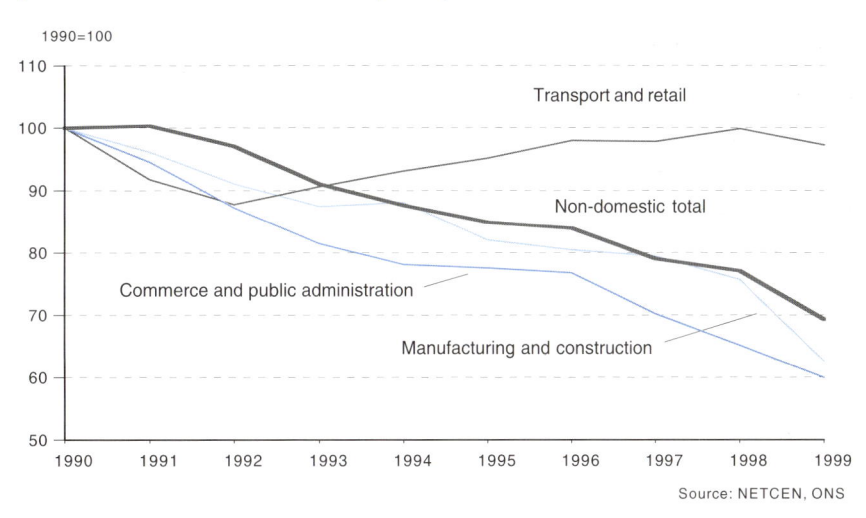

Source: NETCEN, ONS

Components of UK Total Material requirement, 1970-1999

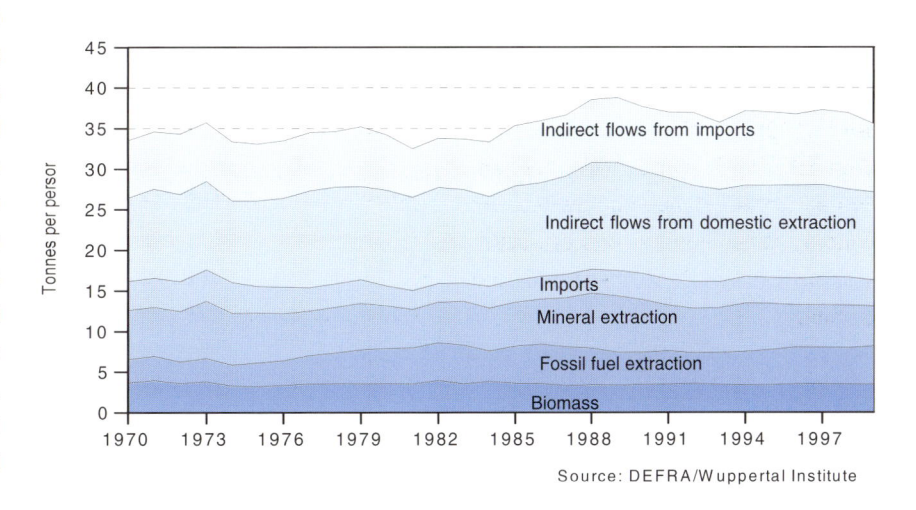

Source: DEFRA/Wuppertal Institute

United Kingdom National Accounts 2001, © Crown copyright 2001

UK Environmental Accounts

Chapter 13:
UK Environmental Accounts

Environmental accounts are "satellite accounts" to the main National Accounts. They provide information on the environmental impact of economic activity (in particular on the emissions of pollutants) and on the importance of natural resources to the economy. Environmental accounts use similar concepts and classifications of industries to those employed in the National Accounts, and they reflect the recommended European Union and United Nations frameworks for developing such accounts.

The accounts are used to inform sustainable development policy, to model impacts of fiscal or monetary measures and to evaluate the environmental performance of different industrial sectors.

Most data are provided in units of physical measurement (volume or mass), although where appropriate some accounts are shown in monetary units.

This chapter updates information published in last year's 'Blue Book' and includes new tables on the value of the UK's oil and gas reserves; waste arisings in the UK in 1998/99, an economy-wide material flow account for the UK, and an account of land cover changes in Great Britain between 1990 and 1998. More detailed information is available on the National Statistics website at http://www.statistics.gov.uk/themes/environment/articles/environmental_accounts.asp.

The diagram below shows how the areas covered by environmental accounts relate to the economy as described by the National Accounts.

Environment and economy interactions

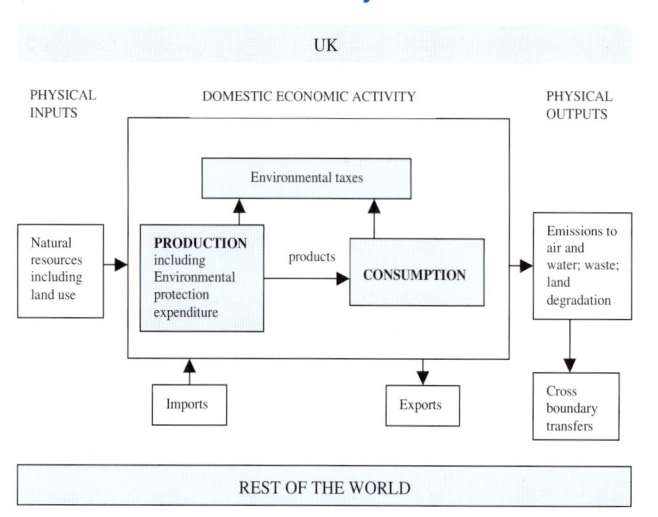

Oil and gas reserves (Tables 13.1 and 13.2)

Definition of oil and gas

Oil reserves include both oil and the liquids and liquefied products obtained from gas fields, gas-condensate fields and from the associated gas in oil fields. Gas reserves are the quantity of gas expected to be available for sale from dry gas fields, gas-condensate fields and oil fields with associated gas. Gas which is expected to be flared or used offshore is not included.

Table 13.1 gives estimates, taken each year from the Department of Trade and Industry's annual "Brown Book"[1], of the level of recoverable oil and gas reserves in the United Kingdom.

Recoverable reserves are classified into two main categories: discovered and undiscovered. The discovered reserves are subdivided into proven, probable and possible. **Proven reserves** are known reserves which, on the available evidence, are virtually certain to be technically and economically producible (i.e. having a better than 90 per cent chance of being produced). **Probable reserves** are known reserves which are not yet proven but which are estimated to have a better than 50 per cent chance of being technically and economically producible. **Possible reserves** are those reserves which, at present, cannot be regarded as 'probable', but are estimated to have a significant but less than 50 per cent chance of being technically and economically producible.

Simulation models using Monte Carlo techniques have been used each year by the DTI to assess the likely existence and size of **undiscovered oil and gas fields** on the UK Continental Shelf (UKCS). The assessments are presented as ranges, but the limits of the ranges should not be regarded as maxima or minima. Estimates of the volume of undiscovered reserves have fluctuated considerably in recent years as new areas of UKCS have been subjected to statistical analysis and older areas have been reassessed.

The lower ends of the ranges of total reserves shown in the table are sums of estimated remaining proven reserves and the lower end of the range of undiscovered reserves for the end of that year. The upper ends of the ranges of total reserves are sums of estimated proven, possible and probable reserves, plus the upper end of the range of undiscovered reserves, for the end of that year.

UK Environmental Accounts

The expected level of reserves is calculated as the sum of proven and probable reserves and the lower bound estimate of the range of undiscovered reserves. Other volume changes are calculated as the difference between the expected level of reserves at the start of the year, less extraction within that year, and the estimated level of reserves at the start of the following year.

Life expectancy is calculated as the expected level of reserves at the end of the year divided by the current level of annual extraction. This calculation gives an indication of the theoretical number of years for which extraction could be sustained at current levels. In practice, towards the end of that period, the rate of extraction is likely to decrease as individual oil and gas fields are exhausted, so the period of extraction will be longer than that implied by the life expectancy calculation.

Monetary valuation of oil and gas reserves

Expressing UK oil and gas reserves in monetary terms allows these subsoil assets to be compared with other economic entities. This provides a means for the commercial depletion of subsoil assets to be set against national income. The results for 1992 to 2000 are presented in Table 13.2 in the form of a balance sheet.

Since observed market values for transactions in the assets in situ are not widely available, the **present value method** is used to put a monetary value on the physical stocks of assets. This is an indirect valuation method measuring the current value of the asset's future streams of income by discounting the expected future rent, often referred to as the **economic rent** or **resource rent.** The method relies on information about the size of resource rent, the number of years for which the rent is to be received and the social discount rate to be applied.

The **resource rent** is the net income from extraction defined as total revenue from sales less all costs incurred in the extraction process i.e. operating costs, depreciation of capital and allowances for decommissioning costs and the return on capital. The rate of return on capital is estimated to be 8 per cent in real terms, in line with Eurostat recommendations[2], but it is worth noting that the resulting valuations are very sensitive to variations in this estimate. Future resource rents can then be calculated using the assumption that the future unit resource rents (i.e. the resource rent per unit of fuel extracted) is constant in real terms and equal to the average of the last three years' unit rents. The estimated values are also very sensitive to this assumption.

In the calculation, it is assumed that the amounts extracted decrease as the reserves are gradually exhausted. The time span until the complete exhaustion of the reserves is the period over which resource rents are discounted, using a social discount rate of 4 per cent, again in line with Eurostat recommendations[2].

Using these assumptions it is possible to calculate a present value of the stocks of oil and gas reserves at the start and end of each year. The accumulation account then breaks down the change between the start-of-year balance and the end-of-year balance. It is worth noting that while physical stocks may change only as a result of extraction and other volume changes such as reassessments, monetary stocks can change for a number of other reasons.

Extraction is equal to the total resource rent for the year, effectively reducing the present value of the stocks by that amount.

Revaluation due to time passing takes account of the fact that, as we move forward in time, the period over which the future rents are discounted is one year less, thereby reducing the effect of discounting future incomes.

Other volume changes are reassessments which change the estimated stock of recoverable reserves.

The **change in the extraction path** sets out in monetary terms the addition or subtraction to the present value arising from a change in the amounts assumed to be extracted each year.

The **change in unit rent** gives the change in the future stream of income resulting from a change in the estimated unit resource rent.

Energy consumption (Table 13.3)

Table 13.3 gives estimates of total energy used by each industrial sector and the proportion of total energy used from renewable resources, for the years 1992 to 1999. Detailed estimates of consumption of different fuel types by each sub-sector are given on the National Statistics website http://www.statistics.gov.uk/themes/environment/articles/environmental_accounts.asp

Unit of measurement

The unit of measurement is tonne of oil equivalent (toe), which enables different fuels to be compared and aggregated. It should be regarded as a measure of energy content rather than a physical quantity. Standard conversion factors for each type of fuel are given in the Digest of UK Energy Statistics (DUKES)[3].

UK Environmental Accounts

Consumption of fossil fuels, energy used in transformation processes and losses in distribution

The consumption of fossil fuels, and the related consumption of energy, can be analysed from a number of different perspectives. In terms of atmospheric emissions, it may be helpful to identify which industrial sectors are actually consuming the fossil fuels that give rise to emissions. From this perspective, fuels used by the electricity generation sector are attributed entirely to that sector, even though some of the energy is transformed into electricity. This analysis is shown in Part 1 of Table 13.3 and is consistent with that used in the atmospheric emissions accounts (see Tables 13.4 and 13.5). Hence the estimated fossil fuel consumption by industry shown in Part 1 of Table 13.3 can be directly related to the estimated emissions of air pollutants.

In terms of energy consumption, it is possible to attribute energy used during the process of transformation into electricity, and the energy lost in distributing electricity to end users, either directly to the electricity generation sector, or indirectly to the consumers of energy. Parts 2 and 3 of Table 13.3 consider energy consumption from both points of view. Part 2 allocates the consumption of energy directly to the immediate consumer of the energy, while Part 3 allocates these "electricity overheads" of the major power producers to the user of the electricity. For this purpose, the consumption of electrical energy produced by autogenerators, either for their own use or supplied directly to other consumers, has been ignored.

Renewable energy sources

Renewable energy is defined to include solar power, energy from wind, wave and tide, hydroelectricity, and energy from wood, straw and sewage gas. Landfill gas and municipal solid waste combustion have also been included with renewable energy for the purposes of defining energy sources in the context of sustainable development policy.

Sources and methods for estimating consumption of energy by industrial sector

Data for estimating fuel consumption by broad industrial sectors are collected by the DTI and are published in DUKES. However, the figures shown in Table 13.3 differ from those given in DUKES in that:

- fuels used by international shipping (marine bunkers) under international bunker contracts are included;

- non-energy uses of fuels for example, chemical feedstocks, solvents, lubricants and road-making material, are excluded;

- the classification of industrial sectors used in environmental accounts differs from that used in DUKES. In particular, the transport sector is defined to include only enterprises that provide transport services to other consumers (i.e. public transport operators, freight haulage companies, etc.). The energy consumed by households' use of private cars is allocated to the domestic sector.

Atmospheric emissions (Tables 13.4 and 13.5)

Tables 13.4 and 13.5 give estimates of pollutants directly emitted to the atmosphere by industrial sector. The figures are on a National Accounts basis and differ from the basis used to monitor progress against the Kyoto protocol in that they include estimated emissions from fuels purchased in the UK and used by international shipping and aircraft on international flights (marine and air bunkers). A further minor difference is that for emissions of hydrofluorocarbons, perfluorocarbons and sulphur hexafluoride, the UK climate change programme uses a 1995 base year in accordance with Article 3.8 of the Kyoto Protocol. Detailed estimates of pollutants for each sub-sector, for the years 1990 to 1999, are given on the National Statistics website at http://www/statistics.gov.uk/themes/environmental/articles/environmental accounts.asp. The website also gives details of other pollutants, such as other heavy metals.

Pollutants and environmental themes

Atmospheric emissions can be aggregated according to their contribution to environmental themes such as greenhouse gases and acid rain. A description of the pollutants covered and the methodology used to calculate environmental themes is given in the annex to these notes.

Attributing emissions to industrial sectors

The disaggregation of national estimates of emissions to industrial sectors is based upon an initial disaggregation provided by the National Environmental Technology Centre (NETCEN) which maintains the National Atmospheric Emissions Inventory (NAEI). Emissions were estimated by multiplying fuel consumption by emissions factors and adding releases unrelated to fuel use such as methane arising from landfill.

The NAEI data is used to identify the main processes and industries responsible for the emissions, which are then allocated to individual sectors on the basis of information from a variety of sources. For example, emissions from DERV (Diesel Engine Road Vehicle) use by heavy goods vehicles, are allocated to sectors using vehicle mileage data from the Department of Transport, Local Government and the Regions. Expenditure information is also used, for example to allocate emissions arising from the use of various industrial coatings (e.g. general industrial, heavy duty and vehicle refinishing) to relevant sectors in proportion to each sector's expenditure on paints, varnishes and similar coatings, printing ink and mastics, using the National Accounts supply-use tables as the main source. A full description of the methods and sources used in these accounts is available on request from the Environmental Accounts branch, Office for National Statistics.

Table 13.4 shows estimates of air pollutants directly emitted by industry in 1999. Emissions generated by the electricity supply industry have not been reallocated to their customers in this analysis. Emissions from road haulage are given on an 'own account' basis, i.e. attributed to the sector owning the transport rather than to the sector of the goods being transported. Similarly emissions from households' use of private cars are allocated to the domestic sector. Figures for total road transport emissions are provided separately.

Table 13.5 shows estimates of emissions of greenhouse gases and acid rain emissions by industrial sector for the years 1992 to 1999.

Waste arisings in the United Kingdom 1998/99 (Table 13.6)

Table 13.6 gives estimates of the total waste arisings in the UK in 1998/99 by industrial sector. The grouping of sectors reflects the variety of sources used to compile the estimates.

The figures for **agricultural waste** arisings in 1999, are based on the results of a research project sponsored by the Department for Environment, Food and Rural Affairs (DEFRA); they include all agricultural waste streams including waste from housed livestock, with liquid volumes converted to tonnes, but they exclude forestry and fishing wastes.

Mining and quarrying waste figures are based on DEFRA estimates of ratios of waste to product[4], with the production data taken from the *UK Minerals Year Book*, published by the British Geological Society.

The Environment Agency survey of commercial and industrial waste arisings in England and Wales in 1998/99 is the main source of information about **waste from the manufacturing sectors.** The figures include power station ash and blast furnace and steel slag. Estimates of waste from the manufacture of coke and petroleum products have been included in with the electricity, gas and water supply sector. The waste is classified according to the type of waste, although "general waste" will include some of the other categories of waste where separation of mixed waste was not possible. The "other waste" category covers contaminated general waste, healthcare risk, chemical and other waste. Approximately 44 per cent of industrial waste arisings is reused or recycled.

The Environment Agency survey for 1998/99 is also the main source of information about **commercial waste.** The definition of the sectors reflects the available information: the Wholesale and Retail sector excludes vehicle repair and maintenance, which is included in with the Transport and Communications sector; travel agents have been included with Finance and Other Services and excluded from Transport and Communications; social work has been included with Finance and Other Services and excluded from the Public Administration, Health and Education sector. The waste services sector was excluded from the survey altogether, in order to avoid double-counting, but separate estimates of dry weight arisings of sewage sludge have been made by Water UK and these are included against the waste water services sector in Table 13.6. The figure for mineral waste for the Transport and Communications sector includes an estimate of the amount of dredged material, based on a Centre for Environment, Fisheries and Aquaculture Science Survey for 1997 covering all UK waters.

Estimates of **household waste** are taken from the DEFRA/National Assembly for Wales survey of Municipal Waste Management in England and Wales[5]. Estimates for paper and card, composting (vegetable waste), glass (mineral waste) and scrap relate to materials separately collected for recycling through kerbsite collection schemes, from civic amenity sites and bring sites. The estimates have been grossed to a UK total using population estimates.

Material Flows (Table 13.7)

Economy-wide material flow accounts record the total mass of natural resources and products that are used by the economy, either directly in the production and distribution of products and services, or indirectly through the movement of materials which are displaced in order for production to take place.

The direct movement of materials into the economy derives primarily from domestic extraction, that is from biomass

UK Environmental Accounts

(agricultural harvest, timber, fish and animal grazing), fossil fuel extraction (such as coal, crude oil and natural gas) and mineral extraction (metal ores, industrial minerals such as pottery clay, and construction material such as crushed rock, sand and gravel).

The direct input of materials from domestic sources is supplemented by the imports of products, which may be of raw materials such as unprocessed agricultural products, but can also be semi-manufactured or finished products. In a similar way the UK produces exports of raw materials, semi-manufactured and finished goods which can be viewed as inputs to the production and consumption of overseas economies.

Indirect flows of natural resources consist of the unused material resulting from domestic extraction such as mining and quarrying overburden and the soil removed during construction and dredging activities. They also include the movement of used and unused material overseas which is associated with the production and delivery of imports. Water – except for that included directly in products – is excluded from the accounts.

Summary aggregates

There are a number of aggregates which can be used to summarise the flows of materials into and out of the economy. Table 13.7 shows three of the main indicators used to measure inputs.

The **Direct Material Input (DMI)** measures the input of used materials into the economy, that is all materials which are of economic value and are used in production and consumption activities (including the production of exports).

Domestic material consumption (DMC) measures the total amount of material directly used in the economy (i.e. it includes imports but excludes exports).

The **Total Material Requirement (TMR)** measures the total material basis of the economy, that is the total primary resource requirements of all the production and consumption activities. It includes not only the direct use of resources for producing exports, but also indirect flows from the production of imports and the indirect flows associated with domestic extraction. Although TMR is widely favoured as a resource use indicator, the estimates of indirect flows are less reliable than those for materials directly used by the economy, and the indicator therefore needs to be considered alongside other indicators.

In summary:
Direct Material Input (DMI) = used domestic extraction + imports
Domestic Material Consumption (DMC) = DMI – exports
Total Material Requirement (TMR) = DMI + indirect flows associated with imports + indirect flows from domestic extraction

Source

The estimates are taken from research carried out by the Wuppertal Institute on behalf of DEFRA[6].

Government revenues from environmental taxes (Table 13.8)

Table 13.8 shows the amounts raised in environmental taxes between 1992 and 2000.

Definition of an environmental tax

An environmental tax is defined as a tax whose base is a physical unit (or a proxy for it) that has a proven specific negative impact on the environment. By convention, in addition to pollution-related taxes, all energy and transport taxes are classified as environmental taxes. This definition has been agreed by international experts and adopted by the Statistical Office of the European Communities (Eurostat) and Organisation for Economic Co-operation and Development (OECD). It enables analysis to be based on the effects of taxes rather than the aims behind their introduction, i.e. the aim of a tax for raising government revenue rather than reducing environmental degradation does not preclude it from being defined as an environmental tax.

Nevertheless, the interpretation and use of measures of environmental taxes need care. In particular, the levels of revenues from environmental taxes do not necessarily indicate the relative importance or the success of environmental policy. High environmental tax revenues can result either from high rates of taxes or from high levels of environmental problems (e.g. pollution) leading to a large tax base. The broad measure of revenues can also fail to capture the effect of the differential rates that encourage a shift away from higher impact behaviour (such as the use of leaded petrol).

Taxes on energy products include duties on hydrocarbon oils used in road vehicles, the main ones being leaded petrol, unleaded petrol, super-unleaded petrol and DERV.

From October 2000, lower rates have been levied on unleaded petrol, super-unleaded petrol, ultra low sulphur petrol. Taxes on energy products also include those used for non-transport purposes (such as industrial gas turbines and heating installations, with a reduced rate for energy saving materials) and the fossil fuel levy (which is levied on sales of electricity from fossil fuels and used to compensate companies producing electricity from non-fossil fuel sources such as nuclear or renewable energy). The climate change levy, which is a tax on non-domestic use of energy, was introduced in April 2001.

VAT on duty is calculated as a fixed proportion (in most cases 17.5 per cent) of the duty paid on hydrocarbon oils. In practice much of this VAT will be reclaimed by business, but it could be argued that the total will eventually be paid when the final product or service is purchased.

Taxes on road vehicles include Vehicle Excise Duty, which owners of motor vehicles pay on an annual basis. There have been various changes to this duty over recent years. Most recently, as from July 2001, most cars with an engine size of up to and including 1549cc qualify for a reduced annual rate. However, new cars first registered from 1 March 2001 will be taxed in a different way, that is according to the level of their carbon dioxide emissions and fuel type.

Air passenger duty was introduced on 1 November 1994. It applies to the carriage from a UK airport of chargeable passengers on chargeable aircraft at two different rates. The lower rate is charged where passengers are travelling to a UK destination or within the European Economic Area, and the higher rate applies in all other cases. The lower rate was £5.00 on the year of introduction, increasing to £10.00 from November 1997. The higher rate of passenger duty was £10.00 in November 1994, increasing to £20.00 from November 1997. The duty was reformed in April 2001, with differential rates for domestic and European flights and economy, first and club class passengers plus some new exemptions.

Landfill tax was introduced in October 1996. It applies to most waste disposed of at registered sites. Types of waste excluded from this tax include dredgings, disposals from mines and quarries, and also waste resulting from the clearance of contaminated land. A standard rate of tax is levied on active waste, this was £7.00 on introduction of the tax, rising to £10.00 in April 1999, and increasing by £1.00 per tonne each year until 2004, when it will be £15.00 per tonne. A lower rate of tax is levied on inert waste, which has remained at £2.00 from the year of introduction.

UK Environmental Accounts

Environmental protection expenditure in 1999 (Table 13.9)

Table 13.9 shows the estimated expenditure on environmental protection by the extraction, manufacturing, energy production and water supply industries in 1999. The estimates should be regarded as approximate orders of magnitude only. Because of this qualification the estimates shown fall outside the scope of National Statistics.

Definition of expenditure

Environmental protection expenditure is defined as capital and operational expenditure incurred because of, and which can be directly related to, the pursuit of an environmental objective. Spending on installations and processes which are environmentally beneficial, but which also produce revenue (or savings) exceeding expenditures, are excluded on the grounds that they are likely to have been carried out for commercial not environmental reasons. The spending falls into five main categories:

- **End-of-pipe-investment** is defined as add-on installations and equipment which treats or controls emissions or reduces waste materials generated by the plant, but which does not affect production processes.

- **Integrated processes** are adaptations or changes to production processes in order to generate fewer emissions or waste materials. Only the additional cost of the adaptation or change for environmental reasons is included.

- **In-house operating expenses** cover operating costs necessary to run end-of-pipe or integrated facilities. The additional cost of the purchase of products with lower environmental impact used as raw materials or as ancillary consumables is also included.

- **Current payments made to others** include all payments to third parties for environmental services, including payments for the treatment or removal of solid waste, water service company charges for sewage treatment, payments to contractors for the removal or treatment of waste waters, and payments made to environmental regulatory authorities.

- **Research and development** expenditure includes both in-house research and development and amounts paid to others such as trade associations and consultants.

UK Environmental Accounts

Source

The results are drawn from a survey for 1999 carried out on behalf of the Department for Environment, Food and Rural Affairs (DEFRA) by URS Dames and Moore[7].

Comparisons with previous surveys

The current study, which gives results for 1999 and is summarised in Table 13.9, is the second in a regular series of surveys. The estimates from this survey and the earlier 1997 survey should be regarded as very approximate and any comparisons between the results should be treated with care.

Land cover account, Great Britain, 1990 to 1998 (Table 13.10)

The estimates are taken from the Countryside Survey 2000 (CS2000), which is a stratified sample survey using detailed field recording and mapping to provide information on the stock and condition of habitats and landscapes in Great Britain in 1998. The survey covered both terrestrial and freshwater habitats but did not cover areas more than 75 per cent built up. A similar Northern Ireland Countryside survey (NICS2000) was also completed, but since comparable estimates for 1990 are not readily available, Table 13.10 only covers Great Britain. More information on the survey, which was funded by DEFRA, the Natural Environment Research Council and other sponsors, can be found in the DEFRA report[8].

Using the results of the 1990 survey and CS2000, it is possible to estimate changes in the stock of land cover types between 1990 and 1998. Table 13.10 sets out a summary of the main changes in land cover over the period, broken down by the type of change in the stock of land. The following notes describe the different land cover types in a little more detail.

Woodland is land which is dominated by trees which are more than 5 metres high when mature and which provide a canopy with a cover of greater than 25 per cent. It is divided between broadleaved and mixed woodland (including yew woodland) and coniferous woodland.

Intensive agricultural land is divided into arable and horticultural land and improved grassland. Arable and horticultural land includes orchards and more specialist operations such as market gardening and commercial flower growing, as well as short-term set-aside. Improved grasslands are often intensively managed using fertiliser and weed control treatments, and are typically used for grazing and silage.

Semi-natural land includes neutral, calcareous and acid grassland (the classification of which depends upon the type of soil and the resulting types of vegetation communities); bracken and dwarf shrub heath (which are lands dominated by bracken, dwarf gorse or heath family species); wetlands such as fen, marsh, swamp and bog; and mountainous and coastal habitats.

The remaining land is classified into water bodies, developed areas covered by the survey which are principally built up areas and gardens, but also include inland rock (such as quarries and excavations as well as cliffs, screes etc) and boundary and linear features such as hedgerows, walls and ditches as well as roads, tracks and railways. Unsurveyed urban land is shown separately, in addition to sea and a small unclassified category.

Annex: Atmospheric pollutants and environmental themes

Greenhouse gases

There is a growing consensus that the rise in concentrations of greenhouse gases in the atmosphere has led to changes in the global climate system. The greenhouse gases included in the atmospheric emissions accounts are those covered by the Kyoto Protocol: carbon dioxide (CO_2), methane (CH_4), nitrous oxide (N_2O), hydrofluorocarbons (HFCs), perfluorocarbons (PFCs) and sulphur hexafluoride (SF_6).

The main source of **carbon dioxide (CO_2)** is from the combustion of fossil fuels, but it is also produced in some industrial processes such as the manufacture of cement. Carbon dioxide is a long-lived gas remaining in the atmosphere for between 50 and 200 years. It is the main anthropogenic greenhouse gas.

Methane (CH_4) is produced when organic matter is broken down in the absence of oxygen. Large quantities are produced by enteric fermentation in cattle and sheep, by the spreading of animal manure and from organic waste deposited in landfill sites. Methane is also emitted in coal mining, oil and gas extraction and gas distribution activities. Methane is a significant greenhouse gas.

Nitrous oxide (N_2O) is released in a few industrial processes and from the soil when nitrogenous fertilisers are applied in agriculture and horticulture. These are the main

UK Environmental Accounts

anthropogenic sources. It is a long-lived pollutant, lasting about 120 years in the atmosphere and is a potent greenhouse gas.

Hydrofluorocarbons (HFCs), perfluorocarbons (PFCs) and sulphur hexafluoride (SF_6) are artificial fluids that contain chlorine and/or fluorine. Because of their low reactivity and non-toxicity they were widely used as refrigerants, foam blowing agents, aerosol propellants and solvents.

To aggregate the greenhouse gases covered in the accounts, a weighting based on the relative global warming potential (GWP) of each of the gases is applied, using the effect of CO_2 over a 100 year period as a reference. This gives methane a weight of 21 relative to relative to CO_2 and nitrous oxide a weight of 310 relative to CO_2. SF_6 has a GWP of 23,900 relative to CO_2. The GWP of the other fluorinated compounds varies according to the individual gas.

Greenhouse gas emissions are sometimes shown in terms of carbon equivalent rather than CO_2 equivalent. To convert from CO_2 equivalent to carbon equivalent it is necessary to multiply by 12/44.

Acid rain precursors

The term 'acid rain' describes the various chemical reactions which acidic gases and particles undergo in the atmosphere. The gases may be transported long distances before being deposited as wet or dry deposition. When deposited, hydrogen ions may be released, forming dilute acids, which damage ecosystems and buildings. The gases covered are sulphur dioxide (SO_2) nitrogen oxides (NO_x) and ammonia (NH_3).

The emissions are weighted together using their relative acidifying effects. The weights, given relative to SO_2, are 0.7 for NO_x and 1.9 for NH_3. This is a simplification of the chemistry involved, and there are a number of factors which can affect the eventual deposition and effect of acid rain. There may be an upward bias on the weights of the nitrogen-based compounds in terms of damage to ecosystems.

Sulphur dioxide (SO_2) is produced when coal and some petroleum products containing sulphur impurities are burnt. Sulphur dioxide is an acid gas that can cause respiratory irritation. It can damage ecosystems and buildings directly and is a major contributor to acid rain.

Nitrogen oxides (NO_x) arise when fossil fuels are burnt under certain conditions. High concentrations are harmful to health and reduce plant growth. Like sulphur dioxide, nitrogen oxides contribute to acid rain; nitrogen dioxide (NO_2) also plays a part in the formation of ground ozone layer.

Ammonia (NH_3) is predominantly emitted from spreading animal manure and some fertilisers.

Other air pollutants

PM_{10}s are smoke particles whose diameter is less than 10 microns. They are regarded as responsible for some physiological damage and have been linked to premature mortality from respiratory diseases.

Carbon monoxide (CO) is produced in small quantities when fossil fuel is burnt with insufficient oxygen for complete combustion. At high concentrations carbon monoxide is toxic.

Non-methane volatile organic compounds (NMVOCs) cover a variety of chemicals, many of which are known carcinogens. Emissions of NMVOCs arise from the deliberate and incidental evaporation of solvents (e.g. in paints and cleaning products), from accidental spillage and from non-combustion of petroleum products. The environmental accounts include natural emissions of NMVOCs from forests. NMVOCs play a role in the formation of ground level ozone, which can have an adverse effect on health. The NMVOC emissions include benzene and 1,3-butadiene.

Benzene is released largely from the distribution and combustion of petrol. It is a carcinogen which has also been found to cause bone-marrow depression and consequent leukopenia (depressed white blood cell count) on prolonged exposure.

1,3-Butadiene is a colourless, gaseous hydrocarbon. It is produced by dehydrogenation of butene, or of mixtures of butene and butane; it may also be made from ethanol. 1,3-butadiene is believed to be a carcinogen, for which the safe level is not known. Emissions of 1,3-butadiene arise from combustion of petroleum products and in its manufacture of synthetic rubber, nylon and latex paints in the chemical industry. 1,3-butadiene is not present in petrol but is formed as a by-product of combustion. The increasing use of catalytic converters through the 1990's has caused a significant reduction in emissions from the road transport sector.

UK Environmental Accounts

Heavy Metals

Lead (Pb) is a heavy metal that is emitted from the combustion of petrol, coal combustion and metal works. Emissions of lead are expected to have fallen to negligible levels in 2000, mainly as a result of the ban on the sale of leaded petrol from 1 January 2000. Lead has been found to inhibit the development of children's intelligence. If the levels of lead are sufficient, lead can cause degenerative processes such as osteoporosis, inhibit many enzyme reactions in the body and cause reproductive disorders such as sterility and miscarriages.

Cadmium (Cd) is a normal constituent of soil and water at low concentrations. Industrially, cadmium is used as an anti-friction agent, in alloys, semi-conductors, control rods for nuclear reactors and PVC and battery manufacture. The main sources of cadmium emissions are from waste incineration, and iron and steel manufacture. Emissions of cadmium have declined over recent years; this is mainly attributable to the decline in coal combustion.

Environmentally, cadmium is dangerous because many plants and some animals absorb it easily and concentrate it in tissues. Cadmium competes with calcium in the body, and if levels are sufficient, it will displace calcium, causing embrittlement of bones and painful deformations of the skeleton. Cadmium also competes with zinc in the body, and if levels of cadmium are high enough, cadmium will also displace zinc from enzymes in the body.

The main sources of **mercury (Hg)** emissions are waste incineration, the manufacture of chlorine in mercury cells, non-ferrous metal production and coal combustion. Emissions of mercury have declined over recent years due to improved controls on mercury cells and their replacement by diaphragm cells and the decline of coal use. Due to the volatility of mercury, if levels are sufficiently high, compounds containing mercury attack and destroy various parts of the body, particularly teeth, lung tissues and intestines.

References

1. Department of Trade and Industry. *Development of UK Oil and Gas Resources (the "Brown Book")*. Various issues (title has changed over the years). HMSO/TSO

2. European Commission. *Accounts for subsoil assets: Results of pilot studies in European countries, 2000*. Office for Official Publication of the European Communities, Luxembourg.

3. Department of Trade and Industry. *Digest of United Kingdom Energy Statistics*. Various issues. HMSO/TSO.

4. Department for Environment, Food and Rural Affairs. *Digest of Environmental Statistics, Chapter 7* on the DEFRA website at http://www.defra.gov.uk/environment/statistics/des/index.htm

5. Department of Environment, Transport and the Regions and the National Assembly for Wales. *Municipal Waste Management 1998/99*. DETR (now DEFRA) September 2000.

6. Wuppertal Institute for Climate, Environment and Energy. *Total Material Resource Flows of the United Kingdom*. February 2001.

7. URS Dames and Moore. *Environmental Protection Expenditure by Industry: 1999 UK Survey*. June 2001.

8. Haines-Young, R.H., et al (2000). *Accounting for Nature: assessing habitats in the UK countryside*. DETR London. See also the Countryside Survey 2000 website at http://www.cs2000.org.uk

UK Environmental Accounts

13.1 Estimates of remaining recoverable oil and gas reserves

End year:	1992	1993	1994	1995	1996	1997	1998	1999	2000
OIL (million tonnes)									
Discovered reserves									
Proven	610	605	575	605	665	690	685	665	630
Probable	755	800	920	765	690	700	575	455	380
Possible	710	690	580	520	670	625	540	545	480
Range of undiscovered reserves									
Lower end	530	560	480	380	285	285	275	250	225
Upper end	3 370	3 355	3 140	2 920	2 700	2 680	2 550	2 600	2 300
Range of total reserves									
Lower end[1]	1 140	1 165	1 055	985	950	975	960	915	855
Upper end[2]	5 445	5 450	5 215	4 810	4 725	4 695	4 350	4 265	3 790
Expected level of reserves[3]									
Opening stocks	1 770	1 895	1 965	1 975	1 750	1 640	1 675	1 535	1 370
Extraction	-94	-100	-127	-130	-130	-128	-132	-137	-126
Other volume changes	219	170	137	-95	20	163	-7	-35	-9
Closing stocks	1 895	1 965	1 975	1 750	1 640	1 675	1 535	1 370	1 235
Life expectancy[4] (years)	20	20	16	13	13	13	12	10	10
GAS (billion cubic metres)									
Discovered reserves									
Proven	610	630	660	700	760	765	755	760	735
Probable	740	805	855	780	660	620	585	500	460
Possible	515	480	400	435	540	600	455	490	430
Range of undiscovered reserves									
Lower end	270	300	430	395	440	500	440	355	325
Upper end	1 277	1 297	1 602	1 412	1 585	1 700	1 595	1 465	1 440
Range of total reserves									
Lower end[1]	880	930	1 090	1 095	1 200	1 265	1 195	1 115	1 060
Upper end[2]	3 142	3 212	3 517	3 327	3 545	3 685	3 390	3 215	3 065
Expected level of reserves[3]									
Opening stock	1 495	1 620	1 735	1 945	1 875	1 860	1 885	1 780	1 615
Extraction	-52	-61	-65	-70	-84	-86	-89	-99	-108
Other volume changes	181	180	280	5	75	117	-9	-66	20
Closing stock	1 620	1 735	1 945	1 875	1 860	1 885	1 780	1 615	1 520
Life expectancy[4] (years)	31	28	30	27	22	22	20	16	14

1 The lower end of the range of total reserves has been calculated as the sum of proven reserves and the lower end of the range of undiscovered reserves.
2 The upper end of the range of total reserves is the sum of proven, probable and possible reserves and the upper end of the range of undiscovered reserves.
3 Expected reserves are the sum of proven reserves, probable reserves and the lower end of the range of undiscovered reserves.
4 Based on expected level of reserves at end year and current extraction rates.

Source: Department of Trade and Industry

UK Environmental Accounts

13.2 Monetary balance sheets for oil and gas reserves[1]

£ million

	1992	1993	1994	1995	1996	1997	1998	1999	2000
OIL									
Opening stocks	16 955	14 897	10 490	16 096	23 955	35 807	39 963	30 200	21 986
Extraction	-1 162	-831	-1 475	-2 424	-3 791	-4 133	-3 407	-2 775	-4 779
Revaluation due to time passing	558	413	671	1 194	1 669	1 643	1 461	1 116	1 871
Other volume changes	1 552	579	129	-4 655	-3 794	1 371	-4 374	-4 268	-6 615
Change in extraction	-774	-931	-5 546	-879	66	730	-1 576	-1 254	5 079
Change in rent	-2 232	-3 636	11 827	14 623	17 702	4 544	-1 866	-1 034	19 705
Closing stocks	14 897	10 490	16 096	23 955	35 807	39 963	30 200	21 986	37 246
GAS									
Opening stocks[2]	-7 318	-4 477	1 943	8 400	15 729	24 951	29 068	32 747	27 836
Extraction[3]	279	-126	-530	-1 053	-1 846	-2 155	-2 563	-2 469	-2 806
Revaluation due to time passing	-163	72	289	676	1 042	1 179	1 465	1 326	1 314
Other volume changes	-514	192	1 408	-794	-294	573	-2 769	-4 164	-2 770
Change in extraction	57	-412	-631	-1 653	-5 859	-702	-1 640	-4 089	-3 898
Change in rent	3 182	6 695	5 920	10 152	16 179	5 221	9 187	4 485	8 912
Closing stocks[2]	-4 477	1 943	8 400	15 729	24 951	29 068	32 747	27 836	28 588

Source: ONS

1. The estimated opening and closing stock values are based on the present value method (see chapter notes for a more detailed description of the methodology used). The estimates are extremely sensitive to the estimated return to capital and to assumptions about future unit resource rents.
2. The negative stock values result from estimated negative resource rents. They could have been set to zero by definition, but have been left in the table in order to show the results of the assumptions made in the calculations.
3. Positive values for extraction are a result of estimated negative resource rents.

UK Environmental Accounts

13.3 Energy consumption

Million tonnes of oil equivalent

	1992	1993	1994	1995	1996	1997	1998	1999
Direct use of energy from fossil fuels								
Agriculture	2.1	2.1	2.1	2.0	2.1	2.0	2.0	1.8
Mining and quarrying	6.2	6.3	6.7	6.5	7.2	7.3	7.7	7.5
Manufacturing	40.5	40.6	41.5	41.5	42.4	42.5	42.5	42.0
Electricity, gas and water supply	53.8	50.7	50.5	51.8	52.8	50.3	52.7	52.0
Construction	1.5	1.5	1.5	1.5	1.5	1.5	1.3	1.5
Wholesale and retail trade	4.6	4.8	4.7	4.7	5.1	5.1	5.4	5.4
Transport and communication	19.8	20.5	21.2	21.9	22.9	23.6	24.7	24.2
Financial intermediation	4.3	4.5	4.7	4.8	5.1	4.6	5.0	5.0
Public administration	3.9	4.0	4.0	4.1	4.1	3.9	3.5	3.4
Education, health and social work	5.4	4.9	4.7	4.7	5.1	5.0	4.8	4.5
Other services	2.0	1.9	1.8	1.8	1.8	1.4	1.3	1.3
Domestic	56.0	57.5	55.3	53.5	59.4	56.7	57.3	57.3
Total use of energy from fossil fuels	200.3	199.3	198.7	198.9	209.6	203.9	208.2	206.1
Energy from other sources[1]	20.4	23.3	23.1	23.3	23.5	24.4	24.7	23.9
Total energy consumption of primary fuels and equivalents	220.7	222.6	221.9	222.2	233.1	228.4	232.9	230.0
Direct use of energy including electricity								
Agriculture	2.5	2.5	2.4	2.4	2.5	2.3	2.3	2.2
Mining and quarrying	6.7	6.8	7.0	6.8	7.6	7.7	8.0	7.8
Manufacturing	47.3	47.9	48.5	48.4	49.4	49.8	49.7	49.3
Electricity, gas and water supply	50.8	50.0	49.9	51.1	51.5	49.6	51.9	50.3
of which - transformation losses by major producers	45.5	45.1	44.5	45.1	45.1	44.0	45.5	43.3
- distribution losses of electricity supply	2.5	2.0	2.3	2.6	2.4	2.5	2.4	2.4
Construction	1.6	1.6	1.6	1.6	1.6	1.6	1.4	1.5
Wholesale and retail trade	6.4	6.7	6.7	6.7	7.1	7.4	7.8	7.8
Transport and communication	20.5	21.5	22.0	22.8	23.9	24.7	25.8	25.3
Financial intermediation	6.2	6.5	6.7	6.9	7.3	7.0	7.4	7.4
Public administration	4.6	4.5	4.7	4.9	4.9	4.6	4.3	4.2
Education, health and social work	6.9	6.1	6.0	5.9	6.3	6.2	6.0	5.7
Other services	2.5	2.4	2.3	2.3	2.3	1.8	1.7	1.7
Domestic	64.6	66.1	63.9	62.3	68.7	65.7	66.7	66.8
Total energy consumption of primary fuels and equivalents	220.7	222.6	221.9	222.2	233.1	228.4	232.9	230.0
Reallocated use of energy								
Energy industry electricity transformation losses and distribution losses allocated to final consumer								
Agriculture	3.0	3.0	3.0	2.9	3.0	2.8	2.9	2.7
Mining and quarrying	7.6	7.6	7.6	7.4	8.2	8.2	8.5	8.3
Manufacturing	58.9	60.0	60.3	60.1	61.0	61.3	61.3	60.3
Electricity, gas and water supply	10.8	9.8	10.2	10.8	11.0	9.9	10.9	11.2
Construction	1.8	1.8	1.8	1.8	1.8	1.7	1.4	1.6
Wholesale and retail trade	9.5	10.1	10.0	10.1	10.6	11.2	11.7	11.5
Transport and communication	21.7	23.1	23.5	24.3	25.4	26.4	27.5	26.9
Financial intermediation	9.4	9.8	10.1	10.5	10.8	10.8	11.2	11.0
Public administration	5.8	5.5	5.8	6.2	6.1	5.7	5.4	5.3
Education, health and social work	9.5	8.3	8.2	7.9	8.4	8.0	7.8	7.5
Other services	3.4	3.2	3.1	3.0	3.0	2.5	2.4	2.3
Domestic	79.3	80.6	78.4	77.2	83.8	79.9	81.9	81.3
Total energy consumption of primary fuels and equivalents	220.7	222.6	221.9	222.2	233.1	228.4	232.9	230.0
Energy from renewable sources[2]	1.4	1.6	2.1	2.1	2.1	2.3	2.7	2.9
Percentage from renewable sources[2]	0.6%	0.7%	0.9%	1.0%	0.9%	1.0%	1.1%	1.3%

1 Nuclear power, hydroelectric power and imports of electricity.
2 Renewable sources include solar power and energy from wind, wave and tide, hydroelectricity, wood, straw and sewage gas. Landfill gas and municipal solid waste combustion have also been included within this definition.

Source: NETCEN, Department of Trade and Industry, ONS

UK Environmental Accounts

13.4 Atmospheric emissions 1999

Thousand tonnes

	Greenhouse gases CO_2, CH_4, N_2O, HFC PFC, SF_6, $KtCO_2$ equiv[1]	Acid rain precursors SO_2, NO_x, NH_3 $K tSO_2$ equiv[2]	PM10[3]	CO[4]	NMVOC[5]	Benzene	Butadiene	Lead (tonnes)	Cadmium (tonnes)	Mercury (tonnes)
Agriculture	56 800	590	20.4	71	149	0.4	0.1	4.3	0.02	0.00
Mining and quarrying	33 700	90	30.7	155	194	0.5	0.1	3.2	0.04	0.02
Manufacturing	132 800	450	32.7	724	483	3.2	0.6	183.7	4.54	3.83
Electricity, gas and water supply	155 700	1 020	19.4	81	30	0.3	0.0	17.8	0.51	1.68
Construction	4 700	30	7.5	183	66	0.6	0.2	2.4	0.01	0.00
Wholesale and retail trade	15 000	40	5.2	178	136	1.4	0.4	14.6	0.03	0.00
Transport and communication	70 300	450	16.6	347	114	2.6	2.3	19.1	0.21	0.02
Financial intermediation	13 400	30	4.0	203	26	1.2	0.2	17.2	0.03	0.00
Public administration	9 000	30	1.3	17	3	0.1	0.0	1.5	0.01	0.05
Education, health and social work	11 100	20	2.1	35	5	0.2	0.0	4.0	0.02	0.09
Other services	20 000	30	1.3	25	17	0.2	0.1	5.5	0.66	2.23
Domestic	147 900	410	48.7	2 849	537	20.3	3.1	281.0	0.50	0.63
Totals	670 400	3 190	189.9	4 868	1 760	31.1	7.3	554.4	6.58	8.55
Of which, emissions from road transport	119 200	550	36.3	3 292	473	21.0	5.3	327.3	0.37	0.00

1 Carbon dioxide, methane, nitrous oxide, hydro-fluorocarbons, perfluorocarbons and sulphur hexafluoride expressed in thousand tonnes of carbon dioxide equivalent
2 Sulphur dioxide, nitrogen oxides and ammonia expressed as thousand tonnes of sulphur dioxide equivalent.
3 PM_{10}s are carbon particles in air arising from incomplete combustion.
4 Carbon monoxide.
5 Non-methane Volatile Organic Compounds including benzene and 1,3-butadiene.

Source: NETCEN, ONS

13.5 Greenhouse gas and acid rain precursor emissions

Thousand tonnes

	1992	1993	1994	1995	1996	1997	1998	1999
Greenhouse gases - CO_2, CH_4, N_2O, HFC, PFCs and SF_6[1]								
Agriculture	58 600	57 200	58 200	58 200	58 900	58 800	58 500	56 800
Mining and quarrying	40 900	39 100	36 800	36 900	38 200	36 800	36 300	33 700
Manufacturing	162 300	159 000	165 500	162 300	166 000	168 100	163 400	132 800
Electricity, gas and water supply	198 600	180 600	177 000	175 800	173 600	159 100	163 700	155 700
Construction	5 000	4 900	4 900	4 800	4 900	4 800	4 400	4 700
Wholesale and retail trade	12 100	12 600	12 700	12 800	13 800	14 100	15 000	15 000
Transport and communication	57 500	59 500	61 400	63 500	66 500	68 700	71 900	70 300
Financial intermediation	11 200	11 600	12 200	12 700	13 400	12 400	13 400	13 400
Public administration	10 900	10 900	10 900	11 000	11 000	10 400	9 300	9 000
Education, health and social work	14 200	12 800	12 200	12 000	12 900	12 600	12 000	11 100
Other services	27 800	26 700	25 800	25 000	24 300	22 700	21 300	20 000
Domestic	144 900	149 100	143 100	137 500	151 900	145 900	147 300	147 900
Total greenhouse gas emissions	744 000	724 000	720 700	712 500	735 400	714 400	716 500	670 400
Of which, emissions from road transport	111 400	113 000	114 100	113 500	118 200	120 100	119 800	119 200
Acid rain precursor emissions - SO_2, NOx, NH_3[2]								
Agriculture	630	620	620	600	590	590	600	590
Mining and quarrying	120	120	120	90	100	100	90	90
Manufacturing	920	900	830	730	670	620	540	450
Electricity, gas and water supply	2 900	2 490	2 140	1 950	1 640	1 290	1 330	1 020
Construction	40	40	40	40	30	30	30	30
Wholesale and retail trade	80	70	70	60	50	50	50	40
Transport and communication	550	540	520	520	520	530	520	450
Financial intermediation	50	50	50	50	50	40	40	30
Public administration	60	60	60	50	50	50	40	30
Education, health and social work	70	70	60	50	40	40	30	20
Other services	50	50	50	50	50	40	40	30
Domestic	620	600	550	500	510	480	440	410
Total acid rain precursor emissions	6 090	5 610	5 110	4 690	4 300	3 860	3 750	3 190
Of which, emissions from road transport	920	860	830	760	720	670	600	550

1 Carbon dioxide, methane, nitrous oxide, hydrofluorocarbons, perfluorocarbons and sulphur hexafluoride expressed in thousand tonnes of carbon dioxide equivalent.
2 Sulphur dioxide, nitrogen oxides and ammonia expressed in thousand tonnes of sulphur dioxide equivalent.

Source: NETCEN, ONS

UK Environmental Accounts

13.6 Total waste arisings in the United Kingdom 1998/9

Million tonnes

	Inert, construction, demolition	Paper, card	Animal and vegetable	General	Metal & scrap equipment	Mineral	Other waste	Total
Agriculture[1]	0.0	0.0	92.5	1.0	0.0	0.0	0.0	93.5
Mining and quarrying[2]	0.0	0.0	0.0	0.0	0.0	119.0	0.0	119.0
Food, drink and tobacco[3]	0.5	0.3	2.3	3.8	0.1	0.0	1.6	8.6
Textiles and clothing etc[3]	0.0	0.1	0.0	0.9	0.0	0.0	0.2	1.2
Paper and printing[3]	0.0	1.8	0.0	2.9	0.0	0.0	0.3	5.0
Chemicals[3]	0.3	0.1	0.0	1.3	0.5	0.2	3.0	5.3
Non-metallic mineral products[3]	1.2	0.2	0.0	1.8	0.1	0.5	0.4	4.3
Metal products[3]	0.2	0.1	0.0	1.2	2.3	7.5	1.8	13.1
Machinery and equipment[3]	0.1	0.1	0.0	1.4	1.0	0.0	0.4	3.1
Transport equipment[3]	0.0	0.0	0.0	0.7	0.8	0.0	1.0	2.5
Other manufacturing[3]	0.0	0.1	0.0	2.3	0.1	0.0	0.3	2.8
Electricity, gas and water supply[4]	0.2	0.0	0.0	0.4	0.1	7.0	0.3	7.9
Construction[5]	78.0	0.0	0.0	0.0	0.0	0.0	0.0	78.0
Wholesale and retail[6]	0.0	1.7	0.3	7.7	0.4	0.0	0.8	10.9
Hotels and catering[6]	0.1	0.1	0.0	3.6	0.1	0.0	0.1	3.9
Transport and communications[6,7]	0.0	0.4	0.2	2.1	0.1	22.3	0.6	25.8
Finance and other services[6]	0.1	0.7	0.0	7.6	0.1	0.1	0.7	9.4
Public administration, health, education[6]	0.1	0.3	0.1	4.2	0.1	0.0	0.2	4.8
Waste water services[8]	0.0	0.0	1.0	0.0	0.0	0.0	0.0	1.0
Households[9]	0.0	0.9	0.6	26.1	0.3	0.4	0.0	28.4
Total waste arisings	80.8	6.9	97.1	69.0	6.0	157.1	11.7	428.6

Source: see Notes 1-9

1. Based on estimate of 87 million tonnes for GB for 1999 (source DEFRA). Grossed to UK total on basis of agriculture GDP for 1997 (source ONS).
2. 1997 figure used as the 1998 figure is still provisional (source DEFRA).
3. Industry figures based on Environment Agency estimates for 1998/99 for England and Wales, controlled to GB total, and grossed to UK total on the basis of estimated manufacturing industry GDP for 1997 (source ONS).
4. Figures based on Environment Agency estimates for 1998/99 for England Wales, controlled to GB industry total and grossed to UK total on the basis of electricity, gas and water supply industry GDP for 1997 (source ONS).
5. Provisional figure based on DEFRA survey for 2000 for England and Wales. Grossed to UK total using 1997 share of Construction Industry GDP (source ONS).
6. Services sector figures based on Environment Agency estimates for 1998/99 for England and Wales, controlled to GB service sector total and grossed to UK total on the basis of service sector GDP estimates for 1997 (source ONS).
7. Mineral waste estimate is for the amount of dredged material, based on Centre for Environment, Fisheries and Aquaculture Science Survey for 1997 for all UK waters
8. Dry weight arisings for 1998/99 (source Water UK). Wet weight can be estimated on the basis of 4% solid content on average giving a total of 26 million tonnes.
9. Household municipal waste 1998/99 for England and Wales (source DETR), grossed to UK total on the basis of population.

UK Environmental Accounts

13.7 Material flows in the UK

Million tonnes

	1970	1980	1990	1991	1992	1993	1994	1995	1996	1997	1998	1999
Domestic extraction												
Biomass												
Agricultural harvest	106	102	100	103	109	102	97	100	109	108	106	107
Timber	3	3	6	6	6	7	8	7	7	7	7	7
Animal grazing	93	92	90	89	89	88	89	89	88	89	90	90
Fish	1	1	1	1	1	1	1	1	1	1	1	1
Total biomass	204	199	196	199	205	199	195	196	204	206	203	204
Minerals												
Ores	12	1	0	0	0	0	0	0	0	0	0	0
Clay	38	25	21	19	16	15	17	18	16	15	16	16
Other industrial minerals	14	11	11	11	10	10	10	10	10	10	9	9
Sand and gravel	122	110	128	103	103	104	113	106	101	103	103	101
Crushed stone	156	150	212	196	190	195	210	200	181	182	182	168
Total minerals	342	298	373	329	319	324	351	334	308	310	310	293
Fossil fuels												
Coal	149	130	94	96	75	69	50	54	51	49	42	38
Natural gas	10	34	46	51	52	61	65	71	84	86	90	99
Crude oil	0	80	92	91	94	100	127	130	130	128	133	139
Total fossil fuels	160	245	232	238	221	230	241	255	265	263	265	276
Total domestic extraction	705	741	801	766	744	752	786	785	778	779	778	773
Imports												
Biomass	15	12	10	10	11	11	11	12	12	12	13	12
Minerals	25	12	22	21	22	22	26	29	26	27	26	22
Fossil fuels	103	60	65	72	73	69	59	57	61	63	59	52
Products	55	55	89	83	85	84	94	90	92	97	103	103
Total imports	197	140	187	185	190	185	190	187	191	200	201	189
Exports												
Biomass	1	4	8	8	7	6	6	6	7	7	7	6
Minerals	8	11	7	8	11	15	15	15	17	16	16	17
Fossil fuels	5	44	58	56	57	64	82	85	80	79	79	84
Products	34	42	44	46	48	66	72	68	70	83	78	77
Total exports	47	101	117	118	124	151	175	174	174	185	181	184
Indirect flows												
- from domestic extraction[1] (excl soil erosion)	574	667	730	724	689	663	657	666	674	671	641	639
- from production of imports	394	384	457	468	522	481	536	527	514	541	553	497
Summary aggregates												
Direct Material Input (domestic extraction + imports)	902	881	988	951	934	937	976	972	969	979	979	962
Domestic Material Consumption (domestic extraction + imports - exports)	855	780	871	833	811	786	801	798	795	793	798	778
Total Material Requirement (direct material input + indirect flows)	1 870	1 932	2 175	2 144	2 145	2 081	2 169	2 165	2 157	2 191	2 174	2 098

1. Indirect flows from domestic extraction relate to unused material which is moved during extraction, such as overburden from mining and quarrying.

Source: Wuppertal Institute

UK Environmental Accounts

13.8 Government revenues from environmental taxes

£ million

		1992	1993	1994	1995	1996	1997	1998	1999	2000
Energy										
Duty on hydrocarbon oils	GTAP	11 281	12 497	13 984	15 360	16 895	18 357	20 996	22 391	23 027
including										
Unleaded petrol	GBHE	3 476	4 242	5 101	5 901	7 043	8 073	9 897	11 952	12 548
Leaded petrol	GBHL	4 661	4 502	4 349	4 088	3 716	3 393	2 984	1 630	7
Ultra low sulphur petrol	ZXTK	–	–	–	–	–	–	–	–	1 162
Diesel	GBHH	2 947	3 484	4 257	5 127	5 888	6 528	7 088	1 274	32
Ultra low sulphur diesel	GBHI	–	–	–	–	–	146	806	7 338	9 061
VAT on duty	CMYA	1 974	2 187	2 447	2 688	2 957	3 212	3 674	3 918	4 030
Fossil fuel levy	CIQY	1 344	1 331	1 355	1 306	978	418	181	104	84
Road vehicles										
Vehicle excise duty	CMXZ	3 113	3 482	3 848	3 954	4 149	4 334	4 631	4 873	4 678
Car tax	GTAT	603	–4	–	–	–	–	–	–	–
Other environmental taxes										
Air passenger duty	CWAA	–	–	33	339	353	442	823	884	940
Landfill tax	BKOF	–	–	–	–	5	378	333	439	461
Total environmental taxes		18 315	19 493	21 667	23 647	25 337	27 141	30 638	32 609	33 220
Environmental taxes as a % of:										
Total taxes and social contributions		8.5	9.0	9.2	9.3	9.5	9.4	9.6	9.7	9.3
Gross domestic product		3.0	3.0	3.2	3.3	3.3	3.3	3.6	3.6	3.5

13.9 Environmental protection expenditure in specified industries, 1999

£ million

	Current expenditure				Capital expenditure			
	In-house operating expenses	Payments made to others	Research and development	Total current expenditure	End-of-pipe investment	Integrated processes	Total capital	Total environmental expenditure
Mining and quarrying	70	40	10	110	40	70	110	230
Food, beverages and tobacco	230	220	10	470	40	150	200	660
Textiles and leather products	20	50	0	80	30	10	30	110
Wood and wood products	20	30	0	50	0	0	0	50
Pulp and paper products, printing and publishing	170	110	10	290	200	20	220	510
Solid and nuclear fuels, oil refining	40	50	10	90	30	10	50	140
Chemicals and man-made fibres	240	170	20	440	60	50	100	540
Rubber and plastic products	70	50	10	130	40	10	50	190
Other non-metallic mineral products	40	40	10	90	30	50	80	170
Basic metals and metal products	180	100	10	300	100	40	140	440
Machinery and equipment	140	80	40	270	40	10	50	320
Electrical and optical equipment	50	50	0	100	10	0	10	120
Transport equipment	70	50	10	120	60	40	100	220
Other manufacturing	10	30	0	40	0	40	40	90
Energy production and water	130	80	0	210	10	100	100	310
Total expenditure in extraction, manufacturing and water supply industries	1 500	1 150	150	2 800	690	610	1 300	4 100

The figures in this table fall outside the scope of National Statistics.

Source: Department for Environment, Food and Rural Affairs

UK Environmental Accounts

13.10 Land cover account, Great Britain 1990-1998

Thousand hectares

	1990 stock	Woodland creation/ rotation	Agriculture creation/ rotation	Semi-natural creation	Semi-natural rotation	Water body creation	Development	Loss to unknown	1998 stock
Broadleaved and mixed woodland	1 371.2	145.9	-22.2	-42.1		-0.8	-12.9	-0.4	1 438.7
Coniferous woodland	1 369.3	53.7	-9.0	-48.3		-0.6	-5.0	0.0	1 360.2
Woodland sub-total	2 740.5	211.6	-31.2	-90.4		-1.4	-17.8	-0.4	2 798.9
Arable and horticultural	5 246.1	-28.8	177.4	-41.4		-1.0	-19.3	-0.2	5 332.9
Improved grassland	5 538.6	-34.1	222.8	-232.0		-0.5	-53.9	-5.3	5 435.5
Intensive agriculture sub-total	10 784.7	-62.8	400.2	-273.4		-1.5	-73.2	-5.5	10 768.4
Neutral grassland	569.5	-24.4	-153.6	238.9	-18.2	-0.5	-33.2	-0.1	578.3
Calcareous grassland	81.4	-1.1	-13.3	3.7	-3.8	0.0	-0.2	0.0	66.7
Acid grassland	1 470.9	-24.0	-133.7	43.3	-34.7	0.0	-4.6	-0.7	1 316.5
Bracken	456.9	-21.8	-8.7	20.4	38.9	0.0	-0.5	0.0	485.1
Dwarf shrub heath	1 487.1	-24.5	-1.2	13.1	-41.4	0.0	-3.3	0.0	1 429.7
Fen, marsh and swamp	456.4	-6.1	-25.1	61.0	71.3	-0.7	-1.2	-0.6	554.9
Bog	2 297.3	-17.9	-0.7	10.5	-10.1	-0.3	-0.2	-0.1	2278.5
Montane	49.8	0.0	0.0	0.0	0.0	0.0	0.0	0.0	49.8
Coastal habitats	274.1	-0.3	-0.8	2.6	-2.0	-0.3	0.0	0.0	273.3
Semi-natural land sub-total	7 143.3	-120.1	-337.2	393.5	0.0	-1.8	-43.2	-1.5	7 032.9
Standing open water and canals	208.4	-0.2	-1.0	-0.9		5.2	-1.2	0.0	210.3
Rivers and streams	66.7	-0.2	-0.1	-1.4		0.3	-0.1	0.0	65.2
Water bodies sub-total	275.1	-0.4	-1.1	-2.3		5.5	-1.2	-0.1	275.5
Inland rock	53.6	-0.6	-2.2	-7.6		0.0	17.0	0.0	60.2
Built up areas and gardens	1 230.4	-14.2	-12.3	-9.4		-0.7	98.3	-1.2	1 291.0
Boundary and linear features	495.0	-1.0	-14.5	-7.8		-0.1	20.2	-0.1	491.7
Developed land sub-total	1 779.0	-15.9	-28.9	-24.8		-0.8	135.5	-1.3	1 842.9
Sea	298.5	0.0	0.0	-0.7		0.0	0.0	0.0	297.8
Unknown	73.9	-0.3	-1.8	-2.0		0.0	0.0	8.8	78.6
Unsurveyed urban land[1]	463.0								463.0
Total land cover	23 557.9	0.0	0.0	0.0	0.0	0.0	0.0	0.0	23 558.0

1. Areas which are more than 75% built up were not covered by the survey.

Source: Department for Environment, Food and Rural Affairs

Glossary

Above the line
Transactions in the production, current and capital accounts which are above the *Net lending (+) / Net borrowing (financial surplus or deficit)* line in the presentation used in the economic accounts. The financial transactions account is *below the line* in this presentation.

Accruals basis
A method of recording transactions to relate them to the period when the exchange of ownership of the goods, services or financial asset applies. (See also *cash basis*). For example, value added tax accrues when the expenditure to which it relates takes place, but Customs and Excise receive the cash some time later. The difference between accruals and cash results in the creation of an asset and liability in the financial accounts, shown as *amounts receivable or payable* (F7).

Actual final consumption
The value of goods consumed by a sector but not necessarily purchased by that sector. See also *Final consumption expenditure, Intermediate consumption*.

Advance and progress payments
Payments made for goods in advance of completion and delivery of the goods. Also referred to as *stage payments*.

Asset boundary
Boundary separating assets included in creating core economic accounts (such as plant and factories, also including non-produced assets such as land and water resources) and those excluded (such as natural assets not managed for an economic purpose).

Assets
Entities over which ownership rights are enforced by institutional units, individually or collectively; and from which economic benefits may be derived by their owners by holding them over a period of time.

Assurance
An equivalent term to insurance, commonly used in the life insurance business.

Balancing item
A balancing item is an accounting construct obtained by subtracting the total value of the entries on one side of an account from the total value for the other side. In the sector accounts in the former system of UK economic accounts the term referred to the difference between the *Financial Surplus or Deficit* for a sector and the sum of the financial transactions for that sector, currently designated the *statistical discrepancy*.

Balance of payments
A summary of the transactions between residents of a country and residents abroad in a given time period.

Balance of trade
The balance on trade in goods and services. The balance of trade is a summary of the imports and exports of goods and services across an economic boundary in a given period.

Balance sheet
A statement, drawn up at a particular point in time, of the value of *assets* owned and of the financial claims (*liabilities*) against the owner of these assets.

Banks (UK)
Strictly, all financial institutions located in the United Kingdom and recognised by the Bank of England as banks for statistical purposes up to late 1981 or as UK banks from then onwards. This category includes the UK offices of institutions authorised under the Banking Act (1987), the Bank of England, the National Girobank and the TSB Group plc. It may include branches of foreign banks where these are recognised as banks by the Bank of England, but not offices abroad of these or of any British-owned banks. An updated list of banks appears in each February's issue of the *Bank of England Quarterly Bulletin*. Institutions in the Channel Islands and the Isle of Man which have opted to adhere to the monetary control arrangements introduced in August 1981 were formerly included in the sector but are not considered to be residents of the United Kingdom under the ESA. Banks are included in the Monetary financial institutions (S.121/S.122) sector.

Bank of England
This comprises S.121, the central bank sub-sector of the *financial corporations* sector.

Bank of England - Issue Department
This part of the Bank of England deals with the issue of bank notes on behalf of central government and was formerly classified to central government though it is now part of the central bank sector. Its activities include, *inter alia*, market purchases of commercial bills from UK banks.

Basic prices
These prices are the preferred method of valuing gross value added and output. They reflect the amount received by the producer for a unit of goods or services *minus* any taxes payable *plus* any subsidy receivable on that unit as a consequence of production or sale (i.e. the cost of production including subsidies). As a result the only taxes included in the basic price are taxes on the production process – such as business rates and any vehicle excise duty paid by businesses – which are not specifically levied on the production of a unit of output. Basic prices exclude any transport charges invoiced separately by the producer.

Below the line
The financial transactions account which shows the financing of *Net lending(+) / Net borrowing (-)* (formerly *financial surplus or deficit*).

Bond
A financial instrument that usually pays interest to the holder, issued by governments as well as companies and other institutions, e.g. local authorities. Most bonds have a fixed date on which the borrower will repay the holder. Bonds are attractive to investors since they can be bought and sold easily in a *secondary market*. Special forms of bonds include *deep discount bonds, equity warrant bonds, Eurobonds*, and *zero coupon bonds*.

British government securities
See *Gilts*.

Building society
Those institutions as defined in the Building Society Acts (1962 and 1986). They offer housing finance largely to the households sector and fund this largely by taking short term deposits from the households sector. They are part of the *monetary financial institutions* sub-sector.

Capital
Capital assets are those which contribute to the productive process so as to produce an economic return. In other contexts the word can be taken to include

Glossary

tangible assets (e.g. buildings, plant and machinery), *intangible assets* and financial capital. See also *fixed assets, inventories*.

Capital formation
Acquisition *less* disposals of *fixed assets*, improvement of land, change in *inventories* and acquisition *less* disposals of *valuables*.

Capital Stock
Measure of the cost of replacing the capital assets of a country, held at a particular point in time.

Capital transfers
Transfers which are related to the acquisition or disposal of assets by the recipient or payer. They may be in cash or kind, and may be imputed to reflect the assumption or forgiveness of debt.

Cash basis
The recording of transactions when cash or other assets are actually transferred, rather than on an *accruals* basis.

Central monetary institutions (CMIs)
Institutions (usually central banks) which control the centralised monetary reserves and the supply of currency in accordance with government policies, and which act as their governments' bankers and agents. In the UK this is equivalent to the Bank of England. In many other countries maintenance of the exchange rate is undertaken in this sector. In the United Kingdom this function is undertaken by central government (part of the Treasury) by use of the *Exchange Equalisation Account*.

Certificate of deposit
A short term interest-paying instrument issued by deposit-taking institutions in return for money deposited for a fixed period. Interest is earned at a given rate. The instrument can be used as security for a loan if the depositor requires money before the repayment date.

Chained index
An index number series which measures changes in consecutive years using weights updated periodically. These periodic changes are linked or chained together to produce comparisons over longer periods.

C.i.f.
The basis of valuation of imports for Customs purposes, it includes the cost of insurance premiums and freight services. These need to be deducted to obtain the f.o.b. valuation consistent with the valuation of exports which is used in the economic accounts.

COICOP (Classification of Individual Consumption by Purpose)
An international classification which groups consumption according to its function or purpose. Thus the heading *clothing*, for example, includes expenditure on garments, clothing materials, laundry and repairs.

Combined use table
Table of the demand for products by each industry group or sector, whether from domestic production or imports, estimated at purchaser's prices. It displays the inputs used by each industry to produce their total output and separates out intermediate purchases of goods and services. This table shows which industries use which products. Columns represent the purchasing industries: rows represent the products purchased.

Commercial paper
This is an unsecured *promissory note* for a specific amount and maturing on a specific date. The commercial paper market allows companies to issue short term debt direct to financial institutions who then market this paper to investors or use it for their own investment purposes.

Compensation of employees
Total remuneration payable to employees in cash or in kind. Includes the value of social contributions payable by the employer.

Consolidated Fund
An account of central government into which most government revenue (excluding borrowing and certain payments to government departments) is paid, and from which most government expenditure (excluding loans and National Insurance benefits) is paid.

Consumption
See *Final consumption, Intermediate consumption*.

Consumption of fixed capital
The amount of capital resources used up in the process of production in any period. It is not an identifiable set of transactions but an imputed transaction which can only be measured by a system of conventions.

Corporations
All bodies recognised as independent legal entities which are producers of market *output* and whose principal activity is the production of goods and services.

Counterpart
In a double-entry system of accounting each transaction gives rise to two corresponding entries. These entries are the counterparts to each other. Thus the counterpart of a payment by one sector is the receipt by another.

Debenture
A long-term bond issued by a UK or foreign company and secured on *fixed assets*. A debenture entitles the holder to a fixed interest payment or a series of such payments.

Depreciation
See *Consumption of fixed capital*.

Derivatives (F.34)
Financial instruments whose value is linked to changes in the value of another financial instrument, an indicator or a commodity. In contrast to the holder of a primary financial instrument (e.g. a government bond or a bank deposit), who has an unqualified right to receive cash (or some other economic benefit) in the future, the holder of a derivative has only a qualified right to receive such a benefit. Examples of derivatives are options and swaps.

DIM (Dividend and Interest Matrix)
The ONS Dividend and Interest Matrix represents property income flows related to holdings of financial transactions. The gross flows are now shown in D4.

Direct investment
Net investment by UK/overseas companies in their overseas/UK branches, subsidiaries or associated companies. A direct investment in a company means that the investor has a significant influence on the operations of the company. Investment includes not only acquisition of fixed assets, stock building and stock appreciation but also all other financial transactions such as additions to, or payments of, working capital, other loans and trade credit and acquisitions of securities. Estimates of investment exclude depreciation.

Glossary

Discount market
That part of the market dealing with short-term borrowing. It is called the discount market because the interest on loans is expressed as a percentage reduction (discount) on the amount paid to the borrower. For example, for a loan of £100 face value when the discount rate is 5% the borrower will receive £95 but will repay £100 at the end of the term.

Double deflation
Method for calculating constant price value added by industry; which takes separate account of the differing price and volume movements of input and outputs in an industry's production process.

Dividend
A payment made to company shareholders from current or previously retained profits. See *DIM*.

ECGD
See *Export Credit Guarantee Department*.

Economically significant prices
These are prices whose level significantly affects the supply of the good or service concerned. Market output consists mainly of goods and services sold at 'economically significant' prices while non-market output comprises those provided free or at prices that are not economically significant.

Enterprise
An *institutional unit* producing *market output*. Enterprises are found mainly in the *non-financial* and *financial corporations* sectors but exist in all sectors. Each enterprise consists of one or more *kind-of-activity units*.

Environmental accounts
Satellite accounts (cf.) describing the relationship between the environment and the economy.

Equity
Equity is ownership or potential ownership of a company. An entity's equity in a company will be evidenced by ordinary shares. They differ from other financial instruments in that they confer ownership of something more than a financial claim. Shareholders are owners of the company whereas bond holders are merely outside creditors.

ESA
European System of National and Regional Accounts. An integrated system of economic accounts which is the European version of the System of National Accounts (SNA).

European Investment Bank
This was set up to assist economic development within the European Union. Its members are the member states of the EU.

European Monetary Cooperation Fund
Central banks of member states of the European Monetary System deposit 20 per cent of their gold and foreign exchange reserves on a short-term basis with the European Monetary Cooperation Fund in exchange for ECUs. The Fund is the clearing house for central banks in the EMS.

European Monetary System
This was established in March 1979. Its most important element is the Exchange Rate Mechanism (ERM) whereby the exchange rates between the currencies of the participating member states (all EU countries except Greece and Portugal) are kept within set ranges. The UK joined the ERM on 8th October 1990. On 16th September 1992 sterling left the ERM and the EMS was suspended.

Exchange Cover Scheme (ECS)
A scheme first introduced in 1969 whereby UK public bodies raise foreign currency from overseas residents, either directly or through UK banks, and surrender it to the *Exchange Equalisation Account* in exchange for sterling for use to finance expenditure in the United Kingdom. HM Treasury sells the borrower foreign currency to service and repay the loan at the exchange rate that applied when the loan was taken out.

Exchange Equalisation Account (EEA)
An account of central government held by the Bank of England in which transactions in the official reserves are recorded. It is the means by which the government, through the Bank of England, influences exchange rates.

Export credit
Credit extended overseas by UK institutions primarily in connection with UK exports but also including some credit in respect of third-country trade.

Export Credits Guarantee Department (ECGD)
A government department whose main function is to provide insurance cover for export credit transactions.

Factor cost
In the former system of national accounts this was the basis of valuation which excluded the effects of taxes on expenditure and subsidies.

Final consumption expenditure
The expenditure on goods and services that are used for the direct satisfaction of individual needs or the collective needs of members of the community as distinct from their purchase for use in the productive process. It may be contrasted with *Actual final consumption*, which is the value of goods consumed but not necessarily purchased by that sector. See also *Intermediate consumption*.

Finance houses
Financial corporations that specialise in the financing of hire purchase arrangements.

Financial auxiliaries
Auxiliary financial activities are ones closely related to financial intermediation but which are not financial intermediation themselves, such as the repackaging of funds. Financial auxiliaries include such activities as insurance broking and fund management.

Financial corporations
All bodies recognised as independent legal entities whose principal activity is financial intermediation and/or the production of auxiliary financial services. However, the United Kingdom currently treats financial auxiliaries as non-financial corporations.

Financial intermediation
Financial intermediation is the activity by which an *institutional unit* acquires financial assets and incurs liabilities on its own account by engaging in financial transactions on the market. The assets and liabilities of financial intermediaries have different characteristics so that the funds are transformed or repackaged with respect to maturity, scale, risk, etc, in the financial intermediation process.

Financial leasing
A form of leasing in which the lessee contracts to assume the rights and responsibilities of ownership of leased goods from the lessor (the legal owner) for

Glossary

the whole (or virtually the whole) of the economic life of the asset. In the economic accounts this is recorded as the sale of the assets to the lessee, financed by an imputed loan (F.42). The leasing payments are split into interest payments and repayments of principal.

Financial Services Adjustment
Now renamed *FISIM* (see below) this is a feature temporarily carried over from the previous system. The output of many financial intermediation services is paid for not by charges, but by an interest rate differential. The value added of these industries is shown including their interest receipts *less* payments, in effect imputing charges for their services. However, GDP in total takes no account of this, and an adjustment is necessary to reconcile the two. For the treatment in the new SNA (to be implemented fully in the EU at a later date) see *FISIM*. Since most output of these industries is intermediate consumption of other industries the difference between the two methods in their effect on total GDP is relatively small.

Financial surplus or deficit (FSD)
The former term for *Net lending(+)/Net borrowing (-)*, the balance of all current and capital account transactions for an institutional sector or the economy as a whole.

FISIM
Financial Intermediation Services Indirectly Measured. The output of many financial intermediation services is paid for not by charges but by an interest rate differential. *FISIM* imputes charges for these services and corresponding offsets in property income. *FISIM*, an innovation of the 1993 SNA, has not yet been fully implemented in the UK economic accounts; the earnings are not yet allocated to the users of the services.

Fixed assets
Produced assets that are themselves used repeatedly or continuously in the production process for more than one year. They comprise buildings and other structures, vehicles and other plant and machinery and also plants and livestock which are used repeatedly or continuously in production, e.g. fruit trees or dairy cattle. They also include intangible assets such as computer software and artistic originals.

Flows
Economic flows reflect the creation, transformation, exchange, transfer or extinction of economic value. They involve changes in the volume, composition or value of an *institutional unit's* assets and liabilities. They are recorded in the *production, distribution and use of income* and *accumulation accounts*.

F.o.b.
Free on board, the valuation of imports and exports of goods used in the economic accounts, including all costs invoiced by the exporter up to the point of loading on to the ship or aircraft but excluding the cost of insurance and freight from the country of consignment.

Futures
Instruments which give the holder the right to purchase a commodity or a financial asset at a future date.

GFCF
See *Gross fixed capital formation*.

Gilts
Bonds issued or guaranteed by the UK government. Also known as gilt-edged securities or British government securities.

Gold
The SNA and the IMF (in the 5th Edition of its Balance of Payments Manual) recognise three types of gold:
- monetary gold, treated as a financial asset;
- gold held as a store of value, to be included in valuables;
- gold as an industrial material, to be included in intermediate consumption or inventories.

This is a significant change from previous UK practice and presents problems such that the United Kingdom has received from the European Union a derogation from applying this fully until the year 2005.

The present treatment is as follows:
In the accounts a distinction is drawn between gold held as a financial asset (financial gold) and gold held like any other commodity (commodity gold). Commodity gold in the form of finished manufactures together with net domestic and overseas transactions in gold moving into or out of finished manufactured form (i.e. for jewellery, dentistry, electronic goods, medals and proof - but not bullion - coins) is recorded in exports and imports of goods.
All other transactions in gold (i.e. those involving semi-manufactures such as rods, wire, etc, or bullion, bullion coins or banking-type assets and liabilities denominated in gold, including official reserve assets) are treated as financial gold transactions and included in the financial account of the Balance of Payments.

The United Kingdom has adopted different treatment to avoid distortion of its visible trade account by the substantial transactions of the London bullion market.

Grants
Voluntary transfer payments. They may be current or capital in nature. Grants from government or the European Union to producers are *subsidies*.

Gross
Key economic series can be shown as gross (i.e. *before* deduction of the consumption of fixed capital or net (i.e. *after* deduction). Gross has this meaning throughout this book unless otherwise stated.

Gross domestic product (GDP)
The total value of output in the economic territory. It is the balancing item on the production account for the whole economy. Domestic product can be measured *gross* or *net*. It is presented in the new accounts at market (or *purchasers'*) prices.

Gross fixed capital formation (GFCF)
Acquisition *less* disposals of *fixed assets* and the improvement of land.

Gross national disposable income
The income available to the residents arising from GDP, and receipts from, *less* payments to, the rest of the world of employment income, property income and current transfers.

Gross value added (GVA)
The value generated by any unit engaged in production, and the contributions of individual sectors or industries to gross domestic product. It is measured at basic prices, excluding taxes *less* subsidies on products.

Hidden economy
Certain activities may be productive and also legal but are concealed from the authorities for various reasons – for example to evade taxes or regulation. In principle these, as well as economic production that is illegal, are to be included in

Glossary

the accounts but they are by their nature difficult to measure.

Holding gains or losses
Profit or loss obtained by virtue of the changing price of assets being held. Holding gains or losses may arise from either physical and financial assets.

Households (S.14)
Individuals or small groups of individuals as consumers and in some cases as entrepreneurs producing goods and market services (where such activities cannot be hived off and treated as those of a *quasi corporation*).

Imputation
The process of inventing a transaction where, although no money has changed hands, there has been a flow of goods or services. It is confined to a very small number of cases where a reasonably satisfactory basis for the assumed valuation is available.

Index-linked gilts
Gilts whose coupon and redemption value are linked to movements in the retail prices index.

Institutional unit
Institutional units are the individual bodies whose data is amalgamated to form the *sectors* of the economy. A body is regarded as an institutional unit if it has decision-making autonomy in respect of its principal function and either keeps a complete set of accounts or is in a position to compile, if required, a complete set of accounts which would be meaningful from both an economic and a legal viewpoint.

Institutional sector
See *Sector*.

Input-Output
A detailed analytical framework based on Supply and Use tables. These are matrices showing the composition of output of individual industries by types of product and how the domestic and imported supply of goods and services is allocated between various intermediate and final uses, including exports.

Intangible assets
Intangible fixed assets include mineral exploration, computer software and entertainment, literary or artistic originals. Expenditure on them is part of *gross fixed capital formation*. They exclude non-produced intangible assets such as patented entities, leases, transferable contracts and purchased goodwill, expenditure on which would be *intermediate consumption*.

Intermediate consumption
The consumption of goods and services in the production process. It may be contrasted with *final consumption* and *capital formation*.

International Monetary Fund (IMF)
A fund set up as a result of the Bretton Woods Conference in 1944 which began operations in 1947. It currently has about 180 member countries including most of the major countries of the world. The fund was set up to supervise the fixed exchange rate system agreed at Bretton Woods and to make available to its members a pool of foreign exchange resources to assist them when they have balance of payments difficulties. It is funded by member countries' subscriptions according to agreed quotas.

Inventories
Inventories (known as stocks in the former system) consist of finished goods (held by the producer prior to sale, further processing or other use) and products (materials and fuel) acquired from other producers to be used for *intermediate consumption* or resold without further processing.

Investment trust
An institution that invests its capital in a wide range of other companies' shares. Investment trusts issue shares which are listed on the London Stock Exchange and use this capital to invest in the shares of other companies. See also *Unit trusts*.

Kind-of-activity unit (KAU)
An *enterprise*, or part of an enterprise, which engages in only one kind of non-ancillary productive activity, or in which the principal productive activity accounts for most of the *value added*. Each *enterprise* consists of one or more kind-of-activity units.

Liability
A claim on an institutional unit by another body which gives rise to a payment or other transaction transferring assets to the other body. Conditional liabilities, i.e. where the transfer of assets only takes place under certain defined circumstances, are known as contingent liabilities.

Liquidity
The ease with which a financial instrument can be exchanged for goods and services. Cash is very liquid whereas a life assurance policy is less so.

Lloyd's of London
The international insurance and reinsurance market in London.

Marketable securities
Securities which can be sold on the open market.

Market output
Output of goods and services sold at *economically significant prices*.

Merchant banks
These are *monetary financial institutions* whose main business is primarily concerned with corporate finance and acquisitions.

Mixed income
The balancing item on the generation of income account for unincorporated businesses owned by households. The owner or members of the same household often provide unpaid labour inputs to the business. The surplus is therefore a mixture of remuneration for such labour and return to the owner as *entrepreneur*.

Money market
The market in which short-term loans are made and short-term securities traded. 'Short term' usually applies to periods under one year but can be longer in some instances.

NACE
The industrial classification used in the European Union. Revision 1 is the 'Statistical classification of economic activities in the European Community in accordance with Council Regulation No. 3037/90 of 9th October 1990'.

National income
See *Gross national disposable income* and *Real national disposable income*.

National Loans Fund
An account of HM Government set up under the National Loans Fund Act (1968) which handles all government borrowing and most domestic lending transactions.

Glossary

Net
After deduction of the consumption of fixed capital. Also used in the context of financial accounts and balance sheets to denote, for example, assets *less* liabilities.

Non-market output
Output of own account production of goods and services provided free or at prices that are not economically significant. Non-market output is produced mainly by the general government and NPISH sectors.

NPISH
Non-profit institutions serving households (S.15). These include bodies such as Charaties, Universities, Churches, Trade Unions or Member's Clubs.

Operating surplus
The balance on the generation of income account. Households also have a mixed income balance. It may be seen as the surplus arising from the production of goods and services before taking into account flows of *property income*.

Operating leasing
The conventional form of leasing, in which the lessee makes use of the leased asset for a period in return for a rental while the asset remains on the balance sheet of the lessor. The leasing payments are part of the *output* of the lessor, and the *intermediate consumption* of the lessee. See also *Financial leasing*.

Ordinary share
The most common type of share in the ownership of a corporation. Holders of ordinary shares receive dividends. See also *Equity*.

Output for own final use
Production of output for *final consumption* or *gross fixed capital formation* by the producer. Also known as *own-account production*.

Own-account production
Production of output for *final consumption* or *gross fixed capital formation* by the producer. Also known as *output for own final use*.

Par value
A security's face or nominal value. Securities can be issued at a premium or discount to par.

Pension funds
The institutions that administer pension schemes. Pension schemes are significant investors in securities. Self-administered funds are classified in the financial accounts as pension funds. Those managed by insurance companies are treated as long-term business of insurance companies. They are part of S.125, the *Insurance corporations and pension funds* sub-sector.

Perpetual Inventory Model (or Method) (PIM)
A method for estimating the level of assets held at a particular point of time by accumulating the acquisitions of such assets over a period and subtracting the disposals of assets over that period. Adjustments are made for price changes over the period. The PIM is used in the UK accounts to estimate the stock of fixed capital, and hence the value of the consumption of fixed capital.

Portfolio
A list of the securities owned by a single investor. In the Balance of Payments statistics, portfolio investment is investment in securities that does not qualify as *direct investment*.

Preference share
This type of share guarantees its holder a prior claim on dividends. The dividend paid to preference share holders is normally more than that paid to holders of ordinary shares. Preference shares may give the holder a right to a share in the ownership of the company (participating preference shares). However in the UK they usually do not, and are therefore classified as *bonds* (F.3).

Prices
See *economically significant prices, basic prices, producers' prices*.

Principal
The lump sum that is lent under a loan or a bond.

Private sector
Private non-financial corporations, financial corporations other than the Bank of England (and Girobank when it was publicly owned), households and the NPISH sector.

Production boundary
Boundary between production included in creating core economic accounts (such as all economic activity by industry and commerce) and production which is excluded (such as production by households which is consumed within the household).

Promissory note
A security which entitles the bearer to receive cash. These may be issued by companies or other institutions. (See *commercial paper*).

Property income
Incomes that accrue from lending or renting financial or tangible non-produced assets, including land, to other units. See also *Tangible assets*.

Public corporations
These are public trading bodies which have a substantial degree of financial independence from the public authority which created them. A public corporation is publicly controlled to the extent that the public authority, i.e. central or local government, usually appoints the whole or a majority of the board of management. Such bodies comprise much the greater part of sub-sector S.11001, public non-financial corporations.

Public sector
Comprises general government *plus* public non-financial corporations *plus* the Bank of England. The concept is not part of the new SNA which includes public corporations with private corporations in the two corporate sectors.

Purchasers' prices
These are the prices paid by purchasers. They include transport costs, trade margins and taxes (unless the taxes are deductible by the purchasers from their own tax liabilities).

Quasi-corporations
Unincorporated *enterprises* that function as if they were corporations. For the purposes of allocation to sectors and sub-sectors they are treated as if they were corporations, i.e. separate units from those to which they legally belong. Three main types of quasi-corporation are recognised in the accounts: unincorporated enterprises owned by government which are engaged in market production, unincorporated enterprises (including partnerships) owned by households and unincorporated enterprises owned by foreign residents. The last group consists of permanent branches or offices of foreign enterprises and production units of foreign enterprises which engage in significant amounts of production in the territory

Glossary

over long or indefinite periods of time.

Real national disposable income (RNDI)
Gross national disposable income adjusted for changes in prices and in the terms of trade.

Related companies
Branches, subsidiaries, associates or parents.

Related import or export credit
Trade credit between related companies, included in direct investment.

Rental
The amount payable by the user of a *fixed asset* to its owner for the right to use that asset in production for a specified period of time. It is included in the *output* of the owner and the *intermediate consumption* of the user.

Rents (D.45)
The property income derived from land and sub-soil assets. It should be distinguished in the current system from *rental* income derived from buildings and other fixed assets, which is included in *output* (P.1).

Repurchase agreement (Repo)
A deal in which an institution lends or 'sells' another institution a security and agrees to buy it back at a future date. Legal ownership does not change under a 'repo' agreement. It was previously treated as a change of ownership in the UK financial account but under the SNA is treated as a collateralised deposit (F.22).

Reserve assets
The UK official holdings of gold, convertible currencies, Special Drawing Rights, changes in the UK reserve position with the IMF and European currency. They include units acquired from swaps with the *European Monetary Co-operation Fund (EMCF)*.

Residents
These comprise general government, individuals, private non-profit-making bodies serving households and enterprises within the territory of a given economy.

Residual error
The term used in the former accounts for the difference between the measures of *gross domestic product* from the expenditure and income approaches.

Rest of the world
This *sector* records the counterpart of transactions of the whole economy with non-residents.

Satellite accounts
Satellite accounts describe areas or activities not dealt with by core economic accounts. These areas/activities are considered to require too much detail for inclusion in the core accounts or they operate with a different conceptual framework. Internal satellite accounts re-present information within the production boundary. External satellite accounts present new information not covered by the core accounts.

Saving
The balance on the *use of income account*. It is that part of disposable income which is not spent on *final consumption*, and may be positive or negative.

Sector
In the economic accounts the economy is split into different institutional sectors, i.e. groupings of units according broadly to their role in the economy. The main sectors are *non-financial corporations, financial corporations, general government, households and non-profit institutions serving households (NPISH)*. The *Rest of the world* is also treated as a sector for many purposes within the accounts.

Secondary market
A market in which holders of financial instruments can re-sell all or part of their holding. The larger and more effective the secondary market for any particular financial instrument the more liquid that instrument is to the holder.

Securities
Tradeable or potentially tradeable financial instruments.

SIC
Standard Industrial Classification. The industrial classification applied to the collection and publication of a wide range of economic statistics. The current version, SIC92, is consistent with *NACE, Rev.1*.

SNA
System of National Accounts, the internationally-agreed standard system for macroeconomic accounts. The latest version is described in *System of National Accounts 1993*.

Special Drawing Rights (SDRs)
These are reserve assets created and distributed by decision of the members of the IMF. Participants accept an obligation, when designated by the IMF to do so, to provide convertible currency to another participant in exchange for SDRs equivalent to three times their own allocation. Only countries with a sufficiently strong balance of payments are so designated. SDRs may also be used in certain direct payments between participants in the scheme and for payments of various kinds to the IMF.

Stage payments
See *Advance and progress payments*.

Stocks, stockbuilding
The terms used in the former system corresponding to *inventories* and changes in inventories.

Subsidiaries
Companies owned or controlled by another company. Under Section 736 of the Companies Act (1985) this means, broadly speaking, that another company either holds more than half the equity share capital or controls the composition of the board of directors. The category also includes subsidiaries of subsidiaries.

Subsidies (D.3)
Current unrequited payments made by general government or the European Union to enterprises. Those made on the basis of a quantity or value of goods or services are classified as 'subsidies on products' (D.31). Other subsidies based on levels of productive activity (e.g. numbers employed) are designated *Other subsidies on production* (D.39).

Suppliers' credit
Export credit extended overseas directly by UK firms other than to related concerns.

Supply table
Table of estimates of domestic industries' output by type of product. Compiled at basic prices and includes columns for imports of goods and services, for distributors' trading margins and for taxes less subsidies on products. The final column shows the value of the supply of goods and services at purchaser's

Glossary

prices. This table shows which industries make which products. Columns represent the supplying industries: rows represent the products supplied.

Tangible assets
These comprise produced fixed assets and non-produced assets. Tangible *fixed* assets, the acquisition and disposal of which are recorded in *gross fixed capital formation* (P.51), comprise buildings and other structures (including historic monuments), vehicles, other machinery and equipment and cultivated assets in the form of livestock and trees yielding repeat products (e.g. dairy cattle, orchards). Tangible *non-produced* assets are assets such as land and sub-soil resources that occur in nature over which ownership rights have been established. Similar assets to which ownership rights have *not* been established are excluded as they do not qualify as economic assets. The acquisition and disposal of non-produced assets in principle is recorded separately in the capital account (K.2). The distinction between produced and non-produced assets is not yet fully possible for the United Kingdom.

Taxes
Compulsory unrequited transfers to central or local government or the European Union. Taxation is classified in the following main groups: taxes on production and imports (D.2), current taxes on income wealth, etc (D.5) and capital taxes (D.91).

Technical reserves (of insurance companies)
These reserves consist of pre-paid premiums, reserves against outstanding claims, actuarial reserves for life insurance and reserves for with-profit insurance. They are treated in the economic accounts as the property of policy-holders.

Terms of trade
Ratio of the change in export prices to the change in import prices. An increase in the terms of trade implies that the receipts from the same quantity of exports will finance an increased volume of imports. Thus measurement of *real national disposable income* needs to take account of this factor.

Transfers
Unrequited payments made by one unit to another. They may be current transfers (D.5-7) or capital transfers (D.9). The most important forms of transfer are taxes, social contributions and benefits.

Treasury bills
Short-term securities or promissory notes which are issued by government in return for funding from the money market. In the United Kingdom every week the Bank of England invites tenders for sterling Treasury bills from the financial institutions operating in the market. ECU-denominated bills are issued by tender each month. Treasury bills are an important form of short-term borrowing for the government, generally being issued for periods of 3 or 6 months.

Unit trusts
Institutions within sub-sector S.123 through which investors pool their funds to invest in a diversified portfolio of securities. Individual investors purchase units in the fund representing an ownership interest in the large pool of underlying assets, i.e. they have an equity stake. The selection of assets is made by professional fund managers. Unit trusts therefore give individual investors the opportunity to invest in a diversified and professionally-managed portfolio of securities without the need for detailed knowledge of the individual companies issuing the stocks and bonds. They differ from *investment trusts* in that the latter are companies in which investors trade shares on the Stock Exchange, whereas unit trust units are issued and bought back on demand by the managers of the trust. The prices of unit trust units thus reflect the value of the underlying pool of securities, whereas the price of shares in investment trusts are affected by the usual market forces.

Use Table
See *Combined Use Table*.

United Kingdom
Broadly, in the accounts, the United Kingdom comprises Great Britain plus Northern Ireland and that part of the continental shelf deemed by International convention to belong to the UK. It excludes the Channel Islands and the Isle of Man.

Valuables
Goods of considerable value that are not used primarily for production or consumption but are held as stores of value over time. They consist of precious metals, precious stones, jewellery, works of art, etc. As a new category in the accounts the estimates for them are currently fairly rudimentary, though transactions are likely to have been recorded elsewhere in the accounts.

Valuation
See *Basic prices, Purchasers' prices, Factor cost*.

Value added
The balance on the production account: output *less* intermediate consumption. Value added may be measured *net* or *gross*.

Value Added Tax (VAT) (D.211)
A tax paid by *enterprises*. In broad terms an enterprise is liable for VAT on the total of its taxable sales but may deduct tax already paid by suppliers on its inputs (*intermediate consumption*). Thus the tax is effectively on the value added by the enterprise. Where the enterprise cannot deduct tax on its inputs the tax is referred to as non-deductible. VAT is the main UK tax on products (D.21).

Index

Figures indicate Table numbers. The letter "G" indicates that the item appears in the Glossary. Where the item is discussed in the section introductions, the appropriate page number is given.

Key for this index

References are either to pages of text or to table numbers.

S   - appears in sector tables which are numbered using the following system:

The table numbering system for the Blue Book shows the relationships between the UK, its sectors and the rest of the world. A 3-part numbering system (e.g. 1.7.2) has been adopted for the accounts drawn directly from the ESA95. The first two digits denotes the UK sector, the third digit denotes the ESA95 account. They are as follows:

    ..0 Goods and services account
    ..1 Production account
    ..2 Generation of income account
    ..3 Allocation of primary income account
    ..4 Secondary distribution of income account
    ..5 Redistribution of income in kind account
    ..6 Use of income account
    ..7 Accumulation account
    ..8 Financial account
    ..9 Financial balance sheet

A

Accounting framework, pp30, 121
Accruals, G
Accumulation accounts, p13
Accuracy, pp31-32
Acquisitions less disposals of valuables, 1.2, 1.3, 2.1, S(0,7)
Acquisitions less disposals of non-produced non-financial assets, S(7)
Actual collective consumption, S(6)
Actual individual consumption, 1.2, 1.3, S(6)
Adjustment to basic prices, 1.1, 1.4
Adjustment for financial services, 1.2, 2.2, 2.3, 2.4
Agriculture, hunting, forestry and fishing, 2.1, 2.2, 2.3, 2.4, 2.5
Air pollution - see atmospheric emissions
Allocation
    of primary income account, p122
    of secondary distribution of income account, p122
Annual chain linking, p30
Atmospheric emissions, pp292-296, 301-302, 13.4

B

Balance sheets (Account IV), pp14, 31, 123 G
Balancing item pp9, 13 G
Base year, p29
Basic prices, p15 G
Bias in estimates, pp31-32
Bonds, S(8,9) G
Borrowing - see net borrowing

C

Capital account (Account III-I), pp13, 123
Capital consumption (fixed), p16, 1.1 ,S(1-4, 6-7) G
Capital formation, G
Capital transfers - see transfers
Cash recording, G
Centre of economic interest, p14
Chain linking, pp29-30
Changes in assets, S(7)
Changes in inventories, 1.2, 1.3, 2.1, 2.2, S(0, 7) G
Changes in net worth, S(7)
Combined use matrix, p88
Compensation of employees, 1.2, 2.1, 2.2, S(2,3)

Index

    employers social contributions, S(2,3,4)
    index numbers, 1.4
    payments to the rest of the world, 1.2
    receipts from the rest of the world, 1.2
    wages and salaries, S(2,3)
Constant prices, pp26-28
Constant prices
    expenditure approach, pp26-28, 1.3
    production (output) approach, p27, 2.4
Construction, 2.1, 2.2, 2.3, 2.4, 2.5
Consumers' expenditure - see Households' final consumption expenditure
Currency, S(8,9)
Current accounts, p9
Current transfers - see transfers

D

Deposits, S(8,9)
Deflation, p28
Disposable income - see gross disposable income Distribution and use of income account, pp13, 120
Double deflation, p27

E

Economic territory, p14
Education, health and social work, 2.1, 2.2, 2.3, 2.4
Electricity, gas and water supply, 2.1, 2.2, 2.3, 2.4
Employers social contributions - see compensation of employees
Employment, pp30, 92, 1.5, 2.5
Employment income from the rest of the world, 1.1
Energy consumption, p291, 13.3
Entrepreneurial income from the rest of the world, 1.1, 1.2
Environmental accounts, pp288-302, 13.1-13.10
Environmental protection expenditure, pp294-295, 12.7
Environmental taxes, pp293-294, 13.8
European community budget, p284, 12.2
Excessive deficit procedure, p284
Exports of goods and services, p26, 1.2, 1.3, 1.4, S(0)

F

Factor cost, p15 G
Final consumption expenditure, p26, S(0, 6) G
    actual individual consumption, 1.2, 1.3, S(6)
    collective government final consumption, 1.2, 1.3, 2.1, S(0,6)
    final consumption of NPISH, 1 2, 1.3, 2.1, S(0)
    household final consumption, 1.2, 1.3, 2.1, S(0)
    implied deflators, p29, 1.4
    index numbers, p29, 1.4
Financial account, pp13, 123
Financial assets, p123, S(9)

Financial corporations, p121 G
Financial derivatives, S(8,9) G, 4.5
Financial intermediation, 2.1, 2.2, 2.3, 2.4 G
Financial services adjustment - see adjustment for financial services G
Fixed capital consumption - see capital consumption

G

General government
    collective final consumption expenditure, 1.2, 1.3, 2.1, S(0)
    individual final consumption expenditure, 1.2, 1.3, S(0)
    net borrowing, p288
    sector, p121
Generation of income account, p122
Gold - see monetary gold
Goods and services account (Account 0), p9, S(0)
Gross capital formation, 1.2, 1.4, 2.1, 2.2, S(0,7) G
    acquisitions less disposals of valuables, 1.2, 1.4, 2.1, 2.2, S(0,7)
    changes in inventories, 1.2, 1.3, 2.1, 2.2, S(0,7)
    gross fixed capital formation, 1.2, 1.3, S(0,7)
    implied deflators, 1.4
    index numbers, 1.4
Gross debt, p288
Gross disposable income, p122, S(4,5,6) G
Gross domestic product, pp25-28, 1.1, 1.2, S(1,2) G
    at 1995 prices, pp28-29, 1.3
    at factor cost, p15
    balancing the annual accounts, pp25, 87, 90
    basic prices - see gross value added
    expenditure approach, pp26-27, 1.2
    headline GDP, p27
    implied deflators, p29, 1.3
    income approach, p25-26, 1.2
    index numbers, 1.4
    output approach, p27, 1.2
    per head, pp24, 30, 1.5
Gross fixed capital formation - see gross capital formation
Gross national disposable income, pp16, 28, 1.1, S(4,5,6) G
    adjusted, S(5,6)
    index numbers, 1.4
Gross national income, pp14, 28, 1.1, 1.2, S(3,4)
    index numbers, 1.4
Gross national product
    continuation on ESA79 basis, p288
Gross operating surplus - see Operating surplus
Gross trading profit - see Operating surplus, gross
Gross trading surplus - see Operating surplus, gross
Gross value added
    at basic prices, p27 G
    at constant basic prices, p27
    by sector, p121

Index

H
Hidden economy, G
Home costs, total, 1.4
Households final consumption expenditure, 1.2, 1.3, 2.1, 6.6- 6.7
Households sectors, p121 G

I
Income from employment - see Compensation of employees
Implied deflator, p29, 1.1, 1.4
Imports of goods and services, p24, 1.2, 1.3, 1.4, S(0)
Index of total home costs, 1.4
Index numbers, 1.4
Individual consumption (actual), 1.2
Industry analysis, pp87-93, 2.1-2.5
Input-output framework, p87
Input-output: balancing process, pp88-89
Insurance
    technical reserves, S(8,9)
    institutional sectors, pp31,121-122
Intermediate consumption, p26, 1.2, 2.2 G
Inventories - see changes in inventories

L
Laspeyres index, p28
Lending - see net lending
Liabilities G
    changes in liabilities and net worth, S(7)
    total financial liabilities, S(9)
Link year, p29
Loans, S(8,9)
Local government final consumption expenditure index numbers, 1.4

M
Make matrix, p88
Manufacturing, 2.1, 2.2, 2.3, 2.4
Market output - see output
Market prices, p13
Mining and quarrying, 2.1, 2.2, 2.3, 2.4
Mixed income G
    gross, p23, 1.2, 1.5, 2.2, S(2,3)
    net, S(2)
Monetary gold, S(8,9) G

N
National disposable income, p13
National income - see gross or net national income
National saving - see saving
Net
    financial assets, S(8,9)
    financial liabilities, S(8,9)
    borrowing, S(7,8)
    domestic product at market prices, p16 1.1
    lending, S(7,8)
    national disposable income at market prices, 1.1, S(4)
    national income at market prices, 1.1, S(3)
    equity of households in pensions funds (adjustment for), S(6)
    worth - see changes in net worth and also liabilities
Non-financial corporations, p121
Non-profit institutions serving households final consumption expenditure, 1.2, 1.4, 2.1
Non-sampling errors, p31
Notional residents, p15

O
Offshore islands, p14
Oil and gas reserves, pp294-295, 13.1
Operating surplus, gross, 1.2, 1.4, 2.1, 2.2 , S(2,3) G
    financial corporations, 1.2
    general government, 1.2
    households and NPISH, 1.2
    non-financial corporations, 1.2
Operating surplus, net, S(2)
Other services, 2.1, 2.2
Output, 1.2, 2.2, S(0,1)
    market output, S(0,1) G
    output for own final use, S(0,1) G
    other non-market output, S(0,1) G

P
Paasche index, p28
Population, p30, 1.5
Price, valuation of economic activity, p15
Producers' prices, pp16, 28
Production account (Account 1), pp7, 122, S(1)
Production boundary, p15
Property and entrepreneurial income, S(3) G
    payments to the rest of the world, 1.2
    receipts from the rest of the world, 1.1, 1.2
Public administration, 2.1, 2.2, 2.3, 2.4
Public expenditure, pp276-277, 11.2, 11.3
Purchasers' prices, p16

R
Real gross domestic income at market prices, p16, 1.1
Real national disposable income, p28, 1.1 G
Rebasing, pp29-30
Rent, G
Residence, p14 G
Rest of the world G
    accounts (Account V), p16
    sector, p121

Index

S

Sampling errors, p31
Satellite accounts, p14
Saving, gross saving, p123, S(6,7) G
    national saving, p13
    net saving, S(6)
Sector accounts, balancing, p123
Securities (other than shares), S(8,9)
Shares and other equity, S(8,9)
Social benefits, S(4,5)
Social contributions (see also compensation of employees), S(4)
Social transfers in kind, S(5)
Special drawing rights (SDR's), S(8,9)
Statistical adjustment items (sector accounts), p123
Statistical discrepancy, pp13, 1.2
    expenditure adjustment, p25, 1.2, 1.3
    income adjustment, p25, 1.2
    sector accounts, p123
Stocks - see Changes in inventories
Stock appreciation adjustment (ESA79), p26
Subsidies G
    on production and imports, 1.2, 2.2, S(2,3)
    on products, 1.2, 1.4, S(0,1,2,3)
Supply matrix, pp87-88

T

Taxes p26, G
    on expenditure - see taxes on production and imports
    on income, wealth etc, S(4)
    on production and imports (D.2), pp26-27, 122
    on products (D.21), p28
    other taxes on production (D.29), p28
    paid by UK residents, 11.1
    value added tax - deductible VAT, p28
Terms of trade effect (trading gain or loss), p28, 1.1
Territorial enclaves, p14
Total home costs - see home costs
Transaction type, pp31, 121
Transfers G
    capital transfers (receivable and payable), p123, S(7) G
    current transfers from the rest of the world, S(2)
    other current transfers, 1.1, S(4)
    Transfer payments, p25
Transport and communication, 2.1, 2.2, 2.3, 2.4

U

Undeclared income, p26
Use of disposable income account, pp122-123
Use matrix, p88

V

Value added taxes - see taxes, 1.2 G

W

Wages and salaries - see compensation of employees
Wholesale and retail trade, 2.1, 2.2, 2.3, 2.4

A Guided Journal to Soaring With God

Copyright © 2021, by Deborah Gall

ISBN: 978-0-578-90051-3

Printed in The United States of America
Published by Selah Press, LLC, selah-press.com
Editor: Loral Pepoon, cowriterpro.com
Cover Art and Interior Art: Deborah Gall
Cover Design and Interior Design: Elena Iria
Interior Icons: Kristi Thomas, designedbykristi.com
Painting Photography: Deborah Gall
Photo Editing: Jesse Gall

Style: Editorial liberties have been taken for emphasis. Names of God and references to Him are capitalized, and satan and the enemy are lowercased.

Unless otherwise noted, scripture quotations are taken from the New American Standard Bible® (NASB), Copyright © 1960, 1962, 1963, 1968, 1971, 1972, 1973, 1975, 1977, 1995 by The Lockman Foundation. Used by permission.www.Lockman.org. Scripture quotations taken from the Amplified® Bible (AMPC), Copyright © 1954, 1958, 1962, 1964, 1965, 1987 by The Lockman Foundation. Used by permission. www.Lockman.org. Scripture taken from the New King James Version. Copyright © 1979, 1980, 1982 by Thomas Nelson, Inc. Used by permission. All rights reserved. Scripture quotations marked TPT are taken from The Psalms: Poetry on Fire. The Passion Translation™, copyright ©2012. Used by permission of 5 Fold Media, LLC, Syracuse, NY 13039, United States of America. All rights reserved. Scripture quotations marked MSG are taken from THE MESSAGE, copyright © 1993, 2002, 2018 by Eugene H. Peterson. Used by permission of NavPress. All rights reserved. Represented by Tyndale House Publishers, Inc. Scripture quotations taken from the Amplified® Bible (AMPC), Copyright © 1954, 1958, 1962, 1964, 1965, 1987 by The Lockman Foundation Used by permission. www.lockman.org.

Notice of Rights: All rights reserved. No part of this book may be reproduced or transmitted in any form by any means, electronic, mechanical, photocopy, recording or other without the prior written permission of the publisher.

ermission: For information on getting permission for reprints and excerpts, contact Deborah Gall at eborah@deborahgall.com.

otice of Liability: The author has made every effort to check and ensure the accuracy of the informa-
n presented in this book. However, the information herein is sold without warranty, either expressed or
plied. Neither the author, publisher, nor any dealer or distributor of this book will be held liable for any
nages caused either directly or indirectly by the instructions and information contained in this book.

laimer: The author and publisher are not engaged in rendering legal or publishing services. Every
has been made to provide the most up-to-date and accurate information possible. Technological
es may occur at any time after the publication of this book. This book may contain typographical
ntent errors; therefore this is only designed as a guide and resource.

ight: In accordance with the U.S. Copyright Act of 1976, the scanning, uploading, and electronic
of any part of this book without the permission of the author is unlawful piracy and theft of the
intellectual property. If you would like to use material from this book (other than for review purpos-
written permission must be obtained by contacting Deborah Gall at deborah@deborahgall.com.
u for your support of the author's rights.

created for so much more

A Guided Journal to
SOARING
WITH GOD

DEBORAH GALL

Selah Press
PUBLISHING
NASHVILLE, TENNESSEE

DEDICATION

With all my love to parents who have walked before me—
Lavern and MaryAnn Franzen
&
Don and Val Gall.

And to the generations that walk after me—
Braden, Haley, Jesse, Hampton, Maren, and Bennett.

May the Lord bless you and keep you in His love.

Aunt Deb
2022

CONTENTS

An Invitation

How to Use This Journal

1. *Created For So Much More* PURPOSE: Affecting Change

    Created On Purpose
    Opening Thoughts: How Do You Feel?
    Soaring With God
        Exercise 1: He Is Who He Says He Is
        Exercise 2: Your Starting Point
    Pause to Ponder and Pray
    Encouragement for Your Journey
        2 Corinthians 12:9

2. *Created For So Much More* FREEDOM: Inspecting Your Instruments

    Check Your Choices
    Opening Thoughts: Checking Your Instruments
    Going Deeper: Co-Laboring With Holy Spirit
    Soaring With God
        Exercise 3: Take Responsibility
        Exercise 4: Putting the Past in the Past
    Pause to Ponder and Pray
    Encouragement for Your Journey
        2 Corinthians 5:17

3. *Created For So Much More* CLARITY: Clearing Out Chatter

    Play to Your Audience of One
    Opening Thoughts: Who Do You Hear?
    Soaring With God
        Exercise 5: Cleaning Your Ears
        Exercise 6: Clearing Out the Chatter
    Pause to Ponder and Pray
    Encouragement for Your Journey
        Hebrews 12:2

4. *Created For So Much More* INTIMACY: Hearing Air Traffic Control

    Learning to Listen
    Opening Thoughts: God Longs To Speak
    Soaring With God
        Exercise 7: Tuning In
        Exercise 8: Recognizing His Voice
        Exercise 9: Application
    Going Deeper
        When God Seems Silent
        Unwrapping God's Message
    Pause to Ponder and Pray
    Encouragement for Your Journey
        Jeremiah 29:13

5. *Created For So Much More* CERTAINTY: Confirming Your Flight

    Clear Confirmation
    Opening Thoughts: Man's Plans, God's Direction
    Going Deeper: Remembering God's Ways
    Soaring with God
        Exercise 10: Confirmations
    Going Deeper: God's Timing
    Soaring With God
        Exercise 11: Asking for Confirmation
    Pause to Ponder and Pray
    Encouragement for Your Journey
        Isaiah 55:8–9

6. *Created For So Much More* IDENTITY: Completing Your Passport

    Heaven's Perspective
    Opening Thoughts: And God Said, "*It is good.*"
    Going Deeper: Labels and Names
    Soaring With God
        Exercise 12: Your Identity
    Going Deeper: Let It Settle In Your Spirit
    Soaring with God
        Exercise 13: Developing Your Life Message
    Pause to Ponder and Pray
    Encouragement for Your Journey
        Philippians 3:13–14

7. *Created For So Much More* VISION: Designing Your Flight Plan

    Dreaming With God
    Opening Thoughts: The Effort of Dreaming
    Going Deeper
        Your Days Are Ordained
        Serving the Kingdom
    Soaring With God
        Exercise 14: Cloud Forming
        Exercise 15: Establishing Your Flight Plan
        Exercise 16: Expanding Your Flight Plan
        Exercise 17: Determining Specific Flight Plan Takeaways
        Exercise 18: Be Strong and Courageous
    Pause to Ponder and Pray
    Encouragement for Your Journey
        1 Thessalonians 5:24

8. *Created For So Much More* UNDERSTANDING: Determining Your Timetable

    Aligning With God's Itinerary
    Opening Thoughts: God's Schedule
    Going Deeper: How Content Are You?
    Soaring With God
        Exercise 19: Seasons and Cycles
    Going Deeper: Aligning With The Lord
    Soaring With God
        Exercise 20: Ten Steps
        Exercise 21: The Next Steps
    Pause to Ponder and Pray
    Encouragement for Your Journey
        Philippians 4:6

9. *Created For So Much More* REST: Enjoying the Layovers

    Making Good Use of Dry Seasons
    Opening Thoughts: Recognizing Your Deserts
    Going Deeper
        Hidden Years
        Lessons Learned in the Wilderness
    Soaring With God
        Exercise 22: Be Still
    Pause to Ponder and Pray
    Encouragement for Your Journey
        Isaiah 30:18

10. *Created For So Much More* PEACE: Navigating Through Storms

    The Path To Peace
    Opening Thoughts: How's Your Peace?
    Soaring With God
        Exercise 23: Storm Tracking
    Going Deeper: What Obstacles Do You Face?
    Soaring With God
        Exercise 24: Tools of the Trade
    Pause to Ponder and Pray
    Encouragement for Your Journey
        Philippians 4:6–7

11. *Created For So Much More* STRATEGY: Unlocking an Amazing Future

    Keys to a Purposeful Life
    Opening Thoughts: Being Proactive
    Soaring With God
        Exercise 25: Which Strategies?
    Going Deeper: Promises of God
    Soaring With God
        Exercise 26: Your Personal Strategies
    Pause to Ponder and Pray
    Encouragement for Your Journey
        Philippians 4:13

12. *Created For So Much More* FLIGHT: Changing Atmospheres

    Soaring With God
    Opening Thoughts: Taking Off
    Going Deeper:
        What Has Changed?
        Where Are You Soaring?
    Soaring With God
        Exercise 27: The Lord's Prayer
        Exercise 28: The 23rd Psalm
    Pause to Ponder and Pray
    Encouragement For Your Journey
        Ephesians 1:15-19

Acknowledgments

About the Author

About the Cover Art

AN INVITATION

Welcome to a life of *so much more*, fellow-traveler!

As you open this journal, you cross a threshold into a hope-filled adventure with the Lord. A future ripe with opportunity and overflowing with promise awaits. It doesn't matter how old you are, where you live, or what you are doing, a future full of greater purpose, intimacy, clarity, peace, and *so much more* is available to you. The lessons in this journal are taken from the most useful and relevant teaching I share with individual clients as well as audiences large and small. This journal is a great tool to help you soar with God into the amazing future He has for you. God—through the exercises in this journal—will empower your vision to live in the sweet spot of your God-given identity and purpose.

Whether you are a new follower of Christ or have known Him for a lifetime, God waits to meet you as you move through the 12 hand-selected lessons. He will transform your life as He reveals *so much more* of who He created you to be and what He created you to do. Whatever your current circumstance is, there is always *so much more* for you because there is always *so much more* of God. That's good news, Dear One.

Your adventure into *so much more* self-discovery begins with a turn of the page. I know our Lord will meet you and speak to you. As you sit at His feet to complete each lesson, you will gain confidence to apply the practical steps God has for you on your unique adventure.

Consider me your adventure guide as you gain greater identity, freedom, understanding, vision, and *so much more*. I am so excited for you! Allow Holy Spirit to be the wind beneath your wings as you soar with God into your amazing future.

May the Lord open your eyes to see, your ears to hear, and your heart to receive as you step into what He has for you each day of your adventure.

Blessings on your amazing journey ahead!

Deborah Gall

Deborah Gall

HOW TO USE THIS GUIDED JOURNAL

You are about to embark on an exhilarating, hope-filled adventure—one created just for you. Gather your willing heart, teachable spirit, your charged computer or device, your Bible, and this journal. Let's get started.

This *Guided Journal to Soaring With God* is a step-by-step manual for discovering the **so much more** that the Lord has for you. You have the freedom to set your own pace as you work through the 12 lessons. You might choose to do a lesson a week—or move through it more quickly or slowly. Allow the Lord to guide your timing. He knows best how the lessons fit in with your current schedule and life events.

Whatever your pace, you have the opportunity to experience the same life changing moments with the Lord as fellow travelers have experienced through *Created For So Much More* conferences and group studies. Within this journal, I have shared many of the ah-ha moments and big takeaways experienced by those who have traveled this adventure before you.

I suggest that after you read the introduction to each of the 12 lessons, you watch the corresponding chapter video before working through the exercises. The videos bring my heart for the material as well as additional scripture, stories, and truth. It is my prayer that the videos will bring **so much more** insight into your adventure with the Lord. The videos can be found on my website—deborahgall.com—which is also listed at the bottom of the first page of each lesson.

As you move into the journaling aspect of each lesson, I invite you to write freely, often, and as much as you desire. I cannot emphasize the importance of doing the work to thoroughly write through each element and lesson of this journal. The exercises and writing prompts are necessary to imprint the material on your heart, mind, and spirit.

Past travelers of the *Created For So Much More* adventure testify that the exercises are what set this book apart. As one traveler said, "When you do the exercises, it is as if you and the Lord are answering the questions together." All of the writing exercises invite you to connect with Heaven and apply God's truth to your daily life. They transform this *Guided Journal to Soaring With God* into a life manual. This journal may be limited to 12 lessons, but the truths and processes you will learn will last a lifetime.

Within each lesson of this journal, you will find four types of writing prompts:
- **Opening Thoughts** give you time and opportunity to pause and consider how you feel or what you think about the video and/or the main point of the lesson.
- **Soaring With God** duplicates the exercises taken from the book. The numbers and titles correspond to the exercises found in the book. Where there are multiple questions within an exercise, I have given you multiple pages with plenty of space to write all that the Lord shows you.
- **Going Deeper** offers an opportunity to spend even more time with the Lord in connection to the lesson's theme. These prompts take you deeper with Holy Spirit as you connect a pertinent truth from the lesson to your own life.
- **Pause to Ponder and Pray** invites you to summarize your experience and write a prayer. I encourage you, as you write, to remind yourself of all of the truths from that lesson and worship the Lord for what He has done. It is also a great time to ask for His assistance with those things that He has pointed out to you.

Finally, you will notice quotes from the book *Created For So Much More* and scripture verses that relate to the material. I suggest you take a few moments to pause, ponder, and write about the thoughts and feelings provoked by the quotes and verses.

Used alone, this journal is a robust tool for transformation. If you are an avid reader and would like even more insight about the lesson topics, as well as more anecdotes from my personal journey, I invite you to purchase the book *Created For So Much More* and read it as well.

Whether you are studying alone or in a group, whether you are reading *Created For So Much More* or not, I trust God will meet you in these pages and bring fresh revelation for your life. You are beginning a life-changing journey. Congratulations! Take flight and soar with God into ***so much more*** intimacy, certainty, rest, peace, and strategy. I know you will experience ***so much more*** excitement, adventure, and love as you embrace who God created you to be and what He created you to do.

Without further ado, get ready to soar with God, Dear One. Your amazing future awaits!

1. PURPOSE

Deborah Gall
Formed, 2012
Acrylic on Canvas
24" x 24"

See ***Formed*** in color at the end of the *Created For So Much More* PURPOSE Video and hear Deborah's prayer and blessing for your upcoming journey.

"**YOU** have the capacity to be the **GATEWAY** that allows others to **EXPERIENCE** God in a deeper manner."

—*Created For So Much More* PURPOSE (Chapter One) Video

1.
created for so much more
PURPOSE:
Affecting Change

Created On Purpose

Your life has a purpose. As we begin our journey, I want to challenge you to recognize and accept that you were created for a purpose. Your purpose is to advance God's Kingdom here on Earth. You were created to serve God and serve others with the unique gifts and talents that God has given you. As you interact with the world around you, God—through you—changes lives and advances His Kingdom.

The exercises in this lesson set the stage for the adventure ahead by laying the foundation and inviting you to reflect on yourself and the Lord. I encourage you to make a note of how you feel today, what your life looks like currently, and where you need God's grace during this season. This adventure is transformative. Considering these aspects of your life brings insight into the transformation that lies ahead. I also encourage you to pause to consider the Lord's character because He is the source of the *so much more* that awaits.

These necessary steps may feel disconnected to identity and purpose. Trust me—the work you will do serves as the chief building block for your God-sized adventure. Trust the Lord—He walks with you every step of the way. Take His hand as He reveals who He created you to be and what He created you to do. Your adventure is just beginning. Get ready to soar with God into your future with *so much more* purpose.

Find out how you can be certain that God has *so much more* for you in the *Created For So Much More* PURPOSE Video, available at deborahgall.com

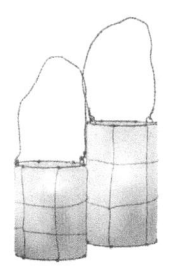

A Guided Journal to Soaring With God

Opening Thoughts: How Do You Feel?

Take a moment to **acknowledge and scribe your emotions** as you consider the journey ahead.

Lesson 1 • PURPOSE

"An amazing future—a future ripe with opportunity and overflowing with promise—lies before you." —Page 1, *Created For So Much More*

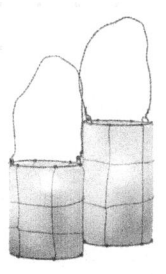

Soaring With God

Exercise 1: He Is Who He Says He Is

As you sit with the Lord to listen, He brings Heaven's perspective to you. As you write your answers to the exercises, you grasp the ***so much more*** of God's love and purpose for you.

This exercise focuses on the ***so much more*** of God. There is always ***so much more*** for your life because God is a never-ending source of love, wisdom, guidance, purpose, and ***so much more***. I offer you several scripture verses that describe the character of God. I recommend that you take the time to look at each scripture verse in your own Bible. Then, **write your answer to the question associated with each verse.**

1. **What does it mean to you that God knew you before He formed you?**

   Before I formed you in the womb I knew you,
   And before you were born I consecrated you (Jeremiah 1:5).

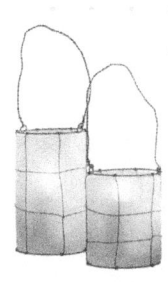

Lesson 1 • PURPOSE

"The fact is there is always ***so much more*** for your life because, this side of eternity, there is always ***so much more*** of God." —Page 11, *Created For So Much More*

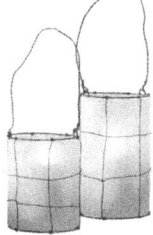

A Guided Journal to Soaring With God

Exercise 1: He Is Who He Says He Is, Continued

2. How does it make you feel that you were formed by God?

*For You formed my inward parts;
You wove me in my mother's womb* (Psalm 139:13).

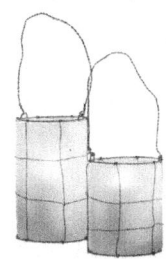

"Like a master chef, God selected the perfect set of ingredients to make the perfect dish that is you."—Page 4, *Created For So Much More*

Exercise 1: He Is Who He Says He Is, Continued

3. **How do you look at your life differently knowing you were created intentionally with a purpose in mind?**

   For we are His workmanship, created in Christ Jesus for good works, which God prepared beforehand so that we would walk in them (Ephesians 2:10).

"Your kingdom purpose is to influence, affect, and change the world right where you are."—Page 11, *Created For So Much More*

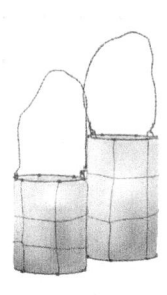

Exercise 1: He Is Who He Says He Is, Continued

4. When have you seen God act in your life to work all things together for your good?

And we know that God causes all things to work together for good to those who love God, to those who are called according to His purpose (Romans 8:28).

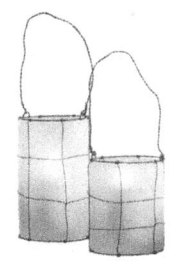

"Living life as a Jesus Follower means trusting God with the "why" of life's occurrences and pursuing His plan and purpose for your life, in spite of how your circumstances look or how you feel on any given day."
—Page 5, *Created For So Much More*

Exercise 1: He Is Who He Says He Is, Continued

5. How does it change your daily choices to know that God is faithful to you and to your purpose?

Faithful is He who calls you, and He also will bring it to pass (1 Thessalonians 5:24).

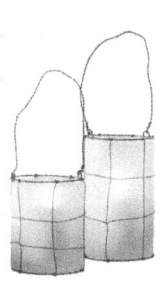

"Purpose is not constrained by age, profession, location, or education. If you are living and breathing on Earth, you have purpose."
—Page 6, *Created For So Much More*

Exercise 1: He Is Who He Says He Is, Continued

6. We all experience God in different ways at different times. What additional characteristics of God are you particularly aware of in your life today? What Bible verses speak of those characteristics? **List the additional characteristics and corresponding Bible verses here.**

***Lesson 1* • PURPOSE**

*So wake up, your living gateways!
Lift up your heads, you ageless doors of destiny!
Welcome the King of Glory, for He is about to come through you!*
(Psalm 24:7, The Passion Translation, TPT).

"You are a living gateway that opens the way for others to be transformed as they encounter Father, Son, and Holy Spirit in you."
—Page 7, *Created For So Much More*

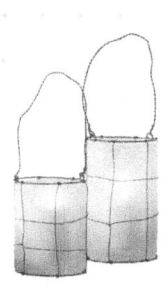

Soaring With God

Exercise 2: Your Starting Point

Every journey has a starting point. Your adventure of self-discovery with the Lord is no different. This exercise establishes your starting point in respect to who God created you to be and what He created you to do. Take a few minutes to consider your current situation and create a written snapshot of your life.

Things you might consider are your marital status, your occupation, and your church involvement. You might also list those things that currently occupy your time. What are the longings of your heart? Make a note of those jobs, tasks, or hobbies you wish you were doing and those roles and jobs you are currently doing. Write about your personality, your gifts, talents, and resources. You have freedom to describe yourself however you wish. Imagine that you are introducing yourself to someone you have never met. **Write your personal snapshot here.**

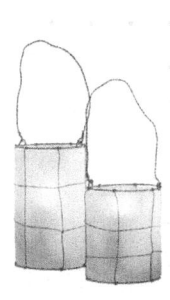

Lesson 1 • PURPOSE

*Thus says the Lord who made you
And formed you from the womb, who will help you,
'Do not fear, O Jacob My servant;
And you Jeshurun whom I have chosen'* (Isaiah 44:2).

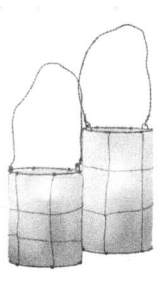

A Guided Journal to Soaring With God

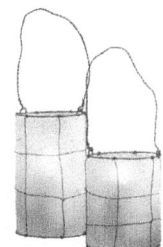

"God longs for you to soar in the sweet spot of your identity and purpose."
—Page 12, *Created For So Much More*

Pause to Ponder and Pray

Before you move on to the next lesson, thank the Lord for where you are today as you begin this journey. **Write your thoughts, feelings, and prayer for the journey ahead** as you ask Father, Jesus, and Holy Spirit to guide you on the path that He has laid before you.

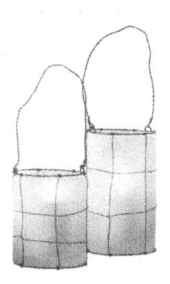

Encouragement for Your Journey

Perhaps you feel overwhelmed by the notion that life is about more than reacting to people and events. Alternatively, you could be thinking, "Okay, I get it. I have **so much more** to learn about my purpose. How am I supposed to find the time to discover it?" Yet another option might find you celebrating because you have sensed there was something more to life, but you didn't know how to find it. All of those responses are authentic reactions to this notion of purpose. You are not alone. I—and those that have traveled before you—have experienced all of these reactions at different times. Wherever you find yourself—disheartened and overwhelmed or full of joy and excitement—you are exactly in the right place.

God's plan for you is to start this journey of discovery today. God's grace is sufficient for you to discover who He created you to be and what He created you to do, regardless of how your life appears at this moment. The apostle Paul offers encouragement for us all in his second letter to the Corinthian church.

> *And He has said to me, "My grace is sufficient for you, for power is perfected in weakness"* (2 Corinthians 12:9).

God hand-picked you for this adventure at this specific time in your life. You have taken the first steps as you completed your first assignments. Congratulations! I'm proud of you. The Lord is proud of you. Pat yourself on the back and celebrate your accomplishment in whatever way you prefer. For me, that might be a cup of espresso and a movie. For you, it might be a walk, a cup of tea, a snuggle with your fur baby, or a visit with a friend. Go ahead. Take the time to celebrate. You deserve it.

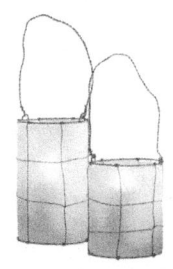

2. FREEDOM

Deborah Gall
Among the Ruins, 2011
Acrylic on Canvas
36" x 24"

See ***Among the Ruins*** in color near the end of the *Created For So Much More* FREEDOM Video and hear the key strategy for life, light, and blessing.

"Allow the Lord to **JETTISON** those things in your past that no longer serve you, and you will **SOAR** into so much more **FREEDOM**."

—*Created For So Much More* FREEDOM (Chapter Two) Video

2.
created for so much more
FREEDOM:
Inspecting Your Instruments

Check Your Choices

Take time to inspect your heart, mind, and spirit, and you will soar with God unencumbered by the weight of the past. At this time, I invite you to take responsibility for the choices you have made and are making. We are each given the power and freedom to choose life, light, and blessing or to choose death, darkness, and destruction. The critical step of inspecting your instrument panel of heart, mind, and spirit, in light of the choices you make, enables you to more freely embrace who God created you to be and what He created you to do.

This lesson's exercises shed light on the choices you have made to date. They ask you to reflect on your past actions and current beliefs. Analyzing your choices, accepting Christ's freedom, taking responsibility, and putting your past in the past are steps that enable you to receive the freedom that the Lord has for you.

Freedom from ALL of your past negative choices is available through Christ's Crucifixion and Resurrection. No matter what has occurred before today, God enables and empowers you to overcome your past and align with His plan and purposes. Do the work suggested in this lesson and you will leave your past where it belongs—in the past. Then you will be ready to embrace ***so much more*** freedom that is available to you.

Let the Lord reveal choices that lead to greater freedom as you watch the *Created For So Much More* FREEDOM Video at deborahgall.com

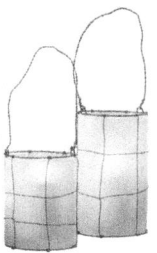

A Guided Journal to Soaring With God

Opening Thoughts: Checking Your Instruments

How does it make you feel when I asked you to look at your past choices? **Make a note of your emotions and write out a prayer for this next step in your journey.**

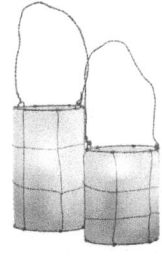

"We co-labor with Holy Spirit and Christ's freedom when we make changes in our words, lifestyles, and actions that reflect the spiritual freedom procured for us."
—Page 17, *Created For So Much More*

Lesson 2 • **FREEDOM**

"God meets you where you are—before you have everything figured out—and He guides you from there."—Page 13, *Created For So Much More*

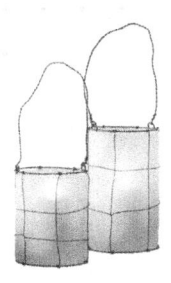

Going Deeper: Co-Laboring with Holy Spirit

Describe a time when you have changed your words, lifestyle, or actions in order to co-labor with God and experience *so much more* freedom.

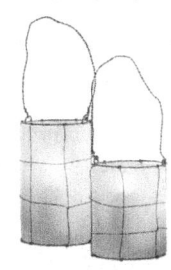

It was for freedom that Christ set us free; therefore keep standing firm and do not be subject again to a yoke of slavery (Galatians 5:1).

Soaring With God

Exercise 3: Take Responsibility

Ask yourself these questions and commit to making the necessary changes that will open the doors to your freedom, abundance, and operating more fully in your gifts and talents.

1. Am I ready to take responsibility for my future?
2. Will I commit to complete the exercises in this book?
3. What choices in my life are hindering my freedom to be who God created me to be?

Write your commitment here. Then turn the page and write out your responses as prompted.

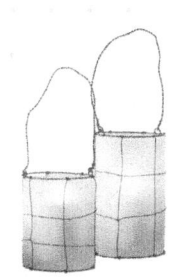

Exercise 3: Take Responsibility, Continued

4. What decisions are you making that are keeping you from stepping into the actions that God is asking you to take?

Exercise 3: Take Responsibility, Continued

5. Now that you have answered the previous questions, **thank the Lord in advance for where He is setting you free and changing your life.**

"Choose LIFE! God gives you the choice to stand in the freedom that Christ offers from the empty tomb, or not to stand in that freedom."
—Page 17, *Created For So Much More*

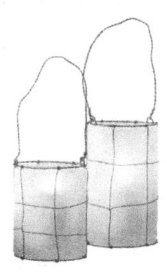

"You have been saved. You are being saved. You will be saved."
—Page 15, *Created For So Much More*

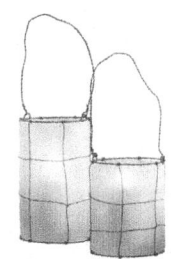

for He says,

*"AT THE ACCEPTABLE TIME I LISTENED TO YOU,
AND ON THE DAY OF SALVATION I HELPED YOU."*

*Behold, now is "THE ACCEPTABLE TIME," behold,
now is "THE DAY OF SALVATION"* (2 Corinthians 6:2).

Soaring With God

Exercise 4: Putting the Past in the Past

Paul wrote in his letter to the Corinthians:

> *"THINGS WHICH EYE HAS NOT SEEN AND EAR HAS NOT HEARD, AND WHICH HAVE NOT ENTERED THE HEART OF MAN, ALL THAT GOD HAS PREPARED FOR THOSE WHO LOVE HIM"*
>
> *For to us God revealed* them *through the Spirit; for the Spirit searches all things, even the depths of God* (1 Corinthians 2:9–10).

Take a moment and ask Holy Spirit to show you what He has prepared for you and your future. What is the new play that He is writing for you? Newly-staged plays cannot be performed with last season's props and costumes. Now is the time to get rid of what has become unnecessary for your future. Let Holy Spirit gently put His finger on those aspects of your life that need to be left behind as you soar into your future.

Ask yourself these questions and scribe what the Lord reveals.

1. What doubts do you need to leave on the altar before the Lord can carry you into your amazing future?

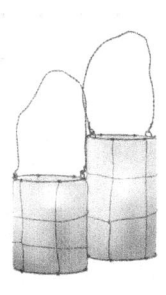

A Guided Journal to Soaring With God

"No matter what has happened in your past, Holy Spirit enables and empowers you to make decisions for your life that align with His purpose and plan."
—Page 19, *Created For So Much More*

Exercise 4: Putting the Past in the Past, Continued

2. When have you taken matters into your own hands and "helped the Lord," when He didn't ask for your help?

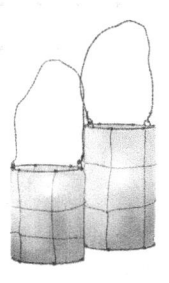

Exercise 4: Putting the Past in the Past, Continued

3. When the giants of your future loom in front of you (see Numbers 13:25–14:10) do you run in fear, or do you rely on the Lord to fight your battle?

Exercise 4: Putting the Past in the Past, Continued

4. What habits or traits that brought you successfully to this point in your life need to be surrendered to the Lord so that you may possess the promises of God?

"The very qualities that brought you to this point may not be the necessary characteristics needed to take you further in your journey."
—Page 22, *Created For So Much More*

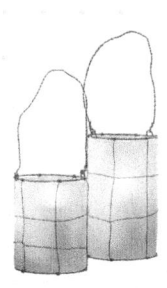

Christ redeemed us from the curse of the Law, having become a curse for us—for it is written, "CURSED IS EVERYONE WHO HANGS ON A TREE"
(Galatians 3:13).

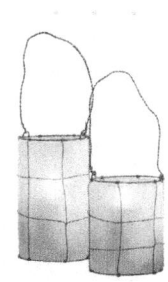

Pause to Ponder and Pray

Before you move on, **write your thoughts, feelings, and a prayer of thanksgiving** for this journey of discovery, even when it hurts a little. Thank the Lord for His transforming freedom procured for you through Christ's death and Resurrection.

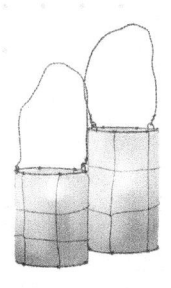

Encouragement for Your Journey

Good work! This chapter is a challenge and can get a little messy. I am so proud of you! I trust that the Lord has lifted your spirit—leaving you free to soar with Him to new heights. Freedom to soar can be an invigorating experience. You may feel lighter as you take responsibility for your choices and put your past in the past. Alternatively, you may be concerned that you are not completely free. The Apostle Paul offers encouragement in one of his letters to the Corinthians when he writes,

> *Therefore if anyone is in Christ, he is a new creature; the old things passed away; behold, new things have come* (2 Corinthians 5:17).

The language in this verse is key. The **old** has **passed**. Your past choices have passed away. They are gone. **They no longer have the power to encumber you or keep you from soaring**. The **new** has come. You are being recreated daily. Glory to God! Christ has replaced your past choices with new choices, attitudes, and insights which open the way to a bright future.

As a new creation in Christ, you have all that you need to take the next step on your transformative journey to live more fully as who God created you to be doing what He created you to do. That's good news, Dear One.

Let me encourage you to take a break if you need to. God has been known to touch deep places of the heart through this lesson. You might need a day or two before moving on to lesson three. Go ahead. Rest in the healing the Lord has done and the newfound—*so much more*—freedom He has procured for you. Take in the Breath of Life—the peace of Christ—and then step into the next lesson.

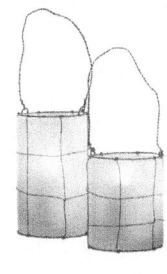

3.
CLARITY

Deborah Gall
New Life, 2021
Acrylic on Canvas
12" x 24"

See ***New Life*** in color near the end of the *Created For So Much More* CLARITY Video and hear about five easy steps to clear out clutter on a path to new life.

"I am **CONFIDENT** of this, that God is at work in you perfecting who He **CREATED** you to **BE** and what He created you to **DO**."

—***Created For So Much More*** CLARITY (Chapter Three) Video

3.
created for so much more
CLARITY:
Clearing Out Chatter

Play to Your Audience of One

Life as a Christ Follower challenges us to stay tuned to the voice of the Lord. He is the One who created you and redeemed you. He guides you to your identity and purpose. This stop in your journey focuses on cleaning out the distracting voices that threaten to override the voice of the Lord.

God is your Audience of One—the only one to "play" to on this stage of life. I want to point out two other voices that threaten to crowd out the voice of your Audience of One. They are your Greek chorus and your negative self-talk. I invite you to take all the time you need to recognize and silence your Greek chorus and your negative self-talk through the exercises in this lesson. I also encourage you to memorize "The Five Rs" I introduce in Exercise 5. Those five "R" words instruct you to take your thoughts captive to the obedience of Christ. These exercises bring even more freedom and greater clarity to your life when used regularly.

I use this lesson's exercises as preparation for teaching and ministry assignments. The steps suggested in these exercises clean my spiritual ears and enable me to follow Holy Spirit as I speak and minister to His children. I recommend that you add the tools offered in this chapter to your travel bag. Use them frequently and you will gain ***so much more*** clarity as you continue your adventure with the Lord.

Find out how to fine-tune your attena to your Audience of One. Watch the *Created For So Much More* CLARITY Video at deborahgall.com

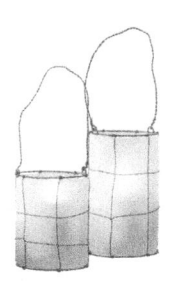

Opening Thoughts: Who Do You Hear?

It might be surprising to realize that you have voices in your head that influence your day-to-day choices and actions. As you think about clearing out the chatter those voices produce, what obstacles do you think you will face? **Make a note of your expectations here.**

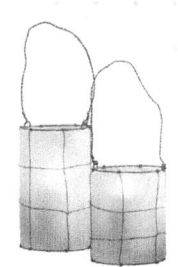

"It is imperative that we take the time to clear out any chatter that interferes with hearing the voice of the One who created you and directs your flight."
—Page 25, *Created For So Much More*

Soaring With God

Exercise 5: Cleaning Your Ears

When you feel stuck on your path, it may be time to clean out your ears. An easy way to cleanse your ears and your heart is to use what I call "The Five Rs." These five "R" words will walk you through a path of healing that opens your spirit, heart, and ears to receive all that the Lord is saying to you about who He created you to be and what He created you to do.

> **Take the time to ponder, pray, and scribe through each of these "Five Rs."**

1. **Recognize** who you need to forgive and what lies you have believed. Then forgive those you need to forgive.

"I call the clamoring voices from various sources the 'Greek chorus' that resides in your head. Your Greek chorus could be made up of teachers, friends, family, colleagues, or mentors."—Page 25, *Created For So Much More*

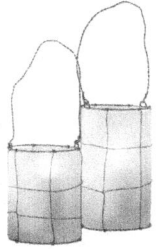

Exercise 5: Cleaning Your Ears, Continued

2. **Repent** of believing the lies of spirits that tell you anything other than the truth that you are a treasured and gifted child of God.

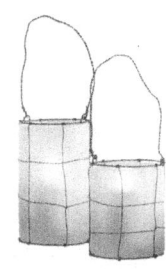

> "You can clear out the chatter of your Greek chorus and the static of your negative self-talk as often as needed through recognizing these interfering voices, repenting of believing them, renouncing lies, receiving God's truth, and replacing your vision with God's vision."
> —Page 31, *Created For So Much More*

Exercise 5: Cleaning Your Ears, Continued

   3. **Renounce** the lies of the enemy.

We are destroying arguments and all arrogance raised against the knowledge of God, and we are taking every thought captive to the obedience of Christ (2 Corinthians 10:5).

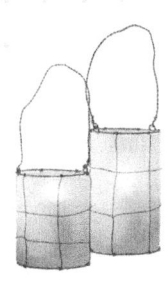

Exercise 5: Cleaning Your Ears, Continued

4. **Receive** the truth of Christ. He is the Way to freedom; He speaks the Truth; He brings Life (John 14:6). Everything you need is found in Him.

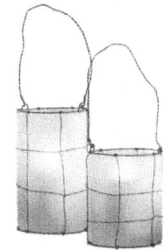

Jesus said to him, "I am the way, and the truth, and the life; no one comes to the Father except through Me" (John 14:6).

Exercise 5: Cleaning Your Ears, Continued

5. **Replace** your view of yourself and your life with God's perspective.

"Taking thoughts captive to the obedience of Christ transforms your self-talk or audience of one (you) to the Audience of One: Christ."
—Page 26, *Created For So Much More*

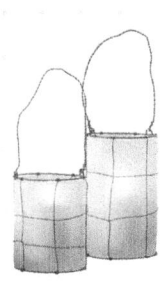

Soaring With God

Exercise 6: Clearing Out the Chatter

Now I want you to take the time to clear out any voices that may interfere with hearing your Audience of One. **Write out your responses as prompted on the following pages.**

1. Whose voice(s) do you repeatedly hear that direct your actions or feelings?

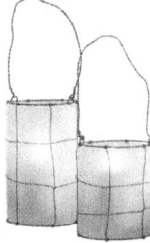

"Knowing the Lord, you learn how to recognize His voice over the voices of your Greek chorus or your self-talk."—Page 29, *Created For So Much More*

Exercise 6: Clearing Out the Chatter, Continued

2. Guilt, shame, and unworthiness often come from your Greek chorus. Identify your Greek chorus by asking yourself who in your life made/makes you feel guilty, shameful, or unworthy. **List the names** of these people or their roles. Be as specific as possible.

3. **Forgive** the people whose voices you hear as part of your Greek chorus for any time that they have spoken negatively about you. Once again, it is helpful to be specific.

"Holy Spirit will direct you to those who will encourage and support you, or He will give you the strength and dedication to withstand criticism and doubt." —Page 29, *Created For So Much More*

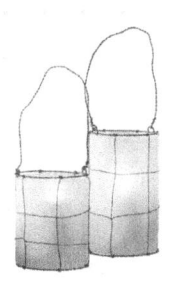

Exercise 6: Clearing Out the Chatter, Continued

4. What negative self-talk do you continually speak/hear? **Write out** who you hear or what you say.

5. Take those thoughts captive to the obedience of Christ. **Speak the words**, "I choose to take these words and thoughts captive to obedience in Christ." Taking thoughts captive often means renouncing the lies you have believed.

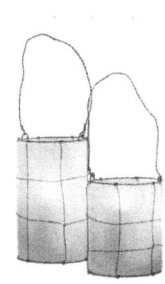

Exercise 6: Clearing Out the Chatter, Continued

6. Now **ask the Lord** to speak the truth about the area where you previously believed lies. Usually, God's truth is the polar opposite of the lie that you believed. For instance, say something like "God's truth says that I am His precious child, and He treasures me. God's truth says that I am worthy of His blessing because I am His child. God's truth says I am a child of King Jesus; therefore, I automatically amount to something."

7. **Write down the truth** that He speaks to you, repeating it out loud, often. Both speaking and writing down His truth are powerful ways to replace lies with God's truth.

"When you play to the Audience of One, you live your life tuned to Heaven's perspective." —Page 27, *Created For So Much More*

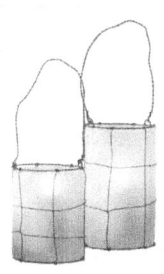

A Guided Journal to Soaring With God

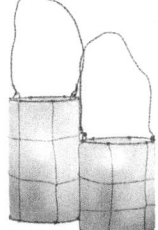

For as he thinks within himself, so he is (Proverbs 23:7).

Pause to Ponder and Pray

Heartache and tears can happen when we "get real" with God. I encourage you to stay in the place of transparency with the Lord and **record your feelings, revelations, and gratitude** for all that He has done through this chapter. Thank Him for a fresh vision for your future and for *so much more*.

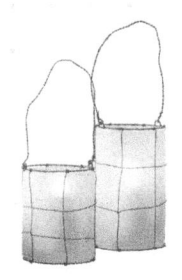

Encouragement for Your Journey

You are a rock star! You made it through what some have considered the most challenging part of this adventure. I am confident the Lord has met you and together you have cleared your mind of any chatter that has interfered with hearing your Audience of One. Allow me to remind you of the following exhortation to help you to keep hearing the Lord:

> *Fixing our eyes on Jesus, the author and perfecter of faith, who for the joy set before Him endured the cross, despising the shame, and has sat down at the right hand of the throne of God* (Hebrews 12:2).

The joy that sets before you is the discovery of the ***so much more*** of your identity and purpose. You may have endured a little discomfort as you cleared out the chatter of your Greek Chorus and negative self-talk, but Holy Spirit never leaves you in that place of discomfort.

There is always life, light, and blessing on the other side of cleaning your conduit to Heaven. The work is done. Take time to acknowledge your hard work and bask in God's love. Close your eyes, lift your face up to Heaven, and feel the warm light of God's love and blessing pouring down upon you. You are awesome! You are a child of the God who loves you with an everlasting love. That unconditional infinite love, Dear One, is worth basking in.

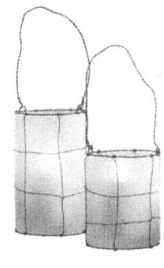

4.
INTIMACY

Deborah Gall
Holy Habitation,
2009
Acrylic on Canvas
48" x 48"

See **Holy Habitation** in color and learn how to implement Heavenly messages by viewing the *Created For So Much More* INTIMACY Video.

"Make time to **SPEND** with the Lord. Just like our **RELATIONSHIPS** here on Earth, it takes **TIME** and effort to go **DEEPER** with God."

—***Created For So Much More*** INTIMACY (Chapter Four) Video

4.
created for so much more
INTIMACY:
Hearing Air Traffic Control

Learning to Listen

When you play to "the Audience of One"—God—you discover He has unlimited ways to communicate with you. In this lesson, I will share tips to recognize the Lord's voice in your daily life. You need faith, an open heart, and courage to acknowledge that God speaks in the many ways He does. Hearing and recognizing the voice of God begins with a relationship with Him.

Conversation with the Lord is born out of intimacy. Getting to know the Lord is as easy as opening your Bible. I suggest you study God's Word to discover His character, His will, and His ways. God loves you and longs to communicate with you.
The universe is God's and He will use whatever is at His disposal to speak with you. Keep in mind that God is Spirit. His language is spirit language. I invite you to open your heart and mind to receive what He speaks, even when His language is unusual and supernatural. You can expand your understanding of God's language by first looking at your own.

The exercises in this lesson invite you to explore your unique means of expression before you turn to memories when you have discerned the Lord's voice and direction. Remembering your past conversations with the Lord opens your heart and mind to embrace ***so much more*** intimacy with Him. Knowing how He has spoken to you in the past also sensitizes you to hear His voice in new ways as you soar into your amazing future of identity and purpose.

Hear more about how God longs to have conversation with you in the *Created For So Much More* INTIMACY Video, found at deborahgall.com

A Guided Journal to Soaring With God

Opening Thoughts: God Longs To Speak

How does it make you feel when you think that the God of the universe desires to speak to you personally? What emotions surface in your heart and spirit? **Write those feelings and ask the Lord to prepare your heart to receive Him.**

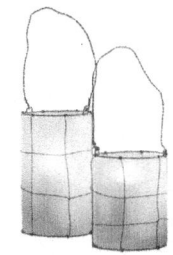

"God desires to speak to all of His children all of the time."
—Page 33, *Created For So Much More*

Soaring With God

Exercise 7: Tuning In

You have freedom to interpret and express yourself through this exercise in any way that moves you. You could grab crayons and draw, write with words, or express yourself through freestyle dance moves. Tap into your inner child—and your childlike faith—and have some fun!

The sky is the limit here. There is only your unique language. Use the words I list as prompts. Pick and choose your favorites and express yourself. For example: What color represents anticipation to you? If you were to dance to express joy what would the movement look like? If you were simply to draw a shape or line to express comfort, what would it look like—curvy, straight, spiral? Ready to try? Go! **Use the next several pages to complete this exercise. Make a note of the word and express away.**

- Anticipation
- Joy
- Comfort
- Anger
- Hope
- Faithfulness
- Control
- Surrender
- God the Father
- Jesus
- Holy Spirit

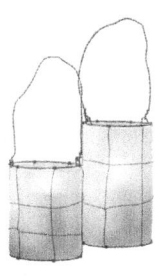

"But when He, the Spirit of truth, comes, He will guide you into all the truth; for He will not speak on His own initiative, but whatever He hears, He will speak; and He will disclose to you what is to come" (John 16:13).

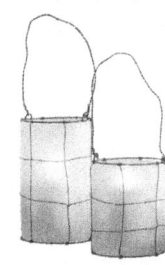

"Experiencing God is how you gain understanding of His language. Dedicate time to reading His Word and sitting in His Presence, and you will become better equipped to hear and know His voice."
—Page 35, *Created For So Much More*

"Like identical twins who often have their own 'twin speak' language, you and the Lord have your own style of communication, developed over your days, weeks, and years of growing in intimacy."
—Page 43, *Created For So Much More*

Soaring With God

Exercise 8: Recognizing His Voice

When God speaks to you, it is as if a message is pulled from Heaven and applied to your daily life. Now I want you to take time to recognize the times, places, and results when you "heard" the Lord. In so doing, you invite Him to speak to you in the future.

1. **Form three columns on your page.** Use the next few pages for this exercise.
2. Ask Holy Spirit to reveal times when you heard from Him. **Write whatever comes to mind in the far-left column.** List as many as you can.
3. With each instance, recall the place and the situation, and **write a brief description of those basics in the middle column.** You might make a note of how you were feeling, where you were, and what you were doing.
4. **Keep the third column blank for now.**

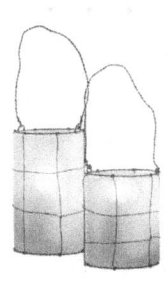

Lesson 4 • **INTIMACY**

"God is always communicating to His children. It is our job to sensitize our antennae to receive what the Spirit is saying. One way we do that is to recall times and situations when we have heard the Lord."
—Page 46, *Created For So Much More*

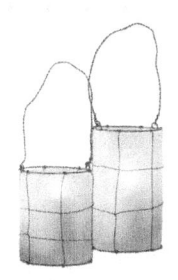

Soaring With God

Exercise 9: Application

Now we will complete the third column of the previous exercise. Consider the times you heard the Lord. How did you apply what you heard? What changed? What action did you take? How did you experience the *so much more* of God and/or the *so much more* for which you were created? Ask the Lord to reveal the results, whether tangible, emotional, or spiritual. **Write the results He shows you in the blank third column.**

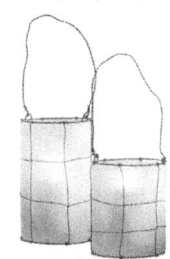

"Revelation or a prophetic word, sign, or message should always lead you closer to the Lord in a way that affects your daily life."
—Page 48, *Created For So Much More*

Going Deeper: When God Seems Silent

Ask Holy Spirit to reveal a time when you have experienced the silence of God. Was there a new "language" God taught you as a result? Were you called to rest in His Presence? Did He speak through music, nature, or His Word in a way He hadn't before? Was there a new language God taught you as a result? **Reflect on the experience, recount it, and scribe the lessons you learned.**

"If God seems silent to you, perhaps He is trying to teach you a different language." —Page 44, *Created For So Much More*

A Guided Journal to Soaring With God

Going Deeper: Unwrapping God's Message

Consider the quote from *Created For So Much More* and the Proverbs 25:2 verse from the following page. **Ask the Lord to reveal when you have experienced searching out a message from Him.** What was the end result of your search? What did the Lord teach you through the process? **Write out your experience and lessons.**

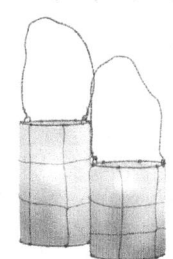

*The heavens are telling of the glory of God;
And their expanse is declaring the work of His hands* (Psalm 19:1).

Lesson 4 • INTIMACY

"God's messages often come wrapped in the mysterious. Like a hidden treasure, His message can require a treasure map and a willingness to search for the meaning."
—Page 41, *Created For So Much More*

*It is the glory of God to conceal a matter,
But the glory of kings is to search out a matter* (Proverbs 25:2).

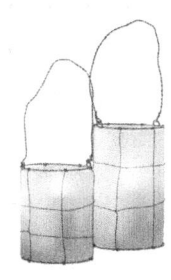

A Guided Journal to Soaring With God

> "Indeed
> God speaks once,
> Or twice, yet no one notices it.
> "In a dream, a vision of the night,
> When sound sleep falls on men,
> While they slumber in their beds,
> Then He opens the ears of men,
> And seals their instruction" (Job 33:14–16).

"The world is God's dictionary, and He will use whatever He needs to get His message across!"—Page 40, *Created For So Much More*

Pause to Ponder and Pray

Take the time to thank the Lord for speaking to you in His unique way. **Sit in His Presence and ponder a specific scripture verse.** What does it tell you about God and your relationship with Him? Ask Him for greater sensitivity to recognize and hear His voice so that you experience *so much more* intimacy with Him.

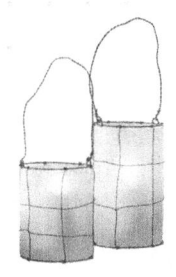

Encouragement for Your Journey

Well done, Dear One! You may feel like you just took a detour from the road of identity and purpose, and maybe you are wondering why it was necessary. Sensitizing your heart and spirit to hear when and what the Lord speaks is an important step to realizing the ***so much more*** that awaits. Rest assured that the Holy Spirit has heightened your sense of His Presence and His voice. Trust that He is developing ***so much more*** intimacy with you as you seek Him. Take heart in the following promise from God that is available to you:

> *You will seek Me and find Me when you search for Me with all your heart* (Jeremiah 29:13).

You have sought the Lord and I trust that you have found Him. He loves you with an intensity that is unshakable. Allow Him to wrap His loving arms around you and whisper words of love and encouragement to you. You are making great progress toward uncovering the ***so much more*** of who God created you to be and what He created you to do.

Congratulations! Take a minute or two to express whatever emotion you are feeling right now. You might sit quietly, take a walk to ponder, or have a dance party. Go ahead. Be real and express yourself. You are in the middle of your journey of self-discovery, and you are doing great! Praise the Lord! Literally, go ahead and worship Him.

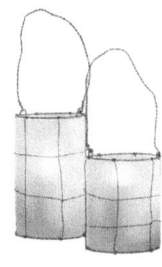

5.
CERTAINTY

Deborah Gall
__Garden's Light__, 2011
Acrylic on Canvas
36" x 18"

See ***Garden's Light*** and God's path to ***so much more*** certainty as Deborah discusses five reasons to confirm God's plan in the *Created For So Much More* CERTAINTY Video.

"There are **TIMES** when the Lord keeps us paused while He **ARRANGES** things around us in our **LIVES**."

—*Created For So Much More* CERTAINTY (Chapter Five) Video

5.
created for so much more
CERTAINTY:
Confirming Your Flight

Clear Confirmation

God is supernatural; we are not. Hearing from Heaven is a supernatural experience that requires confirmation. Waiting for the Lord to confirm His direction ensures that you won't run with a partial vision or run ahead of God's timetable. This lesson suggests several methods that the Lord uses to confirm His word.

Feeling at peace, seeing signs, experiencing the witness of others, finding scripture confirmations, having unexpected divine appointments, and encountering unexpected opportunities are just a few of the many ways God brings confirmation to His children. He is faithful to you and to His word of direction. He will always confirm it.

Confirming God's timing is as important as confirming His word. This lesson strengthens your discernment muscles to bring **so much more** certainty to your relationship with the Lord and the steps He asks you to take.

The exercises in this lesson first invite you to focus on the Lord's confirmations in your past. Then—after you remember and honor the past—you will ask for confirmation for today's direction. This work of remembering past confirmations and waiting for future confirmations brings **so much more** certainty to the flight path before you as you soar into your God-given identity and your purpose.

Find out more about confirming God's direction and timing by watching the *Created For So Much More* CERTAINTY Video, available at deborahgall.com

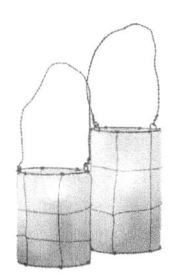

Opening Thoughts: Man's Plans, God's Direction

How does it make you feel to realize that the Lord will direct your steps by confirming His word? **Take the time here and now to write down your emotions and thank the Lord for His direction.**

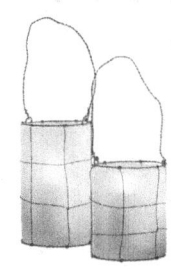

The mind of man plans his way, But the LORD directs his steps (Proverbs 16:9).

"Natural things of the world become supernatural in the hands of the Lord when He chooses to use them to confirm His word."—Page 58, *Created For So Much More*

Going Deeper: Remembering God's Ways

Consider the different ways God has confirmed His next steps for you. Did He use natural things like birds, clouds, sunsets, etc.? Did you come across the perfect passage from Scripture at the just right time? Did a friend or colleague say the exact phrase you were waiting for? Did a request for your services suddenly surface? God uses so many more ways to confirm His direction than could be listed in one chapter. **List some of the specific methods of confirmation you have experienced here.**

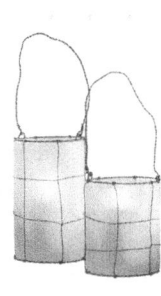

Lesson 5 • **CERTAINTY**

"The Lord will use anything in your life to speak to you and confirm His words to you."—Page 52, *Created For So Much More*

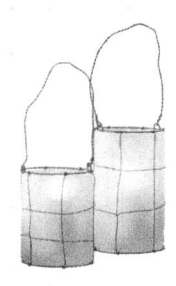

A Guided Journal to Soaring With God

"*Are not two sparrows sold for a cent? And yet not one of them will fall to the ground apart from your Father. But the very hairs on your head are all numbered*" (Matthew 10:29–31).

"Remembering is a way of giving honor and thanksgiving to the Lord for all that He has done in your life."—Page 65, *Created For So Much More*

Soaring With God

Exercise 10: Confirmations

You have already made a list of the ways God has confirmed His word in your life. Now I invite you to connect His way of speaking direction to His way of confirming His word.

Divide the page into three columns

1. In the first column, **list the time/event** when You heard the Lord's word and direction.
2. In the second column, **list the language** the Lord used to speak to you about that event.
3. In the third column, **list the way** in which God confirmed His word or direction for you.

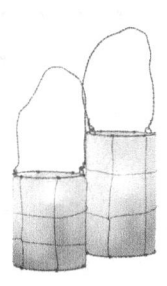

Exercise 10: Confirmations, Continued

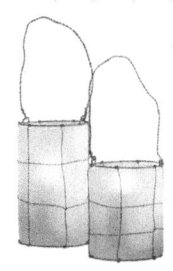

"You can rest in the Lord and trust that He will confirm whatever He wants you to know and do right now."—Page 61, *Created For So Much More*

Lesson 5 • CERTAINTY

*"For as the rain and the snow come down from heaven,
And do not return there without watering the earth
And making it bear and sprout,
And furnishing seed to the sower and bread to the eater;
So will My word be which goes forth from My mouth;
It will not return to Me empty,
Without accomplishing what I desire,
And without succeeding* in the matter *for which I sent it"* (Isaiah 55:10–11).

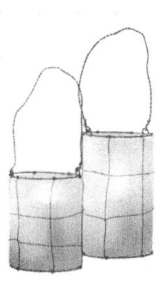

Going Deeper: God's Timing

Sit with the Lord and ask Him to show you when you have run ahead of His timing. Also ask Him if there are other times when you have waited for His confirmation and His timing. **Reflect on the outcomes of both situations and write about the lessons you learned.**

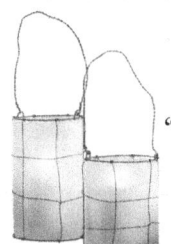

"Once you have heard the Lord, and He has confirmed His word, **go back and ask Him to confirm His timing**."—Page 64, *Created For So Much More*

Lesson 5 • CERTAINTY

"When you don't have a clear picture of direction, asking the Lord for the next step—or the next bread crumb on your path—is a great prayer."
—Page 51, *Created For So Much More*

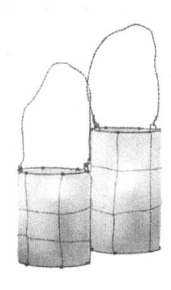

Soaring With God

Exercise 11: Asking for Confirmation

God is faithful to direct and confirm His direction in your life. I invite you to take the time to pause and ask the Lord to confirm what He is saying to you at the present time. Once again, divide the page into three columns.

1. In the first column, **list a directive** that you have felt from the Lord.
2. In the second column, **list how you came to know and understand** this was a directive from the Lord. How did God reveal this to you? What language did He use?
3. **Leave the third column blank.**
4. Look over your list and **seek the Lord**. Ask Him to confirm His directive and give you the timing to begin, work on, and finish what He has called you to do.
5. Over the next days, weeks, or months, keep this list before you, **continuing to pray** for those things not confirmed, and **noting the confirmations** in the third column.

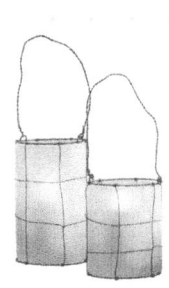

Lesson 5 • CERTAINTY

"Whatever way God chooses to speak and confirm His word, be certain that as you seek your Heavenly Father, He will reveal the *so much more* of who He created you to be." —Page 66, *Created For So Much More*

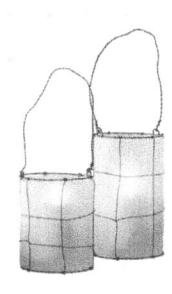

A Guided Journal to Soaring With God

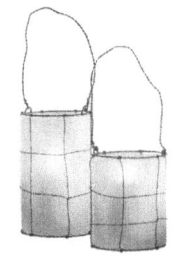

"While you allow God's timing to unfold in your life, diligently pursue the Lord and activate the gifts placed within you."
—Page 62, *Created For So Much More*

Pause to Ponder and Pray

I invite you to **worship the Lord** for all the ways He has spoken to you, whether it is directive or confirming. **Thank Him** for His love and direction that keeps you on His path to *so much more* certainty as you uncover the *so much more* of your identity and purpose.

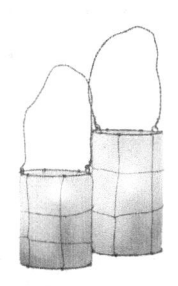

Encouragement for Your Journey

God is faithful to you and to your purpose. He has a plan that is **_so much more_** than you could ever ask or imagine (1 Corinthians 1:9). There are times when you might scratch your head and ask, "Really, Lord?" but I encourage you to wait and then follow when the Lord says, *"Go this way."* The Prophet Isaiah reminds us that we see only from our natural plane when he says:

> *"For My thoughts are not your thoughts,*
> *Nor are your ways My ways," declares the Lord.*
> *"For as the heavens are higher than the earth,*
> *So are My ways higher than your ways*
> *And My thoughts than your thoughts"* (Isaiah 55:8–9).

God operates on the supernatural plane. His plans and His timing might feel a bit out of sync with your thoughts and plans. Trust that He sees things from a broader perspective. I invite you to surrender your plans and timing to God. Allow Him to show and confirm His steps for you. Wait for Him. Do not rush ahead. Trust that He is working on your behalf.

You will experience **_so much more_** certainty as you wait for the Lord before you take the next step in your journey. God's timing for you to discover who He created you to be and what He created you to do is perfect. Trust Him for your steps and rely on Him to confirm them and show you His ideal timetable for taking them. Even now, I recommend that you stop and ask Holy Spirit if you need to pause before moving on to lesson six. He knows what is ahead and will move you forward at the perfect time.

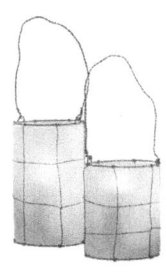

ered with # 6.
IDENTITY

Deborah Gall
Hidden Treasure, 2011
Acrylic on Canvas
36" x 18"

See ***Hidden Treasure*** in color and celebrate that you are a uniquely beautiful treasure as you watch the *Created For So Much More* IDENTITY Video.

"In the **HEAVENLY** realm we are always **EVOLVING** and maturing into **MORE**."

—***Created For So Much More*** IDENTITY (Chapter Six) Video

6.
created for so much more
IDENTITY:
Completing Your Passport

Heaven's Perspective

Although this lesson's title uses the phrase "completing your passport," our Heavenly identity is never fully complete. God is always in the process of refining us and revealing ***so much more*** of our identity. Our Heavenly identity is not based on labels such as where we live, what we do, or how educated we are. These types of labels create boxes that stifle exploration of our identity.

God invites you to break out of the boxes of labels and to soar into the fullness of your name—who He created you to be. He knew you before He formed you (Psalm 139:15). He created you and He called it good (Genesis 1:31). You are fearfully and wonderfully made by a Creator who loves you.

It is time to step into the future and embrace your God-given identity. Soaring with God on the journey of discovering ***so much more*** identity and purpose can get emotional. It can be tough to lay past perceptions of who you are on the line to discover who God says you are. You already took great strides when you took responsibility and put the past in the past in lessons two and three. Allow the Lord to share who HE says you are as you work through this lesson, which has been called life-changing.

I invite you to take as much time as you need to work through the exercises. I am confident that the Lord will speak your name, show you how much He loves you, share what He was thinking when He created you, and ***so much more***. Prepare to soar, Dear One. Father, Jesus, and Holy Spirit are waiting to reveal ***so much more*** of your identity.

Remove labels and realize that only you can bear fruit that is uniquely yours as you watch the *Created For So Much More* IDENTITY Video at deborahgall.com

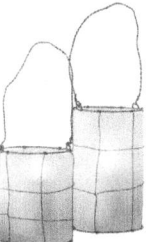

A Guided Journal to Soaring With God

Opening Thoughts: And God Said, *"It is good."*

How does it make you feel to know God says you are fearfully and wonderfully made (Psalm 139:14)? **Write out a prayer sharing your feelings about these words to the Lord and offer thanksgiving to Him for who He created you to be.**

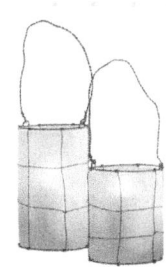

"It is the enemy, through the world around us, who builds the box that labels bring."—Page 71, *Created For So Much More*

Lesson 6 • IDENTITY

And Jesus said to him, "Blessed are you, Simon Barjona, because flesh and blood did not reveal this to you, but My Father who is in heaven" (Matthew 16:17).

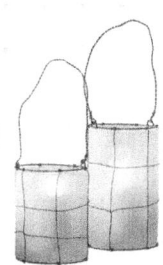

Going Deeper: Labels and Names

Jesus' disciple Simon could have been limited by the labels that his work as an uneducated fisherman implied. Jesus didn't see those labels as limits. He gave Simon a new name. He named him Peter—the Rock—and called him to be the foundation of God's church (Matthew 16:18–19). The world labels; God names.

What labels have you experienced in your life? How did it feel to be put in the box that labels bring? What does the Lord say about that label and box? Ask the Lord to replace the labels you have experienced with the name—your identity—He gave you. **Journal about your experience and what God says about labels and names.**

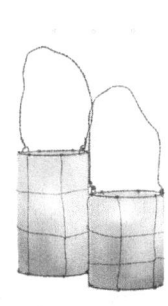

Lesson 6 • **IDENTITY**

"When you, like Peter, keep your spirit tuned to Heaven's perspective, you too break out of the labels that limit you."—Page 72, *Created For So Much More*

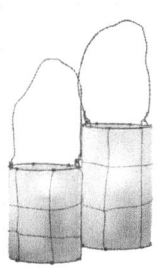

Soaring With God

Exercise 12: Your Identity

I want you to carve out 15–30 minutes for this exercise. Take whatever time you need to ask the Lord the following two questions AND allow Him space and time to answer. Sit quietly in order to tune your spiritual ears to Heaven.

1. Ask the Lord how much He loves you.

    Scribe what you hear Him saying and/or showing you.

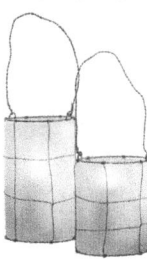

Lesson 6 • IDENTITY

*"Before I formed you in the womb I knew you,
And before you were born I consecrated you;
I have appointed you a prophet to the nations"* (Jeremiah 1:5).

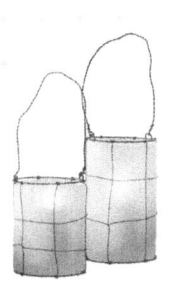

A Guided Journal to Soaring With God

"Your 'true north' for your identity is your God-given identity. Within your identity are the keys that reveal your destination."—Page 75, *Created For So Much More*

Exercise 12: Your Identity, Continued

2. The Psalmist says:

*For You formed my inward parts;
You wove me in my mother's womb* (Psalm 139:13).

Ask, "Father, Jesus, Holy Spirit, what were you thinking when You formed me in my mother's womb?" **Write Their answer.**

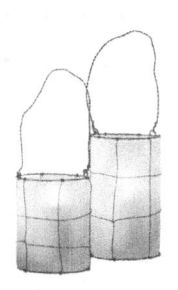

A Guided Journal to Soaring With God

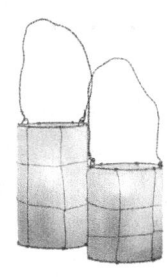

"God is always in process of refining us and pouring more of His identity into us."—Page 75, *Created For So Much More*

Lesson 6 • **IDENTITY**

"Soaring with God means resting in who He created you to be."
—Page 75, *Created For So Much More*

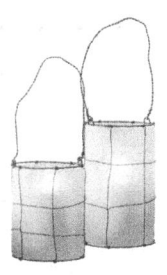

A Guided Journal to Soaring With God

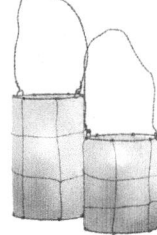

"Knowing who God says you are, and knowing your identity in Christ, is at the root of grasping the **so much more** that the Lord has for you."
—Page 69, *Created For So Much More*

Going Deeper: Let it Settle in Your Spirit

Once you have completed the previous exercise, I recommend that you **ponder what the Lord has revealed to you**. Allow the time to let it settle in your spirit. Even after additional quiet time, it may be time to take a break and perhaps walk around to allow God's truth of who He created you to be to sink deeply into your heart, mind, and spirit. **Jot down any thoughts and feelings that arise here.**

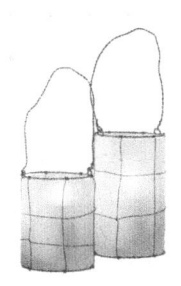

Soaring With God

Exercise 13: Developing Your Life Message

What is your life message? What do you stand for? What do you want people to remember about you? This exercise is not about image. Image is based on labels. This exercise is about God's identity for you and the name/words He speaks over you—character words like faithful, trustworthy, authority, gifted, transparent, or authentic—to name a few.

Take the time to jot a few words down. Combine these with your answers from Exercise 12 to get a more complete picture of who God created you to be.

"Living your message means allowing Holy Spirit to permeate all aspects of your life." —Page 75, *Created For So Much More*

Pause to Ponder and Pray

I invite you to give thanks to the Lord specifically for all of the gifts, talents, and character traits that He gave you. **Worship your Creator as you bask in His love**.

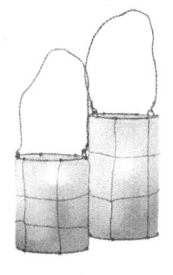

Encouragement for Your Journey

Great job! You are well on your way to a greater understanding of who God created you to be. There is always ***so much more*** for God to reveal about your God-given identity. Rest in what you know today. You are exactly who and where you are supposed to be at this time. This journey of discovering all that you were created to be is never complete. God always reveals ***so much more*** as we allow Him to show us who He is and how we reflect Him through our identity. As we continue on this journey, I recommend that you adopt the mindset and the approach that Apostle Paul shared in his letter to the Philippians:

> *Brethren, I do not regard myself as having laid hold of it yet; but one thing I do: forgetting what lies behind and reaching forward to what lies ahead, I press on toward the goal for the prize of the upward call of God in Christ Jesus* (Philippians 3:13–14).

You, Dear One, are "pressing on toward the goal"; your prize is discovering who God created you to be and what He created you to do. Congratulations. I know Heaven rejoices as you discover and embrace the ***so much more*** of your God-given identity. I am so proud of you. You are getting to the heart of who God created you to be.

Whenever my family vacations together, we live by the phrase, "You do you." I want to encourage you to live by this phrase. Celebrate who God created you to be in whatever way brings joy and delight. That may be dancing, singing, walking, drawing, or sharing your experience with a close friend. Go ahead. Take time to join your praise with Heaven's choir as you worship the loving Creator.

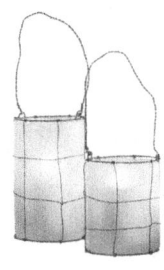

7.
VISION

Deborah Gall
Commanding Presence, 2012
Acrylic on Canvas
30" x 40"

See ***Commanding Presence*** in color in the *Created For So Much More* VISION Video, and get ready to dream with God about your future.

"The sky is **LIMITLESS** and so are God's **POSSIBILITIES** for **YOU**."

—*Created For So Much More* VISION (Chapter Seven) Video

7.
created for so much more
VISION:
Designing Your Flight Plan

Dreaming with God

God created you to soar with vision and purpose. I am so excited to invite you to co-labor with God to develop the plan that empowers your vision and enables your destiny. Having a plan—seeing how things fit together and seeking the Lord for order and direction—keeps you from wandering purposelessly through life.

God knew His plan for you before He formed you. You carry ideas, pictures, visions, and dreams of your destiny—all of which are whispers from Heaven to help you discover your flight plan for the future. The Lord already has the plan and is waiting to share it with you.

The endless work to conjure up your destiny ceases when you look at your future from Heaven's perspective. All that is needed is to dream with God, access His plan, and take notes. When you ask God for His plan, you can stop trying to figure it all out. What a blessing it is to rest in the Lord and scribe His directions as you draw out the flight plan.

The exercises in this lesson are tools to put you in touch with the Lord, who He says you are, and His plan for you. Cloud Forming—what I call brainstorming with God—can be used whenever you want to sort through an idea, project, or assignment from Heaven. Cloud Forming reveals God's plan for your life. You will first form a cloud based on your identity and then you will dream big dreams with God. Finally, you will work small as you ask Him to highlight areas to address now.

Soaring with God to design your flight plan will bring God's vision for your future into focus. You will have **so much more** vision of who God created you to be and what He created you to do as you develop your flight plan with Him.

Hear more about soaring into God's purposes, plans, and promises for your life in the *Created For So Much More* VISION Video at deborahgall.com

Opening Thoughts: The Effort of Dreaming

Ecclesiastes 5:3 says, *"For the dream comes through much effort."* The "effort" I invite you to take in this lesson is to ask the Lord for that dream. What emotions are you experiencing as you think about sitting at the Lord's feet to ask for His vision and dream for your life? **List your emotions and any other thoughts you might have as you begin to brainstorm with Heaven.**

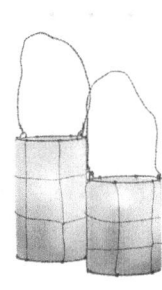

Lesson 7 • **VISION**

"Dear One, God invites you to sit at His feet and ask for His guidance for your future. Providing guidance is one of the reasons He sent the Holy Spirit."
—Page 77, *Created For So Much More*

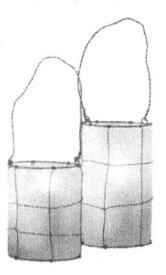

A Guided Journal to Soaring With God

Going Deeper: Your Days Are Ordained

The Psalmist says:

*Your eyes have seen my unformed substance;
And in Your book were all written
The days that were ordained for me,
<u>When as yet there was not one of them</u>* (Psalm 139:16, underlined emphasis mine).

Ponder this verse as you answer the following questions: What does it mean to you that your days were ordained in Heaven before you were born? How does it make you feel that your job is to access what has already been determined in Heaven?

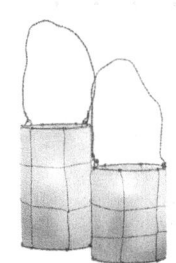

"When you loosen your grip on the future and cease striving to accomplish your vision for your future in your own strength, you open your hand to receive the ***so much more*** of God and what He has for you."
—Page 84, *Created For So Much More*

Lesson 7 • VISION

He said to him again a second time, "Simon, son of John, do you love Me?" He said to Him, "Yes, Lord; You know that I love You." He said to him, "Shepherd My sheep" (John 21:16).

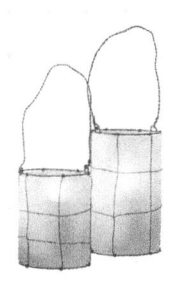

Going Deeper: Serving the Kingdom

Jesus responded to Peter in John 21:16 by saying, *"Shepherd my sheep."* Jesus did not distinguish between a single sheep or a flock of sheep. It makes no difference to the Lord how many people you serve. Your purpose in the Kingdom is not measured by how much you impact the world. **Take a moment to reflect on how you serve God's sheep in your life. Write your reflections here.**

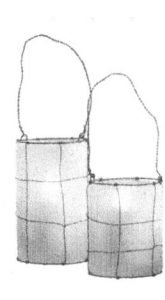

Soaring With God

Exercise 14: Cloud Forming

There is no right or wrong way to do this exercise. Your cloud formation, like you, will be unique. We will start with what you heard Holy Spirit say when you asked Him what He was thinking when He created you in Exercise 12 from the previous lesson. Who did He create you to be?

Step 1: In the center of the page, write your name.

Step 2: Form circles around your name with the interests, talents, characteristics, or gifts that the Lord spoke to you.

For example, during the exercise, the Lord told Susan that He created her to be a mother, teacher, Jesus Follower, leader, and artist. Her cloud formation looks like this.

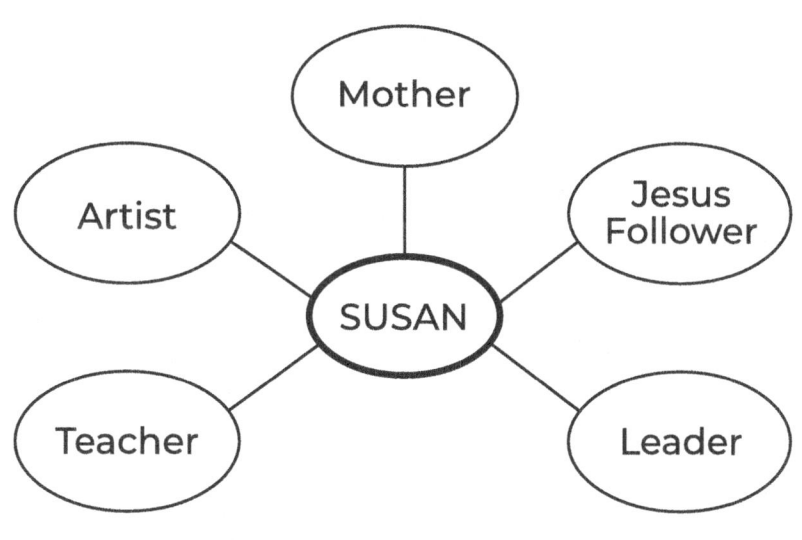

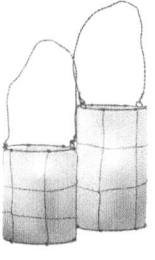

CLOUD FORMING
Steps 1 & 2

- Mother
- Jesus Follower
- Leader
- Teacher
- Artist
- SUSAN

A Guided Journal to Soaring With God

Exercise 14: Cloud Forming, Continued
Draw your formation here.

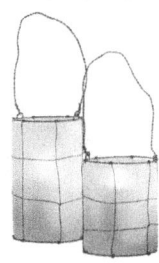

Lesson 7 • VISION

"By soaring with God in who He created you to be and what He created you to do, you are transformed into the best YOU in the whole world, which is exactly what you need to change the world."
—Page 86. *Created For So Much More*

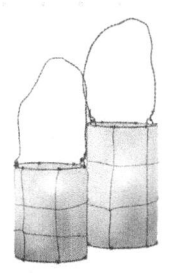

A Guided Journal to Soaring With God

Exercise 14: Cloud Forming, Continued
Continue your cloud formation here.

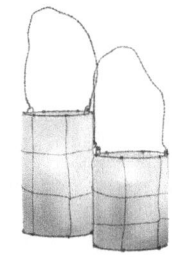

"We know that you were created for a purpose. We know that God placed your purpose within the very characteristics and talents that you possess."
—Page 92, *Created For So Much More*

Exercise 14: Cloud Forming, Continued
Step 3: Take one of those bubbles and drill down a bit.

It is time to be more specific. Remember, we are still asking the Lord to show you who you are. Think of these bubbles like spokes of a wheel coming out from the larger bubble. This exercise is not what you currently do, it is about who you are, what you are passionate about, your gifts, talents, and how God sees you. Here is how Susan's cloud formation is progressing:

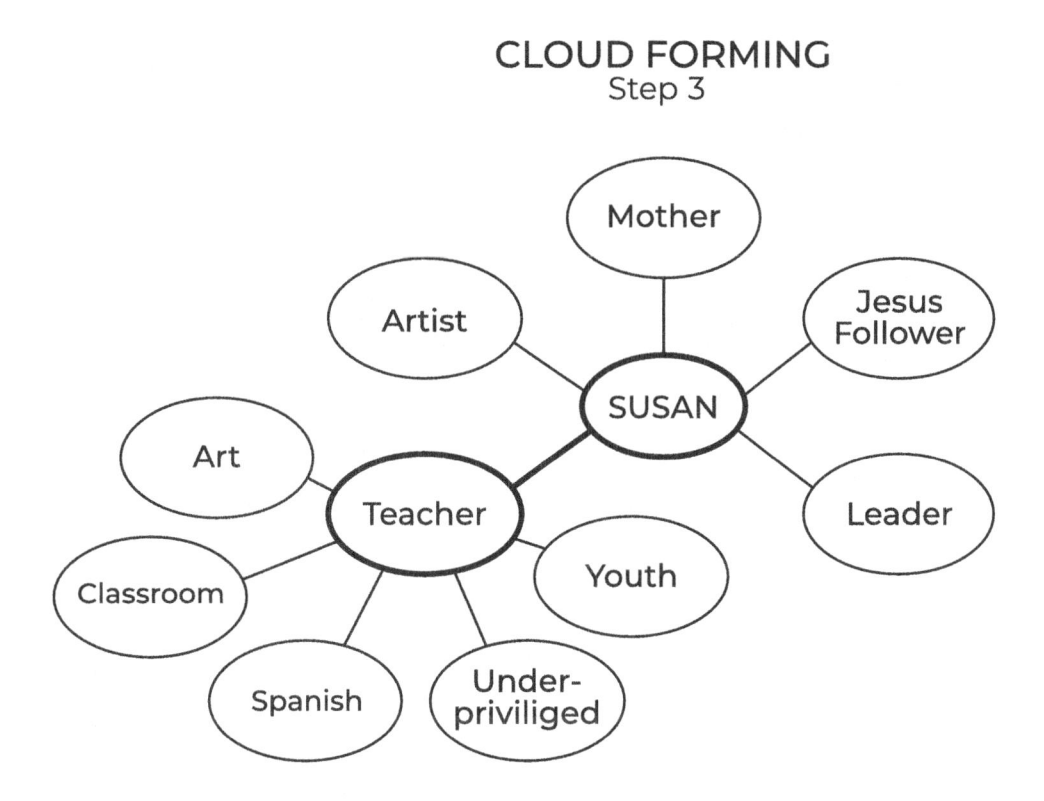

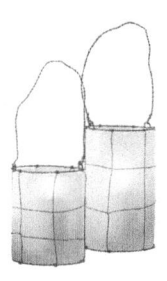

CLOUD FORMING
Step 3

- SUSAN
  - Mother
  - Jesus Follower
  - Leader
  - Youth
  - Teacher
    - Classroom
    - Art
    - Spanish
    - Underpriviliged
  - Artist

Exercise 14: Cloud Forming, Continued

Either go back to your original formation and drill down or use the space here. **Put one characteristic in the middle and then get specific about that characteristic.** In our example, Susan specifically noted she was passionate about teaching art and/or Spanish to underprivileged youth in a classroom.

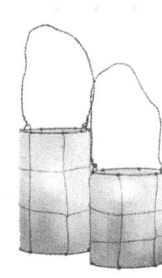

"You carry ideas, pictures, visions, and dreams of your destiny—all of which are whispers from Heaven to help discover your flight plan."
—Page 78, *Created For So Much More*

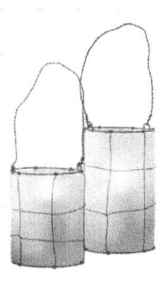

A Guided Journal to Soaring With God

Exercise 14: Cloud Forming, Continued
Continue your cloud formation here:

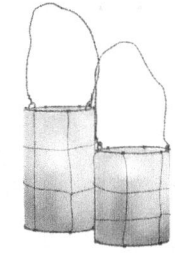

"God knew His plan for you and set you apart for that purpose."
—Page 80, *Created For So Much More*

Soaring With God

Exercise 15: Establishing Your Flight Plan

Your flight plan is God's vision, plan, and purpose for your future. Here we change the focus from who you are to where you are going. I want you to begin with your last cloud formation. Take a moment to ask the Lord to highlight **one aspect** of your identity and seek the Lord for His purposes attached to that aspect. **Take one of your main bubbles from Step 2 from Exercise 14. Place it in the center of the page.**

Now it's time to flesh out specifics and add the details you already know or ask the Lord for fresh revelation about this area of your life. Susan chose to expand on an after-school program. Her flight plan cloud formation looks like this:

CLOUD FORMING
Susan's Flight Plan

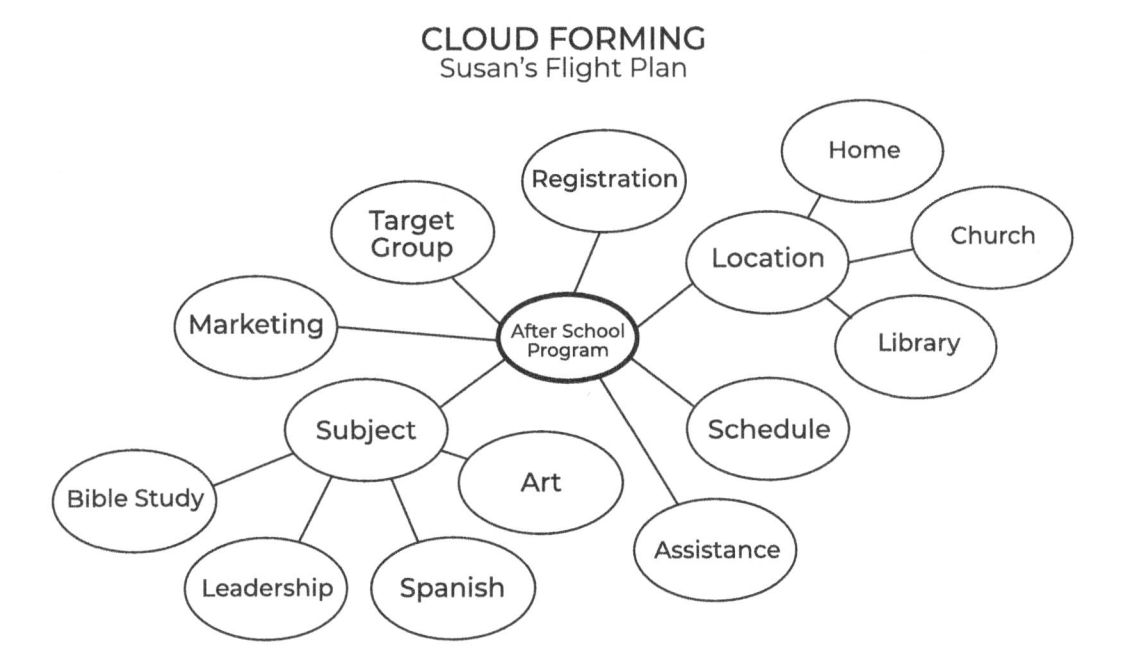

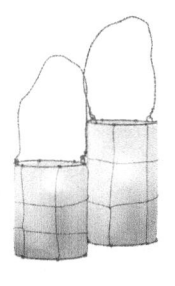

A Guided Journal to Soaring With God

Exercise 15: Establishing Your Flight Plan
Draw your cloud formation here:

Where there is no vision, the people are unrestrained, But happy is he who keeps the law (Proverbs 29:18).

"Do not be afraid to edit your skills, rewrite your script, or do the work to improve your area of expertise."—Page 95, *Created For So Much More*

"Fully embracing the present ignites the passion to live a life fully engaged with God's plan and purpose."—Page 84, *Created For So Much More*

Soaring With God

Exercise 16: Expanding Your Flight Plan

This is the time to continue brainstorming with the Lord. Expand even more from that center bubble and add anything else the Lord shows you. **Write everything down. In essence, you are still brainstorming with Holy Spirit.** This exercise is not meant to be analytical or logical. Just let it flow. There are no right or wrong cloud formations. Let it flow. I often receive huge revelation about projects and areas of my life when I take the additional time to process with the Lord this way.

Expand your flight plan here:

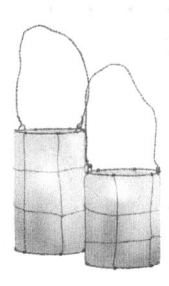

Lesson 7 • **VISION**

"Staying connected with the Lord is how you will know whether it is time to take a leap or time to be still."—Page 85, *Created For So Much More*

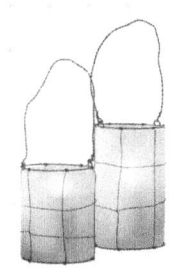

A Guided Journal to Soaring With God

> *If people can't see what God is doing,*
> *They stumble all over themselves;*
> *But when they attend to what he reveals,*
> *They are most blessed* (Proverbs 29:18, The Message Bible).

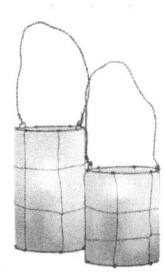

Lesson 7 • **VISION**

"Use the Cloud Forming exercise every time you sense Holy Spirit leading you into something new."—Page 94, *Created For So Much More*

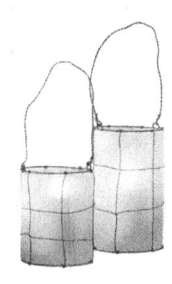

Soaring With God

Exercise 17: Determining Specific Flight Plan Takeaways.

Now I want you to do me a favor. Sit awhile with your pages of cloud formations. Continue to ask the Lord to highlight areas. Ask Him if there are areas you have been neglecting. **Make a list of those areas that Holy Spirit is highlighting to you.**

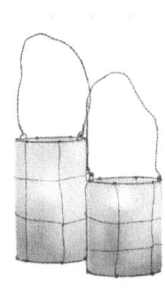

Lesson 7 • **VISION**

"God is a big god. He has big audacious plans for His children. It is often said that if you can accomplish your vision in your own strength, it is not God's vision."—Page 84, *Created For So Much More*

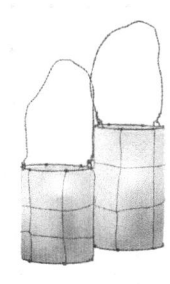

Soaring With God

Exercise 18: Be Strong and Courageous

In Joshua 1:6, 7, and 9, the Lord repeats the phrase, *"Be strong and courageous"* three times, including one that says, *"Only be very strong and very courageous."* The Lord tells Joshua:

> *"Every place on which the sole of your foot tread, I have given it to you, just as I spoke to Moses"* (Joshua 1:3).

For this exercise, I have combined and paraphrased the Lord's message to Joshua as this, "Be strong and courageous, for I have given you the land." We are going to use my paraphrase as the basis of this exercise. It is designed to connect this truth with the cloud you have formed and the big dream you carry within your spirit.

Take the time to settle in with the Lord and let Him finish each sentence as you work through the paraphrased truth of strength, courage, and taking the land.

Fill in the blanks as you are led by the Lord. For instance, today, I would fill in the first line like this: BE: <u>confident that I am working all things together for your good.</u>

BE

BE STRONG

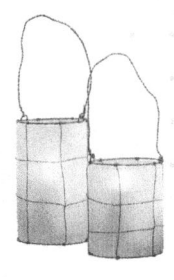

Lesson 7 • **VISION**

BE STRONG AND

BE STRONG AND COURAGEOUS

BE STRONG AND COURAGEOUS FOR

BE STRONG AND COURAGEOUS FOR I

BE STRONG AND COURAGEOUS FOR I HAVE

BE STRONG AND COURAGEOUS FOR I HAVE GIVEN

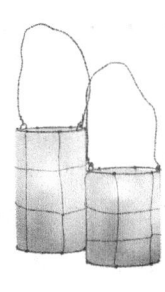

Lesson 7 • VISION

BE STRONG AND COURAGEOUS FOR I HAVE GIVEN YOU

BE STRONG AND COURAGEOUS FOR I HAVE GIVEN YOU THE

BE STRONG AND COURAGEOUS FOR I HAVE GIVEN YOU THE LAND.

Pause to Ponder and Pray

Climbing out of your comfort zone and soaring with God can unleash a host of emotions. **Take the time to write your thoughts and feelings here.** Then thank the Lord for His big audacious dream and ask that He direct your steps as you move forward in your journey.

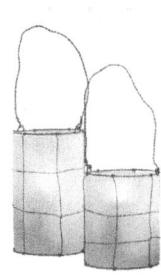

Lesson 7 • VISION

"It is comforting to know that the Lord goes before me. It brings confidence to remind me that He is my Source of strength and courage."
—Page 97, *Created For So Much More*

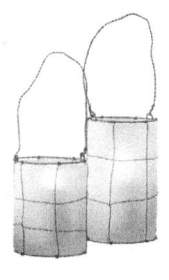

Encouragement for Your Journey

God created all of us to be doing amazing things. That assignment is big. Right about now, you may feel excited, nervous, and even a little anxious as you think about the big audacious dream the Lord revealed. Whenever I feel this kind of tension, it helps me to think of Mary, the mother of Jesus.

When Gabriel visited Mary to bring the news of her pregnancy, Mary first asked, *"How can this be?"* (Luke 1:34). It was faith in God that enabled her to respond, *"May it be done to me according to your word"* (Luke 1:38), just four verses later.

Can you relate to Mary as you think about the God-sized dream the Lord put within you? I encourage you to be strong and courageous and like Mary have faith in the One who gave you your vision. God is faithful to you and to your call. He tells us as much in His Word, when the Apostle Paul writes:

Faithful is He who calls you, and He also will bring it to pass
(1 Thessalonians 5:24).

That verse reveals that it is God's job to bring your dreams to pass. Your job is to say—like Mary—*"May it be done to me according to your word"* (Luke 1:38). Your job is to co-labor with Holy Spirit and take the steps He puts before you. Tune in to Heaven and follow God's direction, knowing that He is God. He will bring **so much more** to your vision as you dream big audacious dreams. He will also bring your vision to pass as you take the steps He highlights.

Through the work you have done in this lesson, you have gained yet another tool for the journey ahead. Cloud Forming is a favorite exercise for those who continue to travel this journey of discovery. Use it often as God reveals **so much more** vision of your identity and purpose. Great job, Dear One! You are well on your way to taking flight to even greater heights as who God created you to be doing what He created you to do.

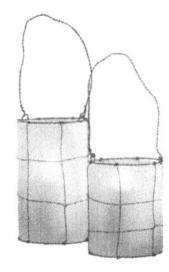

8.
UNDERSTANDING

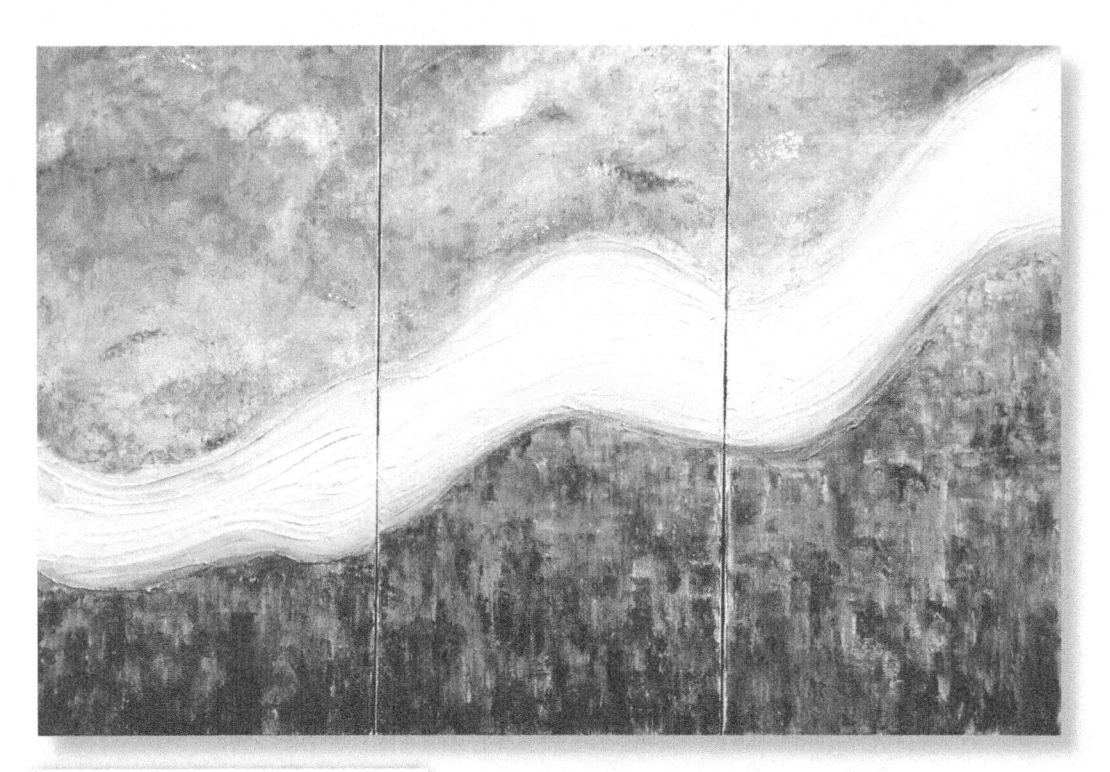

Deborah Gall
Kingdom Come, 2013
Acrylic on Canvas
24" x 36" Triptych

View ***Kingdom Come*** in color during the *Created For So Much More* UNDERSTANDING Video and gain the courage to follow your God-given path—bringing Heaven to Earth.

"What may **SEEM** like an insignificant **STEP** to you, could move **MOUNTAINS** in the Kingdom. You never know."
—*Created For So Much More* UNDERSTANDING (Chapter Eight) Video

8.
created for so much more
UNDERSTANDING:
Determining Your Timetable

Aligning with God's Itinerary

When you work within God's timetable, you live more fully as who He created you to be, and you stay on course pursuing what He created you to do. Staying content, waiting on God, and understanding how God operates through the seasons of life are keys to aligning with God's itinerary.

This lesson uses the story of Peter and the Great Catch of Fish (Luke 5:1–9) as a basis for gaining *so much more* understanding of God's seasons. Methods gleaned from this passage include the following seasons within a cycle of God.

- **Tending the Nets** is a quiet season when the Lord teaches and/or heals you.
- **Launch** is the time when you begin to operate in your purpose and calling.
- **Harvest** is a season that brings Kingdom results from your labors.
- **Needing help** is a time when the Kingdom harvest is so great, you require the help of others.
- **Worship** is meant to be a continuous practice no matter which season you are in.

The exercises in this lesson compare your current situation with the cycle of God to help you understand *so much more* of what the Lord is doing during this season in your life. You will then take a look back at your cloud formation and determine the next steps the Lord has for you. The exercises not only bring *so much more* understanding to God's timetable but they also bring *so much more* contentment and hope.

Hear about how God holds your hands and steadies your steps in the *Created For So Much More* UNDERSTANDING Video, available at deborahgall.com

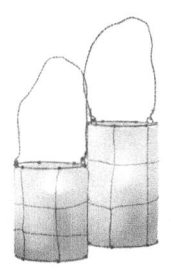

Opening Thoughts: God's Schedule

Take a few minutes to ponder God's schedule for your big dream. How does it make you feel that He's in charge of the timetable for things to unfold in your life? Before digging into the exercises, **note where you see yourself in relation to God's schedule for your big dream.**

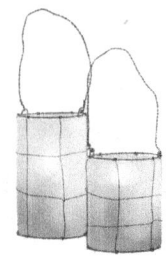

"Just as He [God] has a vision and purpose for your life, He has a schedule set up just for you."—Page 99, *Created For So Much More*

Not that I speak from want, for I have learned to be content in whatever circumstances I am. (Philippians 4:11).

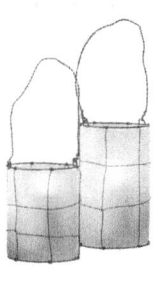

Going Deeper: How Content Are You?

Big dreams cause great frustration when your sense of contentment depends on the fulfillment of those big dreams. Learn to be content wherever you are, and you will discover relief from anxiety and nervousness about the future. Take a few minutes to **jot down your level of contentment on a scale of 1–10** with 10 being peacefully content. **Then make a note of habits** you have in place or need to put into place in order to be content in your current circumstances. Examples of habit include writing a daily gratitude list, scheduling regular prayer time with the Lord, reading a selection of scripture first thing in the morning or before going to bed at night, or playing music that shifts your focus to God. When we take our eyes off of our circumstances and place them on the Lord, we realize greater contentment.

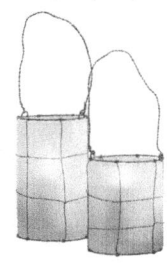

"God has an appointed time for your big dream."
—Page 101, *Created For So Much More*

*"For the vision is yet for the appointed time;
It hastens toward the goal and it will not fail.
Though it tarries, wait for it;
For it will certainly come, it will not delay"* (Habakkuk 2:3).

"Actively waiting on the Lord means taking the time you are given to study, learn, heal, and train."—Page 106, *Created For So Much More*

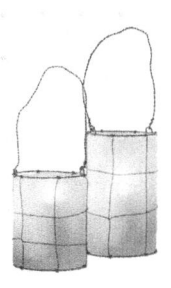

Soaring With God

Exercise 19: Seasons and Cycles

Think about the characteristics of each of the five seasons gleaned from Peter's Great Catch of Fish. Ask yourself the question(s) listed and ask the Lord to show you which season you are currently in.

1. Are you **mending your nets**? Is the Lord asking you to sit quietly and work on heart or character issues? When you were last in this season, what did the Lord teach you?
2. Do you find yourself **launching** out from the shore in God's timing? Have opportunities arisen that require you to take a leap of faith into the deep waters of your calling? If you are launching, what is the pace of your launch?
3. Are you **reaping a harvest?** Do you see results and hear testimonies that what you are doing is bearing fruit in the Kingdom?
4. Do you **need help** because the harvest is more than you can handle?
5. Are you seeing **no results**? Do you feel weary or frustrated? Perhaps you launched outside of God's timetable. Is that where you find yourself?
6. Through it all, have you taken the time to **worship** the Lord in your current season?

Describe your current circumstance in light of God's cycle and seasons. Ask yourself which season you are currently in. Describe other seasons you have experienced.

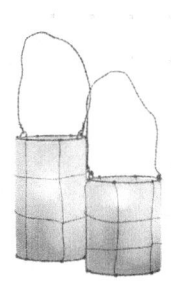

Lesson 8 • **UNDERSTANDING**

"Aligning your choices with your season will propel you forward in your flight path toward the destiny of who God created you to be and what He created you to do." —Page 110, *Created For So Much More*

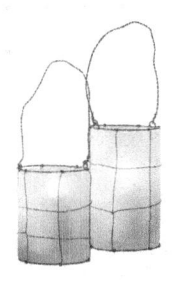

Going Deeper: Aligning with the Lord

Consider your answers from Exercise 19 about where you are currently in God's cycle. **Ask the Lord to show you how you can co-labor with Him.**

1. What are you doing to work with the Lord in your season?
2. How can you multiply what the Lord is doing in your life?

Examples might be setting up meetings with those who could support your work, writing emails of gratitude to those who have assisted you, posting words of encouragement on social media, or setting up an inner healing appointment.

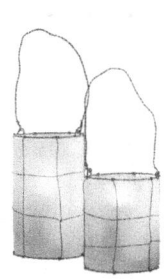

"Each day is a new opportunity to advance your dream, vision, and Kingdom purposes right where you are. As you co-labor with God to accomplish the vision that He planted within you, steps can always be taken today, tomorrow, and this week."
—Page 110, *Created For So Much More*

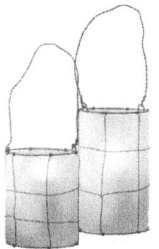

Soaring With God

Exercise 20: Ten Steps

This exercise is a consistent favorite. Don't rush through it.

Go back to the list you created in **Exercise 17: Determining Specific Flight Plan Take Aways** in the previous lesson. Ask the Lord to highlight ten steps from that list that you can take right here in your sacred now. Here are a few things to consider. Think about emails, appointments, workshops, or phone calls that the Lord may be asking you to do. Is it time to volunteer or purchase the needed supplies for your big dream? **Write a list of at least ten things that will help you realize your destiny, with no order of importance.**

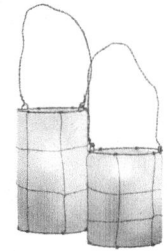

A man's mind plans his way, but the Lord directs his steps and makes them sure (Proverbs 16:9, Amplified Bible, Classic Edition, AMPC).

"As we make plans, we must seek the Lord to ensure the right step is taken at the right time."—Page 112, *Created For So Much More*

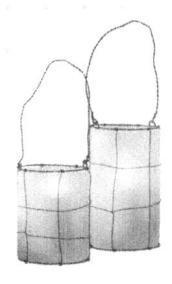

Soaring With God

Exercise 21: The Next Steps

Allowing God to order your footsteps means giving Him time and space to prioritize the tasks and steps before you. Of the ten steps or action items that you listed in the last exercise, ask the Lord to highlight three of them.

1. **Which three is He saying "now" to? List them here.**
2. Next, take a look at those three steps and a look at your calendar. **Next to each of the three steps, write the date by which you will accomplish that step.**

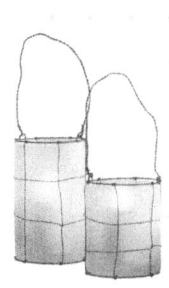

***Lesson 8* • UNDERSTANDING**

"Without clear vision you wander day-to-day doing this and that. With a clear vision and a step-by-step path, you will live joyfully knowing you are operating as who you were created to be, doing what you were created to do."
—Page 115, *Created For So Much More*

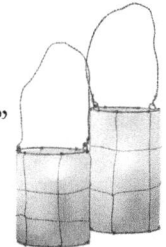

Pause to Ponder and Pray

Worship and give thanks to the Lord for the season you find yourself in. Giving thanks to the Lord creates contentment. Surrender your timetable to the Lord and let Him replace it with His. **Ask Him for His plan and His timetable and write what He says**. Then thank Him for the results that are sure to come.

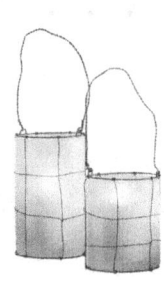

***Lesson 8* • UNDERSTANDING**

*You enlarge my steps under me,
And my feet have not slipped* (Psalm 18:36).

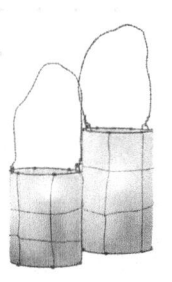

Encouragement for Your Journey

I am so proud of you! Through this chapter, you have taken a leap forward in fulfilling the purpose the Lord has for you. As you align your daily steps with His timetable, you are on the most direct flight path to reach your destination of being all that God created you to be and accomplishing all that He created you to do. God's seasons have purpose and are perfectly timed. Even if you don't immediately experience the results you hoped for, practice thanksgiving and watch contentment grow.

The Apostle Paul gives us a nugget of truth that we can put into action to learn to be content in whatever circumstances we find ourselves. In his letter to the Philippians, he says,

> *Be anxious for nothing, but in everything by prayer and supplication with thanksgiving let your requests be made known to God* (Philippians 4:6).

Allow me to share what I consider the key words in this passage. They are *"in everything"* and *"with thanksgiving."* When we adopt a mindset of gratitude, we are rewarded with contentment. It isn't always comfortable to give thanks, but the reward is worth it.

You might not be thrilled to be in the season you find yourself in, but I assure you that as you spend time to worship the Lord **with thanksgiving**, your heart will lighten as you gain contentment. When you learn to be content in whatever circumstances you are in, the present becomes your sacred now. You will find yourself enjoying life ***so much more*** as you gain understanding and embrace whatever the Lord has for you today.

From that place of contentment, seek the Lord for His timetable and take the step He asks you to take. This step is the quickest and most direct route to fulfilling your big audacious dreams. Enjoy the journey, Dear One. Know that the Lord has your timetable perfectly planned.

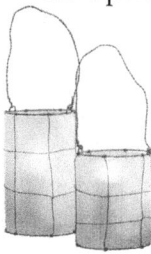

9. REST

Deborah Gall
Transition II,
2012
Acrylic on Canvas
30" x 30"

View *Transition II* in color and learn five practical tips to find rest during your journey in the *Created For So Much More* REST Video.

"When we apply **GRATITUDE** to our lives, it breeds **CONTENTMENT**. Contentment is the foundation of Godly **REST**."

—**Created For So Much More** REST (Chapter Nine) Video

9.
created for so much more
REST:
Enjoying the Layovers

Making Good Use of Dry Seasons

Our loving Father knows we need rest. He will put us through seasons that seem dry and unproductive to bring rest. I call these seasons layovers. They are also known as desert or wilderness seasons. Let's look at these layover seasons with a fresh mindset that trades frustration for enjoyable rest as we co-labor with the Lord. He has a purpose in even the driest of seasons.

God uses wilderness seasons to draw us closer to Himself, to show us which skills need honing, to reveal the heart work that needs to be done, and ***so much more***. This lesson teaches us how to embrace the rest rather than feeling antsy or restless during the seasons when God seemingly has hit the pause button.

If you are in a hidden or layover season, you are in good company. Jesus spent the first 30 years of His life "hidden." David, after being anointed King, was sent back to the wilderness to tend sheep. Both used their layover seasons wisely. The next set of exercises will help you, like Jesus and David, to switch your focus from your situation to Heaven's perspective during these quiet times.

These exercises invite you to both recognize the lessons you have learned through your layover seasons, and to hear what Holy Spirit is saying to you about resting in Him through a Bible verse prompt.

Through recognizing God's hand in your layovers, you put your time to good use and you will enjoy ***so much more*** rest in your life.

Learn about finding joy and contentment in whatever season you are in as you watch the *Created For So Much More* REST Video at deborahgall.com

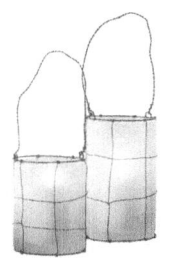

A Guided Journal to Soaring With God

Opening Thoughts: Recognizing Your Deserts

As you consider your past seasons, make a note of when you have felt like you were in a desert or dry season. **List those times here**. How does it feel to know that God works through the desert seasons in your life? **Make a note of your feelings now as well.**

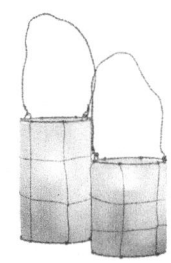

> "As you continue on your journey to realize the ***so much more*** of who you were created to be and what you were created to do, rely on the Lord to show you His plan and purpose or those seasons in your life that may feel dry, dull, and lonely."
> —Page 123, *Created For So Much More*

"He [God] takes you through hidden and wilderness seasons to show you who He is and who you are not. He builds relationship with you in those times because, as I have said before, He is more concerned with being in relationship with you than anything else."—Page 121, *Created For So Much More*

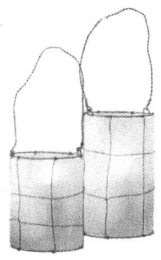

Going Deeper: Hidden Years

We know much more about Jesus' final three years when He was in public ministry than we know of His first 30. Most of His life was lived in a hidden place. Moses, Abraham, Elijah, and David are a few biblical examples of living a life of destiny and hiddenness at the same time. Take a minute to think about your life up to this point. Can you relate to these pillars of the faith who lived in the tension between being hidden and living out their destiny? **If there was a time when have you felt "hidden" while you were also living a life of purpose, describe it. Also list the lessons that come to mind from either biblical examples or from those who have gone before you on the hidden path.**

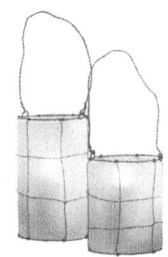

"God was building something even greater than character in David in the wilderness—God was building an intimate relationship with David. The Lord gave David experiences to remember and rely on when FUTURE adversities arose. He does the same for you."
—Page 121, *Created For So Much More*

"Spend layovers working on your heart, restructuring your work, and/or honing your skills. Listen to the Lord for any way that He may want to transform your layover into productive preparation time."
—Page 118, *Created For So Much More*

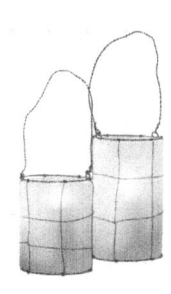

Going Deeper: Lessons Learned in the Wilderness

One purpose of wilderness seasons is that they provide a time and place—without distraction—to listen and hear what the Lord is saying. Take time to sit with the Lord. Ask Him what lessons He has taught or is teaching you in your current season. **Scribe what you have learned.**

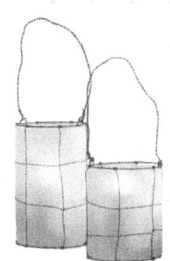

"Sitting with God is never standing still. It is always a means of moving forward." —Page 119, *Created For So Much More*

"God uses the layovers and hidden seasons of our lives to continue the work in, through, and for us."—Page 119, *Created For So Much More*

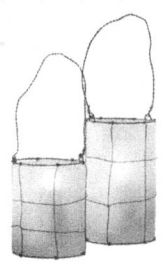

Soaring With God

Exercise 22: Be Still

One interpretation of Psalm 46:10 is *"Be still and know that I am God."* The phrase "be still" can also be translated as "relax, let go, or cease striving." All are powerful phrases to keep in mind as you consider what the Lord is doing in your life. **Use the prompts to fill in the rest of the sentence. Listen to Holy Spirit and let Him fill in the blanks on your behalf.**

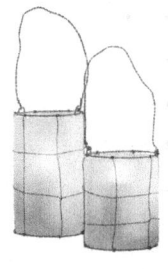

BE

BE STILL

Lesson 9 • REST

BE STILL AND

BE STILL AND KNOW

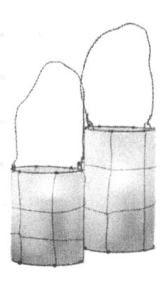

A Guided Journal to Soaring With God

BE STILL AND KNOW THAT

BE STILL AND KNOW THAT I

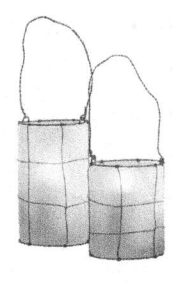

Lesson 9 • REST

BE STILL AND KNOW THAT I AM

BE STILL AND KNOW THAT I AM GOD

*For thus the Lord God, the Holy One of Israel, has said,
"In repentance and rest you will be saved,
In quietness and trust is your strength."
But you were not willing* (Isaiah 30:15).

Pause to Ponder and Pray

It might feel particularly challenging to thank the Lord for a layover or desert season, but I am suggesting you do just that. The lessons learned in the wilderness are priceless and necessary for your journey ahead. **I invite you to scribe your thoughts and a prayer for your ongoing journey, even if you find yourself experiencing a layover.**

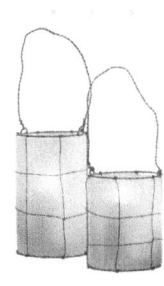

You will keep him *in perfect peace,*
Whose *mind* is *stayed on* You,
Because he trusts in You
(Isaiah 26:3, New King James Version).

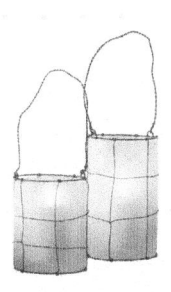

Encouragement for Your Journey

Layovers, pauses, and wilderness seasons are tough for all of us. They are particularly difficult when we are filled with the vision God has for our lives and purposes. As difficult as they may be, the times in our lives when the Lord says, *"Wait a minute"* are important times to align our hearts and spirits with Heaven.

If you find yourself in the middle of a dry season, I want to encourage you to rest in the Lord. Allow God to do any character work that needs to be done so that you will be able to handle the ***so much more*** that He has for your future. The Prophet Isaiah tells us that God waits on high to hear from you and work on your behalf.

> *Therefore the LORD longs to be gracious to you,*
> *And therefore He waits on high to have compassion on you.*
> *For the LORD is a God of justice;*
> *How blessed are all those who long for Him* (Isaiah 30:18).

This verse tells us that we are blessed when we long for God, and I would add that we are doubly blessed when we spend quiet time with Him. Use the lack of distraction that layovers bring to sit at His feet with His Word. The treasures you will discover will equip you for the amazing future He has for you.

Well done! You have come a long way in your journey of discovery. I know that God will do ***so much more***—beyond all that you can ask or think (Ephesians 3:20)—as you rest in Him.

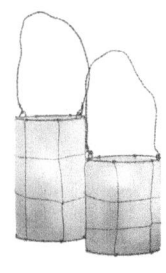

10. PEACE

Deborah Gall
Shifting Moods,
2012
Acrylic on Canvas
36" x 36"

See **Shifting Moods** in color on the *Created For So Much More* PEACE Video, and shift your eyes away from the storm to the One who strengthens you to withstand it.

"When you keep your **MIND** on the Lord and not on the circumstances around you, God **PROMISES** to keep you in **PERFECT** peace."

—*Created For So Much More* PEACE (Chapter Ten) Video

10.
created for so much more
PEACE:
Navigating Through Storms

The Path to Peace

Spiritual and emotional storms in life are inevitable. If you are operating within the fullness of your ***so much more***—who you were created to be and what you were created to do—you will hit opposition. Jesus clearly told us that we would face trials and tribulations (John 16:33). The key to navigating through those trials—otherwise known as the storms of life—is maintaining peace spiritually and emotionally. Allow me to share some of the strategies I use to overcome the difficulties that life's turbulence brings.

One of the keys to understanding obstacles and resistance is to realize that storms in life are often the result of the enemy's actions. Every obstacle you face is rooted in satan's desire to throw you off track. Jesus tells us in John 10:10 that the thief comes to kill, steal, and destroy. I suggest that he is also content to hurt, harm, and hinder God's children and their God-given purpose. It is critical that Jesus Followers build an arsenal of spiritual weapons to counter the attack of the enemy. This chapter suggests several strategies that help defend against and counter the attacks of the enemy.

The exercises in this lesson invite you to recognize the storms in life, ponder the source of the resistance you may be facing, and ask how you can incorporate the 11 strategies to gain peace into your life. One of the upcoming exercises suggests strategies to strengthen yourself in the Lord and co-labor with Him in order to manifest His peace in your heart and life. As the Prince of Peace, Jesus is the ultimate source of the ***so much more*** peace that is available to you.

Hear how Deborah used five of the strategies on how to deal with difficult seasons by watching the *Created For So Much More* PEACE Video at deborahgall.com

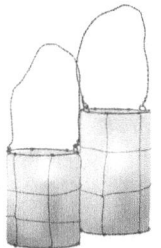

A Guided Journal to Soaring With God

Opening Thoughts: How's Your Peace?

When you consider that storms are inevitable and you make choices that garner peace, ask yourself how peaceful you feel right now? **Make a note of your peace level today.** What emotions are you experiencing when you think about strategies that can help you gain more peace? **Write out your emotions as you consider a more peaceful future.**

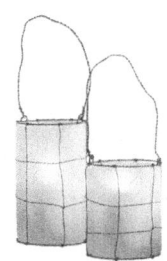

"Storms are inevitable. How you handle them is your choice."
—Page 138, *Created For So Much More*

Lesson 10 • **PEACE**

Moreover David was greatly distressed because the people spoke of stoning him, for all the people were embittered, each one because of his sons and his daughters. <u>But David strengthened himself in the Lord his God</u> (1 Samuel 30:4, underlined emphasis mine).

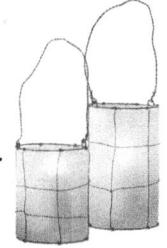

"Peace I leave with you; My peace I give to you; not as the world gives do I give to you. Do not let your heart be troubled, nor let it be fearful" (John 14:27).

Soaring With God

Exercise 23: Storm Tracking

This exercise will heighten your awareness of the spiritual atmosphere in your life at the present time. Set aside some time to ask the Lord where you are in relationship to the storm track. These questions are useful to help you ponder. **Write out your answers.**

1. Are you in the midst of a storm? If so, what does it look like? What challenges do you face?
2. Are you coming out of a storm? Describe your recent season of challenges and how you faced them.
3. Do you see storm clouds brewing? Sometimes the Lord gives us hints that challenges are coming. I do not want you to look for something that is not there, but acknowledge what may be on the horizon.
4. Are you in a season of smooth sailing? That's awesome! Recognize it, treasure it, and give thanks.

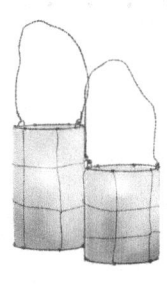

Lesson 10 • PEACE

For our struggle is not against flesh and blood, but against the rulers, against the powers, against the world forces of this darkness, against the spiritual forces of wickedness in the heavenly places (Ephesians 6:12).

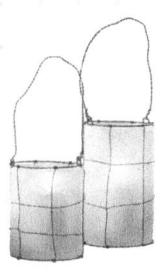

Going Deeper: What Obstacles Do You Face?

Before you go any further, I want you to take a few minutes to give your life a spiritual scan. What resistance and obstacles are you facing? Ask the Lord for the source of these obstacles. Are they a result of your choices or are they resistance from the enemy? It's time to be transparent and brutally honest before the Lord. **Make a note of what the Lord shows you.**

Then move to the next exercise—Tools of the Trade—and apply the necessary strategy to overcome the obstacles you are facing.

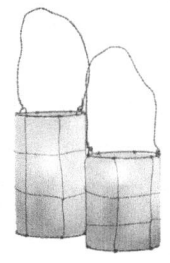

"Make no mistake about it, satan is quite pleased with the complacency and slumber of the children of God. He will bring distraction and resistance when he senses children of the Almighty God waking up to their God-given purpose and destiny." —Page 126, *Created For So Much More*

Lesson 10 • PEACE

"Just as identity and purpose are unique, so are the challenges that we face in life. Do not let others dictate the validity of your 'storm season.'"—Page 138, *Created For So Much More*

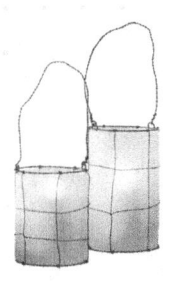

Soaring With God

Exercise 24: Tools of the Trade

In the earlier exercises, you acknowledged the resistance and the storm season you currently face. Now it is time to ask Holy Spirit to show you which strategies would be best to help you navigate through this season and prepare you for the future. As He highlights a strategy, ask Him for a specific way to apply that strategy in your life today. **Ask the Lord for a plan to include these strategies and steps in your daily schedule. Write that plan down and commit to sticking with it.**

    1. **Prayer and Worship**: Have you set aside time to pray and worship?

"A posture of worship acknowledges God for who He is. When you worship and honor Him, you take your hands off the issues of life and give Him control." —Page 127, *Created For So Much More*

Exercise 24: Tools of the Trade, Continued

2. **Take Your Thoughts Captive**: What scriptures can you use to replace your negative thoughts and take them captive to the obedience of Christ?

"Scripture becomes a very handy and useful tool in taking thoughts captive when you replace the lies of the enemy with the truth of God's Word."
—Page 129, *Created For So Much More*

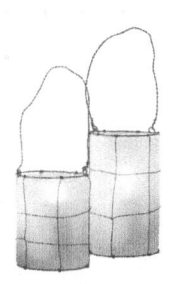

Exercise 24: Tools of the Trade, Continued

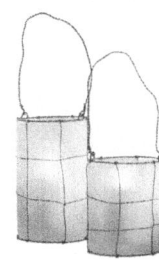

3. **Be absorbed**: Do you diligently remind yourself of the future the Lord has shown you? Are you doing the work necessary to bring it to pass?

"Rereading and praying over your written exercises is a great way to remind yourself that you were created for a purpose, with an identity that fits that purpose, and that God isn't finished with you yet."
—Page 130, *Created For So Much More*

Exercise 24: Tools of the Trade, Continued

4. **Prophetic Promises**: What encouragements have you received from others and from the Lord? Is there a prophetic promise that you need to write out and put where you can read it daily?

"If you have yet to see words from the Lord fulfilled in your life, it may be time to speak them out, to pray them in, and to remind yourself that they are God's truth." —Page 131, *Created For So Much More*

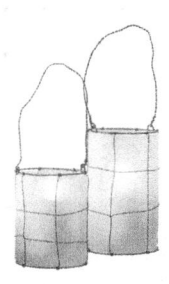

Exercise 24: Tools of the Trade, Continued

5. **Fight the Good Fight**: When spiritual attacks happen, do you use the promises of God to resist the enemy?

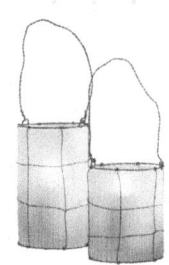

> "We must take authority over our circumstances by reminding ourselves and the powers of darkness of the future that the Lord has shown us through prophecy." —Page 132, *Created For So Much More*

Exercise 24: Tools of the Trade, Continued

6. **Give Thanks in Everything**: Do you live a life full of gratitude? In the midst of a recent or current storm, what is one thing you are thankful for?

Rejoice always; pray without ceasing; in everything give thanks; for this is God's will for you in Christ Jesus (1 Thessalonians 5:16–18).

Exercise 24: Tools of the Trade, Continued

7. **Guard Your Tongue**: What are you speaking over your life?

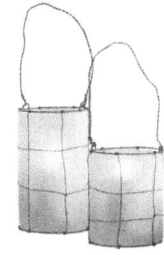

"When you find yourself battling discouragement, take a look at the words you are speaking about yourself and your life."
—Page 134, *Created For So Much More*

Exercise 24: Tools of the Trade, Continued

8. **Guard Your Heart**: Who are the cheerleaders in your life? How can you connect with one or more of these people

"When you feel vulnerable to the attacks of the enemy, being mindful about how you spend your time and with whom is critical."
—Page 135, *Created For So Much More*

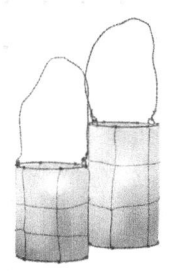

Exercise 24: Tools of the Trade, Continued

9. **Stay Connected**: Is it time to take a vacation or a day off? What can you do to fuel your passion for your God-given purpose?

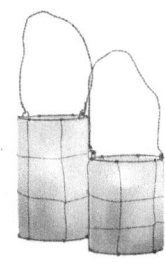

"You stay connected to the Lord by planning, scheduling, and following through on time spent in His Presence and in His Word."—Page 136, *Created For So Much More*

Exercise 24: Tools of the Trade, Continued

10. **Stay Clean Before the Lord**: Who do you need to forgive? When you spend time with God, for what do you need to ask forgiveness?

"There are times when the Lord will slow progress to allow time to do heart business with Him. Harboring unforgiveness or living with unrepented sin can slow progress to a crawl or even a halt."
—Page 137, *Created For So Much More*

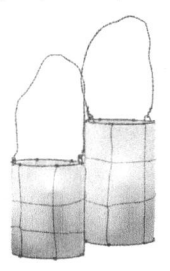

Exercise 24: Tools of the Trade, Continued

11. **Change your "Whys" to Whats"**: Do you need to repent of spending too much time asking the Lord why this storm is upon you? What can you learn from this storm? How can you serve others in the midst of your storm?

"Change your 'Why?' questions to 'What can I learn?', 'What do you want me to do?'. Or 'How can I help someone else?' Asking 'Why?' puts the focus on you and your life. 'What' and 'how' questions remove the poor-pitiful-me attitude and rid you of the evil spirit poised to take you down the slippery slope of despair into the pit of self-pity." —Page 137–138, *Created For So Much More*

Pause to Ponder and Pray

Which of the strategies listed in this chapter were familiar to you? Which were unfamiliar? **Take a moment to write down which strategies you hope to begin to incorporate in your life or to integrate in your life even more. Then ask the Lord to keep you mindful of these strategies as you navigate the storms of life.**

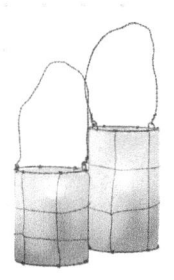

Encouragement for Your Journey

Congratulations! You have filled your travel bag with strategies for the emotional turbulence and spiritual storms that happen on the flight path to your God-given identity and purpose. Remember that the Prince of Peace is your flying companion. He is faithful to show you how to use these strategies when the time arises. Worship is one of the most powerful strategies we have in our arsenal for spiritual warfare.

You don't need to thank the Lord for the storm. However, giving God your sacrifice of praise in the midst of tough times acknowledges His sovereignty and faithfulness. As you, like David, strengthen yourself in the Lord (1 Samuel 30:6), God will bring ***so much more*** peace to you. It is what God promises through the words of the Apostle Paul written to the Philippians.

> *Be anxious for nothing, but in everything by prayer and supplication with thanksgiving let your requests be made known to God. And the peace of God, which surpasses all comprehension, will guard your hearts and your minds in Christ Jesus* (Philippians 4:6–7).

God's promise to you, Dear One, is that He will keep you in perfect peace—the peace which surpasses all human understanding—when you rely on Him. How awesome is that? Use these strategies to stay connected and dependent upon God—even when storm clouds are brewing, or it is thundering all around you. You will find yourself dancing in the midst of the storm as you experience ***so much more*** of His peace.

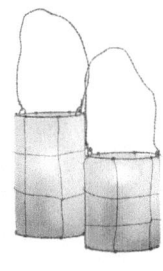

11.
STRATEGY

Deborah Gall
The Road Home,
2014
Acrylic on Canvas
40" x 40"

View **The Road Home** in color in the *Created For So Much More* STRATEGY Video and hear how the Lord uses various strategies at different times to walk you through life.

"Taking **RISKS** is the key to changing your ordinary **LIFE** into an **EXTRAORDINARY** one."

—*Created For So Much More* STRATEGY (Chapter Eleven) Video

11.
created for so much more
STRATEGY:
Unlocking an Amazing Future

Keys To A Purposeful Life

Well done! The toughest part of your journey is over. Now I gather several of the strategic gems from all of the previous material in this journal into one basket. Use these key strategies to apply the truths from *Created For So Much More* to your daily life. They have been refined in the crucible fire of my life and the lives of those I teach, mentor, and coach.

All 12 strategic keys can be summed up in three "master" keys which are: 1) Take Responsibility, 2) Play to the Audience of One, and 3) Dream Big, Work Small. Combined with the remaining nine strategies, these keys bring ***so much more*** strategy for you to be proactive on the journey of self-discovery. All of the key strategies unlock methods to co-labor with God and live as the person He created you to be, doing what He created you to do.

The first exercise for this lesson lists the 12 keys and invites you to ponder which ones to incorporate into your life immediately. Next, you will go deeper by considering the promises from a passage of scripture as they relate to your current situation. Finally, you will be invited to add your unique personal strategy to my list of 12. God gives us each a unique set of keys that unlock doors of opportunity and destiny related truths. Use these key strategies regularly and you will propel your life into ***so much more*** identity and purpose as you unlock your amazing hope-filled future.

To learn more about unlocking the next door and taking the next steps in your journey, watch the *Created For So Much More* STRATEGY Video at deborahgall.com

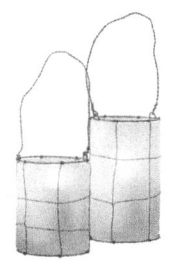

A Guided Journal to Soaring With God

Opening Thoughts: Being Proactive

Keys are useless unless they are used. What are your thoughts and feelings when you consider that you can be more proactive in unlocking an amazing future? **Scribe your thoughts and feelings here.**

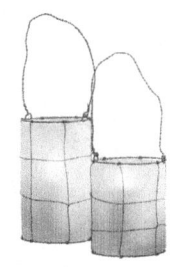

"These keys are meant to be used regularly in your life. They are critical for unlocking the amazing *so much more* that the Lord has for you."—Page 141, *Created For So Much More*

Soaring With God

Exercise 25: Which Strategies?

It is common to use resistance (weights or bands) to strengthen your physical muscles. Strengthening your spiritual muscles requires resistance as well. When snags or resistance surface, the Lord may be saying, *"Let's work on this."*

In this exercise you will review the 12 key strategies that unlock your amazing future. As you consider each key, **ask the Lord** to reveal how that key pertains to your life, what He wants to highlight, and **how you can best implement** that strategy in your life today.

We are never working at 100 percent with these keys; some will need work today and others will need work tomorrow or next week. **Pray through each key**, ask yourself the corresponding questions. Doing so will ingrain the keys in your spirit and make them easier to remember and use.

1. **Take Responsibility.** What choices are you making? Remember sometimes you need more than prayer. Sometimes you need to change your decisions.

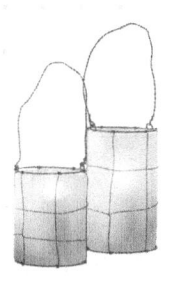

A Guided Journal to Soaring With God

> "*I will give you the treasures of darkness*
> *And hidden wealth of secret places,*
> *So that you may know that it is I,*
> *The LORD, the God of Israel, who calls you by your name*" (Isaiah 45:3).

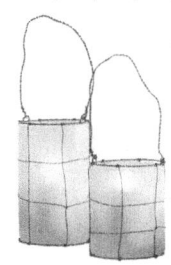

"Remember, sometimes you need more than prayer. Sometimes you need to change your decisions."—Page 142, *Created For So Much More*

Exercise 25: Which Strategies, Continued

2. **Play to the Audience of One**. We all play to some kind of audience. To whom do you listen for your life's decisions?

"'Should' is a judgment word. Change your 'should' to 'I'd like to,' and see what a difference that thought change makes. Your audience of One does not judge you—He invites you to walk with Him to unlock *so much more*."
—Page 142, *Created For So Much More*

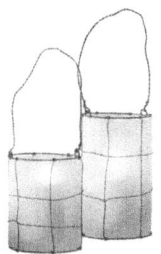

Exercise 25: Which Strategies, Continued

3. **Dream Big, Work Small.** Do you have big audacious dreams and are you taking small steps to accomplish them?

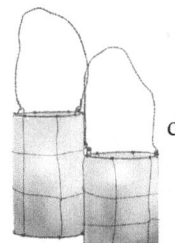

"The second part of this key strategy is just as important as dreaming big dreams. It says: Work Small. In other words, leave the work of unfolding your big dreams into reality to the Lord."—Page 143, *Created For So Much More*

Exercise 25: Which Strategies, Continued

4. **Stay Connected.** Are you putting forth effort to stay in touch with God, family, friends, as well as your inner self?

"This key is all about staying connected to your passion, your tribe, your family, and your God."—Page 143, *Created For So Much More*

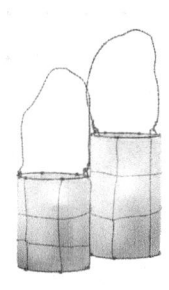

Exercise 25: Which Strategies, Continued

5. **Read the Signs.** What signposts have you noticed along your path? What do they say to you?

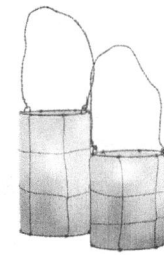

> "Lean in to the Presence of God and rest, knowing that He is trustworthy and that He will bring you signs and peace for your future."
> —Page 144, *Created For So Much More*

Exercise 25: Which Strategies, Continued

6. **Follow Your Path**. Are you staying on the course the Lord has set for you, or are you getting distracted by others?

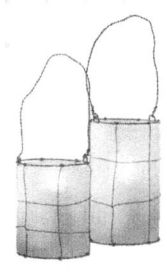

"No one else carries the exact purpose for which you were created."
—Page 144, *Created For So Much More*

Exercise 25: Which Strategies, Continued

7. **Keep Walking.** Have challenges stalled you, or are you continuing to walk at whatever pace the Lord sets?

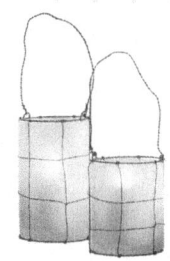

"The Lord knows where you are going and exactly what time you need to arrive at your destination."—Page 145, *Created For So Much More*

Exercise 25: Which Strategies, Continued

8. **Hone your skills.** Learning and practicing isn't striving; it is co-laboring with Holy Spirit. What area of your gifts and talents could be improved?

"Don't settle for ordinary. Don't be content with the status quo. Hone your skills to become extraordinary."—Page 145, *Created For So Much More*

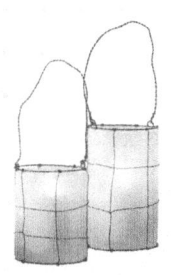

Exercise 25: Which Strategies, Continued

9. **Do the Work.** Doing the work can feel like a small thing. Often it is not fun or comfortable. Have you neglected the nitty-gritty tasks associated with your big dream?

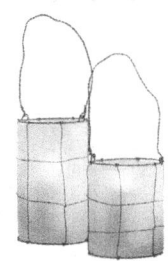

"Doing the work unlocks opportunity, divine appointments, and an amazing future." —Page 146, *Created For So Much More*

Exercise 25: Which Strategies, Continued

10. **Live Now.** Are you living a contented life or are you longingly gazing at the future or at others' successes?

"A mundane meeting can transform into a major opportunity in the Lord's hands."—Page 147, *Created For So Much More*

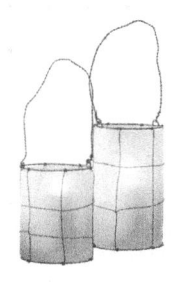

Exercise 25: Which Strategies, Continued

11. **Take Risks.** Have you let fear or anxiety keep you from taking the next step that the Lord has for you to take?

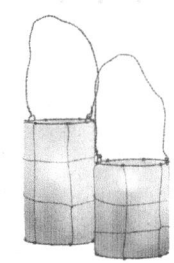

"The Lord knows you better than you know yourself. Although you may face risks, the Lord will not ask you to do anything that does not fit His plan and purpose for your life or who He created you to be."
—Page 148, *Created For So Much More*

Exercise 25: Which Strategies, Continued

12. **Live Your Message**. Does your life exemplify your beliefs, character, and passion?

"What is your life message? How does your life reflect that message? What do your words and actions tell others about you and the God you serve? Do you walk your talk?" —Page 148, *Created For So Much More*

Going Deeper: Promises of God

The following passage offers several promises of God:

> *'For I know the plans that I have for you,' declares the LORD, 'plans for welfare and not for calamity to give you a future and a hope. Then you will call upon Me and come and pray to Me, and I will listen to you. You will seek Me and find Me when you search for Me with all your heart. I will be found by you,' declares the LORD, 'and I will restore your fortunes and will gather you from all the nations and from all the places where I have driven you,' declares the LORD, 'and I will bring you back to the place from where I sent you into exile'* (Jeremiah 29:11–14).

Take a moment to consider each of the promises suggested in the passage. **Then, ask yourself the question connected to the promise. Make a note of your answers on the following pages**. Spend extra time on the promises that feel most relevant to your life today.

1. **Your future is known by God, but you may not see where the Lord is taking you.** How does it change your perspective to know He knows where you are going?
2. **Your future is full of hope. Whether or not you feel hope-filled today, God's promise is that there is hope for you today and tomorrow.** How can you set aside anxiety and reach for hope?
3. **When you call on the Lord, He listens. God knows your heart's desires.** How does that assurance affect your confidence in your prayers?
4. **When you seek God, He will be found. God is always present.** How do you seek and meet God?
5. **Your fortunes will be restored. There is a wealth of peace, joy, hope, and *so much more* that God will restore to you as you sit with Him.** Ask Him to show you a path to restoration.
6. **You will not remain alone on your path—even though it may feel like you are in exile.** How does it make you feel to know that the Lord has others who will walk with you?

Lesson 11 • **STRATEGY**

"When you find yourself alone in your journey, trust the Lord's words spoken through Jeremiah to the exiled leaders of Israel."
—Page 144, *Created For So Much More*

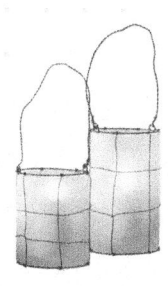

A Guided Journal to Soaring With God

"God is not in a box, He doesn't put His children in boxes either. Get used to living outside the box of normal living" —Page 148, *Created For So Much More*

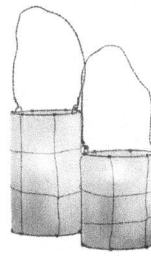

Lesson 11 • STRATEGY

"You are the conductor of your life's symphony."
—Page 151, *Created For So Much More*

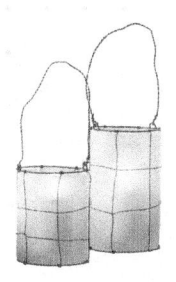

Soaring With God

Exercise 26: Your Personal Strategies

Perhaps, while you have considered my list of key strategies, Holy Spirit has whispered other keys that He has given you for your life and your future. Perhaps you have keys hanging on your key ring that look different than mine. What are your life lessons? Which truths has the Lord highlighted as "words to live by"? **List your personal key strategies here.**

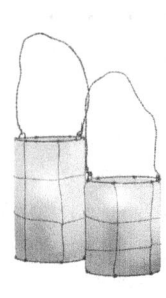

Lesson 11 • **STRATEGY**

"Learning and practicing isn't striving; it is co-laboring with the Holy Spirit." —Page 148, *Created For So Much More*

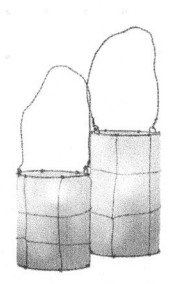

Pause to Ponder and Pray

Now it is time to ponder and pray over what you have learned through this lesson. I would suggest you ask the Lord for guidance to know which key(s) will open the door to immediate opportunities that He has for you. **Write down any insights He gives you.** Thank Him for the strategies that He has taught you throughout your life. **Worship Him as the provider of your amazing future.**

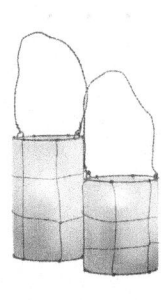

Lesson 11 • **STRATEGY**

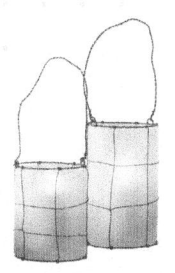

For the dream comes through much effort (Ecclesiastes 5:3a).

Encouragement for Your Journey

I am so proud of you and the work you have done at the Lord's request. An amazing future awaits you today and in all of your tomorrows. Keys come in all shapes and sizes, and they serve many purposes. Continue to ask the Lord which key is needed to unlock the door that leads to your future. Seek Him for which strategy to use to start the engine that will propel you into your destiny. Sit in His Presence to unlock the chest of hidden treasures of truth for the amazing future He has prepared for you.

Even with these keys, a future filled with big vision can feel intimidating. Allow me to share a favorite verse that I rely on whenever I feel inadequate for the tasks that are on my God-breathed to do list. It is another verse the Apostle Paul penned to the church in Philippi.

I can do all things through Him who strengthens me (Philippians 4:13).

The word "all" in this verse means "all, any, or every." That's good news isn't it? What Paul is saying is that, through Christ's spirit working in and through us, we can accomplish all—anything and everything—that the Lord asks. Staying mindful that it is Christ—not me—enabling my work brings rest to my soul.

Remember that Christ walks with you, Dear One; you are not alone. He strengthens your mind, body, and spirit and empowers any strategy you use in your life. In fact, He is the most important key you have. Rest in the Lord as you strategically do the work, take risks, live your message, and keep walking into **so much more** of your God-given identity and purpose.

Father, Jesus, and Holy Spirit are the ones who unlock the **so much more** for your amazing future living as who They created you to be and doing what They created you to do. Glory to God!

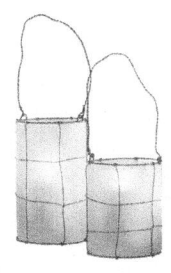

12. FLIGHT

Deborah Gall
New Horizon, 2012
Acrylic on Canvas
30" x 30"

See ***New Horizon*** in color during the *Created For So Much More* FLIGHT Video, and hear about how you become a God-carrier as you soar to new heights.

"Take your next **STEP** to create what God is asking you to **CREATE** because others are **WATCHING** and waiting for you to **TAKE** that step."
—***Created For So Much More*** FLIGHT (Chapter Twelve) Video

12.
created for so much more
FLIGHT:
Changing Atmospheres

Soaring With God

We have come full circle in our journey of discovering **so much more** of your God-given identity and purpose. This entire journey is based on my belief that we, as Children of God, have the power and the responsibility to change the world. When you operate in the purpose for which you were created, you change the atmosphere and advance the Kingdom of God. Every day is an opportunity to soar with God and to take flight into the **so much more** of God and what He has for you.

God uses men and women who dedicate themselves to being excellent at what they do right where they live. He empowers those who are more concerned with bringing glory to Him than to themselves. He strengthens and preserves those who search for the **so much more** of who He is. As God's children seek Him, He pours out **so much more** revelation and knowledge about who He created them to be and what He created them to do.

Your journey of self-discovery is never over. God is always revealing new things. The upcoming exercises invite you to look back, to compare where you are today with when you began this study, and to recognize the transformation that the Lord has done. You will also be urged to look forward and make a note of where you believe God is taking you. Additionally, the exercises share two important Bible passages to use as you soar into your amazing future.

There is always **so much more** for you, your identity, and your purpose because there is **so much more** to learn and embrace about the Lord and what He says about you. Get ready to soar into the **so much more** of who you were created to be and what you were created to do.

Hear Deborah's four reasons for taking your next step and receive her blessing for your ongoing journey during the *Create For So Much More* FLIGHT Video at deborahgall.com

A Guided Journal to Soaring With God

Opening Thoughts: Taking Off

As we come to the end of our time together, how do you feel? Compare and contrast your emotions from Lesson 1 when you began. What is the greatest lesson the Lord has taught you? **Make a note of your feelings and thoughts here.**

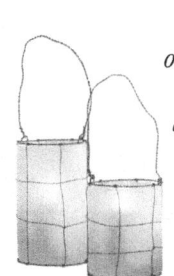

Not that I have already obtained it or have already become perfect, but I press on so that I may lay hold of that for which also I was laid hold of by Christ Jesus. Brethren, I do not regard myself as having laid hold of it yet; but one thing I do: forgetting what lies behind and reaching forward to what lies ahead, I press on toward the goal for the prize of the upward call of God in Christ Jesus (Philippians 3:12–14).

Lesson 12 • FLIGHT

"No matter your age or situation, God is in the business of declaring and doing new things."—Page 154, *Created For So Much More*

Therefore if anyone is in Christ, he is a new creature; the old things passed away; behold, new things have come (Corinthians 5:17).

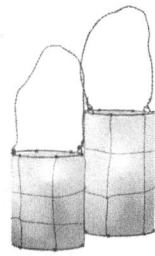

Going Deeper: What has Changed?

Go back to the snapshot you wrote of your life in **Lesson 1, Exercise 2: Your Starting Point.** Now consider where you are right now. Ask yourself and the Lord what has changed. What transformation has occurred as you worked through this book? What transformation is occurring right now in your life? **Write how your life has changed and thank the Lord for His transformative truths.**

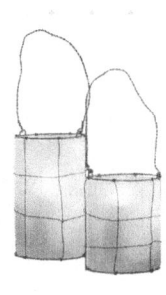

Lesson 12 • **FLIGHT**

"You change the atmosphere by filling your mind, body, and spirit with the ***so much more*** of God. As you breathe in the Breath of Life that comes from Heaven, you become all that the Lord has for you to be and do."—Page 156, *Created For So Much More*

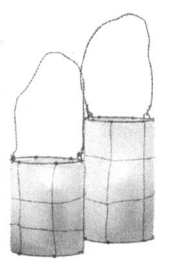

Going Deeper: Where Are You Soaring?

It is time to take flight from this book. Where do you find yourself currently in relation to your God-designed flight plan? What glimpse has the Lord given you for your future? Where are you going from here? **Ponder with Holy Spirit and scribe your responses here.**

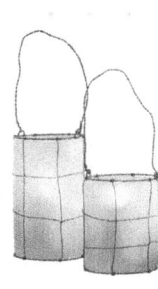

Lesson 12 • FLIGHT

"God uses men and women right where they are, with the tools of their trade, to advance His Kingdom, defeat the enemy, and change the world."
—Page 155, *Created For So Much More*

"You have spheres of influence, lives that you alone touch, and people you singularly come in contact with on a regular basis."
—Page 156, *Created For So Much More*

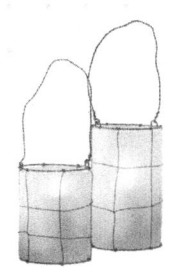

Soaring With God

Exercise 27: The Lord's Prayer

I have timed how long it takes to pray the Lord's Prayer. It takes no more than 30 seconds. That is not a lot of time for such a powerful prayer. Take the time to pray the words the Lord spoke to his disciples. **Then make a note of the phrase or phrases that struck you most today.**

> *'Our Father who is in heaven,*
> *Hallowed be Your name.*
> *'Your kingdom come.*
> *Your will be done,*
> *On earth as it is in heaven.*
> *Give us this day our daily bread.*
> *'And forgive us our debts, as we also have forgiven our debtors.*
> *'And do not lead us into temptation, but deliver us from evil. [For Yours is the kingdom and the power and the glory forever. Amen']*
> (Matthew 6:9–13).

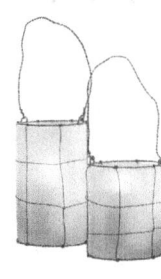

Lesson 12 • **FLIGHT**

"You are the light of the world. A city set on a hill cannot be hidden; nor does anyone light a lamp and put it under a basket, but on the lampstand, and it gives light to all who are in the house. Let your light shine before men in such a way that they may see your good works, and glorify your Father who is in heaven" (Matthew 5:14–16).

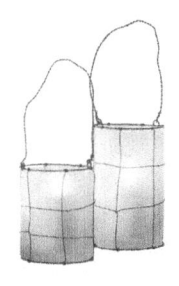

Soaring With God

Exercise 28: The 23rd Psalm

This familiar psalm makes a wonderful prayer that covers almost anything the world or satan can throw at you. Pair it with the Lord's Prayer and you will change the atmosphere surrounding you wherever you are.

Make a note of which phrases hold particular weight for you today.

*The LORD is my shepherd,
I shall not want.
He makes me lie down in green pastures;
He leads me beside quiet waters.
He restores my soul;
He guides me in the paths of righteousness
For His name's sake.*

*Even though I walk through the valley of the shadow of death,
I fear no evil, for You are with me;
Your rod and Your staff, they comfort me.
You prepare a table before me in the presence of my enemies;
You have anointed my head with oil;
My cup overflows.
Surely goodness and loving kindness will follow me all the days of my life,
And I will dwell in the house of the LORD forever*
(Psalm 23:1–6).

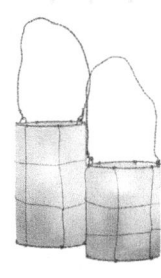

Lesson 12 • **FLIGHT**

"When the Light of Jesus is present, the darkness must flee and the atmosphere changes for Kingdom purposes."—Page 158, *Created For So Much More*

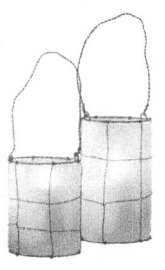

Pause to Ponder and Pray

You are on the runway, ready to take off on your own and soar in your God-given identity and purpose. **Take a few moments to thank the Lord for the transformative power of his Word and Spirit.** Thank Him specifically for the areas that He has touched during our time together. Worship Him as the God of infinite love for you and your future. As you abide in His Presence, and write any final reflections, ask Him to fill you with His atmosphere-changing Spirit of Life and Hope.

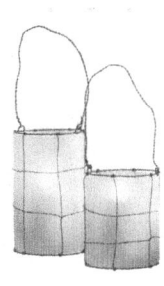

Lesson 12 • FLIGHT

"Everyday is an opportunity to take flight into the ***so much more*** that God has for you." —Page 155, *Created For So Much More*

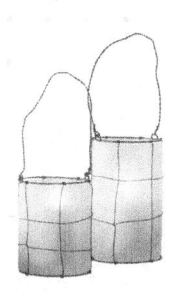

A Guided Journal to Soaring With God

Encouragement for Your Journey

Well done good and faithful servant! You have stewarded you journey into the ***so much more*** of God and the ***so much more*** of your identity and purpose with endurance and perseverance. It may have gotten messy at times, but I know the nitty gritty uncomfortable work is necessary as our gracious and loving Lord brings you into your amazing future. I will say it again—well done!

I want to reiterate what I have said many times, there is ALWAYS ***so much more*** for you because we serve a God that is full of infinite possibilities. He longs to share unimaginable opportunities with His children. He never tires or grows weary. He has ***so much more*** for you when you co-labor with Him as who He created you to be, doing what He created you to do. This may be the end of this book, but it is just the beginning of your big audacious dreams manifesting in your life. You are in my heart, Dear One, as you soar with God.

As we come to the end of our journey together, allow me to thank the Lord for you and your journey as I pray the words that the Apostle Paul wrote to the people in Ephesus,

> *For this reason I too, having heard of the faith in the Lord Jesus which exists among you and your love for all the saints, do not cease giving thanks for you, while making mention of you in my prayers; that the God of our Lord Jesus Christ, the Father of glory, may give to you a spirit of wisdom and of revelation in the knowledge of Him. I pray that the eyes of your heart may be enlightened, so that you will know what is the hope of His calling, what are the riches of the glory of His inheritance in the saints, and what is the surpassing greatness of His power toward us who believe* (Ephesians 1:15–19).

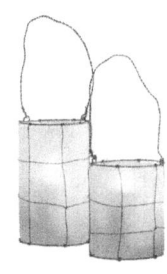

Encouragement for Your Journey, Continued

Remember that the journey of identity and purpose is never over. There is always *so much more*.

Take flight, mighty men and women of God. Now is the time. This is the place.

In some churches, it is typical to hear, "And the people said, Amen! It shall be so" at the end of a prayer or worship service. Let's do that here and now.

Go ahead, declare it out loud to celebrate who God created you to be and what He created you to do. Seal all that the Lord has done by proclaiming your agreement with Heaven. Think about all that has transpired through this journey, then shout, sing, dance and declare:

"Yes, and Amen!
It shall be so!
 Hallelujah!
To God be the glory!"

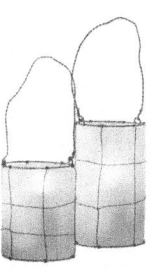

ACKNOWLEDGMENTS

There is no *Guided Journal to Soaring With God* without the God we soar with. Therefore, it is only right that I first acknowledge the Presence and power of the Lord. Father, Jesus, and Holy Spirit drew me back to the computer after I had shelved this project indefinitely. The direction and design morphed from one thing to another as They showed me Their vision for this addition to the *Created For So Much More* program. God's faithfulness to me, my family, and to the ministry causes me to bow down and worship in gratitude and humility. My prayer from the beginning of the *Created For So Much More* program—including this journal—has been that the words contained within the pages and videos would reflect my love for and adoration of my Audience of One. God has used many people here on Earth to be His mouthpiece and hands in the birthing of this book.

Thank you, reader and scribe—you who have walked this guided journey with me. My prayer is that you have met the Lord on your adventure of discovery and are walking closer with Him than ever before. I pray that you are soaring with Him in the amazing life He has for you.

Thank you to the readers of *Created For So Much More* who told me of their ah-ha moments, testimonies of changed lives, and **so much more**. Your willingness to share as well as the transparency of your stories gave me the confidence to keep walking. A special thank you to those who willingly went on record for the testimony videos. You humble me and are often the wind beneath my wings as I continue to soar with the Lord in my calling.

I have always known that it takes a team to publish a book, but that truth has been more pronounced than ever with this journal. Without a writer's challenge issued by my editor and writing coach, Loral Pepoon, in April of 2020—at what would become the beginning of a worldwide pandemic—you would not be holding this book in your hands. Without the obedience of Lori Buzzetti to share her prayer and encouragement for me to get back to writing this journal—at the very same time as Loral's challenge— you would not be holding this book in your hands. Without willing participants to be beta testers of *Created For So Much More* study groups, you would not be holding this book in your hands. Indulge me as I try to acknowledge those to whom I owe a dept of gratitude.

To my team of intercessors who faithfully keep me and this project before the Lord, I thank you. I could not have completed this journal without the faithful prayers of Danielle, Cindy, Lori, Beth, Rick, Barb, Jim, John, Lisa, Sue, Annaleigh, Beth, Loral, Jamie, and Danyalle. Thank you! A special thanks to Cindy Cumbest who kept the team informed when I needed to work on the manuscript rather than write an email with prayer requests.

The study groups of *Created For So Much More* were an integral part of the development and editing of this journal. Thank you to the first participants who heard the material in its rawest state: Loral, Deborah Lee, Beth, Sue, Laurie, Lisa, Jim, Barb, Lori, Danyalle, and Danielle. Not only were you open to receive *Created For So Much More*, your suggestions have improved the program and have built it beyond my original vision.

One of the suggestions the groups shared with me was to create videos to go along with the material. That seemed like walking on water to me, but the Lord breathed life into that suggestion, equipped me, and the videos were born. Thank you for your nudging me to a bigger dream.

Many from the first few *Created For So Much More* groups have taken up the mantel of leadership and are leading study groups of their own. Thank you! I pray that this journal brings added dimension to your studies. It only takes a spark to get a fire going. Thank you for being the sparks that are turning the *Created For So Much More* message into a movement.

A special thank you to Rick, Jesse, Lori, Vertie, and Sherri for helping me with the final read-through and edit of this journal. Your hearts, minds, and spirits helped focus the vision and perfect the finished journal. Thank you for your generosity of time and talent.

The Lord has a way of bringing just the right person in my path to accomplish what He is asking me to do. As I was sharing the idea of videos with my son Jesse, he volunteered to take on the whole video project. He interviewed participants, edited and produced the testimonial video and then took on the *Created For So Much More* chapter videos. He also used his love of photography to transform the art shared in the videos to the dividing pages in the journal. Jess, you brought ***so much more*** to the project than I can ever enumerate here. Your love and support, encouragement, coaching, and attention to excellent detail make me a better speaker, teacher, author, and coach. You have blessed me beyond words and beyond measure. Your willingness to tackle the tough stuff—even graphic design—was inspiring and more than appreciated. I pray that the Lord returns to you all and ***so much more*** that you have freely given.

To my whole family: Rick, Braden, Haley, Maren, Bennett, Jesse, and Hampton, thank you for your inspiration and your gift of time. Hearing "Mom/Gigi needs to work" was a new experience. You have been open, encouraging, and patient with me, and I so appreciate it. Family gatherings and conversations—online or in person around the fire pit—have buoyed me through these past months. I love you and thank the Lord daily for you.

Thank you to my Abiding Writing Warriors group: Beth, Rhoda, Cindy, Loral, and Lori. The power of praying and writing together has gotten me over more than one rough patch. Starting each work week with you mighty women of God always put me in the right frame of mind. Thank you for your continued encouragement to see myself as the writer God created me to be.

I owe a huge debt of gratitude to Loral Pepoon of Cowriterpro. Not only is she the gifted editor of this journal, in the ensuing years from publishing *Created For So Much More* she has become my writing coach and publisher. This journal began in her Cowriting with the Holy Spirit inaugural class in 2018. Since that time, the Lord changed its direction, audience, and format. There have been many times when Holy Spirit used Loral's editing expertise to bring my ideas into alignment with His vision. There were several "iron sharpening iron" moments that we worked through. Loral, through it all, I always knew that you were motivated to publish the Lord's best. I believe we have done just that. Thank you.

Although I carried the Lord's artistic vision, it took several people working together to bring it to fruition. My thanks to Kristi Thomas of Designed by Kristi for taking my paintings and creating icons that represent my style and vision. Your heart connection to my message allowed Holy Spirit to work through you to bring my brand into focus and create a signature logo that looks so much like—only better than—my natural signature. You are a gift.

Another graphic artist who worked to interpret this painter's vision and bring it to print is Elena Iria from the Selah Press team. Thank you for working through all of my specifications for the chapter dividing pages as well as all of the detailed artistic elements for each lesson. Down to the dots on the pages, you have taken my vision and brought it to life.

Selah Press, is far more than a publisher to me; they are a team that makes dreams come true. Owners Loral and Seth Pepoon dedicate themselves to excellence and a high standard of quality in every detail. I am pretty certain I stretched and even challenged you both when it came to working with my vision for the use of my art in this journal. I am happy to say that it was our mutual love and respect for each other and dedication to the Lord that prevailed. Thank you for your patience and willingness to consider my point of view. To see this journal become a reality is indeed a dream come true for me. Thank you.

Last but never least, a huge thank you to my husband Rick. Your unconditional love is something I hope to never take for granted. Thank you for being my sounding board through all of the pivoting and reshaping that I personally went through with the Lord. Thank you also for being a steadying force when the winds of resistance blew. I could always count on you to bring me back to my Center—the Lord and His vision for this book. More than your valuable input for this project, though, I thank the Lord for your willingness to allow me to soar with Him into who He created me to be and what He created me to do. Our schedule changed quite a bit as the Lord called me back to the work of the ministry, and I appreciate your flexibility when I have asked you to cook dinner, watch the girls, or change plans because of my commitments. I love you ***so much more*** than ever! Thank you hardly covers it.

ABOUT THE AUTHOR

Deborah Gall was created to coach others in life's journey of self-discovery. She lives to help fellow travelers discover, embrace, and live fully as who God created them to be, doing what He created them to do. This message of identity and purpose was born out of her own question, "Is this all there is?" God answered her question by taking her on a journey of twists, turns, and "blender moments." Through her own journey, He revealed her God-given identity and purpose as author, teacher, artist, and coach.

Throughout the adventure, the Lord showed Deborah that He advances His Kingdom and changes the world through His Presence in people's lives. In 2013, she began to dedicate more of her time and energy to spread the message of Divine identity and purpose. After hosting many life-changing conferences, she heard Holy Spirit tell her to write *Created For So Much More* based on the conference material.

Since its publication in 2017, Deborah continued to speak and share the message that God created us for ***so much more***. In 2020—in the middle of a worldwide pandemic—the Lord wooed her back to the computer to write a supplement to *Created For So Much More*. Through many months of God-ordained pivots, *A Guided Journal to Soaring With God* was born.

Through the process of penning this work, Deborah hosted online study groups and gained ***so much more*** revelation of the Lord's love and desire for His children to walk fully as who He created them to be, doing what He created them to do. She has seen lives changed by the material—not the least of which is her own—as God deepened her passion for helping others find their way on their own journey of self-discovery.

The Lord continues to take her one step at a time through life's challenges while keeping her on His path for the ***so much more*** that lies ahead. Most days she can be found in her studio writing, hosting groups, training leaders, providing individual counsel and ministry, and/or painting artwork that celebrates the Gospel. Other days find her cooking, traveling, and enjoying her immediate and extended family.

Deborah's previously published books are *Created For So Much More*, *The Color of Embrace*, and *Heartbeat of God*.

Deborah's website is a resource for a lifestyle of *so much more*. Visit www.deborahgall.com to
- Stay up to date with Deborah's ministry
- Hear about what fellow travelers are doing
- Go behind the scenes in Deborah's home studio
- Gain practical tips for living a life soaring with God
- View a current collection of paintings available for purchase
- and *so much more*.

Want to receive regular inspiration from Deborah delivered to your inbox? Sign up for her e-newsletter at www.deborahgall.com.

Join Deborah's tribe for monthly Soaring Into So Much More gatherings for additional teaching and inspiration. Contact Deborah through her website or social media for more information.

Connect with Deborah through social media:

Deborah L Gall

@DeborahLGall

Deborah Gall
HELPING OTHERS FIND THEIR WAY

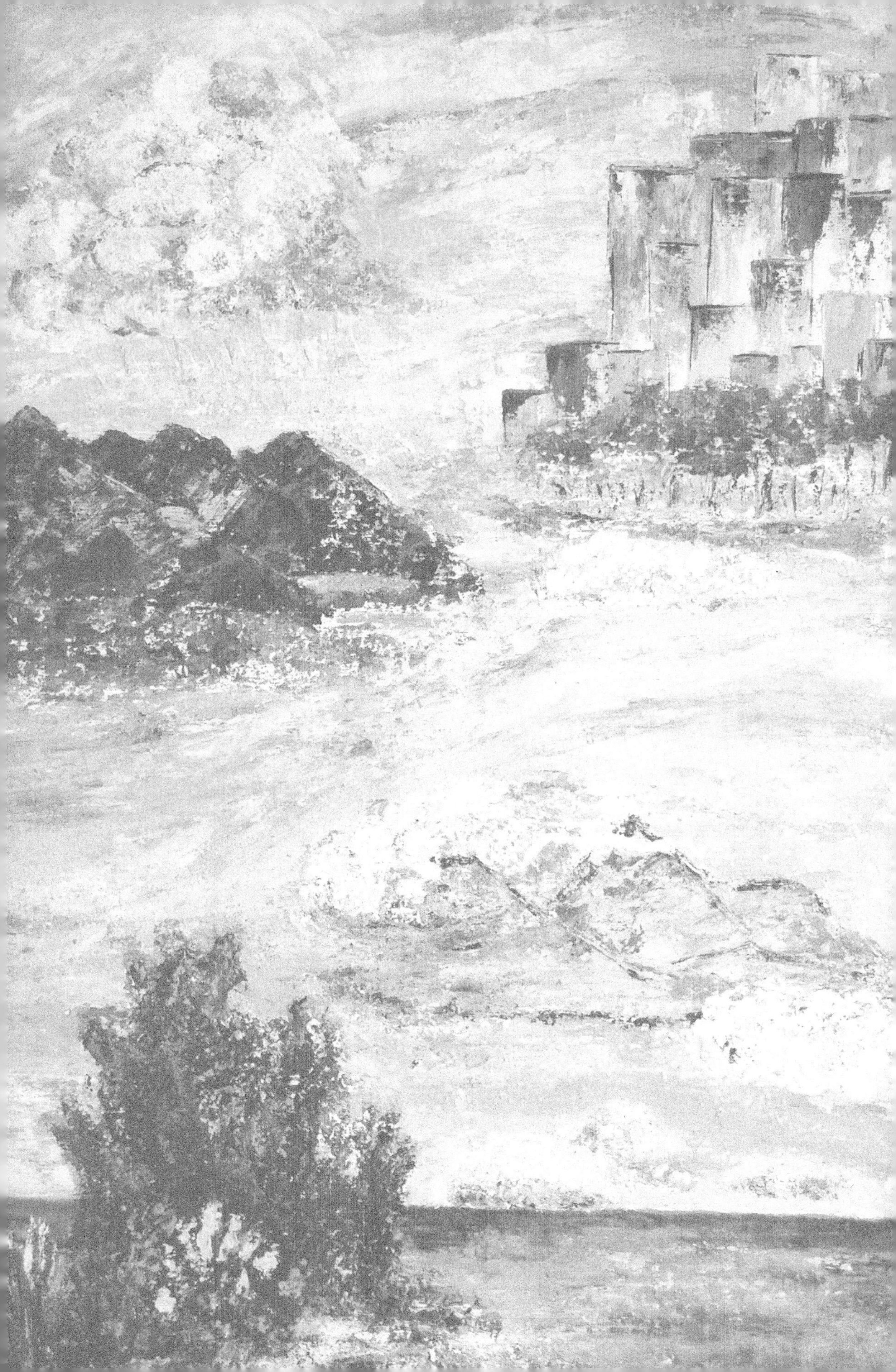

ABOUT THE COVER ART
"Soaring Into So Much More"

*"Soar with Me. Let Me show you **so much more** of
the places you've been and the places you'll go.
Soar with Me from Earth to Heaven
And from Heaven to Earth—"*
Spoken to the heart.

Seen through new eyes—Heaven's perspective

A City—the place of commerce with atmospheres ripe to be changed by
the God Carriers.
Cloud Formations—*"Signs of My Presence and Glory"*
"Reminders that I am always with you."
Mountains—of sin and bondage destroyed at Calvary.
Also symbols of the arduous journey of discovery made every day
to reach the highest height.
Wilderness—desert of the soul.
In desperate times of dryness and loneliness,
The Living Word brings sustenance and hope.
Blossoms in the desert, beauty from ashes, joy in the morning.
Shoreline and Sea—mending and launching,
Reaping abundant harvest.

From city to mountain, sand to sea—
Ever-evolving times and seasons of life.
Glorious Presence and Living Water ever present.
The wind of His Spirit—the flight plan,
His voice—the guide,
*"Take flight and soar, knowing
You were Created For **So Much More**."*